Legal History Library

VOLUME 84

Studies in the History of International Law

VOLUME 31

The titles published in this series are listed at *brill.com/shil*

Carl Schmitt and Francisco de Vitoria

The Paradox of Universalism in International Law

Edited by

José María Beneyto and Ignacio de la Rasilla

BRILL | NIJHOFF

LEIDEN | BOSTON

Cover illustration: Statue of Francisco de Vitoria in Salamanca by Francisco de Toledo, 1975.
Photo: Daniel Quiroga, 18 June 2024.

The Library of Congress Cataloging-in-Publication Data is available online at https://catalog.loc.gov
LC record available at https://lccn.loc.gov/2026904946

Typeface for the Latin, Greek, and Cyrillic scripts: "Brill". See and download: brill.com/brill-typeface.

ISSN 1874-1793
ISBN 978-90-04-75741-7 (hardback)
ISBN 978-90-04-75744-8 (e-book)
DOI 10.1163/9789004757448

This book is printed on acid-free paper and produced in a sustainable manner.

Contents

Acknowledgments

The present volume is the outcome of a sustained editorial effort, during which three academic conferences and numerous passionate intellectual debates were successfully held. The first of these conferences took place at San Pablo CEU University in Madrid in 2021, an international hub for contemporary efforts to shed new light on the rich legacy of Francisco de Vitoria in international law. The second international workshop was held at the University of Salamanca in 2022 – the cradle of the globally celebrated sixteenth- and seventeenth-century School of moral and legal Spanish theologians known as the School of Salamanca. Finally, the third of our international conferences was generously hosted by María Cristina College at El Escorial, a UNESCO World Heritage Site built by order of King Philip II in the sixteenth century near Madrid, in the summer of 2024.

Parts of Chapter 3 were previously published as Jochen von Bernstorff, 'Governing Hegemonic Spaces in Carl Schmitt: Colonialism, Anti-imperialism and the Grossraum Theory', 14 *Humanity* (2023), 369–384. Chapter 19 partly draws on materials previously published as Ignacio de la Rasilla, 'Looking Forward Through and Beyond the Western Classics of International Law', 13 *Asian Journal of International Law* (2023), 146–168.

The editors are deeply grateful to the Royal Institute of European Studies at San Pablo CEU University in Madrid for its institutional support, as well as to its dedicated staff for their personal commitment to this book project, and in particular to Dr. Sandra Galimberti Diaz-Faes, who graciously served as editorial manager in its inception. The editors are also very grateful to Prof. Randall Lesaffer, series editor of *Studies in the History of International Law* – the pioneering book series in the burgeoning field of the history of international law – for providing this volume with an excellent home at Brill/Nijhoff.

Last, but by no means least, the editors wish to once again express their gratitude to all the contributing authors – originating from academic institutions across Europe (including Spain, Portugal, Germany, Belgium, Switzerland, Norway, Italy, and Finland), as well as North America, South America, China, and Australia – for the excellence of their collective efforts to unravel the many concealed mysteries and conceptual paradoxes surrounding the Vitoria–Schmitt nexus in the history and theory of international law.

Ignacio de la Rasilla and José María Beneyto
Wuhan and Madrid, September 2025

Notes on Contributors

Paolo Amorosa

University Lecturer in International Law, Faculty of Law, University of Helsinki. He is the author of *Rewriting the History of the Law of Nations: How James Brown Scott Made Francisco de Vitoria the Founder of International Law* (OUP, 2019).

André Azevedo Alves

Associate Professor in Political Science, Institute for Political Studies at Catholic University of Portugal and Honorary Professor of Political Science and Catholic Social Thought, St. Mary's University, London. His works include *Catholic Social Thought, the Market and Public Policy: Twenty-First-Century Challenges* (ed. with P. M. Booth, St Mary's University Press, 2024), *De Salamanca a Coimbra y Évora: Caminos cruzados de una Escuela Singular* (with J. M. Moreira, Editorial UFV, 2018), and *The Salamanca School* (with J. M. Moreira, Bloomsbury, 2013).

Joseph W. Bendersky

Professor of History, Virginia Commonwealth University. He is author of *Carl Schmitt: Theorist for the Reich* (Princeton, 1983); a translation and scholarly edition of Schmitt's *On the Three Types of Juristic Thought* (Praeger, 2004); *A Concise History of Nazi Germany* (5th expanded ed., Rowman & Littlefield, 2021); and *The 'Jewish Threat': Anti-Semitic Politics of the U.S. Army* (Basic Books, 2000; Finalist for National Jewish Book Award). His works have been translated into six languages. Recent publications include: 'Ausnahmezustand, Staatsnotstandsplan, Ermächtigungsgesetz: Reappraising Carl Schmitt's Political Constitutionalism and the Demise of Weimar' and 'Schmitt a Berlino: 1933–1934'.

José María Beneyto

Jean Monnet Chair and University Professor in International Law, European Law and International Relations at the University San Pablo CEU, Madrid; Visiting Professor, Harvard Law School; and Director of the Royal Institute for European Studies. He is also President of the Institute for Governance and Society and of the Spanish Foreign Policy Association. Among his recent books as author or editor, *EU–China: Comparatives Experiences and Contributions to Global Governance in the Fields of Climate Change, Taxation, Trade, and Competition* (Thomson Reuters, 2024); *Conquest, Empire and Peace: Vito-*

ria and Erasmus before Charles v. (Catedra, 2024); *War or Peace? China, the United States and Europe* (Deusto, 2024); and *Empire, Humanism and Rights: Collected Essays on Francisco de Vitoria* (Springer, 2022).

Ignacio de la Rasilla
Han Depei Chair in International Law and 'One Thousand Talents Plan' Professor, Wuhan University Institute of International Law and Wuhan Academy of International Law and Global Governance. Recent books, as sole author or co-editor, include *The Cambridge Handbook of China and International Law* (CUP, 2024); *International Law and History. Modern Interfaces* (CUP, 2021; Chinese edition, The Commercial Press, 2026); *Experiments in International Adjudication: Historical Accounts* (CUP, 2019); and *In the Shadow of Vitoria: A History of International Law in Spain (1770–1953)* (Bril-Nijhoff, 2018).

Lauren Benton
Barton M. Biggs Professor of History and Professor of Law, Yale University. Benton's recent books include *They Called It Peace: Worlds of Imperial Violence* (Princeton UP, 2024); *Rage for Order: The British Empire and the Origins of International Law, 1800–1850* (co-authored with Lisa Ford, Harvard UP, 2016); and *A Search for Sovereignty: Law and Geography in European Empires, 1400–1900* (CUP, 2010). Benton received the 2019 Toynbee Prize for significant contributions to global history.

Leonor Durão Barroso
Ph.D. in Political Science and International Relations from the Institute for Political Studies of Universidade Católica Portuguesa. She is Visiting Assistant Professor at the Institute for Political Studies of Universidade Católica Portuguesa and a researcher at the Research Centre of the Institute for Political Studies. Her research is mainly on political thought, with a focus on the School of Salamanca and its intersection with international law, modern political philosophy, and the Social Doctrine of the Church. Her works include: 'Limited from the Outside: Francisco Suárez and the External Limits of Political Power', in *Religions*, 15: 259, 2024.

Maximiliano Hernández Marcos
Associate Professor of Philosophy, University of Salamanca. Authors of numerous books in his field of specialization, including *Conceptos en disputa, Disputas sobre conceptos* (Dykinson, 2022).

Ryan Martinez Mitchell
Associate Professor of Law, Chinese University of Hong Kong. He is the author of *Recentering the World: China and the Transformation of International Law* (CUP, 2022).

David Pan
Professor of European Language and Studies at the University of California, Irvine, and editor of the journal *Telos*. He has also served on the Commission on Unalienable Rights at the U.S. State Department. His publications include *Primitive Renaissance: Rethinking German Expressionism* and *Sacrifice in the Modern World: On the Particularity and Generality of Nazi Myth. He* has published essays on Theodor Adorno, Walter Benjamin, Bertolt Brecht, J. W. von Goethe, J. G. Hamann, J. G. Herder, Ernst Jünger, Franz Kafka, Heinrich von Kleist, Friedrich Nietzsche, and Carl Schmitt.

Daniel R. Quiroga-Villamarín
Hauser/Remarque Global Fellow, New York University; Postdoctoral Researcher (habilitand), University of Vienna (Austria). His research is currently being supported by an Ernst Mach fellowship from the Austrian Agency for Education and Internationalisation and a postdoc. Mobility grant from the Swiss National Research Foundation. He holds a Ph.D. in International Law, with a minor in International History and Politics, from the Graduate Institute of International and Development Studies (Geneva, Switzerland) and serves as the managing editor for the *Journal of the History of International Law*.

Juan Pablo Scarfi
Assistant Professor of International Relations, Pontifical Catholic University of Chile. He is the author of *The Hidden History of International Law in the Americas: Empire and Legal Networks* (OUP, 2017) and *El imperio de la ley: James Brown Scott y la construcción de un orden jurídico interamericano* (Fondo de Cultura Económica, 2014); and co-editor (with D. Sheinin) of *The New Pan-Americanism and the Structuring of Inter-American Relations* (Routledge, 2022) and *Cooperation and Hegemony in US–Latin American Relations: Revisiting the Western Hemisphere Idea* (with Andrew Tillman) (Palgrave Macmillan, 2016).

Ville Suuronen
Postdoctoral Research fellow, Turku Institute for Advanced Studies and the Department of Philosophy, Contemporary History and Political Science, University of Turku, Finland. His research interests include twentieth-century

intellectual history and political theory as well as contemporary forms of far-right politics in Europe. He has published peer-reviewed articles in journals such as *Political Theory, Government & Opposition, New German Critique, History of European Ideas, Global Intellectual History, Alternatives, The European Legacy*, and *Contemporary Political Theory*. He is currently finishing a monograph on the political theory of Carl Schmitt and working on a broader research project that analyzes contemporary forms of anti-liberal politics in Europe.

Christopher Rossi
Professor of International Relations and International Law, The Arctic University of Norway. He is the author of *Remoteness Reconsidered: The Atacama Desert and International Law* (University of Michigan Press, 2021); *Whiggish International Law: Elihu Root, the Monroe Doctrine, and International Law in the Americas* (Brill/Nijhoff, 2019), *Sovereignty and Territorial Temptation* (CUP, 2017); and *Broken Chain of Being, James Brown Scott and the Origins of International Law* (Kluwer Law International, 1998).

David Roth-Isigkeit
University Professor of Public Law with specialization on the Law of Digitalization, University of Administrative Sciences Speyer. He is the author of *The Plurality Trilemma: A Geometry of Global Legal Thought* (Palgrave, 2018).

Johannes Thumfart
Researcher at the research group Law, Science, Technology, and Society (LSTS) at Vrije Universiteit Brussels; Ph.D., Humboldt Universität Berlin. He is author of the book *The Liberal Internet in the Postliberal Era* (Palgrave Macmillan, 2024) and a book on Francisco de Vitoria, titled *Die Begründung der globalpolitischen Philosophie* (Kadmos, 2012). His research has been published in the *Journal of Global Security Studies, Global Studies Quarterly, Grotiana*, and *AI and Ethics*. He holds/held teaching positions at Hochschule for Wirtschaft und Recht Berlin, Freie Universität Berlin, Universidad Iberoamericana in Mexico City, and University of Cincinnati.

Jochen Von Bernstorff
Chair for Constitutional law, International Law and Human Rights at the University of Tubingen. He is the author *The Public International Law Theory of Hans Kelsen* (CUP, 2010) and *L'essor et la Chute du Droit International Humanitaire: Une brève Histoire de la Codification de la Protection des Civils en Temps de Guerre* (Pédone Paris, 2023). Recent edited volumes include *The Battle for International Law in the Decolonization Era* (OUP, 2019, together with P. Dann).

Valentina Vadi

Adjunct Professor in International Law at the School of Political Sciences at the University of Florence and Jean Monnet Fellow at the Robert Schumann Center for Advanced Studies at the European University Institute. She is the author of several monographs and more than a hundred articles in peer-reviewed journals on international law. Her recent monographs include: *Proportionality, Reasonableness, and Standards of Review in International Investment Law and Arbitration* (Edward Elgar, 2018); *War and Peace: Alberico Gentili and the Early Modern Law of Nations* (Brill, 2020); and *Cultural Heritage in International Economic Law* (Brill, 2023).

Miguel Vatter

Professor in Political Science School of Humanities and Social Sciences, Deakin University. His most recent books are *The Republic of the Living: Biopolitics and the Critique of Civil Society* (Fordham University Press, 2014); *Divine Democracy. Political Theology after Carl Schmitt* (OUP, 2020); and *Living Law. Jewish Political Theology from Hermann Cohen to Hannah Arendt* (OUP, 2021).

CHAPTER 1

Introduction: The Vitoria–Schmitt Nexus in the History and Theory of International Law

José María Beneyto and Ignacio de la Rasilla

1 Introduction

During the twentieth century, the Dominican friar and chair of theology at the University of Salamanca, Francisco de Vitoria (c. 1483–1546), and the twentieth-century German jurist and political theorist Carl Schmitt (1888–1985) were the embodiments of two almost opposite paradigms in international law. Since the mid-to-late nineteenth century, Vitoria, who presided over the sixteenth- and early seventeenth-century School of Salamanca, was celebrated among international lawyers as the foremost precursor of Hugo Grotius and a venerable founding-father of international law who epitomized a universalist and humanist natural-law-based conception of the *ius gentium*. Moreover, both Vitoria and the tradition of the *seconda scholastica* of the School of Salamanca were influentially reclaimed in the late nineteenth century and the interwar period as forerunners of the tenets of liberal international law and an international-community-centered international legal order.[1] By contrast, Carl Schmitt was set aside by international lawyers as an intellectual outcast whose work was fatally tainted by his anti-Semitism and his association with the Nazi regime and, furthermore, deemed a dangerous exponent of a hyper-realist geopolitical theory of regional state-border-transcending spaces dominated by hegemonic powers with the prohibition of intervention by third countries.

Only in more recent times, influenced by the strategically essentialist re-interpretations of their works put forward by post-colonial and critically oriented international law scholars, the ambivalence of the intellectual constructions that Vitoria and Schmitt bequeathed to international law have been put in starker relief among international law scholars. On the one hand, Vitoria

1 See, more recently, Ignacio de la Rasilla, 'La réception intellectuelle de Francisco de Vitoria chez les juristes internationaux à travers le temps'. *Revue de Synthese* 147 (2025) and José María Beneyto, *La conquista, el imperio y la paz. Vitoria y Erasmo ante Carlos V* (Madrid, Cátedra, 2024).

 | DOI:10.1163/9789004757448_002

has been re-portrayed as an accessory or, even in some cases, as a facilitator or accomplice of European colonialism. According to this late twentieth-century post-colonial reinterpretation, Vitoria would have inaugurated an intellectual justificatory pattern of legalist reasoning through the universalist language of *ius naturale et gentium* that would later become multiple times redeployed by Western imperial powers against non-Western peoples in different waves of colonization and, more broadly, by hegemonic projects of all stripes up to the present day.[2] On the other hand, Schmitt has been re-characterized as an insightful *avant-garde* critic of a just wars-prone US-led liberal international order who was also able to grasp the foundational constitutive role of colonialism for a Eurocentric international legal order and the centrality of the language of international rights and obligations for informal economic imperialism in a globalized capitalist world-system.

Among international law scholars, Carl Schmitt's reflections on the shadow side of contemporary international law went on to gain a great salience in the context of the global war on terror following the terrorist attacks of 9/11 in New York and Washington. Moreover, Schmitt's theoretical constructions are deemed to be regaining again strategic influence amidst troubled geopolitical and geoeconomic contemporary conditions that for many foreshadow the dawn of a second Cold War in international relations. Schmitt's new regained momentum has also fueled a debate on the extent to which he has been unduly 'sanitized' by contemporary thinkers and, therefore, on whether Schmitt should be 'cancelled' from public law and political theory or at least whether academic mentions of his works should always be accompanied by a reference to the indelible association of his legal and political thought with the Nazi horrors.[3]

There is an extremely extensive literature on both Francisco de Vitoria[4] and the School of Salamanca[5] as well as in Carl Schmitt[6] across a great variety of

2 Ironically, this post-colonial interpretation was indirectly influenced by Schmitt's ambivalent supportive views of Western colonialism in the mid-1940s.

3 Joseph Weiler, 'Cancelling Carl Schmitt?' *EJIL:Talk*, 13 August 2021, available at ejiltalk.org/cancelling-carl-schmitt/.

4 Among other recent bibliographies see: Jean Paul Cojou and María Idoya Zorroza-Huarte, (eds.), Bibliografia Vitoriana (Pamplona, Universidad de Navarra, 2014).

5 Among other recent bibliographies, see Celia Alejandra Ramírez Santos, Jose Luis Egío García. *The Research on the School of Salamanca (2008–2019). Conceptual and Multidisciplinary Bibliography.* Max Planck Institute for European Legal History Research Paper Series No. 2020–09: subsidia et instrumenta. 2020, available at https://www.lhlt.mpg.de/2255762/2020-09.

6 See e.g. Jens Meierhenrich, Oliver Simons (eds.), *The Oxford Handbook of Carl Schmitt* (Oxford, Oxford University Press, 2017). See also a fully devoted website to Carl Schmitt's works, Carl-Schmitt-Gesaellschaft e.V. available at https://www.carl-schmitt.de/en/rese

academic disciplines both in the West and, increasingly, elsewhere. In international legal scholarship too, the literature on Francisco de Vitoria,[7] and even on the work of his commentators[8] and the academic debates triggered by their interpretations,[9] has largely expanded in the twenty-first century. Contributing to the rise of interest on Carl Schmitt among international legal theorists and historians were the releases of the Italian (1991), French (1998), Spanish (2002, with a previous edition in 1979), and then the English (2003) and later Portuguese (2014) translations of Schmitt's *Der Nomos der Erde im Völkerrecht des Jus Publicum Europaeum* (1950).[10] In the wake of these translations, some Western international lawyers, notably Peter Haggenmacher and Martti Koskenniemi, began to provide incisive interpretations, largely on the basis of *Der Nomos der Erde,* of the significance of Vitoria's work for Schmitt's theory of international law.[11]

---

arch-2/ with regular updates on publications on his work: https://www.carl-schmitt.de/en/research-2/literature-on-carl-schmitt/.

7 See e.g. Martti Koskenniemi, 'Vitoria and Us. Thoughts on Critical Histories of International Law'. *Rechtsgeschichte: Zeitschrift des Max-Planck-Instituts für europäische Rechtsgeschichte* 22 (2014), 119–139.

8 See e.g. Paolo Amorosa, *Rewriting the History of International Law. How James Brown Scott made Francisco de Vitoria the Founder of International Law* (Oxford, Oxford University Press, 2019).

9 See e.g. Antony Anghie, *Imperialism, Sovereignty and the Making of International Law* (Cambridge, Cambridge University Press, 2005).

10 Carl Schmitt, *Der Nomos der Erde im Völkerrecht des Jus Publicum Europaeum* (Berlin: Duncker & Humblot 1950); Carl Schmitt, *Il nomos della terra nel diritto internazionale dello «Jus publicum europaeum».* F. Volpi (Curatore) E. Castrucci (Traduttore) (Milan: Adelphi, 1991); Carl Schmitt, *Le nomos de la Terre.* Préface. Peter Haggenmacher Traduction. Lilyane Deroche-Gurcel (Paris, Presses Universitaires de France, 1998). Carl Schmitt, *El Nomos de la tierra en el 'Derecho de Gentes del Ius publicum europeaum'.* trad. de Dora Schilling Thou (Granada: Comares, 2002). See previously by the same translator the edition published as Carl Schmitt, *El Nomos de la tierra en el 'Derecho de Gentes del Ius publicum europeaum'.* trad. de Dora Schilling Thou (Madrid: Centro de Estudios Constitucionales, 1979); Carl Schmitt, *The Nomos of the Earth in the International Law of the Jus Publicum Europaeum.* Translated and Annotated by G. L. Ulmen (New York: Telos Press Publishing 2003); Carl Schmitt. *Nomos da Terra no direito das gentes do jus publicum europaeum.* Tradução: Alexandre Franco de Sá, Bernardo Ferreira, José Maria Arruda e Pedro Hermílio Villas Bôas Castelo Branco (Rio de Janeiro, Contraponto 2014).

11 See e.g. Peter Haggenmacher, 'L'itinéraire internationaliste de Carl Schmitt' (Presses Universitaires de France, 1998); Martti Koskenniemi, 'International Law as Political Theology How to Read the *Nomos der Erde'. Constellations* 11 (2004), 492–511; Bardo Fassbender, 'Carl Schmitt', in Bardo Fassbender and Anne Peters (eds.), *The Oxford Handbook of the History of International Law* (Oxford; Oxford University Press, 2012), 1173–1178. See also, previously, Anthony, Carty, 'Carl Schmitt's Critique of Liberal International Legal Order between 1933 and 1945'. *Leiden Journal of International Law* 14 (2001), 25–76.

However, notwithstanding this burgeoning academic literature, there is still no research monograph, and, until this volume, there was not any multi-authored edited volume in English – nor in any other language – which makes its primary aim to further enlarge the study of the Vitoria–Schmitt intellectual nexus in the theory and history of international law in and beyond international law with the inclusion of insights from different disciplines and geographical locations as well as by reference to Schmitt's other works. This volume intends to fill this lacuna and to foster additional analyses and well-contextualized reflections by an interdisciplinary group of authors on the paradox of universalism in international law that is encapsulated at the interface of Vitoria and Schmitt's works on the law – that as Mirabeau once told us – one day will rule the world.

Its editors and contributors have been inspired by the so-called 'turn to the history of international law' among international lawyers, historians of political thought, intellectual historians, and legal historians[12] in the wake of which new 'revisionist' works on the legacy of the Western classics of international law have surfaced. Post-colonial and critical readings of Vitoria's work, in particular, have been at the heart of an impassioned academic debate on historiography and methodology between contextualist historians and post-modern and critical legal historiographical trends. Furthermore, new scholarly writings have unearthed and historically contextualized a complex network of intellectual and biographical academic connections and mutual influences between Vitoria's highly influential international law commentators in the late century, the foundational interwar period, the aftermath of World War II, and beyond. This new research has contributed to unveiling a new intellectual genealogy of the influential uses, abuses, and presentist misuses of Vitoria's foundational works for international law against a diversity of contextually situated historical backgrounds.[13]

Against this backdrop, the purposes of this book were set to achieve, firstly, a critical examination of the reception and influence of both Vitoria and Schmitt's works, and interpretations thereof, on contemporary international legal thought and international relations; secondly, a critical examination of the uses and misuses of Francisco de Vitoria's international thought in different historical contexts and the influence of Vitoria's thought on Carl Schmitt's theoretical constructions about international law; thirdly, a critical examin-

12 Ignacio de la Rasilla, *International Law and History. Modern Interfaces* (Cambridge: Cambridge University Press, 2021).

13 Ignacio de la Rasilla, *In the Shadow of Vitoria – A History of International Law in Spain (1770–1953)* (Leiden: Brill/Nijhoff, 2017).

ation of the contemporaneity of Vitoria and Schmitt in the history and theory of international law including, in particular, for what regards the persistent legacy of imperial-related constructs in the present; and, fourthly, a critical analysis of both the historical and contemporary reception of Carl Schmitt and Vitoria's international legal thought across different geographical locations, namely in Latin-America and China, in starkly diverse political circumstances and historical contexts, amidst increasing polarization in an emerging post-Western-centric international legal order that is structurally deemed to further crystallize in the years and decades to come.

2 Navigating the Contents of the Volume

This section navigates the contributions of authors from different academic traditions, namely those of international law, history, political science, cultural studies, and philosophy to the present volume and explains how they serve its overarching purposes by providing much-welcomed nuance, contextualization, and breadth to the Schmitt–Vitoria nexus in the history and theory of international law. Against the background provided by this introductory Chapter 1, the aim of which is to present the book's main concept, justification, and contribution to the field, this volume is divided into five parts, each of which is in turn – except for the second and the last one – composed of four chapters.

2.1 *The Reception of Francisco de Vitoria and Carl Schmitt in International Legal Thought*

Part 1 is devoted to examining different dimensions of the reception of Vitoria and Schmitt in international legal thought through contributions by José María Beneyto, Jochen von Bernstorff, Lauren Benton, and David Roth-Isigkeit.

In Chapter 2, *José María Beneyto* examines Schmitt's interpretation of Vitoria in light of his critique of James Brown Scott's appropriation of Vitoria's *ius gentium* in the service of American liberal internationalism. Beneyto states that, as an embodiment of natural law, Vitoria's *ius gentium* was common to all humankind and could be recognized by reason, even if it had not been created by the deliberative will of any human legislator. Vitoria no longer thought in terms of a *respublica christiana* but of a *comunitas totius orbis* that both presupposed and articulated consensus. Beneyto analyzes Vitoria as a 'friend–foe' of Carl Schmitt, the author at the heart of Schmitt's seminal international law book *The* Nomos *of the Earth in the International Law of the Jus Publicum Europaeum*. Guided by an intention to develop a theory of 'large spaces' (*Grossräume*) as an alternative to American globalism, Schmitt drew on his reading of Vitoria – mediated through Brown Scott's interpretations since the 1920s – to produce his own re-interpretation and appropriation of Vitoria in opposition to American hegemony and the League of Nations system. Schmitt's reading of Vitoria is thus structurally ambivalent. In his *Glossarium*, Vitoria appears as unsuited to accept the political theology of modernity, its wars of religion, and the need for their 'neutralization' through Schmitt's heavily constructed *jus publicum europaeum* and the formal balance of statehood. According to Schmitt, Vitoria's conception of universal liberties based on a common rationality was overwhelmed by the indeterminacy of law and justice, whereas Schmitt himself opted instead for 'the political', understood as the friend–enemy polarization.

In Chapter 3, *Jochen von Bernstorff* focuses on the relatively little-explored positions of Schmitt on European colonialism and colonial warfare in order to cast light on Schmitt's different attitudes toward two forms of imperialism: 'formal imperialism' and 'informal imperialism', in which the imperial power rather than seeking to 'establish a new colony … seeks domination of a foreign country' by forging 'a clientelist relationship between metropolitan and peripheral elites'. For Von Bernstorff, the interpretive key to understanding Schmitt's positive attitude towards the former and negative attitude towards the latter lies in the extent to which formal imperialism was not just compatible but, in fact, in Schmitt's view, a substantiating factor for the maintenance of Schmitt's idealized *Jus Publicum Europaeum* as – in his view – a well-functioning international legal order in the nineteenth century. By contrast, informal imperialism did not meet the three-tiered requirements of Schmitt's conception of an adequate 'concrete order' underpinned by law. Other than highlighting the influence of Savigny's Historical School of Jurisprudence on Schmitt's romantic attitude towards the *Jus Publicum Europaeum*, Von Bernstorff also explores the different sources of inspiration for Schmitt's laudatory views on Western formal colonialism retracing them to 'thoroughly ideological and ultimately discriminatory and in some usages openly racialized legal justifications' that were relatively standard among nineteenth-century conservative international legal circles. To these justifications, Schmitt utilitarianly added the 'instrumental function' played by an unregulated colonizable territory outside Europe 'in order to shift tensions between the Great Powers to the periphery'. This, in Schmitt's view, served as the ultimate fulcrum of the dissolved *Jus Publicum Europaeum* he yearned for at the dawn of Germany's 'Zero Hour' or *Stunde Null*.

In Chapter 4, *Lauren Benton* focuses on the juxtaposition of Vitoria's and Schmitt's approaches to 'limited war', a topic which was – in her view – 'at the heart of their intellectual agendas' as seen, *inter alia*, for what regards Schmitt, in his *Theory of the Partisan* as her chapter examines. This allows Benton not only to 'expose similarities in approaches to recurring problems' and, therefore, a 'tendency to exaggerate the originality and theoretical coherence of the work of both Vitoria and Schmitt', but also to add 'nuance to our understanding of postwar developments in international law' and to grapple with a persistent 'legacy of empires in global legal thought' both in the twentieth and twenty-first centuries. According to Benton, this legacy continues to surround the 'challenges of defining the legal framework for violence outside Europe', thus placing 'empire, incomplete sovereignty, and atrocity at the very center of the history of international law' from which the traditional focus on other dimensions of Vitoria and Schmitt's nexus in the history of international law had contributed to displace them.

In Chapter 5, *David Roth-Isigkeit* addresses what he regards as the ambivalent reception of Vitoria in the history of international legal thought. According to Roth-Isigkeit, certain approaches that celebrate Vitoria as the father of individual rights humanism stand in obvious contrast to those that present him as a supporter of European imperialism. For Roth-Isigkeit, these alternatives reflect opposite positions in contemporary reflections on international law. His chapter confronts two recent perspectives on Vitoria: for Jürgen Habermas, Vitoria is the first thinker in the Western tradition to have advocated a democratic constitutionalism beyond the state; Martti Koskenniemi, by contrast, portrays Vitoria as the founding father of apologetic economic liberalism. According to Roth-Isigkeit, while the ambivalences of the scholastic method and the tensions within Vitoria's writings may explain these divergent readings, the 'project of critical history' may have largely reached its limits. Over-intensifying the critical perspective, he warns, risks eroding a pragmatic narrative of progress in ways that may ultimately harm the international legal project as a whole. Methodological concerns about whether lawyers are generally equipped to write the history of their own discipline add to the pressing need for an alternative between uncritical systematicity and system-eroding deconstruction. This alternative, however, cannot mean a return to the old idols of universality. Following Habermas, Roth-Isigkeit suggests that it may nonetheless be worthwhile to search for 'splinters of reason' in an undoubtedly dark history of humankind. Ultimately, he concludes, international law needs a powerful conception of just and rightful authority.

2.2 *Conceptual Crossroads in International Law and Political Thought*

Part 2 explore a number of conceptual crossroads in international law and political thought in light of both Vitoria and Schmitt's writings and interpretations thereof. It comprises three contributions by Miguel Vatter, David Pan, André Azevedo Alves, and Leonor Durão Barroso, respectively.

In Chapter 6, *Miguel Vatter* considers the conflict of interpretations in the twentieth century around Francisco de Vitoria's reformulation of *ius gentium* to show the different ways in which the legitimacy of international law is a function of its 'globalization'. By this term, Vatter refers in the first instance to the discursive strategies employed to justify extending a given legal order to cover 'the whole world'. Vatter's hypothesis is that these twentieth-century interpretations of Vitoria's discourse show that the emergence of a 'global' right and a 'global' community relies on a nexus between legal order (*Ordnung*) and localization (*Ortung*) that Schmitt identified as characteristic of the Greek idea of law as *nomos* and associated with the geo-political notion of *Grossraum* and also of empire. The twentieth-century debate on Vitoria indicates that the nexus of spatiality and law can receive antithetical political interpretations, leaving room for a variety of models of global legal order. Thus, Vatter identifies how the discourse of *nomos* functions in a different way in Brown Scott's interpretation of Vitoria as the founding father of liberal internationalism; in how Vitoria was mobilized by Schmitt and Barcia Trelles in a paradoxical neo-imperial and post-colonial direction; and, lastly, in Koskenniemi's account of the Spanish origins of international law as providing a synthesis between the above contrapositions, one that employs the Schmittian notion of *nomos* to argue that Vitoria deploys a subjective understanding of right as *dominium* in order to develop a 'globalized' idea of *ius gentium* as the *nomos* for the emergent global 'liberal' capitalism.

In Chapter 7, *David Pan* examines how both the defenders of a universal international law framework – opposed to Schmitt's critique of such universalism – and the proponents of a Schmittian realism that privileges power to the exclusion of law agree on the basic antagonism between power and law in Schmitt's work. Yet, in his view, both fail to recognize the continuities between Schmitt's writings on political theology and his discussion of international law in *The* Nomos *of the Earth*. For Pan, a better understanding of Schmitt's work requires coming to terms with the fact that, throughout it, the key problem is the way in which power and ideals coincide and reinforce one another. In *Political Theology*, this reinforcing coincidence lies in the political-theological meaning of the decision on the state of exception; in *The* Nomos *of the Earth*, it forms the basis of Schmitt's argument about the essential link between *Ordnung* (order) and *Ortung* (territorialization). According to Pan, this link between law as order and sovereignty as land appropriation forms the basis for Schmitt's interpretation of Francisco de Vitoria's similar approach to international law and sovereignty. Against this conceptual background, Pan traces

Schmitt's development of the connection between order and territorialization, shows how it aligns with Vitoria's conception of sovereignty, and reflects on what this understanding of the relationship between sovereignty and law means for the current *nomos* of the earth.

In Chapter 8, *André Azevedo Alves* and *Leonor Durão Barroso* argue that Vitoria cannot be read simply as a liberal internationalist, following Brown Scott, nor, as Schmitt suggests, as lacking the necessary neutrality and ahistoricism to be fully applicable in a context of sovereign states. Instead, they contend, Vitoria's *ius gentium* possessed a universal character and provided a legal framework that enabled the defense of natural liberties applicable to all nations and all human beings. Vitoria's thought, they note, was specifically intended to apply beyond the context of the *respublica christiana.* In this sense, Vitoria remains relevant today for informing current understandings of universal values in international relations. In the relationship between Vitoria and Schmitt, the latter's treatment of just war theories is crucial for understanding where he situates Vitoria within the development of international legal thought. According to Azevedo Alves and Durão Barroso, Schmitt regarded Vitoria's just war theory – although different from the concept of *justus hostis* proper to the *Jus Publicum Europaeum* – as not the same as that advocated by modern internationalists, building upon Vitoria, during the interwar period. They argue that the neutrality Schmitt attributed to Vitoria does not exhaust his thought, but is nonetheless essential to its understanding. Moreover, while Vitoria undoubtedly held a Christian-centered approach, foundational to his missionary mindset, the neutrality and universalism of his thinking remain unquestionable. As an example, they highlight Vitoria's defense of universal religious liberty and, consequently, his continuing relevance in the context of secular states.

2.3 *Discovery, Nomos, and Conceptions of Space*

Part 3 includes contributions by Ryan Martínez Mitchell, Juan Pablo Scarfi, Valentina Vadi, and Christopher Rossi. It is devoted to the exploration of some central interfaces between Schmitt and Vitoria's works around the essential notions of discovery, *nomos,* and space in their work across faraway geographical locations including China, Latin-America, and the US expansion towards the West of the American continent.

In Chapter 9, *Ryan Martínez Mitchell* explores 'spatiality as a major recurring theme' in the history of Chinese engagements with international law with reference to Vitoria and Schmitt. At different reprises during the Chinese history of international law, including notably in the present, this theme has 'manifested in the tension between advocacy of universal norms or institutions and the countervailing stance of asserting state sovereignty'. Martinez Mitchell explains that 'ideas of natural law have often been invoked by Chinese international legal theorists to support both universal norms and sovereign rights, which, in turn, contributes to significant overlap between Chinese international legal discourse and the claims of leading Western "naturalist" theorists of international law.' While, according to Martinez Mitchell, a 'fruitful comparison can be drawn between the writings of Francisco de Vitoria and other members of the School of Salamanca to China's later defenses of universal norms justifying anticolonial solidarity', Schmitt's work, 'in which natural law-inflected arguments support the sovereign power of the state and the formation of autonomous regional orders, also has echoes in aspects of China's international legal stances.' One interpretative approach to key policy-oriented legal platforms of the PRC, such as the 'Five Principles of Peaceful Coexistence' and, also, the more recent 'Community of Shared Future of Humankind', is, for Martínez Mitchell, to 'see them as vehicles for mediating different strains of thought about the "natural" spaces of international law's binding force, and its limitations'.

In Chapter 10, *Juan Pablo Scarfi* examines Schmitt's understanding of the Monroe Doctrine as a conceptual 'turning-point' for the rise of American Western Hemisphere international law and the gradual decline of European international law. In doing so, he examines Schmitt's related intellectual debt to both Spanish and Latin American authors, ranging from Camilo Barcia Trelles to Alejandro Alvarez. Schmitt's debt to Alvarez lies in that the latter's work served him as an intellectual gateway to the 'exploration of the early twentieth century legal struggle' over the scope and meaning of the Monroe Doctrine. Schmitt's debt to Barcia includes that it was through Barcia's work that Schmitt was able to retrace 'geographical and historical connections between Vitoria and the Monroe Doctrine as the two key points of intersection' for Schmitt between the old European and by then emerging American Western Hemisphere international law. Furthermore, Scarfi's exploration of the main 'two waves of discussions over the Monroe Doctrine in the Americas through the lens of Vitoria and Schmitt', in turn, enables him to trace their intellectual 'resonance and influence in Latin America's intellectual debates' throughout the second half of the twentieth century and the first decades of the twenty-first century.

In Chapter 11, *Valentina Vadi* inspired by her understanding that a *longue durée* historical perspective can contribute to 'nurture the emancipatory potential of international law' through the 'dismantling the remains of colonial injustice by enabling international lawyers to expose the uncertain foundations of specific legal rules, expose their injustice, and develop tools to right historical wrongs', structures her chapter by, first, examining how 'European nations and the Church developed the doctrine of discovery in the early modern period' and examining 'Vitoria's position on this doctrine' before moving forward in time to analyze 'how the 1885 Berlin Conference and Act endorsed the discovery doctrine'. Then, she goes on to elaborate upon how Schmitt himself lent retrospective support to the doctrine of discovery when the turn came for Germany to employ it as part of its imperial project in East Africa. Finally, Vadi compares Vitoria and Schmitt's diverging positions on this issue and examines the 'promises and pitfalls' of adopting a *longue durée* perspective of 'the doctrine of discovery' as an epistemological key 'for the development of international law'.

In Chapter 12, *Christopher Rossi* also 'interrogates the discovery doctrine' as interpreted in Schmitt's Nomos *of the Earth,* connecting it to what he terms 'its controversial, even pernicious reception into the domestic constitutional order of the United States'. This leads Rossi to examine a series of recurrent topics appearing in Schmitt's *The* Nomos *of the Earth,* including Schmitt's 'basic view of spatial study and demarcation, his reading of Vitoria and the Indians, and early nineteenth century American "land hunger" which, in turn, conditioned the US' approach to its expansion towards the West leading ultimately to the forced removal of Indians from their ancestral lands'. According to Rossi, Schmitt's abridgment of the US' treatment of native Americans 'did not have so much to do with an unfamiliarity with United States domestic constitutional and political affairs at that time' as it did with Schmitt's grander twentieth-century narrative. Although Schmitt was 'keenly aware of the federalist mindset and challenges associated with the political consolidation of the new republic,' he decided, according to Rossi, to link 'these antecedent historical considerations to his deep fascination with the Monroe Doctrine and to the epochal new nomos that accompanied the global land and sea dualism arising after WWI between East and West'.

2.4 *Historical and Contemporary Pathways to Vitoria and Carl Schmitt*

Containing works by Joseph W. Bendersky, Daniel R. Quiroga Villamarin, Maximiliano Hernández and Johannes Thumfart Part 4 is devoted to exploring a number of both historical and contemporary related phenomena in the light of Schmitt's writings and their connection with Vitoria's works.

In Chapter 13, *Joseph W. Bendersky* considers Schmitt's understanding of Vitoria as a key element in his conceptualization of the historical development of international law in relation to his theory of a new *Nomos*. In particular, Schmitt's 1944 lectures on Vitoria constitute a case where biography and historical contextualization intersect with theoretical argument. With the outbreak of war, Schmitt shifted his focus from the idea of the Reich as the key element of Grossraum to a more Eurocentric and global emphasis on *nomos*, in which Vitoria emerged as a central figure. According to Bendersky, Schmitt progressively identified himself – like many other Germans – with the Western European rational spirit and tradition, which could not have been completely obliterated or supplanted by Nazi ideology, values, or institutions within the short span of twelve years. For this reason, Bendersky argues, reductionist attempts to subsume Schmitt's significant scholarly contributions under an all-encompassing, ubiquitous anti-Semitic paradigm are untenable. More recent research, he notes, has again demonstrated the complexity of Schmitt's relations with Jews. Despite his official titles and involvement with Nazi leaders, Schmitt's private diaries and correspondence reveal his affinities and intimate connections with the same conservative circles with which he had closely associated before 1933. Bendersky views Schmitt's 1944 Vitoria lectures as a crucial link between his pre–World War II ideas on foreign affairs, war, and international law (including his Grossraum theory) and his postwar private commentaries and writings on these subjects. Nothing in these lectures, he contends, reflects any concurrence with the value system or policies of the Hitler regime. On the contrary, in Bendersky's interpretation, Schmitt's identification with Vitoria's Christian humanism – together with his allusions to the process of dehumanization since the eighteenth century – was inherently antithetical to the wartime actions in the East and to the racial ideology that inspired them.

In Chapter 14, *Daniel R. Quiroga-Villamarin* investigates how, despite the fact that for centuries a central concern for early modern scholars of the *ius gentium* was the body of norms that regulated alliances – and, indirectly, the relations with hostile peoples – which was a topic to which all classic authors of international law devoted attention, by the late nineteenth century, scholarly treatment of the laws of friendship and alliance was far less widespread. Quiroga then goes on to examine Schmitt's *The Concept of the Political* (1932) in tandem with Vitoria's thoughts on the relationship between law and alliances in order to unearth the 'ways in which this early modern concern continues to reverberate in contemporary international legal thought' with reference to historiographical debates that emerged in the wake of the interdisciplinary turn to the history of international law.

In Chapter 15, *Maximiliano Hernández* examines Schmitt's reading of Emer de Vattel as the theoretical culmination of the historical process that led to the constitution of the modern ius gentium europaeum – a process that began at the end of the sixteenth century and resulted in the elaboration of the concept of humanized war. For Hernández, Schmitt, disappointed by the world order that emerged after World War II and the creation of the United Nations, brought Vitoria and Vattel into play as part of a dual intellectual strategy. On the one hand, by situating Vitoria firmly within his concrete medieval roots, Schmitt sought to deprive the new international law – championed by American liberalism – of the abstract, humanitarian-universalist legitimization associated with its presumed founder. At the same time, by claiming Vattel, rather than Kant, as the apex of the ius gentium europaeum, he aimed to justify what Hernández calls his failed plan – conceived in the context of Hitler's expansionism – for a new world order based on a balance between strong, equal powers, each exerting influence over its own large sphere. In this envisioned order, Germany would exercise hegemonic control over Mitteleuropa without external interference, as the United States would in the Americas and the USSR over Eastern Europe. Schmitt thus appeared to find in Vattel's rigorous organization of the modern ius gentium, grounded in state sovereignty, the anchor point for advocating a new international *nomos* of neutrality between continental powers – one that would allow each to freely order its own Grossraum. However, Hernández notes that, contrary to Schmitt's intentions, Vattel's conception of the rights and duties of solidarity among nations established clear natural-law limits to any ius gentium exclusively based on state sovereignty.

In Chapter 16, *Johannes Thumfart* examines the relationship between Vitoria and Schmitt from an uncommon and intriguing perspective: its relevance to contemporary debates on the exercise of state sovereignty in the context of digital technologies. Thumfart regards Vitoria's *ius communicationis* as a precursor to the modern doctrine of the liberal 'free flow of information', a doctrine criticized for promoting 'digital colonialism' through the economic dominance of Silicon Valley's platform economy and the intrusive reach of the US 'cyber-industrial complex'. Schmitt, in turn, has been cited as an intellectual foundation for efforts to counter such 'digital colonialism' by establishing 'digital sovereignty'. In this regard, Thumfart notes, the authoritarian Schmitt holds particular relevance for powers such as China and Russia; Russia's Eurasianist ideologues, in particular, appear to be strongly influenced by Schmittian ideas, including in the digital sphere. Even within the EU, whose goal of achieving *souveraineté numérique* entails a degree of economic protectionism towards US Big Tech, Schmitt is invoked as instrumental to the agenda. Schmitt's rejection of the political neutrality of technology thus acquires unexpected contemporary significance. According to Thumfart, for Schmitt, the historical process of neutralization collapses precisely when societies enter the 'technological age' and become universally technology-driven. Taken to its extreme, technology ceases to have a neutralizing effect and instead exposes the antagonistic power of the political. As a result, the liberal notion of technological neutrality breaks down, and the state is compelled to abandon the concept of neutrality, becoming instead non-neutral and radically partisan – thereby transcending the modern idea of the liberal state. To illustrate this thesis, Thumfart concludes by discussing several concrete EU policies, showing how the development of digital sovereignty reflects, in his view, a symptom of the decay of liberalism in the digital age.

2.5 *Vitoria and Schmitt in the Canon of International Law*

To conclude the book, Part 5 looks into the contemporary status of Vitoria and Schmitt in the intellectual canon and as classics of international law by offering the reader the possibility to juxtapose the analyses on the topic by, on the one hand, Paolo Amorosa and Ville Suuronen, and on the other, Ignacio de la Rasilla.

In Chapter 17, *Paolo Amorosa* and *Ville Suuronen* explore the question of 'whether we should use Schmitt in our disciplinary discourse' by examining 'Schmitt's work, focusing especially on his reading of Francisco de Vitoria and his legacy in the 20th century' in order to show how 'Vitoria emerges as one of the canonical figures' who allows Schmitt 'to rewrite the history of international law from a radically anti-liberal perspective and to whitewash his own Nazi engagement'. In particular, Amorosa and Suuronen 'argue that by criticizing the liberal appropriations of Vitoria in the 20th century', namely that of James Brown Scott, Schmitt offers a 'counter-reading of the history of European international law' inspired by 'core arguments at the heart of his own Nazi writings – in particular the idea that liberalism must be blamed for the breakdown of classical European political rationalism'. Amorosa and Suuronen further assess 'Schmitt's role in the international legal discourse of recent decades through a canonical perspective' analyzing in particular the rationales underlying the 'Schmittian revival of the 21st century' in order to 'disclose the implications of canon-making as a political phenomenon', which has large implications for the continuous reproduction of international law's disciplinary self-image.

Finally, in Chapter 18, *Ignacio de la Rasilla* examines Carl Schmitt's intellectual engagement with the work of Francisco de Vitoria in light of ten distinguishing characteristics that underlie the rise of Vitoria as a global 'classic' of international law. According to De la Rasilla, these ten features are: first, that Vitoria's work has been used as a lens to address larger historical themes; second, his position in the intellectual canon and as a landmark in the historical periodization of international law; third, Vitoria's broad interdisciplinary appeal; fourth, the fact that Vitoria has become identified as the first expounder of international legal ideas and doctrines; fifth, the multiple interpretations and reinterpretations to which Vitoria's oeuvre has been subjected; sixth, that he has been used as a shortcut in an intellectual tradition of thinking about the international; seventh, the fact that he has been turned into an intellectual symbol of cultural patriotism over time; eighth, Vitoria's in part hegemonically induced universal appeal; ninth, the more recent diachronic use to which his works have been put to contextually investigate episodes in the history of international law from the nineteenth century up to the present; and, last but not least, the semi-industrial quantity of academic commentary he has attracted over time. An analysis of the interfaces between this proposed ten-fold list of what makes a global classic of international law and Schmitt's engagement with Vitoria is further complemented by De la Rasilla with references to Schmitt's own contemporary status as a classic legal and political thinker of the twentieth century with regard to each of them. Finally, the conclusion considers the role of Western classics as transmission belts to pass on a deep intellectual disciplinary tradition, but also its embedded critiques, to incoming generations of international legal thinkers.

Bibliography

Amorosa, Paolo. Rewriting the History of the Law of Nations. How James Brown Scott Made Francisco de Vitoria the Founder of International Law (Oxford: Oxford University Press 2019).

Anghie, Antony. Imperialism, Sovereignty, and the Making of International Law (Cambridge: Cambridge University Press 2005).

Beneyto, José María. La conquista, el imperio y la paz. Vitoria y Erasmo ante Carlos V (Madrid: Cátedra 2024).

Carty, Anthony. 'Carl Schmitt's Critique of Liberal International Legal Order between 1933 and 1945'. Leiden Journal of International Law 14 (2001) 25–76.

De la Rasilla, Ignacio 'La réception intellectuelle de Francisco de Vitoria chez les juristes internationaux à travers le temps'. Revue de Synthese 147 (2025).

De la Rasilla, Ignacio. International Law and History. Modern Interfaces (Cambridge: Cambridge University Press 2021).

De la Rasilla, Ignacio. In the Shadow of Vitoria: A History of International Law in Spain 1770–1953 (Leiden: Brill Nijhoff 2017).

Fassbender, Bardo. 'Carl Schmitt', in Bardo Fassbender and Anne Peters (eds.), The Oxford Handbook of the History of International Law (Oxford: Oxford University Press 2012) 1173–1178.

Jean Paul Cojou and María Idoya Zorroza-Huarte, (eds.), Bibliografia Vitoriana (Pamplona: Universidad de Navarra 2014).

Koskenniemi, Martti 'Vitoria and Us: Thoughts on Critical Histories of International Law'. Rechtsgeschichte 22(2014), 119–138.

Koskenniemi, Martti. 'International Law as Political Theology How to Read the Nomos der erde'. Constellations 4 (2004), 492–511.

Meierhenrich, Jens and Oliver Simons (eds.), The Oxford Handbook of Carl Schmitt (Oxford: Oxford University Press 2017).

Peter Haggenmacher, 'L'itinéraire internationaliste de Carl Schmitt', in Schmitt, Carl. Le nomos de la Terre. Préface. Peter Haggenmacher. Traduction. Lilyane Deroche-Gurcel (Paris: Presses Universitaires de France 1998).

Ramírez Santos, Celia Alejandra and Jose Luis Egío García. The Research on the School of Salamanca (2008–2019). Conceptual and Multidisciplinary Bibliography. Max Planck Institute for European Legal History Research Paper Series No. 2020–09: subsidia et instrumenta. 2020, available at https://www.lhlt.mpg.de/2255762/2020-09.

Schmitt, Carl. Der Nomos der Erde im Völkerrecht des Jus Publicum Europaeum (Berlin: Duncker & Humblot 1950).

Schmitt, Carl. El Nomos de la tierra en el Derecho de Gentes del Ius publicum europeaum. trad. de Dora Schilling Thou (Madrid: Centro de Estudios Constitucionales, 1979).

Schmitt, Carl. Il nomos della terra nel diritto internazionale dello «Jus publicum europaeum». F. Volpi (Curatore) E. Castrucci (Traduttore) (Milan: Adelphi, 1991)

Schmitt, Carl. Le nomos de la Terre. Préface. Peter Haggenmacher Traduction. Lilyane Deroche-Gurcel (Paris: Presses Universitaires de France, 1998).

Schmitt, Carl. El Nomos de la tierra en el "Derecho de Gentes del Ius publicum europeaum. trad. de Dora Schilling Thou (Granada: Comares, 2002).

Schmitt, Carl. The Nomos of the Earth in the International Law of the Jus Publicum Europaeum (New York: Telos Press 2003).

Schmitt, Carl. Nomos da Terra no direito das gentes do jus publicum europaeum. Tradução: Alexandre Franco de Sá, Bernardo Ferreira, José Maria Arruda e Pedro Hermílio Villas Bôas Castelo Branco (Rio de Janeiro: Contraponto 2014).

Weiler, Joseph. 'Cancelling Schmitt', 32 European Journal of International Law 2 (2021), 393–395.

PART 1

The Reception of Vitoria and Schmitt in International Legal Thought

CHAPTER 2

Vitoria and Schmitt: Revisiting Political Theology and the Concept of *Grossraum* in the Twenty-First Century

José María Beneyto

1 Vitoria, a 'Friend–Foe' of Carl Schmitt

Francisco de Vitoria occupies a pre-eminent place in Carl Schmitt's thinking on international law. He is the author at the heart of Schmitt's seminal international law work, *The Nomos of the Earth in the International Law of the Jus Publicum Europaeum*.[1] Schmitt devotes an extensive chapter two of his book to the epochal fact of the *Landnahme* of a New World and to the main theorist of the justification of the discovery, the theologian from Salamanca. Vitoria is the initial core from which he develops his conception of the successive historical-formative phases of international law.

Although it is quite certain that Schmitt was familiar with Vitoria's work earlier, the years in which he was most interested in it coincided with the Second World War and the post-war period, from the moment when Germany's defeat became inevitable. Guided by an intention to found a theory of the 'large spaces' or *Grossräume*[2] as an alternative to American globalism, Schmitt used his interpretation of the Vitorian re-readings by James Brown Scott since the 1920s to bring out his own re-interpretation and appropriation of Vitoria as opposed to that of American hegemony and the system of the League of Nations.[3]

1 Schmitt, Carl. *The Nomos of the Earth in the International Law of the Jus Publicum Europaeum*. Translated and annotated by G.L. Ulmen (New York: Telos Press Publishing, 2003).

2 Schmitt, Carl. 'Völkerrechtliche Grossraumordnung mit Interventionsverbot für raumfremde Mächte. Ein Beitrag zum Reichsbegriff im Völkerrecht', in *Staat, Grossraum, Nomos. Arbeiten aus den Jahren 1916–1969*, ed. by Günter Maschke (Berlin: Duncker & Humblot, 1995), 269–371.

3 Brown Scott, James. *The Spanish Origin of International Law. Francico de Vitoria and his Law of Nations* (Oxford: Oxford University Press, 1934). See de la Rasilla, Ignacio. 'Francisco de Vitoria's unexpected transformations and reinterpretations for international law', *International Community Law Review* 15 (2003), 287–318; and Amorosa, Paolo. *Rewriting the History of the Law of Nations. How James Brown Scott made Francisco de Vitoria the founder of International Law* (Oxford: Oxford University Press, 2019).

 | DOI:10.1163/9789004757448_003

Schmitt's reading of Vitoria is structurally ambivalent. On the one hand, he openly rejects what he considers a misrepresentation of Vitoria in Brown Scott's internationalist liberalism. He uses this rebuke to support his own anti-liberal stance. Schmitt rejects the elements of Vitoria's thought that he considers to be precursors of liberalism, such as universalism, the repudiation of war, an anthropology based on positive sociability, and the recognition of fundamental global liberties, principles that, in Vitoria, constitute the centre of his reformulation of *ius gentium.* On the other hand, Schmitt's nostalgia for certain elements of what in recent years Martti Koskenniemi has called Vitoria's 'political theology' is palpable.[4]

Schmitt considers that Vitoria sought 'a-historical objectivity' by claiming to base his reformulation of *ius gentium* on universal human reason. Schmitt's response in *The Concept of the Political*[5] (first published in 1927 and with new revised editions in the critical years of 1932 and 1933) was to reaffirm the Hobbesian *homo homini lupus* as opposed to Vitoria's *homo homini homo.* The basis for Schmitt's definition of 'the political' as an intensity of friend–foe polarisation was a radical version of the theological distinction between bad and good, and thus a theory of absolutist power as opposed to Vitoria's idea of rational justice.

Certainly, unlike Schmitt, Vitoria adhered to the doctrine of the immediate origin of power in the community, a theory that had a long intellectual tradition in the Dominican Order.[6] He projected this notion at a global level by affirming the existence of an implicit consensus between nations that constituted the 'community of the entire globe' (*communitas totius orbis*). This universal community included principalities, peoples and individuals, not only states, the exclusive actors which for Schmitt – as well as for positivism – constituted legitimate subjects of international law.

Regarding the doctrine of just war, in several passages in *The Nomos of the Earth,* Schmitt considers that by not discriminating between Christians and barbarians or infidels, and by not acknowledging the reality of the distinction between friend and foe, Vitoria had moved close to the 'neutralising' concept of *justus hostis.*[7] Non-acceptance of the enemy as such, under the mantle of a humanitarian ideology, entailed its discrimination as an aggressor and ulti-

4 Koskenniemi, Martti. *To the Uttermost Parts of the Earth. Legal Imagination and International Power, 1300–1870* (Cambridge: Cambridge University Press, 2021) 117–211: 'The Political Theology of *Ius gentium*: The Expansion of Spain 1526–1559'.

5 Schmitt, Carl. *The Concept of the Political* (Chicago: The University of Chicago Press, 2007).

6 Tierney, Brian. *The Idea of Natural Rights: Studies on Natural Rights, Natural Law and Church Law, 1150–1625* (Grand Rapids /Cambridge: Eerdmans Publishing, 1997), 290–301.

7 Schmitt, *Nomos of the Earth,* 101–125.

mately its annihilation. Who says 'humanity' – claims Schmitt – wants to deceive. Therefore, in opposition to what Schmitt describes as the 'rationalisation' and 'humanisation' of warfare in the system of *Jus Publicum Europaeum,* Vitoria and Scott's internationalist liberalism are understood to be based on non-recognition and 'criminalisation' of the enemy. According to Schmitt, Vitoria was not responsible for the ideologised and discriminatory concept of a 'war of aggression'. However, Brown Scott's 're-appropriation' of Vitoria would have wrongly treated Vitoria's concept of *bellum justum* as a precursor of the discriminatory doctrine of war.[8] In other passages in *The Nomos of the Earth,* Schmitt, however, seems to go so far as to assimilate Brown Scott's interpretation with Vitoria's in order to argue more forcefully against both of them.

The treatment of Vitoria in *The Nomos* is nevertheless generally respectful. The professor of *Prima* de Salamanca appears as a Spanish Dominican whose *forma mentis* is driven by a need for evangelisation, and who is therefore still a believer in the idea of a *respublica christiana.* However, after defeat in the war, and after confinements and interrogations by the Russians and the Americans, and in a phase of depression,[9] Schmitt wrote the victimhood-ridden autobiographical epigrams of the *Glossarium* between 1947 and 1951.

In these writings, which constitute the esoteric version of his academic publications at the time, Schmitt constructs one of his *personae* with an additional dose of aggression and makes frequent references to Vitoria. In the *Glossarium,* through a personal confrontation with Vitoria, it is as if Schmitt wanted to embody the friend–enemy dialectic as an inescapable anthropological basis. Vitoria appears in these notes as *the enemy,* the intellectual origin of the link between the doctrine of just war and 'the beginning of the epoch of the law of nations, the epiphany of which [...] was organised in Nuremberg'.[10] The Salamanca theologian is no longer an advocate of the medieval doctrine of just war, the framework of which remained the spiritual order of Christianity, but a precursor of the total war unleashed after the end of the Eurocentric conception of international law.

In the *Glossarium,* Vitoria's *homo homini homo* appears to be the antecedent of what Schmitt considers the 'inhumanity of humanitarianism'.[11] This

8 Ibid., 122–123.

9 Schmitt, Carl. Glossarium. *Aufzeichnungen der Jahre 1947–1951* (Berlin: Duncker & Humblot, 1991), 121, annotation of 3.4.48.

10 Schmitt, Glossarium, 186 (entry of 3.8.48). Among many other direct references to Vitoria see also Schmitt's entry of 29.6.48 ('the just war is total war').

11 In his *Gespräch über die Macht und den Zugang zum Machthaber,* first published in 1954, Schmitt ironically expresses himself on the underlying dichotomy with a dialogue:

'Student: Then man is for man a man.

phrase implies not a recognition of *the other* as such, according to Schmitt, but a forceful assimilation. Paradoxically, the affirmation of equal human dignity conceals the maximal discriminatory and annihilatory capacity of the enemy. The enemy is no longer a *justus hostis* but a criminal offender. And Father Vitoria, who was unable to answer the question, 'What happens if both sides consider themselves to have just cause?' turns out to be unable to formally respect the enemy and is even portrayed as an intellectual origin of the destruction of *Deutschland* embodied in the tragedy of *jus publicum europaeum.*

Human anthropology, according to the Schmitt of *Glossarium*, demands a radical political theology which does not admit the medieval remnants of Vitorian thought. Vitoria is inadequate as a fully modern thinker, unsuited to accepting wars of religion and their 'neutralisation' by means of *jus publicum europaeum* and the formal balance of statehood.

What unites both views – the more moderate one of the *Nomos* and the polemical one of the *Glossarium* – in Schmitt's critique is that Vitoria is never a sufficiently 'concrete' and 'political' thinker. Vitoria does not fully belong to the modernity of Hobbes or Bodin. In his thought, neither acceptance of full secularisation nor the advance towards full politicisation that gives rise to the polarising friend–enemy dialectic exists. The political, according to Schmitt, does not admit the 'undecided' equilibrium of Vitoria's thought.

2 The Indeterminacy of Law and Political Theology

It is possible to reconstruct the path to Schmitt's political theology through the evolution of his work. Schmitt develops this concept in the context of his legal decisionism, the theory of 'the political' as a friend–enemy dialectic, and his philosophy of history.

Schmitt's rejection of practical rationality and the possibility of rational justice had its origins very early on in his work. In *Statute and Judgment. An Examination of the Problem of Judicial Praxis*, the published version of his doctoral dissertation of 1912, Schmitt emerges as a strong critic of legal positivism stressing in particular the impossibility of establishing a system of sub-

---

Carl Schmitt: So it is. Certainly always in a very concrete way. This means, for example: the man Stalin is for the man Trotsky a Stalin and the man Trotsky is for the man Stalin a Trostsky'. *Conclusion*, in: Schmitt, Carl, *Dialogues on Power and Space*, ed. by Andreas Kalyvas and Federico Finchelstein, Polity, 2015.

sumption of the concrete case in law without taking into account elements external to the system, such as analogy and the *a contrario* argument.[12]

Seeking a way out of the conundrum of legal interpretation, Schmitt turned to the legal-sociological foundations of law and arrived at a first conclusion in his analysis by observing that judicial decisions are influenced not only by norms but also by many other elements, such as the dominant 'legal conscience' and, above all, by state sanction. The predictability of judicial decisions, therefore, depends as much on the state system as on judicial praxis itself, and Schmitt consequently proposed an application of the sociological-functional method of interpretation.

However, already in this, his first academic publication, Schmitt reduced the legal argumentative process of interpretation to the moment of decision. Ultimately relevant for Schmitt is not what the individual judge considers to be correct, or his normative arguments or psychological or sociological presuppositions, but the decision as such. Schmitt's critique of the positivism of his time finally leads to a radical separation between law and state. Law is what the judge 'creates' with the judicial decision, the legitimacy of which is dependent on the state system as a whole.

Following this emphasis on the autonomous nature of the decision, Schmitt's 1914 habilitation thesis, *The Value of the State and the Significance of the Individual*,[13] analyses the relationship between power and law, resulting in an affirmation of the incompatibility of the two realities. While law belongs to the sphere of norms and so enjoys autonomy from the factual, power is a product of will. Intermediation between power, on the one hand, and the individual, on the other, takes place through the state. Thus, Schmitt, by assimilating power with the state, and despite his attempted critique of positivism, places the state at the centre of his legal theory, as the main instrument for the creation of law.

In Schmitt's 1918 *Political Romanticism*,[14] the primacy of the decision is then spun as the driving thread through the philosophical-cultural origins of mod-

12 Schmitt, Carl. *Gesetz und Urteil. Eine Untersuchung zum Problem der Rechtspraxis* (Berlin: Duncker & Humblot, 2nd. ed., 1969), 26. I analyse the evolution of Schmitt's thinking in more detail in Beneyto, José María. *Politische Theologie als politische Theorie. Eine Untersuchung zur Rechts – und Staatstheorie Carl Schmitts und zu ihrer Wirkungsgeschcihte in Spanien* (Berlin: Duncker & Humblot, 1983), 62–110.

13 Schmitt, Carl. *Der Wert des Staates und die Bedeutung des Einzelnen* (Berlin: Duncker & Humblot, 3rd. ed. 2015). This book and *Gesetz und Urteil* have recently been edited and translated into English by Lars Vinx and Samuel Garrett Zeitlin, in *Carl Schmitt's Early Legal-Theoretical Writings* (Oxford: Oxford University Press, 2021).

14 Schmitt, Carl. *Politische Romantik* (Berlin/Leipzig: Duncker & Humblot, 2nd. edit., 1925). Translated by Guy Oakes as *Political Romanticism* (Cambridge/ MA: The MIT Press, 1986).

ern subjectivity and its ultimate political consequence from Schmitt's perspective, the theory of dictatorship.

This book was the intellectual result of Schmitt's personal experiences in the German army during the First World War and the Bavarian Revolution of 1918–19, from which followed a rejection of the Munich bohemian and expressionist milieus to which he had been strongly attracted in the years before the war. The analytical primacy of decision is transferred in this work to the much broader outlook of political philosophy and the philosophy of history, leading Schmitt to a categorical radicalisation.

Schmitt's amalgam of state, law, power, decision, and reality forced him subsequently to search for new sources of legitimacy. After *Political Romanticism,* decision in its pure form becomes a political category, the dictate of the sovereign. Schmitt constructs the decision of the sovereign, using expressionist emphasis, as a self-founding instance, from which both legitimacy and legality emanate. In a historically biased analysis of the commissarial dictatorship in Rome, Schmitt stylises the decision of the sovereign dictator as 'supra-rationality', which, far from destroying the norm, creates it from the 'zero point' of pre-normativity. As an instance of the creation and application of law, the dictator acts 'within legality'. Law, therefore, emerges from pure power, from the vacuum prior to the creation of the norm. Ultimately, the formal justification of the dictator derives from his capacity, as the highest authority, to suspend the 'normality' of the legal norm, that is, to authorise the state of exception. At the time of the rise of fascism and authoritarian regimes in Europe in the 1920s, Schmitt will have sought to ground the latency of dictatorship behind the norm.

The dialectic between normativity and exceptionality, between law and power, law and decision, in the following step, leads to the question of the highest legal authority and legitimacy, of the supreme *quis judicabit.* Who is the Sovereign? The answer to this question made Schmitt a classic of political theory in the twentieth century: '*Souverän ist, wer über den Ausnahmezustand entscheidet*'[15] – 'Sovereign is he who decides on the state of emergency'. The *political order* must first be established so that the *legal order* can then be inserted into it. The sovereign, as an instance of legitimacy, constitutes and guarantees legality.

Schmitt's objective in his *Political Theology* of 1922 was, then, to grant the decision an ontological quality and, following Hobbes, to overcome the sepa-

---

15 This phrase opens the main work of Schmitt's early phase, *Politische Theologie. Vier Kapitel zur Lehre von der Souveranität* (Munich/Leipzig: Duncker & Humblot, 2nd ed., 1934). Translated into English and with an introduction by George Schwab, with a new

ration between spiritual and state authority, making the former subordinate to the latter.

In this way, Schmitt laid the foundations for the political utilisation of theology and the spiritual realm that made it possible for him to project the maximum level of intensity into decisions and later to derive from this maximum intensity the friend–enemy confrontation.

Schmitt's political theology therefore rests on the non-differentiation between the two 'substances', the political and the theological. It is basically a political use of theological concepts and institutions in order to re-create the model of Hobbesian political-theological absolutism from a Hegelian perspective.

In order to achieve this maximum intensity and friend–enemy dissociation, Schmitt proceeded to eliminate the distinction between the natural and supernatural orders and their link through the *analogia entis* (analogy of beings), which in Vitoria constituted the metaphysical foundation of the bond between natural law and *ius gentium*. From this, Schmitt developed an anti-modern philosophy of history, reducing theology to metaphysics, metaphysics to sociology and finally sociology, to 'the political'. He followed the Hegelian and Comtian schema that the theorists of the counter-revolution, such as De Maistre and De Bonald in France and Donoso Cortés in Spain, had developed in the nineteenth century to lay the foundations of a traditionalist theory of dictatorship.[16]

In particular, Donoso Cortés's evolution from the liberalism of his youth to the anti-parliamentarism and apocalyptic exaltation of dictatorship as a 'decision legitimised from above' in his later years would serve Schmitt to invert the notion of 'analogy' and establish 'structural correlations' between the *theological* world of pre-modernity and the *political* world of modernity. Donoso Cortés established the paradigm of this type of correlation by contrasting the idea of the miracle in the theological sphere with the exception in the juridical-political sphere. Following Donoso Cortés, Schmitt ended up affirming that 'all the main concepts of modern state theory are secularised theological concepts'. The pre-modern world is, therefore, according to Schmitt, one dominated by theology, while modernity defines itself through secularisation and the loss of spiritual substance, in a process of 'neutralisations', a term by which

---

foreword by Tracy B. Strong, *Political Theology. Four Chapters on the Concept of Sovereignty* (Chicago: The University of Chicago Press, 2006).

16 On Donoso Cortés and his radical critique of modernity, see Beneyto, José María. *Apokalypse der Moderne. Die Diktaturtheorie von Donoso Cortés* (Klett-Cotta: Stuttgart, 1988).

Schmitt means the progressive erosion of the absolute power of the state by modern reason and liberalism.

These rather abstract ideas were, in the following decades, transposed by Schmitt into an analysis of the Westphalian system of states and their later replacement by American hegemonic globalism. The subjugation of spiritual power to political power in absolutism would be able to guarantee peace in the state and a balance of power in inter-state relations, thanks to *jus publicum europaeum,* thus bringing to an end the cruel and interminable wars of religion. 'Neutralisation', in the political mythology developed by Schmitt, had decisive consequences for political theory and international law. During the period when the *Nomos* of *ius publicum europaeum* was in force, the unlimited violence of power could be, to a certain extent, 'restrained' (*bändigt*), making possible a 'bracketing' (*Hegung*) of warfare. This balance would be subsequently dismantled by the British domination of the seas, and in the twentieth century by the emergence of American global universalism and its transformation of space.

The doctrine of internationalist liberalism would introduce, according to Schmitt, a new conception of humanity, civilisation and progress, which were no longer European and did not correspond to a European civilisation.[17] This implied the dissolution of the spatial order created by Eurocentric international law.

American globalism was preceded, according to this narrative, by the fact that the belief in the civilising task of Europeans had become a mere façade, at the latest with the Congo Conference of 1878 and its advocacy of the principle of 'effective occupation' as the legal term for territorial appropriation. Instead of clear spheres of influence based on legally defined territorial boundaries, the colonial divisions of the late nineteenth century were nothing more than the expression of a confused hodgepodge of interests dominated by tendentially global economic ambitions that would erode the old order of the European *Nomos.*[18] In the inter-war period, the Briand–Kellogg Pact, with its condemnation of war and the criminalisation of wars of aggression, completed, for Schmitt, the transformation of the law of nations. Quite telling for Schmitt, the introduction by international liberalism (exemplified by James Brown Scott) of a 'discriminatory concept' of war meant a return to the Christian doctrine of just war, i.e., to Vitoria. 'But' – in the words of Schmitt – 'modern trends do not resurrect Christian doctrines'.[19]

17 Schmitt, *Nomos of the Earth*, 227–228.
18 Ibid., 226.
19 Ibid., 321.

The serious shortcomings of Schmitt's historical interpretation, his lack of attention to empirical and sociological details, and the absence of well-founded historiographical analysis have been pointed out by various authors in recent years, for example, Benno Teschke and Thomas Duve.[20]

3 Fleeing Berlin and Positing against American Hegemony

From a biographical perspective, Schmitt's progressive interest in Vitoria was spurred during the journeys he made to Franco's Spain to deliver various lectures in the first half of the 1940s. Schmitt sought to keep a distance from the increasingly occlusive atmosphere in Berlin. After having fallen out of favour with the Nazis, he observed that a growing number of his closer circle took positions opposed to the regime that were increasingly dangerous for his own security. Despite his close friendship with Johannes Poppitz and Ernst Jünger, Schmitt certainly did not share the decision of Poppitz, still Hermann Göring's Finance Minister, or that of Jünger, a staff officer stationed in the German General Headquarter in occupied Paris, to collaborate with the opposition groups, which crystallised in various attempts against Hitler, including that by Stauffenberg. It seems possible that, on the contrary, he sought a way out to Spain if the situation became untenable for him personally.[21]

In April 1941, Antonio de Luna, professor of international law at the University of Granada and co-founder and director of the Francisco de Vitoria Institute in Madrid, sent Schmitt a copy of the new publication of Vitoria's *Relections* edited by Luis Alonso Getino. Schmitt's first visit to Spain took place two years later, between 28 May and 11 June 1943. On a second visit, in the same months before the summer pause of the following year, 1944, he gave three lectures with different titles in various cities in Spain and Portugal: Madrid, Coimbra, Lisbon, Granada, and Barcelona.

It was on this second trip that he delivered the lecture, most of which he would transcribe into *The Nomos of the Earth* and which would also appear as

20 Teschke, Benno. 'Carl Schmitt's Concepts of War: A Categorical Failure', in Jens Meierhenrich and Oliver Simons (eds.), *The Oxford Handbook of Carl Schmitt* (Oxford: Oxford University Press, 2016), 367–400; Duve, Thomas, 'Spatial Perceptions, Juridical Practices, and Early International Legal Thought around 1500: From Tordesillas to Saragossa', in Stefan Kadelbach, Thomas Kleinlein and David Roth-Isigkeit (eds.), *System, Order, and International Law: The Early History of International Law from Machiavelli to Hegel*, (Oxford: Oxford University Press, 2017), 418–442.

21 Mehring, Reinhard. *Carl Schmitt. Aufstieg und Fall. Eine Biographie* (Munich: C.H. Beck, 2009) 488.

a monograph entitled *Francisco de Vitoria and the History of His Fame.*[22] On that same visit, on the occasion of a conference in Granada, he met the Romanist Álvaro d'Ors, who was to become an intellectual companion, both in reaffirming his criticism of Vitoria's 'secularising' universalism and in rejecting the alleged 'manipulation' carried out by Brown Scott and the liberal interpretation of Vitoria.[23]

From 1944 onwards, through Álvaro d'Ors and his successive journeys to Santiago de Compostela, Schmitt came into contact with the work of the international law professor at the University of Santiago Camilo Barcia Trelles. From him he took three essential ideas for his theory of international law and the plea for a *new order* based on a post-Westphalian balance of the great powers endowed with their own spheres of influence.[24]

From Barcia Trelles, Schmitt took the vision of the confrontation between sea and land for the construction of a historical-political mythology, a paradigm of which was the struggle in modern history between the Anglo-Saxon thalassocracies and the European central powers, the political and legal concepts of which were grounded on territoriality of the European Axis powers, and in particular of Germany.

The writings of Barcia Trelles on the dominion of the seas as the origin of modern imperialism led Schmitt to develop his theory of space (*Raum*) as the foundation of international law linked to the idea of a *Nomos* of the earth. If Barcia made a clear distinction between, on the one hand, the structure and nature of the discovery and colonisation of the New World in the sixteenth century and its annexation as a dominion subject to the Spanish Crown, and, on the other hand, later imperialism, Schmitt used this distinction when writing about the right of colonial occupation and its consecration at the Berlin Colonial Conference of 1884–85.[25]

Schmitt's conception of 'Great spaces with a prohibition on intervention by third countries' is uniquely indebted to Barcia Trelles and his interpretation of the Monroe Doctrine. Schmitt, after making direct references to Barcia's work, follows him in detail in his arguments in *The Nomos of the Earth* by emphasis-

22 Schmitt, Carl. 'Francisco de Vitoria und die Geschichte seines Ruhmes', *Die Neue Ordnung. Zeitschrift für Religion, Kultur, Gesellschaft* 4 (1946), 289–313. Most of this text was incorporated in *The Nomos of the Earth.*

23 See the correspondence between Schmitt and Alvaro d'Ors, in Herrero, Montserrat (ed.). *Carl Schmitt and Álvaro d'Ors Briefwechsel* (Berlin: Duncker & Humblot, 2004).

24 Beneyto, José María. 'Camilo Barcia Trelles on Francisco de Vitoria: At the Crossroads of Carl Schmitt's *Grossraum* and James Brown Scott's "Modern International Law"', *European Journal of International Law* 31 (4) (2020), 1477–1492.

25 Schmitt, *Nomos of the Earth*, 38, 214.

ing that the United States used the Monroe Doctrine in an ambiguous way to justify American imperialism.

In his writings of the 1920s and 1930s, Barcia Trelles frequently expressed the view that the Monroe Doctrine had been enunciated to oppose threats of intervention by European powers in the Americas, but that its terms were subsequently reversed with the opposite aim of justifying US interventions in Central and South America, and later in the rest of the world, thus forming the doctrinal backbone of new American imperialist theory. The first and most successful application of the *Grossräume* theory in international law, Schmitt argued, was precisely the Monroe Doctrine, which was designed to act 'spatially globally in a modern sense'. If Vitoria had been the first global international law thinker, the new globalism of American imperialism transformed Vitoria's universalism into a doctrine of imperial hegemony.

4 'Vitoria and Us': International Law as the History of 'Legal Imagination'?

While classical interpretations of Vitoria's work since the sixteenth century have, for the most part, been highly laudatory, if not outright hagiographic, in recent decades post-colonial literature has emphasised the supposed dark side of his thought. In what may amount to an ambitious 'grand narrative' that stretches the vision of the ideological origins of international law, the hesitations and question marks, in short, Vitoria's cautious late-scholastic and sometimes deliberately ambiguous tone has cast suspicion on him as an apologist for empire.[26]

The 'historiographical turn' in international law in recent decades has undoubtedly had the necessary effect of raising the critical and theoretical level of a discipline heavily burdened by formalism and subordinated to practical and technical decisions. The work carried out in this sense by the main protagonists of *Critical Legal Studies*, Martti Koskenniemi and David Kennedy, has brought a breath of fresh air to the discipline.[27] However, as Nehal Butha

26 Anghie, Anthony. *Imperialism, Sovereignty and the Making of International Law* (Cambridge: Cambridge University Press 2004). See the discussion in Fitzmaurice, Andrew. 'The Problem of Eurocentrism in the Thought of Francisco de Vitoria' in José María Beneyto and Justo Corti Varela (eds.), *At the origins of modernity. Francisco de Vitoria and the Discovery of International Law* (Springer International Publishing 2017), 77–94.

27 See in this regard, Beneyto, José María and Kennedy, David (eds.). *New Approaches to International Law. The European and the American Experiences* (TMC Asser Press/Springer: The Hague, 2012).

has put it, do we speak of international law mainly as 'a language' and 'a legal imagination'? Should international law focus primarily on the critical analysis of power?[28]

It might well be that the challenge, at this point, would not be sufficiently addressed by relying merely on a critical attitude, but by suggesting ways that can be constructive in view of the transformation of the international (dis-) order that we are witnessing. In this sense, the programmatic statement 'Vitoria and Us' should imply re-reading Vitoria while trying to separate his thought from the history of his reception. At the origin of his keen interest in Vitoria, Koskenniemi considered that the Dominican could be of some use in the 'gently civilising' task[29] which continues to be reserved for international law in our current historical-political situation.

In this regard, it is very relevant that Jürgen Habermas, in his last major work, again drew attention to the fact that, beyond doubts about the justification of the colonial enterprise in the Americas, the question of whether international conflicts could be settled according to general standards – and not just on Christianity-grounded ones – became central to Vitoria. The discovery of a New World brought to the consciousness of Europeans a clear vision that its territory was only a province in the totality of a global community of nations.[30]

Until Vitoria, natural law was subordinate to divine law. Its content might well be autonomously apprehended, but only when embedded in the Christian ethic did natural law obtain its absolute obligatory character.

Francisco de Vitoria was one of the first to reflect on the limits of this perspective. It is the situation that arises when old empires or kingdoms see themselves as the universe and therefore consider that the rules that are justified for their citizens should also apply to all other people. This way of thinking, which had prevailed up to the time of the discoveries, was then called into question. Vitoria was indeed a pioneer in the search for new legal foundations beyond the limits of the *respublica christiana*.

Without calling natural law into question, Vitoria's intention was to find a principle based on human rationality that was sufficiently abstract and common enough to be extended to infidels as well. On the basis of natural law, he

---

28 Butha, Nehal. 'Let us suppose that universals do not exist: *Bricoleur* and *Bricolage* in Martti Koskenniemi's, *To the Uttermost Parts of the Earth*', *European Journal of International Law* 22 (3) (2021), 943–948.

29 Koskenniemi, Martti. *The Gentle Civilizer of Nations. The Rise and Fall of International Law 1870–1960* (Cambridge: Cambridge University Press, 2001). Among the many publications by Koskenniemi on Vitoria, see 'Vitoria and Us. Thoughts on Critical Histories of International Law', *Rechtsgeschichte. Legal History* 22 (2014), 119–138.

30 Habermas, Jürgen. *Auch eine Geschichte der Philosophie. Die okzidentale Konstellation von Glauben und Wissen*, vol 1 (Berlin: Suhrkhamp, 2nd ed., 2020), 908–918.

developed universal liberties that could be used to critically treat the relationship with non-Christian peoples and principalities. In doing so, he relied on an idea that had been developed in Stoic philosophy. Over and above national borders and cultures there was a basic consensus, norms which derived from the community of the orb and which imposed themselves by their own force of law.

Vitoria was undoubtedly far more original and daring in the questions he asked and in his confrontation with the emperor's claim to be the 'Lord of the Universe' than in the practical consequences he adopted. From our historical perspective he did not escape a complacent view of colonial exploitation. He maintained a naïve attitude towards the characteristics of early commercial capitalism and displayed a remarkable pragmatism about the reality of the conquests, having been highly critical of the abuses of colonisers, as were other missionaries. However, unlike other intellectuals of his time, such as the humanist Sepúlveda, he strongly defended the dignity of indigenous people and their capacity for self-government, even if he did not manage to completely detach himself from the view of the time that they were 'barbarians'. His analysis of justifications for conquest is nevertheless acerbic, as was his relativisation of the existing legal system in favour of the establishment of common standards. The central point of his system was a revision of the concept of *dominium*, with which he succeeded in establishing a link between natural law and positive law.

The concept of *dominium* forms a bridge between Ockham's specific case of *ius utendi* and the more generalised concept of a 'subjective right', without Vitoria ever assuming Ockham's political connotation. Although Vitoria advances the modern concept of *dominium sui et rerum* as an autonomous capacity to act which is sanctioned by state power, and introduces the difference between a private and a public dominium, he interprets liberties as constitutive of the community, i.e., as both individual and subjective, political and organic.

Schmitt was alien to Victoria's construction of justice and liberties grounded in natural law. Although the jurist of *The Nomos of the Earth* remained very attentive to the revival of Vitoria that Barcia Trelles had been leading since the 1920s, his intention was most notably guided by the critical intention to construct an alternative to American liberal internationalism. On quite a number of points, his interpretation of Vitoria was not supported by texts, and on occasions was explicitly contrary to them. This is also the case, more generally, of historical reconstructions carried out in other writings such as *Land and Sea*.[31]

This happens, for example, in the case of the inaccurate assertion that Vitoria described Jews and Muslims as *hostes perpetui* – 'perpetual enemies'. It is also true of Schmitt's contestation that Vitoria must be understood in his concrete political and institutional situation, which implied that his thought was fully subordinate to the mandate to evangelise infidels. According to Schmitt, the aim that subjectively coloured the whole of Vitoria's argumentation was to respond to the dictate of the pope's commission to the Order of Preachers, which therefore constituted in Vitoria's line of argument, the *central* justification of the conquest.

Vitoria undoubtedly defended the freedom to propagate the Christian faith and maintained that denial of this right could be answered with war, but this justification – which was clearly not the main one for him – did not subordinate his theory of *ius gentium* to fulfilment of a papal mandate and neither did it set the conversion of infidels as the all-encompassing aim of his re-working of *ius gentium.* Quite the contrary, a refusal to recognise the universal power of the pope and the emperor and a stern attitude against forced conversions defined Vitoria's position, not only theologically but also juridically. The consequences of rejecting the emperor's universal power were quickly felt. Charles ordered Vitoria's superiors to suppress any further comment by the friars on this matter under threat of punishment.

Paradoxically enough, both Schmitt and Koskenniemi are particularly interested in showing that Vitoria was, above all, a theologian and a friar, not a jurist. The argumentation of the professor of *Prima* of Salamanca, therefore, responded to his institutional enclave and the spiritual objective he was pursuing. Vitoria's doctrines were subordinated to his function as a priest and Dominican, that is, to preaching, the confession of sins, and the moral guidance of the faithful.[32] The political-theological edifice that Vitoria helped to build in his time was principally aimed at responding to the moral questions

---

31 See Schmitt, Carl. *Land and Sea: A World-Historical Meditation* (New York, Telos Press Publishing, 2015); critically, Benton, Lauren. *A Search for Sovereignty: Law and Geography in European Empires, 1400–1900* (Cambridge: Cambridge University Press, 2009); and on the construct of *Jus Publicum Europaeum,* von Bogdandy, Armin and Hinghofer-Szalkay, Stephan. 'Das etwas unheimliche Ius Publicum Europaeum: Begrifsgechichtliche Analysen im Spannungsfeld von europäischen Rechtsraum, droit public de l'Europe und Carl Schmitt', *Zeitschrift für ausländisches öffentliches Recht und Völkerrecht* (*ZaöRV*) 73/2 (2013), 209–248.

32 Schmitt, *Nomos of the Earth,* 110.

raised by the American conquests and the emergence of a new social class of merchants linked to trade.[33]

In the case of Schmitt, this argument is crucial precisely because he wanted to oppose the figure of the 'ecclesiastical theologian' to that of the 'state jurist', two characters which belonged to very different institutional and historical-concrete situations. On the one hand the modern Alberico Gentili, with his claim of 'silence of theologians on matters alien to them' (*Silete theologi in munere alieno!*), and on the other the traditional all-embracing task that Vitoria entrusted to theology. This contraposition was essential for Schmitt in order to make the transition from the medieval theological world to secularised state-centred modernity, as this constitutes the original historical model for his historical dialectic.

For his part, Koskenniemi, by examining the confessional manuals of Vitoria's contemporaries, such as Martín Azpilicueta and Diego de Covarrubias, together with Vitoria's own *Confessional*,[34] leads his readers to contemplate the internal forum at the heart of the process of *juridification of morality* and *moralisation of law* that Koskenniemi identifies with what he considers to be Vitoria's 'political theology'. Therefore, Vitoria's contributions are not juridical principles based on the indissoluble link between *jus naturale* and *jus gentium*, but 'casuistic' answers marked by the probabilism and indeterminacy of the responses given by Spanish theologians and confessors to the doubts of conscience raised by the economic, legal, and political questions of his time.[35]

For Koskenniemi, therefore, in Vitoria there is no law but mere moral casuistry, which, seen through the lens of the analysis of the political theology of Spanish imperial expansion between 1526 and 1592 that he undertakes, concludes with the affirmation that Vitoria's *ius gentium* is, above all, a catalyst of proto-capitalist extraction.

It is, however, doubtful whether this construction does justice to Vitoria's dichotomous conception of *ius naturale-ius gentium*, which allows him to reason as both a theologian and a jurist. On the one hand, according to Vitoria, natural law, thanks to its eternal origin, governs both the Church and the state, in addition to the various peoples of the earth. But the seminal contribution of the Salamanca professor to a universalist conception lay precisely in the non-separation of the principles of natural law from their concretisation through *ius gentium*, thus taking advantage of the flexibility provided by an idea of

33 Koskenniemi, *To the Uttermost Parts of the World*, 181–198.

34 Ibid., 119, 123–130.

35 Ibid., 210.

justice rooted in practical reason. This intellectual achievement substantially influenced the entire history of international law.

5 A New Interpretation of *ius gentium*: The Right to Communicate as the Constitutive Foundation of a Global World

As Vitoria's closest collaborator and disciple Domingo de Soto formulated it, *ius gentium* was not a simple act of will and neither did it merely consist of self-evident principles of natural law reflecting our natural inclinations. The human tendency to realise divine plans was embodied in first principles. However, it was practical reason that was called upon to execute, in every situation, the precise determination of what right was. In this way, the eternal principles of natural law became historical and concrete, and the natural bindingness of law was based on its rationality.

The decisions of princes and the positive law of nations were integrated into a greater moral dimension that depended directly on natural law. Rationality, together with the idea of justice as a social virtue that oriented the law and directed it towards the good, represented for Vitoria and the theologian-jurists of the School of Salamanca an objective dimension capable of tempering the voluntarism of kings and rulers, and at the same time guaranteeing a basis for imagining novel solutions to completely new problems. Vitoria's *ius gentium* was therefore – as Luigi Nuzzo argues – neither pure reason nor pure will, but a process of normative elaboration that combined ethics with new ways of organising power and ensuring the common good of the *respublica*.[36]

Vitoria made the law of nations a positive law that was established on the basis of rationality. This new body of law had a mixed nature, positive and ideal. As an embodiment of natural law, *ius gentium* was common to all mankind and could be recognised by reason, even if it had not been created by the deliberate will of any human legislator.

Vitoria established a theoretical framework that allowed a progressively secular perspective linking the recognition of rights with human rationality.

The unity of Christendom and the unity of humanity were the interrelated foundations on which Vitoria's theory of *ius gentium* was based. These two dimensions were not seen as opposites but as ideas that belonged to each other, so that the re-conceptualisation of *respublica christiana* in the context

36 Nuzzo, Luigi. '"The Law That Wasn't There." Chapter 2: The Political Theology of *Ius Gentium* – The Expansion of Spain 1524–1559', *European Journal of International Law* 32 (3) (2021), 957–964.

of the discovery of the Amerindian cultures and peoples was not opposed to the vision of an orb governed by *ius gentium* but supported it. One dimension was unthinkable without the other. That is to say, the fundamental liberties of the human being that Vitoria associated with *ius gentium* – freedom of communication, freedom of entry and movement, freedom of emigration, freedom of trade, enjoyment of the commons, occupation of uncultivated lands, and free taking of *res derelictae* – were as much the foundation of a just order as the *communitas totius orbis* was the foundation of these fundamental rights.

Vitoria's main concern was to re-imagine a just order (i.e., subject to the *bonum communis*) that would respond to the diversity of different peoples, and in which the ideas of sociability and commutative justice in relation to the basic freedoms of communication and the limitation of war would be more relevant than individual freedom in its modern sense.

Vitoria no longer thought in terms of a *respublica christiana* but of a *communitas totius orbis* that both presupposes and articulates consensus: '*Orbis qui aliquomodo est una respublica*'. For Vitoria, the undivided orb of an interconnected world ontologically and juridically precedes one divided into local kingdoms.

For the Salamanca professor, the law of nations is a law created by an implicit world pact that is capable of clothing this set of rules with a power so superior to that of its origin as to endow it with binding force, a power that derives from natural law but which at the same time possesses autonomy. 'The law of nations' – Vitoria wrote in the famous text of his *De Potestate Civilis*[37] – 'not only has force by virtue of a pact or agreement between men, but also has the force of law [*vim legis*]. In fact, the whole orb, which in a certain sense constitutes a single republic, has the power to promulgate just and convenient laws for all, such as those of the law of nations […] It is not licit for a particular kingdom not to wish to abide by the law of nations, since *it has been promulgated by the authority of the whole world*'.

There is therefore a kind of ontological and legal priority of the world pact that forms the *respublica totius orbis* over individual nations. Certainly, the implicit consent of republics is the basis of the rules that underpin the international order, and therefore there is a dependence of the law of nations on republics. But the hypothetical consent of the greater part of the world has a stronger position than the particular laws of each nation because it aims to

37 Vitoria, Francisco de. 'On Civil Power', *Vitoria Political Writings,* trans. and ed. by Anthony Pagden and Jeremy Lawrance (Cambridge: Cambridge University Press, 1991), 40 (emphasis added).

protect that totality which, insofar as it is composed of individual beings, constitutes humanity before any nation does.[38]

The influence of late medieval nominalism made it possible for the Salamancans to rediscover the subjective dimension of *dominium sui* as the necessary premise for the exercise of *dominium rerum externarum* and, therefore, to conceive a new anthropology founded on exchange and communication.

Quite the contrary, Schmitt's aim was to establish a radical differentiation between the medieval *respublica christiana* and the *jus publicum europaeum* of territorialised sovereign states. The aim was to use the mythology of the *Nomos* as a specifically European construct that confronted a universalist conception in which Europe ceased to be the governing centre of the world.

Vitoria's roots in the European *respublica christiana* did not prevent reconception of it by means of a universalism that ultimately favoured hybridisation between cultures that restricted the violence of colonial imposition. As Anthony Pagden showed years ago, the American conquest brought about an inter-culturalisation that has been considered to be the origin of modern anthropology.[39]

In other words, as Nuzzo has pointed out, the *encomienda* and the strange text of the *requerimiento* were also gateways to other forms of 'legal imagination' that are not exclusively confined to the brutal exploitation of natives subjected to the 'protection' of an *encomendero*, or to the official document that had to be read to the natives before carrying out acts of violence against them to inform them of the existence of the pope, the kings of Spain, and the possibility of their inclusion in the *respublica christiana*.

In the specific context of the discovery of America (and also of an *encounter* between the two worlds), the progress of human relations – what Vitoria called the 'expansion of human sociability' – and the interrelations between institutions and political communities were not only regulated by norms. On the contrary, they still obeyed ethical, moral and religious concepts, such as grace, love, and friendship, which appear as categories that structure and order reality, 'even in exotic locations such as the West Indies'.[40]

In Vitoria, there is no autonomous 'spatial order' that is self-enclosed, that protects itself by prohibiting outside intervention, and declares all outsiders to

38 Beneyto, José María. 'Conquest, Empire, and Peace: Vitoria, Charles v, Erasmus and the Foundations of the Law of Nations', in José María Beneyto (ed.), *Empire, Humanism and Rights. Collected Essays on Francisco de Vitoria* (Cham: Springer Nature, 2022), 1–48, 7.

39 Pagden, Anthony. *The Fall of Natural Man: The American Indians and the Origins of Comparative Ethnology* (Cambridge University Press, Cambridge, 2nd. ed., 1986).

40 Nuzzo, 'The Law That Wasn't There', 961.

be permanent enemies (*hostes perpetui*), as there is in Schmitt. Before the emergence of nations, for Vitoria, there existed a *bond* among mankind established by common human rationality and sociability, from which the specific liberties of individuals are derived.

If it was no longer possible, in the historical context of the expansion of the first modern European states, to have recourse to the authority of the pope or the emperor as *dominus mundi* according to the medieval conception, this could not mean abandoning all order. The *ius gentium*, which in the Middle Ages had possessed the vague contours of a sort of *lex mercatoria* for specific groups or activities (merchants and traders, shipping, etc.), was reactivated as a tool to establish a legal basis for the new reality of (different) individuals and peoples endowed with the same rationality.

Therefore, in Vitoria's formulation, the law of nations had various functions. It was not merely a metaphor but an actual regulating instance of the *totius orbis,* which implied that there could be no legal distinction between Christians and non-Christians. Vitoria's *respublica totius orbis* was intended to overcome the medieval distinction between jurisdiction internal to European Christendom and in relation to the non-Christian territory of the barbarians. The force of law that governed the positive-ideal world of the *respublica totius orbis* was to apply equally to all peoples everywhere. American Indians could not be deprived of their property, their lands (their private domain), or their sovereignty (their public domain) merely because they were pagans. Dominion was an inalienable right derived from natural law, not from grace or spiritual order, and therefore it applied to all peoples regardless of their religious beliefs.[41]

In fact, *dominium,* understood as private property or private appropriation, as Koskenniemi argues, was not the central axis of Vitoria's theory of liberties, but rather *ius communicationis.* Vitoria expanded the idea of hospitality and the concept of natural human sociability of Aristotle and Thomas Aquinas (the *appetitus societatis,* according to the formulation of the latter) into a 'right of natural association and communication' (*ius naturalis societas et communicationis*), which operates not only as the anthropological but also the material and ontological foundation of international political cooperation. As a derivation of both natural law and the law of nations, *ius communicationis*

41 See Pagden, Anthony. 'Introduction: Francisco de Vitoria and the Origins of the Modern Global Order', in José María Beneyto and Justo Corti Varela (eds.), *At the Origins of Modernity. Francisco de Vitoria and the Discovery of International Law* (Springer Nature, Cham, 2017), 1–20, 6.

functions historically in existing social orders, renewing them and adapting them to historical reality according to the regulatory idea of rational justice.

From the way Vitoria defined it, *ius communicationis* seems to have been an original creation of his, and he considered it to be the central argument for legitimisation of the conquest. For the Dominican of San Esteban in Salamanca, *ius communicationis* described a necessary condition of humanity. As Pagden has stressed, 'the fact that such communication was also perceived as a means of civilising the barbarians in no way altered its position as a right'.[42]

'Right of communication' meant many things to Vitoria in addition to free movement: freedom of navigation, the right of innocent passage, the right of immigration, and freedom of trade. Human interconnectivity constitutively preceded property, and the denial of *ius communicationis* by natives to the Spaniards was a legitimate justification for war precisely because it violated justice. If the American Indians prevented the Spaniards from entering their territories without cause or rejected them, then it was possible to wage just war against them on the grounds of the injury caused, i.e., for not having respected their legitimate right.

The right to property, conceived as a *dominium utile*, not as an absolute right, in the unique context of the American discovery also acquired a concomitant utopian dimension. The religious orders responded to the eschatological expectations of the time by activating the utopia of creating a new political and social order in Spanish America, a new Arcadia. Proof of this were the many attempts to create communities in which goods were shared based on the self-government of Native Americans. In Vitoria too, the original biblical vision of the community of goods as a guarantor of peace reappears, a perspective that does not sit well with the thesis that in the final analysis what Vitoria did was endorse the conquest as an exclusive enterprise of material interests, colonial appropriation, and the extension of imperial power.

In the first part of his argument in *De Indis*, the Salamanca professor clearly established the precedence of *ius communicationis* over *dominium*: '(…) at the beginning of the world, when all things were common, everyone was allowed to visit and travel through any land he wished. This right was clearly not taken away by the division of property (*divisio rerum*); it was never the intention of nations to prevent free mutual intercourse of men with one another with this division'.[43]

According to Vitoria, sociability and communication precede power and property, and both *potestas* and *dominium* are instruments for the develop-

42 Ibid., 7.

43 Vitoria, Francisco de. 'On the American Indians', *Vitoria's Political Writings*, 278.

ment of communication. Rights are relevant to the establishment of the new order, but they are not as essential to human nature as the appetite for society and communication. Human relations, like religion, grace, and friendship, go beyond the demands of commutative justice proper to norms. Communication appears to be the defining characteristic of human rationality.

In opposition to Vitoria, for Schmitt, confidence in a supposed objective rationality and in the distinction between just and unjust prevented political decision-making by adopting general and abstract principles that must be applied in each concrete historical case following rules of reason. According to Schmitt, Vitoria's conception of liberties based on a universal and common rationality was overwhelmed by the impossibility of determining in each concrete case the validity or 'justice' of the particular position.

This possibility, which Schmitt denied, however prevented Vitoria from being forced into an existential-political differentiation between the 'civilised' and the 'barbarian', between 'friend' and 'foe', and therefore instrumentalising political-theology as the means to ground extreme polarisation as the basis for 'the political'.

Vitoria did not pronounce whether he approved or condemned morally and legally the actions of individual conquerors, like Pizarro and Cortés, although in his private correspondence his personal position on the so-called *peruleros* is very clear. But in the *Relections*, the argument always unfolds at the abstract level of conditions for just war. This is the pragmatic advantage of Vitorian *jus gentium*. It is anchored in an eternal right and at the same time needs to be applied to the specific circumstances, as opposed to Schmittian decisionism, which permanently needs to stylise the historical situation as confrontation, as extreme polarisation, which requires to the point of exhaustion the strenuous construction of friends and enemies at loggerheads.

Bibiliography

Amorosa, Paolo. *Rewriting the History of the Law of Nations. How James Brown Scott Made Francisco de Vitoria the Founder of International Law* (Oxford: Oxford University Press, 2019).

Anghie, Anthony. *Imperialism, Sovereignty and the Making of International Law* (Cambridge: Cambridge University Press 2004).

Beneyto, José María. 'Conquest, Empire, and Peace: Vitoria, Charles v, Erasmus and the Foundations of the Law of Nations', in *Empire, Humanism and Rights. Collected Essays on Francisco de Vitoria*, ed. José María Beneyto (Cham: Springer Nature, 2022).

Beneyto, José María. 'Camilo Barcia Trelles on Francisco de Vitoria: At the Crossroads of Carl Schmitt's *Grossraum* and James Brown Scott's "Modern International Law"', *European Journal of International Law* 31 (4) (2020), 1477–1492.

Beneyto, José María and Kennedy, David (eds.). *New Approaches to International Law. The European and the American Experiences* (TMC Asser Press/Springer: The Hague, 2012).

Beneyto, José María. *Apokalypse der Moderne. Die Diktaturtheorie von Donoso Cortés* (Stuttgart: Klett-Cotta, 1988).

Beneyto, José María. *Politische Theologie als politische Theorie. Eine Untersuchung zur Rechts – und Staatstheorie Carl Schmitts und zu ihrer Wirkungsgeschichte in Spanien* (Berlin: Duncker & Humblot, 1983), 62–110.

Benton, Lauren. *A Search for Sovereignty: Law and Geography in European Empires, 1400–1900* (Cambridge: Cambridge University Press, 2009).

Brown Scott, James. *The Spanish Origin of International Law. Francico de Vitoria and his Law of Nations* (Oxford: Oxford University Press, 1934).

Butha, Nehal. 'Let Us Suppose that Universals Do Not Exist: *Bricoleur* and *Bricolage* in Martti Koskenniemi's, *To the Uttermost Parts of the Earth*', *European Journal of International Law* 22 (3) (2021), 943–948.

De la Rasilla, Ignacio. 'Francisco de Vitoria's unexpected transformations and reinterpretations for international law', *International Community Law Review* 15 (2003), 287–318.

Duve, Thomas. 'Spatial Perceptions, Juridical Practices, and Early International Legal Thought around 1500: from Tordesillas to Saragossa', in *System, Order, and International Law: The Early History of International Law from Machiavelli to Hegel*, eds. Thomas Kleinlein and David Roth-Isigkeit (Oxford: Oxford University Press, 2017), 418–442.

Fitzmaurice, Andrew. 'The Problem of Eurocentrism in the Thought of Francisco de Vitoria' in *At the origins of modernity. Francisco de Vitoria and the Discovery of International Law*, eds. José María Beneyto and Justo Corti Varela (Springer International Publishing 2017), 77–94.

Habermas, Jürgen. *Auch eine Geschichte der Philosophie. Die okzidentale Konstellation von Glauben und Wissen*, vol 1 (Berlin: Suhrkhamp, 2nd. ed., 2020), 908–918.

Herrero, Montserrat (ed.). *Carl Schmitt and Álvaro d'Ors. Briefwechsel* (Berlin: Duncker & Humblot, 2004).

Koskenniemi, Martti. 'Vitoria and Us. Thoughts on Critical Histories of International Law', *Rechtsgeschichte. Legal History* 22 (2014), 119–138.

Koskenniemi, Martti. *To the Uttermost Parts of the Earth. Legal Imagination and International Power, 1300–1870* (Cambridge: Cambridge University Press, 2021).

Koskenniemi, Martti. *The Gentle Civilizer of Nations. The Rise and Fall of International Law 1870–1960* (Cambridge: Cambridge University Press, 2001).

Mehring, Reinhard. *Carl Schmitt. Aufstieg und Fall. Eine Biographie* (Munich: C.H. Beck, 2009).

Nuzzo, Luigi. '"The Law That Wasn't There." Chapter 2: The Political Theology of *Ius Gentium* – The Expansion of Spain 1524–1559', *European Journal of International Law* 32 (3) (2021), 957–964.

Pagden, Anthony. 'Introduction: Francisco de Vitoria and the Origins of the Modern Global Order', in *At the Origins of Modernity. Francisco de Vitoria and the Discovery of International Law*, eds. José María Beneyto and Justo Corti Varela (Cham: Springer Nature, 2017), 1–20.

Pagden, Anthony. *The Fall of Natural Man: The American Indians and the Origins of Comparative Ethnology* (Cambridge: Cambridge University Press, 2nd ed., 1986).

Schmitt, Carl. *The Concept of the Political* (Chicago: The University of Chicago Press, 2007).

Schmitt, Carl. 'Völkerrechtliche Grossraumordnung mit Interventionsverbot für raumfremde Mächte. Ein Beitrag zum Reichsbegriff im Völkerrecht', in *Staat, Grossraum, Nomos. Arbeiten aus den Jahren 1916–1969*, ed. Günter Maschke (Berlin: Duncker & Humblot, 1995), 269–371.

Schmitt, Carl. Glossarium. *Aufzeichnungen der Jahre 1947–1951* (Berlin: Duncker & Humblot, 1991).

Schmitt, Carl. *Der Wert des Staates und die Bedeutung des Einzelnen* (Berlin: Duncker & Humblot, 3rd. ed., 2015). Edited and translated into English by Lars Vinx and Samuel Garrett Zeitlin, in *Carl Schmitt's Early Legal-Theoretical Writings* (Oxford: Oxford University Press, 2021).

Schmitt, Carl. *Land and Sea: A World-Historical Meditation* (New York: Telos Press Publishing, 2015).

Schmitt, Carl. *Politische Theologie. Vier Kapitel zur Lehre von der Souveranität* (Munich/Leipzig: Duncker & Humblot, 2nd ed., 1934). Translated into English and with an introduction by George Schwab, with a new foreword by Tracy B. Strong, *Political Theology. Four Chapters on the Concept of Sovereignty* (Chicago: The University of Chicago Press, 2006).

Schmitt, Carl. *The Nomos of the Earth in the International Law of the Jus Publicum Europaeum*. Translated and annotated by G.L. Ulmen (New York: Telos Press Publishing, 2003).

Schmitt, Carl. *Politische Romantik* (Berlin/Leipzig: Duncker & Humblot, 2nd. edit., 1925). Translated by Guy Oakes as *Political Romanticism* (Cambridge/Ma.: The MIT Press, 1986).

Schmitt, Carl. *Gesetz und Urteil. Eine Untersuchung zum Problem der Rechtspraxis* (Berlin: Duncker & Humblot, 2nd. ed., 1969).

Schmitt, Carl. *Gespräch über die Macht und den Zugang zum Machthaber* (Pfullingen: Günther Neske, 1954).

Schmitt, Carl. 'Francisco de Vitoria und die Geschichte seines Ruhmes', *Die Neue Ordnung. Zeitschrift für Religion, Kultur, Gesellschaft* 4 (1946), 289–313.

Teschke, Benno. 'Carl Schmitt's Concepts of War: A Categorical Failure', in Jens Meierhenrich and Oliver Simons (eds.), *The Oxford Handbook of Carl Schmitt* (Oxford: Oxford University Press, 2016), 367–400.

Tierney, Brian. *The Idea of Natural Rights: Studies on Natural Rights, Natural Law and Church Law, 1150–1625* (Grand Rapids /Cambridge: Eerdmans Publishing, 1997), 290–301.

Vitoria, Francisco de. 'On the American Indians', *Vitoria Political Writings*, trans. and ed. by Anthony Pagden and Jeremy Lawrance (Cambridge: Cambridge University Press, 1991).

Vitoria, Francisco de. 'On Civil Power', *Vitoria Political Writings*, trans. and ed. by Anthoy Pagden and Jeremy Lawrance (Cambridge: Cambridge University Press, 1991).

Von Bogdandy, Armin and Hinghofer-Szalkay, Stephan. 'Das etwas unheimliche Ius Publicum Europaeum: Begrifsgechichtliche Analysen im Spannungsfeld von europäischen Rechtsraum, droit public de l'Europe und Carl Schmitt', *Zeitschrift für ausländisches öffentliches Recht und Völkerrecht* (*ZaöRV*) 73/2 (2013), 209–248.

CHAPTER 3

Carl Schmitt on Imperialism and International Law

Jochen von Bernstorff

1 Introduction

For over a century, scholars and intellectuals have been fascinated by Carl Schmitt's writings on international law – despite – or perhaps because of – his role as a prominent Nazi legal scholar in Germany during the 1930s.[1] It is not suprising that his views on classic European colonialism and colonial warfare are less well known, given that European colonialism does not feature prominently in Schmitt's complex and enigmatic world of historical and politico-legal concepts. However, Carl Schmitt is renowned for his pioneering critique of early twentieth-century US imperialism. His writings have become a reference point for critical theories on what is currently termed 'informal imperialism' and its associated legal instruments. The term 'informal imperialism' is defined in historiographical scholarship as a modern form of political and economic domination of foreign nations that does not involve territorial annexation.[2] Classic Western colonialism, or formal imperialism, can be defined as the formalized rule of a great power over an overseas territory, with or without the aim of creating settler communities on the claimed territory.

Schmitt considered colonialism, or formal imperialism, to be a historical phenomenon closely linked to the *ius publicum europaeum* in the eighteenth and nineteenth centuries. He regarded the latter as the ideal form of an interstate order. This contribution seeks to synthesize Schmitt's writings on imperialism, encompassing both formal and informal forms. While Schmitt was

1 On Schmitt and international law, see Martti Koskenniemi, 'Carl Schmitt and International Law', in Jens Meierhenrich and Oliver Simons (eds.), The Oxford Handbook of Carl Schmitt (Oxford: Oxford University Press 2017). On Carl Schmitt, colonialism and the Großraum-Theory, see also my partly identical text in Jochen von Bernstorff, 'Governing Hegemonic Spaces in Carl Schmitt: Colonialism, Anti-Imperialism and the Großraum-Theory'. Humanity 14 (2023).

2 John Gallagher and Donald Robinson, 'The Imperialism of Free Trade'. *Economic History Review 6* (1953). https://doi.org/10.2307/2591017.

 | DOI:10.1163/9789004757448_004

highly critical of informal imperialism, he was at best ambivalent about European colonialism (formal imperialism). He portrayed it as a stabilizing element in the eighteenth and nineteenth-century *ius publicum europaeum*. Even in his post–World War II writings, the early era of formal European imperialism is not reconstructed in critical terms but serves an instrumental function for his idealized and by then vanished European inter-state order. Additionally, Schmitt uncritically reproduces the classic nineteenth-century justifications for European colonialism in the *Nomos of the Earth*. This contribution will argue that the tensions between Schmitt as an anti-imperialist and Schmitt as an imperialist can be explained by his concept of an ideal inter-state order projected onto the eighteenth- and nineteenth-century *ius publicum europaeum*. Formal imperialism was compatible with this alleged first emanation of a functioning inter-state order, whereas informal imperialism was not.

2 Formal and Informal Imperialism

To begin with, in line with historiographical research, this contribution will explain in more detail the distinction between historical emanations of formal and informal imperialism.[3] *Formal* imperialism can be equated with nineteenth-century Western colonialism. It is being defined by historians as a situation of formalized rule of a great power over an overseas territory with or without the aim to create settler communities on the claimed territory. In the eyes of European great powers, the colonized territories were not sovereign in the sense of European statehood. The high-water mark of colonialism in the early twentieth century, during the 'Scramble for Africa', was marked by the trend of formally incorporating colonized territories into the state territory of the respective great power. The UK, France, Germany, Portugal, the Netherlands, Spain, Belgium, and the US all maintained formal overseas empires. During the interwar period, approximately two-thirds of the global population resided in these formalised colonies. Colonisers generally framed colonisation as a humanitarian mission, bringing civilisation to the 'uncivilised' and ending the slave trade on the African coast. Given widespread resistance in various forms by local populations in all colonies, the threat and use of military violence was crucial for the metropoles in establishing control and obedience in overseas territories and for protecting their merchants and settlers. Almost all twentieth-century colonial wars were military interventions to police and punish local groups for disobedience and rebellions against the

3 See Gallagher and Robinson, 'The Imperialism of Free Trade'.

metropole. Spurred by anti-colonial resolutions of the United Nations General Assembly most of these colonies emancipated themselves from formal colonial rule in the 1960s and 1970s, often after bloody wars of national liberation, eventually acquiring the desired formal requisites of statehood themselves.

Informal imperialism instead does not seek to establish a new colony but the domination of a foreign country through a clientelistic relationship between metropolitan and peripheral elites.[4] The sovereignty of the client state is not denied by the great power but is officially recognised. Nonetheless, the metropole claims a veto-right with regard to central economic and security-related decisions taken by the client state due to the fact that the 'client state' is situated in a zone of influence defined by the great-power.[5] What distinguishes this form of domination from merely exerting influence via diplomatic means is that the metropole can coerce the client state to accommodate the interests of the metropole, if necessary, by military means. This could be done by gun boats, short military interventions, external regime change, or with the help of interventions by international institutions. Often, 'client states' were also forced to sign so-called intervention treaties, granting the great power a standing right to military intervention.

A paradigmatic case of informal imperialism were the UK–Egypt relations in the second half of the nineteenth century, but it was also the US who systematically resorted to mechanisms of informal empire in declared zones of influence in the late nineteenth and twentieth centuries.[6] Numerous military US interventions in Latin-America in the last three decades before WWI to establish US-friendly regimes or prevent the expropriation of US companies or US banks are a case in point. A famous expression of US informal imperialism in Latin America is the 1904 Roosevelt Corollary to the Monroe Doctrine. It was these US foreign policy-practices in Latin America and the Caribbean, which were analysed in Schmitt's Interbellum theory of informal imperialism. Another example is the joint 1899 intervention of Europe's great powers in China to quell the so-called 'Boxer Rebellion' and to punish the anti-imperial Boxer-movement for the killing and mistreatment of European nationals. Moreover, open or covert regime change through military intervention or

4 For an insightful current historiographical usage of the Gallagher/Robinson concept of 'informal imperialism' by Gallagher and Robinson, see Atul Kohli, *Imperialism and the Developing World* (Oxford: Oxford University Press 2020), 7–8.

5 The term 'client state' was introduced into international legal discourse by Mohammed Bedjaoui in *Towards a New International Economic Order* (Paris: UNESCO; New York: Holmes and Meier 1979), 149–150.

6 See Kohli, *Imperialism*.

other violent acts remained a typical form of great power coercion *vis-à-vis* smaller states throughout the Cold War. After the formal decolonisation of almost all colonised territories in the mid-1970s, great powers could no longer choose between formal and informal imperial domination. Informal imperialism remained the only option to dominate, exploit, and control foreign populations, given that formal colonialism had been entirely discredited through resolutions of the UN General Assembly from the mid-1960s onwards. Access to vital resources for economic and military purposes, such as rubber, oil, copper, or uranium, or to waterways of geopolitical importance (Suez/Panama), remained common twentieth-century motives for great powers in establishing and perpetuating client-governments in certain countries by the threat or use of military force.

3 Carl Schmitt on Formal Imperialism

Schmitt's stance on formal imperialism is challenging to ascertain, particularly considering his reluctance to adopt a definitive and normatively charged stance on both European colonialism and the decolonisation era. Nevertheless, in his post-World War II monograph *The Nomos of the Earth*, Schmitt addresses the function of European colonial empires within the context of his distinctive reconstruction of the *ius publicum europaeum*. In Schmitt's view, the period between 1815 and the 1880s represented a golden age of the *ius publicum europaeum*. During this period, the European order, as Schmitt conceived it, was seen to correspond to his ideal of a good legal order. This ideal was expressed in the concept of the 'unity of order and space' (*Einheit von Ordnung und Ortung*), which he understood as a 'located law' (*geortetes Recht*) or a 'concrete order' (*konkrete Ordnung*). However, this allegedly ideal inter-state order was ultimately replaced in the twentieth century by a 'featureless chaos incapable of containing war'.[7] Schmitt's concept of the 'concrete order', which was developed in the 1930s and was then openly grounded in anti-Semitic ideology, in *The Nomos of the Earth* informs his nostalgic idea of an ideal international legal order. Law constituting order must fulfil three conditions, as outlined by Schmitt. Firstly, it must effectively monopolise the means of violence and constrain its exercise. Secondly, it requires substantive 'spatial principles' (*Raumprinzipien*). Thirdly, it must be based on traditional

7 Carl Schmitt, *Der Nomos der Erde im Völkerrecht des Jus Publicum Europaeum* (Berlin: Duncker & Humblot, 5th ed., 2011), 206, 207, 211–212.

common bonds as a basis for the validity of law. In the context of the *ius publicum europaeum*, these were the 'continuing ecclesiastical, social, and economic traditions' that were allegedly shared by Europeans.[8] In this context, Schmitt's emphasis on societal homogeneity as a cultural foundation for any legal order becomes evident.[9]

Regarding the third point, Schmitt also demonstrates that he is a jurist whose intellectual development was shaped by nineteenth-century German jurisprudential thought, in particular by Savigny's Historical School of Law. Savigny had deeply impacted European legal scholarship in all fields of law during the first half of the twentieth century through a concept of law resting on traditional ties and a common consciousness in the sense of a 'spirit of the people' (*Volksgeist*). Schmitt's 'concrete-order' – ideal draws on the German Historical School's organicist, particularistic, and historicist understanding of law, a perspective that is often overlooked in secondary literature on Schmitt.[10]

This rather conservative assumption of an organic or cultural 'essence' of law, espoused by the Historical School of Law, had also been gradually embraced by influential representatives of the European international law community during the nineteenth century.[11] This trend arguably contributed to the meanwhile notorious parochial nineteenth-century understanding of a distinctively European international law. It triggered the transformation of the received eighteenth-century natural law doctrines and their universalistic framings into an ever more solipsistic approach sharply distinguishing the law of the 'civilised' European nations from legal emanations in non-European and allegedly 'non-civilised' regions of the world. The reception of the Historical

8 Schmitt, *Nomos der Erde*, 120.

9 On homogeneity in Schmitt's thinking, see Richard Wolin, 'Carl Schmitt, Political Existentialism, and the Total State'. *Theory and Society* 19 (1990), 403–404, https://doi.org/10.1007/BF00137619; Chantal Mouffe, 'Carl Schmitt and the Paradox of Liberal Democracy'. *Canadian Journal of Law and Jurisprudence* 10 (1997), https://doi.org/10.1017/S0841820900000217; Rolf Grawert, 'Homogenität, Identität, Souveränität. Positionen jurisdiktioneller Begriffsdogmatik'. *Der Staat* 51 (2012), 192–193, https://doi.org/10.3790/staa.51.2.189; Rüdiger Voigt, 'Mythos Staat. Zum Staatsdenken von Carl Schmitt', in Rüdiger Voigt (ed.), *Denken In Widersprüchen. Carl Schmitt wider den Zeitgeist* (Baden-Baden: Nomos, 2nd ed., 2021), 47–50.

10 Carl Schmitt, 'Die Lage der europäischen Rechtswissenschaft', in *Verfassungsrechtliche Aufsätze aus den Jahren 1924–1954. Materialien zu einer Verfassungslehre* (Berlin: Duncker & Humblot, 4th ed., 2003), 386–429.

11 On the Historical School in general, see Haferkamp, *Die Historische Rechtsschule* (Frankfurt am Main: Vittorio Klostermann 2018); on the Historical School and international law in the nineteenth century, see Robert Schütze, *From Utopia to Apologia: International Normativity in the Long Nineteenth Century* (London: London School of Economics, PhD Thesis, 2019), 67–109.

School in that sense contributed to reducing international law to a law of the so-called 'European Civilised Nations,' resting on a common and allegedly unique European consciousness and on an enlightened European practice.[12]

Schmitt's retrospective reading of the era of *ius publicum europaeum* is characterised by nothing but praise for this mid-nineteenth-century ideological framework. In this sense, these sections of Schmitt's *Nomos* are nostalgic and Eurocentric ruminations, echoing the prevailing view among European scholars in the latter half of the nineteenth century. Notably, Schmitt's idealisation of the nineteenth century also encompasses European colonialism and its contemporary legal justifications. Shortly before the height of the decolonisation era, *The Nomos of the Earth* thus reaffirmed the legitimacy of nineteenth-century European colonialism, albeit implicitly. Peter Uwe Hohendahl has recently drawn attention to these pro-colonial aspects in Schmitt's later writings.[13]

However, let me first return to the opening passages of Schmitt's reflections on European colonialism in *The Nomos of the Earth*. He initiates his discussion of European colonialism with an examination of Vitoria's teachings. In this section, Schmitt draws on contemporary secondary literature on Vitoria from the 1930s, particularly the work of Professor Marcos from Salamanca. Marcos had persuasively demonstrated that, despite his frequently cited critical observations regarding the *conquistadores*, Vitoria ultimately provided a comprehensive justification for the colonisation of Latin America by the Spanish through the *bellum iustum* doctrine.[14] Schmitt concurred with Marcos that, despite Vitoria's emphasis on the equality of the so-called 'Indios' and his assumption of a reciprocal legal relationship between them and the Spanish, the majority of the acts of violence committed by the conquistadores could still be considered lawful according to Vitoria. This is an ex-post critique of the Interbellum revival of Vitoria in Anglo-American scholarship praising the famous neo-scholastic scholar from Salamanca as an early universalist and

12 Luigi Nuzzo, *Lawyers, Space and Subjects. Historical Perspective on the Western Legal Tradition* (Lecce: Pensa MultiMedia 2020), 38–53, 66; Martti Koskenniemi, The Gentle Civilizer of Nations (Cambridge: Cambridge University Press 2001), chapter 1; Jochen von Bernstorff and Max Mayer, 'The Historical School and German International Legal Thought in the 19th Century'. Journal of the History of Internaitonal Law 25 (2023), 316 et seqq. https://doi.org/10.1163/15718050-bja10088.

13 Peter Uwe Hohendahl, *Perilous Futures. On Carl Schmitt's Late Writings* (Ithaca: Cornell University Press 2018), 97–101.

14 Schmitt, *Nomos der Erde*, 77–89; Teodoro Andrés Marcos, *Vitoria y Carlos V en la soberanía hispano-americana* (Salamanca: Sucesores de Rivadeneyra, 2nd ed., 1946), 45–136.

humanitarian thinker. Moreover, Schmitt repudiated all of Vitoria's Christian natural law tenets regarding the equality of all human beings, as well as Vitoria's advocacy for recognising the inherent rights of human beings from non-European or non-Christian populations.[15] Instead, Schmitt replicated the discriminatory justifications for colonialism that were prevalent in Europe during the nineteenth century, which were already being subjected to significant criticism by the 1950s.[16]

How can these concrete nineteenth-century European patterns of justifying the colonial project be summarised? Based on anthropological and racialised assumptions from the early nineteenth century about a graduated capacity of different cultures to reason, which were also propagated in philosophical circles by Kant and Hegel,[17] African societies and indigenous peoples were denied a position as equal legal subjects by European legal scholars. Schmitt explicitly replicated this basic and discriminatory assumption, asserting for Spanish colonialism in the Americas against Vitoria that these societies had indeed lacked the 'knowledge-based power of Christian-European rationality'. He argues that this alleged difference alone justified the Spanish occupation of their territories.[18] Schmitt further asserts that this rationale also applied to nineteenth-century European colonialism in regions of the globe deemed 'uncivilised'. According to Schmitt, European metropoles could legitimately regard the colonial land they had won as 'masterless' in terms of dominium and imperium. This was because indigenous populations allegedly had no property rights or jurisdiction over their own land.[19] This aligns with the controversial and highly apologetic theory of 'masterless sovereignty', introduced by Johann Caspar Bluntschli into German discourse on international law in the mid-nineteenth century. Bluntschli with this concept had countered the

15 Hohendahl, in my view, misunderstands Schmitt's position in these passages as a rejection of the contemporary differentiation between 'civilised' and 'non-civilised' as a justification for European colonialism: Hohendahl, *Perilous Futures*, 100.

16 On the struggle of international legal scholars to abolish the standard of civilisation, see Arnulf Becker–Lorca, *Mestizo International Law. A Global Intellectual History 1842–1933* (Cambridge: Cambridge University Press 2014).

17 For a critical view, see Maureen Maisha Eggers, 'Rassifizierte Machtdifferenz als Deutungsperspektive in der Kritischen Weißseinsforschung in Deutschland. Zur Aktualität und Normativität diskursiver Vermittlungen von hierarchischen aufeinander bezogenen rassifizierten Konstruktionen', in Maureen Maisha Eggers, Kilomba Grada, Peggy Piesche and Susan Arndt (eds.), *Mythen, Masken und Subjekte. Kritische Weißseinsforschung in Deutschland* (Münster: Unrast 2005), 59–61.

18 Schmitt, *Nomos der Erde*, 103.

19 Ibid., 171–172.

position taken by August Wilhelm Heffter and other early nineteenth-century scholars addressing the problem of a missing legally recognised title for peaceful colonial acquisitions in inhabited overseas territories.[20]

But why were peaceful colonial acquisitions, which in practice usually relied on some form of coerced or voluntary consent by local rulers for the presence of Europeans on their land, not considered a legally valid transfer of territory in the eyes of Heffter and other scholars? A legal transfer of territory by the local population to European states through bilateral treaties (consent) could in principle have been regarded as the requisite title. However, contemporary legal scholarship was relatively united in holding that this was not a viable option, as the so-called 'uncivilised' were not considered subjects of international law. In line with the then prevailing 'standard of civilisation', which had been shaped by historicist jurisprudential theories and the abovementioned racialised anthropological concepts, only 'civilised' nations could in the eyes of the Europeans be subjects of international law with treaty-making capacity. Treaties with the local population, of which there were many in this era, were thus considered invalid under international law by the Europeans. In colonial practice, however, they were used instrumentally to facilitate initial cooperation with local elites or to pacify them, as long as these treaties proved useful for this purpose. In later stages of colonial rule, however, the concrete treaty stipulations usually containing reciprocal obligations and delimited jurisdictional rights of the colonisers were often overruled unilaterally by the Europeans referring to their alleged invalidity.[21] In the early stages of colonisation, these treaties were also understood by Europeans as a kind of formalised claim to a certain colony *vis-à-vis* the other European colonial powers.[22] They thus in the eyes of the Europeans primarily had an inner-European legal function. Protectorates could not come into being in most colonial territories for this reason either, as these also required a legally valid treaty between two sovereigns under international law.

Without a treaty-based cessation of territory, early nineteenth-century textbooks agreed that only 'masterless', meaning uninhabited territory (*terra nullius*) could be lawfully occupied in times of peace. Given that in the second half

20 August Wilhelm Heffter and Friedrich Heinrich Geffcken, *Das europäische Völkerrecht der Gegenwart auf den bisherigen Grundlagen* (Berlin: Müller, 8th ed., 1888), 157.

21 On German practice and scholarly debates regarding colonial treaties, see Jochen von Bernstorff, 'Koloniale Herrschaft durch Ambivalenz: Die deutsche Völkerrechtswissenschaft und die Kolonie', in Philip Dann, Isabel Feichtner and Jochen von Bernstorff (eds.), *(Post)Koloniale Rechtswissenschaft* (Tübingen: Mohr Siebeck 2022), 271–296.

22 Norbert Berthold Wagner, *Die deutschen Schutzgebiete. Erwerb, Organisation und Verlust aus juristischer Sicht* (Baden–Baden: Nomos 2002) 111–113.

of the nineteenth century all new colonies had been inhabited at the time of colonisation, all conceivable titles of acquisition under European international law were technically ruled out. Heffter had therefore regarded peaceful acquisitions of inhabited colonial territories by the great powers as unlawful. For this very reason, the above-mentioned doctrine of 'masterless sovereignty' had been developed by Bluntschli, according to which it should be sufficient for lawful occupation if the abstract attribute of sovereignty as such was 'masterless'.[23] Accordingly, it was not the territory or its inhabitants that would be occupied, but the allegedly 'masterless' attribute of sovereignty.[24] Conveniently, the 'non-civilised' peoples by definition lacked the capacity for acquiring 'sovereignty' over their own land in the sense of European international law.[25]

This thoroughly discriminatory and in some usages openly racialised legal justification for nineteenth-century colonial acquisitions is uncritically endorsed by Carl Schmitt in the *Nomos* in 1950. He reproduces the foundational nineteenth-century doctrine of the 'standard of civilisation' without a critical word. According to this doctrine, until the League of Nations era, a hierarchical distinction was made between the Europeans, the 'semi-civilised' states, especially in Asia, and the so-called 'savages' or 'uncivilised' with no legal capacity, especially in Africa.[26] This hierarchy between peoples was an obvious analogy to the family with adults, the semi-adolescents with limited legal capacity and children without legal capacity. From Schmitt's point of view, indigenous rule in the colonial territories had to automatically give way upon contact with the higher 'European rational spirit',[27] as was already the case in Hegel. For Schmitt, '[t]here are no legal limits for European colonial acquisitions under international law'.[28]

Carl Schmitt would not have been Carl Schmitt, however, if he had not added a dialectical train of thought to these nineteenth-century justifications. What is the historical or philosophical train of thought that went beyond the mere reproduction of the contemporary nineteenth-century justifications of

---

23 Johann Caspar Bluntschli, *Das moderne Völkerrecht der civilisirten Staaten* (Nördlingen: Beck 1868), 166. Further, see von Bernstorff, 'Koloniale Herrschaft', 276–284.

24 Jörg Fisch, *Die europäische Expansion und das Völkerrecht. Die Auseinandersetzungen um den Status der überseeischen Gebiete vom 15. Jahrhundert bis zur Gegenwart* (Wiesbaden: Steiner 1984), 300–302.

25 Paul Heilborn, 'Völkerrechtliches und koloniales Protektorat'. *Zeitschrift für Völkerrecht* 8 (1914), 228–229.

26 Schmitt, *Nomos der Erde*, 202–212.

27 Ibid., 103.

28 Ibid., 171.

colonialism? Schmitt was the first legal scholar in the twentieth century to address the constitutive connection between his cherished European spatial order and the allegedly freely occupiable territories outside Europe. He insisted that the *ius publicum europaeum* constructively needed an unregulated space outside of Europe in order to shift tensions between the Great Powers to the periphery and to satisfy expansionist aspirations. For him, this instrumental function was first fulfilled by the European land appropriations in the so-called New World and later in Africa.[29]

This constitutive importance of the 'other' not only for the formation of European identity but also for the displacement of conflicts to the periphery was taken up again by Anthony Anghie in his famous book on European colonialism in 2005; however, unlike in Schmitt's *Nomos*, this time as a critical intervention. Anghie's work marks nothing less than the beginning of the postcolonial turn in international-law scholarship in the twenty-first century. For Schmitt, however, the instrumental connection between colonialism and a supposedly pacified European spatial order was a fortunate and unreservedly positive historical development. It brought into being and stabilised the state-based *ius publicum europaeum*, portrayed by him as a unique civilisational achievement. Schmitt speaks of an inherent 'spatial sense' (*Raum-Sinn*) of the freely occupiable colonies for the *ius publicum europaeum*.[30]

So much, then, for the highly idealised and thoroughly Eurocentric reconstruction of the *ius publicum* and of the supposedly 'good' colonialism in *The Nomos of the Earth*. Not only the perspective of the colonised is missing in Schmitt's nostalgic depiction; also, the perspective of the smaller European states, which in the nineteenth century often became instrumentalised by the European Great Powers and their erratic and at times violent implementation of the balance-of-power principle remains unmentioned. And for whom within European constitutional monarchies could this order be regarded as a 'civilisational achievement'? For monarchical and liberal elites perhaps, but also for the rest of the respective populations?

For Schmitt, a stable international legal order (*konkrete Ordnung*) was an end in itself,[31] particularly as long as this order granted a privileged great-power status to one's own country. To this end, Schmitt willingly subordinates all theoretical questions of justice and legal equality. Where for Hans Kelsen, the formal equality of all states constituted the essence of the international

29 With a critique of this historical argument, see Fisch, *Europäische Expansion*.

30 Schmitt, *Nomos der Erde*, 194.

31 Wolin, 'Carl Schmitt', 393, 395–396; Andreas Heuer, *Carl Schmitt: Die Dialektik der Moderne. Von der europäischen zur Welt-Moderne* (Berlin: Duncker & Humblot 2010); Alexander Lauer, *Carl Schmitts Sicht auf die außereuropäische Welt* (Munich: GRIN 2016), 24–27, 31; Voigt, 'Mythos Staat'.

legal order,[32] Schmitt saw traditional ties, cultural homogeneity and hegemonic leadership as the actual backbone of the international legal order.

4 Carl Schmitt on Informal Imperialism

This leads me to Carl Schmitt's critique of informal imperialism. In his view, the rise of US imperialism coincided historically with an early twentieth-century turn to 'false' European colonialism. Schmitt's laconic affirmation of European colonialism and his criticism of Vitoria's Christian notions of equality between the colonised and the colonisers, however, suggest that Schmitt was himself trapped in nineteenth-century European colonialist thought patterns. These colonial legacies in his writings seem to be at odds with his critical Interbellum theory of legalised US imperialism. A closer look at his critique of US-imperialism however reveals subtle differentiations between 'good' order-stabilising European colonialism during the *ius publicum europaeum* and 'bad' order-undermining informal US imperialism. For Schmitt, the cherished order of the *ius publicum europaeum* perished at the beginning of the twentieth century. It was destroyed by a supposed new order under US hegemony, which is both place- and spaceless (*ort- und raumlos*).[33]

According to Schmitt, the Europeans themselves were also to blame for this development, as they began, towards the end of the nineteenth century, to extend European international law to other regions of the world. Through this expansion, the old cherished order lost its 'spatial sense' or its traditional European ties and homogeneity through the inclusion of new non-European participants. Schmitt also claims in this context that it was a huge mistake by the colonial powers to declare the colonial soil as state territory of the metropole. This legal change in the territorial status of the colonies in the late nineteenth century had been another wrong-headed project of legal positivism in public law. Again, Schmitt's longing for cultural homogeneity and his concrete-order thinking appear to inspire his critique. They can help explain why Schmitt regarded this change of colonial status as a turn towards a 'false' form of European colonialism. In his view, the colonies had now lost their

32 Hans Kelsen, 'Essential Conditions of International Justice'. *Proceedings of the American Society of International Law* 31 (1941), 70–86, https://doi.org/10.1017/S0272503700059097; on Kelsen's theory of international law, see Jochen von Bernstorff, *The Public International Law Theory of Hans Kelsen. Believing in Universal Law* (Cambridge: Cambridge University Press 2010).

33 Schmitt, *Nomos der Erde*, 164–165, 203, 208, 265 et seqq.

stabilising and instrumental function for the *ius publicum europaeum*. Fully integrating the colonies legally into the state-structures of the metropoles after the 1884 Congo Conference, despite their continuing cultural and ethnic alterity, had weakened the *ius publicum europaeum*. Attempts to assimilate other cultures to one's own in his view had to destroy the *Nomos* of a particular legal order.

For Schmitt, the homogeneous spatial order of the old *ius publicum europaeum* was thus replaced at the beginning of the twentieth century by a both 'space- and meaningless universalism' embodied by US foreign policy and later by the Geneva League of Nations.[34] In the interwar period, for him a number of basic doctrinal structures, advanced as elements of a 'universal' law, fostered a global economic and political hegemony of major Western powers by establishing the League of Nations and global capitalist structures. His critical position, however, not accidentally was in line with the German interwar and later Nazi revisionist cause. Schmitt's own anti-Versailles, anti-American, and anti-Semitic agenda in the Interbellum certainly motivated him to unmask the economic dimensions of late nineteenth- and early twentieth-century economic imperialism,[35] which after 1919 – as Schmitt sensed in the 1930s – could no longer openly maintain the civilised/non-civilised dichotomy. American economic imperialism had in his view for that very reason transformed this distinction into the less controversial dichotomy between borrower states and creditor states and continued to deeply intervene in the states belonging to the former category.[36] His often ironically toned writings 'admire' and critically detect how US discursive interventions manage to portray particularistic economic interests as the pursuit of universal values:

> One of the overall most significant phenomena in the legal and intellectual life of mankind is the fact that those who possess true power are themselves able to inherently determine words and concepts. [...] Imperialism creates its own concepts [...].[37]

34 Ibid.

35 Koskenniemi, 'Carl Schmitt', 494.

36 Carl Schmitt, 'USA und die völkerrechtlichen Formen des modernen Imperialismus', in Günter Maschke (ed.), *Frieden oder Pazifismus? Arbeiten zum Völkerrecht und zur internationalen Politik 1924–1978* (Berlin: Duncker & Humblot 2019), 351; on this critique, see Jochen von Bernstorff, 'The critic', in Jean d'Aspremont and Sahib Singh (eds.), *Concepts for International Law. Contributions to Disciplinary Thought* (Cheltenham: Edward Elgar 2019).

37 Schmitt, 'USA und Imperialismus', 364–365.

Schmitt, as a staunch critic of Anglo-American early twentieth-century international political dominance, had an unmatched sense for the power of conceptual representations of violence and economic interests in the language of international law. He acutely analyses how the political aim of creating and penetrating new markets, as well as the robust protection of US banks and investors operating in foreign markets, are being advanced and legitimised as international legal concepts and claims.[38] US imperialism, legitimised by the Monroe Doctrine and numerous intervention treaties with Latin American states, were destroying previously existing 'orders' in the affected states:

> The meaning of this new procedure is the abolition of the located order that had been preserved in the previous form of the state territory. Throughout all the details of the new methods of rule and control, their essential feature is recognisable: territorial sovereignty is transformed into an empty space for economic-social processes. The external territorial stock with its linear borders is guaranteed, but not the social and economic content of territorial integrity, its substance. The area of economic power determines the area of international law. A state whose freedom of action is thus subject to intervention rights is something different from a state whose territorial sovereignty consists in being able to make its own sovereign decisions about the concrete realisation of concepts such as *independence, public order, legality and legitimacy*, or even over its own property and economic constitution [...].[39]

These lucid critical examinations of what can be called informal (economic) imperialism in the language of international law usually end with a lament on how unjust and detrimental the Western-dominated status quo was for Germany after World War I. They do not contradict the idealisation of nineteenth-century European colonialism in *The Nomos of the Earth*. On the contrary: since, for Schmitt, these new discursive structures had contributed significantly to the decline of the glorious *ius publicum europaeum*, they had to be criticised. In other words, the supposedly 'space-related' and thus stabilising European colonialism was good, while the 'space-less' or 'space-destroying' US imperialism of an economic nature was bad.

The normatively charged Schmittian opposition between concrete order and emptied universalism becomes particularly visible here. It also became

38 Schmitt, 'USA und Imperialismus', 358–365.

39 Schmitt, *Nomos der Erde*, 225–226.

the basis of his criticism of the League of Nations. For Schmitt, the League of Nations was not in a position to establish a principle-based order; the very heterogeneity of its members precludes an effective federation of states (*Bund*).

At the same time, he criticised the League of Nations' mandate system with the aim of denouncing English and French hegemonic efforts in the lost German colonies. The mandate system of the League of Nations and the League Covenant, which in Article 22 defined the further development of the former colonies as the 'sacred trust of civilisation', in his words were

> the most concise example of the legitimising function of the dichotomy of civilised and non-civilised nations, which is used by the civilised nations to give themselves the right to "educate", i.e. to control, the less civilised nations in the form of mandates, protectorates and colonies.[40]

These lines sound like a critique of colonial structures, but they were primarily a criticism of French and British hegemonic efforts under the aegis of the League of Nations in the old German colonies. Schmitt, as we have seen above, was not a critic of colonialism *per se*. As concrete evidence for his principled endorsement of European colonialism in the Interbellum can serve Schmitt's remarks in the 1930s on Italy's brutal military annexation of the League member Abyssinia in 1936. When in 1936 Italy annexed Abyssinia, a member of the League of Nations, with colonialist intentions in clear violation of the League covenant, Schmitt found sympathetic words for the justifications of Italian international lawyers, which had referred to the civilisational superiority of Italy.[41] Schmitt even denied Abyssinia's right to exist under international law, saying that Abyssinia had simply not been an entity comparable to the European nations, which had led to its elimination as an independent entity.[42] Again, Schmitt at least implicitly endorsed the nineteenth-century Eurocentric notion of 'civilisation' and its justifications for European colonialism.

---

40 Schmitt, 'USA und Imperialismus', 351.

41 Carl Schmitt, 'Die siebente Wandlung des Genfer Völkerbundes. Eine völkerrechtliche Folge der Vernichtung Abessiniens', in Günter Maschke (ed.), *Frieden oder Pazifismus? Arbeiten zum Völkerrecht und zur internationalen Politik* (Berlin: Duncker & Humblot 2019), 471–472.

42 Carl Schmitt, *Völkerrechtliche Großraumordnung mit Interventionsverbot für raumfremde Mächte. Ein Beitrag zum Reichsbegriff im Völkerrecht* (Berlin: Duncker & Humblot, 4th ed., 2022) 59.

5 Imperial Wars in Schmitt

In Schmitt's writing on war and international law, imperialism does not figure prominently, even though excessive forms of warfare are one of his main concerns in this theory of regulating war through law. For Schmitt, constraining war hinges conceptually on the *iustus hostis* and thus on the overcoming of the scholastic idea of *bellum iustum*. According to Schmitt's plausible insight, so-called 'just wars' against the supposedly unjust enemy had an inner tendency to turn into a war of annihilation, since the reason for the war would be morally exaggerated and the enemy conceptually tends to be placed *hors de la loi*. As Schröder and recently Vergerio have convincingly shown, Schmitt's praise for the restricted warfare between sovereign states as an alleged epochal achievement of a secularised *ius publicum europaeum* has its own blind spots and amounted to an anachronistic idealisation of European absolutism, its wars and some of its scholars.[43] Schmitt used this idealisation in order to construct a negative conceptual shift from the contained or tamed (*gehegt*) old *ius ad bellum* to the aggression and self-defence paradigm in the interwar period as a problematic return of the concept of the 'unjust enemy'. In particular, the League Covenant had stipulated a guarantee of the post – World War I territorial *status quo* and foresaw recourse to collective sanctions against the thus incriminated states violating this order. All of this in the view of Schmitt had destroyed the good old law of neutrality of the *ius publicum europaeum*. Collective sanction-wars against the law-breaking state under a League of Nations' mandate in his view have an inherent tendency to turn into 'wars of annihilation' in the name of universalist values against the alleged lawbreaker, similar to the old just-war doctrine.[44]

For Schmitt, collective enforcement wars were even more problematic in the Interbellum than in the scholastic tradition, given that the League of Nations, due to its heterogeneity, allegedly lacked shared substantive principles according to which territorial disputes could be resolved. So, on the one hand, Schmitt is very concerned about constraining war and the supposed

---

43 With regard to Schmitt's ideological use of Gentili as the father of a secularised European international law, see Claire Vergerio, *War, States, and International Order. Alberico Gentili and the Foundational Myth of the Laws of War* (Cambridge: Cambridge University Press 2022), 213 et seqq.; Peter Schröder, 'Carl Schmitt's Appropriation of the Early Modern European Tradition of Political Thought on the State and Interstate Relations'. *History of Political Thought* 33 (2012).

44 Carl Schmitt, 'Die Wendung zum diskriminierenden Kriegsbegriff', in Günter Maschke (ed.), *Frieden oder Pazifismus? Arbeiten zum Völkerrecht und zur internationalen Politik* (Berlin: Duncker & Humblot 2019), 555–560.

tendency towards unrestrained punitive wars under a universalist *façade*. On the other hand, however, there is not a single critical word in his work about the real wars of extermination of the time, such as the one waged by Germany in South-West Africa before World War I. Like the majority of Western international lawyers at the time, Schmitt does not seem to regard colonial wars as a relevant issue under his intensity theory of constrained and unconstrained war. A number of formal and substantive arguments were raised by contemporary jurists from the metropolitan states in order to deny the applicability of *ius-in-bello* rules in conflicts with 'savages', the most important one being their lack of legal subjectivity as non-sovereign entities and the ensuing non-reciprocity of *ius-in-bello* obligations. That is also why both the UK and the French governments during the Hague Conferences were opposed to opening the conventions for future accessions from countries in the peripheries. As a justification for denying the application of *ius-in-bello* rules, authors could thus cynically point to the fact that the indigenous fighters themselves did not adhere to conventional forms of European warfare.[45] In more concrete terms, a standard practice of Great Powers in warfare against indigenous populations was the strategy of 'attrition', which included the burning of villages, the destruction of crops and the seizure of cattle and foodstuffs as well as summary executions of indigenous fighters.[46]

Excessive violence by regular Western armies *vis-à-vis* civilians often occurred in the form of 'punishment' measures against local insurgents, colonial resistance movements or villagers suspected of having supported them. Whenever rebellions in the colonial peripheries of Great Powers began to pose a real threat to the colonists, reactions by the metropole tended to be particularly harsh, and the measures taken in these so called 'small wars' were usually way beyond recognised inner-European *ius-in-bello* standards. The Italian war fought in Libya in 1911, and the excessive force used by the Italian military are a case in point.[47] Among the many infamous episodes of unregulated colonial violence also stand out the German genocidal reactions to the Herero/Nama

---

45 Various reasons for the non–applicability of humanitarian law for colonial wars were given in Charles Edward Callwell, *Small Wars. Their Principles and Practice* (Lincoln: University of Nebraska Press, 3rd ed., 1996), 21 et seqq; also, assuming the non-applicability of humanitarian law with reference to British and other military manuals, see Elbridge Colby, 'How to Fight Savage Tribes'. *American Journal of International Law* 21 (1927), 279. https://doi.org/10.2307/2189127.

46 Callwell, *Small Wars*, 148.

47 Vanda Wilcox, 'The Italian Soldiers' Experience in Libya, 1911–1912', in Dominik Geppert (ed.), *The Wars before the Great War. Conflict and International Politics before the Outbreak of the First World War* (Cambridge: Cambridge University Press 2015), 41–57.

rebellion in Namibia. One could add the camp system used for prisoners of war and civilians by the British in the Boer War in 1899, and the Spanish repression of anti-colonial rebellions in Cuba between 1868 and 1878.

As for Germany, some of these colonial war patterns would re-appear in both world wars, practised for instance by the German army in occupied territories. Forced labour schemes, wanton destruction of settlements and summary executions of civilians allegedly resisting the advance of the German army in occupied Belgium during World War I in many ways resembled military practices known from colonial warfare.[48] The Nazi government in World War II could no longer build directly on pre-war colonial practices, and it pursued even more radical strategies of terrorisation, enslavement and systematic extermination *vis-à-vis* occupied peoples they regarded as 'inferior races', leading to the introduction and application of the notion of crimes against humanity by the Nuremberg Charter and the invention of the legal concept of 'genocide' by Rafael Lemkin.[49]

Schmitt's complete silence on contemporary colonial German warfare is remarkable, given that these wars – often carried out with utmost brutality and beyond the recognised limits imposed on inner-European wars by the old *ius publicum europaeum* – would have constituted historical evidence of one of the most salient Schmittian theoretical insights: the 'de-humanising' mechanism of putting an enemy '*hors de la loi*'.[50] But Germany in Schmitt's writings exclusively played the role of a 'victim' of Allied hegemony, not the role of a perpetrator of de-humanising war crimes.

Another more exegetical explanation for Schmitt's silence on colonial warfare is his definition of law as necessarily emanating from a 'concrete order'. According to Schmitt's general concrete order-based concept of law, colonial wars must and perhaps also should be legally unrestrained, since they, by definition, took place outside a homogeneous legal order for him. As we have seen above, the colonial space for Schmitt is an unregulated space, which as such stabilised the *ius publicum europaeum* rules between the Europeans on European soil. Even in his *Theory of the Partisan*, Schmitt does not

48 On these violations of *ius-in-bello* rules, see Isabel Virginia Hull, *A Scrap of Paper. Breaking and Making International Law During the Great War* (Ithaca: Cornell University Press 2014), 51 et seqq.

49 Re-narrating Lemkin's struggle is Philippe Sands, *East West Street. On the Origins of Genocide and Crimes against Humanity* (London: Weidenfeld & Nicolson 2016).

50 On these debates, see Frédéric Mégret, 'From "Savages" to "Unlawful Combatants": A Postcolonial Look at International Humanitarian Law's "Other"', in Anne Orford (ed.), *International Law and Its Others* (Cambridge: Cambridge University Press 2006), 265 et seqq.

engage in a normative critique of colonial wars as a space for unregulated violence. His normative position on partisan-warfare remains highly ambivalent throughout the short monograph.[51] All in all, Schmitt seems to have fully endorsed contemporary discriminatory tropes excluding colonial wars from the *ius in bello*. Nor does Schmitt – the self-styled chief critical theorist of wars of annihilation – use the opportunity in the *Nomos* five years after World War II to comment on the Wehrmacht's war of extermination in Eastern Europe during World War II. Schmitt never mentioned Auschwitz or the Holocaust in any of his post-war publications.

Bibliography

Becker-Lorca, Arnulf. *Mestizo International Law. A Global Intellectual History 1842–1933* (Cambridge: Cambridge University Press 2014).

Bedjaoui, Mohammed. *Towards a New International Economic Order* (Paris: UNESCO; New York: Holmes and Meier 1979).

Bluntschli, Johann Caspar. *Das moderne Völkerrecht der civilisirten Staaten* (Nördlingen: Beck 1868).

Callwell, Charles Edeward. *Small Wars. Their Principles* and Practice (Lincoln: University of Nebraska Press, 3rd ed., 1996).

Colby, Elbridge. 'How to Fight Savage Tribes'. *American Journal of International Law* 21 (2) (1927), 279–288.

Eggers, Maureen Maisha. 'Rassifizierte Machtdifferenz als Deutungsperspektive in der Kri-tischen Weißseinsforschung in Deutschland. Zur Aktualität und Normativität diskursiver Vemittlungen von hierarchischen aufeinander bezogenen rassifizierten Konstruktionen', i: Maureen Maisha Eggers, Grada Kilomba, Peggy Piesche and Susan Arndt (eds.), *My-then, Masken und Subjekte. Kritische Weißseinsforschung in Deutschland* (Münster: Un-rast 2005), 56–72.

Fisch, Jörg. *Die europäische Expansion und das Völkerrecht. Die Auseinandersetzungen um den Status der überseeischen Gebiete vom 15. Jahrhundert bis zur Gegenwart* (Wiesba-den: Steiner 1984).

Gallagher, John and Donald Robinson. 'The Imperialism of Free Trade'. *Economic History Review* 6 (1) (1953), 1–15.

Grawert, Rolf. 'Homogenität, Identität, Souveränität. Positionen jurisdiktioneller Begriffs-dogmatik'. *Der Staat* 51 (2) (2012), 192–193.

Haferkamp, Hans–Peter. *Die historische Rechtsschule* (Frankfurt am Main: Vittorio Kloster-mann 2018).

51 Hohendahl, *Perilous Futures*, 103.

Heffter, August Wilhelm and Friedrich Heinrich Geffcken. *Das europäische Völkerrecht der Gegenwart auf den bisherigen Grundlagen* (Berlin: Müller, 8th ed., 1888).

Heilborn, Paul. 'Völkerrechtliches und koloniales Protektorat'. *Zeitschrift für Völkerrecht* 8 (3) (1914), 217–232.

Heuer, Andreas. *Carl Schmitt: Die Dialektik der Moderne. Von der europäischen zur Welt–Moderne* (Berlin: Duncker & Humblot 2010).

Hohendahl, Peter Uwe. *Perilous Futures. On Carl Schmitt's Late Writings* (Ithaca: Cornell University Press 2018).

Hull, Isabel V. *A Scrap of Paper. Breaking and Making International Law During the Great War* (Ithaca: Cornell University Press 2014).

Kelsen, Hans. 'Essential Conditions of International Justice'. *Proceedings of the American Society of International Law at its annual meeting (1921–1969)* 35 (1941), 70–86.

Kohli, Atul. *Imperialism and the Developing World* (Oxford: Oxford University Press 2020).

Koskenniemi, Martti. 'Carl Schmitt and International Law', in Jens Meierhenrich and Oliver Simons (eds.), *The Oxford Handbook of Carl Schmitt* (Oxford: Oxford University Press 2017), 592–611.

Koskenniemi, Martti. *The Gentle Civilizer of Nations* (Cambridge: Cambridge University Press 2001).

Lauer, Alexander. *Carl Schmitts Sicht auf die außereuropäische Welt* (Munich: Grin 2016).

Marcos, Teodoro Andrés. *Vitoria y Carlos V en la soberanía hispano-americana*(Salamanca: Sucesores de Rivadeneyra, 2nd ed., 1946).

Mégret, Frédéric. 'From "Savages" to "Unlawful Combatants": A Postcolonial Look at Inter-national Humanitarian Law's "Other"', in Anne Orford (ed.), *International Law and Its Others* (Cambridge: Cambridge University Press 2006), 265–317.

Mouffe, Chantal. 'Carl Schmitt and the Paradox of Liberal Democracy'. *Canadian Journal of Law and Jurisprudence* 10 (1) (2015), 21–33.

Nuzzo, Luigi. *Lawyers, Space and Subjects. Historical Perspective on the Western Legal Tra-dition* (Lecce: Pensa MultiMedia 2020).

Sands, Philippe. *East West Street. On the Origins of Genocide and Crimes against Humanity* (London: Weidenfeld & Nicolson 2016).

Schmitt, Carl. 'Die Lage der europäischen Rechtswissenschaft', in Carl Schmitt (ed.), *Verfas-sungsrechtliche Aufsätze aus den Jahren 1924–1954. Materialien zu einer Verfassungs-lehre* (Berlin: Duncker & Humblot, 4th ed., 2003), 386–429.

Schmitt, Carl. 'Die siebente Wandlung des Genfer Völkerbundes. Eine völkerrechtliche Folge der Vernichtung Abessiniens', in Günter Maschke (ed.), *Frieden oder Pazifismus? Arbeiten zum Völkerrecht und zur internationalen Politik* (Berlin: Duncker & Humblot 2019), 469–480.

Schmitt, Carl. 'Die Wendung zum diskriminierenden Kriegsbegriff', in Günter Maschke (ed.), *Frieden oder Pazifismus? Arbeiten zum Völkerrecht und zur internationalen Politik 1924–1978* (Berlin: Duncker & Humblot 2019), 518–597.

Schmitt, Carl. 'USA und die völkerrechtlichen Formen des modernen Imperialismus', in Günter Maschke (ed.), *Frieden oder Pazifismus? Arbeiten zum Völkerrecht und zur inter-nationalen Politik 1924–1978* (Berlin: Duncker & Humblot 2019), 349–377.

Schmitt, Carl. *Der Nomos der Erde im Völkerrecht des Jus Publicum Europaeum* (Berlin: Duncker & Humblot, 5th ed., 2011).

Schmitt, Carl. *Völkerrechtliche Großraumordnung mit Interventionsverbot für raumfremde Mächte. Ein Beitrag zum Reichsbegriff im Völkerrecht* (Berlin: Duncker & Humblot, 4th ed., 2022).

Schröder, Peter. 'Carl Schmitt's Appropriation of the Early Modern European Tradition of Political Thought on the State and Interstate Relations'. *History of Political Thought* 33 (2) (2012), 348–371.

Schütze, Robert. *From Utopia to Apologia: International Normativity in the Long Nineteenth Century* (London: London School of Economics, Ph.D Thesis, 2019).

Vergerio, Claire. *War, States, and International Order. Alberico Gentili and the Foundational Myth of the Laws of War* (Cambridge: Cambridge University Press 2022).

Voigt, Rüdiger. 'Mythos Staat. Zum Staatsdenken von Carl Schmitt', in Rüdiger Voigt (ed.), *Denken In Widersprüchen. Carl Schmitt wider den Zeitgeist* (Baden–Baden: Nomos, 2nd ed., 2021), 35–59.

von Bernstorff, Jochen and Max Mayer. 'The Historical School and German International Legal Thought in the 19th Century'. *Journal of the History of International Law* 25 (4) (2023), 1–43.

von Bernstorff, Jochen. 'Governing Hegemonic Spaces in Carl Schmitt: Colonialism, Anti-Imperialism and the Großraum Theory'. *Humanity* 14 (3) (2023), 369–383.

von Bernstorff, Jochen. 'Koloniale Herrschaft durch Ambivalenz: die deutsche Völkerrechts-wissenschaft und die Kolonien', in Philip Dann, Isabel Feichtner and Jochen von Bernst-orff (eds.), *(Post)Koloniale Rechtswissenschaft* (Tübingen: Mohr Siebeck 2022), 271–296.

von Bernstorff, Jochen. 'The critic', in Jean d'Aspremont and Sahib Singh (eds.), *Concepts for International Law. Contributions to Disciplinary Thought* (Cheltenham: Edward Elgar 2019), 154–163.

von Bernstorff, Jochen. *The Public International Law Theory of Hans Kelsen. Believing in Universal Law* (Cambridge: Cambridge University Press 2010).

Wagner, Norbert Berthold. *Die deutschen Schutzgebiete. Erwerb, Organisation und Verlust aus juristischer Sicht* (Baden–Baden: Nomos 2002).

Wilcox, Vanda. 'The Italian Soldiers' Experience in Libya, 1911–1912', in Dominik Geppert (ed.), *The Wars before the Great War. Conflict and International Politics before the Out-break of the First World War* (Cambridge: Cambridge University Press 2015), 41–57.

Wolin, Richard. 'Carl Schmitt, Political Existentialism, and the Total State'. *Theory and Soci-ety* 19 (4) (1990), 389–416.

CHAPTER 4

The Problem of Limited War: Vitoria and Schmitt on Imperial Violence

Lauren Benton

We read the works of Francisco de Vitoria and Carl Schmitt through thick interpretive lenses. Vitoria's place in the canon of international law was profoundly influenced by twentieth- and twenty-first-century efforts to recast the history of international law as a universalist project. Interpretations of Schmitt's texts have spanned the political spectrum, with right-wing critics drawn to his insistence on a muscular state and leftists persuaded by his critique of liberalism. These readings must also contend with political messages that Vitoria and Schmitt themselves inserted into their texts. A careful analysis of their work requires a triple analytical feat: discerning authorial intent, appraising historical contexts and filtering out distortions of ideologically charged commentary.

Keeping these challenges in mind, I propose reading Vitoria and Schmitt as theorists of limited war. The subject is often overlooked in commentary on their work, but both writers placed the definition of limited war at the heart of their intellectual agendas. Both also connected the topic to shared challenges: defining partial or attenuated sovereignty, specifying the legal character of violence short of war, and plotting (or preventing) transitions from limited war to extreme violence or total war. These problems were not merely theoretical. They emerged forcefully in the worlds of violence that Vitoria and Schmitt were observing – in contexts that drew both writers to sketch the legal framework for war beyond Europe. In different ways, each contributed to the development of a theory of limited war, even as their proffered solutions underscored the poverty of available approaches and vocabularies. The project proved remarkably durable across several centuries.[1]

In this chapter, I begin with Vitoria's approach to limited war and then turn to Schmitt's attempts to grapple with the problem. My purpose in juxtaposing the works of these two very different writers is to expose similarities in approaches to recurring problems. As Vitoria and Schmitt sought to describe

1 On the longer tradition of writing on limited war, see Lauren Benton. *They Called It Peace: Worlds of Imperial Violence* (Princeton: Princeton University Press, 2024).

 | DOI:10.1163/9789004757448_005

the nature and limits of war, each represented incomplete or uneven sovereignty as a condition that opened pathways to unruly or annihilating war. Failing to construct a coherent legal framework for violence short of war, each resorted to labelling some peoples and polities as naturally or ideologically inclined toward untamed violence.

These findings suggest the need for several revisions to standard narratives of the history of international law. First, attention to the theme of limited war challenges a tendency to exaggerate the originality and theoretical coherence of the work of both Vitoria and Schmitt. Neither writer arrived at a satisfying solution to the problem of limited war, and neither resolved closely related questions about law and gradations of violence or permutations of sovereignty. Second, tracking commentary on the problem of limited war adds nuance to our understanding of post-war developments in international law. The reception of Vitoria and Schmitt into the canon of international law occurred in the same post-war decades, and that coincidence contributed to a tendency to oversimplify openings to extreme violence or total war. Third, theories of limited war identify the lawfulness of violence in empires as a persistent problem in global legal thought. Although more explicit in Vitoria's texts, challenges in defining the legal framework for violence outside Europe persisted into the twentieth century. The topic concerned Schmitt enough to cause him to think of revising core elements of his theory of the political. Read in combination, Vitoria's and Schmitt's writings on limited war situate empire, incomplete sovereignty and atrocity at the very centre of the history of international law.

1 Just and Limited War

Francisco de Vitoria's paired lectures *De indis* and *De jure belli* have provided material for contrasting interpretations of the 'Dominican moment' and its legacies.[2] Because he recognised the *dominium* of Indigenous Americans, Vitoria is often described, along with other scholastic writers, as a figure

2 I will draw in my discussion from the English translation of these texts, titled 'On the American Indians' and 'On the Law of War' in Anthony Pagden and Jeremy Lawrance (eds.), *Francisco de Vitoria: Political Writings* (Cambridge: Cambridge University Press. 1991), 231–327. On the Latin titles for these works, see Pagden and Lawrance, 233, n.2 and 293. The phrase 'the Dominican moment' is from Annabel Brett, 'Scholastic Political Thought and the Modern Concept of the State', in Annabel Brett and James Tully (eds.), *Rethinking the Foundations of Modern Political Thought* (Cambridge: Cambridge University Press, 2006), 130–148, 141.

whose texts prefigured 'the modern theory of international law as a positive law between sovereign states'.[3] Within this approach, an influential strand of literature identifies Vitoria's reflections on the *ius communicandi*, the right to trade and communication, as foundational to commitments to free trade in the international order. Critics of these views have characterised Vitoria as an apologist of empire. They point out that his commentary on the just titles of Spanish conquest of the Americas enhanced the power of the Spanish crown and justified the exploitation of Indigenous Americans.[4]

Cutting across these interpretations is an emphasis on Vitoria's universalism.[5] Spanish international lawyers celebrated Vitoria as the founder of international law, for example, by highlighting his emphasis on the 'moral unity' of human society.[6] Critics argued that in replacing divine law with the law of nations, Vitoria nevertheless marked some practices as 'limited in scope to the Christian world and therefore inapplicable to the Indians'.[7] In reintroducing imperial practices and Catholic principles as universal, Vitoria constructed an elaborate rationale for European global expansion and imperial violence.

It is helpful to move the assessment of Vitoria's universalism and its influence gently to one side.[8] I want to consider instead how Vitoria approached the paired problems of partial sovereignty and limited war. As Annabel Brett

---

3 Brett, 'Scholastic Political Thought and the Modern Concept of the State', 142.

4 The literature on Vitoria is of course vast. James Brown Scott was influential in claiming a place for Vitoria as a founder of international law and of free trade in the international order. James Brown Scott, *The Spanish Origins of International Law: Francisco de Vitoria and His Law of Nations* (Oxford: Oxford University Press, 1934). Ignacio de la Rasilla traces the multiple phases in the reception and interpretation in Spain of Vitoria as a founding figure in international law. Ignacio de la Rasilla del Moral, *In the Shadow of Vitoria: A History of International Law in Spain (1770–1953)* (Leiden: Brill, 2018). A key work identifying Vitoria as an apologist for empire is Antony Anghie, *Imperialism, Sovereignty and the Making of International Law* (Cambridge: Cambridge University Press, 2004), chapter 1. On private rights in Vitoria's writings, see Martti Koskenniemi, 'Empire and International Law: The Real Spanish Contribution'. *University of Toronto Law Journal* 61:1 (2011), 1–36.

5 An insightful discussion of universalism in European international thought is Jennifer Pitts, 'Empire and Legal Universalisms in the Eighteenth Century', *The American Historical Review*, 117:1 (2012), 92–121.

6 José Yanguas Messía, quoted in de la Rasilla, *In the Shadow of Vitoria*, 175.

7 Anghie, *Imperialism, Sovereignty and the Making of International Law*, 23.

8 This is also a move recommended by Koskenniemi in 'Empire and International Law'. But whereas Koskenniemi highlights Vitoria's take on private rights in natural law, I emphasise representations of authority and place them in relation to rights. See Lauren Benton and Jane Burbank, 'Rights and Empires: Relations of Authority', in Dan Edelstein and Jennifer Pitts (eds.), *The Cambridge History of Rights, Vol. IV* (Cambridge: Cambridge University Press, 2025), 437–462.

has noted, Vitoria was writing in 'a period in which the boundaries of the modern state were not yet fixed'.[9] Composite monarchies were steeped in questions about the jurisdictional scope of multiple legal authorities. Rather than consistently operating as rulers of large states interacting with sovereign equals, imperial sovereigns defined and redefined crown authority in relation to an array of political and religious communities possessing a measure of legitimate local rule and law. But how could the crown be simultaneously dominant and constrained in its power? And how could subordinate political communities be both independent and subject to imperial intervention? Writing in Castile in the shadow of the revolt of the *comuneros*, with its aim of radically recalibrating relations of the nobility to the crown and of the Spanish crown to the Habsburg empire, Vitoria was already immersed in such debates.[10] Instead of posing radically novel challenges, Spanish incursions in the New World gave a new spin to familiar questions.

Indeed, we can read *De indis* and *De jure belli* as exercises in reconciling the empire's pluralism and the Spanish crown's claims to a distinctive kind of power. Vitoria discussed this challenge explicitly in the lecture on war. Here he noted that it was possible for a perfect community – one 'complete in itself' that had 'its own laws, its own independent policy, and its own magistrates' – to be 'subject to a single prince'.[11] He added that this situation was not unique to the Americas, where *indios* possessed dominium but were simultaneously vassals of the Spanish king. The same condition applied to 'the Kingdom of Castile and Aragon and the Republic of Venice and others'.[12] This nod to pluralism matched the practices that Spaniards were deploying to project their power across the Americas. In addition to using force, they engaged in alliance building, truce making and the delegation of authority to local rulers charged with keeping order and delivering tribute to Spaniards.

Vitoria wondered whether and how one might locate the right to make war in composite polities. If 'several such commonwealths of princes share a single prince', Vitoria asked, could such communities 'of themselves wage war without the authority of their supreme sovereign'.[13] In agreement with other scholastics, Vitoria's response was that that the right to make war flowed from the

9 Brett, 'Scholastic Political Thought and the Modern Concept of the State', 142.

10 Brett, 'Scholastic Political Thought and the Modern Concept of the State', 143.

11 Vitoria, 'On the Law of War', 301.

12 Vitoria, 'On the Law of War', 301.

13 Victoria, 'On the Law of War', 301. Fernández-Santamaria regards this position as an indication of Vitoria's desire to replace the model of the empire with another, that of the state (rather than commonwealth or republic), but this interpretation projects the vision of the international community as a collection of sovereign states backward in

natural right to self-preservation, which in turn supported the right to self-defence for all political communities, as for all individuals. It was not possible to strip that right from political communities, regardless of whether they were inside or outside the Spanish orbit.

It remained for Vitoria to explain how it was possible for a polity to simultaneously hold the right to make war and be subject to the Spanish crown's power to limit that right. The answer was multi-layered. Vitoria suggested that not all the political leaders whom Spaniards were encountering in the New World were rulers of perfect communities. Some groups could not lawfully make war because they did not in fact deserve recognition as distinctive political communities. Their leaders might be mere 'princelings' who were 'simply rulers of parts of a greater commonwealth'.[14] Even if polities under a single prince could claim legitimate independence of action in matters of law and war, there could still be limits on that right. Vitoria pointed out, for example, that such communities could not lawfully use force to block Spaniards' 'right to travel and dwell in those countries' so long as travellers or traders were not doing harm to these communities.[15] If locals did obstruct movement or trade, Spaniards could respond to this injury with the just use of force. Later critics, most notably the Jesuit Luis de Molina, questioned this position and suggested that any political community might bar the entry of strangers since their very presence might prove destabilising.[16] As this criticism suggested, Vitoria's position implied that although all individuals and political communities possessed natural rights and *dominium*, their capacity to defend those rights was unequal.

The different legal capacities of political communities came up again when Vitoria discussed, as he did at length, the moral and legal limits on Spanish violence. Although Spaniards could engage in a just war in response to injuries by *indios* and could do so in 'blameless self-defence', Vitoria exhorted them not to extend acts of war beyond the moment of their victory over opponents. Here again, the relative incapacity of *indios* mattered; they had been driven to violence against Spaniards by their innocence and their 'understandable fears'. Vitoria warned that Spaniards should react 'with as little harm to the barbarians as possible' in what was 'merely a defensive war'.[17] Signalling that *indios* were a different kind of enemy who therefore in most (but not all) circum-

---

time. J.A. Fernández-Santamaria, *The State, War and Peace: Spanish Political Thought in the Renaissance 1616–1559* (Cambridge: Cambridge University Press, 1977), 77.

14 Vitoria, 'On the Law of War', 301–302.

15 Vitoria, 'On the American Indians', 282.

16 Brett, 'Scholastic Political Thought and the Modern Concept of the State', 146.

17 Vitoria, 'On the American Indians', 282.

stances deserved a lesser measure of violence, Vitoria stated succinctly that the 'laws of war against really harmful and offensive enemies are quite different from those against innocent or ignorant ones'.[18]

Pushing these arguments still further, Vitoria explained other limits on war by Spaniards. They should avoid punishing entire populations for injuries done by a few; refrain from enslaving or engaging in plunder against non-combatants unless warranted by strict necessity; reject the temptation to inflict violence based solely on revenge, cruelty or terror; and abstain from provocations that would draw opponents into war.[19] Vitoria even recognised the right – indeed, the duty – of the individual to limit personal participation in war if he believed the enemies to be innocent. If a subject judged a war to be unjust, 'he must not fight, even if he is ordered to do so by the prince'.[20]

Notably, Vitoria was concerned not just with limits on Spanish violence but also with defining the conditions under which such limits disappeared. In line with the just war tradition, he assembled a case for lawful extreme violence and described the conditions under which enemies could be treated as something other than enemies in the usual sense. As with the outbreak of just war, Vitoria assigned the responsibility for releasing limits on war to Indigenous Americans.

According to Vitoria, those who made war for defensive purposes, as Spaniards did in the Americas 'to secure [their] safety' and produce 'peace and security', might find their opponents unwilling to make or keep peace after fighting subsided. Such opponents would continue to 'strive to destroy the Spaniards', and their actions would justify Spaniards' extreme violence in response. It would become lawful, Vitoria observed, for Spaniards to cease to treat such opponents as 'innocent enemies', instead regarding them 'as treacherous foes against whom all rights of war can be exercised, including plunder, enslavement, deposition of their former masters, and the institution of new [masters]'.[21] Vitoria was careful to note that violence as punishment did not lie outside the law. A widely accepted doctrine in the law of nations, he explained, held that 'the prince who wages a just war becomes *ipso jure* the judge of the enemy'.[22] That function converted violence into judicial punishment. Having waged a just war, only Spaniards could judge the lawfulness of subsequent violence and fix its appropriate measure. As we shall see, Schmitt

18 Vitoria, 'On the American Indians', 282–83.
19 Vitoria, 'On the Law of War', 315, 317, 318, 320, 323, 326.
20 Vitoria, 'On the Law of War', 307.
21 Vitoria, 'On the American Indians', 283.
22 Vitoria, 'On the American Indians', 283.

later placed the relation of war and punishment at the heart of his critique of a supposed modern turn toward discriminatory war, a variant of war as punishment for criminals rather than engagement with enemies.

Other pathways to unfettered violence might be accidental, according to Vitoria. Killing innocents was permissible if it happened by 'accidental effect', in episodes that created what later war observers came to call 'collateral damage'. Spaniards might be fully aware of the death and destruction their actions were causing among innocents, but these results were necessary in waging war against 'the guilty'.[23] Similarly, Vitoria explained, if the resources of innocents were being used to sustain the enemy, then it would be 'lawful to plunder the enemy indiscriminately, both innocent and guilty'.[24] It was even permissible to wage a war of extermination if the only way to produce peace was by 'the wholesale destruction of the enemy'.[25]

We are now in sight of a dilemma faced by Vitoria. Having argued that *indios* deserved a lesser measure of violence because of their innocence, he now found himself outlining conditions for their lawful extinction. To reconcile these positions, Vitoria ultimately relied on a judgment about differences between Spaniards and non-Christians. Enemies who would not acquiesce after being vanquished in a just war did not share Christians' commitment to peace, he proposed. They were perpetual enemies because they refused to accept defeat and could therefore be judged and punished by Spaniards, and they shared some qualities with rebellious subjects deserving harsh punishment. Perpetual enemies were neither fully inside the empire nor fully outside it. They did not occupy an independent political community with the capacity for waging just war, and they had not fully submitted to the authority of the crown. They might be classed as rebels or enemies.

One way to frame this position would be to regard Vitoria as representing *indios* as possessing the capacity to choose between acquiescence and opposition. This formulation had found expression in the *requerimiento*, the statement drawn up by Juan López de Palacios Rubios, endorsed by the crown and distributed to Spaniards in the New World to read before attacking Indigenous Americans. The statement presented to *indios* the choice to submit or resist and informed them that the consequence of resistance would be that the Spaniards would 'make war' against them 'in all ways and manners'.[26] But in

---

23 Vitoria, 'On the Law of War', 315.

24 Vitoria, 'On the Law of War', 317.

25 Vitoria, 'On the Law of War', 321.

26 The National Humanities Center, Council of Castile (Spain), 'Requerimiento, 1510', 2, available at: https://nationalhumanitiescenter.org/pds/amerbegin/contact/text7/requirement.pdf. For the Spanish text of the *requerimiento*, see Agustín Millares Carlo, ed.,

questioning the usual justifications for Spanish conquest, Vitoria was implicitly critiquing the right of the Spaniards to make such a demand. He instead rested his support for Spanish authority on distinguishing between a singularly powerful crown and the diminished sovereignty of *indios*. Only true sovereigns possessed the capacity to make just war. As Fernández–Santamaria notes, Vitoria was describing 'two forms of sovereignty of vastly different value'. One form comprised 'the overpowering sovereignty of the prince waging a just war'; the other, 'the questionable sovereignty of his victim'.[27] Vitoria was merging the authority of the prince with the regulatory effects of the law of nations.[28]

Here we glimpse another profound tension. For Vitoria, natural law unified political communities because all possessed dominium. One dimension of this unity was the recognition of private rights associated with the liberties of individuals, an effect that Koskenniemi has labelled the creation of an 'empire of private rights'.[29] But we must follow Vitoria a step further and assess the full implications of his perspective, which included the view that natural rights also generated the conditions for human beings *to make other law*. The result was not only a system of private rights but also a system of multiple political authorities. In the phrase an 'empire of private rights' the emphasis belongs on *empire* – understood not as a single political unit but as an assemblage of political communities.[30] Within this pluri-political world, Vitoria found in varieties of sovereignty and in the confusion of enemies and vassals the conditions for violence that reached beyond the limits on war. He observed and accepted these links, even as he recognised that the resulting violence might be so extreme as to border on sin.

Historia de ls Indias, por Fray Bartolomé de Las Casas, Vol 3 (México: Fondo de Cultura Económico, 1951), 26–27. For further discussion of the *requerimiento*, see Benton, *They Called It Peace*, 27–28, 46–50.

27 Fernández-Santamaria, *The State, War and Peace*, 113.

28 Fernández-Santamaria, *The State, War and Peace*, 113. See also Anghie, *Imperialism*, chapter 1. Note that whereas Anghie describes Vitoria as representing a world in which *indios* were '*excluded* from the sphere of sovereignty', Fernández-Santamaria regards Vitoria as relegating them to less powerful political communities (Anghie, *Imperialism*, 27. Emphasis added).

29 Koskenniemi, 'Empire and International Law', 28.

30 Brett notes that for Vitoria, 'an empire can only be a conglomeration of separately formed, territorially limited commonwealths: there is no political unit called "empire" that can be a legitimate holder of political power'. Brett, 'Scholastic Political Thought and the Modern Concept of the State', 144. For a related discussion of the importance of retaining an emphasis on structures of authority in characterising rights in empires, see Benton and Burbank, 'Rights and Empires'.

2 The Paradox of Partisans

Nearly five-hundred years later, another legal writer took up similar questions about limited war. Schmitt's analysis of war has received far less attention than his theories of the political, his decisionist approach to sovereignty or his analysis of concrete spatial orders. Some scholars flag this skewed interpretation as an error and instead suggest that we should regard Schmitt *mainly* as a theorist of war.[31] It was war, after all, that made sense of the friend–enemy distinction at the centre of Schmitt's views of the political. The use of force also defined the land grabs that Schmitt erroneously identified as the point of origin of the *ius publicum europaeum*. The turn toward discriminatory warfare, meanwhile, was for Schmitt a noxious side effect of Anglo-American global power and a phenomenon that provoked and justified the German quest for *Grossraum*. Finally, Schmitt regarded new kinds of wars propelled by partisans as sources of unresolved turmoil in the modern international order.

It is important to recognise Schmitt as a theorist not only of war but also of limited war. Concern with the topic was already present in Schmitt's *The Concept of the Political*.[32] Here he marked the state as a distinctive authority, not one among many authorities in a pluralist order. The state's singularity lay partly in its clear labelling of the enemy, a capacity that Schmitt paired with the decision on emergency or exception as a key to sovereignty. For Schmitt, these insights offered a correction to a dangerous slide toward a world in which defeated enemies found their sovereignty diluted and could even lose their states. Responding to the allied occupation of the Rhineland and other attacks on German sovereignty after WWI and outraged by the treatment of German officials as criminals after WWII, Schmitt regarded such actions as a continuation of war by other names or, more accurately, a type of violence that could not be classed as war. Incursions on German sovereignty 'stopped just short of proper war', but the effects were as devastating as the impact of

31 Johanna Jacques nominates Schmitt as a theorist of war in 'From 'Nomos' to 'Hegung': Sovereignty and the Laws of War in Schmitt's International Order', *The Modern Law Review* 78:3 (2015), 411–430. In a deeply insightful essay, Benno Teschke notes how little sustained critical attention has been given to Schmitt's analysis of war, even though, for Schmitt, 'War defines the very possibility of a political community and constitutes the highest expression of the political'. Benno Teschke, 'Carl Schmitt's Concepts of War: A Categorical Failure', in (eds.) Jens Meierhenrich and Oliver Simons, *The Oxford Handbook of Carl Schmitt* (Oxford: Oxford University Press, 2016), 367–400.

32 Carl Schmitt, *The Concept of the Political* (Chicago: University of Chicago Press, 2007).

war.[33] Here Schmitt was not just analysing historical shifts or devising a theory. He was opposing Anglo-American global power and calling for a new order that would feature a return to a clear division between war and peace, while enabling sharp distinctions between just and absolute enemies.

Schmitt's analysis of limited war was at the heart of this project. The *ius publicum europaeum*, Schmitt argued, had placed limits on war by confining it to conflicts between sovereign states. Conflicts in the *ius publicum europaeum* could not become total wars – not because shared norms or universal principles prevented their escalation on moral or legal grounds but because the concrete spatial order had shifted the locus of unfettered violence outside the order: to the colonial world and to places not yet integrated into Western empires or spheres of influence.

The counterpart to unregulated war in the extra-European realm was, according to Schmitt, the 'bracketing of war' in Europe.[34] Schmitt settled on the word *Hegung* to characterise the process of limiting war. Whereas the word 'bracketing', the usual English translation, implies a setting aside of something, typically within an enclosure, the English word does not capture the association of *Hegung* with the hedging or fencing off of something *for its protection*.[35] For Schmitt, the 'bracketing of war' did not denote a mere division of zones. *Hegung* represented a process for facilitating limited war by protecting warfare among sovereign states:

> The essence of European international law was the bracketing of war. The essence of such wars was a regulated contest of forces gauged by witnesses in a bracketed space. Such wars are the opposite of disorder. They represent the highest form of order within the scope of human power. They are the only protection against a cycle of increasing reprisals, i.e., against nihilistic hatred and reactions whose meaningless goal lies in mutual destruction.[36]

In asserting that the *ius publicum europaeum* constrained war by facilitating it, Schmitt was placing war at the heart of his theory of international order.

33 Jan-Werner Müller, *A Dangerous Mind: Carl Schmitt in Post-War European Thought* (New Haven: Yale University Press, 2004), 26. Müller notes that that Schmitt was operating in 'a culture in which the enemy had become indeterminate, and in which indeterminacy had become the enemy'. Müller, *A Dangerous Mind*, 34.

34 Carl Schmitt, *The Nomos of the Earth in the International Law of Jus Publicum Europaeum* (Candor, NY: Telos Press, 2003), 93.

35 Jacques, 'Sovereignty and the Laws of War', 424.

36 Schmitt, *Nomos of the Earth*, 187.

Limits on war, rather than its prohibition, were the key objects of supra-state ordering.

In Schmitt's telling, claims about liberal international law, exemplified by the Monroe Doctrine, had eroded the European order of limited war. The proliferation of states beyond Europe, moreover, magnified the effects of this trend. The result, Schmitt proposed, was a shift toward discriminatory war, the representation of war as a punitive act to punish criminals rather than to engage the enemy. Paradoxically, for Schmitt that shift had also marked an opening to total war because he could identify no international limits on the treatment of criminal enemies. It is interesting to reflect on Schmitt's equation of policing and the force exercised against criminal enemies since the formula exposes the interpenetration of fascist ideology and Schmitt's approach to international order. Whereas international lawyers at the end of the nineteenth century associated policing with measures short of war, Schmitt characterised policing as a form of hyper-violence that mirrored repression by domestic authority.[37] According to Schmitt, there were no political limits on the use of domestic force, and policing in the international realm similarly faced no constraints.

Schmitt initially made Vitoria a touchstone for describing both the juridical formalisation that produced the bracketing of war and the subsequent shift toward discriminatory war. He noted that for Vitoria, 'even an unjust war was still war'.[38] But also according to Schmitt, the liberal interpreters of Vitoria – and here he had James Brown Scott firmly in mind – had stripped away the theological content of scholastic thought and replaced it with a supposedly neutral juridical approach that narrowed the definition of war and gave rise to 'reversions to civil war and other types of wars of annihilation'.[39] Whereas, Schmitt proposed, the earlier order of limited war had made all non-state forms of fighting illegitimate, including 'rebellion, mutiny, breach of the peace, barbarism, and piracy', these possibilities had come roaring back in the liberal international order.[40] The new order took shape in the absence of a single unifying sovereignty and in the context of proliferating regional spheres populated by part-sovereignties.

This is not the place to detail the significant historical misrepresentations contained in Schmitt's description of the genesis and operation of the *ius pub-*

---

37 Stephen C. Neff, *War and the Law of Nations* (Cambridge: Cambridge University Press, 2005), chapter 6; Benton, *They Called It Peace*, 181.

38 Schmitt, *Nomos of the Earth*, 119.

39 Schmitt, *Nomos of the Earth*, 119, 246.

40 Schmitt, *Nomos of the Earth*, 158.

licum europaeum or embedded in his characterisation of international policing as the exercise of force without limits. But a few key distortions deserve attention since they infused Schmitt's views on violence. One fabrication was Schmitt's wild exaggeration of the degree to which the Europeans regarded violence 'beyond the line' as unregulated.[41] In *Nomos*, he presented a sharp break between the period of the papal donations aimed at containing violence between Iberian powers and the time of overseas expansion by Northern European empires. In the later period, for Schmitt, 'Everything that occurred "beyond the line" remained outside the legal, moral, and political values recognised on this side of the line.'[42] This account confused European discourse about lawlessness outside Europe with accurate historical description.[43] Schmitt could offer only threadbare support for this view since even a cursory examination would have shown that Europeans actively utilised and, indeed, creatively modified law in justifying war and projecting order 'beyond the line'.[44] Imperial legal historians have by now exploded the myth of lawlessness beyond the line and revised the assumption that Europeans followed a clear juridical script in engagements with non-Europeans.[45]

Schmitt apparently had limited access to existing works contradicting his assumptions about the spatial distribution of violence or the operation of law in European empires. Yet he was also blinded by his commitment to pairing limitless violence outside Europe with the ascendance of British global power,

---

41 Schmitt, *Nomos of the Earth*, 92–99.

42 Schmitt, *Nomos of the Earth*, 94.

43 Eliga Gould carefully traces European discourse about this distinction in 'Zones of Law, Zones of Violence: The Legal Geography of the British Atlantic, circa 1772', *William and Mary Quarterly* 60:3 (2003), 471–510. But toward the end of the essay, Gould is also tempted to elide theory and practice.

44 See Lauren Benton and Benjamin Straumann, 'Acquiring Empire by Law: From Roman Doctrine to Early Modern European Practice', *Law and History Review* 28:1 (2010), 1–38; Lauren Benton, 'Interpolity Law', in (eds.) Mlada Bukovansky, Edward Keene, Maja Spanu, and Christopher Reus-Smit, *Oxford Handbook of History and International Relations* (Oxford: Oxford University Press, 2023), 320–333.

45 From this vast literature, some examples of works that document the operation and representation of law in the extra-European world are Lauren Benton, *Law and Colonial Cultures: Legal Regimes in World History, 1400–1900* (Cambridge: Cambridge University Press, 2002); Saliha Belmessous, *Native Claims: Indigenous Law against Empire, 1500–1920* (Oxford: Oxford University Press, 2012); and Martti Koskenniemi, *To the Uttermost Parts of the Earth: Legal Imagination and International Power 1300–1870* (Cambridge: Cambridge University Press, 2021). On the way law functioned as a 'repertoire' rather than a 'script' in European empires, see Benton and Straumann, 'Acquiring Empire by Law'.

and he read available titles selectively.[46] The distortions extended to his representation of liberal internationalism as a continuation of uncontained global violence under Anglo-American hegemony. To make this connection, Schmitt had to ignore a significant record of the twentieth-century campaign for international regulation of war by Western governments. More disturbingly, to represent the spectre of total war as an effect of Anglo-American global power, Schmitt had to ignore the Nazi embrace of total war.[47]

Schmitt's historical errors and omissions represented only one aspect of the ideological constructs undergirding his views on war. We can also pinpoint problems with Schmitt's theory *as theory*.[48] Here Schmitt himself serves as a guide since, beginning in the 1960s, he became increasingly aware of the inconsistencies and problems in his analysis of war. In *The Theory of the Partisan: An Interjection to the Concept of the Political*, first delivered as a lecture at the Spanish War College in Zaragoza in 1962, Schmitt set himself the task of revising the friend–enemy distinction at the heart of his concept of the political. The work's subtitle, 'An Interjection to the Concept of the Political', explicitly marks this goal. Exposing the importance of war to his theory of the political, Schmitt sought to assess the legal and political character of partisans and partisan wars, including 'civil wars and all colonial wars'.[49] *Theory of the Partisan* responded to a world transformed by the defeat of Germany, the Cold War and the proliferation of anti-imperial revolutions. But it was intended, above all, as a theoretical intervention.

---

46 There were, even in Schmitt's time, places to look for the history of law in European empires. One study of legal relations in American colonial society available at the time Charles McLean Andrews's four-volume work on North America, *The Colonial Period of American History* (New Haven: Yale University Press, 1934–1937). Schmitt apparently had access to Lewis Hanke's book, *The Spanish Struggle for Justice in the Conquest of America* (Philadelphia: University of Pennsylvania Press, 1949), cited in *Nomos of the Earth* (101), but he did not take notice of its nuanced discussions of the Spanish recognition of Indigenous polities and law in the New World or the controversies the encounters prompted; on that subject, Schmitt deferred to Vitoria's writings.

47 On both points, see Teschke, 'Carl Schmitt's Concepts of War'.

48 Teschke, 'Carl Schmitt's Concepts of War'.

49 Carl Schmitt, *The Theory of the Partisan: An Interjection to the Concept of the Political*, trans. C.J. Miller (Antelope Hill Publishing, 2020 [1962]), 6. The book was based on two lectures delivered by Schmitt in Spain in the spring of 1962. Antelope Hill Publishing is run by a small group of U.S. white nationalists and publishes works by Nazis and Nazi sympathisers. Michael Edison Hayden and Hannah Gais, Southern Poverty Law Center, 'White Nationalist Group Exploits Amazon to Fund Their Cause', August 23, 2022, available at: https://www.splcenter.org/resources/hatewatch/white-nationalist-group-explo its-amazon-fund-their-cause/.

Schmitt was drawn to the subject of partisans by their in-betweenness. He portrayed them as deeply conservative yet decidedly modern fighters who held strong political allegiances – but not to states.[50] Partisans preserved some elements of an older order while presenting new instabilities. On the one hand, partisans' solidarity, together with their effectiveness as irregular fighters, depended on their unified opposition to a clearly identified enemy, *as if* they were fighting for a state. On the other hand, as irregular fighters whose allegiance was to a cause and not to a state, their subordination to authority was abstract and lay somewhere in the indefinite future. Schmitt followed Clausewitz in treating as paradigmatic the example of Spanish partisans who fought to repel the Napoleonic army between 1809 and 1815. Undoubtedly with his Spanish audience in mind, Schmitt repeated elements of a romantic view of Spanish partisans motivated by strong attachments to land and deep commitments to Catholicism. Spanish partisans had unhesitatingly identified the invading French as 'the enemy', in the process running well ahead of other Spanish factions or leaders, including the king.[51] They were political fighters, but they were not engaged in a classic war between states.

Not all partisans conformed to this model. Particularly vexing to Schmitt was that their in-between condition meant that there was nothing to keep partisan struggles within the bounds of 'tamed and limited warfare'.[52] Partisans might easily aim at 'annihilation' of the enemy.[53] Schmitt did not hide his concern that revolutionary movements in Russia and China, as well as anti-colonial movements in Algeria, Indochina and Cuba, might generate unbridled violence. Such struggles had modified partisan warfare and turned it into a force opposing modernity, capitalism and the liberal state – yet without providing an alternative framework for limiting war. Whereas some varieties of partisanship retained their recognition of subordination to state power, some fighters would fail to distinguish, Schmitt concluded, between 'real enmity' and 'absolute enmity'.[54]

The tension between limited and limitless partisan warfare had taken other forms historically, according to Schmitt. He aligned various phases with the history of the concrete spatial order described in *Nomos*. In the *ius publicum europaeum*, he argued, either partisans operated as marginal fighters whose

50 Muller, *A Dangerous Mind*, 148.

51 Schmitt, *Theory of the Partisan*, 7. Schmitt celebrated – and romanticised – Spanish partisans' 'telluric' character, that is, their deep connections to the land.

52 Quoted in Müller, *A Dangerous Mind*, 148.

53 Schmitt, *The Theory of the Partisan*, 7.

54 Schmitt, *Theory of the Partisan*, 67.

irregularity was of little consequence, or they became criminal outsiders analogous to pirates. In the breakdown of that order, 'different sorts of partisans' emerged, and their iterations blurred distinctions between legality and illegality, and between real and absolute enmity. Because new and emerging orders no longer protected interstate war and harboured varied states of sovereignty, partisans might situate themselves in unpredictable ways within the international order.

Unable to discern a definite pattern, Schmitt turned to ideological aids. In *Theory of the Partisan*, he placed his thumb on the scale as he weighed whether partisan forces of the right or left were more inclined to tip towards annihilating war. Even as Schmitt sought to position himself – possibly with his Spanish audience in mind – outside Cold War alignments, *Theory of the Partisan* remained fundamentally an anti-communist tract. Anti-imperial communist movements, he suggested, could not be relied upon to recognise or conform to limits on war. It was not the structure or the legal underpinnings of the postwar world that set anti-imperial campaigns apart for Schmitt. It was their character as movements and their ideological orientation that altered their legibility as partisan struggles.

Schmitt's ideological aims also shone through another register in which he described limited war: in connection with distinctions between land and sea. Schmitt associated land-centredness with German culture (and with Catholic Spanish society in the example of partisan fighting against the French). In contrast, he linked control of the sea to the global ascendance of Britain and the United States. It should not be forgotten that Schmitt also labelled Jews as 'sea people', a choice based on the notion, expressed with unvarnished antisemitism, that they were wanderers who lacked a home territory.[55] Collapsing discourse about international law from the seventeenth century through the nineteenth century, Schmitt then connected the naval hegemony of Anglo-American powers to Grotius's arguments for freedom of navigation. He contrasted violence on the sea with supposedly more contained kinds of war in

55 *Land and Sea* is one of Schmitt's most blatantly antisemitic texts, even though he worked to cleanse it of its most egregious antisemitic content for postwar publication. See Garrett Zeitlin, 'Propaganda and critique: An Introduction to Land and Sea', in Carl Schmitt, *Land and Sea: A World Historical Meditation*, (Candor, NY: Telos Press, 2015): xxxi-lxix. Schmitt based the tract on a series of articles that appeared in the Nazi weekly publication Das Reich in 1940 and 1941. On the limitations of the work for an understanding of maritime history, see Lauren Benton and Nathan Perl-Rosenthal, 'Land-Sea Regimes in World History', in Lauren Benton and Nathan Perl-Rosenthal (eds.), *The World at Sea: Maritime Practices and Global History* (Philadelphia: University of Pennsylvania Press, 2021), 186–192.

politically and spatially divided land spaces. For Schmitt, piracy was neither interstate war nor partisanship because it aimed at commercial gain; the British were analogous to pirates because of their use of force to spread capitalism.[56] Schmitt was aware that pirates had often sailed with the backing of sovereign sponsors, but he was not interested in the blurred lines separating piracy from privateering, a history that would have placed pirates squarely within the ambit of interstate war. He also adopted a highly simplified view of capitalism as plunder. In the end, Schmitt's portrayal of the British as mere pirates remained a quip rather than a formidable critique.

It is worth noting that Schmitt linked his description of the sea as a site of unlimited violence to his theory of the partisan. Recall his insistence on the 'telluric' character of partisans – an extrapolation from the imagined character of nineteenth-century Spanish partisans. Schmitt could have counted on his Spanish audience to make the connection between his view of land-defending partisans and depictions of Franco's supporters as defenders of order. The kinship to 'telluric' Germans also provided a way of signalling the natural alliance of partisans with forces opposed to liberalism.

Yet partisans were not just defenders of tradition for Schmitt; they might also operate as vectors of a new order. Because partisans engaged in an in-between kind of violence, fighting not as an army but still battling a real enemy, they could help to create the conditions for a new global spatial order, one in which the bracketing of war in the *ius publicum europaeum* might encompass the world. Despite making this inference, Schmitt proved unable either to identify the nature of the limits on partisan warfare or to anticipate its specific effects on global order. Toward the end of *Theory of the Partisan*, he simply reaffirmed the friend–enemy distinction as the central character of the political. Frustrated by elusive patterns of late twentieth-century warfare and driven to defend his portrayal of Anglo-American empires as unique sources of limitless war, Schmitt had to abandon his aim of producing a general theory of limited war, together with his goal of amending his theory of the political.

56 Here, again, Schmitt faulted the liberal international order with setting up the conditions for total war. Again, he had to distort history to do so. For an explanation of how 'pirates' and attempts to curb their activities operated *within* the international legal order, see Lauren Benton, 'Toward a New Legal History of Piracy: Maritime Legalities and the Myth of Universal Jurisdiction', *International Journal of Maritime History* XXIII:1 (2022), 1–15.

3 Conclusion

Separated by centuries, Vitoria and Schmitt were inducted into prominent places in the canon of international law during the same decades, and in the same unexpected place. Having supported the Primo de Rivera dictatorship in 1929 and having taken inspiration for some of his core ideas from the Spanish writer Camilo Barcia Trelles, Schmitt rekindled his connections to Spain and Spanish jurists after World War II.[57] His narrow escape from indictment at Nuremberg pushed Schmitt toward Spain as a refuge and as a promising site of surviving authoritarianism. He was enthusiastically embraced by Spanish Falangist lawyers and jurists – the same group that was working to establish Vitoria as the founder of modern international law. Schmitt responded by attempting to reconcile his views with the dominant themes of the 'Dominican moment'.

Curiously, one result of this coincidence of Vitorian revival and Schmittian ascendance was to help sideline the problem of limited war within the history of international law. The campaign to position Vitoria as a founding figure in international law focused attention on his universalism rather than his writing about types or levels of violence. The reception of Schmitt, meanwhile, overlooked the distortions in his representation of global spatial order and left unexamined his equation of domestic police powers with Anglo-American total war. The result was to push into the background the struggles of these – and other – prominent figures in the history of international law with the problem of limited war.

Yet even across centuries and ideological divides, the problem connected these writers to shared challenges. One question was how to categorise the violence of part-sovereigns. In strikingly different ways, Vitoria and Schmitt addressed at length the capacity of non-sovereign entities to make war. Vitoria's recognition of the *dominium* of American Indians was part of this concern, although what the Dominican gave with one hand he took away with the other. Vitoria described *indios* as 'treacherous foes' whose perpetual failure to make peace opened them to the judgment and punishment of Spaniards. Schmitt, too, struggled to define the violence of polities with imperfect sovereignty, a preoccupation evident in his focus on partisans as a class of fighters

57 José María Beneyto, 'Camilo Barcia Trelles on Francisco de Vitoria: At the Crossroads of Carl Schmitt's Grossraum and James Brown Scott's 'Modern International Law',' in *The European Journal of International Law* 31:4 (2020): 1477–1492; Miguel Saralequi, *Carl Schmitt Pensador Español* (Madrid: Editorial Trotta, 2016).

with legitimate causes who were not serving a sovereign but who operated in the shadow of sovereignty.

Another cross-cutting challenge involved defining violence at the threshold of war. Both Vitoria and Schmitt highlighted distinctions between moderate and extreme use of force. Vitoria, as we have seen, spelled out the conditions under which the limits on violence were released and civilians could be subjected to massacre, pillaging and enslavement. Schmitt distinguished between limited war and wars of annihilation, and he sought to associate particular patterns of each with phases of global ordering. The breakdown of the limited war of the *ius publicum europaeum*, imagined as a controlled regime of war between states, gave way to the supposedly unfettered violence of global policing by hegemonic powers.

Vitoria and Schmitt proposed, in different ways, that the same modalities for containing war could also produce extreme violence. The wider contexts in which they were writing pushed them toward this observation. Vitoria would have known that the violence of conquest in Iberia and the Americas was structured by fragile truces. Pauses in war saved lives and property, but they also sometimes led directly to extreme violence against civilians – justified by the supposed reluctance of opponents to keep the peace.[58] Schmitt described the alternation of limited and limitless war when he pointed out that partisan warfare could give way to unruly reprisal or the limitless violence of rogue actors. This pattern found expression in events that Schmitt was observing outside post-war Europe, especially the large-scale conflicts of anti-imperial revolutions that appeared to spill beyond existing regulatory frameworks and to inform the European response of labelling anti-imperialists as terrorists.

Unable to reconcile these pathways to extreme violence with larger claims about the moral (for Vitoria) and political (for Schmitt) limits on war, both writers characterised some groups and polities as tending, because of ill-defined qualities, toward unruly violence. Vitoria suggested that non-Christians lacked religious and moral commitments that would prevent their engaging in perpetual war against the Spaniards. He classed *indios* as inveterate peace breakers. For Schmitt, those who lacked a political commitment marked by a connection to a territorial homeland hurtled towards unlimited violence. Both writers expressed ambivalence about these judgments. In part to temper the idea that atrocities were inevitable or that all societies observed the same tendencies to extreme violence, they imagined groups moving in and out of enmity and polities moving in and out of sovereignty. There was a flickering

58 On truces as a prelude to extreme violence, see Benton, *They Called It Peace*, 37–44.

quality to limits on war – a temporal instability that marked both the theory and practice of interpolitical violence.

Empires were the settings that most clearly exposed these oscillations. They were assemblages of unequal polities suspended in a state of unstable peace or undefinable war. The structures and practices that held polities within empires also prevented them from engaging in total war or annihilating rebellion. But those same structures and practices gave outsized power to overlords and hegemons that could adopt the harshest forms of reprisal and punishment. Schmitt heaped disdain on Vitoria's theological approach to upholding the justice of such actions, but his own political analysis remained dependent on biases that lay outside the parameters of legal or political analysis. Writing centuries apart, Vitoria and Schmitt tripped over the problems of defining imperfect sovereignty and determining the lawfulness of violence at the threshold of war and peace.

Bibliography

Anghie, Antony. *Imperialism, Sovereignty and the Making of International Law* (Cambridge: Cambridge University Press, 2004).

Belmessous, Saliha. *Native Claims: Indigenous Law against Empire, 1500–1920* (Oxford: Oxford University Press, 2012).

Beneyto, José María. 'Camilo Barcia Trelles on Francisco de Vitoria: At the Crossroads of Carl Schmitt's Grossraum and James Brown Scott's "Modern International Law"', *The European Journal of International Law* 31:4 (2020): 1477–1492.

Benton, Lauren. *They Called It Peace: Worlds of Imperial Violence* (Princeton, NJ: Princeton University Press, 2024).

Benton, Lauren 'Interpolity Law', in *Oxford Handbook of History and International Relations*, Mlada Bukovansky, Edward Keene, Maja Spanu, and Christopher Reus-Smit, eds. (Oxford: Oxford University Press, 2023), 320–333.

Benton, Lauren. 'Toward a New Legal History of Piracy: Maritime Legalities and the Myth of Universal Jurisdiction', *International Journal of Maritime History* XXIII, 1 (2011) 1–15.

Benton, Lauren. *Law and Colonial Cultures: Legal Regimes in World History, 1400–1900* (Cambridge and New York: Cambridge University Press, 2002).

Benton, Lauren and Jane Burbank. 'Rights and Empires: Relations of Authority', in *The Cambridge History of Rights, Vol. IV*, Dan Edelstein and Jennifer Pitts, eds. (Cambridge and New York: Cambridge University Press, 2025), 437–462.

Benton, Lauren and Nathan Perl-Rosenthal. 'Land-Sea Regimes in World History', in *The World at Sea: Maritime Practices and Global History*, Lauren Benton and

Nathan Perl-Rosenthal, eds. (Philadelphia, PA: University of Pennsylvania Press, 2021), 186–192.

Benton, Lauren and Benjamin Straumann. 'Acquiring Empire by Law: From Roman Doctrine to Early Modern European Practice', *Law and History Review* 28:1 (2010): 1–38.

Brett, Annabel. 'Scholastic Political Thought and the Modern Concept of the State', in *Rethinking the Foundations of Modern Political Thought*, Annabel Brett and James Tully, eds. (Cambridge: Cambridge University Press, 2006), 130–148.

Fernández-Santamaria, J. A. *The State, War and Peace: Spanish Political Thought in the Renaissance 1616–1559* (Cambridge: Cambridge University Press, 1977).

Gould, Eliga. 'Zones of Law, Zones of Violence: The Legal Geography of the British Atlantic, circa 1772', *William and Mary Quarterly* 60:3 (2003): 471–510.

Hanke, Lewis, *The Spanish Struggle for Justice in the Conquest of America* (Philadelphia, PA: University of Pennsylvania Press, 1949).

Jacques, Johanna. 'From "Nomos" to "Hegung": Sovereignty and the Laws of War in Schmitt's International Order', *The Modern Law Review* 78:3 (2015), 411–430.

Koskenniemi, Martti. *To the Uttermost Parts of the Earth: Legal Imagination and International Power 1300–1870* (Cambridge: Cambridge University Press, 2021.

Koskenniemi, Martti. 'Empire and International Law: The Real Spanish Contribution', *University of Toronto Law Journal* 61:1 (2011): 1–36.

Millares Carló, Agustín, ed. *Historia de Las Indias, por Fray Bartolomé de Las Casas, Vol 3* (México: Fondo de Cultura Económico, 1951).

Müller, Jan-Werner. *A Dangerous Mind: Carl Schmitt in Post-War European Thought* (New Haven, CT: Yale University Press, 2004).

Neff, Stephen C. *War and the Law of Nations* (Cambridge: Cambridge University Press, 2005).

Pitts, Jennifer. 'Empire and Legal Universalisms in the Eighteenth Century', *The American Historical Review*, 117:1 (2012), 92–121.

Rasilla, Ignacio de la. *In the Shadow of Vitoria: A History of International Law in Spain (1770–1953)* (Leiden: Brill: 2018).

Saralequi, Miguel. *Carl Schmitt Pensador Español* (Madrid: Editorial Trotta, 2016).

Schmitt, Carl. *The Theory of the Partisan: An Interjection to the Concept of the Political*, trans. C. J. Miller (Montgomery County, Pennsylvania: Antelope Hill Publishing, 2020 [1962]).

Schmitt, Carl. *Land and Sea: A World Historical Meditation*, Russell A. Berman and Samuel Garrett Zeitlin, eds. (Candor, NY: Telos Press, 2015).

Schmitt, Carl. *The Concept of the Political* (Chicago: University of Chicago Press, 2007).

Schmitt, Carl. *The Nomos of the Earth in the International Law of Jus Publicum Europaeum* (Candor, NY: Telos Press, 2003).

Scott, James Brown. *The Spanish Origins of International Law: Francisco de Vitoria and His Law of Nations* (Oxford and New York: Oxford University Press, 1934).

Teschke, Benno. 'Carl Schmitt's Concepts of War: a Categorical Failure', in *The Oxford Handbook of Carl Schmitt*, Jens Meierhenrich and Oliver Simons, eds. (Oxford: Oxford University Press, 2016), 367–40.

Vitoria, Francisco de. 'On the Law of War', in *Vitoria: Political Writings*, Anthony Pagden and Jeremy Lawrance, eds. (Cambridge and New York: Cambridge University Press. 1991), 293–328.

Vitoria, Francisco de. 'On the American Indians', in *Vitoria: Political Writings*, Anthony Pagden and Jeremy Lawrance, eds. (Cambridge and New York: Cambridge University Press. 1991), 231–292.

CHAPTER 5

The Founding Father of Imagination: Habermas and Koskenniemi on Vitoria

David Roth-Isigkeit

1 Introduction

It is a quite accepted result of some decades of historical research in international law that historical story-telling may be used to construct political narratives.[1] Behind this background, it is Francisco de Vitoria who occupies a central place in international legal thought. Precisely because Vitoria seems to fit in all shoes, his work has been used for a variety of arguments.

James Brown Scott, for example, made the 'Spanish origin of international law' a cornerstone of his liberal internationalist vision, highlighting in particular the universal community aspect of Vitoria's *totus orbis*.[2] This interpretation was later picked up by influential natural lawyers like Alfred Verdross to promote a visionary international law.[3] Ultimately, even it has been widely characterized as ahistorical,[4] it prepared the pervasive role of an ontological understanding of individual human rights as a core concept. Carl Schmitt, on the other hand, followed Camilo Barcia Trelles in his rather medieval-theological reading of Vitoria to make the point of his Eurocentric philosophy of history.[5]

---

1 Anne Orford, 'On international legal method'. *London Review of International Law* 1 (1) (2003), 170.

2 James Brown Scott, *The Spanish origin of international law* (Oxford: Clarendon Press 1934).

3 Alfred Verdross and Bruno Simma, *Universelles Völkerrecht: Theorie und Praxis* (Berlin: Duncker & Humblot 1984) 8 ff; Alfred Verdross, *Abendländische Rechtsphilosophie Ihre Grundlagen Und Hauptprobleme in Geschichtlicher Schau* (Wien: Springer Verlag 1963) 112–113.

4 Richard Tuck, *The rights of war and peace: political thought and the international order from Grotius to Kant* (Oxford: Oxford University Press on Demand 2001) 11.

5 José María Beneyto, 'Camilo Barcia Trelles on Francisco de Vitoria: At the Crossroads of Carl Schmitt's Grossraum and James Brown Scott's 'Modern International Law'. *European Journal of International Law* 31 (4) (2020), 1481 ff. For a good summary of this argument, see Stefan Kadelbach, 'Mission und Eroberung bei Vitoria. Zur Entstehung des Völkerrechts aus der Theologie', in Kirstin Bunge, Anselm Spindler and Andreas Wagner (eds.), *Die Normativität des Rechts bei Francisco de Vitoria* (Stuttgart: frommann-holzboog Verlag 2011) 294–295. Classically following this: Wilhelm Grewe, *The Epochs of International Law*, trans. by Michael Byers (Berlin: De Gruyter 2000). An early response can be found in

 | DOI:10.1163/9789004757448_006

In his picture, Alberico Gentili rather than Vitoria seemed to be the true founder of modern international law.[6]

In recent years, scholarly appreciations of Vitoria's writings and their reception have grown exponentially, so that there remains barely any news to be told.[7] Vitoria indeed is universally depicted as a founding father, yet of radically different conceptions of international law. Like the colours of a rainbow, his writings are refracted by the prism of today's variety of perspectives. For this purpose, the piece takes two recent critical and intellectual readings of Vitoria as an example. Jürgen Habermas' *This too a History of Philosophy*[8] (Section 2) and Martti Koskenniemi's *To the Uttermost Parts of the Earth*[9] (Section 3) are prime examples how Vitoria is stylized as praetor of an individual contemporary perspective on world order. Taking these interpretations as an example, the paper seeks to explore the openness and textual ambivalences in Vitoria in order to explain its different uses in the history of international law (Section 4).

2 Habermas' Vitoria as the Founding Father of a Democratic *totus orbis*

In his book, *This too a History of Philosophy*, Habermas decides to focus on the fundamental change in perspective that Vitoria's writings offered.[10] He con-

---

Friedrich August Freiherr Von Der Heydte, 'Francisco de Vitoria und die Geschichte seines Ruhmes: Eine Entgegnung'. *Die Friedens-Warte* 49 (4/5) (1949).

6 Carl Schmitt, *The nomos of the earth: In the International Law of the Jus Publicum Europaeum*, trans. by G. L. Ulmen (New York: Telos Press Publishing 2006) 120–121.

7 The discourse on Vitoria has in many respects shifted to the meta-level. See, lately Ignacio de la Rasilla del Moral, *In the shadow of Vitoria: a history of international law in Spain (1770–1953)* (Leiden: Brill 2017). Paolo Amorosa, *Rewriting the history of the law of nations: how James Brown Scott made Francisco de Vitoria the founder of international law* (Oxford: Oxford University Press 2019). It is probably Martti Koskenniemi who started this linkage between Vitoria and a history of the discipline. Martti Koskenniemi, 'Vitoria and Us. Thoughts on Critical Histories of International Law'. *Rechtsgeschichte – Legal History* 22 (2014), available at: https://doi.org/10.12946/rg22/119-138 (last accessed on 7 August 2025).

8 Jürgen Habermas, *Auch eine Geschichte der Philosophie: Band 1: Die okzidentale Konstellation von Glauben und Wissen* (Berlin: Suhrkamp Verlag 2019). English version: Jürgen Habermas, *This too a history of philosophy,* trans. by Ciaran Cronin (Cambridge: Polity 2023).

9 Martti Koskenniemi, *To the Uttermost Parts of the Earth: Legal Imagination and International Power 1300–1870* (Cambridge: Cambridge University Press 2021).

10 See, Habermas, *Auch eine Geschichte der Philosophie: Band 1*, 914 ff. Here, he synthesizes the depictions of Niccolò Machiavelli and Martin Luther together with the arguments of

centrates on the innovatory core, that is his concept of *dominium* that – according to Habermas – paved the way towards the formation of democracy as popular sovereignty on the one hand, and his understanding of international law as a conflict law between largely equal political communities on the other. Such a political vision fits neatly with Habermas' own perspective on the relationship between international law and national democratic communities.

2.1 *The Proto-democratic Reading of* dominium

Habermas locates the quite revolutionary aspect in Vitoria's writings in his proto-democratic reading of the concept of *dominium*.[11] First, Habermas relativizes the Thomist constraints on Vitoria's argumentation style and acknowledges the ongoing emancipation of Spanish late scholastics from Aquinas and his methods.[12] Drawing on a view that highlights in particular the *individual* dimension of the concept of *dominium*, Habermas argues that these essentially mirrored Lutheran/Protestant concepts of voluntarist liberty.

In this interpretation, Vitoria thus would qualify *dominium* as a subjective human right in the form of the capacity of the individual person for self-governance with respect to her actions and property. Habermas goes as far as saying that this original definition of liberty is at the core of the modern

Francisco de Vitoria in a single chapter. All three, according to Habermas, argued in a historical situation where the symbolic power of the church had fundamentally eroded. This departing from universalism, the single point of reference for legitimate authority, allowed for fundamental reconceptions that all three authors used in quite different ways. While Machiavelli's functionalist theory of power seemed to imply its moral neutralization, in particular Vitoria had to deal with the worldly requirements of his theory on the one hand, its rooting in Christian ethics on the other. Both however, write in the role of political experts, mirrors for princes, that should allow to derive practical political guidance in difficult situations. In terms of evidence, Habermas only sparingly uses footnotes. Yet, support for his interpretation comes in particular from the passages in Vitoria, 'On Civil Power', 40. Such a perspective is developed further by Mónica García-Salmones Rovira, 'The Disorder of Economy? The First Relectio de Indis in a Theological Perspective', in Stefan Kadelbach, Thomas Kleinlein and David Roth-Isigkeit (eds.), *System, Order, and International Law* (Oxford: Oxford University Press 2017) 443 ff.

11 For all of the following, see Habermas, *Auch eine Geschichte der Philosophie: Band 1*, 914 ff. Similarly accentuating the innovatory role of Vitoria: Rolf Grawert, 'FRANCISCO DE VITORIA: Naturrecht – Herrschaftsordnung – Völkerrecht'. *Der Staat* 39 (1) (2000), 116 ff. The counter-arguments against this view are summarized by Sergio Dellavalle, *Paradigms of Social Order: From Holism to Pluralism and Beyond* (Cham: Springer International Publishing 2021) 128.

12 Such a view is shared by Rovira, 'The Disorder of Economy? The First Relectio de Indis in a Theological Perspective', 444–448.

concept of individual autonomy. Since the concept of *dominium* was essentially juridical, Habermas' Vitoria becomes a modern human rights advocate.

Further than that, in Habermas' interpretation, this individual liberty offered the sketch for a political model of popular sovereignty.[13] Consequently, *dominium sui et rerum* was the ability of individual self-governance granted by natural law. Only voluntarist political legislation in the form of positive law could potentially set limits to this political liberty.

Habermas encounters the manifestation of this argument in Vitoria's differentiation between *dominium sui* and *dominium civile.* While the latter constituted the right to individual property, the former addressed the question of public authority, that is the legitimacy of public order. All political order, this is the result of this chain of arguments, can only exist *qua positive law* because it is derivative.[14] In that sense, each individual possesses an own voice in the formation of a political commonwealth.[15]

2.2 Ius gentium *as Conflict Law between Equal Political Communities*

According to Habermas, this leads to an unequivocally modern interpretation of international law, as Vitoria proved in *De Indis.*[16] And indeed, here Vitoria is quite unambiguous that the 'Barbarians' were able to exercise this right to self-governance, *dominium sui.* Even if they did not conform to Christian ideals, it could not be put in doubt that before the Spaniards had arrived, they were able to form a political community as has just been described. As this political authority had not been voluntarily transferred in any sort to the colonizers, its initial exercise was wrongful.

With this recognition of the mere possibility of 'other' political communities, Vitoria developed the Roman notion of *ius gentium* destined to describe the relations within one single Empire into an international law that recognized the limits of universal public authority.[17] The Emperor, as Vitoria famously held, was no *dominus mundi,* no ruler of the whole world.

---

13 Habermas, *Auch eine Geschichte der Philosophie: Band 1,* 915. Similar interpretation: Kadelbach, 'Mission und Eroberung bei Vitoria. Zur Entstehung des Völkerrechts aus der Theologie', 312.

14 This does not necessarily mean that there are conditions attached to the rightful exercise of public authority. In that way, Vitoria's view is rather similar to the Hobbesian model than the one of Republican liberties, such as crystallized in Rousseau's social contract.

15 Habermas, *Auch eine Geschichte der Philosophie: Band 1,* 918.

16 Habermas, *Auch eine Geschichte der Philosophie: Band 1,* 916.

17 For this argument, see José María Beneyto, 'Conquest, Empire and Peace: Vitoria, Charles V, Erasmus and the Foundations of the Law of Nations', in José María Beneyto (ed.), *Empire Humanism and Rights* (Cham: Springer Nature 2022) 7. On the importance of

This decentralization of perspectives, according to Habermas, is the root of a modern international law that serves the coordination of different equal political communities.[18] Vitoria's natural law could thus be used to evaluate the rights of 'other' cultures and sharpens the view that the own political community is a mere part of an encompassing whole. It thereby relativizes universality claims of old European Imperialism and paves the way towards intercultural recognition.[19]

This obviously strengthens the role of the *lex humana* and thereby creates inner tension in the system of natural law. In this picture, the universality claims of natural law were increasingly deflected through national perspectives. Accordingly, a method was required to ensure converging interpretations. Vitoria suggested referring to the principle of customary interpretation, *consensus omnium*. Habermas concludes: 'The required global consensus *between* peoples, either constructed as a result of political agreement in the form of accepted custom, reaches beyond the borders of the Christian world as well as beyond the confessionally divided national states. Thereby Vitoria conceptually constructs the basis for a modern international law, even if he is far away from committing to the transition of Christian natural law to a secular law of reason'.[20]

2.3 *Vitoria's Democratic Constitutionalism*

The most powerful support for this view (yet one that Habermas does not invoke) could be found in a side note where Vitoria rejects the proposition that an Emperor could possibly rule the whole world. There, he said, after having rejected all possible divine and natural law titles: 'Nor does the emperor have universal dominion by legitimate succession, gift, exchange, purchase, just war, election, or any other legal title, as is established. Therefore the emperor has never been master of the whole world.'[21] Here, Vitoria acknowledged that it might be theoretically possible that the peoples of the world elect one single Emperor that reforms one single political community.[22] If political authority was in itself derivative and existed only by the grace of self-governing

Roman influences, see Kadelbach, 'Mission und Eroberung bei Vitoria. Zur Entstehung des Völkerrechts aus der Theologie', 306.

18 Habermas, *Auch eine Geschichte der Philosophie: Band 1*, 908. Similar Dellavalle, *Paradigms of Social Order: From Holism to Pluralism and Beyond*, 124.

19 Habermas, *Auch eine Geschichte der Philosophie: Band 1*, 913.

20 Habermas, *Auch eine Geschichte der Philosophie*, 910. My translation.

21 Vitoria, 'On the American Indians', 257–258.

22 Interestingly, Koskenniemi sees this circumstance. Koskenniemi, *To the Uttermost Parts of the Earth*, 172.

communities, then indeed this whole concept could be transferred to a self-governance of peoples in the plural sense.

The vision that comes with such an idea is a quite modern concept of democratic constitutionalism that resonates with Habermas' understanding of a future global order.[23] In line with his argument on Vitoria, Habermas' central concern lies in the legitimacy deficit on the global level. For him, the decisive challenge is 'to *conserve* the great democratic achievements of the European nation-state, beyond its own limits.'[24] That explains his affirmative attitude towards Vitoria's writings.

In that sense, the Vitorian approximation between natural and human law fills a gap that Habermas himself has addressed in a modern form. According to him, legal positivism blinds out the question of justice by either referring to a Kelsenian basic norm or to an adopted custom, such as Hart's rule of recognition. With a mere ahistorical recognition of cosmological constants, natural law does not offer a plausible alternative. In between these seemingly unsatisfying options Habermas develops a third alternative with his procedural concept of law, which explicitly highlights the dimension of collective self-government in the form of law.[25]

The Habermasian interpretation of Vitoria thus supports a conceptual pathway to an (historical) understanding of international law that unsurprisingly aligns with Habermas normative beliefs about international law. These do not necessarily originate in a reading of Vitoria but are grounded in a larger political theory.

3 Koskenniemi's Vitoria as the Founding Father of Apologetic Economic Liberalism

Unsurprisingly the interpretation of Vitoria in Martti Koskenniemi's *To the Uttermost Parts of the Earth* accentuates precisely the part that Habermas deliberately leaves out, namely that the followers of the Salamanca school

---

23 Similar, Pablo Antonio Fernández-Sánchez, 'From Totus Orbis to Global Law', in Giuliana Ziccardi Capaldo (ed.), *The Global Community Yearbook of International Law and Jurisprudence 2015* (New York: Oxford University Press 2016) 113–25. See already with this conclusion, Thomas Kleinlein, *Konstitutionalisierung im Völkerrecht: Konstruktion und Elemente einer idealistischen Völkerrechtslehre* (Berlin/Heidelberg: Springer 2011) 250.

24 Jürgen Habermas, 'Why Europe Needs a Constitution'. *New Left Review* 11 (2001), 5.

25 Jürgen Habermas, *Between facts and norms: Contributions to a discourse theory of law and democracy* (Hoboken: John Wiley & Sons 2015) 123. Jürgen Habermas, *The lure of technocracy* (Hoboken: John Wiley & Sons 2015) 56.

argued in a historical situation where they were essentially advisors of conscience.[26] In this position, their conception of international law required flexibility to respond to pragmatic demands in order to serve as an open tool to justify imperial claims. Koskenniemi arrives at such a conclusion by stressing the economic rather than the political meaning of *dominium*. As a result, the fact that Vitoria recognized the existence of other political communities would rather account for a 'nationalist cult' of the Dominican.[27] This is precisely in line with how Koskenniemi had been describing the state of present-day international law.

3.1 *Vitoria's Method between Apology and Utopia*

Koskenniemi highlights the particular situation of the Salamanca scholars as political advisors at court on the one hand, being tasked with the sacrament of penance on the other hand.[28] In both worldly and theological roles, scholars had a role as modern-day experts. Writing in the mirror-of-princes tradition they would be required to pragmatically deal with moral questions.[29] This ultimately led to a search for a method between positivism and rationalism that allowed for enough leeway to include worldly demands.[30] In Koskenniemi's view, power politics beat the philosophical struggle in the scholastic writings.

In a sophisticated argumentation that intensively draws on the overall context of the Spanish writings on territorial expansion in the Americas, Koskenniemi identifies the central philosophical shift in the turn to 'probabilism.'[31] This method, suggesting that the intentions of the persons taking a decision rather than the objective outcome was central for its moral evaluation, benefited the political role of advisors in two related ways. First, it explained how political decision-makers could get moral relief from following external advice because they could be said to have acted with the best of intentions. Second, it

---

26 See the good discussion by Luigi Nuzzo, 'The Law That Wasn't There: Chapter 2: The Political Theology of Ius Gentium – The Expansion of Spain 1524–1559'. *European Journal of International Law* 32 (3) (2021), 958, available at: https://doi.org/10.1093/ejil/chab076 (last accessed on 7 August 2025).

27 See, in detail below.

28 It is not by accident that Koskenniemi headlines this chapter 'The Political Theology of *ius gentium*.' Indeed, without explicitly acknowledging so, *Koskenniemi* delivers a quite Schmittian interpretation of Vitoria that accentuates the theological aspect of the work. Koskenniemi, *To the Uttermost Parts of the Earth*, 119 ff.

29 Koskenniemi, *To the Uttermost Parts of the Earth*, 124. (with reference to Azpilcueta).

30 Koskenniemi, *To the Uttermost Parts of the Earth*, 121.

31 Koskenniemi, *To the Uttermost Parts of the Earth*, 128.

strengthened the role of advisors because it became morally dangerous not to seek extensive advice.

For the time being, according to Koskenniemi, the scholastic method was a perfect rhetorical technique to accommodate these arguments in *ius gentium*: 'The format of the *quaestio* or the *disputatio*, the reproduction of proof from reason, experience, the Bible and various theological authorities behind the winning proposition, as well as the meticulous statement for the contrary case – all these scholastic techniques tend to obscure the fact that the chain of arguments always juxtaposed something assumed to be evident by revelation with an appeal to a casuistic appreciation of the context.'[32] And this casuistic appreciation, according to *Koskenniemi*, mostly meant sacrificing philosophical clarity at the expense of pragmatic demands.

This assumed structure matches quite precisely Koskenniemi's famous assumption about the argumentative structure of international law. For Koskenniemi, law is a specific technical language rooted in the professional discipline. This legal language is radically indeterminate so that almost everything can be expressed with valid legal arguments. In order to succeed, one has to master the 'grammar' of law, which Koskenniemi describes as 'the system of production of good legal arguments'.[33] This form has a relative emptiness, as Koskenniemi notes: 'A grammar is not what native language-speakers say in fact – it is an account of what it is possible to say in that language.'[34] Whether a justification in terms of law succeeds under the practical circumstances of legal discourse is not a matter of the validity of arguments as *legal* arguments. Rather, 'the argumentative architecture allows any decision, and thus also the critique of any decision without the question of the professional competence of the decision-maker ever arising.'[35] In this picture, Vitoria is one of the first political advisors to have seen this specific legal power of justification: 'though it is partial and subjective, it claims to be universal and objective.'[36]

In his writings on Vitoria, Koskenniemi rediscovers precisely this mechanism. He argues: 'Vitoria and his followers would be able to compensate for the

32 Koskenniemi, *To the Uttermost Parts of the Earth*, 137–138. Support for this argument comes from Nuzzo, 'The Law That Wasn't There: Chapter 2', 960.

33 Martti Koskenniemi, *From Apology to Utopia: The Structure of International Legal Argument* (Cambridge: Cambridge University Press 2006) 568.

34 Koskenniemi, *From Apology to Utopia: The Structure of International Legal Argument*, 589. (emphasis omitted).

35 Ibid.

36 Martti Koskenniemi, *The politics of international law* (London: Hart Publishing 2011) 260.

rigidity of natural law by the much more flexible notion of *ius gentium*.'[37] This flexibility could only be provided by relativizing the formal character of the rules of natural law towards objective considerations of abstract justice on the one hand, a global consensus on the other.[38] Thus constructed, *ius gentium* received an intermediate ('oscillating')[39] character between natural and positive law, between concreteness and normativity, between *Apology* and *Utopia*.

3.2 *The Economic Reading of* dominium

In Vitoria's writings, the concept of *dominium* has a double meaning, including public and private autonomy at the same time.[40] In contrast to Habermas, Koskenniemi reads a hierarchy into the relationship of public and private, accentuating the latter. He finds evidence for this in making Vitoria speak through the writings of Domingo de Soto who argued that a precondition for efficient public governance was the division of property.[41] According to Koskenniemi, Vitoria's methodology put the implementation of economic arguments of necessity in the centre, being able to justify the cutting of individual rights if just the scissor consisting of a sufficiently sophisticated chain of arguments was sharp enough.[42] Vitoria thus turns out as a Catholic Machiavelli.

This reading, however, fits neatly with a circumstance that causes obvious discomfort for Habermas' interpretation, that is Vitoria's writings on the treatment of the New World.[43] Given the economic reading of *dominium*, it does not come as a surprise to Koskenniemi that Vitoria took a rather conformist position with respect to the legal claim of the Spaniards to stay in the Indies.

---

37 Koskenniemi, *To the Uttermost Parts of the Earth*, 143.

38 Koskenniemi, *To the Uttermost Parts of the Earth*, 143–146. For a similar view, see Beneyto, 'Conquest, Empire and Peace', 11.

39 Koskenniemi, *To the Uttermost Parts of the Earth*, 148.

40 Annabel Brett, *Liberty, right and nature: Individual rights in later scholastic thought* (Cambridge: Cambridge University Press 2003) 126 ff. See, for an earlier discussion, Koskenniemi, *To the Uttermost Parts of the Earth*, 150.

41 Koskenniemi, *To the Uttermost Parts of the Earth*, 154. (citing Domingo de Soto, *De iustitia et iure*, III 1.)

42 'imperatives of the human condition': Koskenniemi, *To the Uttermost Parts of the Earth*, 155. Cp. further with regard to the concept of necessity, Ernst-Wolfgang Böckenförde, '§ 14 Die spanische Spätscholastik, II. Francisco de Vitoria', in Ernst-Wolfgang Böckenforde (ed.), *Geschichte der Rechts- und Staatsphilosophie. Antike und Mittelalter* (Tübingen: Mohr Siebeck 2006) 348.

43 Vitoria's line of argument of a possible provocation of just war seems so odd given his previous argumentation that Habermas (with readable feelings of discomfort) chooses to put this dimension aside. Habermas, *Auch eine Geschichte der Philosophie: Band 1*, 917. Similar Dellavalle, *Paradigms of Social Order: From Holism to Pluralism and Beyond*, 125. ('U-turn').

While indeed horrified by the reports about personal abuse, according to Koskenniemi, he nevertheless accepted that 'the Spaniards had a right to travel and trade in the Indies, preach conversion and wage war with their allies against those who obstructed such activities.'[44] Only because the Indians were held fit for self-governance, Koskenniemi adds, does not mean that they were regarded as equals to the Christians.[45]

In such a reading, the part of Vitoria's writings in which he suggested the relativity of the single political commonwealth and the absence of a *legibus solutus* becomes merely a side aspect because it can be explained with economic interests. Koskenniemi writes: 'The determination with which Vitoria and his followers rejected the view that either the pope or the emperor would have universal *dominium* accounts for the nationalist cult of Vitoria.'[46] Part of this cult was the facilitation of economic exploitation overseas. As a second aspect, it prepared an argumentative trait of modern international law. Through the vocabulary of the legitimacy of war, it could provide grounds for belligerent activities in the name of liberty:[47] Here again, the interpretation of Vitoria is quite similar to a Machiavellian perspective.[48]

4 Vitoria's Ambivalences: Text and Method

How can we explain such radically differing interpretations? Both, Habermas and Koskenniemi, undoubtedly speak about the same writings. They are not unduly leaving out parts of Vitoria's argument, nor does it seem odd how they interpret the original writings. Obviously, to state their point, they are accentuating some parts more than others and thereby they are navigating around

44 Koskenniemi, *To the Uttermost Parts of the Earth*, 173.

45 Koskenniemi, *To the Uttermost Parts of the Earth*, 164–65. For this argument, see already Anthony Pagden, *The fall of natural man: the American Indian and the origins of comparative ethnology* (Cambridge: Cambridge University Press 1986) 15 ff. (with reference to the term 'barbarian').

46 Koskenniemi, *To the Uttermost Parts of the Earth*, 167. – citing Ignacio de la Rasilla, *In the Shadow of Vitoria: A History of International Law in Spain (1770–1953) (Leiden: Brill Nijhoff, 2017)*.

47 With regards to Vitoria, Koskenniemi writes: 'The enforcement of *dominium* through just war capped the scholastic system of *ius gentium*. That the just prince acted as a judge over his adversary was a necessary part of this construction, however tenuous it became at a time of the fragmentation of the Christian world.' Koskenniemi, *To the Uttermost Parts of the Earth*, 209.

48 See e.g. Mikael Hörnqvist, *Machiavelli and empire* (Cambridge: Cambridge University Press, 2004) 290.

parts of the writings. Habermas, for example, acknowledges the naïve attitude of Vitoria towards capitalism, yet views this trait as negligible given the great innovations of his theory. Koskenniemi, on the other hand, equally sees the possibility of the democratic interpretation of the *dominus mundi* yet assumes that Vitoria himself considered such global democratic will formation as quite unlikely.

Both arguments thus rest on assumptions in which parts of Vitoria's writings are to be more accentuated than others. Already *Schmitt* noted quite ironically with regard to Vitoria's writings: 'But no thought is safe from reinterpretations, and any argument is subject to a fate that often can be more surprising than is suggested by the well-known expression *fata libellorum*'.[49]

The first reason for such radically differing interpretation paths might be the variety of and the lack of consistency between the texts that Vitoria authored (Section 4.1). A second reason, then, might be that the scholastic method invites such relatively indeterminate conclusions through its combination of systematicity and casuistic reasoning (Section 4.2). With a combination of these reasons, central ambivalences in Vitoria become apparent (Section 4.3).

4.1 *The Variety of Sources*

The main sources for the interpretation of Vitoria's role in the history of international legal thought are three (out of thirteen conserved) lectures, *Relectiones*, that Vitoria prepared for special occasions besides the regular lectures he held for students.[50] These three lectures are titled *De potestate civili* (1527), *De Indis* (1538/39) and *De iure Belli* (1539). In these lectures, Vitoria frequently draws on other parts of his writings, that he then considers as given, such as his commentaries on Aquinas' *Summa theologiae*.[51] Admittedly, in order to assess the role of Vitoria in international legal thought in philosophical terms, this textual basis is not very rich.[52]

Already after his death in 1546, the process of reinterpretation started. Many of his students who served in various governmental and clerical posi-

49 Schmitt, 'The nomos of the earth', 125.

50 I follow here the argument made by Kadelbach, 'Mission und Eroberung bei Vitoria. Zur Entstehung des Völkerrechts aus der Theologie', 293.

51 Daniel Deckers, *Gerechtigkeit und Recht: eine historisch-kritische Untersuchung der Gerechtigkeitslehre des Francisco de Vitoria; 1483–1546* (Freiburg: Herder 1991) 343. (acknowledging that this has lead to misappreciations of his thought).

52 Kadelbach, 'Mission und Eroberung bei Vitoria. Zur Entstehung des Völkerrechts aus der Theologie', 293.

tions worked with Vitoria's writings to make their claims.[53] Both, the spread and the thin content of the writings, allow interpreting lawyers to navigate consciously between the writings, accentuating some aspects over contradicting others and to extract a meaning that would fit their subjective belief.

4.2 *The Open-Endedness of the Scholastic Argumentation Style*

As a second aspect, Vitoria's use of the scholastic method itself does not allow for determinate conclusions. Koskenniemi recognizes here an (intended) argumentation scheme that ultimately leads to the overruling of Thomist philosophical considerations. In his *Nomos,* Schmitt had already noted that the 'modern' style in which Vitoria ordered arguments and conclusions would misleadingly avoid connections between abstract systems and casuistic demands. '[…] Vitoria only examines legal titles and arguments, but does not apply them to concrete circumstances and reach his conclusions on this basis.'[54] Independently of whether one accepts one of the suggested conclusions that Vitoria would either follow a twisted hierarchy between system and individual case (Koskenniemi) or that he would even avoid any methodological connection between the two (Schmitt), the central indeterminacy in the scholastic argumentation style seems to be rooted in the relationship of general norms and their subsequent application.

Against such technical criticism, however, there are good reasons to believe that Vitoria's methods were also a result of the specific context in which he wrote. The rapidly changing political and social circumstances, that is the formation of quasi-nation-state communities, the ongoing confrontation with Islam, the discoveries overseas and in particular the ongoing secularization through the spread of Reformation ideas *necessarily* put the explanatory value of Aquinas' *Summa Theologiae* (that was the standard textbook in Salamanca at the time) under pressure.

As a theologist, Vitoria had to deal with the apparent tension between rapidly changing circumstances that continuously challenged the dogmatic frame of law. Under these conditions, taking a (philosophical) step back towards casuistic reasoning seemed necessary to avoid the conclusion that Catholicism had little to offer with respect to what was going on in the world. Yet, simultaneously, this step back towards casuistry in the *Relectiones* came at a meth-

53 Kirstin Bunge, 'Francisco de Vitoria: A Redesign of Global Order on the Threshold of the Middle Ages to Modern Times', in Stefan Kadelbach, Thomas Kleinlein and David Roth-Isigkeit (eds.), *System, Order, and International Law* (Oxford: Oxford University Press 2017) 50.

54 Schmitt, 'The nomos of the earth', 108.

odological price of a loosening of preassumed hierarchies of religious and worldly spheres, of general norms and their application.

This loosening became visible precisely in the apparently paradox notion of *ius gentium*, located between natural law on the one hand, positive consensus on the other.[55] Natural law was unalterable, unchangeable over time and circumstances. Aquinas had characterized it as the fundamental condition of human sociability.[56] Undoubtedly, Vitoria's general concept of a higher order within and between different political communities belonged to that realm. At the same time, human-made *ius gentium* as a consensus between these communities was an essential part of this order. This *lex humana*, in turn, was not eternal but situated in historical facts rooted in practice.

One may find logical flaws in this reconstruction. Yet, such paradox relationship of *ius gentium* located between cosmological constants and human will (that one may also apply to today's international law) does not make Vitoria's concept of *ius gentium* implausible in itself.[57] Rather, it takes account of the quickly changing political circumstances. Natural law dogmatism cannot plausibly extend to all but only the most fundamental questions of human sociality. Natural law, interpreted in this way, could provide an immutable frame, sometimes considered wider, sometimes narrower, in which human communities could organize themselves.

4.3 *The* orbis *Ambivalence*

The openness of Vitoria's writings has led to key ambivalences in the reception. The most central of these ambivalences concerns Vitoria's concept of *totus orbis*.[58] Undoubtedly, the *orbis* is the nexus of positive legal authority, yet much depends on its precise location. The idealistic interpretation of Vitoria culminates in the *orbis* being a universal community where different peoples

---

55 A precise discussion can be found in Kadelbach, 'Mission und Eroberung bei Vitoria. Zur Entstehung des Völkerrechts aus der Theologie', 310. See further Koskenniemi, *To the Uttermost Parts of the Earth*, 146 ff.

56 See the interpretation by Jean-François Courtine, 'Chapitre V – Vitoria, Suárez et la naissance du droit naturel moderne', in Jean-François Courtine (ed.), *Nature et empire de la loi* (Paris: Éditions de l'Ehess 1999) 135. Similar interpretation, referencing Courtine, Koskenniemi, *To the Uttermost Parts of the Earth*, 147.

57 More critical however, Dellavalle, *Paradigms of Social Order: From Holism to Pluralism and Beyond*, 152–153.

58 I draw here on the view advocated by Kadelbach, 'Mission und Eroberung bei Vitoria. Zur Entstehung des Völkerrechts aus der Theologie', 294. See also, Bunge, 'Francisco de Vitoria: A Redesign of Global Order on the Threshold of the Middle Ages to Modern Times', 44.

are conceived as equal before the law.[59] The other, particularistic interpretation favoured by Schmitt and others emphasizes the meaning of the colonial mission for this project.[60] According to this view, Vitoria still hinges on the universalist dreams of the medieval Empires and the unity of the church, the *tota ecclesia*. For both perspectives, arguments can be found in the writings on the Spanish activities overseas.

In practical terms, certainly the strongest argument for supporters of the Schmittian perspective is the lack of coherence between the theoretical claim of a universal community of peoples and the preferences that Vitoria expresses for the missionary project. How would it be possible that Vitoria derives the right to free trade and missionary activities from the equality of peoples yet reserves this right for Christian communities?[61] Here, Vitoria seems to show a clear preference for the Christian religion.

On the other hand, however, this preference for Christianity seems entirely unrelated to his theoretical premises. Here, Vitoria argues for a far-reaching formal equality of individuals, attributing the capability to non-Christians to govern themselves. Given the tense political situation in which Vitoria wrote (Charles v had already intervened at court),[62] such missing link between premise and conclusion might be understandable. Yet, why, if Vitoria hadn't believed in his theoretical views, did he author them in the first place? It would have been easy for him to justify a difference between 'barbarian' and man based on arguments of tradition.

These obvious ambivalences between theory and practical conclusions became already apparent a few years after Vitoria's death in the *Junta de Valladolid* where *Bartolomé de Las Casas* and *Juan Ginés de Sepúlveda* argued on behalf of Charles v about the treatment of the colonized peoples. While *Las Casas*, drawing on a universalist understanding of Vitoria claimed that any use of violence for the sake of the mission was illegal, *Sepúlveda* equally took Vitoria as the advocate for slavery, forced labour and violence. This irresolvable ambivalence about the interpretation of Vitoria was one of the reasons why the debate remained essentially without a productive result.

59 In addition to Habermas *supra*, see James Brown Scott, *The Spanish origin of international law* (Oxford: Clarendon Press 1934) 278 ff. For a good explanation of the ambivalence between equality before the law and factual inequality, see José Maria Beneyto, 'Conquest, Empire and Peace', 9.

60 Arthur Nussbaum, *A Concise History of the Law of Nations* (New York: The Macmillan Company 1947) 60 ff.

61 Jörg Fisch, *Die europäische Expansion und das Völkerrecht* (Stuttgart: Steiner 1984) 216.

62 For the relationship with Charles v, see Beneyto, 'Conquest, Empire and Peace', 41.

5 Instead of a Conclusion

Generally speaking, it seems that there are two different ways authors approach this recourse to the history of international legal concepts. One method, well exemplified by Habermas' approach, focuses on the contribution of historical thought to the formation of an overarching systematicity of the law. This method is particularly interested in theoretical innovations. For Habermas, it seems more important that Vitoria may have delivered the conceptual sketch for a human rights-based international order than the Dominican's actual conclusions on the colonial project. Such systematic approach would then focus on whether – from a contemporary perspective – interrelations between different entities (individuals, states, global community) in a single author seem plausible and value the importance of that author for a history of international legal thought accordingly.

The value of such systematicity in a legal perspective is it that it implies a context which allows one to derive obligations.[63] In that sense, it theorizes the fitting together of institutions, rules, principles, and precedents that make the law appear as a system. Systematic approaches provide the methodology to contextualize relationships of single norms and hence to resolve tensions between normative ideals such as peace, justice, or liberty. Through offering assumingly *complete* accounts of normativity, only systematic approaches may construct justifications for the exercise of public authority and thereby fill a gap in today's international law. Along these approaches, this trait is the special importance of the *orbis* in Vitoria, Grotius' *foedus arctissimum inter civitates,* Wolff's *civitas maxima* etc. They offer the construction of a universal frame of authority at the highest level of justification.

On the other side of the spectrum, critical accounts of history aim at precisely the opposite, that is the erosion of these narratives of universality by contrasting them with the particularities of their existence conditions.[64] For that purpose, they aim to show how concepts and narratives of international law are related to and deeply rooted in patterns of imperialism and colonial domination. The whole point of the critical reconstruction is not about Vitoria's beliefs as a theorist but about his subsequent role in the discipline. From a critical perspective, 'it matters little whether Vitoria actually felt sympathy

63 H. L. A. Hart, *The concept of law* (Oxford: Oxford University Press 1994) 82–91.

64 Kadelbach, Kleinlein and Roth-Isigkeit, 'Introduction', 6.

towards the Indians; more important is the effect of his teaching on the justification of colonialism.'[65]

However, this characterization leads to a seemingly paradoxical combination of claims. On the one hand, it sacrifices the historical claim by being openly subjective. There is nothing like an objective history. Yet, through this open subjectivity it also impedes on the constructive conceptual claim that history might provide.

Critical accounts do not aim at an alternative account of the universal frame of authority. They do not build an alternative history but are merely cynically directed against what they perceive as the hegemonic narrative. Koskenniemi is quite explicit here: 'There is a systemic or constructive aspect of law, too, that is especially visible in the legal academy. Here the underlying struggle is often hidden in an effort to explain the legal system as coherent and by and large rational. [...] To link legal practices to the stakes they organise and distribute might require leaving the constructivist comfort-zone [...].'[66] In that sense, beyond the polemical use-case to articulate today's injustices, they avoid a theoretical claim of their own. As they believe the systematic approach tends to be used to cement hegemonic practices, they tell the counter-hegemonic story.

That being said, there seem to be absolute methodological limits that prevent the bridge-building between the two camps.[67] The arguments produce a Catch-22. While the critic may discard the systematic approach as ahistorical 'presentism',[68] the critic herself may not be interested in a constructive future for present-day international law. Both sides make their points without clear

---

65 Martti Koskenniemi, 'The Past according to International Law', in Annabel Brett, Martti Koskenniemi and Megan Donaldson (eds.), *History, Politics, Law: Thinking through the International* (Cambridge: Cambridge University Press 2021) 66.

66 Koskenniemi, 'The Past according to International Law', 66.

67 In an earlier work, Stefan Kadelbach, Thomas Kleinlein and I have suggested an approach of 'moderate anachronism', that intended to walk the line between the inner structure of the argument, contextual research and a perspective carefully guided by today's international law. Thereby we tried to get the best of both worlds: to understand how theory responds to a given political context and, in order to make sense of the use of the argument today, to take it out of this original context and reflect upon it in the light of current problems. Trying to implement this approach, however, it quickly turned out that it was little more than a light version of systematicity, that tried to avoid idealizations of founding figures, yet let the interest in the universal narrative largely untouched. Thereby it might serve for a reflexive conception of the discipline of international law, while it will hardly satisfy the fundamental critical intention of post-modern inquiries. Kadelbach, Kleinlein and Roth-Isigkeit, 'Introduction', 6.

68 Anne Orford, *International Law and the Politics of History* (Cambridge: Cambridge University Press 2021) 19. Kleinlein, 'International Legal Thought', 815.

prospect of a productive dialogue between the two. Paradoxically, however, the arguments are meant to convince *vice versa* the opposite side. The narrative of universal authority is supposed to be universal because it is meant to convince even the critic. The critic, in turn, aims at the erosion of the systematic building of thought.

Going back to Vitoria, a central concern of critical scholarship was to erode an assumingly naïve narrative of progress developed in the *League of Nations*-era. For crits, the Habermasian account must have been an appalling return to former times. The sheer imagination that a philosopher who is perceived as one of the most eminent European critical minds accentuates the constructive aspects of Vitorian thought must have been strange, if not disappointing. Why did Habermas take that path?

If one takes the methodological directions as given, this requires implicit assumptions about the distribution of roles between systematic and critical approaches. The 'systematic' is the assumingly hegemonic lead approach while the 'critical' works as a corrective that reveals problematic aspects about the dominant narrative. The critical slashes the marble from the seemingly perfect facade of international public order to show that not everything is as harmonic as it may seem.

These background conditions of a significantly under-theorized international law have been vanishing continuously since the 1990s while with Euro-/US-centric liberal internationalism the preferred target of critical approaches, has experienced considerable external pressure from in – and outside.

In an international law that has come under considerable pressure, lead narratives of progress are largely absent. Given the omnipresence of open violations of international law in political practice, the current hegemony is beyond, rather than in the law. The authoritarian imperialism of our time does not necessarily require the law as a scheme for justification. Yet, fighting against a long-gone 1990s liberal economic imperialism, the crit becomes a modern Don Quijote.[69] This new configuration might flip the interplay of sys-

69 Ironically, *Koskenniemi*'s concluding remarks to his Salamanca treatment might equally hit today's international lawyer: 'The Salamanca scholars tried hard to compromise between received doctrine and a world undergoing rapid economic and cultural transformation. But the more daunting the challenges they faced, the more complex their accommodations became and the less control their proliferating casuistries could have on what was going on, namely a hardening on the practice of government' Koskenniemi, *To the Uttermost Parts of the Earth*, 211.

tematic and critical approaches. At least this is how Niklas Luhmann put it: If there is little left to erode, even the crit owes an alternative.[70]

Following Habermas', it might be worthwhile looking for 'splints of reason'[71] in an undoubtedly dark history of mankind. Even if such narratives of progress are insufficiently reflected in the *status quo*, international law needs a potential conception of just and rightful authority. This pays due regard to the fact that we are certainly not living on a fair, just and equitable planet but we are neither living in the worst of all possible worlds. International law as a discipline and its 'legal imagination' has contributed to both.

Bibliography

Amorosa, Paolo. *Rewriting the History of the Law of Nations: How James Brown Scott made Francisco de Vitoria the Founder of International Law* (Oxford: Oxford University Press 2019).

Beneyto, José María. 'Camilo Barcia Trelles on Francisco de Vitoria: At the Crossroads of Carl Schmitt's Grossraum and James Brown Scott's 'Modern International Law'. *European Journal of International Law* 31 (4) (2020), 1477–1492.

Beneyto, José María. 'Conquest, Empire and Peace: Vitoria, Charles V, Erasmus and the Foundations of the Law of Nations', in José María Beneyto (ed.), *Empire Humanism and Rights* (Cham: Springer Nature 2022), 1–47.

Bhuta, Nehal. '"Let Us Suppose That Universals Do Not Exist": Bricoleur and Bricolage in Martti Koskenniemi's to the Uttermost Parts of the Earth'. *European Journal of International Law* 32 (3) (2021), 943–48, doi: https://doi.org/10.1093/ejil/chab079 (last accessed on 7 August 2025).

Bianchi, Andrea. 'Reflexive Butterfly Catching: Insights from a Situated Catcher', in Joost Pauwely, Ramses Wessel and Jan Wouters (eds.), *Informal International Lawmaking* (Oxford: Oxford University Press 2012), 200–215.

Böckenförde, Ernst-Wolfgang. '§ 14 Die Spanische Spätscholastik, Ii. Francisco de Vitoria', in Ernst-Wolfgang Böckenforde (ed.), *Geschichte der Rechts- und Staatsphilosophie. Antike und Mittelalter* (Tübingen: Mohr Siebeck 2006).

70 Niklas Luhmann, *Soziologische Aufklärung 1. Aufsätze zur Theorie sozialer Systeme* (Wiesbaden: VS Verlag für Sozialwissenschaften 2005) 325.

71 For this early characterization of Habermas' thought, see Dieter Groh, '"Spuren der Vernunft in der Geschichte". Der Weg von Jürgen Habermas zur "Theorie des kommunikativen Handelns" im Schatten Max Webers'. *Geschichte und Gesellschaft* 12 (4) (1986), 448. ('Damit durchbricht die Geschichte den Zirkel der Aporie, der Geschichtsprozeß eröffnet den dialektischen Ausweg').

Brett, Annabel. 'Between History, Politics and Law', in Annabel Brett, Martti Koskenniemi and Megan Donaldson (eds.), *History, Politics, Law: Thinking through the International* (Cambridge: Cambridge University Press 2021), 19–48.

Brett, Annabel. *Liberty, Right and Nature: Individual Rights in Later Scholastic Thought* (Cambridge: Cambridge University Press 2003).

Bunge, Kirstin. 'Francisco de Vitoria: a Redesign of Global Order on the Threshold of the Middle Ages to Modern Times', in Stefan Kadelbach, Thomas Kleinlein and David-Roth-Isigkeit (eds.), *System, Order, and International Law* (Oxford: Oxford University Press 2017).

Chomsky, Noam. *Aspects of the Theory of Syntax* (Cambridge: The M.I.T. Press 1985).

Courtine, Jean-François. 'Chapitre V – Vitoria, Suárez Et La Naissance Du Droit Naturel Moderne', in Jean-François Courtine (ed.), *Nature et empire de la loi* (Paris: Éditions de l'EHESS 1999) 115–161.

Craven, Matthew. 'Theorizing the Turn to History in International Law', in Anne Orford and Florian Hoffmann (eds.), *The Oxford Handbook of the Theory of International Law* (Oxford: Oxford University Press 2016) 21–37.

de la Rasilla, Ignacio. 'The Turn to the History of International Law', in Ignacio de la Rasilla (ed.), *International Law and History: Modern Interfaces* (Cambridge: Cambridge University Press 2021) 11–40.

de la Rasilla, Ignacio. *In the Shadow of Vitoria: A History of International Law in Spain (1770–1953)* (Leiden: Brill 2017).

Deckers, Daniel. *Gerechtigkeit und Recht: eine historisch-kritische Untersuchung der Gerechtigkeitslehre des Francisco de Vitoria; 1483–1546* (Freiburg: Herder 1991).

Dellavalle, Sergio. *Paradigms of Social Order: From Holism to Pluralism and Beyond* (Cham: Springer International Publishing 2021).

Fernández-Sánchez, Pablo Antonio. 'From Totus Orbis to Global Law', in Giuliana Ziccardi Capaldo (ed.), *The Global Community Yearbook of International Law and Jurisprudence 2015* (New York: Oxford University Press 2016).

Fisch, Jörg. *Die europäische Expansion und das Völkerrecht* (Stuttgart: Steiner 1984).

Grawert, Rolf. 'FRANCISCO DE VITORIA: Naturrecht – Herrschaftsordnung – Völkerrecht'. *Der Staat* 39 (1) (2000), 110–125.

Grewe, Wilhelm G. *The Epochs of International Law*, trans. by Michael Byers (Berlin: De Gruyter 2000).

Groh, Dieter. '"Spuren der Vernunft in der Geschichte". Der Weg von Jürgen Habermas zur "Theorie des kommunikativen Handelns" im Schatten Max Webers'. *Geschichte und Gesellschaft* 12 (4) (1986), 443–476.

Habermas, Jürgen. *Auch eine Geschichte der Philosophie: Band 1: Die okzidentale Konstellation von Glauben und Wissen* (Berlin: Suhrkamp Verlag 2019).

Habermas, Jürgen. *Between Facts and Norms: Contributions to a discourse theory of law and democracy* (Hoboken: John Wiley & Sons 2015).

Habermas, Jürgen. *The Lure of Technocracy* (Hoboken: John Wiley & Sons 2015).

Habermas, Jürgen. *This too a History of Philosophy*, trans. by Ciaran Cronin (Cambridge: Polity 2023).

Habermas, Jürgen. 'Why Europe Needs a Constitution'. *New Left Review* 11 (2001).

Haggenmacher, Peter. 'Foreword', in Stefan Kadelbach, Thomas Kleinlein and David-Roth-Isigkeit (eds.), *System, Order, and International Law* (Oxford: Oxford University Press 2017) ix–xi.

Hart, H. L. A. *The Concept of Law* (Oxford: Oxford University Press 1994).

Hörnqvist, Mikael. *Machiavelli and Empire* (Cambridge: Cambridge University Press, 2004).

Hunter, Ian. 'About the Dialectical Historiography of International Law'. *Global Intellectual History* 1 (1) (2016), 1–32, doi: https://doi.org/10.1080/23801883.2016.1155863 (last accessed on 7 August 2025).

Kadelbach, Stefan. 'Mission Und Eroberung Bei Vitoria. Zur Entstehung Des Völkerrechts Aus der Theologie', in Kirstin Bunge, Anselm Spindler and Andreas Wagner (eds.), *Die Normativität des Rechts bei Francisco de Vitoria* (Stuttgart: frommann-holzboog Verlag 2011).

Kadelbach, Stefan, Thomas Kleinlein, and David Roth-Isigkeit. 'Introduction', in Stefan Kadelbach, Thomas Kleinlein and David-Roth-Isigkeit (eds.), *System, Order, and International Law* (Oxford: Oxford University Press 2017).

Kennedy, David. 'The Context for Context: International Legal History in Struggle', in Annabel Brett, Martti Koskenniemi and Megan Donaldson (eds.), *History, Politics, Law: Thinking through the International* (Cambridge: Cambridge University Press 2021) 69–95.

Kleinlein, Thomas. 'International Legal Thought: Creation of a Tradition and the Potential of Disciplinary Self-Reflection'. *Global Community Yearbook of International Law and Jurisprudence* 16 (2016), 811–827, doi: http://dx.doi.org/10.2139/ssrn.2923969 (last accessed on 7 August 2025).

Kleinlein, Thomas. *Konstitutionalisierung im Völkerrecht: Konstruktion und Elemente einer idealistischen Völkerrechtslehre* (Berlin/Heidelberg: Springer 2011).

Kleinlein, Thomas. '"Wollen die leeren Worte kein Ende Haben?" Die Frühe Neuzeit in der heutigen Völkerrechtswissenschaft', Tilmann Altwicker, Francis Cheneval and Oliver Diggelmann (eds.), *Völkerrechtsphilosophie Der Frühaufklärung* (Tübingen: Mohr Siebeck 2015).

Koskenniemi, Martti. 'Between Commitment and Cynicism: Outline for a Theory of International Law as Practice', André Nollkaemper, Jean d'Aspremont, Tarcisio Gazzini and Wouter Werner (eds.), *International Law as a Profession (Cambridge: Cambridge University Press 2017*) 38–66.

Koskenniemi, Martti. 'Expanding Histories of International Law'. *American Journal of Legal History* 56 (1) (2016), 104–112, doi: https://doi.org/10.1093/ajlh/njv011 (last accessed on 7 August 2025).

Koskenniemi, Martti. *From Apology to Utopia: The Structure of International Legal Argument* (Cambridge: Cambridge University Press 2006).

Koskenniemi, Martti. 'Histories of International Law: Dealing with Eurocentrism'. *Rechtsgeschichte – Legal History* 19 (2011), 152–76, doi: https://doi.org/10.12946/rg19/152-176 (last accessed on 7 August 2025).

Koskenniemi, Martti. 'A History of International Law Histories', in Bardo Fassbender and Anne Peters (eds.), *The Oxford Handbook of the History of International Law* (Oxford: Oxford University Press 2012) 943–71.

Koskenniemi, Martti. 'The Past according to International Law', in Annabel Brett, Martti Koskenniemi and Megan Donaldson (eds.), *History, Politics, Law: Thinking through the International* (Cambridge: Cambridge University Press 2021) 49–68.

Koskenniemi, Martti. *The Politics of International Law* (London: Hart Publishing 2011).

Koskenniemi, Martti. '"Stuck in Salamanca": A Response'. *European Journal of International Law* 32 (3) (2021), 1043–1048, doi: https://doi.org/10.1093/ejil/chab073 (last accessed on 7 August 2025).

Koskenniemi, Martti. *To the Uttermost Parts of the Earth: Legal Imagination and International Power 1300–1870* (Cambridge: Cambridge University Press 2021).

Koskenniemi, Martti. 'Vitoria and Us. Thoughts on Critical Histories of International Law'. *Rechtsgeschichte – Legal History* 22 (2014), 119–138, doi: https://doi.org/10.12946/rg22/119-138 (last accessed on 7 August 2025).

Lauterpacht, Hersch. 'The Grotian Tradition in International Law'. *British Yearbook of International Law*. 23 (1946), 1.

Luhmann, Niklas. *Soziologische Aufklärung 1. Aufsätze zur Theorie sozialer Systeme* (Wiesbaden: VS Verlag für Sozialwissenschaften 2005).

Nussbaum, Arthur. *A Concise History of the Law of Nations* (New York: The Macmillan Company 1947).

Nuzzo, Luigi. 'The Law That Wasn't There: Chapter 2: The Political Theology of Ius Gentium – The Expansion of Spain 1524–1559'. *European Journal of International Law* 32 (3) (2021), 957–964, doi: https://doi.org/10.1093/ejil/chab076 (last accessed on 7 August 2025).

Nys, Ernest. 'Introduction', in Ernest Nys (ed.), *Francisco de Vitoria, De Indis et de Iure Belli, Relectiones* (*Classics of International Law*) (Washington: Carnegie Institution 1917).

Orford, Anne. 'On international legal method'. *London Review of International Law* 1 (1) (2003), 166–197.

Orford, Anne. *International Law and the Politics of History* (Cambridge: Cambridge University Press 2021).

Pagden, Anthony. *The Fall of Natural Man: the American Indian and the Origins of Comparative Ethnology* (Cambridge: Cambridge University Press 1986).

Pitts, Jennifer. 'International Relations and the Critical History of International Law'. *International Relations* 31 (3) (2017), 282–298.

Roth-Isigkeit, David. 'The Grammar (s) of Global Law'. *KritV, CritQ, RCrit. Kritische Vierteljahresschrift für Gesetzgebung und Rechtswissenschaft/Critical Quarterly for Legislation and Law/Revue critique trimestrielle de jurisprudence et de législation* (2016), 175–186.

Rovira, Mónica García-Salmones. 'The Disorder of Economy? the First Relectio de Indis in a Theological Perspective', in Stefan Kadelbach, Thomas Kleinlein and David Roth-Isigkeit (eds.), *System, Order, and International Law* (Oxford: Oxford University Press 2017).

Schmitt, Carl. *The Nomos of the Earth: In the International Law of the Jus Publicum Europaeum*. trans. by G. L. Ulmen (New York: Telos Press Publishing 2006).

Scott, James Brown. *The Spanish Origin of International Law* (Oxford: Clarendon Press 1934).

Simpson, Gerry. 'After Method: International Law and the Problems of History', in Annabel Brett, Martti Koskenniemi and Megan Donaldson (eds.), *History, Politics, Law: Thinking through the International* (Cambridge: Cambridge University Press 2021) 96–126.

Skinner, Quentin. 'Meaning and Understanding in the History of Ideas'. *History and Theory* 8 (1) (1969), 3–53.

Skouteris, Thomas. 'The Turn to History in International Law', in *Oxford Bibliographies in International Law*, doi: https://doi.org/10.1093/OBO/9780199796953-0154 (last accessed on 7 August 2025).

Smeltzer, Joshua. 'On the Use and Abuse of Francisco De Vitoria: James Brown Scott and Carl Schmitt'. *Journal of the History of International Law/Revue d'histoire du droit international* 20 (3) (2018), 345–372, doi: https://doi.org/10.1163/15718050-20021052 (last accessed on 7 August 2025).

Tuck, Richard. *The Rights of War and Peace: Political Thought and the International Order from Grotius to Kant* (Oxford: Oxford University Press on Demand 2001).

Vadi, Valentina. 'International Law and Its Histories: Methodological Risks and Opportunities'. *Harvard International Law Journal* 58 (2017), 311.

Vadi, Valentina. 'Perspective and Scale in the Architecture of International Legal History'. *European Journal of International Law* 30 (1) (2019), 53–71, doi: https://doi.org/10.1093/ejil/chz001 (last accessed on 7 August 2025).

Verdross, Alfred, and Bruno Simma. *Universelles Völkerrecht: Theorie und Praxis* (Berlin: Duncker & Humblot 1984).

Verdross, Alfred. *Abendländische Rechtsphilosophie Ihre Grundlagen Und Hauptprobleme in Geschichtlicher Schau* (Wien: Springer Verlag 1963).

Vitoria, Francisco de. 'On Civil Power', in Anthony Pagden and Jeremy Lawrance (eds.), *Vitoria: Political Writings* (Cambridge: Cambridge University Press 1991).

Vitoria, Francisco de. 'On the American Indians', in Anthony Pagden and Jeremy Lawrance (eds.), *Vitoria: Political Writings* (Cambridge: Cambridge University Press 1991).

Von Der Heydte, Friedrich August Freiherr. 'Francisco de Vitoria und die Geschichte seines Ruhmes: Eine Entgegnung'. *Die Friedens-Warte* 49 (4/5) (1949), 190–197.

Whorf, Benjamin Lee. *Language, Thought, and Reality; Selected Writings* (Cambridge: M. I. T. Press 1956).

PART 2

Conceptual Crossroads in International Law and Political Thought

CHAPTER 6

Planetary Enmity, Global Community and International Law: The Case of Vitoria and the Spanish Conquista

Miguel Vatter

1 Introduction: Towards a *Nomos*-based Genealogy of International Law

By definition 'public' enmity is determined by the possibilities inscribed within systems of international law, or what since the ancient Romans is called *ius gentium*, the 'law of peoples'. And since enmity entails the possibility of war, one can understand why Carl Schmitt said that 'in the last instance, all the great questions of international law converge on the concept of the just war'.[1] It is not unusual for philosophical texts to find their moment of legibility in different ages from the one in which they were written. Perhaps Francisco de Vitoria's *Relectio prior de Indis recenter inventis* (Relección primera de los Indios últimamente descubiertos) found its moment of legibility in the 1920s, when Brown Scott used it to support the central principle of liberal internationalism, namely, that wars of aggression were to be considered illegal.[2] Schmitt's own interest in Vitoria was functional to his aim, from the early 1930s onwards, of rejecting this liberal principle and what he took to follow from its spirit, namely, the criminalization of the German *Reich* from the 1919 Treaty of Versailles to the Nuremberg Trials of 1945–6.[3] In opposition to liberal

1 'En última instancia, todos las grandes cuestiones de una ordenación internacional convergen en el concepto de guerra justa'. Carl Schmitt, 'La Justificación de la Ocupación de un Nuevo Mundo (Francisco de Vitoria)'. *Revista Española de Derecho Internacional* 2 (1) (1949), 13–46, 39. All translations from Spanish are mine.

2 'On the American Indians (De Indis)' in Francisco de Vitoria, *Vitoria's Political Writings*, Anthony Pagden and Jeremy Lawrence (eds.), (Cambridge: Cambridge University Press, 1991). For the Spanish translation, Francisco de Vitoria, *Relecciones sobre los Indios y el derecho de guerra* (Madrid: Coleccion Austral, 1946).

3 For a discussion of Schmitt's development of *Grossraum* and *nomos*, see Peter Uwe Hohendahl, *Perilous futures: on Carl Schmitt's late writings* (Ithaca, NY: Cornell University Press, 2018) and Oliver Simons, 'Carl Schmitt's Spatial Rhetoric,' in Jens Meierhenrich and Oliver Simons (eds.), *The Oxford Handbook of Carl Schmitt* (New York: Oxford University Press, 2016), 776–802. On the key 1941 text *Völkerrechtliche Grossraumsordnung: Mit Interventions-*

 | DOI:10.1163/9789004757448_007

conceptions of a global legal community of equal sovereign states, Schmitt sought to formulate a conception of international law that was internally tied to spatial expansion, that is, to the creation and exercise of empire (*imperium*, *Reich*), which cannot occur without war-making and conquest. Starting in the late 1930s, he developed an idea of political space beyond the territorial nation-state, which he called *Grossraum* ('great space'), and he reconstructed a non-liberal concept of law to which he gave the classical Greek name of *nomos* because of its root in the verb *nemein* that contains within it the meanings both of seizure and distribution of land (*Landnahme*).[4] In his post-WWII treatise on international law, *The Nomos of the Earth*, Schmitt argued that *nomos* was best exemplified in the 'land-appropriation of a new world,' that is, in the Spanish Conquista that extended European power and authority over some 'new' part of the surface of the Earth. In this context, his non-liberal interpretation of Vitoria recovered central significance for his attack on liberal international law as having rendered wars both 'global' and 'total'.[5]

In this chapter I consider the conflict of interpretations in the twentieth century around Francisco de Vitoria's reformulation of *ius gentium* to show the different ways in which the legitimacy of international law is a function of its 'globalization'. By this term, I refer in the first instance to the discursive strategies employed to justify extending a given legal order to cover 'the whole world' (as the terrestrial surface came to be figured in and through the discovery of the 'New World' after 1492). For the most part, as I discuss below, the specialized literature tends to see Vitoria's internationalization of law as a

---

verbot für raumfremden Mächte see also Matthew Specter, 'Grossraum and Geopolitics. Resituating Schmitt in an Atlantic Context'. *History and Theory* 56 (3) (2017), 398–406 and Joshua Derman, 'Carl Schmitt on Land and Sea'. *History of European Ideas* 37 (2) (2011), 181–89.

4 See the essays 'Nomos-Nahme-Name' in Carl Schmitt, *Staat, Grossraum, Nomos. Arbeiten aus den Jahren 1916–1969*, Günter Maschke (ed.), (Berlin: Duncker&Humblot, 1995), 'Nehmen-Teilen-Weiden' in Carl Schmitt, *Verfassungsrechtliche Aufsaetze aus den Jahren 1924–1954* (Berlin: Duncker & Humblot, 2003), as well as the discussion in Carl Schmitt, *The Nomos of the Earth in the International Law of Jus Publicum Europaeum* (New York: Telos Press, 2003). On Schmitt's positioning of *Grossraum* with respect to the National Socialist ideology of 'Lebensraum' see Stuart Elden, 'Reading Schmitt geopolitically: Nomos, territory and Großraum,' in Stephen Legg (ed.), *Spatiality, Sovereignty and Carl Schmitt: Geographies of the Nomos* (London: Routledge, 2011), 91–105 and Martti Koskenniemi, 'Letter in Response to Michael Salter's Recent Paper on Carl Schmitt's Grossraum'. *Chinese Journal of International Law* 12 (1) (2013), 201–202. The recovery of Schmitt's *Grossraum* idea for a post-Cold War discourse on 'multipolar' world order is propelled by texts like Chantal Mouffe, 'Schmitt's Vision of a Multipolar World Order'. *The South Atlantic Quarterly* 104 (2) (2005), 245–251. On the concept of *Grossraum* and international political theory, see Carlo Galli, *Political Spaces and Global War* (Minneapolis: University of Minnesota Press, 2010).

5 Hohendahl, *Perilous Futures*, 76–81.

function of his creative adaptation of Roman law categories. My hypothesis is that these twentieth-century interpretations of Vitoria's discourse show that the emergence of a 'global' right and a 'global' community relies on a nexus between legal order (*Ordnung*) and localization (*Ortung*) that Schmitt identified as characteristic of the Greek idea of law as *nomos* and associated with the geo-political notion of *Grossraum* and so also of empire.[6] However, the twentieth-century debate on Vitoria also indicates that the nexus of spatiality and law can receive antithetical political interpretations, leaving room for a variety of models of global legal order. In this chapter, I identify how the discourse of *nomos* functions in Brown Scott's interpretation of Vitoria as the founding father of liberal internationalism, and compare it with how Vitoria was mobilized by Schmitt and Barcia Trelles in a direction that one could paradoxically call both neo-imperial and post-colonial.[7] Lastly, I interpret Koskenniemi's recent account of the Spanish origins of international law as providing a synthesis between the above contrapositions, one that employs the Schmittian notion of *nomos* to argue that Vitoria deploys a subjective understanding of right as *dominium* in order to develop a 'globalized' idea of *ius gentium* as the *nomos* for emergent global 'liberal' capitalism.[8]

By using the concept of *nomos* to analyse these different discourses on the foundations of international law, I argue that one can better appreciate the internal relation between imperialism and international law that is the focus

6 The literature on Schmitt's conception of *nomos* is extensive. See several related chapters in Jens Meierhenrich and Oliver Simons (eds.), *The Oxford Handbook of Carl Schmitt* (New York: Oxford University Press, 2017) and the discussion in Montserrat Herrero, *The Political Discourse of Carl Schmitt. A Mystic of Order* (Lexington: Rowman&Littlefield, 2015). For an alternative reconstruction of the archaic Greek meaning of *nomos* see now Thanos Zartaloudis, *The Birth of Nomos* (Edinburgh: Edinburgh University Press, 2019).

7 I follow here José María Beneyto, 'Camilo Barcia Trelles on Francisco de Vitoria: At the Crossroads of Carl Schmitt's *Grossraum* and James Brown Scott's "Modern International Law"'. *European Journal of International Law* 31 (4) (2021), 1477–1492. For a reading of Schmitt's interpretation of Vitoria as a response to Brown Scott, see Joshua Smeltzer, 'On the Use and Abuse of Francisco de Vitoria: James Brown Scott and Carl Schmitt'. *Journal of the History of International Law* 20 (2018), 345–372. For another reading of Schmitt's approach to Vitoria in the Spanish context, see Miguel Saralegui, *Carl Schmitt pensador español* (Madrid: Trotta, 2013). On Schmitt's account of *nomos* and postcolonialism, see Andreas Kalyvas, 'Carl Schmitt's Postcolonial Imagination'. *Constellations* 25 (1) (2018), 35–53 and Ulrike Kistner, 'In search of a new nomos: Post-colonially'. *Constellations* 27 (2) (2020), 273–284.

8 I mainly address Martti Koskenniemi, 'Empire and International Law. The Real Spanish Contribution'. *University of Toronto Law Journal* 61 (2011), 1–36, but now see the extended version of the argument in the chapter on 'The Political Theology of *Ius Gentium*. The Expansion of Spain 1526–1559' in Martti Koskenniemi, *To the Uttermost Parts of the Earth: Legal Imagination and International Power, 1300–1870* (New York: Cambridge University Press, 2021).

of recent critical theory of international law.[9] In particular, I show that by understanding Vitoria and his twentieth-century interpreters through the conceptual resources of the discourse of *nomos* and its related idea of *Grossraum*, one can articulate the ways in which international law functions as a harbinger of 'peace' only in and through the regulation of planetary enmity, as well as the roles played by the appeal to freedom and religion, indeed to freedom of religion, in this regulation.

While studies on the nexus between liberalism and imperialism have contraposed the ways different Western empires have justified conquest and colonization through their creative use of Roman legal categories starting with Vitoria,[10] at the level of international legal theory the postcolonial perspective has started to examine why and how 'the central doctrines and categories of international law, including, most importantly, the fundamental doctrine of sovereignty, have been shaped by the colonial encounter'.[11] The second hypothesis of this chapter is that the varied and opposed interpretations of Vitoria in the twentieth century also share a further gesture: the simultaneous recognition and sublation, or *méreconnaissance* of Indigenous law, language and culture as a form of ancestral *nomos*. No doubt referring to the problematic of the 'Black Legend' of the Conquista, this constitutive misrecognition of Indigeneity is what Mignolo has referred to as 'the darker side of the Renaissance'.[12] At the other end of this long arc of globalization stands the Australian High Court *Mabo vs Queensland* ruling on the Australian settler colonial use of *terra nullius* to justify its occupation of Aboriginal and Torres Strait Islanders' country in which the above recognition and sublation receives one of its most limpid formulations: as Hegel says, the owl of Minerva flies only at dusk.[13] No

9 For an overview, see Antony Anghie, 'Imperialism and International Legal Theory', in Anne Orford (ed.), *The Oxford Handbook of the Theory of International Law* (New York: Oxford University Press, 2016) 156–172.

10 For the example in relation to *terra nullius* see Lauren Benton and Benjamin Straumann, 'Acquiring Empire by Law: From Roman Doctrine to Early Modern European Practice'. *Law and History Review* 28 (1) (2010), 1–38.

11 Anghie, 'Imperialism and International Legal Theory', 166.

12 Walter Mignolo, *The Darker Side of the Renaissance: Literacy, Territoriality and Colonization* (Ann Arbor: University of Michigan Press, 2003). 'But modernity as such was "born" when Europe was in a position to pose itself against an other, when, in other words, Europe could constitute itself as a unified ego exploring, conquering, colonizing an alterity that gave back its image of itself.... So, if 1492 is the moment of the "birth" of modernity as a concept... it also marks the origin of a process of concealment or misrecognition of the non-European'. Enrique Dussel, 'Eurocentrism and Modernity (Introduction to the Frankfurt lectures)'. *boundary 2* 20 (3) (1993), 65–76, 67.

13 On Indigeneity and law, see Kathleen Birrell, *Indigeneity: Before and Beyond the Law* (New York: Routledge, 2016). For a discussion of ancestral *nomoi* in Australia, see Ste-

genealogy of international law that takes its beginning from Vitoria's discourse can avoid coming to terms with the role played by Indigenous *nomoi* as both a condition of possibility and impossibility of international law.

In the conclusion of the essay, I suggest that the confluence between an approach to international law through the perspective of *nomos* and *Grossraum* and an emerging awareness of the structural reliance of the discourse of international law on ancestral conceptions of *nomos* can be seen at play in the new international law of the global commons, such as it is developed for outer space, the ocean sea-bed, and Antarctica. These are 'great spaces' which, contrary to Schmitt's idea of *Grossraum*, in principle exclude *Landnahme* and sovereign claims and are nominally dedicated to purely peaceful uses. They testify to a pressing need to think about the dependence of international law on non-human Earth systems that make the planet's habitability possible.

2 Brown Scott and the Internationalist Reading of Vitoria

Brown Scott was the motivating intellectual force behind the early twentieth-century push to establish Vitoria as the founder of international law by interpreting his discourse as an argument that makes illegal all wars of aggression.[14] In *The Spanish Origin of International Law* Brown Scott claims that the three

---

phen Muecke, Paddy Roe, and Krim Benterrak, *Reading the Country. Introduction to Nomadology* (Melbourne: re.press, 2014). On international law and settler colonialism, see David Armitage, *Foundations of International Thought* (Cambridge: Cambridge University Press, 2012), Lisa Ford, *Settler Sovereignty: Jurisdiction and Indigenous People in America and Australia 1788–1836* (Cambridge, MA: Harvard University Press, 2010), Duncan Bell, *Reordering the World. Essays on Liberalism and Empire* (Princeton: Princeton University Press, 2016), Mirand Johnson, *The Land is Our History: Indigeneity, Law and the Settler State* (New York: Oxford University Press, 2016), Saliha Belmessous, ed., *Native Claims: Indigenous Law against Empire, 1500–1920* (New York: Oxford University Press, 2012), Laura Benton and Lisa Ford, *Rage for Order: The British Empire and the Origins of International Law* (Cambridge, MA: Harvard University Press, 2016), among many others. With respect to political and legal theory, see James Tully, *Strange Multiplicity: Constitutionalism in an Age of Diversity* (Cambridge: Cambridge University Press, 1995) and Paul Patton, Duncan Ivison, and Will Saunders (eds.), *Political Theory and the Rights of Indigenous Peoples* (New York: Cambridge University Press, 2000), and now in relation to political theology, see Mark Brett, *Indigenous Rights and the Legacies of the Bible: From Moses to Mabo* (New York: Oxford University Press, 2024).

14 See the definitive treatment in Paolo Amorosa, *Rewriting the History of the Law of Nations. How James Brown Scott Made Francisco de Vitoria the Founder of International Law* (New York: Oxford University Press, 2019).

basic 'principles of the law of nations' that sustained the project of the League of Nations were already found in Vitoria's texts that justified the Spanish Conquista. The three principles are, first, that nations are to be recognized insofar as they conform 'states' (by which he means 'modern' territorial states). Second, 'the corner-stone of Vitoria's system was equality of states, applicable not merely to the states of Christendom and of Europe but also to the barbarian principalities in the Western World of Columbus'.[15] The third principle is that states are 'artificial' legal persons through which groups of individuals exercise jurisdiction over a given territory by imposing a rule of law and representative forms of government on themselves.[16] For Brown Scott 'states' are the kind of constitutional polities that came into being first through the English Glorious Revolution and then the American Revolution.[17]

Brown Scott conceives of international law as an extension of the normative order found *within* these kinds of states to the *inter*-state condition. This extension depends on the assumption that the Anglo-American conception of the state is indeed universalizable to all peoples and nations of the world.[18] Since on this model principles of justice that apply within states also apply between states, 'it follows that force between states could only justly be used to redress a wrong, and a resort to force was only to be tolerated because there was no court of the States'.[19] Given that the right to go to war (*ius belli*) was a marker of sovereignty in the *ius publicum europaeum*, only the international-

---

15 James Brown Scott, *Spanish Origin of International Law* (Oxford: Clarendon Press, 1934), 281.

16 Brown Scott, *Spanish Origin*, 281.

17 For the genealogy of this European conception of the state, see Quentin Skinner, 'A Genealogy of the Modern State,' *Proceedings of the British Academy* 162 (2009), 325–370, which does not emphasize its colonial dimension. In *Land and Sea* and *The Nomos of the Earth*, Schmitt claims that this Anglo-American conception of the state should not be equated with the European continental development of the state, the so-called *ius publicum europaeum*. Carl Schmitt, *Land and Sea. A World-Historical Meditation*, Russell A. Berman and Samuel Garrett Zeitlin (eds.) (Candor, NY: Telos Press Publishing, 2015). Schmitt speaks of 'the un-state-like Society-character of English power [*der unstaatliche Societycharakter der englischen Herrschaft*], the excessive use of "indirect" methods of rule, and finally what I would like to call the "de-anchoring" of the island'. Schmitt, *Staat, Grossraum, Nomos*, 419, translation mine.

18 An assumption that is only partially questioned in John Rawls, *The Law of Peoples* (Cambridge: Harvard University Press, 2001) and Philip Pettit, 'A Republican Law of Peoples,' *European Journal of Political Theory* 9 (1) (2010), 70–94.

19 Brown Scott, *Spanish Origin*, 282.

ization of a constitutional scheme that emerged with the American Revolution could make wars of aggression illegal.[20]

Brown Scott advocated for 'the creation of an international court of justice by the States and for the States, in which their controversies would be decided in the same manner as within the State, would render war both unnecessary and unlawful'.[21] For the North American lawyer, the idea of an international court of justice was 'established but a decade ago, upon the *initiative of the successors of Vitoria's aborigines*' (emphasis mine).[22] In this curious formulation, through which Brown Scott refers to Woodrow Wilson's support for the idea of a League of Nations that the United States never joined, one can read different layers of the mis-recognition of an Indigenous *nomos*.[23] For Brown Scott, global international law becomes possible thanks to the 'virtuous' supra-position of three discursive assemblages: Indigenous 'law'; Vitoria's normative justification of the Conquista based on the equal recognition of Indigenous 'sovereignty'; and, last but not least, the evolution of this 'aborigene' sovereignty into the modern state form given to it by the American Revolution and the Constitution of the United States of America.[24] From a postcolonial perspective, on the other hand, one can say that Brown Scott's supra-position hides the effects of two distinct genocidal erasures of the 'aborigines' and their laws, first through the Conquista itself, and second through the Conquest of the 'Far' or 'Wild' West.[25]

---

20 For a critical view of American constitutionalism in light of the European tradition of public law, see now Martin Loughlin, *Against Constitutionalism* (Cambridge: Harvard University Press, 2022).

21 Brown Scott, *Spanish Origin*, 282.

22 Brown Scott, *Spanish Origin*, 282.

23 See the discussion in Amorosa, *Rewriting the History of the Law of Nations*, 159: 'That [Woodrow] Wilson, unknowingly, had recovered the wisdom and the morality of just war theology [as justification for entry into WW I/MV] was, for Scott, reason for both hope and concern.'

24 It is a topos in the historiography of US federalism that some of the thinkers of the American Revolution may have been inspired for their federal designs by the Haudenosaunee (Iroquois) Confederacy. For theoretical treatment of this topos, but without reference to the idea of *nomos*, see Iris Marion Young, 'Hybrid Democracy: Iroquois Federalism and the Postcolonial Project,' in Paul Patton, Duncan Ivison, and Will Sanders (eds.), *Political Theory and the Rights of Indigenous Peoples* (Cambridge: Cambridge University Press, 2000), 237–258 and Tully, *Strange Multiplicity. Constitutionalism in an Age of Diversity*.

25 See Robert A. Williams, *The American Indian in Western Legal Thought. The Discourses of Conquest* (New York: Oxford University Press, 1993) and Edward B. Westermann, *Hitler's Ostkrieg and the Indian Wars. Comparing Genocide and Conquest* (Norman, OK: University of Oklahoma Press, 2016).

Brown Scott deduces a 'global' normative order by applying the jurisprudence of Marbury vs Madison, which assigned 'supremacy' to the Supreme Court over both the executive and the legislative in determining what is law and thus jurisdiction, and projects it onto the international space, in this way anticipating what is now termed 'global constitutionalism'.[26] This 'judicial' formulation of international law rests on Brown Scott's interpretation of Vitoria as the first theorist of a globalized idea of the 'international community': 'Before Columbus discovered the American Indies, the States of Christendom – the European world – was the international community. It was Vitoria's judgement, ever a liberal one, that the American principalities – as equals of the Christian states – should not be excluded from this international community. Therefore in his theory of international law, they were members possessing the same rights and the same duties as the Christian states of Europe'.[27] For Brown Scott, the crucial 'learning process' contained in the 'discovery' of the New World in 1492 was that it allowed Europeans – thanks to the formulations of Vitoria – to become conscious of the *pre-existence* of a truly 'international community' before and beyond the *respublica Christiana*.[28] Since this legal 'equality' between Christian and non-Christian states cannot be established on the basis of a shared Christian religion it would have to receive a 'secular' or 'neutral' foundation. In this sense, Brown Scott dates the European 'Enlightenment' back to Vitoria's *relecciones* on the American Indians, when the encounter in 1492 with an Indigenous *nomos*, recognized as equal to the Christian *nomos* at least in the eyes of Vitoria, eventually led Europeans to a critique of Christianity as the one and only true religion and, ultimately, to the establishment of political society on the principle of freedom of and from religion, best expressed by the US Constitution and its First Amendment.

---

26 For the concept, see Jeffrey L. Dunoff and Joel P. Trachtman (eds.), *Ruling the World? Constitutionalism, International Law, and Global Governance* (New York: Cambridge University Press, 2009), Hauke Brunkhorst, *Solidarity. From Civic Friendship to a Global Legal Community* (Cambridge: MIT Press, 2005) and Chris Thornhill, *The Sociology of Law and the Global Transformation of Democracy* (Cambridge, UK: Cambridge University Press, 2018). For arguments that problematize the co-existence of judicial supremacy and national sovereignty, see Martin Loughlin, *Foundations of Public Law* (New York: Oxford University Press, 2010).

27 Brown Scott, *Spanish Origin*, 282.

28 On the critique of this European Enlightenment 'learning process' from a postcolonial perspective, see now Amy Allen, *The End of Progress* (New York: Columbia University Press, 2015) and Antonio Y. Vázquez-Arroyo, 'Critical Theory, colonialism, and the historicity of thought,' *Constellations* 25 (2018), 54–70.

The principle of disestablishment of religion thus that stands out as the 'spiritual' basis of a 'global' conception of international law in Brown Scott.[29] Brown Scott's axiom of the universal 'equality' between European and non-European nations rests on the universality of the freedom of religion. For Schmitt, on the contrary, Vitoria's idea of *ius gentium* understands the 'freedom of religion' as an internal characteristic of the Christian *nomos*, of the *respublica Christiana*, that partitions the world between unequals, viz. between 'political' friends and enemies on the basis of religious differences with 'pagans and infidels'. Yet, despite their stark political opposition, Brown Scott and Schmitt share the assumption that Vitoria's project to extend *ius gentium* across the 'whole world' is only possible on condition of giving this international law a 'spiritual' ground of authority.[30] Furthermore, the 'spiritual' ground for establishing an over-arching *ius gentium* that would bridge 'pagan' and 'Spanish' republics requires Vitoria to recognize the pre-existence of Indigenous *nomoi*, together with their spiritual beliefs of a polytheistic character.[31]

---

29 For historical discussion of the principle in relation to colonialism and imperialism, see Teresa Bejan, *Mere Civility: Disagreement and the Limits of Toleration* (Cambridge, MA: Harvard University Press, 2017) and Mark G. Brett, *Locations of God. Political Theology in the Hebrew Bible* (New York: Oxford University Press, 2019), ch. 9.

30 I suggest that this is the real ground for the contemporary debate on toleration that emerges with multiculturalism. See Rainer Forst, *Toleranz im Konflikt* (Frankfurt: Suhrkamp, 2003) and Rainer Forst, 'Toleration and Democracy,' *Journal of Social Philosophy* 45 (1) (2014), 65–75, and for a response that emphasizes the 'civilizational' presupposition of toleration, see Wendy Brown, *Regulating Aversion. Tolerance in the Age of Identity and Empire* (Princeton: Princeton University Press, 2008). For a treatment of enmity within monotheism, see Gil Anidjar, *The Jew, the Arab. A History of the Enemy* (Stanford: Stanford University Press, 2003) and Gil Anidjar, *Blood. A Critique of Christianity* (New York: Columbia University Press, 2014).

31 See Dussel's various treatments of Las Casas's defence of paganism and even of cannibalism in his *Apologetica historia* against Gines de Sepulveda. I disagree here with Pagden's claim that 'for Las Casas the entire course of the Spanish overseas empire had been a part of the Lord's design to bring these "countless peoples" into the narrative of the history of Christianity'. Anthony Pagden, 'Legislating for the "Whole World That Is, in a Sense, a Commonwealth". Conquest, Occupation and the "Defence of the Innocent"', in Anthony Carty and Janne Nijman (eds.), *Morality and Responsibility of Rulers. European and Chinese Origins of Rule of Law as Justice for World Order* (New York: Oxford University Press, 2018), 145. Dussel argues that Las Casas develops the first 'anti-modern' discourse of Modernity, and 'anti-modern' precisely in the sense that it employs the legitimacy of paganism and its 'rebirth' (in Renaissance Europe) to dislodge the *nomos* of the *respublica Christiana*. See Enrique Dussel, *El primer debate filósofico de la modernidad* (Buenos Aires: CLACSO, 2020).

3 The Problem of the Legal Authority of the International Community

For Brown Scott, Vitoria replaces the Christian foundation of Western international law in order to conceive of a truly 'global' international law based on a new figure of 'humanity' as co-extensive with an 'international community' that exercises global jurisdiction. 'The international community is not a superimposed state; it is coextensive with humanity – no longer merely with Christianity. It is composed of the state and is their representative; it is likewise the representative of the common humanity rather than of the common religion binding states. It is a union of the states.... Its will is the will of humanity, speaking in terms of peoples; its will is international laws speaking in terms of states'. The key to Brown Scott's interpretation of Vitoria is the belief that there exists an 'international community' which 'possesses the inherent right to impose its will – in the form of law applicable to the individual state – and to punish its violation, not because of a treaty, of a pact or covenant, but because of *an international need*' (emphasis mine).[32] Liberal internationalist readings of Vitoria's justification of the Conquista identify in his novel way of connecting *ius naturale* to *ius gentium* the key conceptual ground of the idea of an international legal community.

The treatment of the connection between natural law and the law of nations in Vitoria's corpus is a complex topic. In this chapter, I am exclusively dealing with the different and incompatible ways in which this connection was reconstructed in the twentieth-century discourse on international law. The central difficulty emerges from the following consideration. The assumption that 'natural law, by definition, was the same for all peoples everywhere' irrespective of their religious beliefs or cultural differences,[33] can be grounded on the proposition, to give an example among many, that all human beings share the same 'natural' drive or need to propagate their species, as do other kinds of animals.[34] But this assumption of a shared natural 'need' does not self-evidently offer the condition of possibility for an 'international legal community' that exercises *dominium* over all states and is endowed with a 'will' to apply a 'uni-

32 Brown Scott, *Spanish Origin*, 283.

33 Pagden, 'Legislating for the "Whole World That Is, in a Sense, a Commonwealth"', 134.

34 For discussion of early modern discourse on natural law, see Annabel S. Brett, *Changes of State: Nature and the Limits of the City in Early Modern Natural Law* (Princeton: Princeton University Press, 2011) and on the Stoic extension of natural law to ideas of world order, see Marcelo D. Boeri, 'Natural law and world order in Stoicism,' in Gabriella Rossi (ed.), *Nature and the Best Life: Exploring the Natural Bases of Practical Normativity in Ancient Philosophy* (Hildesheim: G. Olms, 2013).

versal law' to all states and nations, equally between the Spanish and the French as between the Spanish and the 'American Indians'.[35] How did Vitoria move from one assumption to the other?

Recapitulating the complex scholarship on Vitoria's interpretation of natural law, Geuna suggests that the key novelty lies in Vitoria's emphasis on the concept of *gentes* (nations) over that of *homines* (human beings). Thus, in *On the American Indians* 3.1 Vitoria draws from a passage in the *Institutes* of Gaius, included in the *Digest* in slightly altered form, that refers to both natural law and *ius gentium*: 'the law that natural reason establishes among all mankind [*inter omnes hominem*] is followed by all peoples [*populus*] alike, and is called *ius gentium* as being the law [*iure*] observed by all mankind [*omnes gentes*].'[36] According to Geuna, by emphasizing the idea of nations/*gentes*, Vitoria extends the classical idea of natural law that originally applies to the members of the human species (considered as a natural species) to a modern conception of inter-national law as a *ius inter gentes*, a law applying to all nations (considered politically). On this reading, Vitoria connects natural law to international law through his original suggestion that there exists a *ius* that derives

35 For a discussion of Vitoria's *ius gentium* as being characterized by cultural and religious prejudice, see Antony Anghie, *Imperialism, Sovereignty, and the Making of International Law* (New York: Cambridge University Press, 2005). Pagden, on the contrary, argues that the grounding of *ius gentium* on natural law makes religious differences irrelevant for international law, referring to the passage in *On the American Indians* 1.3: 'unbelief does not cancel either natural or human (civil) law, but all forms of *dominium* derive either from natural or human law'. Vitoria, *Vitoria's Political Writings*, 244. In what follows I take up the interpretation proposed by Marco Geuna, 'Francisco De Vitoria e la questione della guerra giusta'. In *Dalla concordia dei Greci al bellum justum dei moderni*, ed. Giovanna Daverio Rocchi (Milan: Franco Angeli, 2013), 143–74.

36 Gaius, *Institutiones or Institutes of Roman Law by Gaius*, E.A. Whittuck (ed.), trans. Edward Poste, 4th ed. (Oxford: Clarendon Press, 1904), 1. This English translation generates confusion by translating *homines* and *gentes* equally as 'mankind'. The Latin is found in Gaius *Inst.* 1.1 (= *Dig.* 1.1.9): 'Quod vero naturalis ratio inter omnes homines constituit, id apud omnes [populos] peraeque custoditur vocaturque ius gentium, quasi quo iure omnes gentes utuntur'. For discussion see Dante Fedele, 'Ius gentium: The Metamorphoses of a Legal Concept (Ancient Rome to Early Modern Europe)', in Edward Cavanagh (ed.), *Empire and Legal Thought. Ideas and Institutions from Antiquity to Modernity* (Leiden: Brill, 2020) who writes that 'the word 'peoples (populus)', written in square brackets, is only present in the text of the *Institutiones*, whereas it has been expunged from the text included in the *Digesta*'. For an excellent survey of the origins of *ius gentium* in Vitoria, see María Cecilia Añaños Meza, 'El título de "sociedad y comunicación natural" de Francisco de Vitoria. Tras las huellas de su concepto a la luz de la teoría del dominio', *Anuario Mexicano de Derecho Internacional* 12 (2012), 525–592 and for more detailed discussion, see Daniel Deckers, *Gerechtigkeit und Recht: Eine historisch-kritische Untersuchung der Gerechtigkeitslehre des Franciso de Vitoria (1483–1546)* (Freiburg Schweiz: Universitätsverlag, 1991).

from the *naturalis societatis et communicationis* ('right to natural partnership and communication') between nations. Such a right (*ius communicationis*) underlies Vitoria's first legitimate title of conquest: 'Amongst all nations it is considered inhuman to treat strangers and travellers badly without some special cause [*En todas las naciones se tiene por inhumano el recibir y tratar mal a los huéspedes y peregrinos sin motivo especial alguno*], humane and dutiful to behave hospitably to strangers. This would not be the case if travellers were doing something evil by visiting foreign nations'.[37] If a nation violates this *ius communicationis*, then it would be legitimate to make war on them for the sake of upholding the right's universal validity. On this view, the basic 'international need' that requires 'international law' is the counter-factual interest that all peoples on Earth have in exchanging opinions and viewpoints between them, the need for a (communicative) medium that bridges distances in space and makes of the Earth 'one' world. If by 'inhuman' one understands what is contrary to human reason, and so wrong 'by natural law,' then Vitoria's thought could be rendered as follows: all nations agree that it is against natural law to impede communication between human beings, to treat them as enemies without prior cause, because all nations sense that they belong to a world community. This reasoning is crowned by his famous counterposing of Ovid's *homo homini homo* against Plautus's *homo homini lupus*.[38]

Vitoria's new justification for the Discovery and Conquest of the 'new world' could not be based upon an existing, factual 'mutual agreement' or consensus between nations, when these nations were unaware of the existence of each other. That is why the *ius gentium* can only refer to 'a positive law arrived at by a *hypothetical common understanding* between all or most of the peoples of the globe' referring to Vitoria's expression *consensus virtualis totius orbis*.[39] Such an agreement underlying a positive international law would have to be reached through communication between these nations, and what Vitoria needs to justify is a 'universal' a priori 'right' that nations have to communicate with each other and so, counterfactually, be capable of reaching such a mutual understanding. Thus, this universal right must be tied a priori to something about the changed character of the 'whole world,' the change from a 'known' totality such as the *respublica Christiana* to one that now includes an 'unknown' space, and that serves as a new ground for the 'virtual' consent

37 Vitoria, *Vitoria's Political Writings*, 278; Vitoria, *Relecciones sobre los Indios y el derecho de guerra*, 89.

38 See Jacques Derrida, *The Beast and the Sovereign. Volume 1* (Chicago: University of Chicago Press, 2011) on the general problematic of animality and sovereignty.

39 Pagden, 'Legislating for the "Whole World That Is, in a Sense, a Commonwealth"', 138 (emphasis mine).

of nations, or in Pagden's terms, its 'hypothetical' character. The question posed by Vitoria's *ius gentium* is a *quid juris* one: on what ground could such a hypothetical consent be based upon, and what legal force can it have, if not one based on the old political theology of the *respublica Christiana*? The reference to a 'ground' must be understood here at once normatively and spatially: the 'ground' of *ius gentium* must be given in reference to the newly discovered 'fact' that all nations live on the same spherical orb or 'globe,' and to what 'spiritual' consequences are to be drawn from this 'fact'.

Given that human beings do not always behave in humane ways with each other, and indeed can often be like 'wolves' to other human beings, part of the 'international need' that gives rise to international law is the supposed need felt by all peoples of the world for a political organization that can secure peace and justice to any and all in a 'global' setting. This leads to Vitoria's second point, namely, that the *ius gentium* must also be considered a 'positive law' and not simply a moral 'natural law' inherent to human reason. Thus, in *On Civil Power* [*De potestate civili*] 3.4 Vitoria states: 'the law of nations does not have the force merely of pacts or agreements between men, but has the validity of a positive enactment. The whole world, which in a sense is a commonwealth, has the power to enact laws which are just and convenient to all men; and these make up the law of nations [*Ius gentium non solum habet vim ex pacto et condicio inter homines, sed etiam habet vim legis, habet enim totus orbis, qui aliquo modo est una respublica, potestam ferendi leges aequas et convenientes omnibus, quales sunt in iure gentium*]'. The 'positive' nature of *ius gentium* is tied to the sense in which the 'whole world' (*totus orbis*) can be considered 'in some sense a republic' (*aliquo modo est una respublica*) and that the *ius gentium* has jurisdiction over the whole world in virtue of 'the authority of the whole world' (*orbis totius auctoritate*). This is the text that supports Brown Scott's claim that 'the international community is not a superimposed state; it is coextensive with humanity'.

For the *ius gentium* to have the force of positive law (*vis legis*), the newly 'discovered' meaning of *totus orbis*, 'whole world,' is that of 'a single legal person' with *de iure* 'powers of enactment'. But to claim that the 'will' of the international community has a 'force of law' prior to any contract between nations and in the absence of a *de facto* sovereign power that rules over the (new) 'whole world' necessarily entails a discourse about the normativity of spatialization, a discourse on the *nomos* of the Earth. That some normative conception of spatialization or localization is at work in Vitoria is clear from the fact that he adduces, in support of his claim, the Roman law principle that oceans, rivers, airs and forests are 'common goods' (*res communis*) whose common use cannot be prohibited to nations.

At the same time, such a *nomos* of the Earth cannot be divorced from a 'spiritual' conception of inhabiting the Earth. Benton and Straumann have criticized the traditional picture of the justification of conquest by European imperial powers based on the connection between the Roman law category of *res nullius* (a thing belonging to no one) and its extrapolation to *terra nullius* (a land belonging to no one) that seems to underpin the doctrine of discovery.[40] Instead, they suggest that Vitoria, Gentili and Grotius all employ the private law category of *res nullius* in a public law sense, namely, to deny the Papal and Imperial claims to having sovereignty over purportedly unoccupied lands. The argument is that the 'ownership of such *res nullius* was thus limited by control (*custodia*), a condition the Romans [and by extension, the Christian Emperor and the Pope/MV] as a matter of historical fact could simply not meet with regard to the overseas "lands that have just been discovered"'.[41] However, this argument has nothing to say with regard to the point at issue for both Vitoria and Brown Scott, namely, the grounds for considering both Spain and the indigenous nations of the Americas as belonging to one 'international community' with jurisdictional power and authority. From my perspective, what is more decisive in Vitoria's arguments is the assumption that all nations are already 'at home' on the Earth, both in the sense of ancestral *nomoi* that have already distributed these lands (and among which nations are already distributed), and in the sense that what makes these territories 'inhabitable' is the priority of *res communes*, of 'great spaces' on land, on the oceans, and in the air that account for the habitability of the planetary surface and can only be used in common; they are not *res nullius*, not objects for potential seizure and appropriation; and they are the material conditions for the *ius communicationis* between peoples.

These considerations are crucial to understanding Vitoria's point about *ius gentium* having the 'force of law' or *vis legis* without or independently of a world emperor (in this case, the Holy Roman Emperor and its claim to have inherited the title of *dominus mundi* from the Romans). On one side, the claim that *ius gentium* has *vis legis* refers to the 'executive' force that can be relied upon to enact *ius gentium* as a positive international law. This is the traditional way in which Vitoria has been understood. On the other side, the expression *vis legis* refers to a more fundamental problem, which is related to the 'authority' of such international law. This would have to be, following Vitoria, an 'authority' held by the 'whole world' itself, or by the planetary ground that the Earth offers to the community of humans. Here one touches

40 Benton and Straumann, 'Acquiring Empire by Law'.
41 Benton and Straumann, 'Acquiring Empire by Law', 25 citing Vitoria's pupil, de Soto.

on what Derrida has called the 'mystical' foundation of legal authority, which refers to the reason for following law precisely in virtue of its being law, and neither out of some insight into its 'natural morality' nor from the threat of coercion by an established sovereign power in case of non-compliance.[42] The question of the 'mystical' authority or force of *ius gentium* is not often posed by commentators of Vitoria, who simply assume the existence of some global authority with the legitimacy to exercise coercive force. But the problem of the condition of possibility of a global authority must be tied to a consideration of the space, of the globality, that became manifest with the Discovery and Conquest of the New World. The question is: what account of space could justify a 'world community' that makes 'authoritative' law for the whole globe? what conception of space leads to such a 'global' account of justice?

There is one more question left to discuss at this point, namely, the nature of the 'wrong' against *ius gentium* that would justify the use of force by the 'international community'. In order to argue that for Vitoria all 'crimes' against *ius gentium* must be resolved in the same way that crimes are dealt with within a bounded territorial entity like a sovereign state, namely, through some juridical and police action, Brown Scott and Pagden rely on Vitoria's analogy between the 'whole world' or 'globe' and a 'republic' understood in Aristotelian terms, namely, one in which justice is always 'political' (*dikaion politikon*) because it occurs *within the walls of the polis and between its citizens*.[43] Thus, Pagden argues that for Vitoria *any* 'autarchic' republic or principality, not just a Christian one, can in principle act 'as the agents, and by the authority, of a supposed international community, the universal res publica'.[44] The 'just cause' for such a state-based military intervention on behalf of the world legal community is always one and the same: to prevent by force

42 Jacques Derrida, 'Force of Law. The "Mystical Foundation of Authority"', in Gil Anidjar (ed.), *Acts of Religion*, (New York: Routledge, 2001), 230–298.

43 The analogy is obviously problematic, because it assumes that 'the whole world' is somehow contained within the 'walls' of a *polis* with one and the same law applying within this jurisdiction, when in reality the 'space expansion' of western imperialism swept aside such walls. On the problem, see Wendy Brown, *Walled States, Waning Sovereignty* (New York: Zone Books, 2010). For the argument that the processes of globalization have extended law beyond the 'walls' of sovereign, territorial states but in so doing have given rise to 'fragmented' forms of constitutionalising international law, see Guenther Teubner, *Constitutional Fragments: Societal Constitutionalism and Globalization* (New-York: Oxford University Press, 2012).

44 Pagden, 'Legislating for the "Whole World That Is, in a Sense, a Commonwealth"', 139.

the 'wicked from doing harm' to the good.[45] For Pagden, Vitoria's ultimate justification of the Spanish right to intervene militarily in the social and political lives of Indigenous peoples was not to convert them forcefully to the belief that the Christ is the true Saviour, nor to accrue more land, booty and glory for the Spanish prince, but ultimately only because 'it was the harm which the rulers of the "barbarians" were prepared to inflict upon their own subjects [nominally by forcing them to engage in human sacrifices and to practice cannibalism/MV] that constituted a breach not only of the natural law but also of the *ius gentium*. And that would seem to provide grounds for the agents of the "world commonwealth" to intervene on their behalf. We have here in embryonic form a version of the modern concept of "Responsibility to Protect"'.[46] Pagden here expresses the liberal conception of the *nomos* of the Earth according to which the 'whole world,' viz., the globalized conception of the Earth, opens up a space for military (but also humanitarian) 'intervention' into the so-called 'internal' affairs of sovereign peoples. By contrast, the force behind Barcia Trelles's and Schmitt's objections to Brown Scott to be discussed in what follows, argues that the *spatial grounding* of law that is presupposed by any discourse on the 'international community' *necessarily excludes interference* from third powers (rather than calling for it), which is exactly the connection that Barcia Trelles saw between Vitoria and the Monroe Doctrine, and later Schmitt applied to his idea of a Germanic *Grossraum*.[47]

4 Barcia Trelles and the Iberian Origins of the *Grossraum* Doctrine

Contrary to Brown Scott, Barcia Trelles and Schmitt argue that Vitoria's *ius gentium* delineates a 'planetary' *nomos* that divides the Earth along 'spheres of influence,' a 'pluriverse' of normative orders, or *Grossräume*, that *excludes*

45 See also *On Civil Power* 1.4: 'every man has the power and right of self-defence by natural law, since nothing can be more natural than to repel force with force'. Vitoria, *Vitoria's Political Writings*, 11.

46 Pagden, 'Legislating for the "Whole World That Is, in a Sense, a Commonwealth"', 140. He refers to *On the American Indians* 3.5: 'in lawful defence of the innocent from unjust death, even without the pope's authority, the Spaniards may prohibit the barbarians from practising any nefarious custom or rite'. Vitoria, *Vitoria's Political Writings*, 288. On the critique of humanitarianism, see Didier Fassin, *Humanitarian Reason. A Moral History of the Present* (Berkeley, CA: University of California Press, 2012).

47 Schmitt was not alone here, see Kojève's sketch for a French-centered 'Latin Empire'. On these ideas, Nicholas Heron, 'One world: history and space in Schmitt's post-war political theology,' in Mitchell Dean, Lotte List, and Stefan Schwarzkopf (eds.), *Political Theology Today. 100 Years After Carl Schmitt* (London: Bloomsbury, 2022).

the possibility of one common global authority with jurisdiction over the whole Earth, and thus with legitimacy to engage in military interventions and occupations. Schmitt worked out his conception of the *Grossraum* influenced in part by Barcia Trelles's reading of the Monroe Doctrine in *Doctrina de Monroe y cooperación internacional* (1931), whose remote origins the Spanish jurist traces back to Vitoria.[48] Beneyto has argued that Barcia Trelles occupies an intermediary position between Brown Scott and Schmitt. Siding with the former, Barcia Trelles accepts that Vitoria's *ius gentium* sets forward a conception of global justice based on the equality of sovereign states, the existence of an international community with authority to enforce moral rules that apply to these states, and the orientation towards prevention of war between them.[49] What distinguishes Barcia Trelles from Brown Scott, are the spatial features of the 'globe' or 'whole world' that underlie Vitoria's idea of *ius gentium*.

Barcia Trelles argues that the Monroe Doctrine of 'America for Americans' offers a privileged window into how the 'globe' or 'whole world' became a jurisdictional authority after 1492. According to the Spanish jurist, the Monroe Doctrine adopted an Iberian ideal of empire based on the division of the 'whole world' into great spaces that *excluded* intervention from other imperial powers.[50] It was only with the American intervention in World War I that the Monroe Doctrine received a new interpretation that allowed the United States, 'thanks to the domination of the sea', to pivot 'into the global reach of a

---

48 On Barcía Trelles, I follow here Beneyto, 'Camilo Barcia Trelles on Francisco de Vitoria'. See also Hohendahl, *Perilous Futures*, 62ff. who argues that both Schmitt and Hitler employed distorted readings of the Monroe Doctrine that justify aggressive wars of occupation to fashion their conceptions of *Grossraum* and *Lebensraum*, respectively.

49 Beneyto, 'Camilo Barcia Trelles on Francisco De Vitoria', 1487.

50 The literature on the early Modern attempts to divide up the world is enormous. For the Iberian discourses, see Giuseppe Marcocci, 'Iberian Theories of Empire in the Sixteenth and Seventeenth Centuries,' *Journal of the History of Ideas* 83 (4) (2022), 671–683. For some paradoxes of global striated space, and in particular the Treaty of Tordesillas in relation to Indigenous *nomoi*, see David Turnbull, 'Locating, negotiating, and crossing boundaries: a Western Desert land claim, the Tordesillas line, and the West Australian border', *Environment and Planning D: Society and Space* 23 (2005), 757–770. On the political theology of the Spanish Empire, see now José Luis Villacañas Berlanga, *Hispania: de formación imperial a sistema de poderes* (Madrid: Guillermo Escolar editor, 2020). On land and sea empires, with recognition of Schmitt's contribution, see David Armitage, 'The elephant and the whale: Empires of land and sea,' *Journal for Maritime Research* 9 (1) (2007), 23–36.

world police order' along the liberal internationalist lines conceived by Brown Scott.[51]

Barcia Trelles draws the genealogy of the Monroe Doctrine back to the imperial decree of 1519 through which Charles V united 'the American Indian territories to the Spanish Crown and established their perpetual inalienability'.[52] On this view, the Spanish imperial decision to extend and bridge in a permanent fashion the Spanish Empire to the New World subtended the belief in the 'inviolability of the inter-American borders but also the permanent neutrality of the Americas,' eventually giving rise to the universal principle of national 'self-determination' that would become essential to twentieth-century international law and was advocated by Stalin as much as by Woodrow Wilson. This reading of Spanish imperialism was directly opposed to Brown Scott's claim that the principle of self-determination originated with Vitoria's (supposed) rejection of 'the "Spanish Monarchy" as a God-ordained, papally sanctioned state which would continue in its present course until the end of time. No part of it could legally at any time be detached from the whole'.[53]

Barcia Trelles's understanding of Vitoria could not be more different. By justifying the Conquest on new grounds, 'based on the equality of human beings and nations and on Christian solidarity', Vitoria's contribution was precisely to cement the Spanish Crown and American Indian territories and peoples into 'the *same community* as mainland Spaniards'.[54] On this reading, Vitoria did not seek to legitimize the expropriation of Indigenous lands and their forcible incorporation into the Spanish empire. He sought to establish the conditions for the establishment of a trans-Atlantic 'inter-national community' between American Indians and Europeans under the hegemony of the Spanish Crown. This would have been a Latin-based international community rather than the Anglo-American one envisaged by Brown Scott. Barcia Trelles thought that Vitoria's *ius gentium* articulated the potential 'hospitality' of the Spanish empire to the once-and-future republics of 'Latin' America.[55] The key claim is that the openness to and affirmation of 'Indigenous' claims to sover-

51 Beneyto, 'Camilo Barcia Trelles on Francisco De Vitoria', 1490. For a discussion of Vitoria, Schmitt and 'American supremacy' that situates all of them within a 'civilizational' discourse of supremacy that adopts Pagden's view on Vitoria, see William Rasch, 'Human Rights as Geopolitics: Carl Schmitt and the Legal Form of American Supremacy', *Cultural Critique* 54 (2003), 120–147.

52 Cited in Beneyto, 'Camilo Barcia Trelles on Francisco De Vitoria', 1490.

53 Pagden, 'Legislating for the "Whole World That Is, in a Sense, a Commonwealth"', 148.

54 Cited in Beneyto, 'Camilo Barcia Trelles on Francisco De Vitoria', 1490.

55 For a recent, polemical counter-history of this topos, see Miguel Saralegui, *Matar a la madre patria: Historia de una pasión latinoamericana* (Madrid: Tecnos, 2021).

eignty on the part of Vitoria, and notionally of the Spanish Crown, had its spiritual basis 'on the equality of human beings and nations and on Christian solidarity'.

Barcia Trelles's reading of the Spanish Empire as the origin of a new international community had a clear polemical intent. It was meant to distinguish the Spanish Catholic Empire from the Protestant Empires that based their conceptions of international law on the 'freedom' of the high-seas and that eventually led to the nineteenth- and twentieth-century imperialist policies of 'open door' policy in Asia and to the 'scramble for Africa' of the European 'civilizing mission'. Schmitt would extend this claim to the axiom that 'two distinct spatial conceptions of land and sea must correspond to two entirely distinct international legal orders, an international law of the sea and a wholly different international law of the land'.[56] In that sense, Barcia Trelles was intent on turning the 'Black Legend' against the Protestant colonial and imperial powers that had previously exploited it.[57] In Barcia Trelles's opinion, pace Brown Scott, the Anglo-American pursuit of imperialism ignored Vitoria's 'rejection of traditional titles for acquisition of colonial territories' preferring to gain their colonies through the 'power-driven principle of offensive occupation,' something which applied equally to the US 'conquest' of the 'Far West' and accounted for its subsequent history of armed interventions into the political affairs of its Central and Latin American neighbours (not to mention South East Asia and the Middle East).

---

56 Schmitt, *Staat, Grossraum, Nomos*, 407. Translations from the German are mine. 'Naturally, what was decisive is that to the freedom of the seas belongs the freedom to pursue war. As a result the strongest sea power seized the oceans.... Maritime warfare was a commercial war [*Handelskrieg*]. Whoever traded with the competition became an enemy [*In ihm war jeder Feind, der mit dem Gegner Handel trieb*]'. Schmitt, *Staat, Grossraum, Nomos*, 519. The view that the Protestant imperial imagination is a simple function of the 'rationalization of space' is questioned by Benton in her study of European sovereignty and imperial geography. See Lauren Benton, *A Search for Sovereignty: Law and Geography in European Empires, 1400–1900* (Cambridge: Cambridge University Press, 2009). For a more direct attempt at calling into question Schmitt's land/sea axiom, with inconclusive results, see now Lauren Benton and Nathan Perl-Rosenthal (eds.), *A World at Sea: Maritime Practices and Global History* (Philadelphia: University of Pennsylvania Press, 2020).

57 The literature on the 'Black Legend' is enormous. For a good critical overview of the field, see Margaret R. Greer, Walter D. Mignolo, and Maureen Quilligan (eds.), *Rereading the Black Legend: The Discourses of Religious and Racial Difference in the Renaissance Empires* (Chicago: University of Chicago Press, 2007). The debate on the 'Black Legend' continues to rage in Spain, see Elvira Roca Barea, *Imperiofobia y leyenda negra* (Madrid: Siruela, 2016) and José Luis Villacañas Berlanga, *Imperiofilia y el populismo nacional-católico: Otra historia del imperio español* (Madrid: Lengua de Trapo, 2019).

5 Schmitt's Reading of Vitoria: A Public Law Interpretation of *Nomos*

For Schmitt, the history of modern international law begins with the 'conquest of a new world'.[58] This world-historical occurrence poses a new *quid juris*: on what normative basis can one derive 'the justification of the European occupation of those lands'.[59] Schmitt attacks Brown Scott's claim that Vitoria's *ius gentium* established a global, religiously-neutral international law on the basis of the shared 'humanity' of all peoples in the world, and that this international community has the right to impose this law by force over any state that transgresses its prescriptions. Schmitt does not believe in a conception of humanity that lies beyond religious and political differences, and he contests the force of law of the international community since he believes that one particular state could take it upon itself to represent 'all humanity' and by extension whoever this state declares to be 'enemy' would become, eo ipso, the 'enemy of humanity'. From this follows the de-humanization of the enemy as a condition for the perseverance of 'total' warfare without any rules.[60]

Schmitt believes Vitoria's humanism was of a Christian sort, not an Enlightenment one. Both are 'discriminatory,' but in different ways.[61] If an individual or a nation behaves in ways antithetical to the Christian religion, then they should not be treated as Christians, but they remain human beings. Schmitt argues this is not the case with the Enlightenment's 'humanitarian ideology': if a person or nation fails to live up to the Enlightenment picture of 'civilization,' they are not only considered 'barbarian' or 'uncivilized' but also descend to the status of 'not-human' or 'less-than-human'.[62] According to Schmitt, sixteenth-

58 Schmitt, 'La justificación de la ocupación de un nuevo mundo (Francisco de Vitoria)', 13. All translations of the Spanish edition of Schmitt's essay on Vitoria are mine.

59 Schmitt, 'La justificación de la ocupación de un nuevo mundo (Francisco de Vitoria)', 13.

60 This worry came to light post-9/11 and with the Iraq war even in authors, like Derrida or Habermas, who do not share Schmitt's critique of humanism, see Jürgen Habermas, *The Divided West* (Cambridge: Polity Press, 2006). Features of this Schmittian argument seem to have been taken up lately in Samuel Moyn, *Humane: How the United States Abandoned Peace and Reinvented War* (New York: Farrar, Straus & Giroux, 2021), which describes the shift from the criminalization of war to its 'humanization' in carrying out a 'permanent' war.

61 See Habermas's discussion of Schmitt's dictum that 'whoever speaks of "humanity" is a liar' in Jürgen Habermas, *The Inclusion of the Other* (Cambridge: MIT Press, 2001), 188 and Diego Rossello, '"To be human, nonetheless, remains a decision": Humanism as decisionism in contemporary critical political theory,' *Contemporary Political Theory* 16 (4) (2016), 439–458.

62 Sylvia Wynters has mapped a similar distinction in her genealogy of Western humanism, where the Enlightenment picture of Man (characterized by racialization), globalized through capitalism and imperialism, literally erases the plurality of humanity. See Sylvia

century Spaniards were prevented from using humanity in a modern discriminatory fashion when they came into contact with the Indigenous peoples of the New World by 'their Marian piety and devotion to the Virgin, Mother of God'.[63] I shall return to this curious claim in my conclusion.

Unlike the liberal reading of Vitoria, Schmitt argues that the Christian, viz. 'religious' idea of just war still lies at the heart of Vitoria's conception of international law. Schmitt does not deny that Vitoria mobilizes what look like religiously-neutral arguments when he rejects the title of discovery as a legitimate ground of conquest. But his point is that Vitoria mobilizes these religiously-neutral and culturally-relativist claims only because they serve him to legitimate the Conquest 'exclusively through general concepts and with the aid of hypothetical arguments that make a dialectical use of just war'.[64] Vitoria needs to posit the symmetry between the humanity and the rights of Indians and Spaniards in order for the *hypothetical* nature of the argument in favour of just war to work: '*If* the barbarians oppose themselves to hospitality and to the freedom of missionary activity, to the *liberum commercium* and to the free propaganda, then they violate the rights of the Spanish according to *ius gentium*, and *if* the peaceful warnings offered by the Spaniards turn out to have no effect, then the Spaniards have a motive for a just war'.[65] The 'liberal' aspects of Vitoria's discourse are part and parcel of his dialectical use of the concept of just war to legitimate the Conquest. In turn, the conception of a 'just war' that Vitoria mobilizes only makes sense within 'the spatial ordering of the medieval *respublica christiana*, with its distinction between countries inhabited by Christians and countries inhabited by pagans and infidels,' that is, from within the *nomos* of the *respublica christiana*.[66]

For Schmitt, the arguments of the Spanish theologian need to be understood within the historical context marked by the Papal 'donation' of the newly discovered lands to the Crown of Castile, with the duty to preach the Gospel to the Indigenous nations in view of their conversion.[67] 'In fact, the missionary function enjoined by the Pope was the juridical basis of the con-

---

Wynter, *On Being Human as Praxis*, Katherine McKittrick (ed.), (Durham, NC: Duke University Press, 2015) and the essays in Anthony Bogues (ed.), *Caribbean Reasonings: After Man, Towards the Human: Critical Essays on Sylvia Wynter* (Kingston: Ian Randle Publishers, 2005).

63 Schmitt, 'La justificación de la ocupación de un nuevo mundo (Francisco de Vitoria)', 16.

64 Schmitt, 'La justificación de la ocupación de un nuevo mundo (Francisco de Vitoria)', 23.

65 Schmitt, 'La justificación de la ocupación de un nuevo mundo (Francisco de Vitoria)', 23.

66 Schmitt, 'La justificación de la ocupación de un nuevo mundo (Francisco de Vitoria)', 21.

67 For the debate, see Marco Geuna, 'Francisco de Vitoria e la questione della guerra justa,' 150ff. and Marcocci, 'Iberian Theories of Empire in the Sixteenth and Seventeenth Centuries'.

quest'.[68] Vitoria reflects the Christian medieval *nomos* which distinguishes between wars engaged by Christian princes and republics, and wars between Christians and non-Christians. While the Pope could not assign to a Christian king the spiritual mission to conquer another Christian king, 'for those lands whose prince or people were not Christian, the Pope could grant mandates for mission or crusade, and these gave grounds for the justice of the war, and thus for a legitimate territorial appropriation'.[69] In short, the conquest is legitimate because the war to carry it out is legitimate, and this legitimacy has a politico-theological reason, namely, the modalities of mission or crusade through which the Christian 'empire' relates to non-Christian peoples and lands.

Schmitt points out that Vitoria's Catholic Order, the Dominican Order, was precisely the Order charged with 'realizing and supervising the missionary enterprise'.[70] The Dominicans were 'branches of the Papacy and of the Church as the juridical-institutional authority of the *respublica Christiana*'.[71] Schmitt thereby rejects a 'spiritual' authority that would lie in a supposed 'world community,' and that bequeaths any prince, Christian or not Christian, the mission to 'protect the innocents,' as Pagden argued. For Schmitt, the sole 'spiritual' authority of the 'world' community at the time of Vitoria was the Catholic Church: the 'totius orbis' to which Vitoria refers in his texts refers to the same 'orb' over which the Pope has always presided in virtue of being the vicar of Christ. From here the importance that Schmitt gives to the claim that the Spanish 'discovery' of other parts of the same 'orb' was 'the last, great heroic act of the European peoples [that] was not accomplished by the heroes of the Conquista as a mission of the *jus commercii*, but in the name of their redeemed Christ and his holy mother Mary'.[72] Schmitt denies that the 'discovery' of a

68 Schmitt, 'La justificación de la ocupación de un nuevo mundo (Francisco de Vitoria)', 26.

69 Schmitt, 'La justificación de la ocupación de un nuevo mundo (Francisco de Vitoria)', 27.

70 Schmitt, 'La justificación de la ocupación de un nuevo mundo (Francisco de Vitoria)', 27.

71 Dussel has argued that it was not only the Dominicans that arrived to the New World, but also the 'spiritual' sect or wing of the Franciscan Order, heavily persecuted by the Papacy a few centuries before due to their preaching that 'highest poverty' was the most Christian virtue. See Giorgio Agamben, *The Highest Poverty. Monastic Rules and Form-of-Life* (Stanford: Stanford University Press, 2013). According to Dussel, these radical Franciscans saw the possibility of establishing indigenous self-governed 'republics' that would realize the utopian potential found in Saint Francis's Rules and thereby found a true messianic Christian community. The experiment was cut short in 1564 by Philip II. See the discussion in Dussel, *El primer debate filósofico de la modernidad*, 51–56. It is not inconceivable that Dussel's own 'liberation theology' found in these Franciscan and Indigenous communities its remote inspiration.

72 Schmitt, *Nomos of the Earth*, V,2.

New World poses a new limit to the spiritual authority of the Church (which would be a reason to relativize its validity claims).

Only the concrete, at once spiritual, spatial and legal order of the *respublica Christiana* offers the real context from which to understand Vitoria's discourse.[73] According to Schmitt this context sets clear 'limits' to the reach of Vitoria's 'objectivity and neutrality'. The mission to convert the newly discovered and conquered nations to Christianity is the rock against which Vitoria's neutral arguments of equal rights between Indians and Spaniards crash. For in the absence of a distinction between Christian and pagan, understood as a political distinction between friend and enemy, there would be no sense to the Christian mission. Thus, when Vitoria argues that the hypothetical non-recognition on the part of Indigenous nations of *liberum commercium* or *ius communicationis* is a legitimate ground to declare a just war against them, Schmitt argues that these terms do not mean the same as 'the liberal principle of global free exchange and of the free economy in the sense of the "open door" policy of the 20th century.... The freedom of mission, on the contrary, is a *libertas* of the Christian Church, and within the thought and language of the Middle Ages, *libertas* was a synonym for "right"'.[74]

The decisive point is that Schmitt understands the rights of Vitoria's *ius gentium* as functional to the 'public law' mission of the Church which is the spread of Jesus's Gospel 'urbi et orbi'. Indeed, the *ius gentium* grants those 'freedoms' that are required to carry out over the entire globe the moral duties of the Gospel, quite unlike 'modern' rights that offer immunities to individuals from having to carry out a determinate conception of the 'highest good'.[75] Schmitt argues that it is only with Gentili and Grotius that a 'modern' *ius*

---

73 It is symptomatic that Schmitt's recent inclusion into the canon of critical international law occurs thanks to considerations of 'meaning in context' methodology of the Cambridge School. See the essays in Annabel Brett, Megan Donaldson, and Martti Koskenniemi (eds.), *History, Politics, Law: Thinking Through the International* (New York: Cambridge University Press, 2021).

74 Schmitt, 'La justificación de la ocupación de un nuevo mundo (Francisco de Vitoria)', 30.

75 This reading of *libertas* as functional to a Papal 'absolutist' interpretation of the concrete order of the Roman Catholic Church ultimately derives from the claim of *libertas* for the spiritual authority of Church from the power of the Emperor that characterizes the twelfth-century Papal Revolution. See Eugen Rosenstock-Huessy, *Out of Revolution. Autobiography of Western Man* (Norwich, VT: Argo Books, 1969) and Harold Berman, *Law and Revolution. The Formation of the Western Legal Tradition* (Cambridge: Harvard University Press, 1983). Brunkhorst has argued that the Papal Revolution already contained the germs of all future global 'legal revolutions,' including the twentieth century revolutions that would open the way to a true 'world society' with its own 'global constitution' Hauke Brunkhorst, *Critical Theory of Legal Revolutions: Evolutionary Perspectives* (London: Bloomsbury, 2014).

gentium emerges, impulsed by 'jurists of state powers that are confessionally neutral' (by which Schmitt means, those states that follow the principle *cujus regio, eius religio*).[76] Grotius will eliminate the spatial-normative distinction between Christian and non-Christian, and therefore make use of Vitoria's 'neutralizing' arguments for the sake of a different, modern idea of 'freedom'. However, for Schmitt the shift from a medieval to a modern conception of 'freedom' itself presupposes a different spatialization of the *nomos* of the Earth, one that corresponds to the fact that a confessionally 'neutral' conception of the state was coupled with a shift from terrestrial to maritime conceptions of power and law.

The epochal struggle between England, as the emerging sea-power, and Spain, as the premier European land-power, accounts for how a concept of freedom, the Christian *libertas* to preach the Gospel to all and everywhere in the world, which is 'internal' to the concrete order of the 'universal' Church, was turned around by Grotius, Pufendorf and other modern natural law thinkers into an 'external' idea of liberty from interference. This 'negative' conception of freedom was successfully deployed in the conflict against the Spanish terrestrial empire that would lead to the Anglo-American form of imperialism based on the 'freedom of the seas,' and ultimately to the liberal internationalist appropriation of Vitoria in order to justify the criminalization of wars of aggression ('le crime d'attaque').[77] Unlike its liberal internationalist version, 'the medieval theory of just war admits the possibility of a just war of aggression' on the basis of the legitimate finality of 'preaching Christianity in freedom and executing the mission conferred by the Pope'.[78] For this reason, Schmitt would find absurd Pagden's argument that Vitoria could seriously entertain the possibility of the Pope conferring the mission of intervention to a Muslim sultan.[79]

---

76 Schmitt, 'La justificación de la ocupación de un nuevo mundo (Francisco de Vitoria)', 32. On Gentili see Valentina Vadi, *War and Peace. Alberico Gentili and the Early Modern Law of Nations* (Leiden: Brill, 2020). For pre-Enlightenment confessional neutrality as principle of constitutionalism, see Ian Hunter, *Rival Enlightenments. Civil and Metaphysical Philosophy in the Early Modern Germany* (Cambridge: Cambridge University Press, 2001).

77 Schmitt, 'La justificación de la ocupación de un nuevo mundo (Francisco de Vitoria)', 36.

78 Schmitt, 'La justificación de la ocupación de un nuevo mundo (Francisco de Vitoria)', 38.

79 It is interesting to consider the relation between the contemporary, post-liberal 'global' use of 'freedom of religion' for purposes of intervention and regime change and the medieval Christian sense of 'freedom of religion'. On these issues see Winnifred Fallers Sullivan, Elizabeth Shakman Hurd, Saba Mahmood and Peter Danchin (eds.), *Politics of Religious Freedom* (Chicago, IL: University of Chicago Press, 2015) and Elizabeth Shakman Hurd, *Beyond Religious Freedom. The New Global Politics of Religion* (Princeton, NJ: Princeton University Press, 2017).

For the Christian *nomos*, what made for the 'justice' of going to war in a crusade or mission was not whether the war was aggressive or defensive; what mattered was their 'spiritual' or 'religious' authorization for the sake of *augmenting* the *nomos* itself, that is, for spreading Christianity over the 'whole world' and in so doing acquiring more citizens for the *respublica Christiana*. On this view, the 'pagan' is the present 'enemy' but also the future 'friend': there is no 'perpetual enmity' with Indigenous nations.[80] It is only because Jews and Muslims, in principle, excluded their conversion to Christianity and its *nomos* that they were considered to be 'eo ipso perpetual enemies, *hostes perpetui* [of the *respublica christiana*]. All this presupposes the juridical-international authority of a spiritual power, *potestas spiritualis*'.[81] Only a supra-national, and at the same time 'spiritual' authority like that of the Christian Church, could determine the justice of war, and it did so on the basis of the justice of its 'cause,' that is, the salvation of humankind announced by Jesus as the Christ. It is only because of the Christian belief that no human being on the surface of the Earth deserves to be 'lost,' viz., only because Christianity believes that humankind, 'all together' and 'everyone individually' (*omnes et singulatim*), can be saved, that its imperial wars carried out for the sake of conversion qualify as 'just' wars. For Schmitt, Christianity is simply the religion of globalization.[82] By criminalizing wars of aggression, and transforming international war into global police operations, liberal internationalism sought to rule out the Christian idea of just war, believing that they had found an ally in Vitoria. Ironically, Schmitt concludes, in so doing liberal internationalism returned to 'a quasi-theological concept of the enemy; but precisely this shows how opposed [liberal internationalism/MV] is to Vitoria's attitude of non-discriminating reciprocity (brought to an extreme) which is as clear in Vitoria as its Christian roots'.[83]

80 Compare here with Jared Hickman, *Black Prometheus: Race and Radicalism in the Age of Atlantic Slavery* (New York: Oxford University Press, 2016).

81 Schmitt, 'La justificación de la ocupación de un nuevo mundo (Francisco de Vitoria)', 39.

82 This point was picked up and expanded on by Jacques Derrida, 'Faith and Knowledge. The Two Sources of "Religion" at the Limits of Reason Alone', in Jacques Derrida and Gianni Vattimo (eds.), *Religion* (Cambridge: Polity Press, 1998) and Jean-Luc Nancy, *La création du monde ou la mondialisation* (Paris: Galilée, 2002). For the Christian pastoral structure of modern liberal governmentality, see Michel Foucault, *Security, Territory, Population: Lectures at the Collège de France 1977–1978* (New York: Picador, 2009).

83 Schmitt, 'La justificación de la ocupación de un nuevo mundo (Francisco de Vitoria)', 44. For a different articulation of the Christian idea of 'theological' and 'political' enmity, and one which is focused more on the problem of 'infidels' rather than 'pagans,' see Anidjar, *The Jew, the Arab. A History of the Enemy*.

6 Koskenniemi and the Private Law Reading of *Nomos*

For Koskenniemi international law has its roots in the Protestant appropriation, via Grotius, of the Spanish Catholic school of law headed by Vitoria. What appealed to Grotius in Vitoria, so Koskenniemi, is the latter's rejection of the public law justification of the Spanish Conquista and its substitution for a Roman private law justification of empire which takes the form of an 'informal imperial domination that is achieved through a worldwide pattern of acquisition and exchange of private property'.[84] In short, Vitoria's discourse serves as basis to project a global empire of *private* law underpinning capitalist expansion.[85]

The originality of Koskenniemi's thesis, as I interpret it, is that it ascribes to Vitoria the belief that all nations are 'free and equal' because each is characterized by their own *nomos*, and I employ this term now in Robert Cover's celebrated sense, of a narrative of law.[86] This *nomos* is not a law made by sovereigns; it is not 'civil' law. Rather, it should be understood as that (ancestral) legal narrative that accounts for how and why each nation has received its parcel of the Earth that (by natural law) was originally granted in common to humankind. This nomo-centric assumption is then employed by Vitoria as basis to 'deprovincialize' Roman law by offering an interpretation of categories of Roman natural and private law – *dominium, ius gentium*, and *bellum iustum* – in terms of 'subjective right'.[87] The recognition and enactment of this system of individual rights becomes the basis of *ius gentium* as a 'nomos of the Earth' that sets limits to whatever states or empires would otherwise

84 Martti Koskenniemi, 'Empire and International Law. The Real Spanish Contribution.' *University of Toronto Law Journal* 61 (2011), 1–36, 32.

85 For another reading of Vitoria as fitting together with the origins of global capitalism, see Manuel Jiménez Fonseca, 'Jus gentium and the Transformation of Latin American Nature: One More Reading of Vitoria?,' in Martti Koskenniemi, Walter Rech, and Manuel Jiménez Fonseca (eds.) *International Law and Empire: Historical Explorations* (New York: Oxford University Press, 2018), 123–148.

86 Robert Cover, 'Nomos and Narrative,' *Harvard Law Review* 87 (4) (1983–1984), 4–68. It is also possible to add here Deleuze and Guattari's 'nomadic' reading of the ancestral *nomos* according to which nations are distributed over and 'belong' to their planetary locations, rather than land being parcelled out to nations, following an 'agricultural' model of settlement. See John Sellars, 'Deleuze and cosmopolitanism,' *Radical Philosophy* 142 (2007), 30–37. The nomadic vs. agricultural distinction with regard to the original meanings of *nomos* has a long and contested history which I cannot engage in this chapter.

87 For the origins of subjective rights out of medieval interpretations of Roman law, see in general Michel Villey, *La formation de la pensée juridique moderne* (Paris: PUF, 2003) and Brian Tierney, *The Idea of Natural Rights* (Grand Rapids, MI: William B. Eerdmans Publishing Company, 1997).

wish to do to other nations, for instance, wage war on them for purposes of increasing the glory or prestige of their leaders, or force them to convert to the religion of their priests. In this sense, Koskenniemi interprets Vitoria's *ius gentium* as prohibiting the kind of *Grossraum* construction that was advocated, in different ways, by both Barcia Trelles and Schmitt.

Vitoria acknowledged that the 'American Indians' were the lawful owners of their lands and that they lived under legitimate rulers. The starting point of the reasoning is that, by natural law, no human being has a natural title of dominion over another (*non cognoscit jus naturale differentiam inter homines*): everyone who is born on the surface of the Earth is born free and property is common to all in the natural state of humankind.[88] The common possession of the Earth in the 'natural' state of humankind was acknowledged by all parties to the Poverty Controversy initiated by the Franciscan Order a few centuries before Vitoria wrote. It is a well-documented fact acknowledged by most interpreters of Vitoria that in his reformulation of the problem of *dominium* Vitoria drew from these debates.[89] The open question is which of the radically contrasting theoretical standpoints in the Poverty Controversy played a role in Vitoria's reformulation of the *ius gentium*.

While some participants in the controversy tended towards the Augustinian position that private property and state power, though necessary after the 'Fall' of humankind, were still 'sinful,' others like Ockham and Marsilius of Padua, argued that both private and public forms of *dominium* were externalizations of human free will that God granted to all human beings. Like Ockham and Marsilius, Vitoria also found it unacceptable that public power and private property were merely a function of the law of the strongest, and so deemed to be 'evil'. His reasoning seems to have been above all of a juridical kind: for law to command obligation it cannot simply be the same as the law of the strongest. Had he not believed in this, he would have had no arguments against the violence and usurpation of the Conquistadores.

Vitoria's creative interpretation of Roman law categories from the viewpoint of the Poverty Controversy allowed him to discern that the 'discovery' and 'conquest' of the New World brought into evidence that the 'Other' to the

88 See *On Civil Power* 1.4: 'in the absence of any divine law or human elective franchise there is no convincing reason why one man should have power over another'. Vitoria, *Vitoria's Political Writings*, 11.

89 The Poverty Controversy is a much-discussed theme in the history of Western jurisprudence. See Roberto Lambertini, *La povertà pensata. Da Bonaventura a Ockham* (Modena: Mucchi editore, 2000). For a general overview in the English-speaking literature, see Janet Coleman, 'Property and Poverty,' in J.H. Burns (ed.), *The Cambridge History of Medieval Political Thought c.350–c.1450* (New York: Cambridge University Press, 1988), 607–648.

Christian European was *a subject of equal right*, a subject of a *nomos*. Vitoria's answer to the problem of how to justify the division into mine and thine, and also the division into legitimate rulers and legitimate subjects, if the Earth was given in common to all by natural law, was to say that it had been resolved by human beings through their 'ancestral' *nomoi*: at *all times* and in *all places*, human beings had distributed themselves over and parcelled the Earth between them according to a system that was also just.[90] That some things may have remained undivided, that is, *res nullius*, is a consequence of a just division, of a *nomos*, and not its presupposition.[91] More crucially, an essential aspect of these ancestral *nomoi* is their recognition of 'common things,' *res communis*, that cannot be the object of a just division, and thus also of appropriation by anyone, such as the seas and the air and the terrestrial commons, which allow for the movement and exchange between nations. For Vitoria, this very fact of the ancestral *nomos* called for the establishment of a truly 'international' system of law, a *ius gentium*, that could subsume, under some common terms, the *nomoi* of indigenous peoples and the *nomoi* of European states.[92]

The crucial term that allows for this subsumption is *dominium*, now understood as a lawful human power of each individual to appropriate what it needs as a result of a primordial distribution. Natural law does not only consist of 'prohibitive' norms but also of 'permissive' ones: it *does not prohibit* the division of common property and the freedom of individuals to appropriate this or that to satisfy their needs. In addition, for Vitoria, the original or ancestral

90 The need to start here is due to what Luhmann identifies as the need for any legal system to show that its 'right' is not 'wrong', namely, that at the basis of a legal system there is no injustice and domination. Luhmann describes how legal systems addressed the need for '*Entparadoxierung*' (that is, the need to show that determining what is right is not itself done by committing wrong) by adopting solutions coming from the analogous need to explain the origins of exclusive or private property out of 'common ownership' which itself denotes a paradoxical object: a property without property-characteristics [*einem Eigentum ohne Eigentumsmerkmale*]. See Niklas Luhmann, 'Am Anfang war kein Unrecht,' in *Gesellschaftsstruktur und Semantik. Studien zur Wissenssoziologie der modernen Gesellschaft* (Frankfurt: Suhrkamp, 1989), 22.

91 This point seems to have been missed by Benton and Straumann, 'Acquiring Empire by Law', who argue for the foundation of international law as a function of the universalization of arguments about *res nullius* and their adoption into *terra nullius* arguments.

92 I find persuasive Wheatley's argument that the same imperative remains crucial in the *Mabo* judgment and lies at the root of its difficulties. See Natasha Wheatley, 'Legal Pluralism as Temporal Pluralism: Historical Rights, Legal Vitalism and Non-Synchronous Sovereignty,' in Dan Edelstein, Stefanos Geroulanos, and Natasha Wheatley (eds.) *Power and Time. Temporalities in Conflict and the Making of History* (Chicago: University of Chicago Press, 2020), 53–80.

division of the Earth by individuals and nations was done 'by consensus' and became the established normative pattern of acting for subsequent generations. The division did not follow conquest. The partition of the Earth was such that it left everyone satisfied thanks to the pattern of exchanges between individuals. For Vitoria, the content of the ancestral *nomoi*, viz., the appropriation of land, its division into property, and its exchange on fair terms, which is 'permitted' by natural law, takes the form of a *ius gentium*, that is, of a form of justice that is practiced all over the globe ('totius orbis'), and on the basis of which one can infer that the 'the whole world is in a sense a commonwealth'.[93]

Koskenniemi claims this universal idea of justice is tied to *commutative not to distributive justice*. He argues that Vitoria re-interprets *dominium* and *ius gentium* as functions of commutative justice, the justice involved in the exchange of things and services, rather than in the distribution of power and offices. Once *dominium* is a function of commutative justice, Vitoria can then argue that because all human beings have a power of ownership over their actions and things, then the exchange of things and services between people ought to be the basis of their public law relationship. That means, on this reading, that global justice is first of all to be achieved on a free-market basis, and market-based justice is the only one that can be truly globalized. Koskenniemi's interpretation of Vitoria, thus, turns him into the first thinker of '*nomos* of the Earth' as a function of what Hayek will call *catallaxy*, a normative order in which the unrestricted but rule-bound system of exchanges leads to the overcoming of the distinction between friends and enemies in public law.[94] Vitoria's gambit, on this reading, was that the only way to stop the horrifying violence and pillage that the Spanish conquerors were carrying out in the New World was to integrate both conquerors and conquered into a system of free economic exchange (rather than into a *Grossraum* on the model of the Monroe Doctrine as argued by Barcia Trelles and Schmitt). For Koskenniemi, the Salamanca school was the first to set up the juridical basis of capitalist economic transactions and activities; Vitoria and his pupils were the first 'globalists'.[95]

93 For one such hypothesis of primordial anarchism, see David Graeber and David Wengrow, *The Dawn of Everything. A New History of Humanity* (New York: Farrar, Straus and Giroux, 2021).

94 On *nomos* in Hayek see Miguel Vatter, 'Neoliberalism and Republicanism: Economic Rule of Law and Law as Concrete Order (*nomos*),' in Melinda Cooper, Damien Cahill, Martijn Konings and David Primrose (eds.), *The SAGE Handbook of Neoliberalism* (London: Sage, 2018), 370–383 and Jessica Whyte, *The Morals of the Market. Human Rights and the Rise of Neoliberalism* (London: Verso, 2019).

95 Quinn Slobodian, *Globalists: The End of Empire and the Birth of Neoliberalism* (Cambridge, MA: Harvard University Press, 2018).

7 Conclusion: The Persistence of the *Grossraum* in International Law

Today, the *nomos* of globalization stands in crisis, unable to provide solutions to the catastrophe of anthropogenic climate change and its roots in fossil capitalism.[96] Latour has been at the forefront in calling for a new *nomos* of the Earth in the key of Gaia. His proposal adapts Schmitt's understanding of the internal relation between international law and just war by positing that a new planetary enmity is taking place 'between the *nomos* of the Earth conceived as Globe and the *nomos* of the Earth conceived as Gaia – that is, as the anti-Globe'.[97] But Latour calls for a reversal of Schmitt's axiom of land-appropriation, *Landnahme*, so that it 'could begin to mean 'appropriation by the land' – that is, by the Earth. Whereas Humans are defined as those who take the Earth, the Earthbound are taken by it. In both cases, the Earth is still the Mother of their law, but it is not the same mother, it is not the same law, and thus these are not the same humans'.[98] At stake for Latour is inverting the Christian 'spiritual conquest' of Earth, based on the Marian faith, in order to substitute for it a new faith of the Earthbound, which is likewise related to sacred figures of Motherhood, in this case of Pachamama.

However, it may be that international law has already begun to reformulate a new planetary *nomos*, where the oceans, rather than the land, become the new Mother of Law.[99] The entrance of a new 'oceanic' perspective on international law is frequently dated to Arvid Pardo's legendary speech at the UN General Assembly meeting of November 1, 1967. This speech and the United Nations Conferences on the Law of the Sea that followed, culminating in the 1982 Law of the Sea Convention (LOSC), have led him to be called the second 'father' of the Law of the Sea after Grotius.[100] Pardo's argument applies a

96 Andreas Malm, *Fossil Capital. The Rise of Steam Power and the Roots of Global Warming* (London: Verso, 2016).

97 Bruno Latour, *Facing Gaia. Eight Lectures on the New Climate Regime* (Cambridge: Polity Press, 2017), 232. 'I know it is risky to state the problem so bluntly, but I am obliged to say that in the epoch of the Anthropocene the Humans and the Earthbound would have to agree to go to war.' Latour, *Facing Gaia*, 248.

98 Latour, *Facing Gaia*, 251.

99 'In mythical language, the earth became known as the mother of law.… She contains law within herself as a reward of labor, she manifests law upon herself, as fixed boundaries; and she sustains law above herself, as a public sign of order' Schmitt, *The Nomos of the Earth*, 42 cited in Latour, *Facing Gaia*, 249.

100 Arvin Pardo, Speech given at UN General Assembly, 22nd session, First Committee, 1515th Meeting, Wed., Nov.1, 1967. Accessed on 27/10/24 at https://digitallibrary.un.org/record/800578?ln=en&v=pdf. Citations refer to pages of document. On the history of the law of the sea, see R. P. Anand, *Origin and Development of the Law of the Sea* (Leiden:

nomos-based approach to review the Grotian *ius gentium* with respect to the oceanic sea-bed so as to prevent its *Landnahme* 'by those who possess the required technology' (sect. 5). Pardo's intervention pushed back against the attempts at 'enclosure' of the global commons triggered by the Truman Proclamations of 1947 which sought to extend state sovereignty over the continental shelf very much on the basis of an extended Monroe Doctrine applied to the North American continent as a *Grossraum*.[101] Pardo asked that the UN General Assembly – as representative of the 'international community' – designate the sea-bed and ocean floor as a new kind of *Grossraum*. The oceanic sea-bed would be an 'Area' free from state sovereignty and intervention, whose use would be turned over to the finality of peace and development among nations, and would come under a new *ius gentium* principle, the Common Heritage of Mankind.[102]

Pardo's understanding of the Area applies at a planetary level what I have called the *nomos*-centred idea of international law. It is an open argument whether Pardo's proposal and the development of LOSC set in motion a new 'enclosure' of the global commons that is functional to the kind of neoliberal *catallaxy* described by Koskenniemi.[103] This may be the result of the more recent history of interpretation of LOSC, however it *need* not be so. My argument in this chapter indicates that it is perfectly possible for a *nomos*-centred approach to international law, particularly if articulated through indigenous and ancestral *nomoi*, to restructure the idea of international community out of the principle that humankind as a whole is the steward or trustee of the

---

Brill, 1982) and for critical analysis of Pardo's text, see Surabi Ranganathan, 'Global Commons,' *The European Journal of International Law* 27 (3) (2016), 285–308.

101 Pardo argues that the Truman Proclamation 'totally rejected the concept of the continental shelf as *res omnium communis*... and avoided explicitly founding assertion of jurisdiction on the *terra nullius* occupation theory of acquisition of territory, preferring instead to justify the action taken on the assumption that the continental shelf is the geological extension of the littoral state and that the coastal state has a reasonable right to regulate activities on its shores' (p.8).

102 The literature on CHM is vast. See Louis F.E. Goldie, 'A Note On Some Diverse Meanings Of "The Common Heritage Of Mankind"' *Syracuse Journal of International Law and Commerce* 10 (7) (1983), 69–112, Prue Taylor, *An Ecological Approach to International Law: Responding to the Challenges of Climate Change* (London: Routledge, 2008) and Karin Mickelson, 'Common Heritage of Mankind as a Limit to Exploitation of the Global Commons,' *European Journal of International Law* 30 (2) (2019), 635–663 for examples.

103 See Surabhi Ranganathan, 'Sea Change,' in Annabel Brett, Megan Donaldson, and Martti Koskenniemi (eds.), *History, Politics, Law. Thinking Through the International* (New York: Cambridge University Press, 2021), 285–308.

planetary *Grossräume*.[104] This seems to have been the intention behind the advocacy of CHM by Elisabeth Mann Borgese, sometimes referred to as the 'mother' of the new Law of the Sea, when she argued that 'the fundamental concepts, evolved over millennia on land, like sovereignty, geographic boundaries, or ownership, simply will not work in the ocean medium where new political, legal and economic concepts are emerging'.[105] Mann Borgese interpreted LOSC as a 'constitution for the ocean' that could serve as a 'model for a constitution for the world in the next century'.[106] At the heart of this vision was the belief that 'the greater part of ocean economics is based on a non-property and non-sovereignty reality. Ocean economics must incorporate the economics of resources which are the common heritage of mankind and must be managed but cannot be appropriated. The cultural, ethical as well as institutional implication of this need much further study.'[107]

Our current post-Gaia understanding that the Earth's habitability is the result of an assemblage of actants and processes that exercise forms of 'geo-power' which operate beyond 'the time of the living,' beyond the bio-centric distinction of the animate and the inanimate, and on geological time-scales that call into question the temporality associated with modernity.[108] For this reason, Povinelli draws attention to the temporal category of the 'ancestral' which is articulated in the *nomoi* of Indigenous peoples everywhere and at all times. If globalization is indeed driven, at least in part, by the tele-techno-Christian imperative to convert the pagan nations, then the new planetary *nomos* should start by reconsidering jurisgenesis in polytheistic and pantheistic cosmovisions of the relation between religion and nature, transcendence

104 For instance, Klaus Bosselmann, *Earth Governance. Trusteeship of the Global Commons* (Cheltenham, UK: Edward Elgar, 2015).

105 Elisabeth Mann Borgese, *The Oceanic Circle. Governing the Seas as a Global Resource* (Tokyo, New York: United Nations University Press, 1998), 5–6. On Mann Borgese and LOSC, see Tirza Meyer, *Elisabeth Mann Borgese and the Law of the Sea* (Leiden: Brill, 2022) and Prue Taylor, 'The Common Heritage of Mankind: Expanding the Ocean Circle,' in International Ocean Institute (ed.), *The Future of Ocean Governance and Capacity Development: Essays in Honor of Elisabeth Mann Borgese, 1918–2002* (Boston: Brill, 2018).

106 Borgese, *The Oceanic Circle,* 6.

107 Borgese, *The Oceanic Circle,* 12.

108 Elizabeth Povinelli, *Geontologies. A Requiem to Late Liberalism* (Durham, NC: Duke University Press, 2016) and Elizabeth Povinelli, *Between Gaia and Ground. Four Axioms of Existence and the Ancestral Catastrophe of Late Liberalism* (Durham, NC: Duke University Press, 2021). For the planetary turn, see Dipesh Chakrabarty, *The Climate of History in a Planetary Age* (Chicago: University of Chicago Press, 2021). On the development of the motif of 'geopower' in law, see Kathleen Birrell, 'The Anthropocene Archive: Human and Inhuman Subjects and Sediments ' in Peter Burdon and James Martel (eds.), *Routledge Handbook of Ecological Law and the Anthropocene*, (New York: Routledge, 2022).

and immanence.[109] If there is some truth to Latour's claim that the modern scientific picture of nature develops a Gnostic religion of its own, characterized by the 'immanentization' of Heaven such that for it '*there is no longer any accessible Earth*',[110] then a planetary articulation of international law stands to benefit from recovering the ancestral polytheism that was displaced by the Marian conquest of the 'New World'. From this perspective, Vitoria's conception of *ius gentium* does not only contain the justification for the capitalist 'spirit' oriented by an ethos of risk-taking, conquest and appropriation that formed the 'dark side' of the Renaissance. Dormant in its discourse lies a more solar side of the Renaissance that valorizes and adopts a 'return of paganism' and, with it, the 'ancient theology' that had been repressed by the advent of Christianity, from which new insights into the coming politics can still be salvaged.[111]

Bibliography

Agamben, Giorgio. *The Highest Poverty. Monastic Rules and Form-of-Life* (Stanford: Stanford University Press, 2013).

Allen, Amy. *The End of Progress* (New York: Columbia University Press, 2015).

Amorosa, Paolo. *Rewriting the History of the Law of Nations. How James Brown Scott Made Francisco De Vitoria the Founder of International Law* (New York: Oxford University Press, 2019).

Anand, Ram Prakash. *Origin and Development of the Law of the Sea* (Leiden: Brill, 1982).

Anghie, Antony. 'Imperialism and International Legal Theory'. In *The Oxford Handbook of the Theory of International Law*, edited by Anne Orford (New York: Oxford University Press, 2016), 156–172.

Anghie, Antony. *Imperialism, Sovereignty, and the Making of International Law* (New York: Cambridge University Press, 2005).

109 I have argued for this view in Miguel Vatter, '"Only a God can Resist a God." Political theology between Polytheism and Gnosticism,' *Political Theology* 20 (2) (2019), 1–26, and see Mary-Jane Rubenstein, *Pantheologies: Gods, Worlds, Monsters* (New York: Columbia University Press, 2021).

110 Latour, *Facing Gaia*, 200.

111 On polytheism and the racialization of globalization and modern slavery, see Hickman, *Black Prometheus*. For the return of 'ancient theology' in the Renaissance, see Miguel Vatter, 'Machiavelli, "Ancient Theology", and the Problem of Civil Religion,' in Nadia Urbinati, David Johnston, and Camila Vergara (eds.), *Machiavelli on Liberty and Conflict* (Chicago: University of Chicago Press, 2017), 113–38.

Anidjar, Gil. *Blood. A Critique of Christianity* (New York: Columbia University Press, 2014).

Anidjar, Gil. *The Jew, the Arab. A History of the Enemy* (Stanford: Stanford University Press, 2003).

Armitage, David. 'The Elephant and the Whale: Empires of Land and Sea'. *Journal for Maritime Research* 9 (1) (2007), 23–36.

Armitage, David. *Foundations of International Thought* (Cambridge: Cambridge University Press, 2012).

Barea, Elvira Roca. *Imperiofobia y leyenda negra* (Madrid: Siruela, 2016).

Bejan, Teresa. *Mere Civility: Disagreement and the Limits of Toleration* (Cambridge, MA: Harvard University Press, 2017).

Bell, Duncan. *Reordering the World. Essays on Liberalism and Empire* (Princeton: Princeton University Press, 2016).

Belmessous, Saliha, ed. *Native Claims: Indigenous Law against Empire, 1500–1920* (New York: Oxford University Press, 2012).

Beneyto, José María. 'Camilo Barcia Trelles on Francisco De Vitoria: At the Crossroads of Carl Schmitt's *Grossraum* and James Brown Scott's "Modern International Law"'. *European Journal of International Law* 31 (4) (2021), 1477–1492.

Benton, Laura, and Lisa Ford. *Rage for Order: The British Empire and the Origins of International Law* (Cambridge, MA: Harvard University Press, 2016).

Benton, Lauren. *A Search for Sovereignty: Law and Geography in European Empires, 1400–1900* (Cambridge: Cambridge University Press, 2009).

Benton, Lauren, and Nathan Perl-Rosenthal, eds. *A World at Sea: Maritime Practices and Global History* (Philadelphia: University of Pennsylvania Press, 2020).

Benton, Lauren, and Benjamin Straumann. 'Acquiring Empire by Law: From Roman Doctrine to Early Modern European Practice'. *Law and History Review* 28 (1) (2010), 1–38.

Berlanga, José Luis Villacañas. *Hispania: De formación imperial a sistema de poderes* (Madrid: Guillermo Escolar editor, 2020).

Berlanga, José Luis Villacañas. *Imperiofilia y el populismo nacional-católico: Otra historia del imperio español* (Madrid: Lengua de Trapo, 2019).

Berman, Harold. *Law and Revolution. The Formation of the Western Legal Tradition.* Cambridge: Harvard University Press, 1983.

Birrell, Kathleen. 'The Anthropocene Archive: Human and Inhuman Subjects and Sediments'. In *Routledge Handbook of Ecological Law and the Anthropocene*, ed. Peter Burdon and James Martel (New York: Routledge, 2022).

Birrell, Kathleen. *Indigeneity: Before and Beyond the Law* (New York: Routledge, 2016).

Boeri, Marcelo D. 'Natural Law and World Order in Stoicism'. In *Nature and the Best Life: Exploring the Natural Bases of Practical Normativity in Ancient Philosophy*, ed. Gabriella Rossi (Hildesheim: G. Olms, 2013).

Bogues, Anthony, ed. *Caribbean Reasonings: After Man, Towards the Human: Critical Essays on Sylvia Wynter* (Kingston: Ian Randle Publishers, 2005).

Borgese, Elisabeth Mann. *The Oceanic Circle. Governing the Seas as a Global Resource* (Tokyo, New York: United Nations University Press, 1998).

Bosselmann, Klaus. *Earth Governance. Trusteeship of the Global Commons* (Cheltenham, UK: Edward Elgar, 2015).

Brett, Annabel, Megan Donaldson, and Martti Koskenniemi, eds. *History, Politics, Law: Thinking through the International* (New York: Cambridge University Press, 2021).

Brett, Annabel S. *Changes of State: Nature and the Limits of the City in Early Modern Natural Law* (Princeton: Princeton University Press, 2011).

Brett, Mark. *Indigenous Rights and the Legacies of the Bible: From Moses to Mabo* (New York: Oxford University Press, 2024).

Brett, Mark G. *Locations of God. Political Theology in the Hebrew Bible* (New York: Oxford University Press, 2019).

Brown, Wendy. *Regulating Aversion. Tolerance in the Age of Identity and Empire* (Princeton: Princeton University Press, 2008).

Brown, Wendy. *Walled States, Waning Sovereignty* (New York: Zone Books, 2010).

Brunkhorst, Hauke. *Critical Theory of Legal Revolutions: Evolutionary Perspectives* (London: Bloomsbury, 2014).

Brunkhorst, Hauke. *Solidarity. From Civic Friendship to a Global Legal Community* (Cambridge: MIT Press, 2005).

Chakrabarty, Dipesh. *The Climate of History in a Planetary Age* (Chicago: University of Chicago Press, 2021).

Coleman, Janet. 'Property and Poverty'. In *The Cambridge History of Medieval Political Thought C.350–C.1450* ed. J.H. Burns (New York: Cambridge University Press, 1988), 607–648.

Cover, Robert. 'Nomos and Narrative'. *Harvard Law Review* 87 (4) (1983–1984). 4–68.

Deckers, Daniel. *Gerechtigkeit und Recht: Eine Historisch-Kritische Untersuchung der Gerechtigkeitslehre des Franciso De Vitoria (1483–1546)* (Freiburg Schweiz: Universitätsverlag, 1991).

Derman, Joshua. 'Carl Schmitt on Land and Sea.' *History of European Ideas* 37 (2) (2011), 181–189.

Derrida, Jacques. *The Beast and the Sovereign. Volume 1* (Chicago: University of Chicago Press, 2011).

Derrida, Jacques. 'Faith and Knowledge. the Two Sources of "Religion" at the Limits of Reason Alone.' In *Religion*, eds. Jacques Derrida and Gianni Vattimo (Cambridge: Polity Press, 1998), 1–78.

Derrida, Jacques. 'Force of Law. the "Mystical Foundation of Authority"'. In *Acts of Religion*, ed. Gil Anidjar (New York: Routledge, 2001), 230–298.

Dunoff, Jeffrey L., and Joel P. Trachtman, eds. *Ruling the World? Constitutionalism, International Law, and Global Governance* (New York: Cambridge University Press, 2009).

Dussel, Enrique. *El primer debate filósofico de la modernidad* (Buenos Aires: CLACSO, 2020).

Dussel, Enrique. 'Eurocentrism and Modernity (Introduction to the Frankfurt Lectures)'. *boundary 2* 20 (3) (1993), 65–76.

Elden, Stuart. 'Reading Schmitt Geopolitically: Nomos, Territory and Großraum'. In *Spatiality, Sovereignty and Carl Schmitt: Geographies of the Nomos*, ed. Stephen Legg (London: Routledge, 2011), 91–105.

Fassin, Didier. *Humanitarian Reason. A Moral History of the Present* (Berkeley, CA: University of California Press, 2012).

Fedele, Dante. 'Ius Gentium: the Metamorphoses of a Legal Concept (Ancient Rome to Early Moderneurope)'. In *Empire and Legal Thought. Ideas and Institutions from Antiquity to Modernity* ed. Edward Cavanagh (Leiden: Brill, 2020), 213–251.

Fonseca, Manuel Jiménez. 'Jus Gentium and the Transformation of Latin American Nature: One More Reading of Vitoria?'. In *International Law and Empire: Historical Explorations*, eds. Martti Koskenniemi, Walter Rech and Manuel Jiménez Fonseca (New York: Oxford University Press, 2018), 123–148.

Ford, Lisa. *Settler Sovereignty: Jurisdiction and Indigenous People in America and Australia 1788–1836* (Cambridge, MA: Harvard University Press, 2010).

Forst, Rainer. *Toleranz Im Konflikt* (Frankfurt: Suhrkamp, 2003).

Forst, Rainer. 'Toleration and Democracy'. *Journal of Social Philosophy* 45 (1) (2014), 65–75.

Foucault, Michel. *Security, Territory, Population: Lectures at the Collège de France 1977–1978* (New York: Picador, 2009).

Gaius. *Institutiones or Institutes of Roman Law by Gaius*. Trans. Edward Poste. 4th ed. Ed. E. A. Whittuck (Oxford: Clarendon Press, 1904).

Galli, Carlo. *Political Spaces and Global War* (Minneapolis: University of Minnesota Press, 2010).

Geuna, Marco. 'Francisco de Vitoria E La Questione Della Guerra Giusta'. In *Dalla concordia dei Greci al bellum justum dei moderni*, ed. Giovanna Daverio Rocchi (Milan: Franco Angeli, 2013), 143–174.

Goldie, Louis F. E. 'A Note on Some Diverse Meanings of "The Common Heritage of Mankind"'. *Syracuse Journal of International Law and Commerce* 10 (7) (1983), 69–112.

Graeber, David, and David Wengrow. *The Dawn of Everything. A New History of Humanity* (New York: Farrar, Straus and Giroux, 2021).

Greer, Margaret R., Walter D. Mignolo, and Maureen Quilligan, eds. *Rereading the Black Legend: The Discourses of Religious and Racial Difference in the Renaissance Empires* (Chicago: University of Chicago Press, 2007).

Habermas, Jürgen. *The Inclusion of the Other* (Cambridge: MIT Press, 2001).

Habermas, Jürgen. *The Divided West* (Cambridge: Polity Press, 2006).

Heron, Nicholas. 'One World: History and Space in Schmitt's Post-War Political Theology'. In *Political Theology Today. 100 Years after Carl Schmitt*, eds. Mitchell Dean, Lotte List and Stefan Schwarzkopf (London: Bloomsbury, 2022).

Herrero, Montserrat. *The Political Discourse of Carl Schmitt. A Mystic of Order* (Lexington: Rowman & Littlefield, 2015).

Hickman, Jared. *Black Prometheus: Race and Radicalism in the Age of Atlantic Slavery* (New York: Oxford University Press, 2016).

Hohendahl, Peter Uwe. *Perilous Futures: On Carl Schmitt's Late Writings* (Ithaca, NY: Cornell University Press, 2018).

Hunter, Ian. *Rival Enlightenments. Civil and Metaphysical Philosophy in the Early Modern Germany* (Cambridge: Cambridge University Press, 2001).

Hurd, Elizabeth Shakman. *Beyond Religious Freedom. The New Global Politics of Religion* (Princeton, NJ: Princeton University Press, 2017).

Johnson, Mirand. *The Land Is Our History: Indigeneity, Law and the Settler State* (New York: Oxford University Press, 2016).

Kalyvas, Andreas. 'Carl Schmitt's Postcolonial Imagination'. *Constellations* 25 (1) (2018), 35–53.

Kistner, Ulrike. 'In Search of a New Nomos: Post-Colonially'. *Constellations* 27 (2) (2020), 273–284.

Koskenniemi, Martti. 'Empire and International Law. The Real Spanish Contribution'. *University of Toronto Law Journal* 61 (2011), 1–36.

Koskenniemi, Martti. 'Letter in Response to Michael Salter's Recent Paper on Carl Schmitt's Grossraum.' *Chinese Journal of International Law* 12 (1) (2013), 201–202.

Koskenniemi, Martti. *To the Uttermost Parts of the Earth: Legal Imagination and International Power, 1300–1870* (New York: Cambridge University Press, 2021).

Lambertini, Roberto. *La povertà pensata. Da Bonaventura a Ockham* (Modena: Mucchi editore, 2000).

Latour, Bruno. *Facing Gaia. Eight Lectures on the New Climate Regime* (Cambridge: Polity Press, 2017).

Loughlin, Martin. *Against Constitutionalism* (Cambridge: Harvard University Press, 2022).

Loughlin, Martin. *Foundations of Public Law* (New York: Oxford University Press, 2010).

Luhmann, Niklas. 'Am Anfang War Kein Unrecht'. In *Gesellschaftsstruktur und Semantik. Studien zur Wissenssoziologie der modernen Gesellschaft* (Frankfurt: Suhrkamp, 1989), 11–64.

Malm, Andreas. *Fossil Capital. The Rise of Steam Power and the Roots of Global Warming* (London: Verso, 2016).

Marcocci, Giuseppe. 'Iberian Theories of Empire in the Sixteenth and Seventeenth Centuries'. *Journal of the History of Ideas* 83 (4) (2022), 671–683.

Meyer, Tirza. *Elisabeth Mann Borgese and the Law of the Sea* (Leiden: Brill, 2022).

Meza, María Cecilia Añaños. 'El Título De 'Sociedad Y Comunicación Natural' De Francisco De Vitoria. Tras las huellas de su concepto a la luz de la teoría del dominio'. *Anuario Mexicano de Derecho Internacional* 12 (2012), 525–596.

Mickelson, Karin. 'Common Heritage of Mankind as a Limit to Exploitation of the Global Commons'. *European Journal of International Law* 30 (2) (2019), 635–63.

Mignolo, Walter. *The Darker Side of the Renaissance: Literacy, Territoriality and Colonization* (Ann Arbor: University of Michigan Press, 2003).

Mouffe, Chantal. 'Schmitt's Vision of a Multipolar World Order'. *The South Atlantic Quarterly* 104 (2) (2005), 245–251.

Moyn, Samuel. *Humane: How the United States Abandoned Peace and Reinvented War* (New York: Farrar, Straus & Giroux, 2021).

Muecke, Stephen, Paddy Roe, and Krim Benterrak. *Reading the Country. Introduction to Nomadology* (Melbourne: re.press, 2014).

Nancy, Jean-Luc. *La création du monde ou la mondialisation* (Paris: Galilée, 2002).

Pagden, Anthony. 'Legislating for the "Whole World that Is, in a Sense, a Commonwealth". Conquest, Occupation and the "Defence of the Innocent"'. In *Morality and Responsibility of Rulers. European and Chinese Origins of Rule of Law as Justice for World Order*, eds. Anthony Carty and Janne Nijman (New York: Oxford University Press, 2018), 132–148.

Patton, Paul, Duncan Ivison, and Will Saunders, eds. *Political Theory and the Rights of Indigenous Peoples* (New York: Cambridge University Press, 2000).

Pettit, Philip. 'A Republican Law of Peoples'. *European Journal of Political Theory* 9 (1) (2010), 70–94.

Povinelli, Elizabeth. *Between Gaia and Ground. Four Axioms of Existence and the Ancestral Catastrophe of Late Liberalism* (Durham, NC: Duke University Press, 2021).

Povinelli, Elizabeth. *Geontologies. A Requiem to Late Liberalism* (Durham, NC: Duke University Press, 2016).

Ranganathan, Surabhi. 'Sea Change'. In *History, Politics, Law. Thinking through the International*, eds. Annabel Brett, Megan Donaldson and Martti Koskenniemi (New York: Cambridge University Press, 2021), 285–308.

Ranganathan, Surabi. 'Global Commons'. *The European Journal of International Law* 27 (3) (2016), 693–717.

Rasch, William. 'Human Rights as Geopolitics: Carl Schmitt and the Legal Form of American Supremacy'. *Cultural Critique* 54 (2003), 120–147.

Rawls, John. *The Law of Peoples* (Cambridge: Harvard University Press, 2001).

Rosenstock-Huessy, Eugen. *Out of Revolution. Autobiography of Western Man* (Norwich, VT: Argo Books, 1969).

Rossello, Diego. '"To Be Human, Nonetheless, Remains a Decision": Humanism as Decisionism in Contemporary Critical Political Theory'. *Contemporary Political Theory* 16 (4) (2016), 439–458.

Rubenstein, Mary-Jane. *Pantheologies: Gods, Worlds, Monsters* (New York: Columbia University Press, 2021).

Saralegui, Miguel. *Carl Schmitt pensador español* (Madrid: Trotta, 2013).

Saralegui, Miguel. *Matar a la Madre Patria: Historia de una pasión latinoamericana* (Madrid: Tecnos, 2021).

Schmitt, Carl. 'La justificación de la ocupación de un nuevo mundo (Francisco De Vitoria)'. *Revista Española de Derecho Internacional* 2 (1) (1949), 13–46.

Schmitt, Carl. *Land and Sea. A World-Historical Meditation.* Eds. Russell A. Berman and Samuel Garrett Zeitlin (Candor, NY: Telos Press Publishing, 2015).

Schmitt, Carl. *The Nomos of the Earth in the International Law of Jus Publicum Europaeum* (New York: Telos Press, 2003).

Schmitt, Carl. *Staat, Grossraum, Nomos. Arbeiten aus den Jahren 1916–1969.* Ed. Günter Maschke (Berlin: Duncker & Humblot, 1995).

Schmitt, Carl. *Verfassungsrechtliche Aufsätze aus den Jahren 1924–1954* (Berlin: Duncker & Humblot, 2003).

Scott, James Brown. *Spanish Origin of International Law* (Oxford: Clarendon Press, 1934).

Sellars, John. 'Deleuze and Cosmopolitanism'. *Radical Philosophy* 142 (2007), 30–37.

Simons, Jens Meierhenrich and Oliver, eds. *The Oxford Handbook of Carl Schmitt.* New York: Oxford University Press, 2017.

Simons, Oliver. 'Carl Schmitt's Spatial Rhetoric'. In *The Oxford Handbook of Carl Schmitt*, eds. Jens Meierhenrich and Oliver Simons (New York: Oxford University Press, 2016), 776–802.

Skinner, Quentin. 'A Genealogy of the Modern State'. *Proceedings of the British Academy* 162 (2009), 325–370.

Slobodian, Quinn. *Globalists: The End of Empire and the Birth of Neoliberalism* (Cambridge, MA: Harvard University Press, 2018).

Smeltzer, Joshua. 'On the Use and Abuse of Francisco De Vitoria: James Brown Scott and Carl Schmitt'. *Journal of the History of International Law* 20 (2018), 345–372.

Specter, Matthew. 'Grossraum and Geopolitics. Resituating Schmitt in an Atlantic Context'. *History and Theory* 56 (3) (2017), 398–406.

Sullivan, Winnifred Fallers, Elizabeth Shakman Hurd, Saba Mahmood, and Peter Danchin, eds. *Politics of Religious Freedom* (Chicago, IL: University of Chicago Press, 2015).

Taylor, Prue. 'the Common Heritage of Mankind: Expanding the Ocean Circle.' In *The Future of Ocean Governance and Capacity Development: Essays in Honor of Elisabeth Mann Borgese, 1918–2002*, ed. International Ocean Institute (Boston: Brill, 2018), 142–150.

Taylor, Prue. *An Ecological Approach to International Law: Responding to the Challenges of Climate Change* (London: Routledge, 2008).

Teubner, Guenther. *Constitutional Fragments: Societal Constitutionalism and Globalization* (New York: Oxford University Press, 2012).

Thornhill, Chris. *The Sociology of Law and the Global Transformation of Democracy* (Cambridge, UK: Cambridge University Press, 2018).

Tierney, Brian. *The Idea of Natural Rights* (Grand Rapids, MI: William B. Eerdmans Publishing Company, 1997).

Tully, James. *Strange Multiplicity: Constitutionalism in an Age of Diversity* (Cambridge: Cambridge University Press, 1995).

Turnbull, David. 'Locating, Negotiating, and Crossing Boundaries: A Western Desert Land Claim, the Tordesillas Line, and the West Australian Border'. *Environment and Planning D: Society and Space* 23 (2005), 757–770.

Vadi, Valentina. *War and Peace. Alberico Gentili and the Early Modern Law of Nations* (Leiden: Brill, 2020).

Vatter, Miguel. 'Machiavelli, "Ancient Theology", and the Problem of Civil Religion'. In *Machiavelli on Liberty and Conflict*, eds. Nadia Urbinati, David Johnston, and Camila Vergara (Chicago: University of Chicago Press, 2017), 113–138.

Vatter, Miguel. 'Neoliberalism and Republicanism: Economic Rule of Law and Law as Concrete Order (*Nomos*)'. In *The Sage Handbook of Neoliberalism*, eds. Melinda Cooper, Damien Cahill, Martijn Konings and David Primrose (London: Sage, 2018), 370–383.

Vatter, Miguel. '"Only a God Can Resist a God." Political Theology between Polytheism and Gnosticism'. *Political Theology* 20 (2) (2019), 1–26.

Vázquez-Arroyo, Antonio Y. 'Critical Theory, Colonialism, and the Historicity of Thought' *Constellations* 25 (2018), 54–70.

Villey, Michel. *La formation de la pensée juridique moderne* (Paris: PUF, 2003).

Vitoria, Francisco de. *Relecciones sobre los Indios y el derecho de guerra* (Madrid: Coleccion Austral, 1946).

Vitoria, Francisco de. *Vitoria's Political Writings*. Eds. Anthony Pagden and Jeremy Lawrence (Cambridge: Cambridge University Press, 1991).

Westermann, Edward B. *Hitler's Ostkrieg and the Indian Wars. Comparing Genocide and Conquest*. (Norman, OK: University of Oklahoma Press, 2016).

Wheatley, Natasha. 'Legal Pluralism as Temporal Pluralism: Historical Rights, Legal Vitalism and Non-Synchronous Sovereignty'. In *Power and Time. Temporalities in Conflict and the Making of History*, eds. Dan Edelstein, Stefanos Geroulanos and Natasha Wheatley (Chicago: University of Chicago Press, 2020), 53–80.

Whyte, Jessica. *The Morals of the Market. Human Rights and the Rise of Neoliberalism* (London: Verso, 2019).

Williams, Robert A. *The American Indian in Western Legal Thought. The Discourses of Conquest* (New York: Oxford University Press, 1993).

Wynter, Sylvia. *On Being Human as Praxis*. Ed. Katherine McKittrick (Durham, NC: Duke University Press, 2015).

Young, Iris Marion. 'Hybrid Democracy: Iroquois Federalism and the Postcolonial Project'. In *Political Theory and the Rights of Indigenous Peoples*, eds. Paul Patton, Duncan Ivison and Will Sanders (Cambridge: Cambridge University Press, 2000), 237–258.

Zartaloudis, Thanos. *The Birth of Nomos* (Edinburgh: Edinburgh University Press, 2019).

CHAPTER 7

Sovereignty and International Law from Vitoria to Schmitt

David Pan

1 Introduction

Our conceptions about the relationship between sovereignty and law typically set these two ideas against each other as opposites in which the rise of one must coincide with the fall of the other. Thus, in the international arena, the establishment of international law seems to require constraints on state sovereignty. By contrast, an emphasis on state sovereignty is taken to lead to the erosion of international law. This antagonistic relationship between sovereignty and law has led to two opposing interpretations of Carl Schmitt's *The* Nomos *of the Earth*.

On the one hand, defenders of international law as the principle by which the world can suppress armed conflict criticize Schmitt for his rejection of a global legal framework that might limit sovereignty. Those who most emphatically warn of the danger of Schmitt's work are those who defend international law as the basis of world order. They use their reading of *The* Nomos *of the Earth* to better understand how to promote their perspective while taking into account Schmitt's criticisms. Seyla Benhabib, for instance, accepts Schmitt's portrayal of the limitations on international law's ability to establish itself: 'Human rights norms require interpretation and vernacularization; they cannot just be imposed by legal elites and judges upon recalcitrant peoples; rather, they must become elements in the public culture of democratic peoples through their own processes of interpretation, articulation and iteration.'[1] Benhabib recognizes here that international law depends on democratic processes but refuses to grant Schmitt's point that such processes depend on the establishment of sovereignty. Instead of investigating the people's processes of 'interpretation, articulation and iteration' as the origin of sovereignty and then of law, as Schmitt does, Benhabib reverses the causality and refers to the

1 Seyla Benhabib, 'Carl Schmitt's Critique of Kant: Sovereignty and International Law'. *Political Theory* 40.6 (2012), 688–713, 704.

 | DOI:10.1163/9789004757448_008

ways in which laws themselves and legal institutions might affect people and lead them to embrace those laws as legitimate. 'Democratic sovereigntists ignore that international human rights norms can empower citizens in democracies by creating new vocabularies for claim-making as well as by opening new channels of mobilization for civil society actors who then become part of transnational networks of rights activism and hegemonic resistance.'[2] While human rights norms might provide arguments within democracies, Schmitt's point, which Benhabib does not address, is that the establishment of such norms as a practical matter that would drive political action ultimately requires processes by which people develop a sense of their own identity and thus sovereignty. Instead of seeing this development of a collective will of the people as the primary source of ideals, Benhabib attempts to situate international law and human rights principles as the source of the ideals of a particular group. The key point of contention is whether law is a universal context within which the legitimacy of a particular sovereign state can be judged or whether the development of such a state is in the first place the expression of the collective will of the people that forms the basis of its own perspective on the universal.

Martti Koskenniemi is similar to Benhabib in the way that he also adheres to the first conception, in which an over-arching universality is the source of the limits that would constrain the particular sovereignty of state power. He assumes that the focus on sovereignty means a rejection of ideals and a consequent emphasis on pure power as the definer of international relations. He consequently affirms international law as the way to limit such pure power by subjecting it to a universal perspective, not as a positive program but as that which is lacking in particular cultures.

> Through attention to that 'lack', that absence of what a particular feels it should possess in order to be fully itself, focus is directed to its universal aspect: its alleged right to self-determination, a fair distribution of resources, etc. By directing attention to that universality, the particular is opened up, and its communal lien, its shared property or value with other particularities, is revealed. But unlike in imperialism, it is not opened by a positive principle but a negative one: what is it that we lack?[3]

2 Benhabib, 'Carl Schmitt's Critique of Kant', 704. Emphasis in original.

3 Martti Koskenniemi, *The Gentle Civilizer of Nations: The Rise and Fall of International Law 1870–1960* (Cambridge: University of Cambridge Press 2001) 505–506.

In addressing this fundamental lack, international law provides for Koskenniemi, as for Benhabib, the corrective to the particularity of state-based conceptions of identity. The universality of law tempers the focus on pure power, and in this conception, law and power remain in an antagonistic relationship. Because of this presumed inherent antagonism, Koskenniemi takes Schmitt's focus on sovereignty to be fundamentally realist in that it rejects the abstract formalism of an international law framework and only focuses on power relations as the basis of international order. Schmitt becomes the primary source text for Hans Morgenthau's development of this realist perspective that is no longer concerned with issues of ideology and political theology.[4]

We can contrast Benhabib's and Koskenniemi's approach with those who also begin from a basic antagonism between sovereignty and law but then defend Schmitt's realist approach. Martin Loughlin, for instance, situates Schmitt's work within a tradition of political jurisprudence that seeks to understand the workings of political power. In this tradition, including Bodin, Hobbes, Montesquieu, and Hegel, law is 'the product of political power',[5] and these earlier theorists, like Schmitt, work to understand the recurring patterns according to which power functions. Such 'laws' are less prescriptive than descriptive, and Loughlin situates Schmitt as a realist who is not interested in law as such but in the dynamics of political power.[6]

The left-wing version of this realist approach defends Schmitt's critique of liberal internationalism in order to criticize the cosmopolitan dream of a world in which international law replaces war and sovereignty as the basis of relations between nations.[7] Schmitt indicates that liberal internationalism and the discourse of human rights leads, not to the elimination of war, but rather to the intensification of war because it criminalizes the enemy as 'inhuman' and therefore justifies wars of annihilation that remove the limits on warfare established by the *jus publicum europaeum*. Citing this argument, Louiza Odysseos links the cosmopolitan attitude to the US War on Terror by arguing that the latter's demonization of the enemy is in fact a continuation of the logic of liberal internationalism, which seeks to outlaw anti-liberal states and movements. For her, power and law are merged because law is under-

4 Koskenniemi, *The Gentle Civilizer of Nations*, 436–446.

5 Martin Loughlin, 'Politonomy', in Jens Meierhenrich and Oliver Simons (eds.), *The Oxford Handbook of Carl Schmitt* (New York: Oxford University Press 2016), 570–591, 587.

6 Loughlin, 'Politonomy', 587.

7 Louiza Odysseos, 'Crossing the Line? Carl Schmitt on the "spaceless universalism" of cosmopolitanism and the War on Terror', in Louiza Odysseos and Fabio Petito (eds.), *The International Political Thought of Carl Schmitt: Terror, Liberal War and the Crisis of Global Order* (London: Routledge 2007) 124–143, 131–139.

stood to be just a mask for pure power. Ideals have no independent value from this perspective, and any invocation of ideals is seen as a ruse of power.

The defenders of a universal international law framework against Schmitt's critique of such universalism on the one hand and the proponents of a Schmittian realism that focuses on power to the exclusion of law on the other hand are both in agreement about the basic antagonism between power and law in Schmitt's work. Such an approach does not recognize the continuities between his work on political theology and the discussion of international law in *The* Nomos *of the Earth*. Yet, in all of Schmitt's work, the key problem is the way in which power and ideals coincide and reinforce each other. In *Political Theology*, this coincidence lies in the political theological meaning of the decision on the state of exception. In *The* Nomos *of the Earth*, the merging of power and ideals is the basis for Schmitt's argument about the essential link between *Ordnung* (order) and *Ortung* (territorialization). This link between law as order and sovereignty as land appropriation becomes the basis for Schmitt's interpretation of Francisco de Vitoria's similar approach to international law and sovereignty. In what follows, I would like to lay out Schmitt's development of this linking of order and territorialization and the way it accords with Vitoria's conception of sovereignty. At the end, I reflect on what this conception of the relationship between sovereignty and law means for the current *nomos* of the earth.

2 The Continuity between the Decision on the State of Exception and the Land Appropriation

The Nomos *of the Earth*'s theoretical premises, in privileging concrete order, do not diverge from Schmitt's decisionism, as some commentators have suggested. From the time of his book on dictatorship, Carl Schmitt challenged the idea that the primary constraint on sovereign power comes from law. In this book, he describes a commissarial dictatorship as one in which the dictator can suspend the laws in order to preserve the constitutional order as a whole. In such a case, constitutional order maintains its existence as an ideal that motivates the decision-making of the dictator, even when its laws are temporarily suspended in order to defend that order.[8] In making this argument, Schmitt imagines a situation in which power is guided by a set of ideals without, however, being constrained by laws. One might characterize the broad

8 Carl Schmitt, *Dictatorship. From the Origin of the Modern Concept of Sovereignty to Proletarian Class Struggle*, trans. Michael Hoelzl and Graham Ward (Cambridge, UK: Polity 2014) 1–3.

trajectory of his oeuvre as an attempt to understand the origins and nature of this form of sovereign power. In *Political Theology*, the decision on the state of exception defines the sovereign. Yet, this act of sovereignty is not a form of arbitrary violence. 'What characterizes an exception is principally unlimited authority, which means the suspension of the entire existing order. In such a situation it is clear that the state remains, whereas law recedes. Because the exception is different from anarchy and chaos, order in the juristic sense still prevails even if it is not of the ordinary kind'.[9] Schmitt argues that order can emanate from the state, even if law 'recedes', and this ordering capacity of the state comes to the fore in the state of exception. In arguing that the exception is in fact more important than the normal situation of the rule of law, Schmitt indicates that the role of law is not to provide the overarching basis for order. Rather, he reverses the priority to argue that law is a secondary effect of the ordering power of the state. As Thalin Zarmanian formulates it: 'Legal order is, therefore, according to Schmitt, a particular shape given to empirical reality through a sovereign decision'.[10]

If sovereignty has in itself an ordering role, then the next question concerns the source of this order. Schmitt answers this question in *The Concept of the Political*, where he defines the political as based on the friend-enemy distinction. The friend-enemy distinction contains a sense of order because it defines political identity through the contrast with an alternative conception of order that is embodied in the enemy. Even if there is no formal law, the designation of an enemy presupposes some conception of that which is crucial to a collective's identity. As Schmitt indicates, the decision about which aspect of collective identity takes on this defining role is a subjective one and involves a raising up to the level of the political some other type of distinction that might in other cases be considered insignificant for political identity. The political is consequently not a category like all others, but one which measures the political 'temperature' of all other categories.[11] By establishing the most important parameters of collective identity, the designation of an enemy

9 Carl Schmitt, *Political Theology. Four Chapters on the Concept of Sovereignty*, trans. George Schwab (Chicago: University of Chicago Press 2005) 12. See David Pan, 'Carl Schmitt on Culture and Violence in the Political Decision'. *Telos* 142 (Spring 2008), 49–72, 49–51.

10 Thalin Zarmanian, 'Carl Schmitt and the Problem of Legal Order: From Domestic to International'. *Leiden Journal of International Law* 19 (2006), 41–67, 50.

11 Carl Schmitt, *The Concept of the Political*, trans. George Schwab (Chicago: University of Chicago Press 2007) 26–27, 38. See Zarmanian, 'Carl Schmitt and the Problem of Legal Order', 51–53, and David Pan, 'Against Biopolitics: Walter Benjamin, Carl Schmitt, and Giorgio Agamben on Political Sovereignty and Symbolic Order'. *The German Quarterly* 82.1 (Winter 2009), 42–62, 56–59.

becomes the basis for a vision of sovereignty as well as the kind of law that would be appropriate for such a vision. Schmitt's work consequently poses a fundamental challenge to the idea that state sovereignty should be subordinate to the rule of law. In his theory, the establishment of sovereignty, by defining the enemy and thus the key determinants of the political identity of the people, becomes the origin of the legal order.

In *The* Nomos *of the Earth* Schmitt extends this analysis in order to understand the way in which order arises on an international level. As in his earlier work, the establishment of sovereignty is the origin of legal order. Here, he argues that the sovereign decision corresponds in international relations to the land appropriation that simultaneously establishes a set of power relationships in a particular territory and with them a set of rules. The *nomos* links order (*Ordnung*) to territorialization (*Ortung*) through an implicit establishment of social relationships that accompany a land appropriation.

> Not to lose the decisive connection between order and orientation [*Ortung*], one should not translate *nomos* as law (in German, *Gesetz*), regulation, norm, or any similar expression. *Nomos* comes from *nemein* – a [Greek] word that means both 'to divide' and 'to pasture'. Thus, *nomos* is the immediate form in which the political and social order of a people becomes spatially visible – the initial measure and division of pasture-land, i.e., the land-appropriation as well as the concrete order contained in it and following from it. In Kant's words, it is the 'distributive law of mine and thine', or, to use an English term that expresses it so well, it is the 'radical title'. *Nomos* is the *measure* by which the land in a particular order is divided and situated; it is also the form of political, social, and religious order determined by this process.[12]

Schmitt refuses to translate *nomos* as law or norm because this would imply a distinction between an abstract law and a concrete application. Instead, Schmitt sees in the *nomos* an act of land appropriation simultaneously implying political violence and the establishment of a set of social relationships.

> Here, measure, order, and form constitute a spatially concrete unity. The *nomos* by which a tribe, a retinue, or a people becomes settled, i.e., by which it becomes historically situated and turns a part of the

12 Carl Schmitt, *The* Nomos *of the Earth in the International Law of the* Jus Publicum Europaeum, trans. G. L. Ulmen (New York: Telos 2003) 70.

> earth's surface into the force-field of a particular order, becomes visible in the appropriation of land and in the founding of a city or a colony.[13]

Schmitt proposes a structure of order in *The* Nomos *of the Earth* in which there is no separation between the arbitrary violence of land appropriation and the order that it establishes. He opposes this conception of order to the structure presumed by a universal conception of justice, in which order is grounded in the link to natural laws. For Schmitt the concrete order already has a *nomos* structure without necessarily having any explicit laws. 'In its original sense, however, *nomos* is precisely the full immediacy of a legal power not mediated by laws; it is a constitutive historical event – an act of *legitimacy*, whereby the legality of a mere law first is made meaningful'.[14] By insisting that the *nomos* is immediate, Schmitt argues against the idea that the *nomos* would depend on a universal law. *Nomos* comes into being as a contingent act of land appropriation that establishes sovereignty.

By arguing that the state of exception is a condition in which law recedes but order still exists within a structure of sovereignty, Schmitt develops a distinction between *nomos*, the fundamental establishment of order itself by the sovereign, and law as the positive law that is subsequently created by a sovereign power. Such power is not pure violence nor chaotic for Schmitt. Instead, order develops directly out of power relationships for Schmitt in the act of land appropriation, which he understands to be an initial establishment of order. 'At this origin of land-appropriation, law and order are one; where order and orientation coincide, they cannot be separated'.[15] Like the decision on the state of exception, the land appropriation is a singular event that establishes a principle of order in a particular space, in the absence of laws. Yet, Schmitt insists that in this appropriation, order and territorialization coincide. The taking of land already implies an establishment of order and thus a particular conception of order.

3 The Merging of Violence and Order in the Land Appropriation

The argument about the centrality of land appropriation can be understood as an affirmation of violence, but in fact the link between order and territorialization means that land appropriation is an event that combines violence with

13 Schmitt, *The* Nomos *of the Earth*, 70.
14 Schmitt, *The* Nomos *of the Earth*, 73.
15 Schmitt, *The* Nomos *of the Earth*, 81.

a cultural conception. Since land appropriation precedes law, the imagining of an ordering aspect of the appropriation requires Schmitt to differentiate between law on the one hand and a legitimacy that is connected with the *nomos* on the other hand. For Schmitt, this *nomos* is immediate and primary for the constitution of a political order. The 'constitutive historical event' of land appropriation is for Schmitt the foundation of law. Yet, there is a twofold character of land appropriation in which, as 'an original constitutive act of spatial ordering',[16] it is both violent and ordering. It actualizes in reality a concrete order of a society by conquering land. The ordering character of land appropriation is consistent with Schmitt's decisionism because it recognizes that the act of violence can only have a political meaning if it is supported by a cultural context that can define a way of life.

In making the argument that the *nomos* of a particular place is constituted by the act of appropriating the land by force and then drawing lines enforced by violence that enclose this land and determine power relations vis-à-vis neighboring spaces, Schmitt points out that the Spanish and Portuguese conquest of America was predicated on the Catholic missionary task given to Spain and Portugal by the papacy: 'The papal missionary mandate was the legal foundation of the conquista. This was not only the pope's position, but also that of the Catholic rulers of Spain, who recognized the missionary mandate to be legally binding. Above all, they emphasized the duty of the mission in their many instructions and orders to their admiral, Christopher Columbus, and to their governors and officers'.[17] The land appropriation of the New World was not an act without precedent. Rather, it was already embedded within a religious framework. Later on, as the medieval order in Europe began to be replaced by interstate politics, both the idea of freedom and the civilizing mission of Europe became the basis for land appropriation and provided the outline for the *nomos* that governed both European interstate relations and the relations between European powers and the colonies.[18] In these examples, even though the specific power relations defined the way violence was used and contained, these power relations were not 'pure'. Rather, they were always expressed in terms of cultural assumptions about the final goals of conquest and colonization. Violence and power relations provide the limiting factors that determine a *nomos* for a society or for the earth as a whole, but the final form that this *nomos* will take will always result from a cultural medi-

16 Schmitt, *The* Nomos *of the Earth*, 78.

17 Schmitt, *The* Nomos *of the Earth*, 111.

18 Schmitt, *The* Nomos *of the Earth*, 209, 237.

ation of these power relations as expressed in the ideals around which power is being exercised.

Schmitt begins to inquire into the nature of this cultural element when he links the *nomos* to both *Nahme* [appropriation] and *Name*:

> I will say only a few words about the general problem of human thought that is indicated by appropriation, apprehension, perception, understanding, and comprehension. We are concerned with the legal-historical meaning of the relation between *Nahme* and name, power and name-giving, and, in particular, with the formative, even festive processes of many land-appropriations that are able to make *Nahme* a sacred act. A land-appropriation is constituted only if the appropriator is able to give the land a name.[19]

In linking *Nahme* to *Name*, Schmitt recognizes the connection between a cultural marking and a land appropriation and even affirms the crucial importance of the proper name in making the land appropriation possible. This process of name-giving and the ceremony that is connected with it give the land appropriation a specifically cultural character as opposed to a simply violent one. The violence of the land appropriation is not sufficient to establish a *nomos*. Rather, since the land appropriation is constituted only when the appropriation is able to give the land a name, the cultural context is primary. For the naming process is not just a flat positing of something new, but rather an integration of the violent act within a pre-existing cultural tradition that can situate the land within a linguistic and symbolic framework. Because he is willing to see a connection between land appropriation as a historical event and culture as a way of life emanating from a symbolic order, Schmitt's search for the legitimating framework that founds a legal and political order provides the basic theoretical premises for explaining the cultural determination of politics.

At the same time, Schmitt also argues that the historical act of land appropriation defines the character of a culture, presenting an example of how the European amity lines for dividing up the New World influenced European philosophy when he suggests that 'Pascal's meridian is nothing other than the amity lines of his time, which had created an abyss between freedom (the lawlessness of the state of nature) and an orderly "civil" mode of existence'.[20] In this example, along with the examples of Hobbes's 'man is a wolf to

19 Schmitt, *The* Nomos *of the Earth*, 348.
20 Schmitt, *The* Nomos *of the Earth*, 95.

other men' as a description of America and Locke's conception of the 'state of nature', Schmitt tries to show how spatial ordering, such as is embodied in amity lines, creates the framework within which theories gain meaning and significance in a culture.

Moreover, Schmitt emphasizes that the amity line's designation of America as a free space open to conquest was a result of European superiority in power and understanding that had tragic consequences for the cultures of the Americas. A land appropriation will have its own character as a historical event, not just based on the cultural ideals involved but also on the distribution of power. The power relations that are established by a land appropriation may in fact ground a specific form of order, and Schmitt's differentiation of the *respublica Christiana* from the *jus publicum Europaeum* is in part based on the relationships of power established in each. As much as cultural ideals provide the context of goals for land appropriation, the power differentials themselves will also have a decisive impact on the kind of international order that results.

Consequently, sovereignty itself contains an ordering principle that establishes itself in the sovereign act of land appropriation, and 'nomos is precisely the full immediacy of a legal power not mediated by laws; it is a constitutive historical event – an act of legitimacy, whereby the legality of a mere law first is made meaningful'.[21] In establishing land appropriation as that which constitutes law, Schmitt is not simply replacing law with naked power. He is in fact denying the very idea of a pure power that is devoid of any kind of legitimacy, in a similar way to Hannah Arendt's affirmation that power always involves a group of people who are unified by a common purpose.[22] Power only develops with the establishment of such a group, which must involve their commitment to some idea of the basis of their identity as a group that would bind them together and distinguish them from others. At the same time, this group identity cannot become actualized as defining until the group occupies a space in the world. Before that, the group could be something like a set of football fans or a professional association in which the identity of the group is not fundamental politically as the basis for organizing the appropriation and distribution of land. In an imagined beginning of humanity, when land might have been available for occupation with no other competitors, such land appropriation could be carried out peacefully. But at any time afterwards, the decision on the state of exception and the land appropriation coincide because both events arise in a situation when there are two or more groups, each with its own conception of order, that seek to occupy the same space and establish

21 Schmitt, *The* Nomos *of the Earth*, 73.

22 Hannah Arendt, *On Violence* (San Diego: Harcourt Brace Jovanovich 1969) 44–49.

order. The decision and the land appropriation both eliminate other conceptions of order in order to establish a single one. The decision does this through the representational marginalization of an alternative conception of sovereignty and the designation of that alternative as an enemy. The land appropriation carries out a similar establishment of order by displacing or subjugating another group of people with a different form of order.

4 Establishing a *Nomos* of the Earth: Vitoria and Schmitt

When Schmitt turns to international law, he still holds onto the distinction between sovereignty and law. In *The* Nomos *of the Earth*, Schmitt contrasts international law as treaty law between sovereign powers with a *nomos* of the earth, which establishes the basic framework for world order. As in his discussions of state sovereignty, Schmitt links *nomos* at the global level to sovereignty and defines it as the foundational aspect of order, as opposed to law, which derives its legitimacy from an existing *nomos*. Consequently, 'there are two different types of land-appropriations: those that proceed within a given order of international law, which readily receive the recognition of other peoples, and others, which uproot an existing spatial order and establish a new *nomos* of the whole spatial sphere of neighboring peoples'.[23] The *nomos* of the earth is established only in those instances of land appropriation that function like a decision on the state of exception, in which the land appropriation creates new rules for order not just within domestic politics but on the international level as well.

On this international level, Schmitt faces the problem that there is no global sovereign, even if there is still a kind of order that grounds international law. International law, in contrast to domestic law, seems to lack the direct relationship to sovereignty that would be able to create both an enforcement mechanism and a political-theological basis for law's legitimacy. Only a world state would be able to create a world-spanning law, in which case it would no longer be international law, but a form of domestic law. Yet, there also seems to be a kind of order that structures international relationships outside of the rules of treaty law. For Schmitt, the *nomos* of the earth arises directly out of power relationships and the accompanying kinds of behavioral restrictions that those power relationships imply and enforce. The challenge for Schmitt

23 Schmitt, *The* Nomos *of the Earth*, 82.

is to imagine how this ordering of international relations within a particular *nomos* of the earth could establish itself without a global sovereign.

Schmitt addresses this problem by analyzing the establishment of the *nomos* of the earth as another example of the way in which an empire constructs a *nomos* within its part of the world, even when it allows different forms of sovereignty to exist within its spatial area. He demonstrates this relationship in his discussion of the transition from the *respublica Christiana* to the *jus publicum Europaeum* as the two different *nomoi* that structure global relations in the early modern period. The *respublica Christiana* already constituted an ordering of international relations within the space of Latin Europe, even though that space was not dominated by a single sovereign and the state form had not yet fully developed. This *nomos* within the space of Europe was structured by medieval Christianity, which established the theological and institutional arrangements that defined the accepted limits on behavior within that order.

As he argues, Europe's initial colonization of the Americas was carried out as an expansion of this *nomos* of the *respublica Christiana*, and Francisco de Vitoria was crucial for the expansion of the terms of this *nomos* from its development within the space of Europe to the application in the Americas. Schmitt's account of Vitoria's significance as the intellectual architect of the expansion of the *respublica Christiana* across the world as a basis for international relations is opposed to an alternative account by James Scott Brown, who describes Vitoria as the founder of an international law that would transcend sovereignty.[24] In this alternative conception, a universally valid international law establishes a set of rules that should be followed by all of humanity. Such a conception of international law would not necessarily have to replace state sovereignty but could provide a universal moral basis for constraints on state behavior. The question, though, is whether such an understanding of international law is based on a universally valid law of humanity or whether it is based on a specific form of sovereignty that establishes and enforces the international law framework, not as a universally valid set of rules, but as the rules that are being enforced by a dominant sovereign power. The choice between these two options hinges on whether law or sovereignty is primary. Is sover-

24 James Scott Brown, *The Spanish Origin of International Law. Francisco De Vitoria and the Law of Nations* (Oxford: Clarendon Press 1934) 11a, 46. Joshua Smeltzer, 'On the Use and Abuse of Francisco de Vitoria: James Brown Scott and Carl Schmitt'. *Journal of the History of International Law* 20 (2018), 345–372, 351–355. José María Beneyto, 'Camilo Barcia Trelles on Francisco de Vitoria: At the Crossroads of Carl Schmitt's Grossraum and James Brown Scott's "Modern International Law"'. *The European Journal of International Law* 31.4 (2021), 1477–1492, 1487–1492.

eignty based on and legitimated by an adherence to law or is law itself an outgrowth of a particular form of sovereignty? If sovereignty were to be dependent on lawfulness, then one might argue that an offender against international law forfeits the claim to sovereignty based on the unlawfulness of actions according to international law. If on the other hand, law is based on sovereignty, such an offender's sovereignty can be the basis of that offender's own understanding of law, and the offense would be an attempt to establish a particular form of sovereignty as the definer of its own kind of law. The difference between these two understandings leads to two strategies, one legal and one political, for maintaining international order.

The idea of the primacy of law is based on a theory of natural law that originated with Thomas Aquinas and was developed by Francisco de Vitoria into early reflections on international justice. The fundamental premise is that self-preservation is a universally recognized right that can be used as the conceptual basis for establishing what is just and unjust. Vitoria invokes the idea of 'natural and divine law' based on a principle of self-preservation that would transcend the cultural differences between Christian and non-Christian peoples in order to ground a universal understanding of justice.

While he attempts to remain on a theoretical level in his analysis, the issue that haunts Vitoria's analysis is the fact of the military and technological superiority of the Spanish, who had the power to enforce their political will against the Native Americans. Accordingly, Schmitt argues that Vitoria's ideas on international law must be understood within a political framework in which sovereignty becomes a key issue. Even if Vitoria argues for the fundamental legitimacy of the sovereignty of Native American peoples, this legitimacy is not enough to guarantee their sovereignty because sovereignty will also depend on the structure of power relations.

Vitoria himself addresses this issue of the relationship between law and sovereignty in his discussion of capital punishment, whose legitimacy depends upon a higher authority than individual humans. In his 1528 'On Civil Power', Vitoria describes capital punishment as an issue that goes beyond the authority of human laws and can only be justified based on divine and natural law. He first lays out the natural law argument by referring to the 'power and right of self-defence by natural law' and then explains that this right can extend to the commonwealth as a whole. Just as individuals have the right to sacrifice a limb for survival, a commonwealth has the right to sacrifice some of its members in order to assure the survival of the whole. 'Individuals may even risk the loss of a limb if this is necessary to the safety of the rest of the body; and there is no reason why the commonwealth should not have the same power to compel and coerce its members as if they were its limbs for the utility and safety of the common good'.[25] Though Vitoria tries to set up an analogy between the individual's and the commonwealth's right of self-defense, the 'common good' that he invokes establishes a kind of authority that goes beyond the rights of any individual. The individual can be treated like a limb to be cut off to preserve the commonwealth as awhole. Capital punishment presumes that this commonwealth as a whole is the greater entity that transcends the needs of any individual.

Vitoria further elaborates on this transcendent quality of the commonwealth in his description of the way in which it is based on divine law as well as natural law. He highlights two ways in which divine law provides a necessary transcendent basis for capital punishment. In the first place, 'it is prohibited by divine law to kill a fellow man, as clearly stated in the Ten Commandments'.[26] The prohibition against murder is itself part of divine law and therefore cannot be abrogated simply by positive law, that is, by laws created based only on human authority. The law against murder must be an absolute one in order to avoid the possibility that humans might pass laws that would allow murder in some form. 'Therefore the authority to carry out capital punishment must depend on divine law. But the commonwealth has the authority to execute a man, as established by usage and custom; therefore it has the authority by divine law'.[27] But if the law prohibiting murder is itself divine, then capital punishment also cannot be justified by a human law. Because divine law prohibits murder, Vitoria sees the lifting of this prohibition in capital punishment as an indication, not that the commonwealth lacks the authority to carry out executions, but that the commonwealth's authority is not like typical human authority and has its ultimate justification in a divine law that is abrogating itself.

But what does it mean for divine law to abrogate itself? He explains divine law by referring back to the natural law idea that a situation in which the very existence of the commonwealth is threatened constitutes an exceptional case in which a transcendent and absolute law comes into play. It is never lawful for a private individual to kill another 'because a private individual cannot lawfully kill another even if the latter is guilty of a crime'.[28] Because the prohibition on killing is absolute, capital punishment can only be lawful for those cases in which there is divine legitimation. Such situations create a distinction

25 Francisco de Vitoria, *Political Writings*, Anthony Pagden and Jeremy Lawrance (eds.) (Cambridge, UK: Cambridge University Press 1991) 11.

26 Vitoria, *Political Writings*, 11.

27 Vitoria, *Political Writings*, 11.

28 Vitoria, *Political Writings*, 12.

between the normal positive laws of a commonwealth, which cannot justify capital punishment, and the transcendent laws that guarantee the existence of the commonwealth and are grounded in divine and natural law: 'the commonwealth has an authority to take a man's life which the private man does not have, and this right cannot be founded in positive law, and must therefore depend on divine and natural law'.[29] The issue of capital punishment, as a special case that can only be justified through the invocation of such absolute law, brings to the fore a distinction between positive law on the one hand and divine and natural law on the other hand. This distinction makes capital punishment into a limit case, in which its application goes beyond the authority of human laws and provides the link in the legal system on the one hand to an absolute law for humanity and on the other hand to a kind of activity that resembles war more than punishment, in which the commonwealth's use of force is not so much an act of law as a willful form of self-defense.

When the divine law against murder is suspended in order to defend the commonwealth, divine law itself becomes violent and willful. Yet, because Vitoria still maintains that this moment is an expression of natural and divine law, the natural and divine law becomes a form of sovereignty because the violence of capital punishment must be justified based on something prior to its positive laws.

> Furthermore, positive law derives from the commonwealth, therefore the existence of the commonwealth itself and of its power to make laws must precede the existence of positive laws; consequently, it may be deduced that this legislative power itself exists in the commonwealth by divine and natural law.[30]

Vitoria sets up here a distinction between two levels of law. On the one hand, there are positive laws that are created by humans within a commonwealth. On the other hand, there is a divine and natural law that grounds the commonwealth's existence and power. Positive laws can only come into being on the basis of the divine and natural law. Consequently, to the extent that capital punishment occurs, it cannot be a positive law. It is only justified in those cases in which its application is required in order to guarantee 'the existence of the commonwealth itself and of its power'.[31] Vitoria recognizes this foundational power of the commonwealth, expressed in capital punishment, as categoric-

29 Vitoria, *Political Writings*, 12.
30 Vitoria, *Political Writings*, 12.
31 Vitoria, *Political Writings*, 12.

ally different from the normal legislative power. In differentiating between the positive laws of a commonwealth and the source of this commonwealth's existence in divine and natural law, Vitoria insists that the authority for capital punishment must transcend both the simple will of its inhabitants and their adherence to the natural and divine law prohibiting murder. There must be some transcendent sovereign authority that ultimately provides the justification both for the existence of the commonwealth as well as for its ability to carry out capital punishment.

Capital punishment is therefore a unique phenomenon that runs directly to the foundational core of a commonwealth and its very existence. Moreover, it is the point at which the absolute ground of the commonwealth makes itself apparent, separating itself out from the positive laws that make up the everyday fabric of the commonwealth but that are ultimately subordinate to the absolute law that guarantees the existence and authority of the commonwealth as a whole. The question of capital punishment is consequently the question of sovereignty as the power and authority that grounds the existence of the commonwealth.

In recognizing a distinction between the positive laws of a commonwealth and the principle of communal self-preservation that grounds its sovereignty, Vitoria is establishing the priority of sovereignty over law. This sovereignty seems to be arbitrary to the extent that the existence or disappearance of a commonwealth is not guaranteed but is ultimately a consequence of the political contingencies that threaten its survival. At the same time, Vitoria seeks to make this sovereignty of the commonwealth into the basis of a universal principle to the extent that self-preservation of the commonwealth is based in natural and divine law and takes priority over the self-preservation of the individual. As a higher law, natural and divine law can provide the basis for an international law for all of humanity that is based on a natural right of self-preservation. But the slippage between the self-preservation of the commonwealth and the self-preservation of the individual means that the former is not neutral but involves the defense of the particular form of order and sovereignty that the commonwealth represents. In appealing to natural and divine law, Vitoria must turn it into a mode of sovereignty, thereby undermining its status as a universal law.

The difficulty is that the focus on self-preservation of the commonwealth that lies at the basis of this natural and divine law is not just a commitment to the self-preservation of the commonwealth but to the existing order of sovereignty within which the commonwealth exists. If the commonwealth's sovereignty is based on natural and divine order, it may be that this order itself is seeking to preserve itself against alternative justifications of sovereignty. In fact, the linking of sovereignty with natural and divine law must be seen here as a concession to thinkers such as John Wycliffe and Martin Luther, who treat law, not as natural, but as a consequence of God's grace. For Luther, law is much more a product of the will, divine will in the form of God's grace and human will in the form of an act of faith.[32] This conception leads to a practice in which divine and human will can be the only legitimations for law, overriding the notion of a natural law that would be independent of the will. In this conception, the global order is not guaranteed by a natural law of self-preservation that supersedes all existing forms of sovereignty. Instead, the natural law of self-preservation becomes itself subordinate to the idea of the self-preservation of the commonwealth, whose self-preservation is not just about material existence but the preservation of a particular system of order and thus of sovereignty.

In pointing to the ways in which Vitoria is not totally even-handed in his consideration of the relationship between European colonizers and other peoples, Schmitt indicates the ways in which Vitoria's principles of international relations are not a form of universal international law but of the expansion of the *respublica Christiana*, whose claims of universality are belied by the missionary project. Instead of conforming to a rule of self-preservation of individuals, Vitoria maintains the primacy of the project of preserving and expanding Christianity. His attempt to use both arguments leads to a basic contradiction between an idea of a universal natural law and the simultaneous desire to expand the sway of Christianity. By insisting on the universality of natural and divine law, Vitoria seeks to establish an argument for the possibility that both Native Americans and heretics can hold dominion and be sovereign, since they would be participating in the same idea of self-preservation as all others. For Vitoria, the proper reaction to barbarians and heretics would not be to deny their ability to have sovereignty but to affirm that this sovereignty is also grounded in natural and divine law, even if they do not recognize it as such. Yet, this affirmation of the *possibility* of their own sovereignty does not equate to an affirmation of their sovereignty in fact. As a consequence, the strategy that Vitoria takes up for both barbarians and heretics is to persuade them to turn to Catholicism as the true manifestation of natural and divine law.

This is the critique that Carl Schmitt makes of Vitoria's supposedly neutral notion of international law. As Schmitt argues, Vitoria's conception, retaining

32 See David Pan, 'The Transformation of Sovereignty from the Reformation to World War I', in Kai Evers and David Pan (eds.), *Europe and the World. World War I as Crisis of Universalism* (Candor, NY: Telos 2018) 37–62, 44–52.

the medieval idea of a *respublica Christiana*, maintains the legitimacy of a Christian missionary project as the justification for war against non-Christian peoples. In this sense, as Schmitt writes, 'the *papal missionary mandate* was the legal foundation of the *conquista*', also for Vitoria.[33] Though Vitoria attempted to develop an international law that emphasized the reciprocity of rights between Christians and non-Christians in the principle of self-preservation as the basis of natural law, the principle of sovereignty that Vitoria invokes is not in fact neutral in its affirmation of natural and divine law. Vitoria still prioritizes the Christian missionary mandate, and his primary argument justifying the Spanish conquest of the Native Americans hinges on the Christian right to trade and proselytize across the entire world.[34] Yet, these rights are not universal and reciprocal, and Schmitt points out that Vitoria would not have recognized an equal right of the Native Americans to proselytize for their own religions in Spain.[35] This lack of reciprocity provides for Schmitt the key to understanding the type of international order that Vitoria imagined, in which the basis of international order lay in the Catholic Church and its missionary goals: 'the Spanish Conquista was an extension of the concepts of the spatial order of the *respublica Christiana* of the Middle Ages'.[36] For Schmitt, the notion of sovereignty that underlies international law cannot be a universal conception but must ultimately arise out of a specific conception of order, a *nomos*, understood not as law but as a form of sovereignty and thus as an outgrowth of the power relations that allow for land appropriation and the way in which sovereignty is managed globally.

5 The Contemporary *Nomos* of the Earth

The establishment of sovereignty is for Schmitt simultaneously an ordering of domestic space and an attempt to gain recognition within an international space. While the decision on the state of exception determines the basis for order domestically, that same decision must also establish the legitimacy of that form of sovereignty in an external space of international relations.[37] The sovereign must on the one hand contend with alternative conceptions of order in the domestic space and on the other hand establish the legitimacy

33 Schmitt, *The* Nomos *of the Earth*, 111.
34 Vitoria, *Political Writings*, 278–286.
35 Schmitt, *The* Nomos *of the Earth*, 113.
36 Schmitt, *The* Nomos *of the Earth*, 113.
37 Zarmanian, 'Carl Schmitt and the Problem of Legal Order', 59.

of a specific form of sovereignty for other actors within the international space. The character of that space will always be an issue with every establishment of sovereignty as a land appropriation.

Since the *nomos* of the earth will be affected by every establishment of sovereignty in a domestic space, a key aspect of a global *nomos* would be its ability to enforce a particular conception of sovereignty that would not be a threat to the existing international order. Zarmanian characterizes the concern for the organization of international space as linked to an attempt to prevent a descent into a state of nature of unlimited conflict by maintaining an equilibrium between powers that supports the entire system.[38] For him, the solution to this problem that Schmitt identifies in the *jus publicum Europaeum* is that the idea of just war (*bellum justum*) was replaced with the idea of just enemy (*justus hostis*). Schmitt sees here a rationalization of war in which there is no longer a need to eradicate the enemy, but in which the enemy is defined as a similarly organized political entity, a state, against which a war may be fought that follows the rules of war.

> Faced with the problem of these European civil wars, the juridical founders of modern interstate international law – Ayala, Gentili, and Zouch – divorced the question of *bellum justum* proper from that of *justa causa belli*, and made war into a mutual relation between sovereign states in which *justi et aequales hostes* [just and equal enemies] confronted each other indiscriminately.[39]

Replacing the confessional civil wars with a limited concept of war between states reduced the severity of war between European states.

However, just as essential to the *jus publicum Europaeum* was that there was a corresponding lack of recognition of the rights of non-state combatants in the colonial areas, which is to say all peoples outside of Europe, for which the laws of war did not hold. Consequently, the *jus publicum Europaeum* limited war within Europe but allowed unlimited war elsewhere. The shift to the *jus publicum Europaeum* does not replace Christian theology with a secular and non-theological conception of order but rather established a notion of sovereignty based on a European civilizational project which, in establishing a

38 Zarmanian, 'Carl Schmitt and the Problem of Legal Order', 59–62.

39 Schmitt, *The* Nomos *of the Earth*, 124.

seemingly neutral conception of sovereign states, pursued a colonialist project in which non-European peoples could not have sovereign states.[40]

The difficulty in seeking to reestablish the kind of equilibrium of the Westphalian system of nation-states is that its ability to limit warfare by allowing for just enemies was predicated on a European agreement about the permitted forms of political order. The issue is not just about limiting the scope of conflict in the international sphere through an equilibrium between enemies. Rather, the establishment of a *nomos* of the earth involves the definition of the particular types of order that can participate as sovereign entities. The first assumption of the *jus publicum Europaeum* was that there was a line to be drawn between Europe and the rest of the world. While wars within Europe were limited in nature, wars beyond Europe could involve annihilation of the enemy. This distinction was not simply a colonialist one between Europe and the rest of the world. Rather, the basis of the distinction was a particular permitted character of sovereignty within the European dynastic system. One could in fact describe the *jus publicum Europaeum* as a collective defense of absolutist states against all attempts to overthrow this system. This system encompassed both the dynastic monarchies that guaranteed domestic order and a corresponding set of international relationships between the European monarchies. The enemies of this system, against whom war could become total, included both those peoples outside of Europe, who were organized differently than the European monarchies, and also those forces within Europe who sought to undermine the dynastic system, with Napoleon and the French Republic as the first primary examples of this latter possibility. Though Schmitt indicates in *The* Nomos *of the Earth* that the *jus publicum Europaeum* lasted until World War I, he revises this pronouncement in *Theory of the Partisan*, indicating that the Napoleonic Wars were an interruption of the *jus publicum Europaeum* that threatened to dissolve it by introducing a new basis of sovereignty for domestic and international politics.[41]

If liberal internationalism is the target of Schmitt's critique in *The Concept of the Political* and *The* Nomos *of the Earth*, by the time of *Theory of the Partisan*, Schmitt argues that the move toward absolute enemies, signaled during the Napoleonic wars, was a world-wide phenomenon that was not limited to liberal internationalism but also included actors such as Lenin and Mao.[42]

---

40 Andreas Kalyvas, 'Carl Schmitt's Postcolonial Imagination'. *Constellations* 25 (2018), 35–53, 36–40.

41 Carl Schmitt, *Theory of the Partisan: Intermediate Commentary on the Concept of the Political*, trans. G. L. Ulmen (New York: Telos 2007) 9, note 10.

42 Schmitt, *Theory of the Partisan*, 49–61.

In fact, any political movement, including the Nazis (about whom Schmitt remained silent in *The* Nomos *of the Earth*), that made a claim to universal validity could be the basis of the undermining of the limited warfare of the *jus publicum Europaeum*, which itself from this perspective takes on the character of a universalist system that is based on the hegemony of a particular political form of the absolutist state that suppresses all other ones.

From this perspective, there is no escape from absolute enmity, neither through recourse to an international law that would claim to eliminate enmity as such nor through the re-establishment of the *jus publicum Europaeum* and its limited wars. Because this latter system was predicated on total wars outside of Europe that served to maintain the dynastic system against alternative political conceptions for organizing international politics, absolute enmity was in fact never eliminated. It remained as the type of war that was waged when the political-theological foundations for the *nomos* of the earth were seen to be threatened. This was the case with the collective European war against Napoleon as well as the twentieth-century wars against Germany, Italy, and Japan. In all of these cases, the issue was not simply an equilibrium of power but the character of the sovereignty that each enemy represented. If in the nineteenth century the absolutist states were unified in opposing republican nationalism, by the twentieth century there was a unified opposition to the fascism of Germany, Italy, and Japan that threatened a nation-state system based on popular sovereignty. The end of the war established a new basis for the *nomos* of the earth, and the corollary to the allied victory in World War II was consequently the dismantling of the colonial empires that also undermined the principle of popular sovereignty.

Schmitt's interpretation of Vitoria led him to a choice in how to conceive of a contemporary *nomos* of the earth. He could embrace Vitoria's solution, which is to establish rules of international relations that have a universal character but in fact are structured by a particular theological tradition and its conception of order. Yet, Schmitt rejects this conception to the extent that he thought that the US did not act as a guarantor of a nation-state system but rather as a kind of missionary in pursuit of the expansion of liberal democracy. In this view of the US role in international relations, the goal is not simply to maintain the definitions of political sovereignty that ground a nation-state ordering of global relations but to expand liberal democracy as a particular political form that claims universal status. Schmitt criticizes such a structure in his approach to the post-1945 international order because its supposed grounding in a universal principle of non-aggression in fact obscured the underlying sovereignty of US imperialism that sought to universalize liberal democracy. In order to avoid such a form of imperialism, Schmitt imagines, by contrast, a world that might be split up into separate regional blocks (*Grossraum*), each with its hegemon that would establish the political theological basis for order in its own region. The *Grossraum* view of the *nomos* of the earth has become the basis upon which China and Russia seek to establish their own regional hegemony in order to defend their existing state systems. Such a new *nomos* of the earth would break down state boundaries in order to allow great powers to maintain control over neighboring states. Such a development would mean the establishment of a new *nomos* in which the nation-state would no longer be the primary unit of sovereignty but in which each regional hegemon would be the locus of sovereignty in a long-term conflict with other regional powers.

Yet, such a system would not in fact create an equilibrium of enemies because the prerequisite for such an equilibrium would be a basic agreement about the character of sovereignty. Because each regional block is based on its own *nomos* and vision of sovereignty that essentially excludes the others, the *Grossraum* model would institutionalize a permanent situation of absolute enmity. We already see this dynamic unfolding because China, Russia, Iran, and North Korea all see their model of sovereignty as fundamentally threatened by the liberal democratic nation-states that surround them. A proper response would not be to try and establish liberal democracy as such, but to recognize that the key to the current system is the maintenance of the nation-state as the primary unit of sovereignty. The attempt to undermine the nation-state order to establish regional blocs would establish a new global *nomos* that would reject the idea of popular sovereignty that is linked to the nation-state. In order to preserve the nation-state order, though, it is not necessary to deny its implicit political theology but rather to recognize the kind of *nomos* of the earth it imagines in order to argue for the ability of this *nomos* to distribute cultural difference across nation-states, precisely because such a system avoids an endless war between civilizational states, each of which seeks to establish its own form of sovereignty across the world.

The growing importance of ideology as the basis of sovereignty eventually establishes itself in the nation-state as a form of sovereignty that is grounded in the popular will yet allows for the existence of other states based on alternative ideological traditions. The difficulty is that the first nation-states were more than nation-states but in fact nation-empires – France, England, Germany – which denied nation-state status to other peoples.[43] It is only since the end of the Cold War that a truly global nation-state order has been established. While this order is grounded in the sovereignty of the US and its allies, it

43 Pan, 'The Transformation of Sovereignty', 62.

does not necessarily fall into the dynamic of a liberal internationalist creation of enemies of humanity that Schmitt criticizes. Rather, if the nation-state order is based on a particular form of sovereignty, its defense will depend, not on appeals to international law, but on the legitimacy of its political structuring of the *nomos* of the earth, as determined by the political resolution of international conflicts.

One of Carl Schmitt's key theses is that sovereignty itself can establish a framework for order that becomes the basis for law. Schmitt's analysis offers the possibility that forms of order might establish themselves out of conflicts that result in a political agreement about the limits of sovereignty. Today, that would amount to affirming the nation-state basis of international politics with many countries collectively enforcing this system. The collective project would be to defend a Westphalian order in which individual nation-states could be distinctive in their conceptions of sovereignty, while the entire order is dominated by rules regarding the limits of state sovereignty, both domestically and in relations with other states. Such a defense cannot be carried out through the mechanisms of international law but only through a focus by sovereign states on the customs that would structure the use of state power to maintain the global system of state sovereignty. The goal would be to allow for differences between forms of order within each state while at the same time enforcing with sovereign power the habits that would prevent the emergence of absolute enmity in international relations.

Bibliography

Arendt, Hannah. *On Violence* (San Diego: Harcourt Brace Jovanovich 1969).

Beneyto, José María. 'Camilo Barcia Trelles on Francisco de Vitoria: At the Crossroads of Carl Schmitt's Grossraum and James Brown Scott's "Modern International Law"'. *The European Journal of International Law* 31.4 (2021), 1477–1492.

Benhabib, Seyla. 'Carl Schmitt's Critique of Kant: Sovereignty and International Law'. *Political Theory* 40.6 (2012), 688–713.

Brown, James Scott. *The Spanish Origin of International Law. Francisco De Vitoria and the Law of Nations* (Oxford: Clarendon Press 1934).

Kalyvas, Andreas. 'Carl Schmitt's Postcolonial Imagination'. *Constellations* 25 (2018), 35–53.

Koskenniemi, Martti. *The Gentle Civilizer of Nations: The Rise and Fall of International Law 1870–1960* (Cambridge: University of Cambridge Press 2001).

Loughlin, Martin. 'Politonomy', in Jens Meierhenrich and Oliver Simons (eds.), *The Oxford Handbook of Carl Schmitt* (New York: Oxford University Press 2016), 570–591.

Odysseos, Louiza. 'Crossing the Line? Carl Schmitt on the "Spaceless Universalism" of Cosmopolitanism and the War on Terror', in Louiza Odysseos and Fabio Petito (eds.), *The International Political Thought of Carl Schmitt: Terror, Liberal War and the Crisis of Global Order* (London: Routledge 2007) 124–143.

Pan, David. 'Against Biopolitics: Walter Benjamin, Carl Schmitt, and Giorgio Agamben on Political Sovereignty and Symbolic Order'. *The German Quarterly* 82.1 (Winter 2009), 42–62.

Pan, David. 'Carl Schmitt on Culture and Violence in the Political Decision'. *Telos* 142 (Spring 2008), 49–72.

Pan, David. 'The Transformation of Sovereignty from the Reformation to World War I', in Kai Evers and David Pan (eds.), *Europe and the World. World War I as Crisis of Universalism* (Candor, NY: Telos 2018) 37–62.

Schmitt, Carl. *Dictatorship. From the Origin of the Modern Concept of Sovereignty to Proletarian Class Struggle*, trans. Michael Hoelzl and Graham Ward (Cambridge, UK: Polity 2014).

Schmitt, Carl. *Political Theology. Four Chapters on the Concept of Sovereignty*, trans. George Schwab (Chicago: University of Chicago Press 2005).

Schmitt, Carl. *The Concept of the Political*, trans. George Schwab (Chicago: University of Chicago Press 2007).

Schmitt, Carl. *The* Nomos *of the Earth in the International Law of the* Jus Publicum Europaeum, trans. G. L. Ulmen (New York: Telos 2003).

Schmitt, Carl. *Theory of the Partisan: Intermediate Commentary on the Concept of the Political*, trans. G. L. Ulmen (New York: Telos 2007).

Smeltzer, Joshua. 'On the Use and Abuse of Francisco de Vitoria: James Brown Scott and Carl Schmitt'. *Journal of the History of International Law* 20 (2018), 345–372.

Vitoria, Francisco de. *Political Writings*, Anthony Pagden and Jeremy Lawrance (eds.) (Cambridge, UK: Cambridge University Press 1991).

Zarmanian, Thalin. 'Carl Schmitt and the Problem of Legal Order: From Domestic to International'. *Leiden Journal of International Law* 19 (2006), 41–67.

CHAPTER 8

Vitoria on International Law and the Schmittian Critique of the Liberal Order

Leonor Durão Barroso and André Azevedo Alves

1 Introduction: Vitoria's International Thought

From the standpoint of a natural rights-based intellectual mindset, particularly indebted to Thomas Aquinas, the Iberian scholastics of the sixteenth and seventeenth centuries sought to answer pressing ethical, theological, economic, social, and political issues.

One of the main features that characterizes their context and that, therefore, greatly contributed to a scholastic revival was the discovery, by the Europeans, of the American continent. New questions emerged and the masters, especially in the universities, were called upon to elaborate on them.

The impact of such events on the development of international law and international relations has been frequently acknowledged,[1] with the Dominican friar Francisco de Vitoria acquiring a prominent role in the process.

The moral issues brought about by the colonization of America are made clear, for instance, in 1511, before the coronation of Charles V, in the famous condemnation, by the Dominican António de Montesinos, of the harms committed against the native Americans by the *encomenderos* during the process of colonization. In the work *The Salamanca School*, André Azevedo Alves and José Manuel Moreira seek to understand the origins of the polemics regarding the

1 See, for instance, André Azevedo Alves, José Manuel Moreira, *The Salamanca School* (New York: Bloomsbury 2013) 59–65; Ernest Nys (1912), *Le Droit International, Les Principes, Les Théories, Les Faits*, Faits, Volume 1 (Paris: Marcel Rivière 1912) 16–17; Luciano Pereña, 'Estudio Preliminar: Génesis Suareciana del *Ius Gentium*', in Francisco Suárez, *De Legibus* (*II, 13–20*), *De Iure Gentium*, ed. L. Pereña, et al. (Madrid: Consejo Superior de Investigaciones Científicas 1973) LXVII; Teófilo Urdánoz, 'Síntesis Teológico-Jurídica de la Doctrina de Vitoria', in Francisco de Vitoria, *Relectio de Indis o Libertad de los Indios*, ed. Luciano Pereña, J. M. Perez Prendes (Madrid: Consejo Superior de Investigaciones Científicas 1967) LVIII; Malcolm N. Shaw, *International Law* (Cambridge: Cambridge University Press 2014) 16; and Evan Luard (ed.), *Basic Texts in International Relations* (New York: St. Martin's Press 1997) 143–149. On the limits of ascribing the paternity of international law to the late scholastics, see Heinrich A. Rommen, *Die Staatslehre des Franz Suarez S.J.* (New York: Arno Press 1979) 270.

 | DOI:10.1163/9789004757448_009

New World by going back to Montesinos' 'revolutionary sermon in Hispaniola'.[2] It is noted that this condemnation by Montesinos was 'decisive for the reconsideration of the entire colonization process'. In fact, its political impact was such that it prompted the assemblage of the *Junta de Burgos*, followed by the promulgation of the Laws of Burgos, which Lewis Hanke refers to as 'the first detailed regulations to govern relations between Indians and Spaniards'.[3] These dealt with questions regarding the treatment of native Americans by the *encomenderos*, but did not deal with the ethical issue of the conquest itself, as António García y García explains.[4] What ensued was a struggle for justice[5] and, we would now say, for the dignity of the indigenous peoples. Some would even argue that this dispute can be seen as a forerunner of human rights theories.[6]

Francisco de Vitoria will deal with this subject in his *relectiones De Indis* from a theological, moral, and legal point of view. It is due to his treatment of the subject that Vitoria's contribution to international law is broadly recognized.

Notwithstanding this broad recognition, Vitoria's international thought has been interpreted in different ways. Paolo Amorosa points to three contrasting interpretative lines: Vitoria as providing a justification for the conquest; Vitoria as a proponent of universal rights in a 'brave humanitarian stance'; and a third way that rejects readings that seek to interpret Vitoria in light of current concerns, which Amorosa attributes to Koskenniemi.[7] Apart from few exceptions, most commentators do not fit clearly in one, but recognize traces of truth in different accounts.

Carl Schmitt, who would arguably fit into the first of these lines, is one of the authors unequivocally recognizing Vitoria's role in international thought,

---

2 For an account of the impact of this sermon, with a particular focus on its reception in Bartolomé de Las Casas, see Alves, Moreira, *The Salamanca School* 87–90.

3 Lewis Hanke, *All Mankind is One: A Study of the Disputation between Bartolomé de Las Casas and Juan Ginés de Sepúlveda in 1550 on the Intellectual and Religious Capacity of the American Indians* (DeKalb, IL: Northern Illinois University Press 1974) 8.

4 Antonio García y García, 'El Sentido de las Primeras Denuncias', in Demetrio Ramos, et al. (eds.), *Francisco de Vitoria y la Escuela de Salamanca, La Ética en la Conquista de América* (Madrid: Consejo Superior de Investigaciones Científicas 1984) 72. And although the laws resulting from Burgos did not legally ban the enslavement of the Indians, they did aim at protecting them from the inhumane treatment that often came with it: see Oreste Popescu, *Studies in the History of Latin American Economic Thought* (New York: Routledge 1997) 85–86.

5 See Lewis Hanke, *The Spanish Struggle for Justice in the Conquest of America* (Boston, Toronto: Little, Brown and Company 1965).

6 See Alves, Moreira, *The Salamanca School* 89.

7 Paolo Amorosa, *Rewriting the History of the Law of Nations: How James Brown Scott made Francisco de Vitoria the Founder of International Law* (New York: Oxford University Press, 2019) 2.

as shall be made clear later in this chapter. In fact, Vitoria's treatment of the *ius gentium* is particularly relevant to our study because the theme of the discovery of the New World and the reflections it generates regarding the international order is precisely what brings together the sixteenth-century Spanish theologian and the twentieth-century German jurist.

On the other hand, James Brown Scott, a scholar of international law from the United States, and a contemporary of Carl Schmitt, who was Director of the Division of International Law of the Carnegie Endowment for International Peace, has been credited with contributing decisively to Vitoria's positioning as the founder of international law, while associating the Dominican with his own liberal internationalist project.

These contrasting views will be considered in subsequent sections of this chapter. We must now turn first to Vitoria to understand the extent to which he may be considered to have proposed universally applicable principles in his international thought.

In the previously mentioned *relectiones*, Vitoria sets out to argue for the idea that native Americans were subjects of rights, capable of establishing self-governing communities and acquiring private property. Throughout the first *relectio De Indis,*[8] Vitoria champions the equal dignity of Christians and Indians, using reciprocal principles and arguments that will enable his reader to interpret him not only as a champion of the rights of the Indians, but of the rights of every human being.[9]

This reading is further corroborated by considering the contrast between Vitoria's doctrines and those – in Vitoria's view, wrong doctrines – of other thinkers of the time.[10]

The ability of the Indians to exercise dominion is evident, for Vitoria, first of all through empirical evidence. He states that '(...) before the arrival of the Spanish, [the Indians] were in a state of peaceful possession of goods, both publicly and privately'.[11] Natural justice requires that they cannot be deprived

8 Except otherwise stated, all references to and quotations from Vitoria's *relectiones* will be from Teófilo Urdánoz (ed.), *Obras de Francisco de Vitoria, Relecciones Teológicas* (Madrid: Biblioteca de Autores Cristianos 1960).

9 The Dominican theologian Teófilo Urdánoz reads him as such: '[La pregunta de Vitoria en la relección De Indis] equivale a plantear la cuestión de la capacidad jurídica de los indígenas y de todos los hombres en general'. Urdánoz, 'Síntesis Teológico-Jurídica de la Doctrina de Vitoria', LXVII.

10 Most notably, Juan Ginés de Sepúlveda, arguing for the crown, used the distinction, made by Aristotle, between Greeks and natural slaves to account for the Spanish dominion over the Indians.

11 '(...) antequam hispani ad illos venissent illi erant in pacifica possessione rerum, et publice et privatim'. Vitoria, *De Indis* 666. See also Vitoria, *De Indis* 651.

of their goods without a just title for such appropriation, as they had true and legitimate dominion, *sicut christiani*: '(...) the barbarians undoubtedly had a dominion, either public or private, as true as that of Christians'.[12] They had it in the same measure and by the same right as the Christians.

But Vitoria will then look for the legitimacy of his statement, as he grounds dominion on the idea of the *imago Dei*. Being the image of God inevitably common to all human beings by nature, Vitoria does not of course call the Indians sons of God, but the fact that they are the image of God is irrevocable and inalienable.

Thus sin, even mortal sin, cannot hinder civil dominion because man's nature is not destroyed when man parts from God through sin. Vitoria does not mistake mortal sin and infidelity for political disobedience, instead claiming that the political dominion stems from man being made in the image of God and in no way depends upon baptism: 'Dominion is grounded in the image of God. Now man is by nature the image of God (...). Therefore, he does not lose it due to mortal sin'.[13] We are here prompted to recall Aquinas, Vitoria's fellow Dominican, and one of the great authorities on which his thought is grounded. Already for the Angelic Doctor, the absence of faith did not change political power that rests upon natural law.

Dominion thus finds its root in the very nature of men. If we distinguish, as Suárez goes on to do,[14] in his idea of a *status naturae*, the supernatural from the natural, and hypothetically look at nature alone, apart from sin or grace, what we end up with is the separation between sin and grace, on the one hand, and the naturally political life on the other. *Infidelitas*, Vitoria argues, is not an obstacle to true dominion.

If we fast forward a few centuries, to contemporaneity, we may begin to witness the relevance of this conception of man as *imago Dei* to the social sphere besides the Christian-centred world. In fact, this concept is at the core of the Social Doctrine of the Church's personalist principle,[15] which reaffirms the equal dignity of every human being. This principle is, therefore, applicable regardless of faith, culture, or the use of reason.

---

12 '(...) sine dubio barbari erant et publice et privatim ita veri domini sicut christiani'. Vitoria (1960), *De Indis* 665.

13 'Dominium fundatur in imagine Dei. Sed homo est imago Dei per naturam (...). Ergo non perditur per peccatum mortale'. Vitoria, *De Indis* 654.

14 See, for instance, Francisco Suárez, *De Legibus* III, I, 1, in Francisco Suárez, *Tractatus De Legibus ac Deo Legislatore in Decem Libros Distributus* (Nápoles: Ex Typis Fibrenianis 1872)

15 *Compendium of the Social Doctrine of the Church* §105–§109.

It is the same equal dignity that Vitoria is claiming for the discovered peoples. All people – and every community – are, in his view, bound by a common humanity. In Idoya Zorroza's words:

> (…) the community of nature (…) requires a series of considerations regarding the possession of a same ontological and anthropological dignity – against the thesis that argued for the existence of slaves by nature –, that should be the seat for further social and legal recognition.[16]

In this sense, Vitoria's *ius gentium* has a universal character[17] and provides a legal setting that enables the understanding of the defence of natural liberties applicable to all nations and to all human beings *qua homines*, i.e., as human beings.

From this legal equality grounded upon human nature, the Dominican explains that all human beings, as such, are subjects of rights as they are potential objects of injustice and are ends in themselves.

But if one again recalls Aquinas, the fact that the *imago Dei* presupposes reason will not be missed. And sure enough Vitoria does not fail to mention that reason is necessary for the exercise of dominion. The Indians are not, he argues, *a-mentes*, that is, deprived of sanity. They may have, in practice, an inferior capacity to use reason and to govern themselves, he later recognizes, albeit hesitantly.[18] But, in principle, they are as capable as any other people on earth of exercising legitimate dominion – and consequently so. Therefore, the barbarians seem to have sovereign communities that relate to others as equals. The dominion among the Indians is placed at the same level as the dominion among the Christian societies.

The notion of equality among peoples in Vitoria's thought is also present in his *relectio De Temperantia*. There, he argues that in a just war against the Indians it is legitimate to do only what can be done in wars among Christians.[19] Rules of war, as those of property and dominion, apply the same among different peoples, in virtue of a common humanity.

---

16 M. Idoya Zorroza, 'La Ley Natural en el Pensamiento de Francisco de Vitoria', in Laura E. Corso de Estrada, M. Jesús Soto-Bruna, M. Idoya Zorroza (eds.), *Concepciones de la Ley Natural: Medioevo Latino y Escolástica Española e Iberoamericana* (Pamplona: EUNSA 2013) 278.

17 See André Azevedo Alves, 'Vitoria, the Common Good and the Limits of Political Power', in José María Beneyto and Justo Corti Varela, *At the Origins of Modernity, Francisco de Vitoria and the Discovery of International Law* (Cham: Springer 2017) 71.

18 See Vitoria, *De Indis* 723–724.

19 See Francisco de Vitoria, *De Temperantia*, in Francisco de Vitoria, *Obras de Francisco de Vitoria*, ed. T. Urdánoz (Madrid: BAC 1960) 1052.

Vitoria's account of the capacity of the Indians for *dominium* should, in this context, be seen in harmony with an increased autonomy of the political sphere regarding faith and grace. Vitoria explicitly denies a universal power of the Pope in temporal matters.

One could, however, wonder whether the indirect power of the Pope does not end up legitimizing Church authority – and possibly vicarial civil authority – by the Spaniards over the Indians. According to Vitoria's thought, it does not. The temporal power of the Pope, and specifically his coercive power in temporal matters, is understood to be over the baptized, not universal, because it stems, not from nature, but from the spiritual power of the Pope, interpreted within the hierarchy of ends of different realms. The Pope's temporal power is thus ordered only towards the spiritual realm and exists only to such an extent. Now Vitoria argues that the Pope does not have spiritual power over the Indians '(…) and therefore does not have temporal power either'[20] for the latter depends upon the former.

This does not mean that faith and grace do not perfect political communities and governments and that a Christian government is not more perfect than a government by an unfaithful sovereign. Faith and grace contribute to the sound exercise of power and to the prosperity of political communities, directing them to the ultimate end of social beings. But they are no longer conditions for political legitimacy and do not make, from a legal point of view, one government more legitimate than another.

Indeed, the Pope was not, to Vitoria, the ultimate source of all power. The political realm is thus able to detach itself, to some extent, from the spiritual, as Vitoria affirmed its 'independence and autonomy'.[21]

People are governed by a prince, or a public authority, only insofar as it deals with the temporal realm, which is within the scope of the *civitas*. His conscience and the public practice of religion go beyond the temporal sphere.

It is in this sense that Urdánoz states that the scholastics argued against the theories of the medieval *orbis christianus* according to which the Pope had a universal theocratic dominion and was the source of power, leading to a denial of the right of private and public possession of the infidels.[22]

---

20 'Sed non habet potestatem spiritualem in illos (…). Ergo nec temporalem'. Vitoria, *De Indis* 680.

21 See Alves, 'Vitoria, the Common Good and the Limits of Political Power' 73.

22 Urdánoz, 'Síntesis Teológico-Jurídica', LXVII

Also relevant to understanding the universal applicability of Vitoria's writings is his idea of free movement and open trade as natural rights.[23] The disrespect for the rights granted to the Spaniards in Indian territory – but reversible in principle – would justify a war to protect them, provided that nothing short of war worked.

It is precisely this legitimate use of war to reclaim the rights being violated that, according to Schmitt, makes Vitoria's ultimate goal clear: to support and justify the land-appropriation in the American continent. The shortcomings of this reading will be covered in the following

2 Schmitt's Interpretation of Vitoria

Now when we turn to Schmitt's account of Vitoria, we are confronted with a different – in his words 'truer'[24] – view of Vitoria, which has been hinted at in the previous section.

In his 1950 work, *Der Nomos der Erde im Völkerrecht des Jus Publicum Europaeum* (subsequently referred to as *Nomos* in the present chapter), Carl Schmitt devotes a chapter to Vitoria, entitled 'Justification of the Land-Appropriation of a New World: Francisco de Vitoria'.[25] Schmitt begins his account by recognizing the neutral and a-historical character of Vitoria's thought:

> A contemporary reader's *first impression* [emphasis is ours] of Vitoria's *relectiones* is of extraordinary impartiality, objectivity, and neutrality. Consequently, the argumentation no longer appears medieval, but 'modern'. (…) all legal titles of the pope and the emperor deriving from claims to world domination are rejected unconditionally as inappropriate and illegitimate. This impression of total objectivity and neutrality also is sustained elsewhere. In particular, it is emphasized repeatedly that native Americans, though they may be barbarians, are not animals, and are no less human than are the European land-appropriators.[26]

23 On the notions of free movement and free trade in Vitoria, see José Manuel Moreira, André Azevedo Alves, *De Salamanca a Coímbra y Évora: Caminos Cruzados de una Escuela Singular* (Madrid: Editoral Universidad Francisco de Vitoria 2018) 15–22.

24 Carl Schmitt, *The* Nomos *of the Earth in the International Law of the* Jus Publicum Europaeum (USA: Telos Press Publishing 2006) 125.

25 Schmitt, *Nomos* 101–125.

26 Schmitt, *Nomos* 102.

According to Schmitt, it is precisely such (apparent) neutrality that could mislead Vitoria's reader into believing that he would hold a negative view of the conquest and condemn Spanish dominion.

Particularly as regards the reversibility, in Vitoria's mindset, of rights and rules for relations among peoples (rights and rules applying to Indians and Christians alike), Schmitt remarks that '(…) this claim had the ring of an all-too-abstract, neutral, apathetic, and, thus, ahistorical exaggeration'.[27]

And he adds:

> This gives the impression that he no longer saw Europe as the centre of the earth and the source of all standards, that he no longer recognized spatial order of the medieval *respublica Christiana*, with its distinction between the territory of Christian peoples and that of heathens or non-believers.[28]

But Schmitt will immediately dismiss it as just a first impression, arguing that Vitoria actually approved the conquest: '(…) it would be a gross misinterpretation to say that Vitoria had claimed that the great Spanish *conquista* was unjust, although this false assumption certainly is widespread'.[29]

To prove his point, Schmitt singles out what in his view is the main limit of that neutrality: the missionary right, granted by the Pope. It is, according to Schmitt, Vitoria's notion of evangelization, inseparable from his Christian-centred worldview and supported by the threat of just war, that ultimately shows that the Dominican supported Spanish dominion over the Amerindians. Evangelization is the goal and the just war theory the means that enables it.

Schmitt reads Vitoria's international thought as part of the medieval tradition of the *respublica christiana*. The discovery of the New World is pivotal to the inauguration of a new concept of international law – the *ius publicum Europaeum*. But Vitoria is still a part of the previous system of thought, mainly due to his just war theory based on a just cause.

Schmitt's treatment of just war is crucial to understanding where he places Vitoria in the evolution of the international order, as well as what he believes are appropriations of the Dominican's thought.

In Schmitt's reading, Vitoria argued that '(…) the papal missionary mandate, (…), by means of a just war, was the true legal title to the *conquista*'

27 Schmitt, *Nomos* 107.
28 Schmitt, *Nomos* 107.
29 Schmitt, *Nomos* 108.

and that '(...) the Crown of Castile's appropriation of American soil was completely in line with the international law of the Christian Middle Ages. In fact, it was at once its apogee and climax'.[30]

It is true that, if one focuses on the justification of occupation, just war is, to Vitoria, the legal title that may – if other conditions are met – justify land-appropriation. But this cannot be taken to mean that Vitoria argued for a papal mandate as an indirect title of occupation. What Vitoria argued for was the recognition of evangelization as a right stemming from *ius communicationis*, not solely or primarily from divine law, and, in turn, that such a right was enforceable by the threat of war.

And this is the reason why just war theory does not run counter to Vitoria's previous stance on rejecting unjust titles for Spanish land-appropriation, as Schmitt believes when he claims that Vitoria's '(...) lack of presuppositions, his objectivity and neutrality, have their limits, and do not go as far as to disregard the distinction between Christians and non-believers'.[31] However, as has been shown, the just title in itself is not based on Christian superiority, but on a natural right of a community to defend itself and punish offences perpetrated against it.

But it was not only Vitoria's concept of just war what to Schmitt gave away his support for the conquest and closed him in the medieval international order of the *respublica christiana*. It was also crucial to Schmitt's argument that his concept of just war be distinguished from that of the modern international legal scholars.

According to Schmitt, Vitoria's just war theory, with its notion of *justa causa*, albeit divergent from the concept of *justus hostis* of the *ius publicum Europaeum* – the international order that replaced the medieval *orbis christianus* in the sixteenth century – was also not the one that modern internationalists during the interwar period were advocating for, building upon Vitoria. This is so, in Schmitt's view, because of what Vitoria's notion of just war has in common with that of the *ius publicum Europaeum*: the rejection of a discriminatory concept of war, which Schmitt fears modern international law is trying to establish. In his view, this becomes a misuse of Vitoria's doctrine with the aim of calling for the abolition of war and criminalizing aggression, without regard for a true just cause.

At this point, Schmitt is right to distance the idea of the abolition of war from Vitoria's concept of just war. Vitoria would not declare a war illegitimate

30 Schmitt, *Nomos* 112.

31 Schmitt, *Nomos* 113.

or unnecessary in itself without requiring that at least one of the conditions for it to be just was missing.[32]

However, in notes collected in the *Glossarium*, Schmitt does not hide his contempt for Vitoria's *relectio De Indis*. He frequently expresses his impatience with Vitoria's just and unjust titles and particularly with his just war theory, which he considers a terrible abuse, especially because of how it favours criminalization of aggression and, subsequently, leads to total war, due to its focus on a just cause:

> The end of the *primus titulus* [first legitimate title] shows all the sinister reasoning of the just war, the turning of the enemy into a convicted criminal, from *iustus hostis* to *perfidus hostis* treacherous perfidious, the victor as iudex, the absolute disenfranchising.[33]

In another note, from June 1948, and also published in the *Glossarium*, Schmitt acknowledges that he was too prudent and careful in the chapter on Vitoria in the *Nomos*.[34] Here he seems to no longer be separating Vitoria from the twentieth-century recovery of just war and subsequent criminalization of the enemy. The same Schmitt that had argued that '(…) the modern distinction between just and unjust war lacks any inherent relation to medieval scholastic doctrine and to Vitoria'[35] now appears to be dismissing both and for the same reason.

A few months later, in August of the same year, Schmitt refers to Carnegie as a 'foundation for the criminalization of war',[36] and adds that this is the cradle of Vitoria's renewed fame.

According to Schmitt, it was a grave mistake to consider war merely from a punitive lens, and not through the concept of *justus hostis*: 'The enemy became a criminal, and the rest – the deprivation of rights and the plundering of the opponent, i.e., destruction of the concept of the enemy (…) – followed as a

---

32 On the mistake of associating Vitoria's thought with the Kellogg-Briand's pact condemnation of war, see Teófilo Urdánoz, 'Introducción a la relección segunda', in Urdánoz, *Obras de Francisco de Vitoria* 752.

33 'Der Schluß des primus titulus (…) zeigt die ganze unheimliche Logik des gerechten Krieges, die Verwandlung des Feindes in einen verurteilten Verbrecher, vom iustus hostis zum perfidus hostis, der Sieger als iudex, die totale Entrechtung (…)'. Carl Schmitt, *Glossarium, Aufzeichnungen aus den Jahren 1947 bis 1958* (Berlin: Duncker & Humblot 2015) 79. See also Schmitt, *Glossarium* 129.

34 Schmitt, *Glossarium* 130.

35 Schmitt, *Nomos* 122.

36 'Foundation zur Kriminalisierung des Krieges'. Schmitt, *Glossarium* 141.

matter of course'.[37] To Schmitt, this means the rejection of rights to one part of the conflict.

Martti Koskenniemi relates Schmitt's condemnation of the discriminating concept of war and the imperial universalism that spread after World War I to his practical concern for allied control of Germany,[38] as the country was treated as an enemy and justice was being decided by the victorious powers.

That Schmitt has Germany in mind when discussing discriminatory and non-discriminatory concepts of war becomes clear in a chapter of the *Nomos* dedicated to the 'Transformation of the Meaning of War',[39] where the author points out World War I, particularly the peace negotiations that followed, as a turning point in the concept of war, marked by the attempt of criminalizing it.

Furthermore, as we have noted, Schmitt considers that, within Vitoria's thought, Christians and non-Christians are not as equal as they seem, and thus argues that, to Vitoria, non-Christians can never have the same right of intervention and free movement that the Spanish had to further Christianity.

This is, to Schmitt, where the edifice of objectivity collapses – where neutrality ends and partiality is brought forth. This partiality is in Schmitt's Vitoria but a consequence of the Dominican's medieval mindset, which Schmitt refers to as *respublica Christiana*, composed of the *populus Christianus,* the Christian people,[40] which encompassed the European territory, mission territories, and enemy territories.

Here a sharp contrast must be noted between the German political theorist and James Brown Scott, whose interpretation of Vitoria Schmitt sees as inaugurating 'a new stage in the instrumentalization of Vitoria's arguments'.[41]

Whereas Schmitt clearly places Vitoria in the medieval order of the *respublica christiana*, as is clear from what has been said above, Scott considers the Dominican's *relectio De Indis* 'the proclamation of the new international law, and indeed of the law of nations which is yet to be'[42] and 'the first treatise on the modern law of nations'.[43] We shall return to this point in the following section.

---

37 Schmitt, *Nomos* 123.

38 Martti Koskenniemi, 'Carl Schmitt and International Law', in Jens Meierhenrich, Oliver Simons, eds., *The Oxford Handbook of Carl Schmitt* (New York: Oxford University Press 2016) 598–599.

39 Schmitt, *Nomos* 259–280.

40 Schmitt, *Nomos* 58.

41 Schmitt, *Nomos* 119.

42 James Brown Scott, *The Spanish Origin of International Law: Francisco de Vitoria and his Law of Nations* (Union, NJ: Lawbook Exchange, 2000) 95.

43 Scott, *The Spanish Origin of International Law* 96.

For now, it suffices to note that Teofilo Urdánoz, placing, as well as James Brown Scott, Vitoria in the beginning of a new international law, emphasizes the juridical character of Vitoria and his rights-oriented thought.[44] Scott, for his part, stressed the broad concept of theology adopted by Vitoria and others of his time: '(...) it was as necessary for a theologian to be a jurist as it was for a jurist to be a theologian – at least in the days of Victoria'.[45] Schmitt outright dismisses the juridical character of Vitoria, linking his being a theologian with the a-political character of his reasoning:

> (...) the lectures of the great Dominican do not constitute a juridical treatise similar to international law scholarship in the following centuries. Vitoria was a theologian. (...) As a theologian, Vitoria posed the question of the 'right' of the *Conquista* and of the *justa causa belli* from a thoroughly moral-theological standpoint with, at least at first glance, an entirely unpolitical objectivity and neutrality.[46]

From this standpoint Schmitt is able to clarify that Vitoria – the theologian – is to be seen as a representative of the same authority that gave the missionary mandate to the Crown, through which, he argues, land-appropriation is justified. And this is why his just war theory is not as neutral as it seems, once we consider its context, outside of which, Schmitt seems to believe, concepts are deprived of meaning:

> The arguments in favor of just war, which appear to be so general and neutral, obtain their decisive legal force precisely from the missionary mandate; their abstract generality in no way diminishes the existential reality of a concrete historical standpoint.[47]

Schmitt is right in affirming Vitoria mainly as a theologian, ready to counsel on matters of conscience. But that fact, along with his belonging to a specific

---

44 'Vitoria, aunque teólogo, hace aquí el papel primordial de jurista, que funda el orden y relaciones obligadas de los pueblos en el derecho, natural y de gentes'. Teófilo Urdánoz, 'Introducción à la relección primera', in Urdánoz, *Obras de Francisco de Vitoria* 551.

45 James Brown Scott, *The Catholic Conception of International Law* (Clark, NJ: The Lawbook Exchange, 2007) 39.

46 Schmitt, *Nomos* 110–111.

47 Schmitt, *Nomos* 111.

order or to a specific country, does not predetermine his stance on the issues that he discusses.[48]

Reginaldo di Agostino Iannarone, in the introduction to the *relectio de Indis* of the *Corpus Hispanorum de Pace*, while recognizing Vitoria's Catholic and Spanish background, argues that it is not correct to believe that he was constrained by the positions of his Order, and unable or unwilling to think for himself.[49]

There are, indeed, some studies suggesting that Vitoria was not entirely aligned with the Crown. According to Luciano Pereña, Vitoria's *relectio De Indis* may have been the target of censorship. He grounds this assertion on reasons such as the 25-year distance between its writing and its publication in Spain, and the exchange of letters between the emperor and the superior of the Convent of San Esteban, in which the latter is asked to stop the Dominicans within his care (among them was Vitoria) from questioning the right of dominion in America.[50] Such a request is also mentioned by Father Belda Plans, in his monograph on Juan Ginés de Sepúlveda.[51]

Nonetheless, as the same Pereña goes on to clarify, 'it is absurd to imagine a confrontation between Vitoria and Charles V, between the Crown and Salamanca',[52] arguing that Vitoria assumed the legitimacy of the conquest and did not question it.[53] And this is a view, more or less emphatically, but nonetheless commonly held among commentators.

Acknowledging the indebtedness of Vitoria to his context, and regardless of the practical implications or intentions of his argument to the policy of civil and spiritual authorities towards the natives, we must not, however, outright

48 For a brief account of how Vitoria's arguments in the *relectio De Indis* ran counter to those of many contemporary authors, including a fellow Dominican, see Teófilo Urdánoz, 'Introducción a la relección primera'. But it must be noted that, while rejecting the natural slavery of indigenous men, Vitoria does not run counter to the authority of Aristotle. Rather, he interprets the Greek philosopher's theory in a fashion that is compatible with his own position.

49 Reginaldo di Agostino Iannarone, 'Génesis del pensamiento colonial en Francisco de Vitoria', in Francisco de Vitoria, *Relectio De Indis O Libertad de los Indios*, ed. Luciano Pereña, J. M. Perez Prendes (Madrid: Consejo Superior de Investigaciones Científicas 1967) XXXI–XLII.

50 Luciano Pereña, 'La Escuela de Salamanca y la Duda Indiana', in Ramos, et al. (eds.), *La Ética en la Conquista de América* 297.

51 See Juan Belda Plans, *Juan Ginés de Sepúlveda* (Madrid: Fundación Ignacio Larramendi 2016) 39.

52 Pereña, 'La Escuela de Salamanca y la Duda Indiana' 299.

53 'Francisco de Vitoria nunca acusó al Emperador Carlos V, ni cuestionó la legitimidad de la conquista. Era un postulado que daba por supuesto (...)'. Pereña, 'La Escuela de Salamanca y la Duda Indiana' 299.

disregard all his discussion on just and unjust titles, which Schmitt admitted was causing him impatience. A careful reading of Vitoria must focus on the principles and theoretical consequences of his thought.

Schmitt, on the contrary, believes that Vitoria is best understood if enclosed only in his context:

> (…) theoretical conclusions, though they refer only to his arguments and avoid any practical decisions, can be astonishingly provocative and can be misinterpreted, especially when taken out of context (…) and generalized as abstract principles of international law in a manner approaching the completely secularized and neutralized thinking of a modern scholar.[54]

Such a reading risks rendering Vitoria's discussion of the unjust and just titles virtually inconsequential.

It is true that Vitoria's work cannot be understood outside its circumstances. But it is not true that it is not applicable beyond those same circumstances. In fact, Vitoria writes in a period of transition. It is no longer possible that he does not recognize the world is not reduceable to the medieval *respublica christiana*. In the New World and also increasingly so in Europe, on the eve of Westphalia, reality proved otherwise.

This discussion echoes a distinction, eloquently presented by Ramón Hernández in *La Ética de la Conquista de América*, between an *absolute* reading of Vitoria's thought, on the one hand, and a *hypothetical* one, on the other. In the first group are those who see in Vitoria's just titles a real support for the conquest; in the latter, those who read the just titles as merely hypotheses, not applicable to the natives in America.[55]

Significantly, he places in the first group Teodoro Andrés Marcos, to whose interpretation of Vitoria Schmitt refers approvingly more than once.[56]

Schmitt himself would be closer to the first line of interpretation. Although he argues that Vitoria's positive conclusion regarding the justice of the *conquista* 'is reached only by means of general concepts and with the aid of hypothetical arguments in support of a just war', with an 'if-then' structure supported by the title of just war, what he means is that Vitoria was using the artifact of hypothesis to indirectly legitimize conquest.

---

54 Schmitt, *Nomos* 106.

55 Ramón Hernández, 'La hipótesis de Francisco de Vitoria', in Ramos, et al. (eds.), *La Ética en la Conquista de América* 345–347.

56 See, for instance, Schmitt, *Nomos* 108.

Schmitt's reading of Vitoria must also be placed in the broader context of his own thought, particularly in his effort to prove, in the *Nomos of the Earth*, that the stability of the international order, of the old *nomos*, was being destroyed by a non-spatial one, associated with the growing influence of the United States.

The German jurist recognized that the foundations of the *ius publicum Europaeum* had ceased to exist and therefore this European international order had disappeared.[57] The problem, Schmitt argues, was that no coherent system had been thought of that could replace it. In turn, he argues for a '*Großraum* order'.[58]

Vitoria's universalism was being stressed by precisely the ones that were failing to ascribe a notion of space to the new world order. For instance, Scott described Vitoria's international community as one 'without reference to geography', as we shall see. Schmitt's rejection of Vitoria's universalism would thus become instrumental to his rejection of the idea that he was a forerunner of a spaceless, non-Eurocentric order.

Scott associates with Vitoria's founding position, not merely a new international law, but one that is applicable in his day, the fact that 'his was a system that has ceased to be a European but had become a universal law'.[59] And that could help explain its adequacy to Scott's times. Schmitt also agrees that the interwar period saw an irreversible decline of Europe as the centre of the world. But he outright rejected that Vitoria's system had the same global dimension.

Joshua Smeltzer, in an article entitled 'On the Use and Abuse of Francisco de Vitoria: James Brown Scott and Carl Schmitt',[60] argues that Schmitt's interpretation of Vitoria – and his estrangement from Scott and others – is mainly a weapon against 'the liberal internationalist theory of just war'.

Regardless of the practical utility that Schmitt ascribed to his reading of Vitoria, we shall now focus on arguing against what Schmitt believes is the collapse of the edifice of his neutrality, in order to effectively showcase the relevance of Vitoria outside the chains of the medieval order.

---

57 See Schmitt's chapter on the dissolution of the *ius publicum Europaeum*: Schmitt, *Nomos* 227–239.

58 See Carl Schmitt, 'The *Großraum* Order of International Law with a ban on Intervention for Spatially Foreign Powers: A Contribution to the Concept of *Reich* in International Law (1939–1941)', in Carl Schmitt, *Writings on War* (Cambridge: Polity Press, 2011) 77.

59 Scott, *The Spanish Origin of International Law* 163.

60 Joshua Smeltzer, 'On the Use and Abuse of Francisco de Vitoria: James Brown Scott and Carl Schmitt'. *Journal of the History of International Law* 20 (2018), 345–372.

We shall not be looking – or we would be doing so in vain – for an absolute condemnation of the conquest or a plea for the abandonment of the American continent.

What we are looking for in Vitoria's *relectiones* is the establishment of permanent principles that enlighten the relations between peoples – and that, we shall argue, contribute to them in a positive way.

3 Vitoria and the Defence of Religious Liberty

We thus argue that, although Vitoria did in fact have a Christian-centred approach, foundational to his missionary mindset, the neutrality and universalism of his thought are not in question. The reason for this is threefold.

First, the right to evangelize presupposes peaceful evangelization and it requires the evangelizers not to hurt the natives in any way. Second, the conversion to faith is voluntary, which means that the evangelized have the right to reject the faith. And thirdly, the defence of certain principles of religious freedom, although used by Vitoria in the specific context of expanding the Christian faith, reaches beyond that context, and has universal applicability, not explicitly or even intentionally, but as a requirement of some of the principles put forward in his *relectiones*.

3.1 *Peaceful Evangelization*

Within the broader discussion of the legal and anthropological status of the Indians, Vitoria also has a clear position in the debate on whether their evangelization should be pursued only by peaceful means, or if turning to force might be justifiable.

While developing the just and unjust titles of dominion of the Indians by the Spaniards, Vitoria makes an important contribution to the development of a rights-based approach to religious freedom, where the notion of peaceful evangelization becomes particularly illuminating.

Discussing the legitimacy of waging war against the Indians, Vitoria denies the Spanish settlers or kings any right to coerce indigenous peoples in matters of faith. They have merely temporal power and bear no such authority. Furthermore, evangelization through violence contradicts the very essence of faith, that requires freedom of the will, for one may not be said to have faith without true conversion. Sin is, therefore, not a valid motive for war.

This implies that non-believers can never be legitimately coerced to believe. Not only because it is an unjustifiable violence, but also because it is self-contradictory. To believe requires, Vitoria says, an act of the will, while fear decreases the possibility of free choice. Therefore, one may claim to have converted someone by force. But if the will of that person has not moved, then *metanoia*, true conversion of the heart, has not taken place. Fear is driving the exterior actions of the person, but it has no power to convert.

Reason, not violence, is the way to bring souls to Christ. This is not only a proposal of peace, but a solid belief in human reason: Christian faith must be rationally preached; sound reasons for believing must be used in the hope that the pagans can be persuaded. As Teófilo Urdánoz notes, Vitoria is here recognizing the importance of apologetics to Christianity. Forced evangelization is, to Vitoria, not a service to God.

Asking whether the infidels should be forced to convert to the faith (*Vtrum infideles compellendi sint ad fidem*), Vitoria argues that God left it to the free choice of human beings. In his *relectio de Temperantia*, he condemns violent evangelization.[61]

Vitoria was one of the theologians writing a formal approval to the emperor Charles V (in 1543), of the position of Alfonso de Castro in the *Vtrum indigenae noui orbis instruendi sint in mysteriis theologicis et artibus liberalibus* (*Whether the theological mysteries and the liberal arts should be taught to the indigenous of the New World*), where he argues for the capacity of the Indians to use reason and to be taught. This capacity in turn further corroborates the duty of Catholics to evangelize only by peaceful means. It would, in any case, be contradictory to conceive of an evangelization that was not peaceful, as we have seen. But Vitoria also believes that such peaceful conversion is possible and should be pursued because the other side is capable of understanding and being persuaded through reason.

This position had also been sanctioned by the Church authority, in the bull *Sublimis Deus*,[62] where, in 1537, Pope Paul III states that 'all (...), without any exception, (...) are capable of receiving the doctrines of the faith',[63] and that the 'Indians (...), being truly human beings, are capable of [understanding] the Catholic faith'.[64] And he adds:

---

61 Vitoria, *De Temperantia* 1057.

62 Quotations of the Bull from F. A. MacNutt, *Bartholomew de Las Casas, His Life, Apostolate and Writings* (Cleveland: The Arthur H. Clark Company 1909) Appendix II, 426–431, whose Latin version is from C. Gutierrez, *Fray Bartolomé de Las Casas: su tiempo y su apostolado*, Appendix A.

63 'Omnes (...), absque omni deletu, (...) fidei disciplinae capaces [existent]'. Appendix, II 371.

64 'Indos (...), ut (...) veros homines (...) Chistianae Fidei capaces [existent]'. Appendix, II 372.

> (…) the Indians, as well as all other peoples that come to be discovered by the Christian, are not, and can never be, deprived of their freedom or of the possession of their property, even if they are apart from the Christian faith. Besides that, they may, freely and legitimately, use (…) this kind of freedom and dominion and must not be made slaves.[65]

The theologian Teófilo Urdánoz states that, together with the brief *Pastorale Officium*, also from 1537, these documents make up the first *Magna Carta* of the rights of the Indians, of their innate freedom, of the possibility of their salvation, and of the equality of their rights as regards other human beings.[66] García Añoveros further corroborates the idea that, decades after the discovery, the papal bull was confirming, authoritatively, an accepted doctrine within the Church, not creating it.[67]

Lewis Hanke also sees this position in accordance with the ecclesiastical tradition:

> In issuing this bull Paul III was following the established tradition of the Christian church. From its earliest days Christianity had proclaimed in the most solemn and exalted terms the absolute spiritual equality and brotherhood of all men.[68]

By the end of the twentieth century, Pope John Paul II, during his visit to the United States, recalled this ancient position of the Church, referring to the Iberian scholastics:

> Already in 1537, my predecessor Pope Paul III proclaimed the dignity and rights of the native peoples of the Americas by insisting that they not be deprived of their freedom or the possession of their property. In Spain the Dominican priest, Francisco de Vitoria, became the staunch

---

65 '(…) Indos et omnes alias gentes ad notitiam Christianorum imposterum deventuras, licet extra Fidem Christi existant sua libertate ac rerum suarum dominio privatos, seu privandos non esse. Imo libertate et dominio huiusmodi, uti et potiri, et gaudere, libere et licite posse, nee in servitutem redigi debere'. Appendix II, 372

66 '(…) [en el breve Pastorale officium y la bula Sublimis Deus] (…) promulgaba la primera Carta magna de los derechos humanos y cristianos de los indios, su libertad nativa, capacidad de salvación e igualdad de derechos básicos con los demás hombres'. Urdánoz, 'Síntesis Teológico-Jurídica', LXXIII.

67 See Jesús María García Añoveros, 'Carlos V y la Abolición de la Esclativitud de los Indios. Causas, Evolución y Circunstancias'. *Revista de Indias* 60, no. 218 (2000) 83.

68 Lewis Hanke, 'Pope Paul III and the American Indians'. *The Harvard Theological Review* 30, no. 2 (1937), 73.

> advocate of the rights of the Indians and formulated the basis for international law regarding the rights of peoples.[69]

More recently, in July 2022, during the Apostolic Journey of Pope Francis to Canada, in a meeting with the indigenous peoples, the Pontiff recalled the grave evils and justices perpetrated against the indigenous by the policies of assimilation and how they gravely disrespected the identity and dignity of those suffering from them. If one looks at it in this context, from Vitoria, Las Casas, and others, through Paul III, John Paul II and others, to Pope Francis, this visit and attitude was one more instance of a centuries-old tradition.

Las Casas is also a good example of the defence of the indigenous peoples' capacity for reasoning and of their rights more broadly, calling for peaceful evangelization in his Treatise *De Vnico Vocationis Modo*. He states and proves that there is only one, universal way of teaching religion, and that is persuasion of the intellect by means of rational argumentation that brings about voluntary adhesion to faith.[70]

These works are a relevant source of proof of the presence of important principles to the affirmation of religious freedom as a right, violence being rejected as a means to punish strictly religious offences. The matter is different, and significantly so, if those are also offences against natural law.

Beyond religious freedom, Luciano Pereña also argues for the great relevance of the late scholastics to the defence of human rights in general:

> The School of Salamanca upholds the responsibility of peoples against the aggressors of humanity. Against slavery, it affirms the fundamental freedom of the Indians. Against religious repression, it affirms freedom of conscience. It affirms the solidarity and popular sovereignty of the Indigenous peoples. It affirms the protection of the Crown and the right to self-determination. In conclusion, it demands the restitution of their properties and rights unjustly seized during the conquest.[71]

---

69 John Paul II, 'Meeting with the Native Peoples of the Americas: Address of His Holiness John Paul II' (1987).

70 Bartolomé de Las Casas, *Del Único Modo de Atraer a Todos los Pueblos a la Verdadera Religión* (México: Fondo de Cultura Económica 1942) 65.

71 'La Escuela de Salamanca reivindica la responsabilidad de los pueblos contra los agresores de la humanidad. Contra la esclavitud reivindica la libertad fundamental de los indios. Contra la represión religiosa reivindica la libertad de conciencia. Reivindica la solidaridad y soberanía popular de los pueblos indios. Reivindica la protección de la Corona y el derecho de autodeterminación. En conclusión, reivindica la restitución de sus propiedades y derechos injustamente requisados durante la conquista'. Luciano Pereña, 'Estudio Preliminar: Proyecto de Reconversión Colonial', in Luciano Pereña

Now this capability of receiving and understanding the Catholic faith and the rejection of forced evangelization implies that the pagans are under no civil obligation to accept it.

3.2 *Voluntary Conversion*

In Vitoria's doctrine, the right of the Indians to reject the faith is secured and the duty of the Christians not to force them otherwise is stated. In this context, a contribution to a negative concept of religious freedom (clearly stated in the *Compendium of the Social Doctrine of the Church*, §441), emerges, as Indians, in their rationality, endowed with the same dignity as the Christians (based on personalist principles), have a right to choose not to convert.

For instance, Vitoria argues:

> (…) supposing that the barbarians refuse to receive Christ as Lord, yet it is not legitimate to wage war against them or hurt them in any way (…). It is a great absurdity that, being permitted to reject God without punishment, they would be forced to accept his vicar.[72]

When arguing against the fourth unjust title, that is, the fact that the Indians reject the faith of Christ, Vitoria states that ignorance of faith is not, in itself, a sin: 'Before they learned about the faith of Christ, the barbarians did not commit the sin of infidelity (*peccato infidelitatis*) for not believing in Christ'.[73] And from this he deduces consequences for the treatment of the unfaithful, who retain the right to reject the faith.

At this point one may think that this freedom is not satisfiable from a modern standpoint as Vitoria later argues that, if the testimony of faith is truly convincing, and with constancy, those who still reject the faith, incur in mortal sin. Once the conditions are met to consider that the faith was sufficiently communicated, then the Indians have the obligation to accept the Christian faith. The fact was that such conditions had not been met yet. And therefore, no such obligation had arisen.

(ed.), *Carta Magna de los Indios, Fuentes Constitucionales, 1534–1609* (Madrid: Consejo Superior de Investigaciones Científicas, 1988) 10.

72 '(…) dato quod barbari nolint recipere Christum pro domino, non tamen possunt bello peti aut aliquo malo affici. Absurdissimum est autem quod (…), cum possint impune non recipere Christum, teneantur recipere vicarium eius (…)'. Vitoria, *De Indis* 682.

73 'Barbari, priusquam aliquid audissent de fide Christi, non peccabant peccato infidelitatis eo quod non crederent in Christum'. Vitoria, *De Indis* 687.

Such circumstantiality does not mean that Vitoria fails to consequentially argue for a right to reject the faith in a relevant sense applicable to other circumstances. In fact, Vitoria adds the statement that truly establishes the grounds for such a right. He states that such grave sin by the barbarians – that is, to reject the true faith being well presented to them – does not constitute a legitimate title for war and, consequently, for subjugation in the political sphere.

What this in fact implies is that, while the rejection of the faith without the excuse of ignorance has deep spiritual consequences, it does not have political consequences.

3.3 *Right to Evangelize*

On the other hand, while discussing the legitimate titles of dominion, Vitoria affirms the right of the Spanish to evangelize the non-Christian populations, the same right that Schmitt uses to prove the collapse of Vitoria's objectivity. This right implies, according to Vitoria, that if the Spanish are in some way hindered in their peaceful actions as evangelizers, they may thus practice a right to wage a just war in order to guarantee respect for the usurped right of living out their faith in foreign territory. Here the right of the Christians to evangelize and the symmetric duty of the Indians to allow that expression of their faith is defended.

It should be noted that the two rights and the two duties expressed can be read as theoretically interchangeable for they are not human or specifically divine grants, but rather a demand of natural law. Therefore, one may say that the Indians, *sicut Christiani*, would have a right to publicly express their religion and the Christians, as well as the Indians, have a duty to allow it, granted, of course, that its practices are not contrary to natural law.

In fact, if one looks at Vitoria's argument for the right of the Spanish to evangelize the Indians, one is presented with five reasons for it, that may be summarized as follows (although they appear in a different order in the *relectio*): authority of Scripture; the need to be offered the opportunity of salvation; natural law-based fraternal correction; and the right to travel to and trade in those territories. This latter reason is indeed universal, for all enjoy, according to Vitoria, *ius communicationis*.

Furthermore, this suggests that religious freedom is not merely defined as absence of coercion but it acquires here also a positive content, being defended as a right (which is necessarily distinct from viewing this right as a positive claim to be fulfiled by state action which could be used to justify some sort of right on the part of the state to impose an official religion, which Vitoria denies). This is the right that religious people have by nature to publicly pursue their faith and peacefully propose it to others. This idea is, in turn, also present in the Social Doctrine of the Church today.[74] In the Catholic tradition, there is a fundamental, inalienable right to religious freedom that stands in need of protection, and which implies a correlative duty on the part of the state not to obstruct the space of the Church to fulfil its purpose. Here is where Vitoria's approach is particularly useful. Ideally, no preservation would be needed against attacks on religious freedom. However, it is recognized by Vitoria that the possibility of publicly expressing faith – Catholic faith, he means – and thus of evangelizing is necessary for a good society, and not indifferent. He sees religion – again, having in mind Christianism – as a good to be preserved. And it is preserved by the right to religious freedom.

Therefore, if under attack, a right of resistance is defended as peace is at stake. As religious liberty is not merely a freedom to be left alone, but positively demands the recognition by others of the other's right to public profession of faith (within the bounds of civility), and, *men not being angels*, one may find oneself in a situation of being coerced not to publicly live out one's faith, it is only reasonable to provide human beings with mechanisms of defence against unjust external constraints.

It is nonetheless true that Vitoria does not argue that any pagan has the right to promote another faith. But arguing against it might require contradicting himself – in particular, it would probably sacrifice his *ius communicationis*. Maybe Vitoria was ready to sacrifice it, but what is relevant to the present argument is that it would generate such a contradiction.

4 Vitoria as a Liberal Internationalist?

Notwithstanding the universalism and broad applicability of Vitoria's international thought, we must be careful not to read into Vitoria's arguments an exact blueprint for twentieth- and twenty-first-century international order, as James Brown Scott does for his time.

It must be acknowledged that Scott contributed decisively to establishing Vitoria and the late scholastics, and rightly so, as pivotal to the history of international law.[75] But Scott goes further and argues that Vitoria's 'Reading *On the Indians Recently Discovered* is the proclamation of the new inter-

74 *Compendium of the Social Doctrine of the Church* §442.

75 Two major works that contribute to it are: Scott, *The Spanish Origin of International Law*; and James Brown Scott, *The Catholic Conception of International Law.*

national law, and indeed of the law of nations which is yet to be'.[76] Then, in a brief chapter entitled 'The Liberalism of Victoria', Scott argues that Vitoria '(…) was a liberal' and '(…) an internationalist by inheritance', concluding that '(…) his international law is a liberal law of nations'.[77]

As Smeltzer explains, Scott goes beyond recognizing the foundational role of Vitoria's *relectiones* in international law to actually arguing that he is crucial to understanding the principles the present requires to succeed in the international order. He considers that 'Scott's underlying methodological assumption (…) is that it is possible to ascertain the true principles of international law through an archaeology of its founding (…)'.[78] In fact, James Brown Scott presents Vitoria's international community arguably as a model for his times. And these were no easy times in the international realm, as the book was originally published in 1934, i.e., during the challenging interwar period. Nonetheless, Scott argued:

> (…) together with the *Reading De Iure Belli*, [the *De Indis*] did create a law of nations, which is still in existence and which is developing along Victoria's lines, for is not his conception of the international community, possessing the power to make laws and to punish their violation, more than the conception of the Society of Nations in the Covenant of 1920?

This has led some authors to point out problems with his reading, seeing it more as an instrumentalization in favour of an international liberal project. Paolo Amorosa, for instance, in a book on the subject of Scott's inclusion of Vitoria in his theory of international law, argues that Scott uses the Dominican as a 'proxy for his agenda'.[79]

We are not here concerned mainly with Scott's reading or with a possible agenda of his that would call for that instrumentalization. But to understand Schmitt's interpretation of Vitoria and the limits of interpreting the Dominican simply as a modern international law theorist in light of twentieth-century issues, we must look into what Scott means by 'modern law of nations'.

In Chapter XIV of his *Spanish Origin of International Law*, the American scholar describes some of the main features that, in his view, Vitoria's thought and the modern international law conception have in common.

---

76 Scott, *The Spanish Origin of International Law* 95.
77 Scott, *The Spanish Origin of International Law* 280.
78 Smeltzer, 'On the Use and Abuse of Francisco de Vitoria' 351.
79 Amorosa, *Rewriting the History of the Law of Nations* 3.

First of all,[80] the principle of the equality of states. Although Vitoria's concept of a political community is not, as Scott suggests, akin to that of an artificial state, in modern terms, it is true that Vitoria sees international actors as equals. Scott rightly saw Vitoria's notion of *sicut christiani* as conveying the principle of equality between actors in the international sphere. This has been made clear in the aforementioned idea of the reversibility of rights, that Schmitt also acknowledged in Vitoria.

Second, '(...) force between states could only justly be used to redress a wrong'. Scott considers this to be Vitoria's argument and one that his contemporaries should seek to apply. But it is not as clear that Vitoria would subscribe to this view. In fact, although one may argue that Vitoria uses his just war theory as a way of limiting war,[81] he does recognize the legitimacy of a non-defensive war; and it seems too much of a stretch to associate him with the abolition or criminalization of war.

Lastly, Scott argues that both Vitoria and his contemporaries have a conception of the international community as 'composed of states without reference to geography, race, or religion', that in Vitoria's conception 'replaces the large but still limited international community coextensive with Christendom'.[82] It must be noted in this regard that, as Teófilo Urdánoz argues, Vitoria's international community did not do away with the *respublica christiana* but incorporated it: 'He integrates [the *respublica christiana*] in a larger [community], in the community of humanity, conceived of as a new international order (...).'[83]

To fully present Vitoria's idea of an international community and the extent to which it coincides with Scott's liberal idea would require a thorough analysis of Vitoria's concepts of a political community and of the international community, grounded in common humanity, which is not the object of this chapter.

However, the principles of Vitoria's international thought that have been presented in the previous pages constitute an important first step in that analysis. We have seen that Vitoria's thought does offer some relevant ideas for a principle-based approach to international relations. And this has conse-

80 This is not an exhaustive enumeration of Scott's features, which can be read in Scott, *The Spanish Origin of International Law* 281–283. We have selected that ones that are most relevant to the purpose of this study.

81 See Leonor Durão Barroso, André Azevedo Alves, 'Vitoria and Erasmus on the Justice of War', José María Beneyto (ed.), *Empire, Humanism and Rights, Collected Essays on Francisco de Vitoria* (Cham: Springer, 2022) 171–187.

82 Scott, *The Spanish Origin of International Law* 283.

83 See Urdánoz, 'Introducción a la relección primera' 573.

quences that affect how states relate to each other and how the international community is to be organized.

We see an instance of what is at stake in the fact that democracies of the twenty-first century tend to be faced with a choice of how to relate to certain states that do not abide by the same rules, but with whom they need to engage to tackle common challenges.

There are instances in international relations when a balance has to be found between cooperation, on the one hand, and greater autonomy on the other as guarantee of security. To what extent this can be done while incorporating Vitoria's notion of a common humanity, of the borderless ties that unite human beings and call for action when one's dignity is at stake, is a question for subsequent research.

In any case, this shows that concepts expounded by Vitoria as the solidarity among peoples and human beings or the right to wage a defensive war are not obsolete, but central to current international politics. The *societas humana* that is the basis of the right to evangelize, as we have seen, is the same that justifies the defence of the innocent, suffering at the hands of tyranny or unjustified war, regardless of state borders.

But the answers to current challenges need to be thought of in the current context, as spheres of influence and great power politics have returned to the forefront of international debates. The *unipolar moment* as we knew it has ended, and we are now faced with increasing challenges from authoritarian powers that are determined – and, at least in the case of China, increasingly capable – to undermine the international rules-based order, led by the United States.

It is useful to note, and open to further research, the fact that Schmitt has recently been the object of greater interest within China, as some Chinese thinkers and decision-makers look for theories of sovereignty that may provide alternatives to liberalism.[84]

One additional promising path for future research would be to build upon the contrast between Schmitt and Vitoria on universality by exploring how a contemporary influential liberal theorist of law – Friedrich A. Hayek – himself contrasts with Schmitt and the extent to which differences between the two in this regard can be traced back to the same issues raised by Schmitt's reading and critique of Vitoria. It is worth noting that Hayek recognized the influence

84 On this, see, for instance, Chang Che (2020, December 1), 'The Nazi Inspiring China's Communists', in *The Atlantic*. Timothy Snyder notes that Schmitt also influenced contemporary Russia's thinking of 'great spaces' through Alexander Dugin: Timothy Snyder, *The Road to Unfreedom, Russia, Europe, America* (Vintage 2019) 88–90.

of the late Iberian scholastics in his own thought, particularly in his later works, precisely those where Hayek also devotes more attention to the philosophy of law.

In this regard, not only Vitoria's international thought, but another doctrine of his proves relevant: his limits on the power of the state and his concept of popular sovereignty.

Vitoria's internationalism is, in fact, grounded upon the notion of a self-governing community that relates to other communities in a rights-based but apolitical approach. For while Vitoria envisages a human community united by the bond of mere humanity, he cannot be associated with a kind of internationalism that is linked to a specific political regime. He argues for intervention to protect human rights against atrocities but does not extend it to the creation of alliances to defend political stability or promote political change.

However, although he cannot be said to argue for a specific type of political regime as the basis of an international order, the universality of his principles and the connectedness of all peoples subject to natural law is affirmed.

To go back to Schmitt's claim in the *Nomos*, previously mentioned in this chapter, that a reader's first impression of Vitoria may be one of neutrality, one is tempted to remember that first impressions can often be correct. The neutrality that Schmitt first notes in Vitoria does not exhaust his thought. But it is nonetheless essential to its understanding. And even Schmitt, in a note from February 1948, now published in the *Glossarium*, referring to an article by Alfred Verdross-Drossberg, explains that what in his view was Vitoria's temptation was his 'neutralizing humanization'.

It is through principles expressed in Vitoria's universality that liberty and dignity have been granted the conditions to no longer be the prerogative of some – those professing true religion or those in a more advanced civilizational status, within a certain culture – and can now be applied to all human beings indistinctly. This in turn makes the defence of liberty in face of superior powers independent from the contingent circumstances and the faith they profess.

Bibliography

Alves, André Azevedo and José Manuel Moreira. *The Salamanca School* (New York: Bloomsbury, 2013).

Alves, André Azevedo, 'Vitoria, the Common Good and the Limits of Political Power', in *At the Origins of Modernity, Francisco de Vitoria and the Discovery of Inter-*

national Law, eds. José María Beneyto and Justo Corti Varela (Cham: Springer, 2017), 63–75.

Amorosa, Paolo, *Rewriting the History of the Law of Nations: How James Brown Scott made Francisco de Vitoria the Founder of International Law* (New York: Oxford University Press, 2019).

Barroso, Leonor Durão, and André Azevedo Alves. 'Vitoria and Erasmus on the Justice of War', in *Empire, Humanism and Rights, Collected Essays on Francisco de Vitoria*, ed. José María Beneyto (Cham: Springer 2022), 171–187.

Belda Plans, Juan. *Juan Ginés de Sepúlveda* (Madrid: Fundación Ignacio Larramendi, 2016).

Che, Chang. 'The Nazi Inspiring China's Communists'. *The Atlantic* (1 December 2020) Accessed online (on 21 October 2022): https://www.theatlantic.com/international/archive/2020/12/nazi-china-communists-carl-schmitt/617237/.

García Añoveros, Jesús María, 'Carlos V y la Abolición de la Esclavitud de los Indios. Causas, Evolución y Circunstancias'. *Revista de Indias* 60(218) (2000), 58–84.

García García Y, Antonio.' El Sentido de Las Primeras Denuncias', in *La Ética en la Conquista de América*, eds. Demetrio Ramos, et al. (Madrid: Consejo Superior de Investigaciones Científicas, 1984) 67–115.

Hanke, Lewis. *All Mankind is One, A Study of the Disputation between Bartolomé de Las Casas and Juan Ginés de Sepúlveda in 1550 on the Intellectual and Religious Capacity of the American Indians* (DeKalb, IL: Northern Illinois University Press, 1974).

Hanke, Lewis. 'Pope Paul III and the American Indians'. *The Harvard Theological Review* 30(2) (1937), 65–102.

Hanke, Lewis, *The Spanish Struggle for Justice in the Conquest of America* (Boston; Toronto: Little, Brown and Company, 1965).

Hernández, Ramón. 'La Hipótesis de Francisco de Vitoria', in *La Ética en la Conquista de América*, eds. Demetrio Ramos, et al. (Madrid: Consejo Superior de Investigaciones Científicas, 1984), 345–382.

Iannarone, Reginaldo di Agostino. 'Génesis del pensamiento colonial en Francisco de Vitoria', in *Relectio De Indis O Libertad de los Indios*, Francisco de Vitoria, eds. L. Pereña, J. M. Perez Prendes (Madrid: Consejo Superior de Investigaciones Científicas, 1967), XXXI–XLII.

Koskenniemi, Martti. 'Carl Schmitt and International Law', in *The Oxford Handbook of Carl Schmitt*, eds Jens Meierhenrich and Oliver Simons (New York: Oxford University Press, 2016), 592–611.

Las Casas, Bartolomé de. *Del Único Modo de Atraer a Todos los Pueblos a la Verdadera Religión* (México: Fondo de Cultura Económica, 1942).

Luard, Evan, ed. *Basic Texts in International Relations*. (New York: St. Martin's Press, 1997).

MacNutt, F. A. *Bartholomew de Las Casas, His Life, Apostolate and Writings* (Cleveland: The Arthur H. Clark Company, 1909), Appendix II, 426–431.

Moreira, José Manuel, and André Azevedo Alves. *De Salamanca a Coímbra y Évora: Caminos Cruzados de una Escuela Singular* (Madrid: Editoral Universidad Francisco de Vitoria, 2018).

Nys, Ernest. *Le Droit International, Les Principes, Les Théories, Les Faits*, vol. 1 (Paris: Marcel Rivière, 1912).

Pereña, Luciano, ed. *Carta Magna de los Indios, Fuentes Constitucionales, 1534–1609* (Madrid: Consejo Superior de Investigaciones Científicas, 1988).

Pereña, Luciano. 'La Escuela de Salamanca Y La Duda Indiana', in *Francisco de Vitoria y la Escuela de Salamanca, La Ética en la Conquista de América*, eds. Demetrio Ramos, et al. (Madrid: Consejo Superior de Investigaciones Científicas, 1984), 291–344.

Popescu, Oreste. *Studies in the History of Latin American Economic Thought* (New York: Routledge, 1997).

Ramos, Demetrio, et al., eds. *Francisco de Vitoria Y La Escuela de Salamanca*, *La Ética en la Conquista de América* (Madrid: Consejo Superior de Investigaciones Científicas, 1984).

Rommen, Heinrich A. *Die Staatslehre des Franz Suarez S.J.* (New York: Arno Press, 1979).

Schmitt, Carl. *Glossarium, Aufzeichnungen aus den Jahren 1947 bis 1958* (Berlin: Duncker & Humblot, 2015).

Schmitt, Carl. 'the *Großraum* Order of International Law with a Ban on Intervention for Spatially Foreign Powers: a Contribution to the Concept of Reich in International Law (1939–1941)', in *Writings on War* (Cambridge: Polity Press, 2011), 75–124.

Schmitt, Carl. *The* Nomos *of the Earth in the International Law of the* Jus Publicum Europaeum (New York: Telos Press Publishing, 2006).

Scott, James Brown. *The Catholic Conception of International Law* (Clark, NJ: The Lawbook Exchange, 2007).

Scott, James Brown. *The Spanish Origin of International Law: Francisco de Vitoria and his Law of Nations* (Union, NJ: Lawbook Exchange, 2000).

Shaw, Malcolm N. *International Law* (Cambridge: Cambridge University Press, 2014).

Smeltzer, Joshua, 'On the Use and Abuse of Francisco de Vitoria: James Brown Scott and Carl Schmitt'. *Journal of the History of International Law* 20 (2018), 345–372.

Snyder, Timothy, *The Road to Unfreedom, Russia, Europe, America* (Vintage Publishing, 2019).

Suárez, Francisco. *De Legibus (II 13–20), De Iure Gentium*, ed. Luciano Pereña et al. (Madrid: Consejo Superior de Investigaciones Científicas, 1973).

Suárez, Francisco. *Tractatus De Legibus ac Deo Legislatore in Decem Libros Distributus* (Nápoles: Ex Typis Fibrenianis, 1872).

Urdánoz, Teófilo, ed. *Obras de Francisco de Vitoria, Relecciones Teológicas* (Madrid: Biblioteca de Autores Cristianos, 1960).

Urdánoz, Teófilo. 'Síntesis Teológico-Jurídica de la Doctrina de Vitoria', in *Relectio De Indis O Libertad de los Indios*, Francisco de Vitoria, eds. Luciano Pereña nad J. M. Perez Prendes (Madrid: Consejo Superior de Investigaciones Científicas, 1967), XLIII–CXLII.

Vitoria, Francisco de. *Obras de Francisco de Vitoria, Relecciones Teológicas*, ed. Teófilo Urdánoz (Madrid: Biblioteca de Autores Cristianos, 1960).

Vitoria, Francisco de. *Relectio De Indis, O Libertad de los Indios*, eds. Luciano Pereña and J. M. Perez Prendes (Madrid: Consejo Superior de Investigaciones Científicas, 1967).

Zorroza, M. Idoya. 'La Ley Natural En El Pensamiento de Francisco de Vitoria', in *Concepciones de la Ley Natural: Medioevo Latino y Escolástica Española e Iberoamericana*, eds. Laura E. Corso de Estrada, M. Jesús Soto-Bruna, M. Idoya Zorroza (Pamplona: EUNSA, 2013), 265–284.

Other documents

Pontifical Council for Justice and Peace, *Compendium of the Social Doctrine of the Church.* Accessed online: https://www.vatican.va/roman_curia/pontifical_councils/justpeace/documents/rc_pc_justpeace_doc_20060526_compendio-dott-soc_en.html

John Paul II, 'Meeting with the Native Peoples of the Americas: Address of His Holiness John Paul II' (Vatican City: Libreria Editrice Vaticana, 1987).

PART 3

Discovery, Nomos, and Conceptions of Space

CHAPTER 9

The Spatial Imagination of International Law in China

Ryan Martínez Mitchell

1 Introduction

China's comprehensive incorporation into the international legal order occurred between the early nineteenth to mid-twentieth centuries.[1] Throughout this period, and across highly varying regimes and situations, domestic officials and intellectuals had to grapple with the question of how to fit their state and its zones of rule into foreign legal frameworks, or decide how best to resist them when necessary. Certain themes became consistently significant in Chinese discussions regarding international law. One of the most important of these themes has been that of space.[2]

Historical Chinese encounters with international law often involved shifts in the spatial conceptions of the state's domestic political order, territory, and place in the world.[3] Above all, they entailed a gradual, far-reaching redefinition of China as a nation-state with delimited boundaries and formalized

1 For recent discussions of China's role in international law, historically and currently, see Xue Hanqin, "Chinese Contemporary Perspectives on International Law: History, Culture and International Law," *Recueil Des Cours* 355 (2011): 41–233; Congyan Cai, *The Rise of China and International Law: Taking Chinese Exceptionalism Seriously* (Oxford University Press, 2019); Ryan Martínez Mitchell, *Recentering the World: China and the Transformation of International Law* (Cambridge University Press, 2022); *The Cambridge Handbook of China and International Law*, eds. Ignacio de la Rasilla and Congyan Cai (Cambridge University Press, 2024).

2 Cf. Jiang Shigong, "Ludi Yu Haiyang: 'Kongjian Geming' Yu Shijie Lishi De 'Maijinde Shidai' [Land and Sea: Spatial Revolution and the Mackinder Age of World History]," *Kaifang Shidai* [Open Times] (2018): 103–127, 127 ('The rise of China calls for not only universal thinking of political philosophy, but also global geopolitical awareness. We must not only think about geopolitical strategies, but also the intrinsic connection between geography and human history in which may lie the fundamental principle of human historical development.').

3 Richard J. Smith, *Mapping China and Managing the World: Culture, Cartography and Cosmology in Late Imperial Times* (Routledge, 2013), 83–84 ("[I]t was the Sino-Japanese War of 1894–1895 that sounded the death knell of traditional Chinese cartography ... From this time onward, Chinese nationalism affected in fundamental ways the rendering of geographical space by cartographers in China.").

 | DOI:10.1163/9789004757448_010

rights and obligations.[4] However, it would be a mistake to characterize this as merely a passive flow of 'norm-taking', in which China has gradually been socialized into a pre-existing Western (and 'Westphalian') order.[5] From the period of the first Chinese uses of international legal argument to the present day, there have been creative readings of legal norms and attempts to define new doctrines to serve local aspirations.[6] In this vein, spatial conceptions have chiefly arisen in two competing forms: on the one hand, calls for a more genuine globalized universalism than that invoked by great powers in the course of China's, and other 'peripheral' states', historical experiences of subjugation; on the other hand, assertions of local sovereign and regional collective rights against external interventions.

This chapter makes the argument that different ways of imagining political and legal space have been a vitally important element in shaping China's role in and discourse on the global legal order. First, it describes the diversity in traditional Chinese views on the spatial dimension of state authority, which ranged from moral universalism to pragmatic and concrete approaches to statecraft. Then, it connects these traditional perspectives with the new thematic explorations that entered Chinese intellectual life in the process of receiving Western international law. In China as elsewhere, 'naturalist' conceptions of law, in various guises, have often served as a corrective to the pure positivist focus on doctrines established by authoritative instruments.[7]

With respect to the topic of law's spatiality, variations of natural law-tinged argumentation (from Confucian to Kantian to socialist) have been used to justify the righteousness of anticolonial resistance, solidarity amongst formerly marginalized peoples, and peaceful coexistence. Yet they have also, separately, informed assertions about the natural rights of sovereigns to maintain

---

4 Cf. Immanuel C. Y. Hsü, *China's Entrance into the Family of Nations: The Diplomatic Phase, 1858–1880* (Harvard University Press, 1960), 133.

5 China's potential status as a 'norm-maker' versus 'norm-taker' is a major topic of ongoing discourse, particularly in the field of international relations. See, for example, Chris Alden and Daniel Large, "On Becoming a Norms Maker: Chinese Foreign Policy, Norms Evolution and the Challenges of Security in Africa," *The China Quarterly* 221 (2015): 123–142.

6 For one early example of such contestation concerning the different ways of arguing over 'sovereignty', see Amanda J. Cheney, "Tibet Lost in Translation: Sovereignty, Suzerainty and International Order Transformation, 1904–1906," *Journal of Contemporary China* 26 (2017): 769–783.

7 Stephen Hall, "The Persistent Spectre: Natural Law, International Order and the Limits of Legal Positivism," *European Journal of International Law* 12, no. 2 (2001): 269–307; G. M. Gordon, "Natural Law in International Legal Theory: Linear and Dialectical Presentations," in *Oxford Handbook of the Theory of International Law*, in Anne Orford, Florian Hoffmann, and Martin Clark (Oxford University Press, 2016), 279–305.

their territory, freedom from interference, and the regional arrangements suitable to their own particular, concrete historical contexts. As will be argued, the natural law tradition of the School of Salamanca and those it inspired, along with the contrasting but also naturalistically styled 'geojurisprudence' of Carl Schmitt, may be particularly useful comparative lenses for interpreting these two poles in Chinese approaches to international law.[8]

As the concluding sections of the chapter will argue, these competing strains of naturalist legal thought have continued to operate in the international initiatives of the People's Republic of China. The main platforms of China's stances on international law, the Five Principles of Peaceful Coexistence and the more recent Community of Shared Future for Humankind, can be interpreted as vehicles for mediating the opposing logics of universal norms and sovereigntist 'concrete order.' As foreign policy agendas encompassing a wide range of positions, they work towards reconciling different visions of the spatiality of the global legal order.

2 Early Antecedents of Competing Chinese Spatial Conceptions of Global Legal Order

The most globally famous Chinese spatial concept today, and the one most often invoked in discussions about distinctively Chinese notions of law and politics, is the notion of *Tianxia*, literally referring to 'All Under Heaven'.[9] Since its very earliest uses, this traditional term has always had at least two

8 Carl Schmitt's legal thought is often described, especially by recent interpreters, as 'decisionist' or even 'nihilistic'. See, for example, Robert Howse, "Schmitt, Schmitteanism and Contemporary International Legal Theory," in *Oxford Handbook of the Theory of International Law*, eds. Anne Orford, Florian Hoffmann, and Martin Clark (Oxford University Press, 2016), 212–230. However, despite major decisionist elements, much of his thought in fact turned on invocations of 'natural' norms and categories, and indeed he explicitly identified the political philosophers Jean Bodin and Thomas Hobbes, both of whom had developed their own idiosyncratic accounts of natural law, as models. On Schmitt's critique of international law's 'spacelessness', and its association with his version of naturalist legal thought, see Carl Schmitt, *Der Nomos der Erde im Völkerrecht des Jus Publicum Europaeum* (Duncker & Humblot, 1974), 64–65 (describing how his intellectual predecessor Thomas Hobbes, like Vitoria, 'speaks of the "state of nature"', but unlike Vitoria and his generation of natural lawyers, does so in a way that is 'by no means in the sense of a spaceless utopia'). At the time when Schmitt was writing, he was also frequently thought of as adopting a variant of natural law argumentation. See, for example, Virginia L. Gott, "The National Socialist Theory of International Law," *American Journal of International Law* 32, no. 4 (1938): 704–718.

9 See Yuri Pines, "Changing Views of 'Tianxia' in Pre-imperial Discourse," *Oriens Extremus* 43 (2002): 101–116.

possible referents: either the practical realm of political rule by China's central authorities or the world as a whole.[10] That overlap of meanings, and the fact that traditional Chinese thought usually did not find it necessary to explicitly distinguish between these two usages, contrasts with the territorially delimited notion of the modern nation-state.[11]

However, despite the presence of a longstanding official discourse of universal moral authority, in terms of which the Chinese Emperor was conceived to stand at the center of cosmic order, the realities of statecraft also at times involved concessions to the precise opposite idea. Chinese rulers regularly established ad hoc, idiosyncratic relationships with kingdoms, peoples, and communities, based on principles of spatial and cultural or moral distance. Limits to the reach or ambitions of central authority could frequently be justified on the basis of notions of exclusivity. Rather than a potentially all-encompassing *Tianxia*, differentiated notions such as *Hua–Yi* (roughly equivalent to 'civilized' and 'non-civilized') or *Zhong–Wai* ('central' and 'outer') were frequently invoked in order to explain both Chinese cultural supremacy and the acceptability of limits to direct Chinese rule.[12] They could also be invoked in order to explain specific policies of distancing, such as the famous Ming Dynasty ban on sea traffic, that would otherwise compromise the premise of the Emperor as a source of universal moral influence.[13]

Although it is impossible to capture the full range and complexity of traditional spatial discourses in the course of a brief description, it is sufficient to note the longstanding tension between the ideas of *Tianxia* and *Zhong–Wai* as forming the basis for later tendencies. As early as China's Warring States era, these ideas formed the basis for the different views of competing political theorists regarding the proper scope for the application of legal norms. While thinkers in what would later be called the 'Confucian' (or *Rujia*) tradition tended to emphasize the universal applicability of ethical rules and standards, regardless of political or territorial context, those associated with 'Legalism' (*Fajia*), adopted starkly different views.[14]

10 Ibid.

11 Ibid., for a modern reconceptualization, see Zhao Tingyang, *All Under Heaven: The Tianxia System for a Possible World Order* (University of California Press, 2021).

12 See, e.g. *China among Equals: The Middle Kingdom and Its Neighbors, 10th–14th Centuries*, ed. Morris Rossabi (University of California Press, 1983).

13 Cf. Yiu Siu, "Maritime exclusion policy in Ming China and Chosŏn Korea, 1368–1450: dynastic authority, national security, and trade," PhD diss., University of Oxford, 2022.

14 On the origins of Confucianism or Rujia as a category, see Michael Hunter and Martin Kern, *Confucius and the Analects Revisited: New Perspectives on Composition, Dating, and Authorship* (Brill, 2018).

By the time that the Qing polity under its Manchu rulers began coming under intense pressure from Western empires seeking to open its markets to foreign commerce, these ancient spatial themes of universalism and particularity were both susceptible to being invoked. Each had long traditions of conceptualization as well as recent practical examples of implementation. For example, under the early Qing rulers the Chinese realm (*dulimbai gurun*) could extend its power to intervene against regional peoples such as the inhabitants of what are now Vietnam, Myanmar, and Central Asian territories, among others, on the basis of claims to universal authority and notions that local rulers were failing to provide due prestige to the imperial center.[15] At the same time, more pragmatic and self-limiting approaches to territoriality were also not infrequent. Longstanding Chinese policies of *de facto* non-intervention against regional kingdoms maintaining 'respectful' tributary relationships reflected this tendency. So too, still more clearly, did episodes such as the seventeenth-century formation of a treaty-based relationship with the Russian Empire, as mediated by Jesuit missionary interlocutors.[16] Indeed, the Qing course of dealing with respect to Western merchants was almost always characterized more by its association with the '*Zhong–Wai*' framework of strategic inclusion and exclusion of outside influences, rather than by the aspiration towards universal incorporation and rule.[17] The great distance of Western states, and their association with precarious sea travel, contributed to their characterization as peripheral elements in the Sinocentric 'world system'.[18]

Of course, the advent of Western military pressure and incursion would lead to numerous crises, and would fundamentally reshape many aspects of China's political and legal thought. With regard to the issue of the spatial framework for state and interstate order, however, there would be some meaningful continuities. The reception of Western international law doctrine from the mid-nineteenth century onward provided an *en masse* influx of new conceptual influences, but these, arguably, came to resemble in important

15 Dai Yingcong, "A Disguised Defeat: The Myanmar Campaign of the Qing Dynasty," *Modern Asian Studies* 38, no. 1 (2004): 145–189.

16 V. S. Frank, "The Territorial Terms of the Sino-Russian Treaty of Nerchinsk, 1689," *Pacific Historical Review* 16, no. 3 (1947): 265–270.

17 Fang Weigui, "Yi, Yang, Xi, Wai and Other Terms: The Transition from 'Barbarian' to 'Foreigner' in Nineteenth-Century China," in *New Terms for New Ideas*, eds. Michael Lackner, Iwo Amelung, Joachim Kurtz (Brill, 2001), 95–123.

18 See Giovanni Arrighi and Beverly J. Silver, *Chaos and Governance in the Modern World System* (The University of Minnesota Press, 1999), 248–249 (describing the eventual "formal dissolution" of a Sinocentric world system due to European imperial expansion).

ways the traditional dynamic of tension between universalistic/moralistic and pragmatic/situational/interest-based ideas of state jurisdiction.

3 The Issue of Space within the Early Reception of Western Legal Thought

The reception of Western international legal thought in China occurred in various phases, during which translated texts and imported ideas were gradually diffused first among a small network of elite actors, then through a broader community of politically engaged intellectuals, and finally through large segments of the broader population. The earliest translations were of brief segments of Emer de Vattel's *Droit des Gens*, produced under the direction of the imperial commissioner for Southern China, Lin Zexu, during the course of the First Opium War.[19] These sections were translated for the pragmatic purpose of attempting to use Western norms to justify Chinese policies of autonomous local jurisdiction and the ability for states to restrict trade at their own discretion. Indeed, Vattel's account of international law doctrine made allowances for such rights on the part of individual states and did not support the legal interpretations being advanced by the British side, which justified military coercion as a legitimate form of reprisal for the interruption of commerce.[20] In this encounter, the British 'imperialism of free trade' represented a more extreme form of universalism than China's claims to exceptional moral authority, which avoided attempts to assert actual universal rule.[21]

However, already in this earliest attempt to make use of Western international legal argumentation in order to advance distinctive Chinese interests, the problematic of spatial differentiation was beginning to play a role. For, in order to convey China's arguments about the legitimacy of excluding foreign trade in opium, Lin and others arguing the Chinese position had to employ the Western legal framework of a specifically delimited territorial administration. The role of Western natural law theories in such encounters was two-fold, for they provided both a universal frame of reference – the idea

19 See Rune Svarverud, "The Notions of 'Power' and 'Rights' in Chinese Political Discourse," in *New Terms for New Ideas*, eds. Michael Lackner, Iwo Amelung, Joachim Kurtz (Brill, 2001), 125–143.

20 See, e.g., accounts of the relevant parliamentary debates in Stephen R. Platt, *Imperial Twilight: The Opium War and the End of China's Last Golden Age* (Vintage, 2019).

21 Cf. Ronald Robinson and John Gallagher, "The Imperialism of Free Trade," *Economic History Review* 6, no. 1 (1953): 1–15.

of 'natural' ethical categories, such as the state, the ruler, and the individual commercial actor – and at the same time allowed for the exclusion of outsiders as a natural prerogative of the individual state.[22] This was, of course, a different position from that which had been advanced by earlier natural law theorists, including Francisco de Vitoria, Alberico Gentili, and Hugo Grotius, who had emphasized a 'right of intercourse' (*ius communicationis*) that encompassed both missionary activities and trade.[23]

Natural law-based accounts of the law of nations in the West had always exhibited their own internal tension between ethical universalism and concrete pragmatic concerns. Vitoria, for example, had, according to Martti Koskenniemi, sought to provide 'a vocabulary that would accept the basic contemporary forms of territorial government, private ownership, and war but that would nevertheless restate the unity of humankind under God.'[24] The subsequent conceptual vocabulary of also Western international law reflected these dueling motivations.[25] In the Sino-Western encounters of the early nineteenth century, both sides sought to assert natural rights – either to access markets for trade, or to restrict foreign access to one's own territory – in support of their own national positions with diametrically opposing spatial conceptions.

Although Lin's Vattel translation was an episode with limited immediate relevance to the course of the Opium War, it was emblematic as the start of a broader pattern in which Chinese officials, diplomats, and intellectuals would find themselves increasingly turning to Western international legal argument in defense of China's interests. These efforts were subdued until roughly the 1860s-1980s period following the so-called Second Opium War or 'Arrow War', during which officials engaged in self-strengthening (*ziqiang*) policies began to place more emphasis on an assertive diplomacy that made use of Western international legal argumentation and the invocation of customary rights.[26] By this point, more recent international law authorities, in particular the textbooks of Henry Wheaton and Johann Kaspar Bluntschli, were being used as

22 See Emer de Vattel, *Le droit des gens* (Carnegie institution of Washington, 1916).

23 Cf. François Rigaux, "Aux origines du droit international: la conquête de l'Amérique," in *The Roots of International Law/Les fondements du droit international: Liber Amicorum Peter Haggenmacher*, eds. Pierre-Marie Dupuy and Vincent Chetail (Brill Nijhoff, 2014), 641–648.

24 See Martti Koskenniemi, "Empire and International Law: The Real Spanish Contribution," *University of Toronto Law Journal* 61, no. 1 (2011): 1–36.

25 Ibid.

26 Stephen R. Halsey, *Quest for Power: European Imperialism and the Making of Chinese Statecraft* (Harvard University Press, 2015).

key reference points in place of earlier natural law-oriented theorists.[27] A major aspect of the changes was the adoption of a stricter doctrine of civilizational differences and an exclusionary conception of the 'Family of Nations' comprising the (Eurocentric) international legal community, for which China and its region were clearly identified as peripheral.[28]

With regard to the category of norms dealing with state authority, the newer, more positivist legal texts emphasized criteria of effective occupation and administration as prerequisites for jurisdiction.[29] For Chinese readers of such texts, the emerging notions of effective occupation as a heuristic for genuine territorial title served to spur a sense of crisis over the vulnerability of China's integrity as a political unit. It was primarily after the intensified reception of Western legal texts, including via the diplomatic encounters of the 1860s and after, that Qing officials began to emphasize policies of military deployment to ensure counter the encroachment of Western empires (and Japan) into vulnerable and far-flung frontier regions. These Qing attempts to shore up territorial integrity echoed the pattern of legal practice on a global scale, as the same concepts were being deployed globally in order, according to Duve *et al.*, 'to legitimize the acquisition of territory by European states from non-European entities and to regulate the relations between the European states.'[30] This further consolidated the turn from a more 'Vitorian' naturalistic discourse of the rights of states and peoples to one emphasizing positive criteria of administration and the pre-emption of foreign claims over particular spaces.

Not only the descriptions and justifications for the acquisition and retention of territory, but the broader legal dimensions of diplomatic relations among states as well, were being redefined during this period. As Martti Koskenniemi writes:

> … [A] new generation of activist lawyers and academics sought a more progressive type of legal engagement with what they felt was an increasingly modern, internationalising and integrating world. Members of this new generation were keen to contribute to the consolidation of peaceful relations and the expansion of liberal legislation in Europe as well as to civilising the colonies. Their ambitions were universal, but they assumed

27 See Mitchell, *Recentering the World*, 80.

28 Lassa Oppenheim, *International Law*, Volume 1 (Longmans, Green & Co., 1912), 33.

29 Cf. Andrew Fitzmaurice, "Liberalism and empire in nineteenth-century international law," *The American Historical Review* 117, no. 1 (2012): 122–140.

30 Thomas Duve, et al., *Entanglements in Legal History: Conceptual Approaches* (Max Planck Institute for Legal History and Legal Theory, 2014).

> that what 'universality' meant was represented by the 'civilised world' of Europe and the United States.[31]

International law's 'standard of civilization' was thoroughly consolidated by the end of the nineteenth century, and China was among the states hierarchically subordinated on its basis.[32] Relatedly, the use of the international conference form as a diplomatic setting for the formulation of new norms had major repercussions for determining the spatial dimension of international law's authority and the nature of its relation to China and other non-Western polities. With respect to major new initiatives such as the reallocations of territorial and sovereign rights via the Congress of Paris (1856), the Congress of Berlin (1878), and the Berlin Conference of 1884–1885, among others, non-Western states were, in general, excluded from any position of meaningful agency.[33] The same was true with respect to the development of specific new initiatives in norm-legislation, such as the Geneva Conventions and subsequent efforts to codify the laws of war. Even the ostensibly global Hague Peace Conferences of 1899 and 1907 appeared to Chinese and other 'peripheral' participants as meetings of great powers for the administration of the globe, division of its territories, and decisions upon rules of competition.[34]

In terms of China's own domestic reception of international law discourse during this late nineteenth- to early twentieth-century period, there was correspondingly a turn away from the ethically inflected argumentation of previous decades and, instead, an appreciation for the close correlation between national power and the authority a state could exert within the international system. By the crucial turning point of the late 1890s, as Japan and other foreign empires began to exert increasing pressure against the Qing realm in the attempt to carve out new territorial and jurisdictional rights, Chinese activist intellectuals had firmly embraced the new discourse of 'state sovereignty' as the metric for political agency and equality with foreign states.[35] The continued sense of the vulnerability of the vast Qing realm, and the examples of

31 Martti Koskenniemi, "International Law in 1873," in *Au Service du Droit International: Les 150 ans de l'Association de droit international*, eds. Catherine Kessedjian, Olivier Descamps et Teodolinda Fabrizi (Éditions Panthéon-Assas, 2023), 167–197.

32 Gerrit W. Gong, *The Standard of "Civilization" in International Society* (Clarendon Press, 1984).

33 Ryan Martinez Mitchell, "International Law as Project or System?," *Georgetown Journal of International Law* 51, no. 3 (2019): 623–689.

34 See Ryan Martínez Mitchell, "China's Participation in the Second Hague Conference and the Concept of Equal Sovereignty in International Law," *Asian Journal of International Law* 11, no. 2 (2021): 351–371.

35 Wang Hui, *Zhongguo Xiandai Sixiang de Xingqi*, Volume 1 (Sanlian Shudian, 2004).

India and other regions which had become fully subject to foreign colonial domination, became the spurs for a newly geopolitically oriented way of thinking about legal norms at the interstate level.

The discourse of national rights had shifted markedly, with reform activists of the 1890s beginning to volubly criticize the unequal character of China's treaties with Western powers, its loss of national autonomy in domains such as independent economic policy, and its risk of becoming 'another India or Poland' should Western imperial penetration continue to intensify.[36] Rather than a general emphasis on argumentation in terms of universalized ethical conceptions, the discourse of national power as the determining factor in establishing the rights of a member of the international order began to gain prominence. It was also only from this period that international law texts began to be received in large quantities in Chinese society, primarily via the medium of translations from Japanese editions.[37] International law appeared to many Chinese observers as the discursive regime of expanding empires in constant communication to codify new norms of conduct and territorial administration – rather than as a universally applicable ethical normative system – informed views among the nationalist activist movement in China that rapidly grew in the early years of the twentieth century.

4 International Law as 'Discourse of Equals' or Vehicle for Hegemony?

By the turn of the twentieth century, the Qing Dynasty was already nearing the point of collapse in the wake of its crisis of legitimacy following Japan's successful annexation of territories during the First Sino-Japanese War of 1894–1895 as well as other episodes of national subordination. Awareness of international law's connection with initiatives for hegemonic control over 'peripheral' regions of the world was also reinforced in the course of China's participation in the Hague Conferences of 1899 and 1907. During the first of these, the leading Qing delegate, Yang Ru, was confronted with Western delegates who explicitly rejected the notion that China could contribute as an equal to the formulation of new legal norms. He and his translator/co-dele-

36 Xiong Xiling, "Wei Xiangsheng Xing Lun Cheng Zhang Zhidong [Memorial to Zhang Zhidong on Allowing Steamboat Travel in Hunan] (1896)," in *Hunan Weixin Yundong Shiliao* [*Historical Materials on the Hunan Restoration Movement*], ed. Yi Feizhou (Yuelu Shushe, 2013): 223–230.

37 Rune Svarverud, *International Law as World Order in Late Imperial China* (Brill, 2007).

gate, Lu Zhengxiang, sought to draw explicit attention to Western abuses of the universal rights associated with the *ius communicationis*, which proclaimed the ability for Western missionaries to penetrate throughout Chinese territory and then, when they encountered local resistance, legitimated violent reprisals that severely impaired Chinese sovereignty. Yang articulated the growing cynicism regarding the Western discourse of international law with his comment that Western lawyers should come up with a formula for how much of China's land to seize every time a missionary died on its soil.[38]

China's participation in the 1899 conference did not establish it as an equal and homogenous member of the global community.[39] Instead, the ensuing Boxer uprising of 1899–1901 entailed dramatic experiences of invasion and occupation by the collective forces of the great powers of the 'West', as well as the imposition of equally remarkable limits upon Chinese sovereignty via the Boxer Protocol that restricted the state's ability to independently set tariff rates, required the repayment of a vast reparations sum, and subjected broad swathes of territory to foreign military presence, among other obligations.[40] Both experiences, the collective 'reprisal' undertaken by the great powers in disregard of Chinese territorial autonomy and the subsequent collectively imposed treaty terms, reinforced the trend towards skepticism of international law's normative validity and proclivity to view it as a tool for intervention by foreign empires.

At the 1907 Second Hague Conference, Lu Zhengxiang served as the primary delegate for China and was able to exert a role of meaningfully greater (if still limited) agency. In response to Western proposals on a number of topics, Lu and other delegates of 'peripheral' states, particularly those of Latin America, were able to coordinate common positions that imposed some constrains on initiatives spearheaded by the great powers. These included, in particular, plans for the establishment of an international prize court as well as a potential permanent international court of general jurisdiction. In opposition to the new court's membership arrangement, which was to be determined on the basis of a ranking system in which China (and other 'minor' states) would

38 Mitchell, *Recentering the World*, 86–88.

39 Ibid., cf. Friedrich von Martens, *La Conférence de la Paix á La Haye: Étude d'Histoire Contemporaine* (Arthur Rousseau, 1900): 18; F. de Martens, "How the Chinese Question Should Be Solved," *The Advocate of Peace*, 62, no. 11 (1900): 240–241; Julius Hirschfeld, "Current Notes on International Law," *Law Mag. & Rev. Quart. Rev. Juris. 5th ser.* 26 (1900): 335; Alfred Thayer Mahan, *The Problem of Asia and Its Effect Upon International Policies* (Sampson, Low, Marston and Co., 1900): 167.

40 "International Protocol (1901), Article VI," in *Treaties, Conventions, etc., Between China and Foreign States* (Maritime Customs Service, 1917): 301–345.

only be classed as a 'third-class power', Lu and other delegates were able to successfully stymy the proposal.[41]

With regard to this major shift in the dynamic as compared to the 1899 conference, Carl Schmitt was later to write that this had marked a profoundly important turning point for international law itself: instead of a spatially determined order imposed by a central European conclave upon the peoples of the rest of the world, the 1907 Second Hague Conference had seen the inclusion of non-European peoples that had played a meaningful role.[42] This was, in his view, a breakdown of the logically consistent and 'natural' international legal order of the nineteenth-century *jus publicum Europaeum* – a 'concrete order' of law developed among European empires – and a turn towards a new form of 'spaceless' (*raumlos*) universalism.[43]

For Schmitt, writing in the 1930s and 40s, these were developments to be condemned. They pointed the way towards an incoherent and universal interventionism, which, in his view, would be a stand-in for Anglo-American efforts at global hegemony.[44] Yet from the Chinese perspective, the Second Hague Conference marked the first time that the state's representatives had been able to affect the outcome of international legal discourse in a meaningful way. While nationalist activists continued to express deep-seated doubts and suspicions about Western rules of international law and their ongoing role in limiting Chinese sovereignty, elite officials and jurists in the following years became for the first time genuinely integrated into an international law profession that now began to seem like a potential constraint on foreign incursions into China. The first generation of fully trained Chinese international lawyers, correspondingly, tempered their keen awareness of the geopolitical framework within which international law operated in the early years of the twentieth century, with a rejuvenated dedication to the aspirational rhetoric of universalism and attempts at ethical engagement with global peers.

This position was represented by figures such as Wellington Koo, who during his studies at Columbia University for his 1912 PhD in political science and international law under John Bassett Moore advocated for China's national

41 Mitchell, "China's Participation in the Second Hague Conference," 370–371.

42 Cf. Martha Finnemore and Michelle Jurkovich, "Getting a Seat at the Table: The Origins of Universal Participation and Modern Multilateral Conferences," *Global Governance: A Review of Multilateralism and International Organizations* 20, no. 3 (2014): 361–373.

43 Schmitt, *Der Nomos der Erde*, 204–05.

44 Indeed, one way to interpret Schmitt's own critique of this shift is that it comprised an abandonment of a concrete "*Zhong-Wai*" model in which Europe was the "Center", replacing it with a spaceless moral universalism. He did not, of course, use this terminology.

rights, the end of Western extraterritorial consular jurisdiction, and the fair treatment of Chinese immigrants abroad, among other issues, primarily by reference to developing standards of fair and equal treatment.[45] A similar, universalist approach was adopted by Zhou Wei (aka Tchéou Wei), whose studies at the University of Paris and at Fribourg became the basis for his 1917 monograph on 'the legal organization of international society.'[46] In this book, Zhou joined the just-emerging discourse aiming to design and establish a new international organization. He argued for a universal League that would enjoy powers of legislation, adjudication, and execution of the law standing above the authority of the state.[47] Also active beginning in the 1910s was Zhou Gengsheng, who invoked notions of the natural rights of peoples to equal membership in the international system, and was a leader in framing the doctrine of the repudiation of 'unequal treaties.'[48]

For each of these significant early jurists, as well as for several others in the community of Chinese lawyers, the 'regaining' of national sovereignty was thought of as being compatible with a commitment to international organization. Fundamental norms of the *ius communicationis*, such as those involving market access and openness to foreign missionaries, could be accepted, even if the outrages that had been committed by foreign powers in retaliation for alleged violations of those rights in China ought to be rejected. The solution for establishing China as a more equal player within the international system, capable of enjoying its own collective rights on par with the states of the West, would be in the turn towards an intensified legal organization of the international community, and an embrace of the naturalistic ethical discourse of equality among nations. The theme of equality, indeed, was one that Western international lawyers increasingly associated with China and the task of determining its place within international legal order. Progressive lawyers such as Max Huber discussed China's role in international law since the Second Hague Conference as embodying a 'problem of equality' (*Gleichheitsproblem*) that had to be addressed in order to ensure the continued viability of the normative system as a whole.[49] By the time of the Paris Peace Conference, Chinese

45 V.K. Wellington Koo, *The Status of Aliens in China* (Columbia University Press, 1912).

46 S. Tchéou Wei [Zhou Wei], *Essai sur l'organisation juridique de la Société international* (Libraire Atar, 1917).

47 Ibid.

48 Gengsheng [Zhou Gengsheng], "Zongzhuquan Lun [The Theory of Suzerainty]," *Taipingyang* 1, no. 10 (1918); Zhou Gengsheng, *Bupingdeng Tiaoyue Shijiang* [Ten Lectures on Unequal Treaties] (Taipingyang Shudian, 1928).

49 Max Huber, "Die Gleichheit der Staaten," in *Rechtswissenschaftliche Beiträge: Juristische Festgabe des Auslandes zu Josef Kohlers 60. Geburtstag, 9. März 1909*, ed. Fritz Berolzheimer (Scientia Verlag, 1981) (original publication 1909).

lawyers, diplomats, and scholars were expressing with increasing frequency their commitment to the idea of China as an integral member of the international legal community. The nineteenth-century 'standard of civilization' was by no means completely abandoned even during the League of Nations years of the 1920s–1930s, with non-Western states continuing to be marginalized.[50]

5 Spatial Imagination during China's Mid-Twentieth-Century Transition to Great Power Status

The competing trends of viewing international law as a vehicle for the concrete exertion of state power, particularly that of foreign empires, or alternatively as a global ethical discourse among equals, continued to exhibit tension throughout the interwar period. The potentialities of a universal applicability of legal norms were represented with particular vividness by China's inclusion as a major constituent member of the League of Nations. Indeed, its delegates, including Wellington Koo, were able to take up rotating positions as leaders within the organization. For some onlookers both Chinese and Western, there could hardly be a more potent embodiment of the international legal order's aspiration to universality than a Chinese (or Japanese) diplomat chairing a commission to decide an intra-European interstate dispute.[51] Chinese delegates also pioneered the norm of 'continental' representations within the League Council, which has remained a key feature of international organizations to this day.[52]

A number of states, including the United States and Japan, were particularly concerned with the preservation of 'regional arrangements' such as the Monroe Doctrine under the new rules of the League Covenant that purported to restrict recourse to interstate uses of force. Washington's hegemonic position in the Americas, and Tokyo's often-stated aspirations for a similar role in East Asia, risked being found to be conflict with the principles of formal (if not practical) legal equality among states upon which the League was supposed to be based.[53] For some Chinese diplomats and international lawyers, correspondingly, the Monroe Doctrine and the general principle of regional hegem-

50 Gong, *The Standard of "Civilization"*, 124–128.

51 Cf. Alison Adcock Kaufman, "In Pursuit of Equality and Respect: China's Diplomacy and the League of Nations," *Modern China* 40, no. 6 (2014): 605–638.

52 Mitchell, *Recentering the World*, 146, 163, 263.

53 See Ryan Martínez Mitchell, "Monroe's Shadow: League of Nations Covenant Article 21 and the Space of Asia in International Legal Order," *TWAIL Review* 2 (2021): 200–231.

ony it justified came to be a target for increasing critique.[54] The continuation of foreign empires' ability to exert unequal rights of jurisdiction deep within Chinese territory due to the continuation of the unequal treaties signed under the Qing Dynasty, however, was a far greater subject of concern. Chinese jurists wrote extensively on the illegitimacy of foreign constraints on the national sovereignty, and advocated principles of popular diplomacy in combining official action with popular boycotts and protests to attempt to exert pressure on foreign powers to give up their unequal rights in China.[55]

There were thus many varieties of 'revisionism' with respect to the status quo of the League of Nations and the international order it undergirded. The Soviet Union, for example, rejected many aspects of the international economic order as well as the positions of foreign states whose legitimacy it called into question on the basis of their alleged exploitation of the proletariat; in turn, it was unrecognized by Washington and several other Western powers until the 1930s.[56] Chinese international lawyers were increasingly influenced by the Soviet model of critique of Western legal standards, which they depicted as in line with 'natural' justice.[57] However, similar themes were also articulated by other strains of international legal thought, including by non-Marxist scholars who turned instead to Kantian variants of natural law.[58]

Another major variant of natural law-inflected critical international law discourse during this era was that coming from the extreme right. For German critics such as Schmitt, for example, the League had to be condemned as a vehicle for a 'universal interventionism' that could comprise humiliating episodes such as the Franco-Belgian occupation of the Ruhr, exorbitant reparations demands, limits on national autonomy with respect to military policy and interstate relations, etc.[59] The idea that the German people possessed a

54 Ibid.

55 Cf. Wang Zheng, *Never Forget National Humiliation: Historical Memory in Chinese Politics and Foreign Relations* (Columbia University Press, 2014).

56 Edwin D. Dickinson, "The Recognition of Russia," *Michigan Law Review* 30, no. 2 (1931): 181–196.

57 See, for example, Li Dade, "Guanyu Zhou Gengsheng Hu Shi zhi de Lunzhan: Tongyi Zhou Gengsheng Kanfa, Hu Shi zhi You 'Kong Su Bing' [On the War of Words Between Zhou Gengsheng and Hu Shi: Agreeing with Zhou Gengsheng, Hu Shi Has 'Sovietphobia'']," *Zhongyang Zhoukan* 10, no. 9 (1948).

58 Thomas E. Greift, "The Principle of Human Rights in Nationalist China: John CH Wu and the Ideological Origins of the 1946 Constitution," *The China Quarterly* 103 (1985): 441–461; Weng Hekai, "Zhanhou Zhang Junmai De Shehuizhuyi Xin Sikao [Zhang Junmai's New Postwar Thought About Socialism]," *Shixue Yuekan* 6 (2008): 62–67.

59 Carl Schmitt, *Frieden oder Pazifismus? Arbeiten zum Völkerrecht und zur internationalen Politik 1924–1978*, ed. Gunther Maschke (Duncker & Humblot, 2005).

'natural' historical and natural claim to autonomy became closely associated with discussions of spatial themes, including with ideas of 'living space' (*Lebensraum*) advocated by Karl Haushofer and other geopoliticians as well as with Schmitt's discussions of the 'great space' (*Großraum*) as the fundamental constituent unit of international legal order.[60] As a critique of the purportedly 'spaceless' international legal order developing at Geneva, these positions gained considerable influence, becoming increasingly dominant by the Nazi era, and gaining attention abroad.[61]

Chinese critical discourse on international law, however, was never quite as radical as that. Although also a revisionist power with respect to key aspects of the status quo, which often operated in favor of great powers and at China's expense (especially in terms of jurisdictional questions) Chinese lawyers also saw in the League order one of the few possible guarantors for the preservation of China's political existence and territorial integrity. They thus tended to put great emphasis on the pursuit of change via the processes of the League itself as well as argument premised on the broad acceptance of most of the universal norms of international law being developed in contexts such as the Permanent Court of International Justice (PCIJ).[62] Certainly, radical movements of both the right and the left expressed strong critiques of the League, and not infrequently portrayed it as a vehicle for Western domination. However, the basic commitment to both the League and its successor the United Nations, as designed with Chinese input at the conferences of Dumbarton Oaks and San Francisco, continued to typify widely shared Chinese stances, despite the many dramatic occurrences of the interwar period.[63]

Instead of rejecting these international norms and organizations, Chinese statesmen and international lawyers generally sought to make them more representative of peripheral peoples. Officials and lawyers of the Guomindang, for example, appealed to ideas of regional solidarity in Asia to articulate their support for the independence of India and other colonized societies.[64] Intel-

---

60 On Haushofer, see Hans-Adolf Jacobsen, "'Kampf um Lebensraum': Zur Rolle des Geopolitikers Karl Haushofer im Dritten Reich," *German Studies Review* 4, no. 1 (1981): 79–104; Matthew Specter, *The Atlantic Realists: Empire and International Political Thought Between Germany and the United States* (Stanford University Press, 2022).

61 Lawrence Preuss, "National Socialist Conceptions of International Law," *American Political Science Review* 29, no. 4 (1935): 594–609; Schmitt, *Der Nomos der Erde*, 64–65.

62 See, for example, Ole Spiermann, "Judge Wang Chung-hui at the Permanent Court of International Justice," *Chinese Journal of International Law* 5, no. 1 (2006): 115–128.

63 Mitchell, *Recentering the World*, 181–190.

64 See, for example, Zhou Gengsheng, "Zhou Gengsheng Lun Taipingyang Yongjiu Zhixu; Bixu Wanquan Jiechu Riben Wuzhuang; Zhuzhang Chengli Taipingyang Lianheguo [Zhou Gengsheng Writes on a Permanent Order for the Pacific; Japan Must be Perman-

lectuals associated with the Communist Party, the ruling Guomindang, and even the Japanese collaboration regime invoked notions of regionalism and the autonomy of Asian peoples in order to criticize Western imperialism and phenomena such as the unequal treaties. Indeed, these criticisms formed one of the few shared positions that united interlocutors across otherwise vast ideological gulfs. International lawyers, like other intellectuals, often found themselves having to choose sides amidst the geopolitical chaos of the period. Yet essentially all of this community, including those who remained loyal to the Guomindang until its defeat in 1949 and exile to Taiwan, as well as those who joined the Communist Party–led People's Republic of China (PRC) shared critiques of Western interventionism in China's history.[65]

These critiques continued after the welcome final relinquishment of Western extraterritorial rights in China by the United States and the United Kingdom in 1942 (following earlier renunciations by other powers).[66] During the course of the intra-Allied discussions regarding post-war order in 1941–1944, for example, Chiang Kai-shek had demanded Chinese participation in the key planning meetings and warned that they would otherwise 'lose relevance' for Asia.[67] Guomindang officials even contemplated the possibility of pursuing the establishment of a regional organization in the form of a 'United Nations of the Pacific', in order to establish the autonomy of their region and its peoples and to try to attain 'leadership/hegemony over the Far East' (*yuandong lingdaoquan*).[68] While the very notion of 'Asia' as a region was in many respects a neologism, the aim for regional unity and the exclusion of 'external' influences was a relatively widely shared one among many intellectuals by the mid-twentieth century.[69] The notion of a 'natural' familial relationship among Asian peoples had been instrumentalized by many political forces, not least Japanese imperialists, but at the same time it was part of a broader set of views on the just character of anticolonial struggle.[70]

---

ently Disarmed; Advocates Setting Up a United Nations of the Pacific]," *Zhongyang Ribao Saodang Bao Lianhe Ban* (8 January 1943).

65 See, for example Wang Tieya, "Dulumenzhuyi Yu Menluozhuyi' [The Truman Doctrine and the Monroe Doctrine]," *Minzhu Luntan* 1, no. 9 (1947).

66 Quincy Wright, "The End of Extraterritoriality in China," *American Journal of International Law* 37, no. 2 (1943): 286–289.

67 Mitchell, *Recentering the World*, 176–78.

68 Ibid., 182.

69 Prasenjit Duara, "The Discourse of Civilization and Pan-Asianism," *Journal of World History* 12, no. 1 (2001): 99–130.

70 Ibid., 110 FN8 ("Born in reaction to both the Western and imperialist character of Civilization [discourse], the idea of an 'Asian' civilization necessarily possessed an anti-

6 The People's Republic of China and the Universality of International Law

The United Nations was founded with China's consent being provided via a joint delegation including both Guomindang and Communist Party representatives.[71] The Vitorian tradition of international law's universality seemed to have received new confirmation and legitimacy. Many Chinese participants in this process also demonstrated a commitment to 'spaceless' universal norms. For example, Chinese representatives supported and contributed to the norms on broad jurisdiction for the International Court of Justice (ICJ), the development of the Universal Declaration of Human Rights (UDHR), and the drafting of the Genocide Convention, among many other such activities in the immediate post-war years.[72]

Yet, at the same time, many factors also soon served to reinject problems of spatial differentiation, hierarchy, and resistance into perceptions of the new global legal order. The question of decolonization and the scope of the norm of self-determination was one that was heavily contested from the beginning of the UN system. Very soon, Chinese views on this topic came to once again embody a strong stance of anticolonial resistance.[73] Another aspect that restored spatial difference and struggle to the core of international law engagement was, of course, the advent of the Cold War. China's own resumed civil war between 1945 and 1949 was one of the first sites of the world's division into competing ideological blocs, and the intense geopolitical struggles soon to unfold across numerous proxy wars and stand-offs.[74]

Following the establishment of the PRC in 1949, it continued to endorse in principle the universalist UN system and to seek legitimation within it.[75] However, it was excluded due to the US policy of non-recognition, which was combined with a comprehensive economic embargo.[76] Exclusion from the UN, and from the resumption of normal trade relations, greatly facilitated the PRC's further development of close ties with the Soviet Union as its pri-

imperialist rhetoric and egalitarianism that was often in tension with the celebration of Asian traditionalism.").

71 Mitchell, *Recentering the World*, 189–190.

72 Ibid., 195.

73 Ibid., 203–204.

74 Xue, "Chinese Contemporary Perspectives," 58.

75 Ibid.

76 Ti-chiang Chen, "The People's Republic of China and Public International Law," *Dalhousie Law Journal* 8, no. 1 (1984): 3–31; Shu Guang Zhang, *Economic Cold War: America's Embargo against China and the Sino-Soviet Alliance, 1949–1963* (Stanford University Press, 2001).

mary source of international support. After 1950, the outbreak of the Korean War and the US entry into it on the side of the South intensified a stance of resistance against a Western 'imperialism' that was portrayed by PRC legal scholars as continuous with Japan's attempts to dominate China and the Asian continent.[77] While the US condemned China's forces assisting North Korea as committing an act of 'aggression', the PRC position was that the US itself, as a spatially 'outside' power, had first violated the Korean people's rights by intervening in support of the South – and had waged aggression against China by military intervention to protect the KMT forces on Taiwan.[78]

Despite the intensely agonistic character of this period in international law, China following the end of the Korean conflict in 1953 soon turned towards redoubled efforts at promoting peace and international solidarity. This was especially manifested in its diplomatic efforts towards close neighbors that had recently emerged from colonial rule. The most important of these initiatives was the 'Five Principles of Peaceful Coexistence,' a brief program of international legal norms premised on mutual respect for sovereignty, non-interference,g and peaceful cooperation.[79] Formulated via China's diplomacy under Premier Zhou Enlai along with Prime Ministers Jawaharlal Nehru of India and U Nu of Burma (Myanmar), the Five Principles platform was intended to facilitate the 'newly independent nation-states in Asia and Africa ... to safeguard independence and sovereignty, resist aggression and outside interference, cultivate equal relations with other countries, and secure an international environment of peace to develop their national economies.'[80]

The Five Principles agenda was also directly aimed against the US efforts to form an 'Asian NATO', which had already succeeded to the extent of establishing the Southeast Asian Treaty Organization (SEATO) as a nascent regional collective security arrangement.[81] Fearful that this initiative would be used to contain China and potentially offer a springboard for regime change operations, Beijing's policy of Third World solidarity took shape in part as a way to counter what it viewed as US attempt to exert hegemony over Asia.[82] Indeed,

77 Chen Tiqiang, "Wei Shenme Bixu Queding Qinlüe Dingyi? [Why Is It Necessary to Define Aggression?]," *Shijie Zhishi* 2 (1953): 9–10.

78 Ibid.

79 Boutros Boutros-Ghali, "The Five Principles," *Chinese Journal of International Law* 3, no. 2 (2004): 373–378.

80 Wen Jiabao, "Carrying Forward the Five Principles of Peaceful Coexistence in the Promotion of Peace and Development," *Chinese Journal of International Law* 3, no. 2 (2004): 363–368.

81 Ronald C. Keith, *The Diplomacy of Zhou Enlai* (Springer, 1989): 80.

82 Ibid.

both Soviet and Chinese scholars at times associated the US efforts of 'expansionism' via NATO and SEATO as resembling the imperialist efforts of Germany and Japan in the 1930s.[83] The ultimate failure of SEATO was closely tied to the success of the PRC's diplomatic efforts.

The African-Asian Conference at Bandung, in 1955, was a related major initiative that brought Zhou Enlai's diplomacy together with that of regional neighbors (and similarly situated postcolonial states elsewhere) to promote peaceful cooperation and oppose external interventions by Western powers.[84] Although explicit references to natural law were not prominent during the conference, it did in many respects embody a widely shared position as to the 'natural' and innate character of the rights to self-determination and non-interference.[85] Rather than justifying particular *interests* of the state, Chinese international law discourse of the early and mid-1950s focused on principles of political autonomy and identification of unjust forms of coercion as expressions of the interests of the oppressed classes.[86] Amidst the Sino-Soviet split beginning in the late 1950s, meanwhile, the universalist dimension of China's anticolonial international legal discourse also embodied a resistance to the Soviet Union as a practitioner of 'socialist imperialism' through its interventions in satellite states.[87]

The Cultural Revolution era (1966–1976) could be considered as the high point of China's international anticolonial activism in the geopolitical sphere, although international law itself was largely marginalized as a 'bourgeois' discipline.[88] The commitment to 'Asia–Africa–Latin America' (*Yafeila*) cooperation during this period was also associated with a newly intensified notion of Chinese moral leadership.[89] For Lin Biao, who was a dominant figure during the latter half of the 1960s, this leadership role was associated with an idiosyncratic geopolitical imaginary in which North America and Western Europe were the 'cities of the world' while the formerly colonized periphery formed

83 Cf. Chen, "Wei Shenme Bixu Queding Qinlüe Dingyi?".

84 See "Asian-African Conference Bulletin 5," Ministry of Foreign Affairs, Republic of Indonesia, April 20, 1955, 17.

85 Cf. Partha Chatterjee, "The Legacy of Bandung," in *Bandung, Global History, and International Law: Critical Pasts and Pending Futures*, eds. Luis Eslava, Michael Fakhri, and Vasuki Nesiah (Cambridge University Press, 2017): 657–674.

86 Chen, "The People's Republic of China and Public International Law," 16–17.

87 See Suzanne Ogden, "Sovereignty and International Law: The Perspective of the People's Republic of China," *NYU Journal of International Law and Politics* 7, no. 1 (1974): 1–32, 12.

88 Ibid.

89 Yu Miin-ling, "From Two Camps to Three Worlds: The Party Worldview in PRC Textbooks (1949–1966)," *The China Quarterly* 215 (2013): 682–702.

the 'countryside of the world'.[90] Ultimate victory in socialist and anticolonial struggle would arise from resistance action somehow resembling Mao Zedong's strategy of (in Mao's case, literally) 'surrounding the cities from the countryside' during the Chinese Civil War.[91] This invocation of 'natural' physical aspects of geopolitical hegemony resembled, to an appreciable degree, an inversion of the German geopoliticians' notions of Europe as the central axis of world politics.[92]

Nonetheless, both before and after Lin's period of ascendance, the more important and lasting theme of Chinese spatial imagination remained territorial integrity and its 'sacred' role. Indeed, the PRC's most significant armed conflicts after the Korean War have been its clashes with three fellow self-described socialist states: India (1962), the Soviet Union (1969), and Vietnam (1979), of which the former two turned on territorial disputes as well as worries over vulnerability to future invasions. The latter, meanwhile, was connected with regime change and proxy conflict in Cambodia, along with associated conflicts along frontier zones including the South China Sea. The inherited 'geobody' of the Qing *Tianxia*, to its maximum extent, continued to form the imagined borders of the Chinese polity and its internal space.[93]

The late phase of the Cultural Revolution saw vast changes, including the fall of Lin, the reassertion of Zhou Enlai's influence, the attainment of the PRC to the position of China's recognized government in the UN, and the normalization of relations with the USA, among other major shifts.[94] From the mid to late 1970s, the agenda of normalization and a return to economic reform became the basis for Deng Xiaoping's reformulation of many aspects of PRC policy. In the sphere of international law, a reassertion of the importance of

---

90 Ibid., 696.

91 Ibid.

92 Notably, Lin's doctrine was specifically identified by many contemporary Western commentators as reminiscent of radical German geopolitical thought. See, for example, Lin Piao, *Long Live the Victory of the People's War: Red Chinese Blueprint* (Armed Forces Information and Education, Department of Defense, 1965), i ('Experts on Red China consider this article a highly significant statement of policy. It has been compared with Hitler's *Mein Kampf*'); Hans J. Morgenthau, "The United States and China," *International Studies* 10, no. 1–2 (1968): 23–34, 25 ('Lin Piao's manifesto is not the Chinese equivalent of *Mein Kampf*, for the simple reason that even a Chinese Hitler would be incapable of putting it into practice. Completely lacking in even the most elementary understanding of the outside world, it rather reminds one, if one needs a historical analogy, of the eccentricities of German geopolitics.').

93 William A. Callahan, "The Cartography of National Humiliation and the Emergence of China's Geobody," *Public Culture* 21, no. 1 (2009): 141–173.

94 See Xue, "Chinese Contemporary Perspectives," 54–55, 69.

the Third World as 'the main progressive force to move world history forward against imperialism, colonialism and the superpowers' despite the new aim to integrate into the UN and other global institutions having finally achieved China's 'natural' place in international society.[95] During the ensuing period known as 'Reform and Opening-Up', beginning in 1978, the economic opening of China to foreign investment and increasingly capitalistic trade relations was associated with a new emphasis on joining treaties and adhering to international norms.[96] Rather than a manifestation of a Western imperial 'center' oppressing a subjugated 'periphery', or a tool for the periphery to assert its autonomy from the center, international law was now depicted as an array of universal norms promoting peaceful development.[97]

7 Spatial Organization in the PRC's Policy-Oriented International Legal Platforms

Following four decades of Reform Era policies, China today is now the largest or second-largest economy in the world depending on the form of measurement used, and is also deeply embedded in almost all existing major international organizations. It is also a member of a vast number of international treaty regimes, and is a frequent participant in international adjudication and dispute resolution processes, particularly in the realm of international economic law.[98] In many ways, China's deep level of global integration now surpasses that of any previous period in its history, arguably bringing it closer than ever before to a situation in which its favored norms can be viewed as expressing a 'Vitorian' ethical universalism.

Since 2015, the affirmation of 'international law with the UN at its core' has been one of the major principles of China's new comprehensive policy platform for international relations, the 'Community of Shared Future for Man-

95 Zhang Yongjin, *China in International Society since 1949: Alienation and Beyond* (Springer, 1998): 2–5, 76 (describing China as being "gradually yet inexorably incorporated into the present-day international society").

96 Xue, "Chinese Contemporary Perspectives," 193 ("China also gradually took part in all treaty making processes, transforming itself from a silent observer to an active participant.").

97 Ibid., 90–91.

98 See, for example Wang, Jiangyu. "China and International Trade Law: Rising from Within the System or Always an Outlier?" In *The Cambridge Handbook of China and International Law*, eds. Ignacio de la Rasilla and Congyan Cai (Cambridge University Press, 2024): 397–422.

kind' (*renlei mingyun gongtongti*) (CSFM).[99] Like the previous platform of the Five Principles of Peaceful Coexistence, which it in part incorporates, the CSFM also includes a strong affirmation of the rights of sovereign states and a rejection of intervention and interference. As expressed in 2023 by the State Council Information Office, it CSFM includes the positions that 'No country has the right to dominate global affairs, dictate the future of others, or monopolize development advantages'; that 'Countries should safeguard the international order based on international law, uphold the authority of the international rule of law, and ensure equal and unified application of international law'; and that 'The practice of double standards or selective application of law should be rejected', among numerous other stances favoring egalitarian interstate norms.[100]

This platform is also associated with China's embrace of not only centralized economic governance via the World Trade Organization (WTO) but also even of some 'neoliberal' phenomena such as Investor-State Dispute Arbitration (ISDS). ISDS, which serves to 'pierce the veil' of national sovereignty in the favor of foreign investors operating under relevant bilateral investment treaties, can be interpreted as a modern continuation of the (Vitorian) theme of a *ius communicationis* imbuing universal protections to cross-border commerce.[101] In the face of a major sovereigntist and protectionist turn in a number of major Western states, especially the USA, the fate of the WTO, free trade agreements, and other pillars of a universalist international economic order are often seen as resting on China's shoulders.[102]

99 See de la Rasilla, Ignacio and Yayezi Hao. "The Community of Shared Future for Mankind and International Law." In *The Cambridge Handbook of China and International Law*, eds. Ignacio de la Rasilla and Congyan Cai (Cambridge University Press, 2024): 49–72. Notably, the Chinese term translated as 'community of shared future', *mingyun gongtongti*, itself originates as a translation from the earlier German term *Schicksalsgemeinschaft*, which was invoked by sociologists, economists, and political theorists to describe innate, 'natural' forms of political community. On this point, see Mitchell, Ryan Martínez. "The Human Community of Fate: A Conceptual History of China's Ordoglobal Idea," *Humanity: An International Journal of Human Rights, Humanitarianism, and Development* 13, no. 2 (2022): 175–195.

100 "A Global Community of Shared Future: China's Proposals and Actions," The Third Belt and Road Forum for International Cooperation, accessed September 15, 2025, http://www.beltandroadforum.org/english/n101/2023/1010/c127-916.html.

101 Li Yuwen and Cheng Bian, "China's Stance on Investor-State Dispute Settlement: Evolution, Challenges, and Reform Options," *Netherlands International Law Review* 67, no. 3 (2020): 503–551.

102 Cf. "Farewell speech of Appellate Body member Prof. Dr. Hong Zhao," World Trade Organization, accessed September 15, 2025, https://www.wto.org/english/tratop_e/dispu_e/farwellspeechhzhao_e.htm.

At the same time, however, the contrasting theme of regional autonomy and the exclusion of outside influences remains of great importance, and arguably has renewed significance. Beijing has, for instance, taken a strong position on the rejection of military alliances and collective security arrangements by which Western powers, above all the United States, have sought to extend their normative influence into the Asia-Pacific region. Also in the realm of security and military policy, China's historically strong commitment to the UN Charter prohibitions on the use of force has nonetheless been tested with regard to the example of conflicts within the imagined 'security space' (*anquan kongjian*) of its close international partner, Russia.[103] China's own regional encounters in contested frontier zones, though of far lesser gravity, also exhibit an intense focus on national security and spaces of vulnerability.[104]

In other settings, Beijing also frequently seeks to promote regional unity as well as a sense of solidarity among peoples of the 'Global South', conceived of as a majority of the world's states rejecting interventionism and unequal relations with the wealthy states of the Global North. Although extending beyond the immediate region, the Global South concept does form another spatialized reframing of international legal order that can be used to justify limits on the applicability of universal norms.[105] Meanwhile, China tends to reject the extension of monitoring jurisdiction for bodies such as the Human Rights Council into the domestic territory of states in contravention of the express consent of their governments.[106]

Even within the realm of trade and development, the Belt and Road Initiative (BRI) also includes a significant emphasis on the 'great spaces' of Chinese geoeconomic influence. Although not conceived as a realm of hegemonic domination, patterns of massive investment and lending, infrastructure con-

---

103 See, e.g. "Ji Ya Eluosi Anquan Kongjian Beiyue Huo Xian Zhong Dong Ou Paiqian 4000 Ren Zuozhan Budui [Putting the Squeeze on Russia's Security Space, NATO May Deploy 4000 Armed Personnel to Central and Eastern Europe]," *Xinhua* (17 February 2022).

104 Toby Dalton and Tong Zhao, *At a Crossroads?: China-India Nuclear Relations after the Border Clash* (Carnegie Endowment for International Peace, 2020).

105 Cf. Emma Mawdsley, "Human Rights and South-South Development Cooperation: Reflections on the 'Rising Powers' as International Development Actors," *Human Rights Quarterly* 36, no. 3 (2014): 630–652.

106 Dai Ruijun, "China and International Human Rights Law," in *The Cambridge Handbook of China and International Law*, eds. Ignacio de la Rasilla and Congyan Cai (Cambridge University Press, 2024), 261–283, 267 ('China claims that international human rights protection should abide by the principle of sovereignty'); Mitchell, Ryan Martínez. 'The Emerging Chinese Model of Statist Human Rights'. *American University International Law Review* 37, no. 3 (2023): 617–71.

struction, and private commercial flows do tend to reinforce a central position for Beijing vis-à-vis BRI partners.[107] Related platforms such as the Shanghai Cooperation Organization (SCO) and the BRICS grouping of states, also serve to promote efforts towards regional or 'Global South' alternatives to 'hegemonic' groupings, such as the G7, and phenomena such as the US dollar's global reserve currency status.[108] The call for an 'Asia run by the peoples of Asia' has also been a recurring theme of the annual Bo'ao conference on regional economic issues.[109] These reassertions of the particular, and the central role of the regional superpower, remain exceptions to a broader globalist orientation.

The law of the sea, as a major field of international legal ordering bridging both economic and security-related topics, serves as perhaps the most vivid expression of this split approach. On the one hand, Beijing has become over the last three decades a major constituent and supporter of the UN Convention on the Law of the Sea (UNCLOS) and many of its established norms and institutions. It has, for example, expressed support for the mechanisms of dispute resolution under the auspices of the International Tribunal on the Law of the Sea (ITLOS), and for a variety of UNCLOS-based norms regarding issues such as deep seabed mining, the regulation of fishing in international waters, and defense of marine ecosystems.[110] At the same time, it has tested the boundaries of UNCLOS-based norms regarding the extent of maritime jurisdiction in terms of its arguments regarding unique 'historic rights' in the South China Sea, and rejection of the jurisdiction of a PCA arbitration panel on the basis of its express reservation against arbitration on matters of territorial sovereignty.[111]

In sum, the spatiality of international law continues to be a topic of great concern for Beijing when it comes to the application of norms either to China's internal territory or to important considerations of either security or hegemonic contestation within its immediate region. At the global level, however, the universalist motivation of the CSFM is manifested in a vast and grow-

---

107 Thomas P. Narins and John Agnew, "Missing from the Map: Chinese Exceptionalism, Sovereignty Regimes and the Belt Road Initiative," *Geopolitics* 25, no. 4 (2020): 809–837.

108 Cf. "Joint Statement of the BRIC Countries' Leaders," BRICS Information Centre, University of Toronto, accessed September 15, 2025, http://www.brics.utoronto.ca/docs/090616-leaders.html.

109 Callahan, William A., "China's 'Asia Dream' the Belt Road Initiative and the New Regional Order," *Asian Journal of Comparative Politics* 1, no. 3 (2016): 226–243.

110 See, e.g. Zou Keyuan and Qiang Ye, "The relationship between UNCLOS and Customary International Law: Some reflections," *Marine Policy* 154 (2023): 105–691.

111 Ibid.

ing variety of instances of international organization and cooperation, as well as in an interest in expanding international legal regulation of various aspects of global governance. The field of international environmental law, with its necessary incorporation of a global elements, offers apt insights into China's current balancing of sovereignty and universality.[112]

For example, China's embrace of the United Nations Framework Convention on Climate Change (UNFCCC), the Paris Agreement, and other related environmental measures such as the Convention on Biological Diversity are frequently tied to the 'naturalist' conceptions of innate solidarity embodied in the CSFM platform.[113] The 2022 Kunming-Montreal Global Biodiversity Framework, aiming to halt and reverse biodiversity loss by 2030, also reflects the kind of coordination-based and 'policy-oriented' agreement that Beijing often favors.[114] Within the arenas where Beijing has identified common interests for all states around the globe, as in the regulation of free and orderly commerce and the protection of the environment, its universalist initiatives appear to be growing in number and importance.

8 Conclusion

This chapter has recounted the recurring themes of universalism and particularism in the spatial conceptions attached to international law topics in Chinese discourse. Beginning with a brief overview of traditional political phenomenology, it has explained that the apparent cosmic authority associated with the *Tianxia* concept of imperial China was at times paired with alternative vocabularies implying a more modest, spatially limited, scope of state power. As with the Western natural law tradition, which could encompass theorists as dramatically disparate as Vitoria and Schmitt, China's domestic naturalist discourses varied greatly.

Later, when Chinese scholars and officials first began to adopt the concepts of Western international law, they found themselves part of the latter field's own rapid transition from a traditional universalist orientation to a new, positivist preoccupation with formalized hierarchies and criteria for territorial

---

112 See Xue, "Chinese Contemporary Perspectives," 178–83.

113 Cf. Fuwen Wei, Shuhong Cui, Ning Liu, Jiang Chang, Xiaoge Ping, Tianxiao Ma, Jing Xu, Ronald R. Swaisgood, and Harvey Locke, "Ecological Civilization: China's Effort to Build a Shared Future for All Life on Earth," *National Science Review* 8, no. 7 (2021): 1–5.

114 See "Kunming Declaration", accessed 15 September 2025, at https://www.cbd.int/doc/c/99c8/9426/1537e277fa5f846e9245a706/kunmingdeclaration-en.pdf ('Ecological Civilization: Building a Shared Future for All Life on Earth').

dominium. Preserving China's sovereignty and territorial integrity became the overriding preoccupation of successive generations of politicians and lawyers. By the early to mid-twentieth century, various forms of natural law-inflected critique of international legal norms and institutions had proliferated globally, and were also participated in by many Chinese jurists, seeking to assert a more genuine universalism than that proclaimed by the hierarchical and imperialist Eurocentric legal order.

Anticolonialism and peaceful coexistence among sovereign states became the key elements of China's post-1949 engagements with international legal order, with the strategies pursued towards these ends varying greatly during the Cold War period. In recent decades, however, there has been a consistent embrace of universal norms and institutions across important areas ranging from economic regulation to important aspects of domestic and global governance related to the environment, health, transnational crime, and many other domains. Despite this globalizing disposition, embodied most authoritatively in the CSFM, there remain various areas within which China's particular territorial and regional security concerns dictate a continued emphasis on the ability to exclude external forms of interference. The mostly retained borders of the Qing realm continue to delineate a spatial barrier within which 'global' authority, including that of some international legal norms or of institutions claiming to apply them, is at times viewed as embodying threats of domination by outside powers. The natural unity of humanity proclaimed by the CSFM may, nonetheless, imply that solutions even to longstanding territorial or security disputes should in principle be achieved by methods that are multilateral and embody international norms, while still respecting the sovereignty of the state.

Bibliography

"A Global Community of Shared Future: China's Proposals and Actions," The Third Belt and Road Forum for International Cooperation, accessed September 15, 2025, http://www.beltandroadforum.org/english/n101/2023/1010/c127-916.html.

Alden, Chris and Daniel Large. "On becoming a norms maker: Chinese foreign policy, norms evolution and the challenges of security in Africa." *The China Quarterly* 221 (2015): 123–142.

Arrighi, Giovanni and Beverly J. Silver. *Chaos and Governance in the Modern World System* (The University of Minnesota Press, 1999).

"Asian-African Conference Bulletin 5," Ministry of Foreign Affairs, Republic of Indonesia, April 20, 1955, 17.

Boutros Boutros-Ghali. "The Five Principles." *Chinese Journal of International Law* 3, no. 2 (2004): 373–378.

"Joint Statement of the BRIC Countries' Leaders," BRICS Information Centre, University of Toronto, accessed September 15, 2025, http://www.brics.utoronto.ca/docs/090616-leaders.html.

The Cambridge Handbook of China and International Law, eds. Ignacio de la Rasilla and Congyan Cai (Cambridge University Press, 2024).

Cai, Congyan. *The Rise of China and International Law: Taking Chinese Exceptionalism Seriously* (Oxford University Press, 2019).

Callahan, William A. "China's 'Asia Dream' the Belt Road Initiative and the new regional order." *Asian Journal of Comparative Politics* 1, no. 3 (2016): 226–243.

Callahan, William A. "The cartography of national humiliation and the emergence of China's geobody." *Public Culture* 21, no. 1 (2009): 141–173.

Chatterjee, Partha. "the Legacy of Bandung." In *Bandung, Global History, and International Law: Critical Pasts and Pending Futures*, eds. Luis Eslava, Michael Fakhri, and Vasuki Nesiah (Cambridge University Press, 2017): 657–674.

Chen, Ti-chiang. "The People's Republic of China and Public International Law." *Dalhousie Law Journal* 8, no. 1 (1984): 3–31.

Chen, Tiqiang. "Wei Shenme Bixu Queding Qinlüe Dingyi? [Why Is It Necessary To Define Aggression?]" *Shijie Zhishi* 2 (1953): 9–10.

Cheney, Amanda J. "Tibet lost in translation: sovereignty, suzerainty and international order transformation, 1904–1906." *Journal of Contemporary China* 26 (2017): 769–783.

China among Equals: The Middle Kingdom and Its Neighbors, 10th-14th Centuries, ed. Morris Rossabi (University of California Press, 1983).

Dai, Ruijun. "China and International Human Rights Law." In *The Cambridge Handbook of China and International Law*, eds. Ignacio de la Rasilla and Congyan Cai (Cambridge University Press, 2024), 261–283.

Dai, Yingcong. "A disguised defeat: The Myanmar campaign of the Qing dynasty." *Modern Asian Studies* 38, no. 1 (2004): 145–189.

Dalton, Toby and Tong Zhao. *At a Crossroads?: China-India Nuclear Relations After the Border Clash* (Carnegie Endowment for International Peace, 2020).

de la Rasilla, Ignacio and Yayezi Hao. "the Community of Shared Future for Mankind and International Law." In *The Cambridge Handbook of China and International Law*, eds. Ignacio de la Rasilla and Congyan Cai (Cambridge University Press, 2024): 49–72.

de Martens, F. "How the Chinese Question should be Solved." *The Advocate of Peace*, 62, no. 11 (1900): 240–241.

Dickinson, Edwin D. "The Recognition of Russia." *Michigan Law Review* 30, no. 2 (1931): 181–196.

de Vattel, Emer. *Le Droit des Gens* (Carnegie institution of Washington, 1916).

Duara, Prasenjit. "The discourse of civilization and Pan-Asianism." *Journal of World History* 12, no. 1 (2001): 99–130.

Duve, Thomas, et al. *Entanglements in Legal History: Conceptual Approaches* (Max Planck Institute for Legal History and Legal Theory, 2014).

Fang, Weigui. "Yi, Yang, Xi, Wai and Other Terms: The Transition from 'Barbarian' to 'Foreigner' in Nineteenth-Century China." In *New Terms for New Ideas*, eds. Michael Lackner, Iwo Amelung, Joachim Kurtz (Brill, 2001): 95–123.

"Farewell speech of Appellate Body member Prof. Dr. Hong Zhao," World Trade Organization, accessed September 15, 2025, https://www.wto.org/english/tratop_e/dispu_e/farwellspeechhzhao_e.htm.

Finnemore, Martha and Michelle Jurkovich. "Getting a Seat at the Table: The Origins of Universal Participation and Modern Multilateral Conferences." *Global Governance: A Review of Multilateralism and International Organizations* 20, no. 3 (2014): 361–373.

Fitzmaurice, Andrew. "Liberalism and Empire in Nineteenth-Century International Law." *The American Historical Review* 117, no. 1 (2012): 122–140.

Frank, V. S. "The Territorial Terms of the Sino-Russian Treaty of Nerchinsk, 1689." *Pacific Historical Review* 16, no. 3 (1947): 265–270.

Gengsheng [Zhou Gengsheng]. 'Zongzhuquan Lun [The Theory of Suzerainty]'." *Taipingyang* 1, no. 10 (1918).

Gong, Gerrit W. *The Standard of "Civilization" in International Society* (Clarendon Press, 1984).

Gordon, G. M. "Natural Law in International Legal Theory: Linear and Dialectical Presentations." In *Oxford Handbook of the Theory of International Law*, in Anne Orford, Florian Hoffmann, and Martin Clark (Oxford University Press, 2016): 279–305.

Gott, Virginia L. "The National Socialist Theory of International Law." *American Journal of International Law* 32, no. 4 (1938): 704–718.

Greift, Thomas E. "The principle of human rights in Nationalist China: John CH Wu and the ideological origins of the 1946 constitution." *The China Quarterly* 103 (1985): 441–461.

Hall, Stephen. "The persistent spectre: natural law, international order and the limits of legal positivism." *European Journal of International Law* 12, no. 2 (2001): 269–307.

Halsey, Stephen R. *Quest for Power: European Imperialism and the Making of Chinese Statecraft* (Harvard University Press, 2015).

Hirschfeld, Julius. "Current Notes on International Law." *Law Mag. & Rev. Quart. Rev. Juris. 5th ser.* 26 (1900): 335.

Howse, Robert. "Schmitt, Schmitteanism and Contemporary International Legal Theory." In *Oxford Handbook of the Theory of International Law*, eds. Anne Orford, Florian Hoffmann, and Martin Clark (Oxford University Press, 2016): 212–230.

Hsü, Immanuel C. Y. *China's Entrance into the Family of Nations: The Diplomatic Phase, 1858–1880* (Harvard University Press, 1960).

Huber, Max. "Die Gleichheit der Staaten." In *Rechtswissenschaftliche Beiträge: Juristische Festgabe des Auslandes zu Josef Kohlers 60. Geburtstag, 9. März 1909*, ed. Fritz Berolzheimer (Scientia Verlag, 1981).

Hunter, Michael and Martin Kern. *Confucius and the Analects Revisited: New Perspectives on Composition, Dating, and Authorship* (Brill, 2018).

"International Protocol (1901), Article v." In *Treaties, Conventions, etc., Between China and Foreign States* (Maritime Customs Service, 1917): 301–345.

Jacobsen, Hans-Adolf. "'Kampf um Lebensraum': Zur Rolle des Geopolitikers Karl Haushofer im Dritten Reich." *German Studies Review* 4, no. 1 (1981): 79–104.

"Ji Ya Eluosi Anquan Kongjian Beiyue Huo Xian Zhong Dong Ou Paiqian 4000 Ren Zuozhan Budui [Putting the Squeeze on Russia's Security Space, NATO May Deploy 4000 Armed Personnel to Central and Eastern Europe]." *Xinhua* (17 February 2022).

Jiang, Shigong. "Ludi Yu Haiyang: 'Kongjian Geming' Yu Shijie Lishi De 'Maijinde Shidai' [Land and Sea: Spatial Revolution and the Mackinder Age of World History]." *Kaifang Shidai* [Open Times] (2018): 103–127.

Kaufman, Alison Adcock. "In pursuit of equality and respect: China's diplomacy and the League of Nations." *Modern China* 40, no. 6 (2014): 605–638.

Keith, Ronald C. *The Diplomacy of Zhou Enlai* (Springer, 1989).

Koo, V. K. Wellington. *The Status of Aliens in China* (Columbia University Press, 1912).

Koskenniemi, Martti. "Empire and International Law: The Real Spanish Contribution." *University of Toronto Law Journal* 61, no. 1 (2011): 1–36.

Koskenniemi, Martti. "International Law in 1873." In *Au Service du Droit International: Les 150 ans de l'Association de droit international*, eds. Catherine Kessedjian, Olivier Descamps et Teodolinda Fabrizi (Éditions Panthéon-Assas, 2023), 167–197.

"Kunming Declaration", accessed 15 September 2025, https://www.cbd.int/doc/c/99c8/9426/1537e277fa5f846e9245a706/kunmingdeclaration-en.pdf.

Li, Dade. "Guanyu Zhou Gengsheng Hu Shi zhi de Lunzhan: Tongyi Zhou Gengsheng Kanfa, Hu Shi zhi You 'Kong Su Bing' [On the War of Words Between Zhou Gengsheng and Hu Shi: Agreeing with Zhou Gengsheng, Hu Shi Has 'Sovietphobia']." *Zhongyang Zhoukan* 10, no. 9 (1948).

Li, Yuwen and Cheng Bian. "China's stance on investor-state dispute settlement: evolution, challenges, and reform options." *Netherlands International Law Review* 67, no. 3 (2020): 503–551.

Lin, Piao. *Long Live the Victory of the People's War: Red Chinese Blueprint* (Armed Forces Information and Education, Department of Defense, 1965).

Mahan, Alfred Thayer. *The Problem of Asia and its Effect Upon International Policies* (Sampson, Low, Marston and Co., 1900).

Mawdsley, Emma. "Human rights and south-south development cooperation: Reflections on the "rising powers" as international development actors." *Human Rights Quarterly* 36, no. 3 (2014): 630–652.

Mitchell, Ryan Martínez. "China's participation in the second Hague conference and the concept of equal sovereignty in international law," *Asian Journal of International Law* 11, no. 2 (2021): 351–371.

Mitchell, Ryan Martinez. "International Law as Project or System?," *Georgetown Journal of International Law* 51, no. 3 (2019): 623–689.

Mitchell, Ryan Martínez. "Monroe's Shadow: League of Nations Covenant Article 21 and the Space of Asia in International Legal Order." *TWAIL Review* 2 (2021): 200–231.

Mitchell, Ryan Martínez. *Recentering the World: China and the Transformation of International Law* (Cambridge University Press, 2022).

Mitchell, Ryan Martínez. "The Emerging Chinese Model of Statist Human Rights." *American University International Law Review* 37, no. 3 (2023): 617–671.

Mitchell, Ryan Martínez. "The Human Community of Fate: A Conceptual History of China's Ordoglobal Idea," *Humanity: An International Journal of Human Rights, Humanitarianism, and Development* 13, no. 2 (2022): 175–95.

Morgenthau, Hans J. "The United States and China." *International Studies* 10, no. 1–2 (1968): 23–34.

Narins, Thomas P. and John Agnew. "Missing from the map: Chinese exceptionalism, sovereignty regimes and the Belt Road Initiative." *Geopolitics* 25, no. 4 (2020): 809–837.

Ogden, Suzanne. "Sovereignty and International Law: The Perspective of the People's Republic of China." *NYU Journal of International Law and Politics* 7, no. 1 (1974): 1–32.

Oppenheim, Lassa. *International Law*, Volume 1 (Longmans, Green & Co., 1912).

Pines, Yuri. "Changing views of 'Tianxia' in pre-imperial discourse." *Oriens Extremus* 43 (2002): 101–116.

Platt, Stephen R. *Imperial Twilight: The Opium War and the End of China's Last Golden Age* (Vintage, 2019).

Preuss, Lawrence. "National Socialist Conceptions of International Law." *American Political Science Review* 29, no. 4 (1935): 594–609.

Rigaux, François. "Aux Origines Du Droit International: La Conquête de L'Amérique." In *The Roots of International Law/Les fondements du droit international: Liber Amicorum Peter Haggenmacher*, eds. Pierre-Marie Dupuy and Vincent Chetail (Brill Nijhoff, 2014), 641–648.

Robinson, Ronald and John Gallagher. "The Imperialism of Free Trade." *Economic History Review* 6, no. 1 (1953): 1–15.

Schmitt, Carl. *Der Nomos der Erde im Völkerrecht des Jus Publicum Europaeum* (Duncker & Humblot, 1974).

Schmitt, Carl. *Frieden oder Pazifismus? Arbeiten zum Völkerrecht und zur internationalen Politik 1924–1978*, ed. Gunther Maschke (Duncker & Humblot, 2005).

Siu, Yiu. "Maritime exclusion policy in Ming China and Chosŏn Korea, 1368–1450: dynastic authority, national security, and trade." PhD diss., University of Oxford, 2022.

Smith, Richard J. *Mapping China and Managing the World: Culture, Cartography and Cosmology in Late Imperial Times* (Routledge, 2013).

Specter, Matthew. *The Atlantic Realists: Empire and International Political Thought Between Germany and the United States* (Stanford University Press, 2022).

Spiermann, Ole. "Judge Wang Chung-hui at the Permanent Court of International Justice." *Chinese Journal of International Law* 5, no. 1 (2006): 115–128.

Svarverud, Rune. *International Law as World Order in Late Imperial China* (Brill, 2007).

Svarverud, Rune. "The Notions of 'Power' and 'Rights' in Chinese Political Discourse." In *New Terms for New Ideas*, eds. Michael Lackner, Iwo Amelung, Joachim Kurtz (Brill, 2001), 125–143.

Tchéou Wei, S. [Zhou Wei]. *Essai sur l'organisation juridique de la Société international* (Libraire Atar, 1917).

von Martens, Friedrich. *La Conférence de la Paix á La Haye: Étude d'Histoire Contemporaine* (Arthur Rousseau, 1900).

Wang, Hui. *Zhongguo Xiandai Sixiang de Xingqi*, Volume I (Sanlian Shudian, 2004).

Wang, Jiangyu. "China and International Trade Law: Rising from within the System or Always an Outlier?" In *The Cambridge Handbook of China and International Law*, eds. Ignacio de la Rasilla and Congyan Cai (Cambridge University Press, 2024): 397–422.

Wang Tieya. "Dulumenzhuyi Yu Menluozhuyi' [The Truman Doctrine and the Monroe Doctrine]." *Minzhu Luntan* 1, no. 9 (1947).

Wang, Zheng. *Never Forget National Humiliation: Historical Memory in Chinese Politics and Foreign Relations* (Columbia University Press, 2014).

Wei, Fuwen, Shuhong Cui, Ning Liu, Jiang Chang, Xiaoge Ping, Tianxiao Ma, Jing Xu, Ronald R. Swaisgood, and Harvey Locke. "Ecological civilization: China's effort to build a shared future for all life on Earth." *National Science Review* 8, no. 7 (2021): 1–5.

Wen, Jiabao. "Carrying forward the five principles of peaceful coexistence in the promotion of peace and development." *Chinese Journal of International Law* 3, no. 2 (2004): 363–368.

Weng, Hekai. "Zhanhou Zhang Junmai De Shehuizhuyi Xin Sikao [Zhang Junmai's New Postwar Thought About Socialism]." *Shixue Yuekan* 6 (2008): 62–67.

Wright, Quincy. "The End of Extraterritoriality in China." *American Journal of International Law* 37, no. 2 (1943): 286–289.

Xiong, Xiling. "Wei Xiangsheng Xing Lun Cheng Zhang Zhidong [Memorial to Zhang Zhidong on Allowing Steamboat Travel in Hunan] (1896)." In *Hunan Weixin Yundong Shiliao* [*Historical Materials on the Hunan Restoration Movement*], ed. Yi Feizhou (Yuelu Shushe, 2013): 223–230.

Xue, Hanqin. "Chinese Contemporary Perspectives on International Law: History, Culture and International Law." *Recueil Des Cours* 355 (2011): 41–233.

Yu, Miin-ling. "From two camps to three worlds: The party worldview in PRC textbooks (1949–1966)." *The China Quarterly* 215 (2013): 682–702.

Zhang, Shu Guang. *Economic Cold War: America's Embargo against China and the Sino-Soviet Alliance, 1949–1963* (Stanford University Press, 2001).

Zhang, Yongjin. *China in International Society since 1949: Alienation and Beyond* (Springer, 1998).

Zhao, Tingyang. *All Under Heaven: The Tianxia System for a Possible World Order* (University of California Press, 2021).

Zhou, Gengsheng. *Bupingdeng Tiaoyue Shijiang* [Ten Lectures on Unequal Treaties] (Taipingyang Shudian, 1928).

Zhou, Gengsheng. "Zhou Gengsheng Lun Taipingyang Yongjiu Zhixu; Bixu Wanquan Jiechu Riben Wuzhuang; Zhuzhang Chengli Taipingyang Lianheguo [Zhou Gengsheng Writes on a Permanent Order for the Pacific; Japan Must be Permanently Disarmed; Advocates Setting Up a United Nations of the Pacific]." *Zhongyang Ribao Saodang Bao Lianhe Ban* (8 January 1943).

Zou, Keyuan and Qiang Ye. "The relationship between UNCLOS and Customary International Law: Some reflections." *Marine Policy* 154 (2023): 105–691.

CHAPTER 10

The Monroe Doctrine and the Influence of Vitoria and Carl Schmitt in Latin America

Juan Pablo Scarfi

1 Introduction

Originally enunciated in 1823 as a US unilateral foreign policy declaration, the Monroe Doctrine was reframed since the late nineteenth and early twentieth centuries in connection with the emerging policy of Pan-Americanism and the rise of the US as an informal empire in Latin America, especially its interventionist policies in Central America and the Caribbean. The doctrine became in turn a continental and global subject of debate to the extent that Latin American jurists promoted Pan-American redefinitions of the doctrine as a multilateral legal principle and condemned it at the same time as an elastic tool to legitimize US interventions in the region. These transformations of the meaning and scope of the Monroe Doctrine motivated broader continental discussions across the Americas, as well as in Europe and Asia, over the doctrine in connection with the Spanish conquest of America, the roots of the European law of nations, and the foundations of international law in the Americas. These discussions, and the revival of just war theory in the 1920s and 1930s, generated a renaissance of the interest in the international legal thought of Francisco de Vitoria and the conquest of America in Latin America, the US and Europe. In this specific context, Carl Schmitt began to conceive and formulate his own interpretation of the Monroe Doctrine as an American Großraum and the Ius Publicum Europaeum, which led in turn to his influential and controversial work, *The Nomos of the Earth* (1950).[1] It is no coincidence that he regarded the Monroe Doctrine as a central turning-point feature in the transformations and notably the decline of European international law. While he regarded Vitoria as one of the most eloquent epitomes of the early modern version of the Ius Publicum Europaeum and European law of nations, Schmitt also famously excavated on the international legal struggles over the Monroe Doctrine and developed the notion of Großraum, arguing that the formulation

1 Carl Schmitt, *The Nomos of the Earth in the International Law of the Jus Publicum Europaeum* (New York: Telos Press, 2003).

 | DOI:10.1163/9789004757448_011

of the doctrine and its global resonances contributed to the progressive decline of the European law of nations. The debates over the Monroe Doctrine and the legacy of Vitoria in the Americas were thus revisited and re-signified by Schmitt, generating another wave of discussions and influences of his work – and that of Vitoria – in Latin America throughout the second half of the twentieth century. This chapter explores these two waves of discussions over the Monroe Doctrine in the Americas through the lens of Vitoria and Schmitt, focusing on the resonances and influence of their work in Latin America throughout the twentieth century. The chapter argues that these debates over the meaning and scope of the Monroe Doctrine in the early twentieth century contributed to structuring and re-signifying the legacy and influence of Vitoria and Schmitt in Latin America to the extent that a second wave of discussions over the doctrine and these related issues centered around international law and political theology adopted a new striking tone in the second half of the twentieth century and even in our twenty-first century of humanitarian wars. It also argues that Schmitt regarded Vitoria as a foundational figure of the European Law of Nations, but, unlike James Brown Scott and Camilo Barcia Trelles, he resisted any attempt to canonize its contribution and legacy. By contrast, he portrayed Vitoria as the central point of intersection between the European Law of Nations and the concept of the Western Hemisphere, the Old World, and the New World. While the Monroe Doctrine was for Alejandro Alvarez the pillar of Western Hemisphere American international law, in the mind of Schmitt, Vitoria was essentially the aleph of international law, a unique point of convergence in which the rise and decline of the European Law of Nations, its past and future, could be ciphered.

In the early twentieth century, Latin American jurists promoted pioneeringly a debate over the meaning and scope of the Monroe Doctrine and proposed contending Pan-American and critical anti-imperialist interpretations of the doctrine. As such, they contributed to reviving the Monroe Doctrine approaching its centenary. As will be shown in the first section of this chapter, Schmitt was attentive to these debates to the extent that they resonated in his approach to Vitoria, the evolution of the European Law of Nations, and the disruptive notion of the Western Hemisphere as addressed in the original Monroe Doctrine. On the one hand, Luis María Drago and Alejandro Alvarez, sought to redefine the Monroe Doctrine as a Pan-American a shared hemispheric multilateral legal principle of non-intervention to safeguard the region from European interventions. On the other hand, a small group of anti-imperialist Latin American jurists, diplomats, and intellectuals, including Fabela and Roig de Leuchsenring, denounced the flexibility and elasticity of the Monroe Doctrine and its adaptation to US imperial and interventionist aspirations and its inconsistency as a proper principle of international law. Schmitt was aware of the existence of contending interpretations and usages of the Monroe Doctrine both in the US and Latin America and thus sought to forge a consistent view of the meaning and scope of the doctrine in the Western Hemisphere and its implications.

As the second section of this chapter shows, the debates over the meaning of the Monroe Doctrine stimulated Schmitt to advance a reflection about the connections between imperialism and international law, and the argument that the Monroe Doctrine consolidated itself in the inter-war period and the second half of the twentieth century as an American Großraum in the Western Hemisphere. The third section of this chapter briefly examines the influence of Vitoria and Schmitt in Latin America in an attempt to make sense of the hidden history and overlooked importance of the Spanish and Latin American origins of Schmitt's approach to Vitoria and the European Law of Nations.

2 The Monroe Doctrine and the Foundations of International Law in the Western Hemisphere

If one recovers the central debates about the history and theory of international law in the Americas, the Monroe Doctrine emerges as a core notion entangled in the practice of international law and diplomacy across the Americas. Enunciated in the US at the time of the aftermath of independence of the Americas from Great Britain and Spain, the Monroe Doctrine soon became a tenet for envisioning a regional and continental approach to international law, especially one that associated the region and the continent to the principle of non-intervention. In its original proclamation in 1823, the Monroe Doctrine emerged as a US unilateral anticolonial and anti-interventionist principle condemning European interventions in the Americas formulated essentially by Secretary of State John Quincy Adams and President James Monroe as regards to Europe. At the same time, even though the US was not a great power in the Americas by any means in 1823, the doctrine asserted verbally US supremacy in the Americas as the guardians of the continent, since it stated that any European intervention in any country of the Americas was a threat to US national interests. In this regard, the doctrine was imperial since it entailed a verbal assertation of US imperial dominance with regards to Latin America. As such, the Monroe Doctrine became a principle of "imperial anticolonialism" and generated the tenets for envisioning the Americas as a continent organized through political and legal traditions radically differently from those of

Europe and notably around the principle of non-intervention as a regulating foundational norm.[2] As is well-known, the Monroe Doctrine had its roots in Thomas Jefferson's notion of Western Hemisphere exceptionalism and his idea that the Americas were "a hemisphere to itself,"[3] that is, it was grounded on the idea that the Americas were organized around different political and legal principles that distinguished them radically from its former European colonial powers. This idea of hemispheric uniqueness was explicitly addressed in the original formulation of the doctrine. The idea of the Western Hemisphere as a separate unit was envisioned before the Monroe Doctrine was conceived as such, but the formulation of the doctrine a few years later consolidated Jefferson's initial assertation.

Following the US – Mexican War, especially by the time when the US became a new empire and a clear hegemon in the Americas, the Monroe Doctrine began to adopt a much clearer imperialist feature to the extent that it was progressively transformed into an interventionist principle, legitimizing US special and exclusive right to intervene in Latin America. This was anticipated by US Secretary of State Richard Olney famous declaration in the context of the British–Venezuelan boundary dispute over British Guiana (1895–1896, affirming US regional political and economic hegemony categorically when he asserted "Today the United States is practically sovereign on this continent and its fiat is law."[4] However, this was formally consolidated with the so-called Roosevelt Corollary of the Monroe Doctrine. In his Presidential address, Roosevelt famously asserted:

> Chronic wrongdoing, or an impotence which results in a general loosening of the ties of civilized society, may in America, as elsewhere, ultimately require intervention by some civilized nation, and in the Western Hemisphere the adherence of the United States to the Monroe Doctrine may force the United States, however reluctantly, in flagrant cases of

2 Juan Pablo Scarfi, "The Monroe Doctrine in the Americas: Towards a Hemispheric Intellectual History," *Diplomatic History* 47(5) (2023): 738–763; Jay Sexton, *The Monroe Doctrine: Empire and Nation in Nineteenth-Century America* (New York: Hill and Wang, 2011), 5–8, William Appleman Williams, *The Tragedy of American Diplomacy* (New York: Norton, 2009).

3 Thomas Jefferson to Alexander von Humboldt, 6 December 1813, in *The Writings of Thomas Jefferson*, vol 14, ed. Andrew A. Lipscomb (Washington, DC: The Thomas Jefferson Memorial Association of the United States, 1904), 22.

4 Richard Olney to Bayard, July 20, 1895, *Papers Relating to the Foreign Relations of the United States*, 1895, 1, 545–562, quoted in Jay Sexton, *The Monroe Doctrine*, 203.

> such wrongdoing or impotence, to the exercise of an international police power.[5]

Therefore, in the early twentieth century, the meaning and scope of the Monroe Doctrine was sharply redefined by the US in connection the dollar diplomacy and the Roosevelt Corollary as a principle, which essentially legitimized US civilizing interventions in Latin America. A doctrine originally formulated and defined unilaterally in anti-colonial and anti-interventionist terms, became in turn a crude interventionist principle.

The Pan-American movement emerged by 1890s in the very same context in which the US became an imperial hegemon across the Americas and began to intervene on a regular basis, but since it emerged as a US-led policy of economic, legal, political, and intellectual cooperation towards Latin America, several jurists and diplomats from the region were stimulated and inspired by this cooperative turn in US foreign policy. They sought to promote the US Monroe Doctrine in its original version as a principle of non-intervention, giving it a twist of Pan-American solidarity and cooperation as a truly shared multilateral principle. As such, they contributed to Pan-Americanizing the Monroe Doctrine as a multilateral principle of international law. In the context of the 1902 European intervention of Great Britain, Germany in Venezuela for the collection of public debts, the Argentine Minister of Foreign Affairs Luis María Drago invoked the Monroe Doctrine as a common continental principle, condemning the resort to interventions for the collection of public debts categorically. Like the jurist Carlos Calvo, Drago sought to demolish the doctrine of diplomatic protection, prompting European nations to sort out the claim for the collection of public debts in local Latin American tribunals. Although he originally sent his note to the Argentine Minister in Washington D.C. and failed to get support from the US Secretary of State John Hay, Drago's appropriation of the Monroe Doctrine is indicative of how it was used to forge regional legal principles and doctrines of international law and diplomacy that became part of the canon of Western Hemisphere international law.[6]

---

5 Theodore Roosevelt, "Annual Message of the President to Congress," December 6, 1904, United States, *Papers Related to the Foreign Relations of the United States* (Washington, DC: Government Printing Office, 1904) XLI.

6 Luis María Drago to Martín García Mérou, Argentine Minister in Washington D.C., 11 March, 1903, *Archivo del Ministerio de Relaciones Exteriores y Culto, República Argentina*, Buenos Aires, Doctrina Drago, Legajo, 33. See also Luis María Drago, Luis María Drago, "State Loans in Their Relation to International Policy," *American Journal of International Law* 1(3) (1907), 692–726; and Juan Pablo Scarfi, *The Hidden History of International Law in the Americas: Empire and Legal Networks* (New York: Oxford University Press, 2017), 71.

This was a first manifestation of the extent to which the Monroe Doctrine began progressively to be deployed among Latin American jurists as a foundational principle of Western Hemisphere international law.

Yet no Latin American jurist made a much stronger case than Alejandro Alvarez for the reconfiguration of the Monroe Doctrine as a foundation principle of Western Hemisphere international law. As is well-known, in his most famous book and in a series of influential articles, Alvarez made a strong case for redefining the US unilateral Monroe Doctrine as a core foundational principle of what he termed continental American international law. He reconfigured the Monroe Doctrine as both a Pan-American and international law principle, transforming a unilateral political doctrine into a multilateral international law principle. According to Alvarez, the Monroe Doctrine was foundational of American international law in three important ways. Firstly, it rejected European interventions in the Americas and asserted that the Americas were not *terra nullius*. Secondly, it affirmed that "*no one of the two continents* [Europe and the Americas] may intermeddle in the affairs of the other, and on this all America stands united," and thus the Monroe Doctrine "is the expression of the will of America."[7] Thirdly, the doctrine formulated a foundational distinction between Europe and the Americas, and their respective approaches to international law, according to which the former approach was based on monarchical regimes, imperial competition, the balance of power, war and armed peace and interventionism, whereas the latter one was grounded on republican regimes, solidarity, peace, the peaceful and legal settlement of international disputes and non-intervention. In its original version, the Monroe Doctrine addressed the basis of this general distinction between the Western Hemisphere and Europe and Alvarez sought to reinforce and expanded it further to the field of international law and diplomacy.

However, as has been already noted, a specific group of Latin American jurists questioned the attempts to redefine the Monroe Doctrine as a principle of international law and stressed the extent to which it was deployed as an elastic and flexible principle legitimizing US unilateral interventions in Latin America. The fact that they sought to denounce its legal legitimacy could be regarded as a symptom of the prominence it acquired in legal debates among international lawyers. The debate over the foundations of international law in the Western Hemisphere was grounded essentially on a discussion about the nature and scope of the Monroe Doctrine. It is no coincidence that in the

---

7 Alejandro Alvarez, "Latin America and International Law," *American Journal of International Law* 3(3) (1909), 269–353, 311, 313. See also, Alvarez, *Le droit international américain: son fondement, sa nature* (Paris: A. Pedone Éditeur, 1910).

context of these hemispheric debates US President Woodrow Wilson invoked by 1917 the Monroe Doctrine as a global "doctrine of the world."[8] More importantly it was legitimized and consolidated a few years later by 1920 as a principle of Western Hemisphere international law because of its inclusion of as article 21 into the Covenant of the League of Nations. Article 21 famously stated: "Nothing in this Covenant shall be deemed to affect the validity of international engagements, such as Treaties of Arbitration, or regional understandings like the Monroe Doctrine, for securing the maintenance of peace."[9] Latin American anti-imperialist jurists, notably Isidro Fabela and Emilio Roig de Leuchsenring, denounced the elasticity and flexibility of the Monroe and its US instrumentalization as a principle to legitimize interventions in Latin America, arguing that this plasticity and hegemonic instrumentalization made evident that it could not be considered a legitimate principle of American Western Hemisphere international law. They both rejected categorically the view of Alvarez, putting forward "a critique of the legitimacy of the Monroe Doctrine" as a principle of international law.[10] In particular, in the face of the US unilateral and interventionist version of the Monroe Doctrine under the Roosevelt Corollary, Fabela played a pivotal role in formulating the so-called Carranza Doctrine and dissemination it in South America in the context of the Mexican Revolution.[11] According to Fabela, the Carranza Doctrine entailed a rejection of the Monroe Doctrine as an arbitrary protectorate with no juridical legitimacy and no reciprocity, creating the conditions for validating US arbitrary interventions across the region, but it was at the same time grounded in previous Latin American legal doctrines of non-intervention and the resolution of disputes over the collection of public debts in national courts, as formulated by the Argentine jurist Luis María Drago.[12] More importantly, Fabela and Roig de Leuchsenring became especially concerned about the dis-

---

8 Woodrow Wilson, "Address to the Senate, 22 January 1917," in *Papers of Woodrow Wilson*, Vol. 40, November 20, 1916-January 23, 1917, ed. Arthur Link (Princeton, NJ: Princeton University Press, 1982), 538–539.

9 F. S. Northedge, *The League of Nations: Its Life and Times, 1920–1946* (Leicester: Leicester University Press, 1988), 324.

10 Juan Pablo Scarfi, "Denaturalizing the Monroe Doctrine: The Rise of Latin American Legal Anti-imperialism in the Face of the Modern US and Hemispheric Redefinition of the Monroe Doctrine," *Leiden Journal of International Law* 33(3) (2020), 541–555, 550.

11 Juan Pablo Scarfi, "Mexican Revolutionary Constituencies and the Latin American Critique of US Intervention," in *Revolutions in International Law: The Legacies of 1917*, ed. Anne Orford, Kathryn Greenman, Anna Saunders and Ntina Tzouvala (Cambridge: Cambridge University Press, 2021), 218–241.

12 Fernando Serrano Migallón, *Isidro Fabela y la diplomacia mexicana* (México: Fondo de Cultura Económica, 1981), 154.

ruption introduced by the Monroe Doctrine into the sovereignty and territorial integrity of Latin American states as a result of its subsequent inclusion as article 21 of the League Covenant and the legitimacy it provided to an unilateral principle in the form of a law or norm by 1920. While Fabela believed this inclusion implied "that the majority of the European countries was comfortable with letting the United States to play a hegemonic role in the Americas,"[13] Roig de Leuchsenring was even more categorically since this institutionalization created a state of exception for the US in international organizations and international law. He thus affirmed: Article 21 was "converting into law an international policy of the American Continent, accepted and recognized by all the nations of the Old and New World, a contract that, though bilateral, in reality was, as it is today, simply unilateral, dictated by one part, which is at the same time executor and judge, and applied and imposed to others."[14] All in all, although the Monroe Doctrine, according to Roig and Fabela, could not be conceived as a legal principle and advanced a critique of its plastic nature, it was formally recognized as a regional understanding of the Western Hemisphere. Like Roig and Fabela, Schmitt was well-aware of its importance and subsequent consolidation as a regional norm of Western Hemisphere international law to the extent that he took even more seriously this transformation of the doctrine and its double implications for the consolidation of the Western Hemisphere as a separate entity and the progressive decline of European international law.

3 Francisco de Vitoria and the Foundations of the European Law of Nations: The Idea of the Western Hemisphere and the Monroe Doctrine according to Carl Schmitt

In the 1920s and 1930s, there was an important revival of just war theory, motivating a renaissance of the interest in the international legal thought of Francisco de Vitoria and the conquest of America, notably in the US, but also in Latin America and Europe. At the same time, the conquest of America and the work of Vitoria gained special prominence in US, Latin American and Spanish historiography since the 1930s and 1940s, giving birth to an important historical renovation around debates about the comparative history of the

13 Isidro Fabela, *Los Estados Unidos contra la libertad: Estudios de historia diplomática americana* (Barcelona: Talleres gráficos "Lux", 1920), 306.

14 Emilio Roig de Leuchsenring, *La Doctrina de Monroe y el Pacto de la Liga de las Naciones* (La Habana: Imprenta El Siglo XX, 1921), 43.

Americas, that is, the common histories of the US and Latin America. These important global debates over the work of Vitoria and the conquest of America, along with the debates over the meaning and scope of the Monroe Doctrine for international law, as shown in the previous section, were to inform Carl Schmitt's interest in the work of Vitoria, the historical and geopolitical foundations of the European law of nations and notably shaping the formation of his own conception of the Monroe Doctrine as an American Großraum and its implications for the crisis and subsequent dissolution of the European Law of Nations (the Ius Publicum Europaeum). Schmitt's reflections on these matters led in turn to a series of writings, the most notable of which was his influential and controversial work, *The Nomos of the Earth* (1950).

In the 1920s and 1930s, when Schmitt began to envision *The Nomos of the Earth*, he reacted critically to the revival of just war theory and the renaissance of work of Vitoria and wrote two important essays about the Monroe Doctrine as an American Großraum and the connections between modern US imperialism and international law. In the mind of Schmitt, all these questions were inter-connected and thus shaped his own conception of the rise and decline of the European law of nations from Vitoria and the conquest and land-appropriation of America to the emergence of the Monroe Doctrine and the progressive separation of the Western Hemisphere from the rest of the world. According to Schmitt, this latter question which acquired special prominence through the quest made by Alejandro Alvarez in 1910 for an American Western Hemisphere international law. The extent to which the revival of just war theory in the US shaped the renaissance of Vitoria in US international legal thought was one of Schmitt's greatest obsessions. In fact, Schmitt felt especially motivated to react critically to some canonical and highly influential interpretations of the work of Vitoria through the prism of US just war theory, especially those that emerged from the work of the renowned jurist James Brown Scott and the important collections he himself launched, published, and sponsored on the Classics of International Law through the Carnegie Endowment for International Peace.[15] In an influential study published in 1934 and included in this book series on the Classics of International Law, Scott portrayed Vitoria as the founder of the modern law of nations and famously presented a teleological and anachronic interpretation of the work of the Spanish theologian, projecting his contribution into the present and

15 James Brown Scott, Editorial Note, "The Classics of International Law," *American Journal of International Law* 3(3) (1909), 701–707.

even the future of international law.[16] Scott regarded Vitoria as a liberal internationalist and prophet of doctrines, international law principles and institutions of the future, such as the League of Nations, the Court of International Justice, the US Declaration of Independence, Woodrow Wilson's Fourteenth Points and Franklin Delano Roosevelt's Good Neighbor Policy.[17] Scott thus affirmed: "Vitoria was a liberal. He could not help being a liberal. He was an internationalist by inheritance. And because he was both, his international law was a liberal law of nations."[18] Yet Schmitt was primarily obsessed with the revival of just war theory as promoted in the US by Scott along with the renaissance of the work of Vitoria. In this regard, according to Schmitt, Scott's revival of Vitoria was extremely problematic, since he found "a great resource" for exploring just war theory and legitimizing the modern criminalization of war in a classic canonical figure as Vitoria and in other Spanish theologians.[19] In a clear attempt to delink Vitoria's just war theory from US and Scott usages of it, Schmitt, by contrast, presented Vitoria's approach in a radically different light, as essentially ahistorical and objective. He argued that Vitoria's style of argumentation was "modern," since it created an impression of "impartiality, objectivity and neutrality."[20] Indeed, he went as far as to affirm that "Vitoria's exposition is completely ahistorical."[21] Interestingly, he regarded this feature as a merit, since because he was ahistorical he ignored and disregarded the humanitarian notion of discovery and humanitarian approaches to history, which became prominent in the nineteenth century. In short, if Vitoria was regarded as the father of just war theory and a humanitarian jurist, it was because US jurists, notably Scott, projected their humanitarian criminalization of war into the Spanish theologian. Rather than condemning and questioning Scott for being anachronic regarding Vitoria's humanitarian discourse, Schmitt sought to save Vitoria's ahistorical objectivity from any US humanitarian and instrumental manipulation of history and just war theory. Moreover, Schmitt was convinced that Vitoria and the global line of the Western Hemisphere were central to the formation and subsequent evolution of the

16 James Brown Scott, *The Spanish Origin of International Law: Francisco de Vitoria and His Law of Nations* (Oxford: Clarendon Press, 1934). See also Juan Pablo Scarfi, "Francisco de Vitoria and the (Geo)politics of Canonization in Spain/America," *Leiden Journal of International Law* 35(3) (2022), 479–495, and Juan Pablo Scarfi, *El imperio de la ley: James Brown Scott y la construcción de un orden jurídico interamericano* (Buenos Aires: Fondo de Cultura Económica, 2014).

17 See Scarfi, "Francisco de Vitoria," 489–490.

18 Scott, *Spanish Origin*, 280.

19 Schmitt, *The Nomos of the Earth*, 119.

20 Schmitt, *The Nomos of the Earth*, 102.

21 Schmitt, *The Nomos of the Earth*, 109.

European law of nations following the conquest of America to the extent that he framed and presented the main arguments of his *Nomos* around these two foundational legal features. In other words, the work of Vitoria in the context of the discovery and conquest of America and the incorporation of the Western Hemisphere as a global line into the European orbit were two inter-connected foundational tenets for the rise and decline of the European Law of Nations. While Vitoria crystalized as the epitome and most eminent example representing the foundation of the European Law of Nations as an act of land-appropriation and modern international law as such, the Western Hemisphere and the birth of the New World were also central to the formation and especially the subsequent evolution and decline of the European Law of Nations.

Schmitt was also aware and especially inspired by the renaissance of the work of Vitoria as the founder of international law in European and Spanish international legal thought, in particular by the work of Camilo Barcia Trelles, whose lectures on Vitoria "constituted the strongest breakthrough for the world at large."[22] Therefore, Schmitt was not compelled to react critically to this Spanish recovery, as he did with the US one inspired by humanitarian motivations and an adherence to just war theory, since in this case he shared important common grounds with Barcia Trelles, notably certain nostalgia for the past legacy of Vitoria and the early modern European law of nations. Schmitt was quite explicit about the influence of Barcia Trelles on his work in the afterword of *The Nomos of the Earth*, for he went as far as to affirm, "I agree with Camilo Barcia Trelles, an important scholar of contemporary international law, who has also dealt with the theme of land and sea."[23] More importantly, when envisioning *The Nomos of the Earth*, Schmitt drew on Barcia's idea that Vitoria was a precursor of the Monroe Doctrine and that there was a connection between the conquest of America and the progressive demarcation of the Western Hemisphere as a global line that "was no longer Eurocentric."[24] This new global line was finally consolidated in international law with the formulation of the Monroe Doctrine in 1823, which made explicit reference to the geopolitical notion of the Western Hemisphere. Barcia was convinced that the Western Hemisphere or what he termed a specific continental "American system" was a distinct and separate entity from that of Europe. "According to Barcia Trelles, the Americas formed a specific continental 'American system', which was based on three interconnected core principles: (i) the Americas should not be a subject of future colonization; (ii) the political

22 Schmtt, *The Nomos of the Earth*, 118.
23 Schmitt, *The Nomos of the Earth*, 38.
24 Schmitt, *The Nomos of the Earth*, 281.

system of the New World was both different and incompatible with that of Europe; (iii) Europe should not intervene in the Americas."[25] The Monroe Doctrine, as Barcia observed, had a prehistory which stemmed from the precedent of Vitoria. Schmitt drew on Barcia's take on the prehistory of the Monroe Doctrine and especially on the premise that the work of Vitoria in the context of the conquest of America contributed to demarcating for the first time the "American system" as a separate and distinct unit from Europe.[26] Yet Schmitt replaced it for the term Western Hemisphere, which was deployed and used in the original formulation of the Monroe Doctrine. According to Schmitt, Vitoria was central not only for the formation of the European Law of Nations, but also for the demarcation of the Americas as a distinct global line from that of Europe. Such distinction was to acquire much wider implications and connotations for the Americas following the formulation of the Monroe Doctrine in 1823. There were strong common grounds regarding the work of Vitoria, but there were some important differences between Schmitt and Barcia. As I have argued elsewhere, Barcia was more of a romantic jurist than Schmitt, since he maintained also a significant and peculiar nostalgia for the lost unity of international law in the Americas, according to which the legal divisions between the US and Latin America since the formulation of the US unilateral Monroe Doctrine dismantled the unity of the Americas that had persisted since the 'discovery' and conquest of the Americas and the times of Vitoria.

Schmitt's approach to Vitoria and the conquest of America was not only informed by the renaissance of the work of the Spanish theologian in US and European international law, but also by the important renovation of the historical scholarship on the conquest of America in the US and Latin America which took shape in the 1930s and 1940s. The work of US historian Lewis

25 Juan Pablo Scarfi, "Camilo Barcia Trelles on the Meaning of the Monroe Doctrine and the Legacy of Vitoria in the Americas," *European Journal of International Law* 31(4) (2020), 1463–1475.

26 Camilo Barcia Trelles, *Doctrina de Monroe y cooperación internacional* (Madrid: Editorial Mundo Latino, 1931). For a detailed overview of the international legal thought and the contributions of Camilo Barcia Trelles to international law, see Ignacio de la Rasilla, "Camilo Barcia Trelles in and beyond Vitoria's Shadow (1888–1977)," *European Journal of International Law* 31(4) (2020), 1433–1450, Randall Lessafer, "The Cradle of International Law: Camilo Barcia Trelles on Francisco de Vitoria at The Hague (1927)," *European Journal of International Law* 31(4) (2020): 1451–1462, José María Beneyto, "Camilo Barcia Trelles on Francisco de Vitoria: At the Crossroads of Carl Schmitt's Grossraum and James Brown Scott's 'Modern International Law,'" *European Journal of International Law* 31(4) (2020), 1477–1492, and Juan Pablo Scarfi, "Camilo Barcia Trelles on the Meaning of the Monroe Doctrine and the Legacy of Vitoria in the Americas," *European Journal of International Law* 31(4) (2020), 1463–1475.

Hanke, *The Spanish Struggle for Justice*, published in 1949, renovated significantly the debates about the conquest of America, since it famously stressed the rather advanced and humanist approach of Vitoria and Bartolomé de Las Casas as compared to Juan Ginés Sepúlveda, who regarded the American Indians as savages and barbarians lacking the right to equal treatment.[27] Although Schmitt did not shared Hanke's approach to the subject in its full length, he drew on this important premise and the idea that Vitoria was radically modern in his solid and robust treatment of the rights of American Indians as rational human agents. While it is hard to know whether Schmitt was in tune with the important historiographical renovation of the study of Vitoria and the conquest of America in the US and Latin America, his own approach to Vitoria was in syntony with the scholarly contributions of Hanke, Herbert Bolton and Arthur Whitaker in the US and Silvio Zavala in Mexico, among others, and the discussions generated by Herbert Bolton's thesis over the existence of a common history of the Americas and the polemics it provoked.[28] It is not a coincidence that Arthur Whitaker's important book, *The Western Hemisphere Idea*, which was a late response to the Bolton's thesis, came out a few years after the original publication of *The Nomos of the Earth*.[29] It is clear that in the late 1940s and 1950s, the debates about the existence of the Western Hemisphere as a separate unit from Europe reached their peak. *The Nomos of the Earth* contributed to expanding these discussions further by arguing that Vitoria's contribution was not only fundamental for how it helped to frame the European modern law of nations in its territorial boundaries, but also because it was foundational in envisioning and structuring the territorial division of the Western Hemisphere as a separate and distinct geographical entity.

As has already been noted, Schmitt's approach to the Monroe Doctrine, its configuration as an American Großraum and the concept of the Western Hemisphere was originally envisioned in a series of essays written in the

27 Lewis Hanke, *The Spanish Struggle for Justice in the Conquest of America* (Philadelphia: University of Pennsylvania Press, 1949). See also Hanke, *Aristotle and the American Indians: A Study in Race Prejudice in the Modern World* (Chicago: Henry Regnery Company, 1959).

28 For a good and brief overview of this historiographical renovation recovered and presented a few years later by Hanke, see Lewis Hanke (ed.), *Do the Americas have a Common History? A Critique of the Bolton Theory* (New York: Alfred A. Knopf, 1963).

29 See Arthur P. Whitaker, *The Western Hemisphere Idea: Its Rise and Decline* (Ithaca: Cornell University Press, 1954). For a recent reassessment of Whitaker's approach, see Juan Pablo Scarfi and Andrew Tillman (eds.), *Cooperation and Hegemony in US-Latin American Relations: Revisiting the Western Hemisphere Idea* (New York: Palgrave Macmillan, 2016).

1930s as a response to the rise of US imperialism in Latin America and its imperial usages of international law. On the one hand, in these essays, long before the so-called historical turn began in the first two decades of the twenty-first century to place a strong emphasis on the connection between international law and imperialism, Schmitt argued seventy years ago that the US imperial usages of the Monroe Doctrine were an emblematic testament of how the language of international law was deployed by the US in the Western Hemisphere for imperial purposes. Schmitt concluded his essay, famously stressing that "for an historically significant imperialism, not only military and naval, not only economic and financial wealth, but also this capability to determine the content of political and legal concepts... A people is only conquered when it subordinates itself to the foreign vocabulary, the foreign construction of what law, especially international law, is."[30] On the other hand and more importantly, in another early writing devoted to explore the international legal struggle over the Monroe Doctrine, Schmitt advanced for the very first time his interpretation of the Monroe Doctrine as a US-led American Großraum in the Western Hemisphere, a separate and well-define unit, in which extra-regional powers [notably Europe] may not interfere."[31] He proved to be well-aware of the debates about the meaning and scope of the Monroe Doctrine in the Americas, especially about Latin American specific contributions to these discussions and the important contributions of Alvarez in particular. He thus acknowledged that "a strong Ibero-American school of thought is working to [re-]establish the specifically Western Hemispheric and [purely] defensive character of the Monroe Doctrine against such imperialistic [US] abuses, and thus to salvage its original meaning."[32] The redefinition of the Monroe Doctrine as a multilateral principle of continental American international law advanced by Alvarez generated a strong tension with the progressive US redefinition of the doctrine as an American Großraum in the Western Hemisphere. Schmitt took these battles over the meaning of the doctrine seriously because he identified important implications for the meaning and fate of international law. He acknowledged that the quest for redefining the doctrine as a principle of American international law epitomized one of the most ambitious attempts to transform an imperial American Großraum in the West-

30 Carl Schmitt, "Forms of Modern Imperialism in International Law" (1933), in *Spatiality, Sovereignty and Carl Schmitt: Geographies of the Nomos*, ed. Stephen Legg (New York: Routledge, 2011), 44–45.

31 Carl Schmitt, "Großraum versus Universalism: The international legal struggle over the Monroe Doctrine" (1939), in *Spatiality, Sovereignty and Carl Schmitt: Geographies of the Nomos*, ed. Stephen Legg (New York: Routledge, 2011), 46.

32 Schmitt, "Großraum versus Universalism," (1939), 47.

ern Hemisphere into the language of international law. Yet he was aware of the fact that in the last instance, only the US would have the final word over what the Monroe Doctrine should entail and how it could be used, since "the Monroe Doctrine is a monopoly of the United States of America" and thus "it cannot be transferred to other political or geopolitical situations, or can only be transferred with the permission and approval of the United States."[33] The quest of Alvarez might be valuable, but in the end, according to Schmitt, it was useless in the face of US hegemony in the Western Hemisphere. In any case, it was an emblematic testimony of the struggle over the meaning and scope of the Monroe Doctrine in the Americas and beyond. Indeed, Schmitt referred explicitly to Alvarez in *The Nomos of the Earth*, but he proved to be even more eclectic by 1950 of the quest of Alvarez for an American international law. Schmitt thus asserted: "only in 1910 did a pioneering book by Alejandro Alvarez appear that opposed the universalistic international law and outlined the characteristics of an American international law."[34] All in all, the opposition to a universalist notion of international law was regarded by Schmitt as one important move towards the crisis and progressive decline of the European law of Nations. Therefore, through the redefinition of the Monroe Doctrine as a hemispheric principle and the quest for an American international law, Alvarez could be legitimately blamed for the crisis of the European Law of Nations.

As a critic of the elasticity and flexibility of the Monroe Doctrine for US imperial interventionist policies in Latin America, like the Mexican and Cuban jurists Fabela and Roig de Leuchsenring, Schmitt was particularly concerned with the inclusion of the doctrine as article 21 of the League Covenant since the 1930s, recognizing the Monroe Doctrine as a "regional understanding." Although it was not originally formulated as an international legal principle and it emerged instead as a US unilateral political declaration, the Monroe Doctrine was especially relevant for international law, and it was incorporated in textbooks and debates about international law. Along with the Alvarez quest for an American international law, its inclusion into the League Covenant made it especially meaningful in a quite concrete manner to the language of international law and organizations. Schmitt acknowledged its importance in his early writings to the extent that he went as far as to affirm that since the "American Monroe Doctrine" is "recognized in article 21 of the Covenant of the League of Nations," it has primacy and "pre-

33 Schmitt, "Großraum versus Universalism," (1939), 48.

34 Schmitt, *The Nomos of the Earth*, 229.

cedence over the League Covenant and prevents the interference of the Geneva League in American affairs" in the Western Hemisphere.[35] As has been already noted, Fabela and Roig de Leuchsenring regarded the inclusion of article 21 into the League Covenant as an extremely problematic outcome for Latin American states, since it was a formal symptom of the global acceptance of the Monroe Doctrine by European nations and international norms and institutions. In this regard, although it is hard to affirm that he read and was aware of the work and contributions of such jurists, these Latin American critical visions of the Monroe Doctrine were in tune with Schmitt's broader critique of US usages of the Monroe Doctrine. Schmitt and these Latin American jurists regarded the inclusion of article 21 into the Covenant as one of the most problematic evolving developments of the Monroe Doctrine.

The Western Hemisphere was after all, according to Schmitt, a concept articulated and ciphered firstly by Vitoria in the early modern world and a notion originally deployed in the original formulation of the Monroe Doctrine in 1823. Yet while the latter made an explicit reference to the notion of the Western Hemisphere, Vitoria never used this term in *De Indis*, that is, on his lectures "On the American Indians."[36] Like Barcia Trelles, who established a strong connection between Vitoria and the Monroe Doctrine, Schmitt sought to trace certain connections in terms of languages and territorial boundaries between the idea of the Western Hemisphere and the international legal thought of the Spanish theologian. Since he was obsessed with the rise and decline of the European Law of Nations, Schmitt long remained fixed with the idea of the Western Hemisphere as a key geographical unit contributing to the decline of the former. By contrast, because Alvarez remained fixed with American international law and the Western Hemisphere, he was also especially concerned with the European law of nations as a distinct notion from Western Hemisphere American international law.

4 The Influence of Vitoria and Schmitt in Latin America: The Hidden History of Spanish and Latin American Influences on Schmitt's Approach to the European Law of Nations (and Vitoria)

When thinking about the historical and geopolitical foundations of international law, Schmitt took the Western Hemisphere, the US and notably

35 Schmitt, "Forms of Modern Imperialism," 40.

36 See Vitoria, "On the American Indians," in *Vitoria: Political Writings*, ed. Anthony Pagden and Jeremy Lawrance (Cambridge: Cambridge University Press, 1991), 231–292.

Latin America, more seriously than it has often been regarded. This section examines the influence of Vitoria and Schmitt in Latin America, but also how the construction of the idea the Western Hemisphere in general and the region of Latin America in the nineteenth century contributed to shaping new regional Spanish Americanist and Latin Americanist interpretations of Vitoria and Schmitt's historical and geopolitical approach to international law, as outlined in *The Nomos of the Earth*. More importantly, this section shows that to fully understand why Vitoria and Schmitt generated resonances and were influential in Latin America, it is worth exploring the influence and resonances that Spanish and Latin American authors and contributions generated on Schmitt's sophisticated conception of Vitoria and the European Law of Nations, as addressed in *The Nomos of the Earth*. All these questions are somehow inter-connected and will be examined as such throughout this section. In fact, the Spanish and Latin American origins of Schmitt's approach to Vitoria and the European Law of Nations has been largely glossed over among scholars and experts on the work of Schmitt. As has been shown in the previous sections of this chapter, Schmitt was well-aware and indeed influenced by Spanish and Latin American approaches to Vitoria and American Western Hemisphere international law. In short, Spanish, and Latin American jurists, politicians, diplomats, and political thinkers proved to be an important source for Schmitt when he envisioned and dealt with these important questions, because they touched on the struggles over the Monroe Doctrine and the idea of the Western Hemisphere, and their visions have important implications for making sense and grasping the nature of the European Law of Nations. It was through Vitoria and these Spanish and Latin American contributions that Schmitt could inter-connect the Old War and the New World and understand the importance of the delimitation of the Western Hemisphere as a global line.

The work of Vitoria generated a first important wave of resonances in the context of Latin American independences, especially for those who were active political actors in this context and in the political and legal thought of politicians and prominent figures in the early nineteenth century. Important leaders of the revolutions of independence relied on the intellectual contributions of Vitoria when advancing a modern vision about the rights of indigenous peoples and self-government, including the liberator Simón Bolívar and the ideologue of the revolution in the Viceroyalty of the River Plate, Mariano Moreno, among others. Early modern Spanish political traditions and the ideas of Vitoria and Suárez generated an important ideological precedent and a window of opportunities for the emergence of the revolutions of independence, republican conceptions of self-government and the myth of revolutionary ideologies, which were informed by these previous well-established Spanish traditions.[37] In this regard, one of the first legacies and influences of Vitoria was the progressive germination and elaboration of modern and rational conceptions of natural law, reason and self-government, which stressed the rights of creole elites and indigenous peoples, creating the grounds for the emergence of "creole patriotism," an ideology associated to the independence movement that could be traced also back to Vitoria's political and legal vision about the rights of American Indians.[38] The revival of Spanish Americanism in the late nineteenth century and early twentieth century contributed to a first revival of the work of Vitoria in Spain and in Latin America.[39] In this regard, the quest of Barcia Trelles for presenting Vitoria as the founder of international law played a central role and had reverberations and resonances among Latin American jurists and intellectuals throughout the twentieth century.[40]

While the work of Vitoria generated different and concrete waves of influence and revival across Latin America in the nineteenth and twentieth centuries, the work of Schmitt generated an important impact in Latin America throughout the twentieth century, but only recently scholars have begun to examine it and get a concrete sense of his legacy and influence across the region. As is well-known, Schmitt established close contacts with Spanish jurists and political theorists and had some contact with very specific figures in Latin America. In Argentina, Schmitt's influence and the discussions provoked by his work, especially his writings on political theology, Hobbes, and the concept of the political, generated important and lasting resonances to the extent that Argentine political philosopher Jorge Dotti wrote a masterful and erudite account of the intellectual history of his influence in Argentina throughout the twentieth century.[41]

---

37 This is the argument of Argentine historian Tulio Halperin Donghi. See, for instance, Tulio Halperin Donghi, *Tradición política española e ideología revolucionaria de mayo* (Buenos Aires: Centro Editor de América Latina, 1985).

38 These connections and this long evolution of Spanish American and Latin American political thought has been elegantly grasped in the masterful study by Anthony Pagden, *Spanish Imperialism and the Political Imagination* (New Haven: Yale University Press, 1990).

39 See Camilo Barcia Trelles, *Francisco de Vitoria, fundador del Derecho Internacional moderno* (Madrid: Reus, 1928).

40 Barcia Trelles, *Francisco de Vitoria.*

41 See Jorge E. Dotti, *Carl Schmitt en Argentina* (Rosario: Homo Sapiens Ediciones, 2000). See also Jorge E. Dotti, "From Karl to Carl: Schmitt as a Reader of Marx" in *The Challenge of Carl Schmitt*, ed. Chantal Mouffe (London: Verso, 1999), 92–117.

What has been often glossed over about Schmitt is that his interest in Spanish and Latin American legal traditions and legacies informed and primarily influenced the elaboration and evolution of his own idea about the rise and decline of the European Law of Nations and the rather negative impact of the Monroe Doctrine, US hegemony and the consolidation of the notion of the Western Hemisphere in this latter trajectory. In order to grasp and make sense of this broader question and its global implications, Schmitt drew on the contributions and ideas of Spanish and Latin American jurists, notably on Alvarez. Like Alvarez, he learned that in order to understand the uniqueness of American Western Hemisphere international law, it was central to grasp and compare it with the European Law of Nations. It has been overlooked the extent to which Schmitt's Eurocentric approach to international law was rooted in a sophisticated but somehow overlooked and hidden interpretation of the importance of Latin America and Western Hemisphere continental ideals and contributions to American international law for the foundations of the modern European Law of Nations. Yet it was not only a question of interest and interpretation, but also an imperative necessity. If one is to understand Western Hemisphere international law, it is worth understanding the European Law of Nations, and the other way around. In other words, consciously or unconsciously, implicitly or explicitly, Schmitt followed the circular analysis of Alvarez, but he inverted the terms to arrive to a rather different conclusion. Western Hemisphere international law and the US Monroe Doctrine generated the grounds and causes for the decline of the European Law of Nations. In his pursuit of making a case in defense of European international law, Schmitt was perfectly well-aware that it was worth understanding the foundations and nature of Western Hemisphere international law. In a similar vein, so was Alvarez well-aware of the importance of understanding the nature of European international law when he sought to make a case for American – Western Hemisphere – international law. All in all, it does not come as a surprise that Schmitt took the quest of Alvarez for American international law and a multilateral Monroe Doctrine very seriously since the 1930s up to the elaboration and completion of *The Nomos of the Earth* in 1950. Schmitt was conscious that to fully understand and grasp the importance and decline of the European Law of Nations it was worth analyzing the connections between the Old and the New World, in other words, American international law, the emergence of the Western Hemisphere and the work of Vitoria.

Moreover, Schmitt drew on Barcia's Spanish Americanist approach to Vitoria. Barcia regarded Vitoria as the true intellectual progenitor of the notion outlined in the original principles associated to the Monroe Doctrine, according to which the New World and the Americas should be a separate continental entity safeguarded from European interventions and colonial aspirations. The trouble with the Monroe Doctrine, in the mind of Barcia, was that it advanced this notion through a unilateral and selfish US declaration, rather than as a proper principle of international law. Although Schmitt had no intention in constructing an innocent and benevolent meaning for the original Monroe Doctrine, he drew on Barcia's connection between Vitoria and the Monroe Doctrine to the extent that the notion of the New World and the idea of the Western Hemisphere, according to Schmitt, was a historical and geopolitical configuration that could be traced back to Vitoria, the lands discovered by Columbus and the conquest of the New World and was reinforced with the Monroe Doctrine. In the mind of Schmitt, if the notion of the Western Hemisphere was originally envisioned alongside the conquest of America and the contribution of Vitoria, the Monroe Doctrine consolidated this notion and made of it a case for an exceptional US-led American Großraum. For Barcia, Vitoria was an epitome and founder of Spanish American international law and international law as such. In other words, in its origins and roots international law was essentially a Spanish American invention, since it was consolidated through the encounter between the Old and the New World. By contrast, for Schmitt Vitoria was the foundational and most eminent example of the European law of nations.

Although he did not prove to be aware and informed about Latin American anti-imperial critiques of the Monroe Doctrine, such as those advanced by Fabela and Roig, Schmitt shared many of their concerns, especially their obsession with the plasticity of the Monroe Doctrine and the negative implications of its inclusion as article 21 into the League Covenant, consolidating it as a global norm. Latin American conceptions of international law and their broader global implications were somehow present in Schmitt's vision of the decline of the European Law of Nations. He proved to have taken these conceptions more seriously than those of US international lawyers, such as James Brown Scott, especially if they were supportive of just war theory, which Schmitt rejected categorically. While these Latin American jurists were not central references for Schmitt, their concerns were more consistent and meaningful for exploring the crisis of the European Law of Nations and its progressive dissolution through the emergence of the Monroe Doctrine and the global line of the Western Hemisphere.

All in all, Schmitt made used of Spanish Americanist and Latin American contributions to explore the decline of the European Law of Nations and the disruption introduced by the concept of the Western Hemisphere, which was central to this evolution. By contrast, the notion of Latin America was insignificant to this process. What it is often overlooked is that in the exploration of the crisis of European law of nations, Schmitt drew and was convinced that Spanish Americanist and Latin American jurists were relevant observers and it was worth drawing on their multiple and contradictory diagnosis of the Monroe Doctrine as a principle of Western Hemisphere international law, its plastic and interventionist usages by the US and its inclusion as a global norm in the League of Nations Covenant.

5 Conclusion

While Scott and Barcia contributed to the canonization of Vitoria as the founder of international law, a few years later Schmitt portrayed Vitoria not only as a foundational figure in international law, the one who advanced the European justification of the land-appropriation of the New World, but more importantly as the historical and geographical point of intersection between the rise of the European Law of Nations and the idea of the Western Hemisphere, the Old and the New World, Europe and the Americas. In *The Nomos of the Earth*, Vitoria was not portrayed as a canonical author by any means, but instead as the central aleph in the overall geographical and historical architecture of Schmitt's conception and interpretation of the tragic evolution of international law. In the mind of Schmitt, Vitoria and the Monroe Doctrine were inter-connected, since the notion of the New World, which emerged as the distinctive community composed of American Indians in the times of Vitoria, consolidated itself as a separate entity known as the Western Hemisphere only in the early nineteenth century, creating the grounds for envisioning the US Monroe Doctrine in the nineteenth century and Western American international law in the twentieth century, as proposed by Alvarez. In other words, Schmitt's understanding of the European Law of Nations was somehow circular: Vitoria was the epitome of the European Law of Nations and at the same time the one who ciphered the historical and geopolitical delimitations of the New World as a distinctive entity, creating the conditions of possibility for its decline, through the European discovery and land-appropriation of the New World, the subsequent rise of the idea of the Western Hemisphere and the deployment of the US Monroe Doctrine in the nineteenth century.

This chapter has shown that through the reading and interpretation of Spanish and Latin American authors, ranging from Barcia Trelles to Alejandro Alvarez, and the categorical rejection of US dominant interpretations of Vitoria through the prism of just war theory, such as those advanced by James Brown Scott, Schmitt was able to make sense and envision significant connections between the European Law of Nations and American Western Hemisphere international law and explore the rise and decline of the former through the emergence of the latter. Since he was convinced that the pillar of the European Law of Nations was Vitoria and his justification of the European land-appropriation of the New World, he sought to find the foundations of American Western Hemisphere international law in the Monroe Doctrine and the international legal struggle over its meaning and scope to understand the crisis of the European Law of Nations. Thanks to Alvarez – and the exploration of the legal struggle over the Monroe Doctrine – Schmitt became aware of its relevance not only as a pillar of Western Hemisphere international law, but also as the central motive for the crisis of the European Law of Nations. Thanks to Barcia, Schmitt was able to trace geographical and historical connections between these two important legal pillars, Vitoria, and the Monroe Doctrine as key points of intersection between Europe and the Americas, the Old and the New World, European and American Western Hemisphere international law. If the Monroe Doctrine was the pillar of American Western Hemisphere international law, Vitoria was the initial and most important precedent, a unique point of convergence between the European Law of Nations and Western Hemisphere international law, the New World and the Old World, Europe and the Americas, the past and the future of international law as such.

Bibliography

Alvarez, Alejandro. *Le droit international américain: son fondement, sa nature* (Paris: A. Pedone Éditeur, 1910).

Alvarez, Alejandro. "Latin America and International Law," *American Journal of International Law* 3(3) (1909), 269–353.

Archivo del Ministerio de Relaciones Exteriores y Culto, República Argentina, Doctrina Drago (Buenos Aires, 1903).

Barcia Trelles, Camilo. *Doctrina de Monroe y cooperación internacional* (Madrid: Editorial Mundo Latino, 1931).

Barcia Trelles, Camilo. *Francisco de Vitoria, fundador del Derecho Internacional moderno* (Madrid: Reus, 1928).

Beneyto, José María. "Camilo Barcia Trelles on Francisco de Vitoria: At the Crossroads of Carl Schmitt's Grossraum and James Brown Scott's 'Modern International Law,'" *European Journal of International Law* 31(4) (2020), 1477–1492.

De la Rasilla, Ignacio "Camilo Barcia Trelles in and beyond Vitoria's Shadow (1888–1977)," *European Journal of International Law* 31(4) (2020), 1433–1450.

Dotti, Jorge E. *Carl Schmitt en Argentina* (Rosario: Homo Sapiens Ediciones, 2000).

Dotti, Jorge E. "From Karl to Carl: Schmitt as a Reader of Marx" in *The Challenge of Carl Schmitt*, ed. Chantal Mouffe (London: Verso, 1999), 92–117.

Drago, Luis María. "State Loans in Their Relation to International Policy," *American Journal of International Law* 1(3) (1907), 692–726.

Fabela, Isidro. *Los Estados Unidos contra la libertad: Estudios de historia diplomática americana* (Barcelona: Talleres gráficos "Lux", 1920).

Halperin Donghi, Tulio. *Tradición política española e ideología revolucionaria de mayo* (Buenos Aires: Centro Editor de América Latina, 1985).

Hanke, Lewis. *Aristotle and the American Indians: A Study in Race Prejudice in the Modern World* (Chicago: Henry Regnery Company, 1959).

Hanke, Lewis. *The Spanish Struggle for Justice in the Conquest of America* (Philadelphia: University of Pennsylvania Press, 1949).

Hanke, Lewis (ed.). *Do the Americas Have a Common History? A Critique of the Bolton Theory* (New York: Alfred A. Knopf, 1963).

Lipscomb, Andrew A. (ed.). *The Writings of Thomas Jefferson*, vol 14 (Washington, DC: The Thomas Jefferson Memorial Association of the United States, 1904).

Lessafer, Randall. "The Cradle of International Law: Camilo Barcia Trelles on Francisco de Vitoria at The Hague (1927)," *European Journal of International Law* 31(4) (2020), 1451–1462.

Link, Arthur (ed.). *Papers of Woodrow Wilson*, Vol. 40 (Princeton, NJ: Princeton University Press, 1982).

Northedge, F. S. *The League of Nations: Its Life and Times, 1920–1946* (Leicester: Leicester University Press, 1988).

Pagden, Anthony. *Spanish Imperialism and the Political Imagination* (New Haven: Yale University Press, 1990).

Papers Related to the Foreign Relations of the United States (Washington, DC: Government Printing Office, 1904).

Roig de Leuchsenring, Emilio. *La Doctrina de Monroe y el Pacto de la Liga de las Naciones* (La Habana: Imprenta El Siglo XX, 1921).

Scarfi, Juan Pablo. "The Monroe Doctrine in the Americas: Towards a Hemispheric Intellectual History," *Diplomatic History* 47(5) (2023), 738–763.

Scarfi, Juan Pablo. "Francisco de Vitoria and the (Geo)Politics of Canonization in Spain/America," *Leiden Journal of International Law* 35 (2022), 479–495.

Scarfi, Juan Pablo. "Mexican Revolutionary Constituencies and the Latin American Critique of US Intervention," in *Revolutions in International Law: The Legacies of 1917*, ed. Anne Orford, Kathryn Greenman, Anna Saunders and Ntina Tzouvala (Cambridge: Cambridge University Press, 2021), 218–241.

Scarfi, Juan Pablo. "Camilo Barcia Trelles on the Meaning of the Monroe Doctrine and the Legacy of Vitoria in the Americas," *European Journal of International Law* 31(4) (2020), 1463–1475.

Scarfi, Juan Pablo. "Denaturalizing the Monroe Doctrine: The Rise of Latin American Legal Anti-imperialism in the Face of the Modern US and Hemispheric Redefinition of the Monroe Doctrine," *Leiden Journal of International Law* 33(3) (2020), 541–555.

Scarfi, Juan Pablo. *The Hidden History of International Law in the Americas: Empire and Legal Networks* (New York: Oxford University Press, 2017).

Scarfi, Juan Pablo. *El imperio de la ley: James Brown Scott y la construcción de un orden jurídico interamericano* (Buenos Aires: Fondo de Cultura Económica, 2014).

Scarfi, Juan Pablo and Andrew Tillman (eds.). *Cooperation and Hegemony in US-Latin American Relations: Revisiting the Western Hemisphere Idea* (New York: Palgrave Macmillan, 2016).

Schmitt, Carl. *The Nomos of the Earth in the International Law of the Jus Publicum Europaeum* (New York: Telos Press, 2003).

Schmitt, Carl. "Forms of Modern Imperialism in International Law" (1933), in *Spatiality, Sovereignty and Carl Schmitt: Geographies of the Nomos*, ed. Stephen Legg (New York: Routledge, 2011), 29–47.

Schmitt, Carl. "Großraum versus Universalism: the International Legal Struggle over the Monroe Doctrine" (1939), in *Spatiality, Sovereignty and Carl Schmitt: Geographies of the Nomos*, ed. Stephen Legg (New York: Routledge, 2011), 48–54.

Scott, James Brown. *The Spanish Origin of International Law: Francisco de Vitoria and His Law of Nations* (Oxford: Clarendon Press, 1934).

Scott, James Brown, Editorial Note, "The Classics of International Law," *American Journal of International Law* 3(3) (1909), 701–707.

Serrano Migallón, Fernando. *Isidro Fabela y la diplomacia mexicana* (México: Fondo de Cultura Económica, 1981).

Sexton, Jay. *The Monroe Doctrine: Empire and Nation in Nineteenth-Century America* (New York: Hill and Wang, 2011).

Vitoria, Francisco de, "on the American Indians," in *Vitoria: Political Writings*, ed. Anthony Pagden and Jeremy Lawrance (Cambridge: Cambridge University Press, 1991), 231–292.

Whitaker, Arthur P. *The Western Hemisphere Idea: Its Rise and Decline* (Ithaca: Cornell University Press, 1954).

Williams, William Appleman. *The Tragedy of American Diplomacy* (New York: Norton, 2009).

CHAPTER 11

Beyond Discovery: Decolonizing International Law through Long-Term Historical Analysis

Valentina Vadi

1 Introduction

About 70 percent of the world's population before WWI was subject to foreign rule.[1] At the end of WWII, nearly a third of the world's population, or 750 million people, resided in colonies.[2] Eighty former colonies have achieved independence since the end of WWII.[3] Less than two million people now reside in the seventeen remaining non-self-governing territories.[4] While most former colonies have gradually achieved their political independence, the decolonization process remains incomplete.[5] International law oscillates between inclusion and exclusion, recognition and rejection, universality and particularity.[6] Moreover, economic, social, and cultural decolonization remains a work in progress, particularly in knowledge systems where colonial epistemologies persist.[7]

Decolonization is more than political emancipation. Among the de-colonial strategies, the de-colonization of knowledge is an epistemological approach

1 Marion Mushkatt, 'The Process of Decolonization International Legal Aspects' (1972) 2 *University of Baltimore Law Review* 16, 16.

2 United Nations, 'Global Issues: Decolonization', https://www.un.org/en/global-issues/decolonization (last visited 10 July 2025).

3 Id.

4 Under of the Charter of the United Nations, the Non-Self-Governing Territories are defined as 'territories whose people have not yet attained a full measure of self-government'. Non Self-Governing Territories include Western Sahara, Anguilla, Bermuda, British Virgin Islands, Cayman Islands, Falkland Island (Malvinas), Montserrat, Saint Helena, Turks and Caicos Islands, United States Virgin Islands, Gibraltar, American Samoa, French Polynesia, Guam, New Caledonia, Pitcairn. United Nations, 'Non-Self-Governing Territories', https://www.un.org/dppa/decolonization/en/nsgt (last visited 10 July 2025).

5 See e.g. ICJ, *Legal Consequences of the Separation of the Chagos Archipelago from Mauritius in 1965*, Advisory Opinion, 25 February 2019.

6 See Jochen Von Bernstorff and Philipp Dann (eds) *The Battle for International Law in the Decolonization Era* (Oxford: Oxford University Press 2019).

7 Sundhya Pahuja, *Decolonising International Law: Development, Economic Growth and the Politics of Universality* (Cambridge: Cambridge University Press 2011) 12.

 | DOI:10.1163/9789004757448_012

that aims to overcome the monopolization of knowledge production by colonial powers.[8] Colonial powers historically marginalized the forms of knowledge of the colonized cultures to validate colonial domination. The decolonization of knowledge entails undoing historical epistemological frameworks and diversifying the production of knowledge by putting into conversation differing cultural systems.[9] It aims at recognizing the different ways of knowing by which peoples across the globe run their lives and provide meaning to their existence. The chapter aims to contribute to the decolonization of international law by deconstructing and examining the long-term history of the concept of discovery and contrasting Vitoria (1483–1546) and Schmitt's (1888–1985) antithetical positions on the issue.

The doctrine of discovery (*ius inventionis*) played a central role among the arguments supporting the European conquest.[10] Sovereigns often employed this doctrine to justify imperial expansion, claiming rights to territory on the basis of discovery. For instance, Spain based its claim to the New World on the argument of discovery. Although the concept of discovery was instrumentally used to justify European seizure of Indigenous lands, already in the early modern period Vitoria and other scholars rejected the epistemological fallacy and injustice of discovery. Adopting a long-term historical perspective can help international lawyers decolonize international law, exposing the uncertain foundations and injustice of specific legal rules and developing tools to right historical wrongs. Thus, it can nurture the emancipatory potential of international law.

The chapter proceeds as follows. Section 1 investigates how European nations and the Church developed the doctrine of discovery in the early modern period. Section 2 zooms in Vitoria's position on this doctrine. Section 3 examines how the 1885 Berlin Conference endorsed the discovery doctrine. It also examines how Schmitt supported the doctrine that Germany had used in East Africa. Lastly, Section 4 compares Vitoria and Schmitt's diverging positions. Section 5 discusses the promises and pitfalls of adopting the long view on the doctrine of discovery for contributing to the decolonization and development of international law. Given the violence of the colonial encounter, the chapter argues for jettisoning the discovery doctrine, dismantling colonial frameworks

---

8 Water D. Mignolo, 'Epistemic Disobedience, Independent Thought and Decolonial Freedom' (2009) 26 *Theory, Culture & Society* 159–181.

9 *See generally* Boaventura de Sousa Santos, *The End of the Cognitive Empire: The Coming of Age of Epistemologies of the South* (Durham, North Carolina: Duke University Press 2018) 8.

10 Giuseppe Tosi, 'La Teoria della Guerra Giusta in Francisco de Vitoria e il Dibattito sulla Conquista' (2006) *Jura Gentium* 1–17, 3.

in international law, and developing new, ethical, and intercultural ways of understanding space, sovereignty, and justice.

2 The Doctrine of Discovery in the Early Modern Period

The doctrine of discovery was one of the legal grounds that European colonizers used to claim lands beyond the European continent since the fifteenth century. Under this doctrine, land was considered vacant (*terra nullius*) if it was unclaimed by other Christian rulers.[11] Such vacant lands could be 'discovered' and, as a result, sovereignty, title, and jurisdiction could be claimed. The doctrine made its way into international law to justify state occupation, colonization, and sovereignty acquisition.

After Columbus' voyage in 1492 resulted in Europe learning of the existence of the Americas, Pope Alexander VI (1431–1503) issued a declaration that set the ground for the doctrine of discovery. The papal bull *Inter Caetera* (1493)[12] conferred the Americas to Spain and African and Asian territories to Portugal. The bull established that the meridian (in Spanish, *raya*) passing 100 leagues west from the Azores Islands constituted the border between the lands belonging to Spain, west of the meridian, and those belonging to Portugal, east of the meridian. Spain and Portugal argued that the mere discovery of new lands within their spheres of influence established their sovereignty over the lands. They thus displayed symbolic acts of possession.[13]

While most other European powers disagreed with the surrender of entire continents to the Spanish and Portuguese empires, they agreed with the idea of claiming land for their nations by 'discovering' vacant lands. For instance, Queen Elizabeth I's (1533–1603) Charters to the adventurers Sir Humphrey Gilbert (1539–1583) and Sir Walter Raleigh (1552–1618) also relied on arguments of discovery, almost paraphrasing the papal bull in some respects.[14]

---

11 Shane Chalmers, '*Terra Nullius*? Temporal Legal Pluralism in an Australian Colony' (2019) 8 *Social & Legal Studies* 1–23.

12 Alexander VI, bull *Inter Caetera*, 4 May 1493 ('should any of said islands have been found by your envoys and captains, [we] give, grant, and assign to you and your heirs and successors … forever, together with all their dominions, cities, camps, places, and villages, and all rights, jurisdictions, and appurtenances, all islands and mainlands found and to be found, *discovered* and to be *discovered* towards the west and the south' [emphasis added]).

13 Robert J. Miller and Olivia Stitz, 'The International Law of Colonialism in East Africa: Germany, England, and the Doctrine of Discovery' (2021) 32 *Duke Journal of Comparative & International Law* 1–59, at 12.

14 Queen Elizabeth's Charter to Sir Humphrey Gilbert of 11 June 1578 granted him 'all the soil of all such lands, countries and territories to be *discovered* … with full power to

While the Queen rejected the validity of the bull's donation of the New World to the Iberian Empire, her charters still relied on arguments of discovery. Similarly, the 1606 Virginia Charter established that land would belong to James I (1566–1625), with the Virginia Company as the King's tenant, and the settlers as subtenants provided that the grantees 'could establish settlements on lands which [were] not actually possessed by any Christian prince'.[15] The charter determined that the colony would be subject to English sovereignty; its inhabitants and their children would remain English subjects and have to comply with the common law of England. The Charter proclaimed colonial rule in manifest disregard of Indigenous sovereignty, conflating occupation of territories by private parties with acquisition of property and sovereignty by the British ruler. These charters disregarded Indigenous realms, rights, and interests as if they did not exist. The official policy was that by discovering and occupying land, the colonists extended the private property and territorial sovereignty of the home country. According to the discovery theory, territories could be occupied if they did not already belong to another state, whether they were uninhabited, or inhabited by people whose community was not regarded as a state.[16] *Terra nullius* was a legal fiction, a legal weapon, a principle of violence.

Early modern sovereigns transferred the concept of *terra nullius* from Roman law to the law of nations. However, this legal transfer altered the original meaning of *terra nullius*. In Roman law, the concept of *res nullius* denoted movable property without an owner.[17] Under Roman law, movable objects without owners (*res nullius*) could be acquired by anybody though possession.[18] Wild animals (*ferae naturae*) and objects left abandoned (*res derelictae*) were both *res nullius* open to anyone's seizure and claim. However, under

---

dispose thereof … according to the order of the laws of England' [emphasis added]. Only 'remote, heathen, and barbarous lands, countries and territories not actually possessed of any Christian prince or people' were targeted. See Elizabeth I, Charter to Sir Humphrey Gilbert of 11 June 1578, reprinted in William S. Powell, 'An Elizabethan Experiment', in Lindley S. Butler and Alan D. Watson (eds) *The North Carolina Experience: An Interpretive and Documentary History* (Chapel Hill: University of North Carolina Press 1984) 29–52, 36.

15 Elizabeth Mancke, 'Chartered Enterprises and the Evolution of the British Atlantic World', in Elizabeth Mancke and Carole Shammas (eds) *The Creation of the British Atlantic World* (Baltimore: Johns Hopkins University Press 2015), 237–262, 241.

16 Robert Jennings, Arthur Watts (eds) *Oppenheim's International Law, Vol. I, Peace* (Burnt Mill: Longman 1982) 687.

17 Lauren Benton and Benjamin Straumann, 'Acquiring Empire by Law: From Roman Doctrine to Early Modern European Practice' (2010) 28 *Law and History Review* 1, 6.

18 Id. 14–15.

Roman law, the concept of *res nullius* did not apply to land. It did not justify the acquisition of land or sovereignty. In fact, only movable objects (*mobiles res*) opposed to immovable objects like lands and buildings could be lawfully appropriated under Roman law.[19] In the context of European expansion 'the question arose whether all things in the [Americas and other continents] had, upon the arrival of the Europeans, the status of *res nullius*', or whether Indigenous peoples had any sovereignty and property claims over the newly discovered lands.[20]

Already in the early modern period several scholars examined the *terra nullius* argument and judged it to have questionable validity and applicability. As a result, they opposed the use of *terra nullius* for justifying conquest. The philosopher and theologian Domingo de Soto (1494–1560), for example, contended that Spain had no claim to the Americas because the continent was not *res nullius* at the time of discovery.[21] The philosopher, theologian, and jurist Francisco de Vitoria similarly contended that Indigenous peoples had private ownership and sovereign control over their territories, and that the Spaniards had no legal right to acquire these lands through simple discovery.[22]

In his 1598 *De Jure Belli Libri Tres*, Alberico Gentili (1552–1608), a religious refugee and Regius Professor at the University of Oxford, rejected the argument of *terra nullius*. He recognized that 'we are by nature all akin' and acknowledged the sovereignty and property rights of Indigenous peoples.[23] Gentili asserted that other nations can 'live in a manner different from that which we follow in our own country'.[24] As such, no one should be offended by the fact that someone else follows a different religion or lives by different customs. Gentili saw the occupation of vacant lands as a tool to gain property there, rather than sovereignty.[25] For him, full sovereignty over these lands remained with Indigenous sovereigns who could provide safe space to immigrants 'if it [could] be offered without too much inconvenience'.[26] In other

---

19 Lorenzo Cotula, 'Land, Property, and Sovereignty in International Law' (2017) 25 *Cardozo Journal of International & Comparative Law* 229.

20 Benton and Straumann, 'Acquiring Empire by Law' 20.

21 Id. 23–25.

22 Francisco de Vitoria, 'On the American Indians', in *Political Writings*, Anthony Pagden (ed.) (Cambridge: Cambridge University Press 1991) 264.

23 A. Gentili, *De Iure Belli Libri Tres* [1612] (On the Law of War) J. C. Rolfe transl. (Oxford: Clarendon Press 1933) Book I, Chapter 12, p. 54.

24 Gentili, *De Iure Belli Libri Tres*, Book I, Chapter 9.

25 Valentina Vadi, *War and Peace – Alberico Gentili and the Early Modern Law of Nations* (Leiden: Brill 2020) 301.

26 Gentili, *De Iure Belli Libri Tres*, Book I, Chapter 17, p. 80.

words, the immigrants would become subjects of the host Indigenous governments while the host states would retain control over them and could restrict access to their territories for legitimate reasons.[27] As is known, Gentili's writings did not have much influence on this point of law as his views were out of sync with contemporary expansionism.

There was a clear divide between theory and practice. Powerful states articulated arguments of discovery and *terra nullius* despite fierce Indigenous opposition and granted territorial concessions over land they did not own. Colonial rule disregarded Indigenous sovereignty, conflating private occupation of territories with public acquisition of sovereignty, something that the legal discourse had neatly distinguished.[28] Colonists in this way became proprietors of given land while remaining subjects of their homeland.[29] While 'the various European powers made different claims as to the basis of the acquisition of territory ... there was one thing in which they all agreed, that of almost entirely disregarding the right of the native inhabitants of these regions'.[30] In fact the concepts of discovery and *terra nullius* 'not only disregard[ed] the will of the conquered original inhabitants of the land, but treat[ed] them, in essence, as legally irrelevant'.[31] Such theories advanced the idea that European peoples, culture and religion were superior to all others. Colonial powers viewed Ireland, the Americas, and most of the African and Australasian territories as ownerless lands; for the native inhabitants were counted as nothing.[32] By depicting local people as 'barbarous and uncivil people', domestic charters handed foreign land to the colonists.[33]

---

27 Vadi, *War and Peace*, 224.

28 Anthony Pagden, 'Empire and Its Anxieties' (2012) *American Historical Review* 141–148, 146.

29 Vadi, *War and Peace*, 361.

30 Steven Wheatley, 'Conceptualizing the Authority of the Sovereign State over Indigenous Peoples' (2014) 27 *Leiden Journal of International Law* 371–396, 380.

31 Siegfried Wiessner, 'Indigenous Sovereignty: A Reassessment in Light of the UN Declaration on the Rights of Indigenous Peoples' (2008) 41 *Vanderbilt Journal of Transnational Law* 1141, 1153.

32 Petra Gümplová, 'Rights of Conquest, Discovery and Occupation, and the Freedom of the Seas: A Genealogy of Natural Resource Injustice' (2021) 54 *Isonomia. Revista de Teoria y Filosofia del Derecho* 1–36 (analyzing the colonial origins of the right of discovery and occupation and exposing their 'morally arbitrary origins') at 7–8 (noting that the doctrine of discovery and occupation became expansion tools by enclosing 'land that seemed to belong to nobody or was used ineffectively').

33 Valentina Vadi, 'The Power of Scale: International Law and Microhistories' (2018) 46 *Denver Journal of International Law & Policy* 315, 337.

The absence of Western agricultural practices was factored in the *terra nullius* argument.[34] Indigenous peoples practiced slash-and-burn agriculture: they burned forests to nourish the soil and create fields. They used these fields for a few seasons before leaving them to revert to forests. This cyclical agriculture helped preserve the natural landscape and allowed the soil to recover. Yet, colonists did not recognize and respect Indigenous lifestyles and farming and pastoralist methods.[35] Rather, they replaced traditional Indigenous practices with intensive agriculture.[36] They conceived nature in economic terms and conceptualized intensive agriculture as the best interplay between man and nature and a legitimate tool to appropriate natural resources and acquire land. Not only did they clear forests to transform land into agricultural fields, but they also adopted the monoculture plantation model to produce sugar, tea, coffee, cocoa, and cotton in Asia, the Americas, and Africa to maximize yields and profits. By increasing production, this extractive vision of nature damaged the ecosystem and destroyed biodiversity. Moreover, the products of plantations were for distant European markets and not for local consumption. As the colonists brought laborers to plantations from different continents under abject conditions, colonial agriculture caused the global displacement of many people. This instrumental view of the environment remains embedded in international law[37] that should be rethought in more sustainable ways.[38]

---

34 Martti Koskenniemi, *To the Uttermost Parts of the Earth – Legal Imagination and International Power 1300–1870* (Cambridge: Cambridge University Press 2021), 256–257 (referring to Irish colonization).

35 Gümplová, 'Rights of Conquest, Discovery and Occupation, and the Freedom of the Seas', 8–9.

36 Consider, for instance, the Hobbesian concept of settlement. In the Hobbesian theory, there was no reference to the sovereignty and property rights of Indigenous peoples; and there was no reference to the possibility that the local ruler might oppose or limit immigration on legitimate grounds and exercise self-defense. Thomas Hobbes, *Leviathan* [1651], C.B. Macpherson (ed.) (London: Penguin Books 1985) Chapter 30.

37 Anna Chadwick, *Law and the Political Economy of Hunger* (Oxford: Oxford University Press 2019), 19–53 (locating the origins of the contemporary global food system in the period of European colonialism, exploring the role of international law in creating conditions of food insecurity through international trade between colonial powers and colonized peoples, and enabling the perpetuation of colonial dynamics).

38 Karin Mickelson, 'The Maps of International Law: Perceptions of Nature in the Classification of Territory' (2014) 27 *Leiden Journal of International Law* 621–639.

3 Against Discovery: Francisco de Vitoria

Early modern theologians, philosophers, and lawyers engaged in complex debates on how to best govern interactions among peoples. Early modern international law emerged as a response to the challenge of cultural diversity.[39] Most attempts to address such challenge oscillated between tolerance, paternalism, and repression.[40] Two main attitudes emerged: 'others' were either considered as human beings and were thus expected to assimilate, or they were perceived as inferior.[41] Rather than accurately understanding other cultures, Europeans framed the others as 'imperfect' versions of themselves.[42]

Active in the sixteenth century until the early seventeenth century, the Spanish School of Salamanca emphasized the primacy of theology among the various fields of knowledge. For instance, one of its founders and main proponents, the theologian Francisco de Vitoria (1483–1546), stated that 'the duty and calling of a theologian is so wide that no argument, no discussion or controversy on any subject can be considered foreign to his profession ... Theology is ... the ... first of all sciences and disciplines in the world'.[43] Accordingly, theology extended so broadly to cover almost any field of inquiry including global governance and the emerging law of nations.[44]

Canon lawyers had debated the question as to whether legitimate possession and property (*dominium*) 'depended upon being in the state of grace'.[45] If *dominium* depended on grace, 'only Christians could legitimately hold property and self-government'.[46] Therefore, 'this theory would justify Christian conquest of any territory possessed by non-Christians'.[47] Vitoria rejected this the-

---

39 Antony Anghie, 'Francisco De Vitoria and the Colonial Origins of International Law' (1996) 5 *Social and Legal Studies* 321–336, 321.

40 Martti Koskenniemi, *The Gentle Civilizer of Nations. The Rise and Fall of International Law 1870–1960* (Cambridge: Cambridge University Press 2001) 88–97.

41 Tzvetan Todorov, *The Conquest of America–The Question of the Other* (Norman: University of Oklahoma Press 1999) 42.

42 Anghie, 'Francisco De Vitoria and the Colonial Origins of International Law', 323–325.

43 Diego Panizza, 'Political Theory and Jurisprudence in Gentili's *De Iure Belli*: The Great Debate between Theological and Humanist Perspectives from Vitoria to Grotius', in Pierre-Marie Dupuy and Vincent Chetail (eds) *The Roots of International Law* (Leiden: Brill 2014) 211–247, 215.

44 Peter Haggenmacher, 'Il Diritto della Guerra e della Pace di Gentili. Considerazioni Sparse di un Groziano' in VVAA, *Il Diritto della Guerra e della Pace di Alberico Gentili* (Milano: Giuffrè 1995), 26.

45 James Muldoon, 'Medieval Canon Law and the Conquest of the Americas', *Jarbuch für Geschichte Latinamerikas* (Köln: Böhlau Verlag 2000) 9–22, 20.

46 Id.

47 Id.

ory; the heathens legitimately possessed land and owned property. Therefore, there existed no general right to invade their lands. In this regard, Vitoria held that 'the Indians [could] not be deprived of their lands merely by virtue of their status as unbelievers'.[48] Rather, as Indigenous societies had 'properly organized cities, ... magistrates..., laws, industries, and commerce',[49] they had rights 'to their freedom, their property, their territories, and their self-governance'.[50] Not only did Indigenous chiefs rightly exercised jurisdiction over their tribes,[51] but Indigenous peoples were 'true masters' (*veri domini*) of themselves, their land, and their property (*dominium sui et rerum*).[52] Accordingly, Vitoria recognized that Indigenous peoples were sovereign in their territories and were entitled to their lands. Therefore, they should not be deprived of their sovereignty and property because of their different religious beliefs. For Vitoria, 'religion is a matter of will' and religious diversity did not justify war.[53]

Like other early modern scholars, Vitoria also questioned the distinct albeit related theory of discovery. Could European powers claim sovereignty because of discovery?[54] He rejected this doctrine, claiming that discovery could not be a lawful argument for conquering lands.[55] The mere fact of discovering a territory did not mean that such territory belonged to none. Because Indigenous peoples were true sovereigns and owners of their lands (*barbari erant veri domini et publice et privatim*), such territories were not nobody's thing (*res nullius*), and the Europeans could not appropriate them on this basis.[56] In conclusion, for Vitoria the argument of discovery provided no support for the acquisition of the New World, 'any more than it would if [Indigenous peoples] had discovered us' (*non plus quam si ipsi invenissent nos*).[57]

While Vitoria rejected discovery to justify the conquest of the New World, other arguments could indirectly and insidiously support colonization. For

48 Anghie, *Imperialism, Sovereignty, and the Making of International Law*, 18.

49 Vitoria, 'On the American Indians', question 1 art. 6, para. 23, 250 (also denying that the Spaniards had any right to occupy Indigenous lands).

50 Ramon Hernandez, 'The Internationalization of Francisco De Vitoria and Domingo De Soto' (1991) 15 *Fordham International Law Journal* 1031–1059, 1040.

51 Benton and Straumann, 'Acquiring Empire by Law', 21.

52 Vitoria, 'On the American Indians', question 1, conclusion, para. 23.

53 Id. question 2, article 4, para. 39.

54 Andrew Fitzmaurice, 'Discovery, Conquest, and Occupation of Territory' in Bardo Fassbender and Anne Peters (eds) *The Oxford Handbook of the History of International Law* (Oxford: Oxford University Press 2012) 840–859, 841.

55 Benton and Straumann, 'Acquiring Empire by Law', 15.

56 Vitoria, 'On the American Indians', question 2, article 3.

57 Id.

Vitoria, under the law of nations, human beings also possessed the right to travel and dwell in foreign countries or freedom of movement (*ius peregrinandi et degendi*) due to their natural kinship (*cognatio*), if they did not cause any harm. Vitoria did not adhere to the Plautus' maxim 'a man is a wolf to another man' (*homo homini lupus*); rather, his maxim 'a man is a man to another man' (*homo homini homo*) is based on the assumption that 'all men seem to seek the good' (*omnes appetere bonum videntur*).[58] For Vitoria, the right to travel was a natural right that belonged to all: as citizens of the world, human beings could travel from one province to another.[59] He thus postulated international hospitality (*hospitalitas*) as one special interaction among individuals of different societies, political communities, and cultures. He considered 'humane and dutiful to behave hospitably to strangers'[60] and considered amity (*amicitia*) between human beings 'part of natural law'.[61]

Vitoria also maintained the legitimacy of the right to preach the gospel (*ius praedicandi*). As a theologian, not only did he believe in the truth of his faith, but he was also deeply concerned about the soul's salvation. He thus considered preaching the gospel as a Christian duty. Although forced conversions of the heathens had been commonplace since antiquity,[62] Vitoria argued against the forced conversion of Indigenous peoples. In parallel, for Vitoria, the Spaniards did not have the authority to wage war on these peoples if they refused to accept Christianity.

Yet, Vitoria postulated the free movement of persons and proselytism as rules of international law, expressing the right of universal communication between people (*ius communicationis*).[63] Accordingly, the law of nations gave people the right to travel and enter other states, look for natural resources there, and share the gospel with locals. He also argued that 'the barbarians

58 Cfr. Fr. Baconis, *De Augmentiis Scientiarum Libri ix* (Amstelaedami: Ioannis Ravesteinii 1662) Book vi, p. 502 (endorsing the axiom *homo homini lupus* and arguing that justice should be done so that man could be a god to another man (*iustitia debetur, quod homo homini sit Deus*).

59 Annabel S. Brett, *Changes of State: Nature and the Limits of the City in Early Modern Natural Law* (Princeton: Princeton University Press 2011) 29 (referring to Vitoria).

60 Vitoria, 'On the American Indians', question 3, Art. 1, para. 2.

61 Vincent Chetail, 'Sovereignty and Migration in the Doctrine of the Law of Nations: An Intellectual History of Hospitality from Vitoria to Vattel' (2017) 27 *European Journal of International Law* 901–922, 904.

62 Mercedes García-Arenal and Yonatan Glazer-Eytan (eds) *Forced Conversion in Christianity, Judaism and Islam – Coercion and Faith in Premodern Iberia and Beyond* (Leiden: Brill 2020).

63 Chetail, 'Sovereignty and Migration in the Doctrine of the Law of Nations', 901 and 903.

would do wrong to the Spaniards if they were to bar them from their lands'.[64] The Spaniards had the right to defend themselves and wage a just war against those Indigenous peoples who denied them the exercise of the *ius peregrinandi*. For Vitoria, a justified fear of the armed Spaniards could lead Indigenous peoples to wage war against them.[65] Nonetheless, for Vitoria, this was not a case of legitimate self-defense; such fear did not justify war; rather, it made it only apparently just on both sides.[66] Moreover, this special case confirmed the medieval notion of just war that war could be just on one side only.[67] According to Vitoria, 'if ... both parties ha[d] right and justice on their side, they [could not] lawfully fight each other'.[68]

More fundamentally, Vitoria supported the concept of guardianship or tutelage to justify the Spanish rule in the Americas. For Vitoria, Indigenous peoples were unable to govern themselves.[69] He considered them as 'unsuited' to setting up or administering a legitimate and ordered state due to 'their lack of letters, ... of systematic agriculture, of manufacture' and concluded that 'for their benefit' the Spanish sovereigns 'might take over their administration'.[70] For Vitoria, 'those who are by nature less intelligent ... need others to govern and direct them ... like children [are subordinate] to their parents until they reach adulthood, and like a wife to her husband'.[71] Moreover, he argued that it was legitimate to defend 'innocents' from 'tyranny and oppression' and 'save' Indigenous inhabitants from harmful rulers.[72]

Whether Vitoria's theory was a way to justify colonial expansionism or limit imperialist ambitions remains controversial. Postcolonial scholars have highlighted that despite his best intentions, his paternalistic theory provided indirect and 'insidious' justifications for the Spanish conquest, presenting the replacement of local sovereigns with Christian rulers to allegedly benefit Indi-

---

64 Vitoria, 'On American Indians', q. 3. Art. 1, para. 2.

65 Giuseppe Tosi, 'La Teoria della Guerra Giusta in Francisco de Vitoria e il Dibattito sulla Conquista' (2006) *Jura Gentium* 1–17, 4.

66 Id.

67 G. I. A. D. Draper, 'Grotius' Place in the Development of Legal Ideas about War', in Hedley Bull, Benedict Kingsbury, and Adam Roberts (eds.) *Hugo Grotius and International Relations* (Oxford: Clarendon Press 1990) 177–207, 188.

68 Francisco de Vitoria, *On the Law of War* [*De Indiis Relectio Posterior, sive De Iure Belli*, 1539], in Francisco de Vitoria, *Political Writings*, Anthony Pagden and Jeremy Lawrance (eds) (Cambridge: Cambridge University Press 1991) 312–313.

69 See generally Vitoria, 'On the American Indians'.

70 Id. question 3, article 8 para. 18

71 Id. question 1, conclusion, para. 23.

72 *See generally* Vitoria, *On the Law of War*.

genous peoples.[73] In fairness, Vitoria was nonetheless 'distressed by the news of the horrible deeds of the *conquistadores* and the destruction of the Indians'.[74]

4 Discovery in the Modern and Contemporary World

Discovery 'became the single most important justification for European empire over the five centuries following the discoveries by Columbus'.[75] For the colonizers, discovery and occupation of land did not just constitute a means to acquire private property but a tool to gain sovereignty. No consideration was given to local rulers except if such rulers were Christian. As an international legal principle, discovery 'facilitated the colonization of distant people, their territories and lands' and the institutionalization of systems of political domination and economic exploitation.[76] Imperial powers granted land to the colonists if it was 'not yet cultivated' even in those regions that were inhabited by Indigenous peoples.[77] The agriculturalist argument that by not incorporating labor to the soil, Indigenous peoples had not appropriated land, corroborated colonial expansion to the detriment of nomadic civilizations.[78] It expressed the royal support of active colonial expansion in the form of acquisition of property and sovereignty of new lands through the exploitation of natural resources.[79]

In the eighteenth and nineteenth centuries, the discovery and occupation doctrines were codified as tools to acquire sovereignty.[80] At the domestic level, in 1823, the United States Supreme Court formally acknowledged the doctrine of discovery in *Johnson v. M'Intosh*.[81] While 'the outcome of the case

73 Anthony Anghie, *Imperialism, Sovereignty, and the Making of International Law* (Cambridge: Cambridge University Press 2005) 28.

74 Alexis Heraclides and Ada Dialla, *Humanitarian Intervention in the Long Nineteenth Century* (Manchester: Manchester University Press 2015) 20.

75 Fitzmaurice, 'Discovery, Conquest, and Occupation of Territory', 852.

76 Gümplova, 'Rights of Conquest, Discovery and Occupation, and the Freedom of the Seas', at 1.

77 David Armitage, *Foundations of Modern International Thought* (Cambridge: Cambridge University Press 2013) 110.

78 Fitzmaurice, 'Discovery, Conquest, and Occupation of Territory', 852 and 853.

79 Merete Borch, 'Rethinking the Origins of Terra Nullius' (2001) 32 *Australian Historical Studies* 222–239, 238.

80 Andrew Fitzmaurice, 'The Genealogy of *Terra Nullius*' (2007) 129 *Australian Historical Studies*, 1–15, 8.

81 US Supreme Court, *Johnson v. McIntosh*, [a] 21 U.S. (8 Wheat.) 543 (1823).

has come to be viewed with disapproval in law school', this case has joined a few others 'to form a small canon (or maybe an anti-canon) of famous cases students are taught to criticize'.[82] This doctrine was used by the governments, judicial systems, and settlers in Australia, Canada, New Zealand, and the United States, having a significant impact on these legal systems.[83]

At the international level, the 1885 Berlin Conference, which determined the partition and colonization of Africa under European rule,[84] substantially codified the doctrine of discovery.[85] It reflected the scramble for Africa and its exploitation through the colonial system.[86] No African political entities 'were invited to provide their view of the legality of colonization or, put differently, the loss of sovereignty over their societies'.[87] To justify such control and conquest, European powers divided countries into civilized and uncivilized nations and viewed the Christian states as superior and deserving of special treatment.[88] At the Berlin Conference, they regarded Africa as '*terra nullius*, subject to the possession of the European power exercising effective authority. They never took into account that there were people of vastly different backgrounds and cultures living on the continent'.[89]

The 1945 United Nations Charter[90] and the 1948 Universal Declaration of Human Rights[91] provided some legal basis for the decolonization process by firmly recognizing the right to self-determination. The 1960 Declaration for the Granting of Independence to Colonial Countries and Peoples also affirmed the right of all peoples to self-determination and called for ending colonial rule, characterizing 'foreign rule as a violation of human rights'.[92] Notoriously, both the 1966 Covenants recognize the right to self-determination.

---

82 Stuart Banner, *How the Indians Lost Their Land: Law and Power on the Frontier* (Harvard University Press 2005) 11–12.

83 Robert Miller, Jacinta Ruru, Larissa Behrendt, Tracey Lindberg, *Discovering Indigenous Lands: The Doctrine of Discovery in the English Colonies* (Oxford University Press 2010).

84 The Act of Berlin, 26 February 1885, 10 Martens Nouveau Recueil (2 ser.) 200 (1853–1885); The Act and General Declaration of Brussels, 2 July 1890, 16 Martens Nouveau Recueil (2 ser.).

85 Miller and Stitz, 'The International Law of Colonialism in East Africa', 15.

86 Mushkatt, 'The Process of Decolonization International Legal Aspects', 18.

87 Makau Mutua, 'Why Redraw the Map of Africa: A Moral and Legal Inquiry' (1995) 16 *Michigan Journal of International Law* 1113, 1127.

88 Bernard Röling, *International Law in an Expanded World* (Amsterdam: Djambatan 1960) 21.

89 Mutua, 'Why Redraw the Map of Africa', 1135.

90 Charter of the United Nations, 26 June 1945, in force 24 October 1946, 1 UNTS XVI.

91 Universal Declaration of Human Rights (UDHR), 10 December 1948, GA Res. 217 (III) UNGAOR 3rd Sess. UN Doc. A/810 (1948).

92 Declaration for the Granting of Independence to Colonial Countries and Peoples, adopted on 14 December 1960, A/RES/1514(XV), resolution 1514 (XV). For commentary,

More recently, in 2023, a Joint Statement from the Holy See's Dicastery for Culture and the Dicastery for Integral Human Development formally repudiated 'concepts that fail to recognize the inherent human rights of indigenous peoples, including ... the legal and political doctrine of discovery'.[93] The statement acknowledges that 'papal bulls did not adequately reflect the equal dignity and rights of indigenous peoples' and that 'the contents of these documents were manipulated for political purposes by competing colonial powers'.[94]

In the twentieth century, several domestic and international cases rejected the applicability of discovery and *terra nullius* severing the connection with the common law tradition and halting its sedimentation.[95] For example, the High Court of Australia determined that the continent was not *terra nullius* at the time of settlement in the famous *Mabo v. Queensland* case.[96] In this case, the Indigenous plaintiffs, who inhabited the Mer Islands situated in the Torres Strait between Australia and Papua New Guinea sought declarations that they were entitled to such islands 'as owners; as possessors; as occupiers; or as persons entitled to use and enjoy the said islands'.[97] The High Court rejected the argument of *terra nullius* advanced by the defendant and recognized that the Mer Islanders had a pre-existing system of law, which remained in force under the new sovereign except where specifically modified or extinguished by legislative or executive action.[98] Accordingly, the islands' natives were entitled to possess, use, and enjoy their islands.[99] The Court famously held that 'Whatever the justification advanced in earlier days for refusing to recognize the rights and interests in land of the indigenous inhabitants of settled colonies, [the] unjust and discriminatory doctrine of [*terra nullius*] can no longer be accepted'.[100] The Court added that 'international law is a legitimate and import-

see Adom Getachew, *Worldmaking after Empire: The Rise and Fall of Self-Determination* (Princeton, New Jersey: Princeton University Press 2019) 14.

93 Holy See Press Office, Joint Statement of the Dicasteries for Culture and Education and for Promoting Integral Human Development on the "Doctrine of Discovery", 30 March 2023, para. 7, available at https://press.vatican.va/content/salastampa/en/bollettino/pubblico/2023/03/30/230330b.html.

94 Id. para. 6.

95 Supreme Court of Canada, *Delgamuukw v. British Columbia*, [1997] 3 S.C.R. 1010.

96 High Court of Australia, *Mabo v. Queensland* (No 2) (1992), 175 CLR 1, 3 June 1992.

97 Valentina Vadi, 'Spatio-temporal Dimensions of Indigenous Sovereignty in International Law' in Antonietta Di Blase and Valentina Vadi (eds) *The Inherent Rights of Indigenous Peoples in International Law* (Rome: University of Rome III Press 2020) 104.

98 Id. 104.

99 *Mabo v Queensland* (No 2) (1992) 175 CLR 1, 3 June 1992, 217, also 76 (Brennan J).

100 Id. para. 42.

ant influence on the development of the common law, especially when international law declares the existence of universal human rights. A common law doctrine founded on unjust discrimination in the enjoyment of civil and political rights demands reconsideration'.[101] In conclusion, 'political imperatives force[d] the legal system to jettison … the … doctrines [of discovery and *terra nullius*] which [had] enabled it to ignore accepted history in [other cases]'.[102]

On the international level, the International Court of Justice discarded the concept of *terra nullius* in its 1975 Western Sahara Opinion.[103] In this case, the Court did not recognize original title obtained by occupation of *terra nullius*. Instead, it held that agreements between Indigenous peoples and states were 'derivative roots of title'. As the inhabitants of Western Sahara were nomadic but politically organized at the time of Spanish colonization in 1884, the land was not *terra nullius*.

5 Carl Schmitt on Discovery

One of the most significant and divisive political theorists and jurists of the twentieth century, Carl Schmitt (1888–1985) criticized Vitoria's rejection of discovery as a legitimate title for acquiring property and sovereignty over other continents. A prominent member of the Nazi Party, Schmitt supported activities like burning books by Jewish authors and 'anti-German' material[104] and held a chair at the University of Berlin from 1933 until the end of World War II.[105] His engagement with National Socialism 'was aligned with his own inclinations and was not something … forced upon him'.[106] Unrepentant for his role in the creation of the Nazi state, he refused denazification, which excluded him from academic posts after WWII.[107]

For decades, international lawyers have seen Carl Schmitt as an intellectual outcast irremediably stained by his racist Nazi beliefs. Nonetheless, his work

---

101 Id.

102 Gerry Simpson, 'Mabo, International Law, *Terra Nullius*, and the Stories of Settlement: An Unresolved Jurisprudence', (1993) 19 *Melbourne University Law Review* 195–210, at 210.

103 ICJ, *Western Sahara*, Advisory Opinion (1975) ICJ Report 12, 16 October 1975.

104 Claudia Koonz, *The Nazi Conscience* (Boston: Harvard University Press 2003) 58.

105 Gopal Balakrishnan, *The Enemy – An Intellectual Portrait of Carl Schmitt* (Verso 2000) 183–184.

106 Raphael Gross, 'The True Enemy: Antisemitism in Carl Schmitt's Life and Work' in Jens Meierhenrich and Oliver Simons (eds) *The Oxford Handbook of Carl Schmitt* (Oxford: Oxford University Press 2014) 96–116, 108.

107 Lars Vinx, 'Carl Schmitt', in Edward N. Zalta (ed.) *Stanford Encyclopaedia of Philosophy* (Stanford, California: Stanford University Press 2019).

has recently inspired not only conservative thinkers but also postcolonial analyses.[108] A 'divisive and polarizing thinker', intellectually brilliant but morally untenable, Schmitt 'has been admired and praised by some, and sharply criticized and even condemned by others'.[109] This raises the question of 'why should such a man have a prominent place in contemporary debates and discourses about international law' and whether scholars can truly detach his insights into international legal history and theory from his troubling political beliefs and biography.[110] As political goals motivated his partisan narration of the history of international law,[111] it does not seem possible, plausible, or desirable to separate the man from his work. Therefore, it seems apposite when citing his works to contextualize them.[112] With this warning in mind, this section briefly explores Schmitt's theory of international law in general and discovery in particular.

Schmitt's vision of international law builds upon, but also diametrically opposes, that of Vitoria. While the unity of humankind is the conceptual foundation of Vitoria's work, and for Vitoria *homo hominis homo*, Schmitt has a pessimistic view of human nature.[113] He regards man as evil and human nature as greedy, aggressive, and dangerous.[114] For Schmitt, men naturally seek trouble, war, and hegemony. Their troubled nature thus requires the creation of a strong state that can compel people to behave properly.[115] In his 1938

---

108 See *ex multis* Jens Meierhenrich and Oliver Simons (eds) *The Oxford Handbook of Carl Schmitt* (Oxford: Oxford University Press 2016); Matilda Arvidssen, Leila Brännström and Panu Minkkine (eds) *The Contemporary Relevance of Carl Schmitt: Law, Politics and Theology* (Routledge 2015). See also Jan-Werner Müller, *A Dangerous Mind: Carl Schmitt in Post-War European Thought* (New Haven: Yale University Press 2003).

109 Bardo Fassbender, 'Carl Schmitt (1888–1985)' in Bardo Fassbender and Anne Peters (eds) *The Oxford Handbook of the History of International Law* (Oxford: Oxford University Press 2012) 1173–1178, 1173.

110 Robert Howse, 'Schmitt, Schmitteanism, and Contemporary International Legal Theory', in Anne Orford and Florian Hoffmann (eds) *The Oxford Handbook of the Theory of International Law* (Oxford: Oxford University Press 2016) 212–230, 212.

111 Joseph W. Bendersky, *Carl Schmitt: Theorist for the Reich* (Princeton: Princeton University Press 1983).

112 See Joseph Weiler, 'Cancelling Carl Schmitt?', (2021) 32 *European Journal of International Law* 393–395, at 395.

113 Peter Schröder, 'Carl Schmitt's Appropriation of the Early Modern European Tradition of Political Thought on the State and Interstate Relations' (2012) 33 *History of Political Thought* 348–371, 350.

114 Carl Schmitt, *The Concept of the Political*, G Schwab (trans) (Chicago: Chicago University Press 1996) 58.

115 Schröder, 'Carl Schmitt's Appropriation of the Early Modern European Tradition of Political Thought' 356.

work *The Leviathan in the State Theory of Thomas Hobbes*, Schmitt explores the concept of sovereignty and the modern state through the lens of Thomas Hobbes's philosophy and examines how the Leviathan, Hobbes' symbol of a powerful, unified state, can both protect and potentially fail its citizens. Although Schmitt identifies the modern state's tendency to evolve into something that might betray its initial purpose of providing security and order,[116] he considers decisive leadership necessary to recover from years of directionless democracy.[117] As a positivist, Schmitt does not believe in natural law; rather, for him, 'there exists no law before and outside the state'.[118]

Schmitt's view of international legal history and theory reflected his existential pessimism and centered on war. For Schmitt, after the Age of Discovery, a new legal order, the Nomos of the Earth, a global system of international law gradually emerged. Among European nations, the European Law of Nations (*ius publicum europaeum*) replaced the medieval just war theory (*iustum bellum*) and transformed war 'into a relation of mutually equal and sovereign states'.[119] Under the just war theory, war could be waged only to ensure justice and peace and only one party had the right to wage the war.[120] Instead, the modern theory of the legal equality of warring parties (*aequalitas hostium*) rationalized and humanized war by presupposing that both parties had grounds for waging war and preventing military methods of annihilation.[121] Both belligerents had the same rights.

Schmitt considers colonial wars outside this law[122] as pursued against 'wild peoples'.[123] He sees the New World 'as free space, an area open to European occupation and expansion'.[124] Accordingly, Schmitt defends European colonialism, the conquest of other continents, and colonial rule based on discovery. For Schmitt, discovery presupposes a dynamic of difference and the inevitable cultural and political superiority and hegemony of civilized nations over the

116 Carl Schmitt, *The Leviathan in the State Theory of Thomas Hobbes* (Chicago: University of Chicago Press 2008).

117 Koontz, *The Nazi Conscience*, 163.

118 Schröder, 'Carl Schmitt's Appropriation of the Early Modern European Tradition of Political Thought' 357.

119 Carl Schmitt, *The Nomos of the Earth in the International Law of the Ius Publicum Europaeum*, G. L. Ulmen (trans.) (New York: Telos Press 2004) 309.

120 Giuseppe Tosi, 'Carl Schmitt Interprete di Francisco de Vitoria sulla Guerra Giusta' in Mario Longo and Giuseppe Micheli (eds), *La Filosofia e la Sua Storia – Studi in Onore di Gregorio Piaia*, volume II (Padua: Cleup 2017) 345–360, 724–725.

121 Schmitt, *The Nomos of the Earth*, 142.

122 Id. 309

123 Id. 142.

124 Id. 87.

uncivilized. In his controversial *The Nomos of the Earth*, he unveils the racism that underpinned European colonial expansion.[125] For Schmitt, discovery constituted the most powerful argument supporting European conquest and colonization. Schmitt regarded discovery as the only legal title to confer the sovereignty of such places to European powers. For him, such discoveries did not require the authorization of the people who were discovered because any act of discovery implies the superiority of the discoverer. In Schmitt's twisted view, only predators who know their prey better than the prey knows itself can capture and subdue it, using their superior knowledge.[126]

Schmitt dedicated an entire chapter of *The Nomos of the Earth* to Francisco de Vitoria, criticizing him for not endorsing the doctrine of discovery. For Schmitt, the Vitorian concept that man is a man to man (*homo hominis homo*) is a tautology. Schmitt highlights that while Vitoria considers Indigenous peoples as human beings, he fails to consider them equal or respect their cultural, legal, and political diversity. Schmitt concludes that even for Vitoria Indigenous peoples needed some guidance.[127] Schmitt aptly captures Vitoria's contradiction: on the one hand, the theologian highlighted the common humanity of human beings and promoted the idea of peaceful relations among nations. On the other hand, he patronizingly regarded Indigenous peoples as similar to 'minors' or 'women' to be subject to the patriarchy of empire for their own benefit, devaluing their political, economic, social, and cultural systems, when comparing them to their European counterparts.

At the same time, however, Schmitt's theory was not neutral.[128] Carefully crafted, his arguments are simultaneously ambivalent and deceptive. Not only does his endorsement of discovery reveal his racism, but it also highlights Schmitt's nostalgia for the German empire and his contempt for the Nuremberg trials. Schmitt's theory reflects a 'personal drama' as he resented the treatment of Germany in the interwar period and the loss of its colonies.[129] The 1885 Berlin Act enabled Germany to build the fourth-largest colonial empire at

---

125 *See generally* Schmitt, *The Nomos of the Earth.*

126 Carl Schmitt, *Il Nomos della Terra nel Diritto Internazionale dello Jus Publicum Europaeum*, Emanuele Castrucci (trans.) F. Volpi (ed) (Milan: Adelphi 1991) 150.

127 Id. 109–110.

128 Anna Jurkevics, 'Hannah Arendt reads Carl Schmitt's *The Nomos of the Earth*: A Dialogue on Law and Geopolitics from the Margins' (2017) 16 *European Journal of Political Theory* 345–366 (reporting that Arendt deemed Schmitt's theory to be imperialist and contradictory).

129 Peter Haggenmacher, 'Présentation: L'Itinéraire Internationaliste de Carl Schmitt', in Carl Schmitt, *Le Nomos de la Terre dans le Droit de Gens du Jus Publicum Europaeum* (Paris: PUF 2001) 1, 40.

the time, after the British, French, and Dutch empires.[130] German colonies included parts of present-day Burundi, Rwanda, Tanzania, Namibia, Cameroon, Gabon, Congo, Central African Republic, Chad, Nigeria, Togo, and Ghana. Although it lasted a mere three decades, the German empire 'was a significant and integral part' of the imperialism before the First World War.[131] After WWI, the Allies claimed that Germany had misgoverned its colonies and thus should not retain them. The 1919 Treaty of Versailles, which ended World War I between Germany and the Allied Powers, mandated that Germany cede its colonies, significantly reducing its military power. These colonies were then placed under the administration of the League of Nations. The Treaty of Versailles thus halted German imperial ambition. Schmitt criticizes the treaty for sanctioning the end of Europe's centrality in the world and of the *ius publicum europaeum*.[132] The emergence of international organizations like the Society of Nations aimed to guarantee peace and proscribe war as a tool for settling international disputes. For Schmitt, the criminalization of the war of aggression amounted to a return of the medieval just war theory.

Finally, Schmitt instrumentally criticized Vitoria's just war theory to implicitly object to the United States' rise to power and the Allies' criminalization of the enemy in the aftermath of WWII. Schmitt came close to being a defendant in a case related to propaganda and education before the Nuremberg Military Tribunals.[133] In 1945, the United States Military Government arrested him and confined him in a detention camp in Berlin and then in Nuremberg.[134] While he was ultimately acquitted, he considered the Nuremberg Trials as an expression of victor's justice and as a new type of just war that dehumanized and criminalized the vanquished. Yet, both historians and international lawyers find it surprising that Schmitt omitted any reference to the genocide, war crimes, and crimes against humanity committed by the Nazi regime while he criticized the humanitarian intervention of the Allies.[135]

130 Sebastian Conrad, *German Colonialism: A Short History*, Sorcha O'Hagan (trans.) (Cambridge: Cambridge University Press 2011) 1–14.

131 Id. 1.

132 Schröder, 'Carl Schmitt's Appropriation of the Early Modern European Tradition of Political Thought' 370–371.

133 Kevin Jon Heller, 'Carl Schmitt's Nuremberg Near-Miss', *Opinio Juris*, 10 January 2010.

134 Fassbender, 'Carl Schmitt (1888–1985)' 1175.

135 Tosi, 'Carl Schmitt Interprete di Francisco de Vitoria', 737–738.

6 Long-Term Perspectives to the History of International Law

What does this long view on the discovery doctrine entail for international lawyers? First, this short examination demonstrates that already in the early modern period, Vitoria and other scholars rejected the epistemological fallacy and injustice of discovery and *terra nullius*. Adopting a long-term historical perspective can help dismantle the remains of colonial injustice, by enabling international lawyers to expose the shaky foundations of specific legal rules, expose their injustice, and develop tools to right historical wrongs.[136] Thus, it can nurture the emancipatory potential of international law.

Second, by adopting a long-term and intercultural lens, it is possible to jettison discovery and draw on concepts used by other civilizations. Indigenous peoples, for example, demand that their laws, philosophy, and knowledge be given a more prominent place in the history and theory of international law.[137] They call for filling the empty space of *terra nullius* and the predatory time of discovery with Indigenous law, history, and theory as well as adopting decolonial strategies to foster intercultural dialogue and understanding.[138] Adopting a long-term historical perspective enables international lawyers to unveil long-neglected legal histories. Indigenous peoples' histories date back hundreds, if not thousands of years before the colonial encounter. For thousands of years prior to colonial times, First Peoples governed their territories in a sustainable manner.[139] Their laws dictated how land should be treated.[140] The land itself contains evidence of Indigenous histories. Ancient rock art, engravings, inscriptions, and the like reveal deep time histories. Geographical, cultural, and historical conditions have shaped forms of law ordering that are worthy of investigation. Indigenous legal systems are not mere customs, stories, and songs. Such legal systems reflect Indigenous peoples' complex,

---

136 Valentina Vadi, 'From Here to Eternity? Time, History, and International Law' (*forthcoming* 2026) *Michigan State University International Law Review*; Valentina Vadi, 'Il Mare Come Storia: Diritto Internazionale, Tempo e Storia' 30 *Ars Interpretandi* (2025) 125–140.

137 Irene Watson, 'Re-centering First Nations Knowledge and Places in a *Terra Nullius* Space' (2014) 10 *AlterNative: an International Journal of Indigenous Scholarship* 508–520, 508.

138 Id. See also Eric R. Wolf, *Europe and the People Without History* (Oakland, California: University of California Press 2010) (challenging the colonial view that non-European cultures and peoples were isolated and static entities before the advent of European imperialism and showing that these societies possessed perpetually changing cultures and 'were indeed just as intertwined into the processes of the pre-Columbian global economic system as their European counterparts').

139 Watson, 'Re-centering First Nations Knowledge and Places in a *Terra Nullius* Space'.

140 Id.

nuanced, and multilayered cosmologies and worldviews. Adopting an intercultural approach to international law would require considering these systems for the emergence of general principles of international law.

Third, a long-term view of international legal history also reveals that extractivism, that is, the 'destructive process' of natural resources exploitation,[141] constitutes a form of neo-colonialism[142] and perpetuates the practices of discovery and *terra nullius* by 'creat[ing] space for the tangible expansion of the (settlers') world' while simultaneously erasing or minimizing the existence of other (Indigenous) worlds.[143] Most industrial development projects take place in Indigenous peoples' lands. Such developments are often incompatible with Indigenous cultures and worldviews based on practices of sustainability, stewardship, reciprocity, regeneration, conservation, and intergenerational equity.

Finally, by putting into an imaginary dialogue Vitoria and Schmitt on the debated discovery doctrine, the promises and pitfalls of international law come to the fore. On the one hand, international law promises to build peaceful, just, and prosperous relations among nations, building imaginary bridges among different civilizations. It constitutes 'an important instrument for the realization of valuable purposes', offering 'a useful platform to channel disagreement' and a site for resolving tensions.[144] On the other hand, it also displays some weaknesses. It remains an imperfect system that predatory states have instrumentalized to pursue imperialist goals, territorial aggrandizement, and political, cultural, and economic hegemony. While Vitoria endorses an optimistic approach to human nature and international law, seeing the former as innately good and the latter as a natural expression of human sociability, Schmitt epitomizes a pessimistic, some would argue realist, approach to human nature and international law. For Schmitt, human beings are natural troublemakers. As a result, at the domestic level, he endorsed anti-democratic tendencies, being one of the intellectual gravediggers of the Weimar Republic

141 Christopher W. Chagnon et al., 'From Extractivism to Global Extractivism: The Evolution of an Organizing Concept' (2022) 49 *Journal of Peasant Studies* 760–792.

142 Eduardo Faleiro, 'Colonialism, Neo-Colonialism, And Beyond' (2012) 16 *World Affairs: The Journal of International Issues* 12–17; Philippe Ardant, 'Le Néo-colonialisme: Thème, Mythe et Réalité' (1965) 15 *Revue Française de Science Politique* 837–855.

143 Mario Blaser and Marisol de la Cadena, 'Introduction: Pluriverse – Proposals for a World of Many Worlds' in Marisol de la Cadena and Mario Blaser (eds), *A World of Many Worlds* (Durham and London: Duke University Press 2018) 1–22, at 3.

144 Martti Koskenniemi, 'Carl Schmitt and International Law' in Jens Meuerhenrich and Oliver Simons (eds) *The Oxford Handbook of Carl Schmitt* (Oxford: Oxford University Press 2013) 592–611, 607.

and favoring the rise of the Third Reich.[145] At the international level, he argued that international law inevitably reflects power politics and struggles for hegemony.

Combining powerful 'analytical brilliance' and 'rhetorical magnificence' with awkward generalizations,[146] Schmitt highlights the contradictions of Vitoria's theory. On the one hand, Vitoria rejected the validity of the discovery doctrine for imperial expansion. On the other hand, he supported proselytism and did not respect the cultural diversity, epistemologies, and worldviews of Indigenous peoples. Admittedly, 'he never depicted Indians at the same level as the Spaniards'.[147] Rather, he considered them to be like minors and women in need of Spanish guardianship. At the same time, Schmitt's enthusiastic endorsement of the discovery doctrine is based on racist, colonialist, and self-serving assumptions that cannot but repulse contemporary readers. While his arguments vividly highlight the aporias of Vitoria's theory, they betray opportunistic and predatory worldviews. Nonetheless, 'bringing into the picture a dense, difficult, and controversial thinker like Schmitt' helps consider the promises and pitfalls of international law.[148] In conclusion, this chapter argues that the time has come to jettison the concept of discovery once and for all, and envisage new, ethical and intercultural approaches for charting the future of international law.

Bibliography

Anghie, Antony. 'Francisco De Vitoria and the Colonial Origins of International Law' (1996) 5 *Social and Legal Studies* 321–336.

Anghie, Anthony. *Imperialism, Sovereignty, and the Making of International Law* (Cambridge: Cambridge University Press, 2005).

Ardant, Philippe. 'Le Néo-colonialisme: Thème, Mythe et Réalité' (1965) 15 *Revue Française de Science Politique* 837–855.

145 But see Joseph W. Bendersky, *Carl Schmitt: Theorist for the Reich* (Princeton University Press 1983)(arguing that Schmitt's late Weimar writings were directed at preventing rather than encouraging the Nazi acquisition of power.)

146 John P. McCormick, 'Identifying or Exploiting the Paradoxes of Constitutional Democracy? – An Introduction to Carl Schmitt's Legality and Legitimacy', in Carl Schmitt, *Legality and Legitimacy*, Jeffrey Seitzer (trans.) (Durham, North Carolina: Duke University Press 2004) i, xxiii.

147 Koskenniemi, 'Carl Schmitt and International Law', 602.

148 Howse, 'Schmitt, Schmitteanism, and Contemporary International Legal Theory', 226.

Armitage, David. *Foundations of Modern International Thought* (Cambridge: Cambridge University Press, 2013).

Arvidssen, Matilda, Leila Brännström and Panu Minkkine, eds. *The Contemporary Relevance of Carl Schmitt: Law, Politics and Theology* (London: Routledge, 2015).

Baconis, Fr. *De Augmentiis Scientiarum Libri ix* (Amstelaedami: Ioannis Ravesteinii, 1662).

Balakrishnan, Gopal. *The Enemy – An Intellectual Portrait of Carl Schmitt* (London: Verso, 2000).

Banner, Stuart. *How the Indians Lost Their Land: Law and Power on the Frontier* (Cambridge, MA: Harvard University Press, 2005).

Bendersky, Joseph W. *Carl Schmitt: Theorist for the Reich* (Princeton: Princeton University Press, 1983).

Benton, Lauren and Benjamin Straumann. 'Acquiring Empire by Law: From Roman Doctrine to Early Modern European Practice' (2010) 28 *Law and History Review* 1–38.

Blaser, Mario, and Marisol de la Cadena, 'Introduction: Pluriverse – Proposals for a World of Many Worlds' in Marisol de la Cadena and Mario Blaser, eds. *A World of Many Worlds* (Durham and London: Duke University Press, 2018) 1–22.

Brett, Annabel S. *Changes of State: Nature and the Limits of the City in Early Modern Natural Law* (Princeton: Princeton University Press, 2011).

Borch, Merete. 'Rethinking the Origins of *Terra Nullius*' (2001) 32 *Australian Historical Studies* 222–239.

Chadwick, Anna. *Law and the Political Economy of Hunger* (Oxford: Oxford University Press, 2019).

Chagnon, Christopher W. et al., 'From Extractivism to Global Extractivism: The Evolution of an Organizing Concept' (2022) 49 *Journal of Peasant Studies* 760–792.

Chalmers, Shane. '*Terra Nullius*? Temporal Legal Pluralism in an Australian Colony' (2019) 8 *Social & Legal Studies* 1–23.

Chetail, Vincent. 'Sovereignty and Migration in the Doctrine of the Law of Nations: An Intellectual History of Hospitality from Vitoria to Vattel' (2017) 27 *European Journal of International Law* 901–922.

Conrad, Sebastian. *German Colonialism: A Short History*, Sorcha O'Hagan (trans.) (Cambridge: Cambridge University Press, 2011).

Cotula, Lorenzo. 'Land, Property, and Sovereignty in International Law' (2017) 25 *Cardozo Journal of International & Comparative Law* 219–286.

de Sousa Santos, Boaventura. *The End of the Cognitive Empire: The Coming of Age of Epistemologies of the South* (Durham, North Carolina: Duke University Press, 2018).

de Vitoria, Francisco. 'On the American Indians', in *Political Writings*, Anthony Pagden, ed. (Cambridge: Cambridge University Press, 1991).

de Vitoria, Francisco. *on the Law of War* [*de Indiis Relectio Posterior, Sive de Iure Belli*, 1539], in Francisco de Vitoria, *Political Writings*, Anthony Pagden and Jeremy Lawrance (eds) (Cambridge: Cambridge University Press, 1991).

Draper, G. I. A. D. 'Grotius' Place in the Development of Legal Ideas about War', in Hedley Bull, Benedict Kingsbury, and Adam Roberts, eds. *Hugo Grotius and International Relations* (Oxford: Clarendon Press, 1990) 177–207.

Faleiro, Eduardo. 'Colonialism, Neo-Colonialism, And Beyond' (2012) 16 *World Affairs: The Journal of International Issues* 12–17.

Fassbender, Bardo. 'Carl Schmitt (1888–1985)' in Bardo Fassbender and Anne Peters, eds. *The Oxford Handbook of the History of International Law* (Oxford: Oxford University Press, 2012) 1173–1178.

Fitzmaurice, Andrew. 'Discovery, Conquest, and Occupation of Territory' in Bardo Fassbender and Anne Peters, eds. *The Oxford Handbook of the History of International Law* (Oxford: Oxford University Press, 2012) 840–859.

Fitzmaurice, Andrew. 'The Genealogy of *Terra Nullius*' (2007) 129 *Australian Historical Studies*, 1–15.

García-Arenal, Mercedes and Yonatan Glazer-Eytan, eds. *Forced Conversion in Christianity, Judaism and Islam – Coercion and Faith in Premodern Iberia and Beyond* (Leiden: Brill, 2020).

Gentili, Alberico. *De Iure Belli Libri Tres* [1612] (On the Law of War) J. C. Rolfe transl. (Oxford: Clarendon Press, 1933).

Getachew, Adom. *Worldmaking after Empire: The Rise and Fall of Self-Determination* (Princeton, New Jersey: Princeton University Press, 2019).

Gross, Raphael. 'the True Enemy: Antisemitism in Carl Schmitt's Life and Work' in Jens Meierhenrich and Oliver Simons, eds. *The Oxford Handbook of Carl Schmitt* (Oxford: Oxford University Press, 2014) 96–116.

Gümplová, Petra 'Rights of Conquest, Discovery and Occupation, and the Freedom of the Seas: A Genealogy of Natural Resource Injustice' (2021) 54 *Isonomia. Revista de Teoria y Filosofia del Derecho* 1–36.

Haggenmacher, Peter. 'Il Diritto Della Guerra E Della Pace Di Gentili. Considerazioni Sparse Di Un Groziano' in VVAA, *Il Diritto della Guerra e della Pace di Alberico Gentili* (Milano: Giuffrè, 1995).

Heller, Kevin Jon. 'Carl Schmitt's Nuremberg Near-Miss', *Opinio Juris*, 10 January 2010.

Heraclides, Alexis, and Ada Dialla, *Humanitarian Intervention in the Long Nineteenth Century* (Manchester: Manchester University Press, 2015).

Hernandez, Ramon. 'The Internationalization of Francisco De Vitoria and Domingo De Soto' (1991) 15 *Fordham International Law Journal* 1031–1059.

Hobbes, Thomas. *Leviathan* [1651], C. B. Macpherson (ed.) (London: Penguin Books, 1985).

Howse, Robert. 'Schmitt, Schmitteanism, and Contemporary International Legal Theory', in Anne Orford and Florian Hoffmann, eds. *The Oxford Handbook of the Theory of International Law* (Oxford: Oxford University Press, 2016) 212–230.

Jennings, Robert, Arthur Watts (eds) *Oppenheim's International Law, Vol. I, Peace* (Burnt Mill: Longman, 1982).

Jurkevics, Anna. 'Hannah Arendt reads Carl Schmitt's *The Nomos of the Earth*: A Dialogue on Law and Geopolitics from the Margins' (2017) 16 *European Journal of Political Theory* 345–366.

Koonz, Claudia. *The Nazi Conscience* (Boston: Harvard University Press, 2003).

Koskenniemi, Martti. *To the Uttermost Parts of the Earth – Legal Imagination and International Power 1300–1870* (Cambridge: Cambridge University Press, 2021).

Koskenniemi, Martti. *The Gentle Civilizer of Nations. The Rise and Fall of International Law 1870–1960* (Cambridge: Cambridge University Press, 2001).

Koskenniemi, Martti. 'Carl Schmitt and International Law' in Jens Meuerhenrich and Oliver Simons (eds) *The Oxford Handbook of Carl Schmitt* (Oxford: Oxford University Press, 2013) 592–611.

Mancke, Elizabeth. 'Chartered Enterprises and the Evolution of the British Atlantic World', in Elizabeth Mancke and Carole Shammas, eds. *The Creation of the British Atlantic World* (Baltimore: Johns Hopkins University Press, 2015), 237–262.

McCormick, John P. 'Identifying or Exploiting the Paradoxes of Constitutional Democracy? – an Introduction to Carl Schmitt's Legality and Legitimacy', in Carl Schmitt, *Legality and Legitimacy*, Jeffrey Seitzer (trans.) (Durham, North Carolina: Duke University Press, 2004).

Meierhenrich, Jens and Oliver Simons (eds) *The Oxford Handbook of Carl Schmitt* (Oxford: Oxford University Press, 2016).

Mickelson, Karin. 'The Maps of International Law: Perceptions of Nature in the Classification of Territory' (2014) 27 *Leiden Journal of International Law* 621–639.

Mignolo, Walter D. 'Epistemic Disobedience, Independent Thought and Decolonial Freedom' (2009) 26 *Theory, Culture & Society* 159–181.

Miller, Robert J. and Olivia Stitz. 'The International Law of Colonialism in East Africa: Germany, England, and the Doctrine of Discovery' (2021) 32 *Duke Journal of Comparative & International Law* 1–59.

Miller, Robert, Jacinta Ruru, Larissa Behrendt, Tracey Lindberg, *Discovering Indigenous Lands: The Doctrine of Discovery in the English Colonies* (Oxford: Oxford University Press, 2010).

Müller, Jan-Werner. *A Dangerous Mind: Carl Schmitt in Post-War European Thought* (New Haven: Yale University Press, 2003).

Muldoon, James. 'Medieval Canon Law and the Conquest of the Americas', *Jarbuch für Geschichte Latinamerikas* (Köln: Böhlau Verlag, 2000).

Mushkatt, Marion. 'The Process of Decolonization International Legal Aspects' (1972) 2 *University of Baltimore Law Review* 16–34.

Mutua, Makau. 'Why Redraw the Map of Africa: A Moral and Legal Inquiry' (1995) 16 *Michigan Journal of International Law* 1113–1176.

Pagden, Anthony. 'Empire and Its Anxieties' (2012) *American Historical Review* 141–148.

Pahuja, Sundhya. *Decolonising International Law: Development, Economic Growth and the Politics of Universality* (Cambridge: Cambridge University Press, 2011).

Panizza, Diego. 'Political Theory and Jurisprudence in Gentili's *de Iure Belli*: the Great Debate between Theological and Humanist Perspectives from Vitoria to Grotius', in Pierre-Marie Dupuy and Vincent Chetail, eds. *The Roots of International Law* (Leiden: Brill, 2014) 211–247.

Röling, Bernard. *International Law in an Expanded World* (Amsterdam: Djambatan, 1960).

Schmitt, Carl. *The Concept of the Political*, G Schwab (trans) (Chicago: University of Chicago Press, 1996).

Schmitt, Carl. *The Leviathan in the State Theory of Thomas Hobbes* George Schwab and Erna Hilfstein (trans.) (Chicago: University of Chicago Press, 2008).

Schmitt, Carl. *The Nomos of the Earth in the International Law of the Ius Publicum Europaeum*, G. L. Ulmen (trans.) (New York: Telos Press, 2004).

Schmitt, Carl. *Il Nomos della Terra nel Diritto Internazionale dello Jus Publicum Europaeum*, Emanuele Castrucci (trans.) F. Volpi (ed) (Milan: Adelphi, 1991).

Schröder, Peter. 'Carl Schmitt's Appropriation of the Early Modern European Tradition of Political Thought on the State and Interstate Relations' (2012) 33 *History of Political Thought* 348–371.

Simpson, Gerry. 'Mabo, International Law, *Terra Nullius*, and the Stories of Settlement: An Unresolved Jurisprudence', (1993) 19 *Melbourne University Law Review* 195–210.

Todorov, Tzvetan. *The Conquest of America–The Question of the Other* (Norman: University of Oklahoma Press, 1999).

Tosi, Giuseppe. 'La Teoria della Guerra Giusta in Francisco de Vitoria e il Dibattito sulla Conquista' (2006) *Jura Gentium* 1–17.

Tosi, Giuseppe. 'Carl Schmitt Interprete Di Francisco de Vitoria Sulla Guerra Giusta' in Mario Longo and Giuseppe Micheli, eds. *La Filosofia e la Sua Storia – Studi in Onore di Gregorio Piaia*, volume II (Padua: Cleup, 2017) 345–360.

Vadi, Valentina. *War and Peace – Alberico Gentili and the Early Modern Law of Nations* (Leiden: Brill, 2020).

Vadi, Valentina. 'The Power of Scale: International Law and Microhistories' (2018) 46 *Denver Journal of International Law & Policy* 315–348.

Vadi, Valentina. 'Spatio-Temporal Dimensions of Indigenous Sovereignty in International Law' in Antonietta Di Blase and Valentina Vadi, eds. *The Inherent Rights of Indigenous Peoples in International Law* (Rome: University of Rome III Press, 2020) 91–119.

Vadi, Valentina. 'From Here to Eternity? Time, History, and International Law' (*forthcoming* 2026) *Michigan State University International Law Review*;

Vadi, Valentina. 'Il Mare Come Storia: Diritto Internazionale, Tempo e Storia' (2025) 30 *Ars Interpretandi* 125–140.

Vinx, Lars. 'Carl Schmitt', in Edward N. Zalta and Uri Nodelman, eds. *Stanford Encyclopaedia of Philosophy* (Stanford, California: Stanford University Press, 2019).

Von Bernstorff, Jochen and Philipp Dann, eds. *The Battle for International Law in the Decolonization Era* (Oxford: Oxford University Press, 2019).

Watson, Irene. 'Re-centering First Nations Knowledge and Places in a *Terra Nullius* Space' (2014) 10 *AlterNative: an International Journal of Indigenous Scholarship* 508–520.

Weiler, Joseph. 'Çancelling Carl Schmitt?', (2021) 32 *European Journal of International Law* 393–395.

Wheatley, Steven. 'Conceptualizing the Authority of the Sovereign State over Indigenous Peoples' (2014) 27 *Leiden Journal of International Law* 371–96.

Wiessner, Siegfried. 'Indigenous Sovereignty: A Reassessment in Light of the UN Declaration on the Rights of Indigenous Peoples' (2008) 41 *Vanderbilt Journal of Transnational Law* 1141–1176.

Wolf, Eric R. *Europe and the People without History* (Oakland, California: University of California Press, 2010).

Table of Cases

International

ICJ, *Legal Consequences of the Separation of the Chagos Archipelago from Mauritius in 1965*, Advisory Opinion, 25 February 2019.

ICJ, *Western Sahara*, Advisory Opinion (1975) ICJ Report 12, 16 October 1975.

Domestic

Australia, High Court, *Mabo v. Queensland* (No 2) (1992), 175 CLR 1, 3 June 1992.

Canada, Supreme Court, *Delgamuukw v. British Columbia*, [1997] 3 S.C.R. 1010.

US Supreme Court, Johnson v. McIntosh, [a] 21 U.S. (8 Wheat.) 543 (1823).

Legal Instruments

International

Act of Berlin, 26 February 1885, 10 *Martens Nouveau Recueil* (2 ser.) 200 (1853–1885).

Act and General Declaration of Brussels, 2 July 1890, 16 *Martens Nouveau Recueil* (2 ser.).

Charter of the United Nations, 26 June 1945, in force 24 October 1946, 1 UNTS XVI.

Universal Declaration of Human Rights (UDHR), 10 December 1948, GA Res. 217 (III) UNGAOR 3rd Sess. UN Doc. A/810 (1948).

UN Declaration for the Granting of Independence to Colonial Countries and Peoples, adopted on 14 December 1960, A/RES/1514(XV), resolution 1514 (XV).

Municipal

Holy See, Joint Statement of the Dicasteries for Culture and Education and for Promoting Integral Human Development on the 'Doctrine of Discovery', 30 March 2023, available at https://press.vatican.va/content/salastampa/en/bollettino/pubblico/2023/03/30/230330b.html

Pope Alexander VI, bull *Inter Caetera*, 4 May 1493.

Queen Elizabeth's Charter to Sir Humphrey Gilbert of 11 June 1578, reprinted in William S. Powell, 'An Elizabethan Experiment', in Lindley S. Butler and Alan D. Watson, eds. *The North Carolina Experience: An Interpretive and Documentary History* (Chapel Hill: University of North Carolina Press, 1984) 29–52.

CHAPTER 12

The Extravagant Pretension: Schmitt, Vitoria, the Discovery Doctrine, and the Trail of Tears

Christopher R. Rossi

This chapter interrogates the discovery doctrine as interpreted by Carl Schmitt (1888–1985) in *Nomos of the Earth*[1] and connects it to its controversial, even pernicious[2] reception into the domestic constitutional order of the United States.[3] Schmitt's retrospective reading of the discovery doctrine fundamentally bore connection to the federalist mindset associated with the "most important Indian rights opinion ever issued by any court of law in the United States"[4] – the (in)famous *Johnson v. M'Intosh* case (1823).[5] This case was the first of three cases involving the Cherokee Nation that the United States Supreme Court decided over the turbulent course of nine years.[6] The preeminent federalist architect of American constitutional nation-building, Chief Justice John Marshall (1755–1835), penned each main decision.[7] The ruling

1 Carl Schmitt, *The Nomos of the Earth in the International Law of the Jus Publicum Europaeum* (Candor, N.Y.: Telos Press Publishing 2006).

2 Michael C. Blumm, 'Retracing the Discovery Doctrine: Aboriginal Title, Tribal Sovereignty, and Their Significance to Treaty-Making and Modern Natural Resources Policy in Indian Country'. *Vermont Law Review* 28 (2004) 713–777, at 715.

3 *See, e.g.*, Stuart Banner, *How the Indians Lost Their Land: Law and Power on the Frontier* (Cambridge, M.A.: Harvard University Press 2005); Robert J. Miller, *Native America, Discovered and Conquered: Thomas Jefferson, Lewis & Cark, and Manifest Destiny* (Foreword by Elizabeth Furse; Westport, Conn.: Praeger 2006); Steven T. Newcomb, *Pagans in the Promised Land: Decoding the Doctrine of Christian Discovery* (Golden, Co.: Fulcrum Publishing 2008); Lindsay G. Robertson, *Conquest by Law: How the Discovery of America Dispossessed Indigenous Peoples of Their Lands* (Oxford: Oxford University Press 2005); Robert A. Williams, Jr., *The American Indian in Western Legal Thought: The Discourse of Conquest* (New York: Oxford University Press 1990).

4 Williams, Jr., *The American Indian in Western Legal Thought* 289.

5 Johnson & Graham's Lessee v. M'Intosh, 21 U.S. (8 Wheat.) 543, 574 (1823) [Johnson v. M'Intosh].

6 *See also* Cherokee Nation v. Georgia, 30 U.S. (5 Pet.) 1 (1831); Worcester v. Georgia, 31 U.S. (6 Pet.) 515 (1832).

7 Taken together, the three cases are known as the Marshall Trilogy. He penned the main opinion in each case. The Trilogy has been described as incorporating "the seeds of the entire catalog of the current doctrines making up American Indian law" including the plenary power of Congress to legislate in respect to Indian tribes, state authority in Indian

 | DOI:10.1163/9789004757448_013

facilitated the forced removal of between 100,000 to 125,000 Natives from their ancestral homelands of the southeastern United States to the Oklahoma Territory,[8] a wilderness beyond the westernmost demarcation line of civility, the Mississippi River. The doctrine remains at the heart of the diminishment of Native property rights in the United States and it launched a world-wide "Trail of Tears" involving Indigenous legal deprivations across English-speaking settler nations, including Australia, Canada, and New Zealand.[9]

Notwithstanding the "seeds of [cultural] extinction" planted by America's founding fathers, the rationalism of Jeffersonian philanthropy at times envisioned "only a minor transition" for the Native – a paternalistic assimilation "from the wilderness to the garden" of European civility.[10] This transition ambivalently incorporated the discovery doctrine into American jurisprudence and yet anticipated and possibly informed Schmitt's vocabulary and reflection about land appropriation, which he would elevate to a global spatial platform from its early nineteenth-century America formation. However, Schmitt's treatment of the discovery doctrine within the context of United States

---

Country, the special canon of construction for Indian treaties ("interpreting terms as the Indians themselves would have understood them"), the doctrine of implicit divestiture, the trust doctrine, and the guardianship–ward status of the federal government and the Indian tribes. Matthew L.M. Fletcher, 'The Iron Cold of the Marshall Trilogy'. *North Dakota Law Review* 82(3) (2006), 625–696, 628–629.

8 The southeastern Tribes – the Cherokees, Creeks, Chickasaws, Choctaws, and Seminoles – were forcibly relocated to what is now Oklahoma by 1842. Some individual Natives fled into the southeastern hills; many Seminoles resisted and penetrated deeply into the swamps of Florida. These tribes were known as the Five Civilized Tribes, an anachronistic term applied by white settlers in recognition of some Natives' conversion to the agricultural technologies and sartorial styles of white settlers. Many other tribes including the Pamunkey of Virginia, the Lumbee and Catawba of the Carolinas, the Piankashaws in Indiana, the Kaskaskias of central Mississippi, and the Peorias and Cahokias in Illinois – were also forced into western migration through land sales. *See* Christopher R. Rossi, 'The Blind Eye: *Jus Soli* and the "Pretended" Treaty of New Echota'. *American Indian Law Journal* 8(2) (2021), 403–433, 421–22. *See also* Robertson, *Conquest by Law*, 143.

9 Anthony W. Hobert, Locke's '"Wild Indian" in United States Supreme Court Jurisprudence', 12(2) *American Indian Law Journal* 12(2) 1–38, 4. *See generally* Blake A. Watson, 'The Impact of the American Doctrine of Discovery on Native Land Rights in Australia, Canada, and New Zealand'. *Seattle University Law Review* 34 (2011), 507–551; Robert J. Miller, Jacinta Ruru, Larissa Behrendt and Tracey Lindberg (eds.), *Discovering Indigenous Lands: The Doctrine of Discovery in the English Colonies* (Oxford Academic Books, 2010).

10 Bernard W. Sheehan, *Seeds of Extinction: Jeffersonian Philanthropy and the American Indian* (Chapel Hill: University of North Carolina Press 1973) 10. *See also* Thomas Jefferson, 'From Thomas Jefferson to William Henry Harrison, 27 February 1803'. *Founders Online, National Archives*, https://founders.archives.gov/documents/Jefferson/01-39-02-0500 (providing 'a more extensive view of our policy respecting the Indians').

jurisprudence also admitted to a type of overgeneralized abridgement that he complained about with regard to anachronistic readings of Vitoria. The discovery doctrine presented an ambivalent and sometimes inconvenient simulacrum for sovereignty's purportedly uninterrupted transmission of the European chain of title to the New World.

Schmitt's reading of the discovery doctrine most certainly abridged discussion about the fate of the American Indians even though much discussion in *Nomos* squarely focused around early nineteenth-century America, when their fate was sealed. However, *Nomos* clearly reflected his acute study of United States history. He was a preeminent scholar of constitutional theory,[11] which naturally attracted him to the study of United States constitutive documents and the founders who created them. In *Nomos*, he cited the American Bill of Rights and the United States Constitution[12] and referenced Tocqueville's *Democracy in America* (1835), which is replete with references to the plight of North American Natives and their engagement with early nineteenth-century white settlers.[13] He cited James Kent's *Commentaries on American Law* (1828), which contained a detailed restatement of the discovery doctrine as well as a detailed discussion of Indian title and *Johnson v. M'Intosh*.[14] He referenced Henry Wheaton's *History of the Law of Nations in Europe and America* (1842) and his most influential *Elements of International Law*, where Wheaton discussed *Cherokee Nation v. Georgia* (1831), the Supreme Court case recognizing Natives' "independence and right to self-government."[15] He also cited to Marshall's greatest federalist contemporary and ally on the bench, Justice Joseph Story (1779–1845),[16] whose constitutional commentary helped frame Tocqueville's

11 *See* Carl Schmitt, *Constitutional Theory* (Durham and London: Duke University Press, 1983 [1928]. *See also* Ernst-Wolfgang Böckenförde, *State Society and Liberty: Studies in Political Theory and Constitutional Law* (J.A. Underwood trans.; Berg 1991) 89.

12 Schmitt, *Nomos*, 288 (Bill of Rights), 293 (Constitution).

13 Tocqueville referred to Native Americans as "the first and the legitimate master of the American continent." Alexis de Tocqueville, *Democracy in America* (ed Eduardo Nolla, trans James T. Schleifer; Indianapolis: Liberty Fund, 2012) 1304. Much and wide-ranging scholarly discussion attaches to Tocqueville's perceptions of Native Americans. For more, see Raúl Rodríguez, 'Tocqueville and Native Americans'. *American Political Thought: A Journal of Ideas, Institutions, and Culture* 13(2) 2024, 216–238.

14 *See* James Kent, *Commentaries on American Law* (New-York: O. Halsted, 1828) 307–321 (Of the Foundation of Title to Land, And herein of Indian Rights and titles). Kent's discussion of *Johnson v. M'Intosh* begins on 309. Schmitt cited to the 12th edition edited by Oliver Wendell Holmes. Schmitt, *Nomos*, 287 n. 11.

15 Schmitt, *Nomos*, 228–29. Henry Wheaton, *Elements of International Law* (8th ed., Boston: Little, Brown and Company 1866) 30.

16 Schmitt, *Nomos*, 286. Schmitt cited Story's seminal decision in *United States v. Le Jeune Eugénie*, 26 F. Cas. 832 (C.C.D. Mass. 1822) (no.15,551), which affirmed the universal

work.[17] He also referenced correspondences of Thomas Jefferson,[18] George Washington's Farewell Address (1796),[19] and Benjamin Franklin's dazzling ambassadorship in France (1776–1785), which represented the spirit of a land not yet spoiled "by the corruption of over-civilized Europe".[20] He extended his discussion of the formative influences of the American character up to 1890, impliedly referencing Frederick Jackson Turner's thesis connecting American democracy to the closing of the American frontier.[21]

Understanding Schmitt's reading of the discovery doctrine, so animated with regard to Vitoria yet so abridged with regard to the juridical and constitutional treatment of American Aborigines, involves an interrogation of recurrent topics appearing in *Nomos*: Schmitt's basic view of spatial study and demarcation, Schmitt's reading of Vitoria and the Indians, and early nineteenth-century American land hunger, which conditioned its approach to Western expansion and ultimately Indian removal. Schmitt's abridgment of this latter history did not have so much to do with an unfamiliarity with United States domestic constitutional and political affairs at that time as it did with the grander twentieth-century story he aimed to tell. He was keenly aware of the

---

nature of international law by ruling that the slave trade violated the law of nations. Marshall would come to the opposite conclusion three years later in *The Antelope*, 23 U.S. (10 Wheat.) 66 (1825), essentially affirming according to positive law that international law permitted the trade. The ambivalence with which the Marshall Court dealt with the slave trade was also apparent in Story's decision in *Le Jeune Eugénie*. The schooner belonged to a French slaver, and instead of condemning the vessel, which would have most probably roiled relations with France and undercut the status of the judiciary in relation to the executive and legislative branches of government, he transferred the vessel to the French king as a measure of international comity. *See generally* Christopher R. Rossi, 'Slaves, Indians, and Legal Formalism in 19th Century America', in Cornelia Navari and Yannis A. Stivachtis (eds.), *Nineteenth Century America in the Society of States: Reluctant Power* (Routledge Press, 2024) 110–128.

17 *See* Giulia Oskian, 'Tocqueville and the Legal Culture of Jacksonian Democracy.' *Journal of the Early Republic* (39)(1) (2019) 135–44, 136.

18 Schmitt, *Nomos*, 287 (quoting Jefferson's letter to John Crawford in 1812: "When our strength will permit us to give the law of our hemisphere, it should be that the meridian of the mid-Atlantic should be the line of demarcation between war and peace"); 288 (quoting Jefferson's letter to William Short, "The day is not distant, when we may formally require a meridian of partition through the ocean which separates the two hemispheres, on either side of which no European gun shall ever be heard, nor an American on the other").

19 Schmitt, *Nomos*, 281.

20 Schmitt, *Nomos*, 289.

21 Schmitt, *Nomos*, 293 ('Around 1890, the freedom of internal land-appropriation in the United States ended'). *See also* Frederick Jackson Turner, 'The Significance of the Frontier in American History 1893'. *American Historical Association*, 12 July 1893.

federalist mindset and challenges associated with the political consolidation of the new republic. But he ultimately linked these antecedent historical considerations to his deep fascination with the Monroe Doctrine (1823) and to the epochal new *nomos* that accompanied the global land and sea dualism arising after WWI between East and West.[22] These considerations are taken up in turn.

1 Schmitt's Telluric Worldview

Schmitt had a binary penchant to demarcate spatial order. He based this distinction on opposable concepts, such as friend and enemy, amity and enmity, and the decaying *jus publicum Europaeum* versus the rising *jus publicum Americanum*. This latter contrast reflected his primary objective of establishing a historico-geospatial explanation of the international order. Further complicating this retrospective discussion of the discovery doctrine was Schmitt's embrace of a vocabulary replete with telluric metaphor. He employed this vocabulary to demarcate land and apportion space. This point was central to his concept of *nomos* and central to his understanding of "every historical epoch."[23]

His imagery and prose burst with references to earth, soil, and "physical inscriptions" on virginal land.[24] In one dense paragraph, Schmitt made seventeen references to "soil," "earth," "virgin[ity]," and "unspoiled," "not yet infested," "[un]corrupt," "pure" spatial orders of the earth.[25] According to François Debrix, "perhaps no modern theorist of international relations invigorated a closer connection of international law to the earth than Schmitt."[26] Evidence for this association appears throughout *Nomos* but perhaps never more emphatically than in America's posture toward its "wide-open spaces."[27]

Drawing from John Locke (1632–1704) and Immanuel Kant (1724–1804), Schmitt asserted that "the occupation of a country is subjugation by whoever has jurisdiction over the soil."[28] Every legal order projected land appropriation "as its precondition," noting that "every commonwealth, every empire," and

22 Schmitt, *Nomos*, 354.
23 Schmitt, *Nomos*, 78.
24 François Debrix, 'The Virtual Nomos?', in Stephen Legg (ed.), *Spatiality, Sovereignty and Carl Schmitt: Geographies of the Nomos* (London: Routledge 2011) 220–226, 220.
25 Schmitt, *Nomos*, 289.
26 Debrix, 'The Virtual Nomos?', 220. Debrix noted that 'perhaps no modern theorist of international relations invigorated a closer connection of international law to the earth than Schmitt'.
27 Schmitt, *Nomos*, 286–291.
28 Schmitt, *Nomos*, 47.

the "history of every *settled* people" was based on a terrestrial form of land appropriation.[29] "Land-appropriation is always the ultimate legal title," wrote Schmitt.[30] Tillage, enclosure, and mixing land and labor provided for Locke the basis of land appropriation: "[F]or I ask, whether in the wild woods and uncultivated waste of America, left to nature, without any improvement, tillage or husbandry, a thousand acres yield the needy and wretched inhabitants as many conveniences of life, as ten acres of equally fertile land do in Devonshire, where they are well cultivated?"[31] Emer de Vattel (1714–1767), whose *Le droit de gens* (1758) most influentially shaped the mindset of the American founders,[32] seconded this view: "[W]hen the Nations of Europe, which are too confined at home, come upon lands which the savages have no special need of and are making no present and continuous use of, they may lawfully take possession of them and establish colonies in them."[33] The American founder, Thomas Paine (1737–1809) embraced this evolutionary movement from a natural state to a civilized state through the process of land cultivation. Foreshadowing Marshall's discovery doctrine and the assignment of *dominium* to those who "*made it,*" Paine wrote that "the additional value made by cultivation ... became the property of those who *did it.*"[34] However, the Natives did

29 Schmitt, *Nomos*, 48–49. The italics indicate Schmitt's implied distinction between settler societies, which are based on agrarianism, and Native nomadic societies, which are impliedly abridged in his reconstruction of history.

30 Schmitt, *Nomos*, 328.

31 John Locke, *Second Treatise of Government*, Of Property, ch. v, sec 37.

32 *See generally* Emer de Vattel, *Le droit des gens, ou, Principes de la loi naturelle appliqués à la conduit et aux affaires des nations et des souverains* (Charles G. Fenwick trans., Classics of International Law; Washington: Carnegie Institution 1916 (1758). *See also* Schmitt, *Nomos*, pt. IV, ch. 5. Vattel's construction of his Law of Nations highlighted an emerging international society based on freedom, sovereignty, and independence. Peter and Nicholas Onuf labeled his influence on the American founders "The Vatellian World"; David Armitage noted his imprint on the United States' seminal independence decree; Sominik Andréas Gerber and William Ossipow credited Vattel with providing 'American revolutionary discourse with the language and conceptual tools to think of the colonies no longer as subordinate entities of the Crown', and 'offering successive governments and the Supreme Court guidance on may sectoral problems in international law'. *See generally* Peter S. Onuf and Nicholas Greenwood Onuf, *Federal Union, Modern World: The Law of Nations in an Age of Revolutions 1776–1814* (Madison, Wis.: Madison House, 1993); David Armitage, *The Declaration of Independence: A Global History* (Cambridge, MA: Harvard University Press, 2007); Dominik Andrés Gerber and William Ossipow, 'The Reception of Vattel's Law of Nations in the American Colonies: From James Otis and John Adams to the Declaration of Independence'. *American Journal of Legal History* 2017, 1–35, at 35.

33 Vattel, 85.

34 Rossi, 'The Blind Eye', 416 (quoting Paine's 1797 view on agrarian justice) (emphasis added).

not *make*, improve, or settle on the earth. Therefore "their natural right to occupancy could not stand in the way of those who added value to soil through cultivation."[35] Thus, land inscription became loosely conflated with discovery and together these concepts became associated with ownership.

2 Schmitt on Vitoria and the Discovery Doctrine

In *Nomos*, the discovery doctrine occupied a concern in his treatment of the great Dominican friar, Franciso de Vitoria (1483–1546).[36] Schmitt believed that Vitoria had been misread by modern scholars. They had scripted an explanation of the moral and legal basis for the Spanish conquest of the Americas based on the discovery doctrine. They attributed this viewpoint to Vitoria but Schmitt criticized this rendering as overly generalized and divorced from Vitoria's time.[37]

Schmitt adamantly maintained that for Vitoria, the discovery doctrine was "not a legitimate title of acquisition ... for the New World."[38] It would become recognized as the basis between the sixteenth and eighteenth centuries,[39] once the Enlightenment project of the sovereign, territorial state of the *jus publicum Europaeum* fully replaced the spatial order of the *respublica Christiana* of the European Middle Ages.[40] This transposition uprooted the moral–theological doctrines of Vitoria and the Roman Church with the mindset of secular jurists, who advanced a vocabulary of legitimacy based on international law. Schmitt credited Jean Bodin as the "real founder" of this turn toward the secular state-centered law of sovereignty,[41] although he substantially credited the Spanish crown defender, Balthazar de Ayala (1548–1584) with taking the "decisive step" out of the Middle Ages.[42] Ayala designated private or civil wars as non-wars, thus classifying insurrectionists as outlaws.[43]

35 Rossi, 'The Blind Eye', 416.
36 Schmitt, *Nomos*, 101.
37 Schmitt, *Nomos*, 105–106.
38 Schmitt, *Nomos*, 106.
39 Schmitt, *Nomos*, 106. *See also* 111–112 ("discovery and occupation were for [sovereign states] the only legal title for land-appropriation").
40 Schmitt, *Nomos*, 113.
41 Schmitt, *Nomos*, 152.
42 Schmitt, Nomos, 152.
43 *See* Schmitt, *Nomos*, 152–153. Ayala served as the Spanish crown's Judge-Advocate-General during the Dutch revolt. *See generally* Balthazar Ayala, *De Jure et Officiis Bellicis et Disciplina Militari*, Vol. 1 (edited by John Westlake, trans. by John Pawley Bate; Classics of International Law; Washington: Carnegie Institution 1912 [1582]).

Bodin's idea of absolute sovereignty lay at the base of Schmitt's recurrent theme of a *bracketed*, global set of lines (*rayas geograficas*) that moderated neighborly European understandings of armed conflict. These demarcations affixed armed conflict to the status of rightful enemies (*justi hostes*), meaning proper sovereigns. Every other form of conflict, even conflicts over new spaces, fell beyond the line of state-sponsored amity. To Schmitt, "the essence of *hostis"* required "*aequalitas*" (equality) between combatants.[44] Nonprotected conflicts, which Schmitt enumerated as involving "[r]obbers, pirates, and rebels" became private conflicts. They did not give rise to a public cause of action or a public right of restoration (*jus postliminii*) because they did not involve a true and mutually recognized enemy.[45] These conflicts were purely internal matters and in no sense involved the law of nations or foreign involvement.[46] The question of American Indians did not fall categorically within the subaltern domestic world of robbers, pirates, and rebels. It required a decades-long removal campaign predicated doctrinally on the discovery doctrine but incongruously dependent on alliances and treaties with Natives – coerced, broken, and even pretended[47] – but nevertheless perfected in pursuit of territorial claims. This reliance on Native assistance recognized a degree of Native sovereignty or distinctiveness identified by Vitoria. Schmitt's reading of the discovery doctrine in America's constitutional jurisprudence abridged the political, legal, and moral disruptions of its application.

By the late eighteenth century, this subaltern view had discernably entered into the mindset of America's founding fathers, who had demanded independence from British rule and recognition as an equal among states. The twenty-seventh bill of indictment in the United States Declaration of Independence (1776), personally drafted by Thomas Jefferson (1743–1826),[48] had

44 Schmitt, *Nomos*, 153.

45 Schmitt phrased the concept of mutually recognized enemies in accordance with the principle of "non-discrimination," "parity" and "*bellum utrimque justum*," or just war on both sides. Schmitt, *Nomos*, 153.

46 Schmitt, *Nomos*, 153.

47 *See generally* Rossi, 'The Blind Eye' (discussing the Treaty of New Echota and the United States recognition of a minority faction of Cherokees as the official signing party notwithstanding the majority opposition led by the Cherokee Principal Chief, John Ross). *See* 'Treaty with the Cherokee, 1835' [Treaty of New Echota] *Indian Affairs. Laws and Treaties.* Vol. II (Charles J. Kappler ed; Washington: Government Printing Office, 1904) 439–49.

48 *See* Sidney Kaplan, 'The "Domestic Insurrectionists" of the Declaration of Independence'. 61(6) *The Journal of Negro History* 61(6) (1976), 243–255, at 246 (noting that Jefferson himself penned the words that King George III "excited domestic insurrections amongst us").

charged British king George III (1738–1820) with interference by inciting wanton frontier attacks by the '*domestic* insurrections amongst us ... the merciless Indian savages'.[49] Jefferson's recognition of the domestic nature of Indian affairs implied that the status of the American Natives occupied a jurisdictional world below the level of the international, outside the purview of external concern, and, given his identification of Aboriginal savagery, beneath the Anglo-European standard of civilization.[50]

Vitoria's great contribution to the modern history of the law of nations began with his interrogation of the temporal power that Spain could rightly exercise over the Indians of the Americas. By what right could such jurisdiction be asserted? This gateway question into the sixteenth century occupied the scholastic mind following Columbus' landing in the place he christened San Salvador (the Bahamas) in 1492. Vitoria began a conversation about *dominion* (ownership) in the New World that separated questions of *imperium* (rulership) from rights established by public and private law. He questioned the governing view that divine law established the temporal authority of the pope. He asserted that the rational capacity of all people, whether Spanish or Native, governed their actions, even slyly chiding some of his Spanish peasant-compatriots (*rustici*) for exhibiting behavior "little different" from the ascribed animalism of Natives.[51] He further lectured that any ascription of barbarity commonly attaching to the Indians would also attach to the enemies of Christianity, meaning Saracens (Muslims) and Jews. However, Vitoria noted that even they were not denied the right of their humanity and ownership (*dominium rerum*) over lands unless they had been improperly taken from Christians by conquest.[52] He concluded that the Indians, before the arrival of

49 'Declaration of Independence, July 7, 1776'. *America's Founding Documents, National Archives*, https://www.archives.gov/founding-docs/declaration-transcript (emphasis added). The term "domestic insurrectionists" also applied to slaves, who had been incited to leave their masters and fight with the British. *See* John Murray [Lord Dunmore], 'Lord Dunmore's Proclamation (1775)'. *Encyclopedia Virginia*, https://encyclopediavirginia.org/primary-documents/lord-dunmores-proclamation-1775/.

50 The phrase obviously implied the inclusion of American founders in the Anglo-European view of civilization. *See* Schmitt, Nomos, 286 ("From the outset, the American impulse was directed much more at being a representative of European civilization and European international law").

51 Anthony Pagden and Jeremy Lawrance, *Vitoria: Political Writings* (Cambridge: Cambridge University Press, 1991) 249.

52 Pagden and Lawrance, *Vitoria, Political Writings*, 250–251.

the Spaniards, undoubtedly exercised and possessed true *dominium* over both their public and private property.[53]

Schmitt praised Vitoria for specifically and systematically addressing the "basic problem" covering the 400-year development of European international law from the sixteenth to the twentieth century – the "justification of European land appropriations" originating from the conquest of the New World.[54] However, Schmitt's "scorn" of the Enlightenment project contributed to his need to set the record straight. Central to Schmitt's interpretation was the meaning of land appropriation (*Landnehmen*). According to Schmitt, Vitoria "explicitly reject[ed] discovery and occupation as the legal title for land appropriation, because, for him, the territory of America was neither free nor unclaimed,"[55] a view belatedly addressed by the Supreme Court in the third of Marshall's Cherokee Trilogy, *Worcester v. Georgia*.

While Vitoria recognized four conditions that could possibly deprive the Natives of their mastery over their domain – sin (*peccatores*), unbelief (*infideles*), insanity (*amentes*), or lack of consciousness (*insensati*), he nevertheless dismissed these possibilities in answer to the question of Spain's legal title to the peoples and lands of the New World.[56] He definitively concluded that the Indians exercised judgment and order over their affairs.[57]

Vitoria ultimately provided a justification for the conquest of the Indians based on papal missionary mandate, yet his two primary *relectiones*[58] on the Indians have been dissected and variously interpreted as support for the proto rights of humans,[59] justification for the enslavement actions by colonists,[60]

---

53 Pagden and Lawrance, *Vitoria: Political Writings*, 250.

54 Schmitt, *Nomos*, 101.

55 Schmitt, *Nomos*, 112.

56 Schmitt, *Nomos*, 240.

57 Schmitt, *Nomos*, 250.

58 As is well known, Vitoria never published anything. His teachings filter down through history from his students' notes taken from his lectures (*relectiones*) at Salamanca. Two of his most important surviving lectures were *De Indis Recenter Inventis* (1538) and *De Indis sive de Iure Belli Hispanorum in Barbaos* (1539). *See* Anthony Pagden, 'Gentili, Vitoria and the Fabrication of a Natural Law of Nations', in Benedict Kingsbury and Benjamin Straussmen (eds.), *Roman Foundations of the Law of Nations: Alberico Gentili and the Justice of Empire* (New York: Oxford University Press, 2010) 340–362, 342.

59 *See generally* James Brown Scott, *The Spanish Origin of International Law: Francisco de Vitoria and His Law of Nations* (London: Humphrey Milford, 1934); Christopher R. Rossi, *Broken Chain of Being: James Brown Scott and the Origins of Modern International Law* (The Hague, London, Boston: Kluwer Law International, 1998).

60 *See generally* Antony Anghie, *Imperialism, Sovereignty and the Making of International Law* (Cambridge: Cambridge University Press, 2007).

and advocacy for an informal worldwide empire of capitalistic exchange and private property.[61] These entangling reflections of Vitoria are irresolvable unless interpreted as insights and "bewildering antinomies."[62]

Schmitt took care to correct what he considered to be rampant historical misuses and misreadings of Vitoria, particularly through liberal appropriations of his name.[63] Schmitt argued that "the great jurist must not be situated in the empty space of a neutral objectivity in the modern sense."[64] He must be "seen in his historical context and … in his thoroughly concrete thinking as a representative of the Roman Catholic Church" and as an agent "from which the Crown of Castile received … legal title for the great land-appropriation" of the New World.[65]

Yet Schmitt complained that Vitoria's teachings had been carelessly lifted out of their time and place, that his ideas had become "divorced from the concrete unity of [their] complex intellectual structure and from the concrete historical situation,"[66] and they had been anachronistically "transplanted" with "almost mythical renown" "in certain ['freethinking'] quarters."[67] Could the same be said of the discovery doctrine in United States jurisprudence? Schmitt had come into agreement with Vitoria's fundamental and blurred historical point about the seminal question of the early sixteenth century.[68] It would be a "gross misinterpretation to say that Vitoria had [proclaimed] the

61 Martti Koskenniemi, 'Empire and International Law: The Real Spanish Contribution'. *University of Toronto Law Journal* 61(1) (2011), 1–32, 32.

62 Karl Popper's reflection on Kant and the growth of knowledge as applied mostly to scientific method but intentionally directed toward the study of politics and history is helpful in assimilating various interpretations of Vitoria. *See generally* Karl Popper, *Conjectures and Refutations: The Growth of Scientific Knowledge* (London and New York; Routledge Classics, 2002 [1963]) 240–242. The Vatican denounced the discovery doctrine in 2023, protesting that claims attributing its basis to papal documents (such as the Bulls *Dum Diversas* (1452), *Romanus Pontifex* (1455) and *Inter Catera* (1493)) reflected political manipulations by 'competing colonial powers in order to justify immoral acts against Indigenous Peoples'. 'Joint Statement of the Dicasteries for Culture and Education and for Promoting Integral Human Development on the "Doctrine of Discovery", 30.03.2023'. *Holy See Press Office 2023*, https://press.vatican.va/content/salastampa/en/bollettino/pubblico/2023/03/30/230330b.html.

63 *See* Orlando Bentacor, 'Francisco de Vitoria, Carl Schmitt, and Originary Technicity'. *Politica Común* 5 (2014), 5.

64 Schmitt, *Nomos*, 111.

65 Schmitt, *Nomos*, 111.

66 Schmitt, *Nomos*, 115.

67 Schmitt, *Nomos*, 115.

68 Peter Uwe Hohendahl, *Perilous Futures: On Carl Schmitt's Later Writings* (Ithica and New York: Cornell University Press 2018) 99.

great Spanish *conquista* ...unjust."[69] Despite a concern for Vitoria's ahistorical exposition,[70] Schmitt agreed with Vitoria that the colonial domination of the Indians reflected the spatial order of a *respublica Christiana*.[71] It amounted to "the *fait accompli* of Christianization"[72] based on a legal foundation to wage just war on grounds of *jus gentium*, meaning the right of free passage (*jus peregrinandi*), free commerce (*liberum commercium*), and papal missionary mandate.[73]

Schmitt blamed Hugo Grotius (1583–1645) for the first and almost immediate reworking of Vitoria's thought. In his pamphlet, *Mare Liberum* (1609), Schmitt claimed Grotius:

> adopted Vitoria's arguments on *liberum commercium* and the freedom of missions. That same *freedom* that Vitoria sanctioned for Spanish Catholics vis-à-vis heathen Indians, Grotius advanced for Dutch and English Protestants vis-à-vis Portuguese and Spanish Catholics. Thus, a train of thought that a Spanish theologian had expounded as an altogether internal, Spanish-Catholic matter within the firm framework of the Dominican order and within the political unity of the Spanish-Catholic empire, was used only a few decades later against Spain by a polemical jurist of a hostile country as propaganda in European trade wars.

Schmitt's attempt to reclaim Vitoria's name from the "heterogeneous uses," to "strip his image of added layers of false veneer"[74] promulgated by acolytes such as Ernest Nys (1851–1920), Camilo Barcia Trelles (1888–1977), Alejandro Alvarez (1868–1960), and James Brown Scott (1866–1943),[75] intended to instrumentalize the truer tone of his voice.[76] Schmitt interpreted Vitoria's voice as contributing to the epochal shift in world history brought on by the discovery of the New World. It had become lost in the din of a paternity debate about the

69 Schmitt, *Nomos*, 108. *See also* 113 ("It is necessary to reiterate that Vitoria did not present the Spanish conquest of the Americas as 'unjust'").

70 Schmitt, *Nomos*, 109.

71 Schmitt, *Nomos*, 112.

72 Schmitt, *Nomos*, 109.

73 Schmitt, *Nomos*, 109 (free passage and commerce), and 111 ("The arguments in favor of just war ... obtain their decisive legal force precisely from the missionary mandate; ... The *papal missionary mandate* was the legal foundation of the *conquista*").

74 Schmitt, *Nomos*, 125.

75 *See* Schmitt, *Nomos*, 117–19.

76 *See* Schmitt, *Nomos*, 125. According to Schmitt, "[o]ur intention is not to polemicize...but to restore to his words their true meaning. His reputation loses noting in the process. The less shrill the resonance, the truer the sound."). Schmitt, *Nomos*, 125.

origins of modern international law. The discovery doctrine would also involve an entangled paternity debate.

3 *The Precursor to* M'Intosh*: The Discovery Doctrine, Native American Sovereignty, and the 1763 Proclamation*

Within the United States historical context, Native sovereignty and self-determination represented a recognized but often underdiscussed third sovereign sphere in the mindset of early American founders. These spheres not only divided federal power among nascent executive, judicial, and legislative branches, they also involved limitations of federal power in relation to states' rights and a complicated federal–state interface with Indian Tribes.[77]

Tensions involving the American interface with Native Tribes accelerated immediately after the French and Indian War (1754–1763), when the victorious British Crown began to pragmatically recognize Tribal sovereignty over the Ohio Valley interior as a means of consolidating imperial rule over land vacated by France. In fact, the British had recognized Tribal autonomy leading into the Ohio Valley in 1758 with the Easton Treaty. This treaty forged an alliance with Natives in western Pennsylvania in exchange for Native assistance against the French. The British guaranteed the protection of Indigenous lands beyond the Allegheny Mountains in Pennsylvania from Anglo-American colonial encroachment. The treaty involved five hundred and seven chiefs from fifteen Woodland Peoples. By withdrawing their support for the French, they helped the British take control of the strategic Fort Duquesne (renamed Fort Pitt).[78] Native participation intended to convert the fort into a trading post once the British retreated back across the Appalachian Divide. They laid siege to the fort after the British betrayed their promise and strengthened it as a military garrison.[79]

---

77 The United States Constitution references Indian Tribes in art. I, sec 2, cl 3 (excluding Indians not taxed); art. I, sec 8, cl 3 (regulating commerce with Indian tribes); and amendment XIV, sec 2 (regarding apportionment, excluding Indians not taxed).

78 'The Minutes of a treaty held at Easton, in Pennsylvania, in October, 1758. By the lieutenant governor of Pennsylvania, and the governor of New-Jersey; with the chief sachems and warriors of the Mohawks, Oneydos, Onondagas, Cayugas, Senecas, Tuscaroras, Tuteloes, Nanticokes and Conoys, Chugnuts, Delawares, Unamies, Mohickons, Minisinks, and Wapings'. University of Michigan Library, https://quod.lib.umich.edu/e/evans/N06429.0001.001/1:2?rgn=div1;view=fulltext.

79 *See* 'The Siege of Fort Pitt-1763'. *Society of Colonial Wars in the Commonwealth of Pennsylvania*, https://colonialwarspa.org/siege-fort-pitt-june-1763/.

In 1627, French king Louis XIII had claimed that French Jesuits discovered all land west of the Appalachian Mountains, north of the Ohio River, south of the Great Lakes and east of the Mississippi River, as "no Christian had ever been [here]."[80] Britain's fifty-year campaign to expel France from North America and claim title by conquest resulted in 1763 in an asserted land acquisition "greater than that of imperial Rome" but hugely contested given raging and successful Tribal rebellions in the Great Lakes region (Pontiac's War, 1763-1766), and pressures from land-hungry speculators and frontier expansionists.[81] On the brink of bankruptcy, king George III "attempted to impose a new imperial order in North America" with the Royal Proclamation of 1763,[82] which enjoined American colonists from jumping over the crest of the Appalachian Mountains and "mak[ing] any purchase from … Indians of any Lands … not having been ceded to or purchased by Us."[83]

The proclamation sought to protect an empire Britain lacked the resources to defend by forestalling the colonists' expansion into the heartland, a move perceived as potentially threatening to Britain's economic and inchoate sovereign interests.[84] Britain's previous assurances to respect Native interior lands once the war was won used these promises as a buffer against claim-jumping colonists to assert an imperial domination based on agreements that "they should not be molested or disturbed."[85]

Land-hungry frontiersmen ignored the proclamation. Upwards of 80,000 colonists poured into the backwoods of the Ohio Valley between 1775 and 1790.[86] That number would increase to 200,000 by the end of the century.[87] This tide of American expansionism fomented by the myth of exceptionalism and Manifest Destiny prompted historian Greg Grandin to conclude "[t]here was not problem caused by expansion that couldn't be solved by more expansion."[88] However, this expansion at the same time threatened future British

80 Miller, et al., *Discovering Indigenous Lands* 17.

81 Colin G. Calloway, *The Scratch of a Pen: 1763 and the Transformation of North America* (Oxford University Press, 2006) 4.

82 Calloway, *The Scratch of a Pen*, 92.

83 'By the King. A Proclamation [7 October 1763]'. *Avalon Project* https://avalon.law.yale.edu/18th_century/proc1763.asp [The Royal Proclamation of 1763].

84 *See* Calloway, *The Scratch of a Pen*, 92–93.

85 The Royal Proclamation of 1763; Calloway, *The Scratch of a Pen*, 93.

86 Colin G. Calloway, '"We Have Always Been The Frontier": The American Revolution in Shawnee Country'. *American Indian Quarterly* 16(1) (1992) 39–52, 47.

87 'Kentucky'. *History.com* (9 November 2009), https://www.history.com/topics/us-states/kentucky.

88 Greg Grandin, *The End of the Myth: From the Frontier to the Border Wall in the Mind of America* (New York: Metropolitan Books 2019) 270.

mercantile interests with the possible growth of commercial agriculture in the Ohio Valley. England attempted to restrict this growth through established restrictions imposed by Navigation Acts, but these impediments added to colonial resentment over restrictions on Western free space,[89] and ultimately stirred rebellious passions.[90]

Cross-cutting imperial policies in the New World complicated the question of sovereignty. In 1609, King James issued charters to New World trading companies, which extended their western limits to the South Sea (Pacific Ocean), or at least to the Mississippi River.[91] Although rescinded in 1624, Virginia's landed gentry claimed that their forbearers never consented to the relinquishment of their charter rights, which substantially overlapped with Pennsylvanian claims and other poorly defined claims stretching throughout the Great Lakes and Ohio Valley. By this time, sovereignty was contested by Pennsylvania, Virginia, France, Britain, the confederation of Iroquois, the Lenape (Delaware) and smaller Tribes. By the 1760s, Virginians, none more heavily involved than George Washington (1732–1799) (himself a surveyor by trade), had begun engaging in ventures involving the sale of millions of acres of interior land partly in pursuit of speculative deals and partly as remuneration to veterans of the French and Indian War.[92] Washington simultaneously petitioned Virginia to release tracts of land to veterans while lobbying the Crown to accommodate speculators' interest in pushing the borders farther west.[93]

The frontier migration incited the Shawnee and other nations to align with the British during the Revolutionary War, and again under Chief Tecumseh (*Tekoomsē*, 1768–1813) during the War of 1812.[94] Overlapping westward claims secured by company speculators' land purchases from tribes provoked Virginia's annexation of Kentucky (1776), followed by Kentucky's separatist movement resulting in statehood in 1792.

---

89 Noeleen McIlvenna, *A Very Mutinous People: The Struggle for North Carolina, 1660–1713* (Chapel Hill: University of North Carolina Press, 2009) 46–70 (discussing the Navigation Acts and Culpeper's Rebellion).

90 'Proclamation Line of 1763'. *George Washington Presidential Library*, https://www.mountvernon.org/library/digitalhistory/digital-encyclopedia/article/proclamation-line-of-1763.

91 'Motion Regarding the Western Lands, [6 September]1780'. *Founders Online, National Archives*, https://founders.archives.gov/documents/Madison/01-02-02-0051; Christopher R Rossi, *Whiggish International Law: Elihu Root, the Monroe Doctrine, and International Law in the Americas* (Leiden, Boston: Brill/Nijhoff, 2019) 67.

92 'Proclamation Line of 1763'. George Washington Presidential Library.

93 'Proclamation Line of 1763'. George Washington Presidential Library.

94 *See* Rossi, 'The Blind Eye', 418.

Scholars disagree on whether the proclamation recognized or undermined Tribal sovereignty. Some scholars claim it regulated Indian regulations with settlers, not the crown. Others associate the crown's claim with the discovery doctrine, and still more associate the proclamation with the implied or even explicit but possibly limited recognition of Native legal autonomy.[95] Native scholars note the formality of the proclamation's conclusion at the Council of Niagara (1764),[96] where the exchange of the Covenant Chain wampum belt (*dehudadnetsháus/teHonane:tosho:t*) – as significant in Native semiotics as a European royal seal and signature on treaty parchment – affirmed that the proclamation was not a unilateral declaration but a ratified document in recognition of mutual interests and Native rights.[97] Similar solemnities had accompanied the conclusion of the Treaty of Easton.

In the western mind, sovereignty cannot be held in abeyance. It must always seamlessly vest somewhere. However, it seems that in the Ohio Valley the British began to learn "what the French had known, that in Indian country imperial policies often depended on negotiation and agreement,"[98] particularly after the Anishinabe and other Nations had overtaken all but three of eight British garrisons on the Great Lakes and killed and expelled thousands of settlers from much of the territory during Pontiac's War.[99] The 1763 Proclamation Line had to be modified multiple times to resolve concerns of settlers and land speculators on the one hand, and competing Native and federal–

---

95 Calloway, *The Scratch of a Pen*, 96 (canvassing the disparate views of L.C. Green, Olive Dickerson, Robert Williams, Anthony Pagden, and Gregory Dowd).

96 To secure peace in the Ohio Valley, the British dispatched Sir William Johnson, superintendent of Indian Affairs, to negotiate the Proclamation with an assemblage of 2000 First Nation attendees from 24 Indigenous Nations stretching from the Mississippi River to the southern end of Hudson Bay (James Bay) to the Atlantic. *See* Bradley Clements, 'From the GKS: Niagara Conference Minutes, July 28, 1764'. *GRASAC Great Lakes Research Alliance* (1 August 2021) https://grasac.artsci.utoronto.ca/?p=1508.

97 John Borrows, 'Wampum at Niagara: The Royal Proclamation, Canadian Legal History, and Self-Government', in Michael Asche (ed), *Aboriginal and Treaty Rights in Canada* (Vancouver: University of British Colombia Press, 1977) 155–72,162–63.

98 Calloway, *The Scratch of a Pen*, 96.

99 *See* 'The Covenant Chain, Royal Proclamation and Treaty of Niagara'. *Canadian Museum of History*, https://www.historymuseum.ca/history-hall/covenant-chain-royal-proclamation-treaty-niagara/. The British held Fort Detroit, Fort Pitt. Fort Niagara fell but was reclaimed. *See* 'Pontiac's War: 23 May-28 November 1783'. *The Loyal Edmonton Regiment Military Museum*, https://www.lermuseum.org/imperial-rivalry-1731-1763/pontiacs-war-23-may-28-nov-1763; 'Old Fort Niagara's Long History', *Old Fort Niagara* (30 May 2024), https://www.oldfortniagara.org/old-fort-niagara-s-long-history.

state interests on the other.[100] From 1774 until 1833, treaties became the method for establishing land holdings, entitlements, and borders between individual sovereign American Nations and the United States government. During this period, special commissioners acting for the Continental Congress, the Congress of the Confederation, and the United States President under the supervision of the Secretary of War negotiated 374 treaties with Native Tribes. The form and procedures for putting them into effect were the same as for foreign nations.[101]

4 The M'Intosh Decision

Much of this land confusion would come to a head in the first half of the nineteenth century, beginning with the *Johnson v. M'Intosh* case. In *M'Intosh*, the heirs of a British citizen, Johnson, contested M'Intosh's 1818 purchase of eleven thousand acres of Virginia land from the United States government. Johnson's heirs had purchased the land from the Piankeshaw and Illinois Natives in 1775, a transaction that had occurred during the rampant speculative period prior to the existence of the United States. They based their title on the 1763 Proclamation. The Marshall Court ruled Johnson's preexisting claim invalid because the Natives never had good title to sell the land; it belonged to its discoverer.[102] The discoverer maintained the exclusive power to extinguish the right of the soil (*jus soli*) that the Natives admittedly possessed.

In *M'Intosh*, Marshall wrote that the Natives lacked capacity to sell their land to private speculators in part because they were "fierce savages ... whose subsistence was drawn chiefly from the forest," and because, citing to Locke, they did not exclusively "improve the land" but "[left] the country a wilderness."[103] The "lands occupied by [them] were not used by them in such a manner as to prevent their being appropriated by a people of cultivators."[104] As

100 The 1768 Treaty of Hard Labor with the Cherokee set a western boundary line different than the Treaty of Fort Stanwix (1768), signed with the Six Nations (Iroquois), forcing a renegotiation with the Cherokee regarding the Hard Labor line (see the 1770 Treaty of Lochaber). *See* '1768 Boundary Line Treaty of Fort Stanwix'. *National Park Service* (2023), https://www.nps.gov/articles/000/1768-boundary-line-treaty-of-fort-stanwix.htm.

101 Christopher R. Rossi 'The Widening Gyre: Legal Formalism and International Law's Sense of Place. *Notre Dame Journal of International and Comparative Law* 11(1) (2021), 107–137, 133–134. *See also Ratified Indian Treaties 1722–1869*, National Archives Microfilm Publications (Washington: General Services Administration, 1973) 1.

102 Johnson v. M'Intosh, 574.

103 Johnson v. M'Intosh, 590.

104 Johnson v. M'Intosh, 570.

they never possessed a fee title to convey, and despite numerous real property interests secured by parchment, they acquired only an "impaired" occupancy interest. Similar to Vitoria's reasoning in *De Indis*, Marshall held that the discovery doctrine did not dispossess Natives of all rights of *dominion*:

> In the establishment of these relations [between the discoverer and the Natives], the rights of the original inhabitants were, in no instance entirely disregarded; but were necessarily, to a considerable extent, impaired. The were admitted to be the rightful occupants of the soil, with a legal as well as just claim to retain possession of it, and to use it according to their own discretion; but their rights to complete sovereignty, as independent nations, were necessarily diminished, and their power to dispose of the soil at their own will, to whomsoever they pleased, was denied by the original fundamental principle, that *discovery gave exclusive title to those who made it.*[105]

The Natives of North America were no more than tenants in common.[106] The opinion was in line with an 1822 Indian Commission Madison Administration report, which held that the Natives held a qualified occupancy of the land with no power to convey or own. "The right of soil, or the absolute property, belong[ed] to the Sovereign, or State under whose authority the discovery and settlement were made."[107]

According to Marshall, "The history of America, from its discovery to the present day" proved the "universal recognition" of the principle "that discovery gave exclusive title to those who made it."[108] Natives were not allowed to alienate property alienated to them by treaty in full recognition that their possessory interest predated European discovery.

Marshall sensed that this circumstance strained credulity to present a "rational system of land acquisition in the United States."[109] He nevertheless invoked the discovery doctrine as a *deus ex machina* to mask federal–state tensions developing elsewhere in the young republic. Sovereignty vested som-

---

105 Johnson v. M'Intosh, 574 (emphasis added).

106 Johnson v. M'intosh, 549–550, 595.

107 Jedidiah Morse, *A Report to the Secretary of War of the United States on Indian Affairs, comprising a narrative of a tour performed in the summer of 1820 under a commission from the President of the United States, for the purpose of ascertaining, fir the use of the government, the actual state of the Indian tribes in our country* (New Haven: Printed by S. Converse, 1822) 279.

108 Johnson v. M'Intosh, 574.

109 Robertson, *Conquest by Law*, xiii.

ewhere between the state and the federal government, but not with the Indians. To conclude otherwise would be to undo the proprietary interests of the supervening power ("great[er] mass of community"), uproot "sustained" practices (*stare decisis*), and impermissibly call into question the "law of the land."[110] In *M'Intosh*, the Marshall Court could not dispute the pretense that seemingly upheld the foundation of the republic, a pretense that supported the proprietary interests secured over time by its settler population.[111] Even so, Marshall felt compelled to admit: "However extravagant the pretension of converting the discovery of an inhabited country into conquest may appear, if the principle has been asserted in the first instance, and afterwards sustained; if a country has been acquired and held under it; if the property of the great mass of the community originates in it, it becomes the law of the land, and cannot be questioned."[112] Kathleen Birrell reduced Marshall's formalistic reasoning to its irreducible core meaning: "The law could not dispute, and must therefore uphold, the means of its own foundation."[113]

The Marshall Court ruling adopted the discovery doctrine as a matter of federal common law. It was a ruling from a federal court that did not trace to a traditional method of interpretation arising from a federal statutory provision or constitutional command.[114] According to the Chief Justice, "It has never been doubted, that *either* the United States, or the several States, had a clear title to all the lands ... subject only to the Indian right of occupancy, and that the exclusive power to extinguish that right, was vested in that government which might constitutionally exercise it."[115] This assertion of the power to preempt lesser claims would explode in ways Marshall did not foresee. His

110 Johnson v. McIntosh, 590.

111 *See* Kathleen Birrell, *Indigeneity: Before and Beyond the Law* (Milton Park and New York: Routledge, 2016) 148.

112 Johnson v. M'Intosh 591.

113 *See* Kathleen Birrell, *Indigeneity: Before and Beyond the Law* (Milton Park and New York: Routledge, 2016) 148.

114 Common law is the system of law developed from the practices and legal precedents of the English court system arising from civil law traditions. It implicitly emphasizes court (judge-made) decisions, as opposed to code-based or statutory laws. Federal common law admits to various definitions but one standard usage means "federal rules of decision whose content cannot be traced by traditional methods of interpretation to federal statutory or constitutional commands." Richard H. Fallon, Jr. et al., *Hart and Wechsler's The Federal Courts and the Federal System* (5th ed.; Foundation Press 2003) 685.

115 Johnson v. M'Intosh, 584–585 (emphasis added). Determining where proper sovereign authority vested prompted dramatic constitutional confrontations between federal authority and states' rights. Marshall's dictum as to the political authority vested in the power to exercise jurisdiction was turned against the federal government in 1830, when the Georgia Supreme Court cited *M'Intosh* to uphold Georgia's statutory extension

dictum held in abeyance whether the power to preempt vested with the state or with the federal government.

Jefferson had laid the foundation for this doctrine during his tenure as Secretary of State (1790–1793). In correspondence, he articulated the doctrine of preemption to foreclose any other nation's attempt to challenge United States supremacy to rights over the Indian soil "in lands west of the Appalachia and Allegheny Mountains."[116] He asserted for the United States the "sole and exclusive right of purchasing" this land "should they be willing to sell."[117] As president (1801–1809) he repeated the preemption doctrine to Native delegations, explaining that they owned their land and had legal rights of use and occupancy; however the United States was the only qualified purchaser of land they wished to alienate.[118] Following the Louisiana Purchase (1803) from France, Jefferson dispatched the Corps of Discovery Expedition (1804–1806) under the direction of Meriwether Lewis and William Clark partly to find an all-water route from the Missouri River to the Pacific Ocean (which did not exist) and to deliver messages and tokens to the Indian Nations of the interior that the United States was the new authority over them.[119]

5 After M'Intosh

M'Intosh emboldened certain states to assert rights vis-à-vis the federal government and it directly reinforced the legal foundation for the passage of the

---

of jurisdiction over the Cherokee Nation. The Cherokee had formed their own republican constitution in 1827, which enraged Georgia's interest in adjacent Cherokee Territory. Furthermore, Georgia's land hunger for Cherokee Territory would intensify the following year, when gold was discovered in Cherokee land. Matters came to a head in 1830 when Georgia put on trial a Cherokee national accused of murdering another Cherokee in what it deemed as sovereign Cherokee Territory. Corn Tassel contested the jurisdiction of the State of Georgia, claiming a right to be tried in the courts of his nation. The United States Supreme Court granted his writ in error and served notice to Georgia to show cause for proceeding. Georgia's legislature disregarded the service, refused to recognize the jurisdiction of the Supreme Court, refused to send counsel to argue the case before the Court, and executed Corn Tassel. In essence, Georgia preempted the federal government's attempt to preempt the state action, calling into question the rightful jurisdictional authority over power conferred by the doctrine of discovery. *See* The State v. George Tassels, 1 Ga. Rep. Ann. 478, 1 Dud. 229 (1830).

116 Miller et al., *Discovering Indigenous Lands* 66–67 (referencing an exchange with English diplomat Sir George Hammond).

117 Miller et al., 'The Doctrine of Discovery', 67 (quoting Jefferson).

118 Miller et al., 'The Doctrine of Discovery', 69.

119 Miller et al., 'The Doctrine of Discovery', 70.

Indian Removal Act (1830).[120] Tendentious relations between states and the federal government had already surfaced. In 1828, South Carolina attempted to nullify as unconstitutional federal protectionist tariff authority.[121] It would do so again with the Nullification Crisis of 1832. Seizing on the *M'Intosh* language that Natives were tenants at will, the Georgia State Legislature passed laws to squeeze the Cherokee off their Tribal territory and out of Georgia.[122] Georgia's claim of authority traced from its cession of chartered land back to the United States in 1802, which stipulated that the federal government "extinguish the Indian title so soon only as it could be done peaceably."[123] These titles had been established by treaty with Natives and negotiated by the trustees of the Georgia Colony Charter,[124] which had been granted by King George II in 1732.[125] Having failed for decades to perform under terms of the Compact, Georgia undertook unilateral action to reclaim its sovereign state interest. The Cherokee contested the constitutionality of the state laws on the basis of Art III of the Constitution, which vested original jurisdiction in the Court over cases "between a State or the citizens thereof, and foreign states." Marshall's decision in *Cherokee Nation v. Georgia* rejected the argument that the Cherokee Nation was a *foreign* state, "more correctly …denominat[ing it as a] domestic dependent nation … in a state of pupilage … resemble[ing] that of a ward to his guardian."[126] Consequently, the Court did not have jurisdiction to hear the Cherokee complaint because the Cherokee Nation was not a foreign state within the meaning of the United States Constitution.

---

120 *See* An Act to provide for an exchange of lands with the Indians residing in any of the states or territories, and for their removal west of the river Mississippi. *US Statutes at Large*, Vol 4 (1824–1835), 19th through 23 Congress, May 28, 1830, 411 [Indian Removal Act]. Indian Removal Act hugely controversial. Passed the Senate comfortably (28 to 19) but the House margin was slender (102–197).

121 The so-called Tariff of Abominations would threaten the union and is regarded as an important precursor to the Civil War. The crisis would arise again in 1832. *See* 'Andrew Jackson & the Nullification Crisis'. *Andrew Jackson's Hermitage*, https://thehermitage.com/andrew-jackson-the-nullification-crisis.

122 Cherokee Nation v. Georgia, 7; Sheila Simon, 'Johnson v. M'Intosh: 200 Years of Racism that Runs with the Land'. *Southern Illinois University Law Journal* 47 (2023) 311–352, 344.

123 Cherokee Nation v. Georgia 8. *See also* 'Articles of Agreement and Cession, 24 April 1802'. https://amindians.tripod.com/18022.htm.

124 'Establishing the Georgia Colony, 1732–1750', *Library of Congress*, https://www.loc.gov/classroom-materials/united-states-history-primary-source-timeline/colonial-settlement-1600-1763/georgia-colony-1732-1750/.

125 'Charter of Georgia:1732'. *The Avalon* Project, https://avalon.law.yale.edu/18th_century/ga01.asp.

126 Cherokee Nation v. Georgia, 2.

Had the Court ruled in favor of jurisdiction, it would have been presented with a "politically explosive" question of the "highest degree," for it would have invited "the sovereign state of Georgia into federal court," prompted the likelihood that "Georgia would simply decline to appear," force a default judgment, and risk that the executive would not enforce the Court's decision.[127] Such a series of events would seriously diminish the institutional integrity of the judiciary in the formative years of its founding. It would also affirm that sovereignty conveyed by discovery passed originally to the colonies, which later confederated and later still unionized. This prospect was no mere conjecture in the mind of the Court. Georgia had refused to recognize the Supreme Court's jurisdiction in the *Case of Corn Tassel* (1830),[128] which presented a constitutional crisis only mooted out by Georgia's swift execution of the Cherokee petitioner.

Two years later Marshall's attempted bold reworking of *M'Intosh* in *Worcester v. Georgia* followed a Vatellian pathway that emphasized that Indian Nations "had always been considered as distinct, independent political communities retaining their original natural rights as undisputed possessors of the soil from time immemorial."[129] Quoting Vattel, Marshall noted that "Tributary and feudatory states ... do not thereby cease to be sovereign and independent states."[130] As a distinct community occupying its own territory, "the laws of Georgia can have no force ... but with the assent of the Cherokees themselves or in conformity with treaties and the acts of Congress."[131] Moreover, the charters granted by the king "before possession was taken of any part of the country" ... "were well understood to convey the title which ... they might rightfully convey, and no more. This was the exclusive right of purchasing such lands as the natives were willing to sell. The Crown could not be understood to grant what the Crown did not affect to claim." Amending language introduced in *M'Intosh*, Marshall wrote: "The extravagant and absurd idea that the feeble settlements made on the seacoast, or the companies under whom they were made, acquired legitimate power by them to govern the people, or occupy the lands from sea to sea, did not enter the mind of any man." Here, the discovery doctrine reduced to "the exclusive right of purchasing such lands as the

127 William F. Swindler, 'Politics as Law: The Cherokee Cases'. 3(1) (1975) *American Indian Law Review* 7–20, 12 (referencing as well concerns of Marshall's close associate on the bench, Justice Joseph Story).

128 *See* note 115.

129 Worcester v. Georgia, 559.

130 Worcester v. Georgia, 561.

131 Worcester v. Georgia, 561.

natives were willing to sell."[132] His reworking of the discovery doctrine doubtless infuriated President Andrew Jackson, who had made Indian removal *the* object of his presidency. The decision allegedly prompted Jackson to opine: "John Marshall has made his decision; now let him enforce it."[133]

As noted by Lindsay Robertson, the *Worcester* reformulation came all too late. Marshall died in 1835. Andrew Jackson's appointed successors to the Court closed the door on Marshall's repudiation of the discovery doctrine, "and the US inherited a legal regime 'dependent on their subsequent politically driven resurrection of a wrongly decided, collusive case'."[134]

The Indian Removal Act actually proffered guarantees for "such tribes or nations of Indians *as may choose* to exchange the lands where they now reside."[135] Marshall later lamented the hollowness of upholding the Natives' right not to sell or assimilate.[136] Marshall, like the presidencies of Jefferson (1801–1809) and Monroe (1817–1825),[137] had believed in the philanthropic mission of assimilating conquered people, "[where] the distinction between [Natives and settlers] is gradually lost and they make one people."[138] However, assimilation had a turbulent seventeenth-century history marked by the thirty-seven year war between the Powhatans and the English colonists in tidewater Virginia and Maryland,[139] the Pequot War against the English Puritans in Massachusetts and the Connecticut River Valley (1636–1637),[140] the Susquehannock War

132 Worcester v. Georgia, 517.

133 Swindler, 'Politics as Law', 7.

134 Robertson, *Conquest by Law*, xii.

135 Indian Removal Act sec 1, 412 (emphasis added).

136 Swindler, 'Politics as Law, 12 (quoting Marshall: 'Humanity must bewail the course which is pursued' by the Act).

137 *See* 'Indian Treaties and the Removal Act of 1830'. *Office of the Historian*, https://history.state.gov/milestones/1830-1860/indian-treaties.

138 Johnson v. M'Intosh, 589. Native American assimilation became a pragmatic option of appeasement for tribes, none more so than the Cherokee. The Eastern Cherokee converted toward agrarianism during the Monroe presidency (1817–1825). They accepted Christian missionary schools, developed their own alphabet in 1821, openly adapted European conventions and sartorial dress, converted matrilineal clan-based decision-making into representative councils and constitutional government, established newspapers, a diplomatic corps, and even slave-based plantations with a bourgeois aristocracy. *See* Rossi, 'The Blind Eye' 422; Mary Young, 'The Exercise of Sovereignty in Cherokee Georgia'. *Journal of the Early Republic* 10(1) (1990), 43–63, 49 ('bourgeois planter aristocracy').

139 The Powhatan wars began in 1609 and ended in 1646 and are sometimes divided into three most active stages of open warfare (1609–1614, 1622–1632, and 1644–1646). *See generally* Alfred A. Cave, *Lethal Encounters: Englishmen and Indians in Colonial Virginia* (Lincoln: University of Nebraska Press, 2011).

140 Alfred A. Cave, *The Pequot War* (Amherst: University of Massachusetts Press, 1996).

straddling Maryland and Virginia (1675),[141] and the Pueblo Revolt against the Spanish colony at Santa Fe (1680).[142]

The seamless transfer of title, later speciously mythologized by the United States Supreme Court in the *Curtiss-Wright* case (1936: "Sovereignty is never held in suspense")[143] focused on the transfer of power from the British Crown to the American colonists, once the American colonists gained control of the eastern seaboard region from the French in the Lake Champlain region (1775), the Dutch in Hudson Bay and New Amsterdam (1664), Spanish interests in Florida (1819), and French control of the Mississippi River and Louisiana Territory (1803). The sovereignty acquired among European powers and ultimately ceded to the British meant to preclude "the idea of any other sovereignty existing within the same limits,"[144] never contemplating the principle establish by President Washington at the Fort Haramar Treaty (1789), which placed Indian treaties on par with the formal ratification "solemnities [i.e., advice and consent] as afforded to treaties with European sovereigns."[145] The discovery doctrine formed in American jurisprudence to assert an *ab initio* sovereignty claim devolving from the mythos of an uninterrupted transfer of title from

---

141 *See* Matthew Kruer, 'Bloody Minds and Peoples Undone: Emotion, Family, and Political Order in the Susquehannock-Virginia War'. *The William and Mary Quarterly* 74(3) (2022), 401–36.

142 Robert Mario Salmon, *Indian Revolts in Northern New Spain: A Synthesis of Resistance (1680–1786)* (Lanham, MD: University Press of America, 1991). *See also* John Schmal, 'An Entire Frontier in Flames: The Regional Implications of the Pueblo Revolt (1680–1696)'. *Indigenous Mexico*, https://www.indigenousmexico.org/articles/an-entire-frontier-in-flames-the-regional-implications-of-the-pueblo-revolt-1680-1696 (noting that the Pueblo Revolt 'was actually part of a larger regional rebellion against Spanish rule').

143 In the famous, albeit historically contorted Curtiss-Wright decision, which has never been overruled, Mr. Justice Sutherland's wrote: As a result of the separation from Great Britain by the colonies acting as a unit, the powers of external sovereignty passed from the Crown not to the colonies severally, but to the colonies in their collective and corporate capacity as the United States of America. Even before the Declaration, the colonies were a unit in foreign affairs, acting through a common agency – namely the Continental Congress.... Rulers come and go; governments and forms of governments change; but sovereignty survives ... Sovereignty is never held in suspense. When, therefore, the external sovereignty of Great Britain in respect of the colonies ceased, it immediately passed to the Union. United States v. Curtiss-Wright Export Corporation, 299 U.S. 304, 316–17 (1936).

144 Sarah H. Cleveland, 'Powers Inherent in Sovereignty: Indians, Aliens, Territories, and the Nineteenth Century Origins of Plenary Power over Foreign Affairs'. *Texas Law Review* 81 (1) (2002), 3–284, 32.

145 Cleveland, 'Powers Inherent in Sovereignty' 30. *See also* US Constitution art II, sec 2 (the president 'shall have Power, by and with the Advice and Consent of the Senate, to make Treaties, provided two-thirds of the Senators present concur'.

England. However, the first major Native land transfer to the federal government of southeastern ancestral homeland resulted from war.[146]

6 Conclusion

Schmitt's story of epochal change began with the discovery of the New World and resulted in the nihilistic *jus publicum Americanum* wrought of the Monroe Doctrine. It discretely hinged on the telluric significance of *nomos* and the powerful metaphor of discovery, often inconsistently mixed with conquest.[147] Schmitt's usage of this discovery metaphor was unexceptional and understandable given its deeply rooted connection to Vitoria and the early sixteenth-century debate about the Indians. It is an enshrined metaphorical signpost in the sequential presentation of the late scholastic transition to modernity.[148] It ultimately steered the United States toward its land appropriation scheme of a Western Hemispheric *Großraum*, which intrigued and analogously inspired Schmitt to justify one for Nazi Germany over Central Europe.

If signposts allow the storyteller to tell the "usual kind of story … that is *going* somewhere,"[149] this is the direction Schmitt wanted to go. In telling this story, however, Schmitt navigated shortcuts through the discovery doctrine's history in its North American graveyard. He would do the same with his decidedly illiberal explication of the Monroe Doctrine. Whatever ruptures in continuity the question of Indians posed for the European mindset, the pathway put forward from the introduction of the discovery doctrine was not as straightforward as Schmitt's abridged storytelling detailed. Marshall's Cherokee Trilogy, apart from the aftermath involving a worldwide Trail of Tears, reflected a prob-

146 The Upper Creek Nation (Red Sticks) was the first to effectively resist American land encroachments into the North American Southeast. They were defeated at the 1814 Battle of Horseshoe Bend by Major General Andrew Jackson's troops and a confederacy of other southeastern Tribes. The Upper Creeks later surrendered by treaty half of future Alabama and one-fifth of present-day Georgia (over twenty-million acres, or eight million hectares). Their defeat forced Native Tribes to consider strategies of appeasement with the greater power, however practically all Tribes were removed within thirty years. *See* Christopher G. Marquis, 'Reckoning at Horseshoe Bend'. *Warfare History Network*, https://warfarehistorynetwork.com/article/reckoning-at-horseshoe-bend/.

147 *See* Nicholas Onuf, 'Metaphoricizing Modernity'. *Contexto Internacional* 46(1) (2024), 1–23, 2.

148 *See generally* Onuf, 'Metaphoricizing Modernity'.

149 Onuf, 'Metaphoricizing Modernity' 7.

lematic interface between discovery and the seamless transfer of sovereignty to newborn territory, a transfer aided by an extravagant pretension.

Bibliography

"1768 Boundary Line Treaty of Fort Stanwix". *National Park Service* (2023), available at: https://www.nps.gov/articles/000/1768-boundary-line-treaty-of-fort-stanwix.htm (last accessed on July 11, 2025).

An Act to provide for an exchange of lands with the Indians residing in any of the states or territories, and for their removal west of the river Mississippi. *US Statutes at Large*, Vol 4 (1824–1835), 19th through 23 Congress, May 28, 1830, 411 [Indian Removal Act].

"Andrew Jackson & the Nullification Crisis". *Andrew Jackson's Hermitage*, available at: https://thehermitage.com/andrew-jackson-the-nullification-crisis (last accessed on July 11 2025).

Anghie, Antony. *Imperialism, Sovereignty and the Making of International Law* (Cambridge: Cambridge University Press, 2007).

Armitage, David. *The Declaration of Independence: A Global History* (Cambridge, MA: Harvard University Press, 2007).

"Articles of Agreement and Cession, 24 April 1802," available at: https://amindians.tripod.com/18022.htm (last accessed on 11 July 2025).

Asche, Michael, ed. *Aboriginal and Treaty Rights in Canada* (Vancouver: University of British Colombia Press, 1977).

Ayala, Balthazar. *De Jure et Officiis Bellicis et Disciplina Militari*, Vol. 1 (edited by John Westlake, trans. by John Pawley Bate; Classics of International Law; Washington: Carnegie Institution 1912 [1582]).

Banner, Stuart. *How the Indians Lost Their Land: Law and Power on the Frontier* (Cambridge, MA: Harvard University Press 2005).

Bentacor, Orlando. "Francisco de Vitoria, Carl Schmitt, and Originary Technicity." *Politica Común* 5 (2014), available at: https://quod.lib.umich.edu/p/pc/12322227.0005.002/–francisco-de-vitoria-carl-schmitt-and-originary-technicity?rgn=main;view=fulltext (last accessed on July 11, 2025).

Birrell, Kathleen. *Indigeneity: Before and Beyond the Law* (Milton Park and New York: Routledge, 2016).

Blumm, Michael C. "Retracing the Discovery Doctrine: Aboriginal Title, Tribal Sovereignty, and Their Significance to Treaty-Making and Modern Natural Resources Policy in Indian Country." *Vermont Law Review* 28 (2004), 713–777.

Böckenförde, Ernst-Wolfgang. *State Society and Liberty: Studies in Political Theory and Constitutional Law* (J.A. Underwood trans.; Berg 1991).

Borrows, John. "Wampum at Niagara: The Royal Proclamation, Canadian Legal History, and Self-Government," in Michael Asche (ed), *Aboriginal and Treaty Rights in Canada* (Vancouver: University of British Colombia Press, 1977) 155–172.

"By the King. A Proclamation [7 October 1763]." *Avalon Project*, available at: https://avalon.law.yale.edu/18th_century/proc1763.asp [The Royal Proclamation of 1763] (last accessed on July 11, 2025).

Calloway, Colin G. *The Scratch of a Pen: 1763 and the Transformation of North America* (Oxford University Press, 2006).

Calloway, Colin G. "We Have Always Been The Frontier": The American Revolution in Shawnee Country." *American Indian Quarterly* 16(1) (1992), 39–52.

Cave, Alfred A. *Lethal Encounters: Englishmen and Indians in Colonial Virginia* (Lincoln: University of Nebraska Press, 2011.

Cave, Alfred A. *The Pequot War* (Amherst: University of Massachusetts Press, 1996).

"Charter of Georgia: 1732." *The Avalon* Project, available at: https://avalon.law.yale.edu/18th_century/ga01.asp (last accessed on July 11, 2025).

Cherokee Nation v. Georgia, 30 U.S. (5 Pet.) 1 (1831).

Clements, Bradley. "From the GKS: Niagara Conference Minutes, July 28, 1764." *GRASAC Great Lakes Research Alliance* (August 1, 2021), available at: https://grasac.artsci.utoronto.ca/?p=1508 (last accessed on 11 July 2025).

Cleveland, Sarah H. "Powers Inherent in Sovereignty: Indians, Aliens, Territories, and the Nineteenth Century Origins of Plenary Power over Foreign Affairs." *Texas Law Review* 81(1) (2002), 3–284.

Debrix, François. "The Virtual Nomos?", in *Spatiality, Sovereignty and Carl Schmitt: Geographies of the Nomos*, ed. Stephen Legg (London: Routledge 2011), 220–226.

"Declaration of Independence, July 7, 1776." *America's Founding Documents, National Archives*, https://www.archives.gov/founding-docs/declaration-transcript.

Establishing the Georgia Colony, Library of Congress, available at: https://www.loc.gov/classroom-materials/united-states-history-primary-source-timeline/colonial-settlement-1600-1763/georgia-colony-1732-1750/ (last accessed on July 11, 2025).

Fallon, Jr. Richard H., John F. Manning, Daniel J. Meltzer and David L. Shapiro, eds. *Hart and Wechsler's The Federal Courts and the Federal System* (5th ed.s; Foundation Press 2003).

Fletcher, Matthew L. M. "The Iron Cold of the Marshall Trilogy." *North Dakota Law Review* 82(3) (2006), 625–696.

Gerber, Dominik Andrés and William Ossipow, "The Reception of Vattel's Law of Nations in the American Colonies: From James Otis and John Adams to the Declaration of Independence." *American Journal of Legal History* 2017, 1–35.

Grandin, Greg. *The End of the Myth: From the Frontier to the Border Wall in the Mind of America* (New York: Metropolitan Books 2019).

Hobert, Anthony W. Locke's "'Wild Indian' in United States Supreme Court Jurisprudence," *American Indian Law Journal* 12(2) (2024), 1–38.

Hohendahl, Peter Uwe. *Perilous Futures: On Carl Schmitt's Later Writings* (Ithica and New York: Cornell University Press 2018).

Holy See Press Office. "Joint Statement of the Dicasteries for Culture and Education and for Promoting Integral Human Development on the 'Doctrine of Discovery,' 30.03.2023," available at: https://press.vatican.va/content/salastampa/en/bollettino/pubblico/2023/03/30/230330b.html (last accessed on July 11, 2025).

"Indian Treaties and the Removal Act of 1830." *Office of the Historian*, available at: https://history.state.gov/milestones/1830-1860/indian-treaties (last accessed on July 11, 2025).

Jefferson, Thomas. "From Thomas Jefferson to William Henry Harrison, 27 February 1803." *Founders Online, National Archives*, available at: https://founders.archives.gov/documents/Jefferson/01-39-02-0500 (last accessed on July 11, 2025).

Johnson & Graham's Lessee v. M'Intosh, 21 U.S. (8 Wheat.) 543 (1823) [*Johnson v. M'Intosh*].

Kaplan, Sidney. "The 'Domestic Insurrectionists' of the Declaration of Independence." *The Journal of Negro History* 61(6) (1976), 243–255.

Kent, James. *Commentaries on American Law* (New-York: O. Halsted, 1828).

"Kentucky." *History.com* (November 9, 2009), available at: https://www.history.com/topics/us-states/kentucky (last accessed on July 11, 2025).

Kingsbury, Benedict and Benjamin Straussmen, eds. *Roman Foundations of the Law of Nations: Alberico Gentili and the Justice of Empire* (New York: Oxford University Press, 2010).

Koskenniemi, Martti. "Empire and International Law: The Real Spanish Contribution." *University of Toronto Law Journal* 61(1) (2011), 1–32.

Kruer, Matthew. "Bloody Minds and Peoples Undone: Emotion, Family, and Political Order in the Susquehannock-Virginia War." *The William and Mary Quarterly* 74(3) (2022), 401–436.

Legg, Stephen, ed. *Spatiality, Sovereignty and Carl Schmitt: Geographies of the Nomos* (London: Routledge 2011).

Locke, John. *Second Treatise of Government*, Of Property, ch. V, sec 37.

Marquis, Christopher G. "Reckoning at Horseshoe Bend." *Warfare History Network*, available at https://warfarehistorynetwork.com/article/reckoning-at-horseshoe-bend/ (last accessed on July 11, 2025).

McIlvenna, Noeleen. *A Very Mutinous People: The Struggle for North Carolina, 1660–1713* (Chapel Hill: University of North Carolina Press, 2009).

Miller, Robert J. *Native America, Discovered and Conquered: Thomas Jefferson, Lewis & Cark, and Manifest Destiny* (Foreword by Elizabeth Furse; Westport, Conn.: Praeger 2006).

Miller, Robert J., Jacinta Ruru, Larissa Behrendt and Tracey Lindberg (eds.), *Discovering Indigenous Lands: The Doctrine of Discovery in the English Colonies* (Oxford Academic Books, 2010).

Morse, Jedidiah, *A Report to the Secretary of War of the United States on Indian Affairs, comprising a narrative of a tour performed in the summer of 1820 under a commission from the President of the United States, fir the purpose of ascertaining, fir the use of the government, the actual state of the Indian tribes in our country* (New Haven: Printed by S. Converse, 1822).

"Motion Regarding the Western Lands, [6 September]1780." *Founders Online, National Archives*, available at: https://founders.archives.gov/documents/Madison/01-02-02-0051 (last accessed on July 11, 2025).

Murray, John [Lord Dunmore], "Lord Dunmore's Proclamation (1775)." *Encyclopedia Virginia*, https://encyclopediavirginia.org/primary-documents/lord-dunmores-proclamation-1775/.

Navari, Cornelia and Yannis A. Stivachtis, eds. *Nineteenth Century America in the Society of States: Reluctant Power* (London and New York: Routledge Press, 2024).

Newcomb, Steven T. *Pagans in the Promised Land: Decoding the Doctrine of Christian Discovery* (Golden, Co.: Fulcrum Publishing 2008).

"Old Fort Niagara's Long History," *Old Fort Niagara* (May 30, 2024), available at: https://www.oldfortniagara.org/old-fort-niagara-s-long-history (last accessed on July 11, 2025).

Onuf, Nicholas. "Metaphoricizing Modernity." *Contexto Internacional* 46(1) (2024), 1–23.

Onuf, Peter S. and Nicholas Greenwood Onuf, *Federal Union, Modern World: The Law of Nations in an Age of Revolutions 1776–1814* (Madison, Wis.: Madison House, 1993).

Oskian, Giulia. "Tocqueville and the Legal Culture of Jacksonian Democracy." *Journal of the Early Republic* (39)(1) (2019), 135–144.

Pagden, "Gentili, Vitoria and the Fabrication of a Natural Law of Nations," in *Roman Foundations of the Law of Nations: Alberico Gentili and the Justice of Empire*, eds. Benedict Kingsbury and Benjamin Straussmen (New York: Oxford University Press, 2010), 340–362.

Pagden, Anthony and Jeremy Lawrance, *Vitoria: Political Writings* (Cambridge: Cambridge University Press, 1991).

"Pontiac's War: 23 May-28 November 1783." *The Loyal Edmonton Regiment Military Museum*, available at: https://www.lermuseum.org/imperial-rivalry-1731-1763/pontiacs-war-23-may-28-nov-1763 (last accessed on July 11, 2025).

Popper, Karl. *Conjectures and Refutations: The Growth of Scientific Knowledge* (London and New York; Routledge Classics, 2002 [1963]).

"Proclamation Line of 1763." *George Washington Presidential Library*, available at: https://www.mountvernon.org/library/digitalhistory/digital-encyclopedia/article/proclamation-line-of-1763 (last accessed on July 11, 2025).

Ratified Indian Treaties 1722–1869, National Archives Microfilm Publications (Washington: General Services Administration, 1973).

Robertson, Lindsay G. *Conquest by Law: How the Discovery of America Dispossessed Indigenous Peoples of Their Lands* (Oxford: Oxford University Press 2005).

Rodríguez, Raúl. 'Tocqueville and Native Americans'. *American Political Thought: A Journal of Ideas, Institutions, and Culture* 13(2) 2024, 216–238.

Rossi, Christopher R. 'Slaves, Indians, and Legal Formalism in 19th Century America', in *Nineteenth Century America in the Society of States: Reluctant Power*, eds. Cornelia Navari and Yannis A. Stivachtis (London and New York: Routledge Press, 2024), 100–117.

Rossi, Christopher R. 'The Blind Eye: *Jus Soli* and the "Pretended" Treaty of New Echota'. *American Indian Law Journal* 8(2) (2021), 403–433.

Rossi Christopher R. 'The Widening Gyre: Legal Formalism and International Law's Sense of Place'. *Notre Dame Journal of International and Comparative Law* 11(1) (2021), 107–137.

Rossi, Christopher R. *Whiggish International Law: Elihu Root, the Monroe Doctrine, and International Law in the Americas* (Leiden, Boston: Brill/Nijhoff, 2019).

Rossi, *Broken Chain of Being: James Brown Scott and the Origins of Modern International Law* (The Hague, London, Boston: Kluwer Law International, 1998).

Salmon, Robert Mario. *Indian Revolts in Northern New Spain: A Synthesis of Resistance (1680–1786)* (Lanham, MD: University Press of America, 1991.

Schmal, John. 'An Entire Frontier in Flames: The Regional Implications of the Pueblo Revolt (1680–1696)'. *Indigenous Mexico*, available at: https://www.indigenousmexico.org/articles/an-entire-frontier-in-flames-the-regional-implications-of-the-pueblo-revolt-1680-1696 (last accessed on 11 Julys 2025).

Schmitt, Carl. *The Nomos of the Earth in the International Law of the Jus Publicum Europaeum* (Candor, NY: Telos Press Publishing 2006).

Schmitt, Carl. *Constitutional Theory* (Durham and London: Duke University Press, 1983 [1928]).

Scott, James Brown. *The Spanish Origin of International Law: Francisco de Vitoria and His Law of Nations* (London: Humphrey Milford, 1934).

Sheehan, Bernard W. *Seeds of Extinction: Jeffersonian Philanthropy and the American Indian* (Chapel Hill: University of North Carolina Press, 1973).

Simon, Sheila. 'Johnson v. M'Intosh: 200 Years of Racism that Runs with the Land'. *Southern Illinois University Law Journal* 47 (2023), 311–352.

Swindler, William F. 'Politics as Law: The Cherokee Cases'. *American Indian Law Review* 3(1) (1975), 7–20.

The Antelope, 23 U.S. (10 Wheat.) 66 (1825).

'The Covenant Chain, Royal Proclamation and Treaty of Niagara'. *Canadian Museum of History*, available at: https://www.historymuseum.ca/history-hall/covenant-chain-royal-proclamation-treaty-niagara/ (last accessed on 11 July 2025).

'The Minutes of a treaty held at Easton, in Pennsylvania, in October, 1758. By the lieutenant governor of Pennsylvania, and the governor of New-Jersey; with the chief sachems and warriors of the Mohawks, Oneydos, Onondagas, Cayugas, Senecas, Tuscaroras, Tuteloes, Nanticokes and Conoys, Chugnuts, Delawares, Unamies,

Mohickons, Minisinks, and Wapings'. University of Michigan Library, available at: https://quod.lib.umich.edu/e/evans/N06429.0001.001/1:2?rgn=div1;view=fulltext (last accessed on 11 July 2025).

The State v. George Tassels, 1 Ga. Rep. Ann. 478, 1 Dud. 229 (1830).

'The Siege of Fort Pitt-1763'. *Society of Colonial Wars in the Commonwealth of Pennsylvania*, available at: https://colonialwarspa.org/siege-fort-pitt-june-1763/ (last accessed on 11 July 2025).

Tocqueville, Alexis de. *Democracy in America* (ed. Eduardo Nolla, trans James T. Schleifer; Indianapolis: Liberty Fund, 2012).

'Treaty with the Cherokee, 1835' [Treaty of New Echota], in *Indian Affairs. Laws and Treaties*. Vol. II, ed. Charles J. Kappler (Washington: Government Printing Office, 1904), 439–449.

Turner, Frederick Jackson. 'The Significance of the Frontier in American History 1893'. *American Historical Association*, 12 July 1893, available at: chrome-extension: //efaidnbmnnnibpcajpcglclefindmkaj/https://<uri>www.usmcu.edu/Portals/218/Turner%20Thesis%2C%20Frederick%20Jackson%20Turner.pdf (last accessed on 11 July 2025).

United States Constitution

United States v. Curtiss-Wright Export Corporation, 299 U.S. 304 (1936).

United States v. Le Jeune Eugénie, 26 F. Cas. 832 (C.C.D. Mass. 1822) (no.15,551).

Vattel, Emer de. *Le droit des gens, ou, Principes de la loi naturelle appliqués à la conduit et aux affaires des nations et des souverains* (Charles G. Fenwick trans., Classics of International Law; Washington: Carnegie Institution 1916 [1758]).

Vitoria, Francisco de. *De Indis Recenter Inventis* (1538).

Vitoria, Francisco de. *De Indis sive de Iure Belli Hispanorum in Barbaos* (1539).

Watson, Blake A. 'The Impact of the American Doctrine of Discovery on Native Land Rights in Australia, Canada, and New Zealand'. *Seattle University Law Review* 34(2) (2011), 507–551.

Wheaton, Henry. *Elements of International Law* (8th edn ., Boston: Little, Brown and Company 1866).

Williams, Jr., Robert A. *The American Indian in Western Legal Thought: The Discourse of Conquest* (New York: Oxford University Press 1990).

Worcester v. Georgia, 31 U.S. (6 Pet.) 515 (1832).

Young, Mary. 'The Exercise of Sovereignty in Cherokee Georgia'. *Journal of the Early Republic* 10(1) (1990), 43–63.

PART 4

Historical and Contemporary Pathways to Vitoria and Carl Schmitt

CHAPTER 13

Tyrannum licet deciper: 'The mind has its ineluctable freedom…even in the claws of the Leviathan'

Vitoria as Clue to Schmitt's Concepts of Grossraum, *Race, and War during World War II*

Joseph W. Bendersky

1 Vitoria and the *Grossraum* Controversy

Among the scholars of public law in the sixteenth and seventeenth centuries Carl Schmitt claimed to know quite well and respect he highlighted the names Francisco de Vitoria, Alberico Gentile, and Hugo Grotius. 'I love them', he wrote, as 'they belong without a doubt to our camp.' Nonetheless, he felt much closer to Jean Bodin and Thomas Hobbes;[1] and besides the sections on Vitoria in *The Nomos of the Earth* and *Glossarium*, Schmitt's references to Vitoria are sparse and infrequent. Yet the Vitoria section in *Nomos* is quite significant. It encapsulates Schmitt's understanding and interpretation of Vitoria, and is a key segment in Schmitt's theoretical conceptualization of the historical development of international law in relationship to his general theme of a new *Nomos*. And Vitoria is the means through which Schmitt contests James Brown Scott's arguments on international law. Moreover, Schmitt's original 1944 Vitoria lectures also reveal crucial insights into his own thoughts and attitudes on the wartime situation in which he composed and articulated his ideas on these subjects. However, these latter illuminating aspects of Schmitt's mindset regarding *Grossraum* and the war in the East have long been neglected.

Though certainly quite important, recent scholarship on Schmitt and Vitoria generally continues to overlook the significance of Schmitt's wartime thoughts and attitudes for an accurate understanding of his overall political and legal thinking, focusing instead on whether Schmitt's interpretation of Vitoria or Scott withstands critical scrutiny. Some question whether Schmitt's

1 Carl Schmitt, *Ex Captivitate Salus*, ed. Andreas Kalyvas and Federico Finchelstein (Cambridge, UK: Polity Press 2017), 52.

 | DOI:10.1163/9789004757448_014

theoretical edifice on the development and nature of international law has fundamental flaws. Others raise doubts about whether his historical facts and narratives embody the requisite degree of accuracy to substantiate his arguments and buttress his theoretical structure.[2] Certain scholarship offers a more positive perspective in contending that Schmitt's writings on these subjects were intellectually indebted to a Spanish school of thought on international law.[3] Of particular contemporary relevance are those publications on Vitoria, and directly or indirectly related to Schmitt, that trace the legal foundations of modern imperialism, especially informal empire, to the Salamanca School.[4] Such aspects of the Schmitt-Vitoria intellectual nexus have long been points of contention, and will remain so into the foreseeable future

Nonetheless, Schmitt's 1944 lectures on Vitoria constitute a case where biography and historical contextualization intersect with theoretical and intellect formulations and arguments. This is especially significant in Schmitt's Vitoria discussions on humanity – the human vs inhuman; of total enemies and total wars of annihilation of entire peoples. For these concepts are flash points in the debates not only over Schmitt's *Grossraum* theory but also generally over the anthropological foundations and implications of his political thinking on humanity and war. And, like so many of the controversies surrounding him, these, too, eventually pivot in one way or another toward his relationship with the National Socialist regime. Despite evidence already available in the early 1980s that the Nazis explicitly rejected Schmitt's *Grossraum* theory for lacking the essential biological racial foundations,[5] articles continued to appear in

2 Joshua Smelser, 'On the Use and Abuse of Francisco de Vitoria: James Brown Scott and Carl Schmitt'. *Journal of the History of International Law* 20, 3 (December 2018), 345–372; Peter Schröder, 'Carl Schmitt's Appropriation of the Early Modern European Tradition of Political Thought on the State and Interstate Relations'. *History of Political Thought* 33, 2 (Summer 2012), 348–371; David Chandler, 'The Revival of Carl Schmitt in International Relations: The Last Refuge of Critical Theorists?' *Millennium: Journal of International Studies*, 37 (August 2008), 27–48.

3 In this regard see the recent illuminating article by José Maria Beneyto, 'Camilo Barcia Trelles on Francisco de Vitoria: At the Crossroads of Carl Schmitt's Grossraum and James Brown Scott's Modern International Law'. *European Journal of International Law* XX (2021), 1–16.

4 Martti Koskenniemi, 'Empire and International Law: The Real Spanish Contribution'. *University of Toronto Law Journal* 61 (2011), 1–36. Antony Anghie, *Imperialism, Sovereignty and the Making of International Law* (New York: Cambridge University Press 2004). On the specific relationship of Schmitt and Vitoria to American foreign policy see William Rasch, 'Human Rights as Geopolitics: Carl Schmitt and the Legal Form of American Supremacy'. *Cultural Critique* 54 (Spring 2002), 120–147. Particularly insightful is Rasch's discussion of the 'other' as barbarians from the era of Spanish conquest to the contemporary world.

5 On the criticism by National Socialist jurists of Schmitt's *Grossraum* theory for its non-racial essence see Werner Best, 'Völkische Grossraumordnung'. *Deutsches Recht* 10, 25 (22 June

major journals linking his ideas to Nazi racial theory and racist occupation policies in the East. Although these articles usually conceded that Schmitt's arguments are fundamentally 'geopolitical' in nature, they nevertheless associate these either with the transition to Nazi racist *Lebensraum* theory and practice,[6] or claim that his theories bore an 'ambivalent' relationship to these, even asserting that 'Schmitt shared the dominant Darwinian ethos' of the regime regarding peoples and states in the East.[7] In the most recent version of this kind of interpretation, the highly respected Peter Hohendahl contends that Leftist and Rightist scholars have 'sanitized', 'dehistoricized', and normalized Schmitt's late writings, including those on *Grossraum*. In the process, they have supposedly lost sight of the real 'historical Schmitt', whose original purpose was allegedly to advance Nazi expansionism and who after World War II provided a 'positive defense of colonialism'. To Hohendahl, Schmitt's actual National Socialist affiliations belie the inaccurate interpretations of him as a modern, secular, realist thinker. Moreover, Hohendahl warns that this sanitized version of Schmitt hides the inherently dangerous nature of his thinking, with horrific consequences if these ideas are permitted to affect policies in the twenty-first century.[8]

2 Negotiating the Leviathan: Outer Conformity and Inner Classical Conservatism

Since so much of Schmitt's writings from Weimar until his final years address critical contemporary questions within specific 'concrete situations', his ideas do, indeed, require historical contextualization. But, in this regard, a determining factor to consider in his Vitoria lectures, as well as his *Grossraum* writ-

1940), 1006–07; Roger Diener, 'Reichsverfassung und Grossraumverwaltung im Altertum'. *Reich, Volksordnung, Lebensraum*, I (1941), 177–229; Günther Küchenhoff, 'Grossraumgedanke und völkische Idee im Recht'. *Zeitschrift für ausländisches öffenliches Recht und Völkerrecht* XII, 1 (September 1944), 34–82.

6 Dan Diner, 'Rassistisches Völkerrecht: Elemente einer nationalsozialistischen Weltordnung'. *Vierteljahreshefte für Zeitgeschichte* 37, 1 (1989), 23–56.

7 Peter Stirk, 'Carl Schmitt's Völkerrechtliche Grossraumordnung', *History of Political Thought* 2 (Summer 1999), 357–74.

8 See Peter Uwe Hohendahl, *Perilous Futures: Carl Schmitt's Late Writings* (Ithaca & London: Cornell University Press 2018). For an especially egregious version of this type of interpretation that links Schmitt to the 'cultural genocide' and ethnic cleansing of Jews and Slavs in the East see Timothy Nunan's Translator's Introduction to Carl Schmitt, *Writings on War* (Malden Ma: Polity Press 2011), 1–26.

ings, is that in 1943–44 Schmitt could not speak, write, or publish candidly about the real total, ideologically driven war in the East and its integral policies of subjugation and genocide. But he could project his sentiments and thoughts through the seemingly distant and unrelated historical era of early Spanish colonization of the New World. It is also relevant that he introduced these ideas not in Germany but in the more sympathetic intellectual milieu of Spain. Although this was, of course, not his only or primary purpose in addressing Vitoria, it remains an important dimension of this work, especially given some of the recent condemnatory interpretations of his *Grossraum* writings.

Schmitt's veiled approach was a necessary ploy when conducting intellectual activity under the scrutiny of the totalitarian Nazi terror state. Schmitt had lived and worked under its suspicious gaze since its condemnation of him during his early years of collaboration. And the wartime situation greatly aggravated his already precarious position. This was complicated by the fact that the attitudes, perceptions, and goals of many Germans, particularly conservative theorists such as Schmitt, overlapped with certain foreign policy initiatives of Hitler that corresponded to the traditional national interests of Germany, though not with Nazi racial ideological objectives, policies, and actions.

Schmitt's postwar claims regarding his complicated, though still perilous, relationship with the Third Reich, particularly in the wartime situation, cannot be merely dismissed as an attempt to evade responsibility or rehabilitate his reputation. The evidence suggests an essential continuity between his private wartime attitudes and his postwar accounts. His identification with Benito Cereno in his wartime discussions with Ernst Jünger corresponds quite well with his explanations to Robert Kempner during his postwar Nuremberg interrogations, as they do with his musing in *Ex Captivitate Salus*. Moreover, there exists a factual consistency between what Schmitt stated in his wartime lectures on Vitoria regarding the potential destructive division of humans vs inhumans, and his clear position on these subjects in his writings years before the Nazis were a significant political factor in Weimar, as well as what he wrote before the outbreak of war.

Thus, these sections of Schmitt's writings on Vitoria can fruitfully be examined through the situation he describes in his response to the radio address by Karl Mannheim while still interned in 1945–1946. Schmitt identified himself and many Germans with the western European rational spirit and tradition that could not have been completely obliterated or supplanted by Nazi ideology, values, or institutions within a mere twelve years. He noted, in particular, the limited impact of the Nazi-inspired mentality on the intellectual essence of the Christian churches and Marxism.[9] Beneath the surface of the external terror state, with its slogans and obligatory public affirmations, other intellectuals and artists continued to exercise a substantial degree of valuable creativity. Schmitt wrote:

> The mind has its pride, its tactics, its ineluctable freedom… and it has all this not merely in emigration but also inwardly, even in the claws of the Leviathan itself. In Europe, the mind has known until now how to find its crypts and catacombs, its new methods and forms.[10]

He described the persistence of such intellectual individualism in the face of a 'perfunctory conquest'. It was a dissonant dual existence of 'withdrawal to a private interiority…along with a great readiness for conscientious cooperation with whatever the current legal government mandated'. There emerged a 'complete disjunction between inside and outside'. Suppressing this inner essence and thought proved far more difficult than the 'smooth and easy' Nazi external *Gleichschaltung* of the educated class. After all, Schmitt interjected, '*Tryrannum licet decipere* ["one is allowed to deceive a tyrant"]'.[11]

Even during his most active years of collaboration between 1933 and 1936, Schmitt had actually employed 'multiple forms of politeness, correctness, and irony…against the clamor of public activity'.[12] His diaries from 1933 to 1934 confirm this dissonance, just as his writings from this period manifest a tense balance between accommodations to Nazi political and legal dictates and his deep-seated classical conservatism. After writing his initial draft of the *Reichstatthaltergesetz* that the Nazis would invoke to subdue state governments, Schmitt noted in his diary: 'depressed, because I cannot believe that the Nazis would understand [it]'. Indeed, the Nazis forced him to revise the law to their suiting. A similar dissonance is quite observable in his major publica-

9 Although recent literature such as Robert P. Ericksen's *Complicity in the Holocaust: Churches and Universities in Nazi Germany* (Cambridge: Cambridge University Press 2012) correctly highlight the reprehensible compromises the churches made with National Socialism, the Christian religion and value systems remained, nonetheless, strong moral and ideological competitors to the regime's *Weltanschauung*. On Christian morality as primary motivations for the actions of prominent anti-Nazi resistors see Peter Hoffmann, *The History of the German Resistance, 1933–1945* (Montreal & Kingston: McGill-Queen's University Press 2012).

10 Schmitt, *Ex Captivitate Salus*, 18.

11 *Ibid.*, 18, 20.

12 Ibid., 21.

tions from this period: *Staat, Bewegung, Volk*; *On the Three Types of Juristic Thought*, and *Staatsgefüge und Zusammenbruch des Zweiten Reiches*.[13]

Much of the historiography of this era over the past few decades has focused increasingly on the extensive acquiescence and consent of various segments of German society to the Nazi regime.[14] And certainly, Schmitt's anti-Semitism fits into such critical analyses, where a deep-personal, often coarsely expressed personal anti-Semitism gradually evolved into more and more concessions to the Nazis on the so-called 'Jewish Question', culminating in the 1936 conference on 'Purging the Jewish Spirit from German law'. The brief but not unimportant negative references to Jews in his subsequent *Grossraum* publications are a similar case in point.[15] But untenable reductionist attempts to subsume Schmitt's significant scholarly contributions under an all-encompassing, ubiquitous anti-Semitic paradigm have failed to impact the major interpretive debates. More recent research has once again demonstrated the complexity of Schmitt's relationship to Jews. It is now evident that in the 1920s and 1930s Schmitt received an enthusiastic reception among cer-

13 Carl Schmitt, *Staat, Bewegung, Volk: Die Dreigliederung der politischen Einheit* (Hamburg: Hanseatische Verlagsanstalt 1933); *On the Three Types of Juristic Thought*, trans. Joseph W. Bendersky (Westport, CT: Praeger 2004); and *Staatsgefüge und Zusammenbruch des Zweiten Reiches: Der Sieg des Bürgers über den Soldaten* (Hamburg: Hanseatische Verlagsanstalt 1934). As Volker Neumann has recently documented, Schmitt's Concrete-Order and Institutional theory had very limited resonance in the Third Reich; it was, with very few exceptions, either severely criticized or ignored. Thus, 'Schmitt did not advance institutional legal thought, but rather brought it into disrepute under the name Concrete-Order Thinking'. See *Carl Schmitt als Jurist* (Tübingen: Mohr Siebeck 2015), 372–374.

14 See for example, Robert Gellately, *Backing Hitler: Consent and Coercion in Nazi Germany* (Oxford: Oxford University Press 2001); and Peter Fritzsche, *Life and Death in the Third Reich* (Cambridge, MA: Harvard University Press 2008).

15 For a thorough examination of the revealing anti-Semitic expressions in Schmitt's private notations see Joseph W. Bendersky, 'Schmitt's Diaries,' *The Oxford Handbook of Carl Schmitt*, ed. Jens Meierhenreich and Oliver Simons (New York: Oxford University Press 2016), 117–146. A comprehensive and convincing study of Schmitt's anti-Semitism is yet to be published. Neither the earlier widespread interpretation of Schmitt's Nazi era anti-Semitism as mere opportunism nor the more recent argument of Raphael Gross that all of Schmitt's political and legal theory is inherently anti-Semitic can withstand critical scrutiny in light of extant documentation. See Gross, *Carl Schmitt and the Jews: The "Jewish Question," the Holocaust, and German Legal Theory*, trans. Joel Golb (Madison, WI: University of Wisconsin Press 2007). For a significant revision in my own earlier 'opportunism' interpretation see Joseph W. Bendersky, 'Underestimating German Anti-semitism: The Case of Carl Schmitt, the Frankfurt School, and Weimar Jewish Elites', in *Antisemitism: From the 1930s to Today*, ed. Ari Kohen and Gerald J. Steinacher (Lincoln: University of Nebraska Press 2021), 23–45.

tain European Zionists who internalized his major works in support of their arguments about the present and future of European Jews. And during attempts to construct a constitution for the new state of Israel in the late 1940s, Jewish jurists paid serious attention to the insights and arguments in Schmitt's *Constitutional Theory* and *Nomos of the Earth*.[16]

The fact remains that a duality continued between traditional German society and the all-embracing revolutionary transformation pursued by the Nazis. Despite his official titles, and involvements with institutional leadership, Schmitt's private diaries and correspondence clearly indicate that his proclivities, intimate confidences, and Berlin life revolved around the same conservative circles with which he had closely associated before 1933. The Schmitt home remained a center for confidential discussions among the Jünger and Popitz families, Catholic publicists such as Paul Adams, anti-Nazi conservatives such as Wilhelm Stapel, and the modernist artist Werner Gillis, whose art was publicly defamed and banned by the Nazis. The only two major Nazi leaders with whom he had an association, Hans Frank and Hermann Göring, never integrated him into their Nazi circles. And even those relationships, dissipating already by 1934, lapsed completely after 1936. Privately despairing throughout these years, he found solace not in Nazified Germanic literature but escaped into the classics, reading the Greek Plutarch and the Frenchmen Maurice Hauriou.[17]

3 Recoiling from the Dehumanization of Ideological Total War

The debate over whether Schmitt's late 1930s and early 1940s writings on *Grossraum* encouraged or legitimized Hitler's expansionist foreign policy is beyond the scope of this study. However, as Reinhard Mehring's masterful biography confirms, with substantial archival evidence, Schmitt's attitudes dramatically altered with the outbreak of war.[18] He shifted his focus from the concept of the

16 See Andrés Rosler, "It Had to Be You: Carl Schmitt on Exclusion and Political Reasoning," *Philosophies* 9, 48 (April 2024), 1–26. And Wojciech Engelking, 'The Jewish *Verfassung*, the Israeli *Nomos*: the constitutional situation of the beginnings of the State of Israel in the context of Carl Schmitt's political and legal philosophy'. *International Journal of Law in Context* (2021), 1–21.

17 See in particular Schmitt's diary entries for January and February 1934 in *Carl Schmitt Tagebücher 1930 bis 1934*, ed. Wolfgang Schuller (Berlin: Akademie Verlag 2010), 316–331.

18 Reinhard Mehring, *Carl Schmitt: A Biography*, trans. Daniel Steuer (Cambridge, UK: Polity Press, 2014), 370.

Reich as a key element of *Grossraum* to a more Euro-centric and global emphasis on 'nomos', in which Vitoria emerged as a key figure. Schmitt published very little and no major work after 1940. Even his short *Land and Sea* and its various published excerpts reflect the perspective of traditional conservative foreign policy attitudes toward Britain and the United States that one could already find in Friedrich Meinecke's 1924 book on *raison d'état*.[19] According to Mehring, *Land and Sea* 'represented Schmitt's literary distancing from National Socialism',[20] which is also corroborated by his correspondence with Ernst Jünger and Ernst Rudolf Huber. Emblematic of the duality of Schmitt's concessions to outer dictates, and the struggle to maintain an inner intellectual autonomy, is the 1943 excerpt from *Land and Sea* published in the *Deutsche Kolonialzeitung*. Although situated between texts and photos propagandizing Nazi Nordic ideological interpretations of ancient Egypt and Persia, Schmitt's piece is completely devoid of racial factors in analyzing British and American sea power and the recent catastrophic exercise of air power.[21] It is quite difficult to associate Schmitt with any Nordic ideology or foreign policy objectives.

Even his undeniable German nationalism was tempered by his deep personal affinities for Latin and Slavic culture, as exemplified by his two Serbian wives and his youthful diary expressions of empathy and identity with them, as opposed to the cold, 'barbarism' of Prussianism, especially its militarism.[22] Throughout his life he relished his visits to Italy and Spain in whose stimulating cultural and intellectual milieu he found some of the most impressive and enduring creativity of classical western civilization. That he focused so much of his wartime work through Spain and Spanish thinkers strongly suggests a continuity in such sentiments. His effusive admiration for French and Italian legal thinkers such as Maurice Hauriou and Santi Romano after 1933 reflects a similar affinity, as does the crucial impact of Donoso Cortés on this thinking.[23] Schmitt also acknowledged the influence of Camilo Barcia Trelles on his inter-

19 See Friedrich Meinecke, *Machiavellism: The Doctrine of Raison d'état and Its Place in Modern History* (New Haven: Yale University Press 1962), 210, 392–431.

20 Mehring, *Carl Schmitt*, 374.

21 See Carl Schmitt, 'Behemoth, Leviathan und Genf: Vom Wandel der Herrschaftsformen'. *Deutsche Kolonialzeitung* 55 (1943), 30–33, and surrounding photo articles.

22 Diary entry 1 August 1914, in *Carl Schmitt Tagebücher, Oktober 1912 bis Februar 1915*, ed., Ernst Hüsmert (Berlin: Akademie Verlag, 2003), 173. Diary entry 2 May 1915 in *Carl Schmitt: Die Militärzeit 1915 bis 1919*, ed., Ernst Hüsmert and Gerd Giesler (Berlin: Akademie Verlag, 2005), 55–56.

23 Schmitt, *On the Three Types of Juristic Thought*, 57, 59, 86–89. Mehring contends that Schmitt often used Cortés as a mask for surreptitiously expressing his own political perspectives. See *Carl Schmitt*, 198.

pretation of Vitoria in the context of his general conceptualization of *Grossraum*.[24]

Likewise, Schmitt's prewar lecture (published in 1942) on 'The Forming of the French Spirit via the Legists' exhibits a mastery and profound appreciation of French history, literature, and juridical thought, with particular praise for his intellectual brother Jean Bodin.[25] That piece again embodies the duplicity he had to engage in throughout all of his writings during the Nazi dictatorship. Like several of his publications of this period, he invoked the brief obligatory reference to 'race', while the essence of the piece is on culturally, historically, and juridically conditioned 'national character'. As Schmitt phrased it:

> Homogeneity, without which there is no commonwealth, is here defined neither by religion nor race; it lies in a juristically defined '*régime civil*.' The *régime civil* is the presupposition for the *citoyen*, the state citizen. The state of modern civilization, the modern state simply is the consciousness of the Frenchman a juristically composed *état civil* in opposition to all that is uncivilized. A Negro tribe as well as a feudal or clerical rule, a military or civil-servant state as well as a dictatorship falls under this negative category.[26]

What Schmitt criticized was the 'tragic' subjugation of this distinctly and admirable French characteristic to interventionist 'universal world politics' advancing and legitimizing hegemonic English imperialism.[27] As in his general *Grossraum* concept, here too, Schmitt reveals himself as an international cultural pluralist.

From the start of the war, and not in response to the military reversals after 1942, Schmitt's university lectures likewise revealed an even greater souring on the regime, with his cosmic pessimism about the conflict intensifying already with the invasion of Russia, despite the regime's euphoria emanating from its initial successes.[28] However, until publication of Schmitt's wartime diaries, his intimate wartime correspondence with Ernst Jünger, together with the latter's journals, provide the best evidence of his true mood and sentiments. Though

24 See Beneyto, 'Camilo Barcia Trelles', 6–7.

25 Carl Schmitt, 'The Forming of the French Spirit via the Legists', in *The Tyranny of Values & Other Texts*, ed. Russell Berman & Samuel Zeitlin (Candor, NY: Telos Press Publishing 2018), 73–79.

26 Ibid., 84–85.

27 Ibid., 86–87.

28 Mehring, *Carl Schmitt*, 370.

often veiled in cryptic references and esoteric symbolism, their thoughts and perspectives clearly disassociate them from the ideological thrust and occupation of the Nazi war in the East. It is a disassociation consisting of both omission of anything even implicitly favorable to the latter, and a distinct redirection toward non-German intellectual and cultural figures to whom they turn for solace as well as understanding of the catastrophe of their time. Their most candid confidential exchanges occurred during their private meetings in Paris, Berlin and Kirchhorst between 1941 and 1944. The excerpts from Schmitt's incomplete, unedited, and unpublished 1943 diary entries also corroborate the evidence in these sources.

Even before the invasion of Russia, they turned to the American Herman Melville not only regarding '*Benito Cereno* as *Situations*-Symbol' so indicative of the well-known controversies over Schmitt's predicament in the Third Reich, but to Melville's other works such as *Billy Budd* and *Moby Dick*. With the invasion of Russia, Edgar Allan Poe emerges as 'one of the greatest prophets of this age' and the essence of the 'dangerous world' who offered the most 'moral clarity'. Schmitt and Jünger continually returned to the bible and readings of the radical Catholic publicist Leon Bloy, whose apocalyptic theological prognostications helped explain, while reinforcing, their dread of a cosmic nihilism underlying the events they witnessed.[29]

As the war reached greater and greater heights of destruction and inhumanity, the paintings of Hieronymus Bosch, depicting fantastic nightmarish scenes of hell and earthly brutality and cruelty, became for Schmitt and Jünger the prophetic artistic manifestation of the 'Großkatastrophen' of their contemporary world. Jünger turned to Bosch in attempting to convey to Schmitt the gravity of the reality of war and barbarism he witnessed in the '*Osten*' in late 1942. Compared to the 'particular cruelty of our time', Jünger lamented, the Inquisition was humane. In this life and death struggle of two 'nihilisms' – one Asian and the other European – there was an incomparable convergence of 'mechanical processes crystalizing in pure violence' and killing with the complete 'metaphysical' extinguishing of the 'other' to be destroyed.[30] Just days after writing that letter, Jünger learned at a New Year's Eve party of the 'monstrous atrocities' of the SS against Jews in Kiev, of trains transporting them, and of gassings. Undoubtedly, he wrote in his journal, 'extermination is certainly

29 In particular, see their correspondence between February 1941 and November 1943, in *Ernst Jünger-Carl Schmitt Briefe 1930–1983*, ed. Helmuth Kiesel (Stuttgart: Klett-Cotta 1999), 114–115, 127, 129, 161, 173.

30 Ibid., 152–153, 171–177.

occurring on a huge scale'.[31] A few weeks later, Jünger stayed with Schmitt in Berlin, where these details were certainly conveyed. By the end of 1943, Jünger had more explicit details of the Ghetto suffering and 'butchering' methods of shootings and 'death chambers....which not even Dostoevsky could have predicted'. And in February 1944, Jünger again lived with Schmitt in Berlin.[32] From the invasion of Russia through the collapsing eastern front by December 1943, Schmitt's students serving in that theatre of war also kept him well aware of the realities of that struggle. From '[Herbert] Gremmels I received news about Russia', Schmitt wrote to Jünger in September 1941.[33] In March 1942, Schmitt had conversations with Gremmels in a Berlin field hospital. Although, as Mehring noted, these letters were so heavily censored that they often conveyed a comic quality in their positive formulaic expressions of the conditions soldiers faced, Schmitt had sufficient personal contacts over time to confirm his expectations of impending collapse. And occasionally, reality broke through, as in a letter from Günther Schwarz in October 1943 foreseeing a short end to the war – a soldier, he wrote, lived 'like a wild animal. It is terrible'.[34] It was, Walter Golombek wrote after the war, 'a question of naked survival'. Golombek's postwar letter bears an important correlation to Schmitt's 1944 lectures in Spain on Vitoria, where Schmitt emphasized 'moral and legal questions'. While serving in the desperate conditions of the eastern front, Golombek 'realized one thing especially during these times: how much fundamental...human and moral values emanated from your work in jurisprudence, also where it touched upon the level of politics'.[35] Dread over the loss of morality, as well as of Christian and idealistic values, also pervaded the Jünger-Schmitt exchanges. Such horrific destruction and 'mass exterminations' can only occur, Jünger wrote, with 'a change in the world of morality' and a debasement in the value of humans.[36]

Schmitt was also privy to the knowledge of the mass atrocities in the East from his personal contacts with members of the resistance. Although Schmitt never joined the resistance, since the late 1930s he had been present during the discussions on removing Hitler held by his close friends and confidents Johannes Popitz, Wilhelm Ahlmann, and Jens Jessen, all of whom sacrificed

31 Ernst Jünger, *A German Officer in Occupied Paris, The War Journals, 1941–1945*, Trans. Thomas S. Hansen & Abby J. Hansen (New York: Columbia University Press 2019), 151–152.

32 Ibid., 182–183, 190–191, 209, 287, 298.

33 *Jünger-Schmitt Briefe*, 128–130.

34 Cited in Mehring, *Carl Schmitt*, 381–382.

35 Cited in Mehring, *Carl Schmitt*, 371.

36 Jünger, *War Journals*, 264. Euphemistically referring to Hitler and the Nazis, Jünger also held their 'vulgar instincts' and satanic will 'responsible for the blood of millions', as they take 'cold pleasure in destroying human beings, perhaps even humanity', 49.

their lives as major conspirators.[37] As Jünger noted several times, 'Anyone who knows...Popitz, and Jessen...has a picture of the *Fronde*. One can see the moral element – not the political – is ready to make its move.'[38] And one could confidently assume that the intimate conversations in these circles not only conveyed information about the horrific wartime situation in the East, but echoed even more explicitly the apocalyptic *Angst* of the Jünger-Schmitt letters. Through Jünger, Schmitt had also established in Paris a close personal and intellectual relationship with General Hans Speidel, a pivotal figure in several early plots against Hitler culminating in the July 20, 1944, assassination attempt.[39] The Schmitt-Speidel bond lasted into their old age.[40]

Schmitt's closest confidant among the conspirators was Popitz, with whom he had worked to prevent the Nazi seizure of power in late Weimar, and who thereafter had brought Schmitt into institutional collaboration with the Third Reich.[41] During the preparation for the invasion of the Soviet Union, Popitz was among those who futilely hoped that army commanders would disobey Hitler's order for the brutal suppression of Russians and Jews that soon unleashed the atrocities. Despite general knowledge of the mass killings of Jews over the next two years, it was only in 1943 that a full picture of systematic murder emerged. And it was, in fact, Popitz who informed Ulrich von Hassell, a conspiracy leader, of the mass gassings of Jews.[42] During conversations with Popitz and Carl Brinkmann on March 18, 1943, Schmitt learned of the 'rumors about the treatment of the Jews'.[43] A few months later, Schmitt discussed the

37 Carl Schmitt to Ernst Rudolf Huber, 25 August 1948, *Carl Schmitt-Ernst Rudolf Huber Briefwechsel, 1926–1981* (Berlin: Duncker & Humblot 2014), 339–342. See also Mehring, *Carl Schmitt*, 364. Schmitt later dedicated *Ex Captivitate Salus* to Wilhelm Ahlmann, and *Verfassungsrechtliche Aufsätz aus den Jahren 1924–1954: Materialien zu einer Verfassungslehre* (Berlin: Duncker & Humblot 1958) to Johannes Popitz.

38 The *Fronde* was a code word for the German resistance. See Jünger, *War Journals*, 47, 307, 315.

39 All indications are, however, that Schmitt remained completely unaware of the specific 'July 20th Plot'. That he was in Spain as that plot unfolded probably explains why these associations did not lead to his arrest.

40 *Jünger-Schmitt Briefe*, 123, 135, 145–146, 176–177; Jünger, *War Journals*, 26, 49, 315–316. See also the Schmitt-Hans Speidel Correspondence, 1947–1978, Carl Schmitt Nachlass, RW 265, 15553–15576, Landesarchiv, Nordrhein-Westfalen, Duisburg. Hoffmann, *German Resistance*, 279–280, 351–354, 375, 388, 471–474.

41 Schmitt, *Tagebücher, 1930 bis 1934, passim*. The most recent biography of Popitz is Anne C. Nagel, *Johannes Popitz (1884–1945) Görings Finanzminister und Verschwörer gegen Hitler: Eine Biographie* (Cologne: Böhlau Verlag 2015)

42 Hoffmann, *German Resistance*, 269; Hans Mommsen, *Alternatives to Hitler: German Resistance under the Third Reich* (Princeton: Princeton University Press 2003) 265.

43 Schmitt diary entry 18 March 1943, Schmitt Nachlass RW 265 19618.

ss in Poland as related by student stationed there, who also mentioned the 'Evacuation [*Evakuierung*] of the Ghetto of Warsaw'.[44] Although corroborating documentation is not yet available, Mehring makes a convincing argument that 'There is no doubt that Schmitt considered genocide and the Holocaust as crimes.'[45] That these revelations from Popitz and others coincided with Schmitt's preparation for his Spanish excursions adds a circumstantial but highly probable indication of a relationship to his Vitoria lectures. In fact, in July 1943, Schmitt had a nice discussion about Vitoria with Jessen.[46]

In June and August of 1943, Schmitt had earlier delivered lectures in Madrid and Salamanca on topics related to his ideas on *Nomos* and *Grossraum*. As noted above, his intellectual work at this time had a distinctive traditional conservative tone and focus in its argumentation. Of course, considering the terror of the totalitarian Nazi state, especially in such a desperate, deteriorating wartime phase as 1943–1944, one would not expect any explicit criticism of the Hitler regime or its wartime policies. But conspicuous by its absence is even any neutral references to the racial explanations and justifications of the war constantly propagated by the Nazi regime. It is quite telling, in fact, that he had actually eschewed any substantive discussion of a German hegemonic *Grossraum* similar to what he had argued in his writings before 1940. Instead, he spoke only of the 'substance of Europe' defending itself against the 'boundless imperialism of the capitalist west and Bolshevik east'. Referencing the current year, 1943, he cited specifically US secretary of war Henry L. Stimson's doctrine of global 'pan-interventionism' and the 'American century'.[47] Here, Schmitt continued the line of argumentation he had developed since the 1920s regarding Anglo-Saxon imperialism.[48] He had provided substantial elaboration of this in his late 1930s writings on just war theory, discriminatory war, and the criminalization of war.[49]

44 Ibid., 28 June 1943.

45 Mehring, *Carl Schmitt*, 395–396.

46 Schmitt diary entry 19 July 1943.

47 Carl Schmitt, 'Cambio de Estructura del Instituto de Estudios Politicos'. Instituto de Estudios Politicos Berlin 1943 35–36. See related German renditions 'Die letzte globale Linie'. *Marine-Rundschau*, 8 (1943), 521–527, and 'Die letzte Globale Linie'. *Völker und Meer: Aufsätze und Vorträge*, ed. Egmont Zechlin (Leipzig: Verlag Otto Harrassowitz 1944), 342–49.

48 See Carl Schmitt, *Die Kernfrage des Völkerbundes* (Berlin: Dummler 1926); and 'USA und die völkerrechtlichen Formen des modernen Imperialismus', in *Die Vereinigten Staaten von Amerika*, ed. Hans Rothfels (Köningsberg: Albertus-Universität 1933), 117–142.

49 Carl Schmitt, *Die Wendung zum diskriminierenden Kriegsbegriff* (Munich: Duncker & Humblot 1938); and 'Über des Verhältnis der Begriffe Krieg und Feind (1938)', in *Positio-*

4 Vitoria Lectures as Manifestation of Schmitt's Inner Sentiments on Humanity and War

Schmitt pursued these same themes in his 1944 lectures on Vitoria. And much of what Schmitt wrote on Vitoria was likewise aimed at the prospects of Allied victors who would justify their postwar policies on discriminatory and criminal concepts of enemies and war. These aspects would be integral parts of his fully developed 1950 book *The Nomos of the Earth*. What is distinctive about his wartime Vitoria lectures is the fundamental theme of humanity and the division of it into humans and non-humans; and the consequential implications of such divisions for both just war theory and actual wars and conquests. This turn toward Vitoria's stance on the questions of the humanity or inhumanity of the Indians of the new world did not signify an attempt by Schmitt to disassociate himself from the war crimes of the Nazi regime when its defeat appeared imminent. These were themes he had already explicitly discussed in the 1927 and 1932 editions of his *The Concept of the Political*.

To appropriate and invoke the concept of humanity, Schmitt had written, 'has certain incalculable effects, such as denying the enemy the quality of being human and declaring him to be an outlaw of humanity; and a war can thereby be driven to the most extreme inhumanity'.[50] Foreshadowing what he later elaborated in his Vitoria work, Schmitt illustrated the inherent dangers of such a concept by footnoting Samuel Pufendorf's favorable reference to Francis Bacon that 'specific peoples are "proscribed by nature itself"; e.g., the Indians because they eat human flesh. And in fact the Indians of North America were then exterminated. As civilization progresses and morality arises, even less harmless things than devouring human flesh could qualify as deserving to be outlawed in such a manner.'[51] Thus, 'the concept of humanity is an especially useful ideological instrument of imperialist expansion'.[52]

In these early works, Schmitt also envisaged the catastrophic possibility of a total war of annihilation of a people by a power that appropriates the concept of humanity for itself, and conducts a war in its name. Schmitt never advocated the annihilation of the enemy, an erroneous allegation that still surfaces in public and scholarly discourses to this day. Quite the contrary, as clearly exemplified by Schmitt's indignant response to the Social Democratic theorist Her-

---

nen und Begriff im Kampf mit Weimar – Genf – Versailles, 1923–1939 (Hamburg: Hanseatische Verlagsanstalt 1940), 244–251.

50 Carl Schmitt, *The Concept of the Political*, trans. George Schwab (Chicago: University of Chicago Press, expanded ed. 2007), 54.

51 Ibid., 54–55.

52 Ibid., 54.

mann Heller's accusation that he espoused an irrational political theory that reduced politics to a 'naked power struggle' and called for the 'existential annihilation of the enemy'. Heller, Schmitt retorted, had completely misrepresented the entire thrust of his arguments. Not only was the very 'idea of such annihilation foreign and disgusting to me', Schmitt wrote, but he was actually warning against those tendencies leading toward total wars of annihilation by political entities that usurped such concepts as universal humanity, morality, or historical inevitability as justification for their self-interested actions or their ideological crusades. Enmity, conflict, and war remained unfortunate perpetual realities. Yet Schmitt still hoped these could be restrained in terms of the limited wars of the *jus Publicum Europaeum*, in which the enemy is not denigrated as morally evil subject to annihilation, but rather remains merely the existential other who must be combatted to defend one's own way of life, with this latter objective as the only legitimate justification for war.[53] 'Such annihilation [of the enemy] only results from a false moralization', Schmitt asserted, 'the refutation of which [my] entire essay is dedicated.'[54] 'Such a war is necessarily unusually intense and inhumane.'[55] It morally debases the people deemed an enemy of humanity. It transforms that people into 'a monster that must not only be defeated but also utterly destroyed…he is an enemy who no longer must be compelled to only retreat into his own borders'.[56]

Schmitt continued this argument in his writings on war in the late 1930s, where he foresaw an 'ultimate final war of humanity' as a more intensified 'total war' in which the pursuit of the 'universal end goal' sharpened the distinction between friend and enemy.[57] Such a 'total war' would necessarily expand quantitatively and qualitatively beyond purely military dimensions. Abolishing the distinction between combatants and non-combatants, this 'totalization' and 'intensification of *Feindschaft*' would extend into the economic as well as the psychic and moral energy of the non-combatants.[58]

By 1941, an analogous situation existed on the eastern front. There, two enemies confronted each other, driven by the irreconcilable ideological dictates of conflicting universalist, one might argue, utopian visions. Each had

53 Hermann Heller, 'Bemerkungen zur staat- und rechtstheoretischen Problematik der Gegenwart'. Archiv für öffentlichen Rechts, 16, 3 (1929), 338. See also Schmitt to Heller, 18 December, and Heller to Schmitt, 20 December, 1928, in Carl Schmitt, *Tagebücher 1925 bis 1929*, ed. Martin Tielke and Gert Giesler (Berlin: Duncker & Humblot 2018), 500–502.

54 Schmitt to Heller, 22 December 1928, ibid., 503.

55 Schmitt, *Concept of the Political*, 36.

56 Ibid.

57 Schmitt, *Die Wendung zum diskriminierenden Kriegsbegriff*, 49–50.

58 Schmitt, 'Über das Verhältnis der Begriffe Krieg und Feind', 249–250.

appropriated for itself the mantel of an absolute righteousness and political necessity transcending the longstanding norms of traditional theories of the state and war in favor of world dominating crusades. A communist world revolution for humanity confronted an equally dogmatic racial struggle for the survival of a higher Nordic civilization. Both ideological dogmas had universalistic tendencies supposedly compelled and justified by the course of history as well as scientific certainty. Under such circumstances neither the international class enemy nor the racial enemy could be given any quarter. Preceding a later discussion of Vitoria in his postwar *Glossarium*, Schmitt wrote of those utopian visions in which the path to this paradise could be accelerated by the 'quick and radical removal of the final obstacle – the capitalists, the Jews, the Jesuits, or Hitler'.[59]

Writing in the final stages of World War II, Schmitt praised the 'intellectual courage' of Vitoria and his 'extraordinary impartiality, objectivity, and neutrality'.[60] But it was inaccurate to see in these virtues, or Vitoria's arguments, the precursor of a modern juridical thinker on international law. Schmitt insisted that Vitoria remained a medieval theological thinker whose ideas must be interpreted in terms of this medieval Christianity. And within this historical context, Vitoria served primarily as a 'moral counsellor' to those exercising political power. That Vitoria always spoke from a 'thoroughly moral-theological standpoint' of medieval Christianity revealed the limitations of his neutrality and objectivity as well as of the impossibility of transferring his ideas to a modern historical context.[61]

---

59 Entry 10.2.48, Carl Schmitt, *Glossarium: Aufzeichnungen der Jahre 1947–1951*, ed. Eberhard Freiherr von Medem (Berlin: Duncker & Humblot 1991), 94.

60 Schmitt originally published his Vitoria interpretation as 'Francisco de Vitoria und die Geschichte seines Ruhmes'. *Die Neue Ordnung: Zeitschrift für Religion, Kultur, Gesellschaft* 3, 4 (July 1949), 289–313. References here are to G. L. Ulmen's English translation of 'Justification of the Land-Appropriation of a New World: Francisco de Vitoria', in Carl Schmitt, *The Nomos of the Earth in the International Law of the Jus Publicum Europaeum* (New York: Telos Press 2003), 101–102. I am indebted to William Rasch for reminding me of the tension-ridden ambiguous, even contradictory, serious second thoughts on Vitoria Schmitt expressed, often quite fervently, in his private notes at the time he published his article in *Die Neue Ordnung*, and the unaltered text of this article that that appeared as a chapter in *Der Nomos der Erde* (1950). See Schmitt, *Glossarium*, 172–173, 200. For an in-depth analysis of Schmitt's conflicting published and private perspectives on Vitoria requiring reconciliation in any valid interpretation of Schmitt and Vitoria see Joseph W. Bendersky, 'Regrets and Resentment: Carl Schmitt's *Glossarium* Critique of Vitoria in Historical, Theoretical, and Personal Context,' International Workshop, Vitoria and Carl Schmitt: Discussing Universalism in International Law, El Escorial, Madrid 20–22 June, 2024.

61 Schmitt, *Nomos of the Earth*, 105–106, 110–111, 113.

Schmitt devoted substantial parts of his piece on Vitoria to disassociating this Dominican theologian from modern concepts of rational natural law theory and from Enlightenment notions of humanitarianism and civilizational progress. The latter, Schmitt argued, led to the modern concept of discriminatory war that transformed the enemy into a criminal aggressor, who had to be completely subdued if not eradicated.[62] In stark contrast, Vitoria remained adamant that even aggressive wars or crusades against non-Christians, 'such as Jews and Saracens', must treat these enemies as a 'justis hostis' – the 'just enemy'. One had to defeat such non-Christian enemies, but not dehumanize them, subject them to punitive action, or annihilate them.[63]

What Schmitt found most courageous in Vitoria was his relentless stand, not just against the jurists of his age, but against the dominant position of his fellow theologians who dehumanized the Indians. Here Schmitt was quite explicit in his praise: 'With the purest motives of a moral-theological objectivity, Vitoria rejected any discrimination on the basis of Christian and non-Christian, civilized and barbarian, European and non-European.'[64] In that laudatory statement Schmitt identified himself with that historical sense of Christian morality that Vitoria represented. In 1944, that assertion by Schmitt also implicitly rejected the ideological impetus and justification for Nazi racial policies and actions.

Although Schmitt never abandoned his own Hobbesian anthropology of the *homo homini lupus* in political theory, at the fundamental level of the value of human beings he clearly concurred with Vitoria's concept of the *homo homini homo*. From this distinct Christian concept of the *homo homini homo* stemmed Vitoria's broader theological interpretation, not only regarding the Indians of the New World, but of non-Christians and non-Europeans generally.[65] Vitoria's major adversary, Juan Gines Sepúlveda, had defined the Indians as savages and barbarians, who by their very nature were as inferior to Europeans as apes were to humans. Sepúlveda, and other like-mind theologians and jurists, depicted the Indians variously as idol worshipers, practitioners of human sacrifices, cannibals, and criminals who stood beyond the pale of civilization and law. This denial of 'human qualities' not merely justified but compelled the subjugation of such beings. Schmitt argued that Sepúlveda's use of Aristotle's

62 Ibid., 108, 117–119.
63 Ibid., 120–124.
64 Ibid., 115.
65 Ibid., 104–105.

pronouncements on the inferiority of barbarians further dehumanized the Indians and underscored the 'higher humanity of the conqueror'.[66]

Schmitt then deviated from his discussion of Vitoria and Sepúlveda by interjecting an elaboration of the footnote to the humanist Francis Bacon in his Weimar treatise *The Concept of the Political*.[67] Schmitt argued that Bacon had developed the 'classic formulation' of the inhumanity of the Indians as cannibals by their very nature. By defining the Indians beyond the scope of humanity, it followed from Bacon's assertion that they had no claim to the rights of humanity or civilization. Yet Schmitt qualified his argument by noting that the distinction between the inhuman and the human was not as salient in the era of Vitoria and Sepúlveda as it would be in later centuries. The sixteenth and seventeenth centuries remained 'too deeply Christian', still abiding the notion of the Indians as having immortal souls.[68]

From Schmitt's perspective, the significant transformation in the discrimination between the 'human and the inhuman' emerged with the humanitarian ideology of the eighteenth-century Enlightenment. It was a division pregnant with 'political meaning'. The triumph of the 'philosophy of absolute humanity' deposed the medieval Christian view of man. However, inherent in this new philosophy of the celebrated human was its contentious other–the '*inhuman*'. To Schmitt, the identification of the inhuman other constituted a 'new enemy' whose expulsion was a prerequisite for the fulfillment of the humanitarian philosophy.[69]

The next phase in Schmitt's historical argument – the nineteenth century – offers a key insight into his thoughts and sentiments while composing his Vitoria lectures. The dominant intellectual tendencies of that century, he argued, had significantly widened the Enlightenment division between the human and inhuman. That century introduced the new discriminatory category between the *Übermenschen* and 'its hostile twin' the *Untermenschen*. This entire section on the evolution of the discriminatory division between the human and the inhuman, and ultimately between the superhuman and subhuman, had immense contemporary relevance in 1944. In this regard, Schmitt's brief interjection of comments on 'discrimination based on biological arguments' is particularly noteworthy. Although such biological distinctions between humans and inhumans had been foreign to the mentality of Vitoria's era, Hugo Grotius had, already in 1642, racially identified the North

66 Ibid., 102–103.

67 Schmitt, *Concept of the Political*, 54–55.

68 Schmitt, *Nomos of the Earth*, 103–104.

69 Ibid., 104.

American Indians as descendants of Scandinavians. Nonetheless, Schmitt concluded, Grotius' treatise 'did not protect them from extermination'.[70]

That Schmitt did not elaborate further was probably due to his cautious awareness of the dangers of overtly contesting, or even rationally discussing, the pervasive ideology of the Nazi regime, thereby incurring the wrath of the dictatorship's ubiquitous security apparatus. He later described the precarious circumstances of the time in which 'one no longer knows where even his closest friend really stands'.[71] Nonetheless, as he would also note, one had the 'right to deceive a tyrant'.[72] And in doing so, the mind resorts to new intellectual tactics and forms. And what Schmitt omitted to say was as revealing as the fact that he injected these brief comments on superhumans, subhumans, and biological determinants at all. For so much of significance was implied in these specific passages as well as in the general thrust of his arguments.

Throughout his entire historical discourse, Schmitt had empathized with Vitoria's Christian sensibilities about humans. Schmitt clearly lamented the loss of this kind of religious humanism as these fundamental concepts of humanity and inhumans evolved through the eighteenth and nineteenth centuries.[73] His critique of the secular humanism of the eighteenth-century Enlightenment was, of course, typical of his longstanding conservative thinking, as was his implied reproach of the scientific materialistic trends of the nineteenth century. He had warned against the dehumanizing implications of the latter since World War I. 'The very age of humanity', he had written, 'prides itself on destroying everything anthropomorphic in human form…the result is the machine, which destroys the human countenance….In the name of humanity one destroys the very image of the human being.'[74] By its very essence, his brief and

70 Ibid.

71 Schmitt, *Ex Captivitate Salus*, 21–22.

72 Ibid., 18.

73 Schmitt's deep personal identification with Christian values and culture does not in any way relate to the 'theological twist' in Schmitt historiography that interprets him primarily as a 'political theologian', as argued in Andreas Koenen, *Der Fall Carl Schmitt: Sein Aufstieg zum "Kronjuristen des Dritten Reiches"* (Darmstadt: Wissenschaftliche Buchgesellschaft 1995) and Heinrich Meier, *Carl Schmitt und Leo Strauss: The Hidden Dialogue* (Chicago: University of Chicago Press 1995); and *The Lessons of Carl Schmitt: Four Chapters on the Distinction between Political Theology and Political Philosophy* (Chicago: University of Chicago Press 1998). For the doubt that Schmitt's diaries cast up these interpretations see Bendersky, 'Schmitt's Diaries', 122–123. For a systematic refutation of the arguments of Koenen, Meier, and other representative of the 'theological twist', see Aaron B. Roberts, 'Carl Schmitt – Political Theologian'? *The Review of Politics*, 77, 3 (Summer 2015), 449–474.

74 Schmitt, *Tagebücher Oktober 1912 bis Februar 1915*, 91.

somewhat surreptitious questioning of the rise of superhumans and subhumans in the nineteenth century signified a rejection of the scientific racism on which the entire National Socialist ideological edifice rested. The Nazi doctrine of *Lebensraum* emanated from this, as did Hitler's general foreign policy and his wartime strategic thinking regarding the war of extermination in the East.

Throughout 1943, Schmitt and his conservative cohorts privately display nothing but disdain for Hitler, the Nazis, and the prosecution of the war and other actions in the East. Schmitt was much more candid in his diary notations than he was in his public lecture on Vitoria. He lamented the materialistic-mechanistic course of natural science in the nineteenth century from Helmholtz to Darwin's evolutionary theory (descending from apes and gorillas) that reduced man to a mere animalistic creature. He explicitly rejected the theories of the major Nazi eugenicist Eugen Fischer. Schmitt held special contempt for Nietzsche's nihilism – the 'will to power' and concept of the *Übermensch* that he saw as the culmination of these naturalistic intellectual currents. What appeared in his Vitoria lectures on superhumans and subhumans had clearly been developed in his private thoughts about what he referred to as the dialectical relationship between *'Mensch-Unmensch; Übermensch-Untermensch'*. The dire consequences of this dehumanization of man were self-evident in the hellish catastrophe across the wartime world that so obsessed him and Jünger.

From his youth, Schmitt had dismissed racial thinking. Likewise, his fundamental political philosophy best articulated in *The Concept of the Political*, to which so much of all his other work related, was intrinsically non-racial. The same was true of his *Grossraum* theory, around which major debates still erupt over its relationship to Hitlerian foreign policy. Although Schmitt observed the emergence of a European-wide *Grossraum* under German hegemony, his theory bore no relationship to biological racial concepts or wars to establish *Lebensraum*, and certainly not to ethnic cleansing and genocide. In various conferences and publications, the leading Nazi theorists admonished Schmitt and dismissed his theory precisely for its lack of a racial essence.[75] Werner Daitz, the prominent Nazi theorist of a racially based economic *Grossraum*, also made it eminently clear personally to Schmitt almost a year before the invasion of the Soviet Union. Rejecting Schmitt's use of the American Monroe Doctrine as a template for a 'political concept' of *Grossraum*, Daitz proclaimed a 'racist Monroe Doctrine'. 'For me', Daitz told Schmitt, 'Europe, East Asia,

75 Volker Neumann categorically establishes that 'The distance between [Schmitt's] *Grossraum* thinking and the *Lebensraum* doctrine is unmistakable....The difference between Imperialism and *Lebensraum* is also the difference between disenfranchisement and murder. Despite heavy criticism from his SS adversaries, Schmitt stuck to this distinction'. See *Carl Schmitt als Jurist*, 489.

America, or India are not geographical spaces, but biologically founded living spaces.'[76] As he was preparing for his lecture in Salamanca, Schmitt wrote in his diary on 25 July 1943, 'Harrowing desolation…the poisonous sauce of race theory. Orgiastic beacon of Nordic megalomania.'[77]

5 Conclusion

In general, Schmitt's Vitoria lectures of 1944 were a crucial link between his pre-World War II ideas on foreign affairs, war, and international law (including his *Grossraum* theory) and his postwar private commentaries and writings on these subjects. In particular, Schmitt's interpretation of Vitoria's stance on the humanity of the Indians, and on the concept of *justus hostis* in war, possesses a distinctive importance. However, an appreciation of the tone and content of Schmitt's presentations on Vitoria, including revelatory nuances, requires contextualizing them into the concrete historical situation of those years, as well as within the general long-term trajectory of Schmitt thinking on these subjects. Functioning under the restraints on intellectual expression imposed by the dictatorial regime, Schmitt found Vitoria a valuable intellectual and historical conduit through which cautiously to reveal some of his true sentiments and ideas.

On the surface, his statements reviling the concepts of the criminalization of war and punitive actions against wars of aggression were quite consistent with his published work since the 1920s. Particularly noteworthy were his visceral condemnations of American and British wartime justifications and policies. These reproaches were also compatible with the wartime predicament of a faltering regime, and a German nation, facing the impending prospects of 'unconditional surrender', punishment, and retribution. However, nothing in Schmitt's Vitoria lectures reflects any concurrence with the value system or policies of the Hitler regime. On the contrary, Schmitt's identification with Vitoria's Christian humanism, like his allusions to the dehumanization pro-

76 Werner Daitz to Carl Schmitt, 5 October 1940, Schmitt Nachlass RW 265–2740. Volker Neumann cited Daitz's dogmatic assertion that 'According to historical experience, the annihilation and displacement of alien *Volkstum* does not contradict the laws of life'. The theoretical debate, Neumann documents, was between the alternatives of Schmitt's '*Grossraum* ideology or the *völkische Raum* concepts' of Best and Schmitt's SS critic Reinhard Höhn, with 'the majority of theorists siding with the murderous line of Best and Höhn'. See *Carl Schmitt als Jurist*, 488–489.

77 Schmitt unpublished diary, 25 July 1943. Schmitt Nachlass RW 265, 19618.

cess since the eighteenth century, was inherently antithetical to the wartime actions in the East and the racial ideology that spawned these.

The legal brief Schmitt wrote in the summer of 1945 contesting the crime of aggressive war under international law was quite consistent with his earlier writings on these subjects. Equally consistent was his vigorous condemnation of what he perceived as the actual wartime atrocities of the non-military 'systematic murders and inhuman cruelty, whose victims were defenseless human beings'. The 'abnormity', 'brutality and bestiality of these monstrous crimes' of Hitler, the SS, and Gestapo were, he exclaimed, so unique and of such unspeakable magnitude – *'scelus infandum'* – that 'mankind is obliged to pass a sentence' upon them that 'must be solemny [*sic*] in its form and striking in its effects'.[78] However, though non-military in nature, these abominations bore a distinct relationship to the war. These crimes emanated from the long historical development of a 'distinctive inhuman mentality that culminated in the World War of 1939'.[79] Under the guise of the distant time and place of the Spanish Colonial Conquest of the New World, Schmitt had already articulated these basic sentiments a year before in his Vitoria lectures.

Bibliography

Anghie, Antony, *Imperialism, Sovereignty and the Making of International Law* (New York: Cambridge University Press 2004).

78 Carl Schmitt, *Das internationale Verbrechen des Angriffskrieges und der Grundsatz "Nullum crimen, nulla poena sine lege"*, ed. and commentary by Helmut Quaritsch (Berlin: Duncker & Humblot 1994), 16; and the 'Note' in English of 25 August 1945 that Schmitt attached to this *Gutachten*, wherein he stated that these crimes were so horrific that they 'cannot be classified in their real essence by the rules and the categories of the usual positive law; neither with...the old municipal criminal or constitutional law, nor...present international law, that has its origins in the jus publicum Europaeum, i.e. the relations between the christian Souvereigns [*sic*] of Europe from the sixteenth to the nineteenth century', 80–81.

79 Ibid. These comments should not be read as an attempt at a personal preemptive exculpation by Schmitt. For at the time of writing this brief Schmitt had no reason to assume that he personally would be in any legal jeopardy that required this kind of defense against war crimes. The sincerity and veracity of these statements is clearly substantiated by the wartime Schmitt-Jünger correspondence and Jünger's wartime journals. It would, in fact, be a month after he submitted his legal brief before various OMGUS officials even initiated new interrogations of him leading to his internment. See Joseph W. Bendersky, 'Carl Schmitt's Path to Nuremberg: A Sixty-Year Reassessment'. *Telos* 139 (Summer 2007), 6–34. See also Carl Schmitt, *Antworten in Nürnberg*, ed. Helmuth Quaritsch (Berlin: Duncker & Humblot 2000).

Bendersky, Joseph W, 'Carl Schmitt's Path to Nuremberg: A Sixty-Year Reassessment'. *Telos* 139 (Summer 2007), 6–34.

Bendersky, Joseph W. *Carl Schmitt: Theorist for the Reich* (Princeton: Princeton University Press, 1983).

Bendersky, Joseph W. 'Schmitt's Diaries,' *The Oxford Handbook of Carl Schmitt*, eds. Jens Meierhenreich and Oliver Simons (New York: Oxford University Press 2016), 117–146.

Bendersky, Joseph W. 'Underestimating German Antisemitism: the Case of Carl Schmitt, the Frankfurt School, and Weimar Jewish Elites', in *Antisemitism: From the 1930s to Today*, eds. Ari Kohen and Gerald J. Steinacher (Lincoln: University of Nebraska Press 2021), 23–45.

Beneyto, José Maria, 'Camilo Barcia Trelles on Francisco de Vitoria: At the Crossroads of Carl Schmitt's Großraum and James Brown Scott's Modern International Law'. *European Journal of International Law* XX (2021), 1–16.

Best, Werner, 'Völkische Großraumordnung'. *Deutsches Recht* 10, 25 (22 June 1940), 1006–1007.

Chandler, David, 'The Revival of Carl Schmitt in International Relations: The Last Refuge of Critical Theorists?'. *Millennium: Journal of International Studies*, 37 (August 2008), 27–48.

Diener, Roger, 'Reichsverfassung und Großraumverwaltung im Altertum'. *Reich, Volksordnung, Lebensraum*, I (1941), 177–229.

Diner, Dan, 'Rassistisches Völkerrecht: Elemente einer nationalsozialistischen Weltordnung'. *Vierteljahreshefte für Zeitgeschichte* 37, 1 (1989), 23–56.

Engelking, Wojciech, 'The Jewish *Verfassung*, the Israeli *Nomos*: the constitutional situation of the beginnings of the State of Israel in the context of Carl Schmitt's political and legal philosophy'. *International Journal of Law in Context* (2021), 1–21.

Ericksen, Robert P. *Complicity in the Holocaust: Churches and Universities in Nazi Germany* (Cambridge: Cambridge University Press 2012).

Fritzsche, Peter. *Life and Death in the Third Reich* (Cambridge, MA: Harvard University Press 2008).

Gellately, Robert. *Backing Hitler: Consent and Coercion in Nazi Germany* (Oxford: Oxford University Press 2001).

Gross, Raphael. *Carl Schmitt and the Jews: The "Jewish Question," the Holocaust, and German Legal Theory*, trans. Joel Golb (Madison, WI: University of Wisconsin Press 2007).

Heller, Hermann, 'Bemerkungen zur staat- und rechtstheoretischen Problematik der Gegenwart'. Archiv für öffentlichen Rechts, 16, 3 (1929), 338.

Hoffmann, Peter. *The History of the German Resistance, 1933–1945* (Montreal & Kingston: McGill-Queen's University Press 2012).

Hohendahl, Peter Uwe, *Perilous Futures: Carl Schmitt's Late Writings* (Ithaca & London: Cornell University Press 2018).

Jünger, Ernst. *A German Officer in Occupied Paris, The War Journals, 1941–1945*, Trans. Thomas S. Hansen & Abby J. Hansen (New York: Columbia University Press 2019).

Jünger, Ernst, Schmitt, Carl. *Ernst Jünger-Carl Schmitt Briefe 1930–1983*, ed. Helmuth Kiesel (Stuttgart: Klett-Cotta 1999).

Koenen, Andreas. *Der Fall Carl Schmitt: Sein Aufstieg zum "Kronjuristen des Dritten Reiches"* (Darmstadt: Wissenschaftliche Buchgesellschaft 1995).

Koskenniemi, Martti, 'Empire and International Law: The Real Spanish Contribution'. *University of Toronto Law Journal* 61 (2011), 1–36.

Küchenhoff, Günther, 'Großraumgedanke und völkische Idee im Recht'. *Zeitschrift für ausländisches öffenliches Recht und Völkerrecht* XII, 1 (September 1944), 34–82.

Mehring, Reinhard. *Carl Schmitt: A Biography*, trans. Daniel Steuer (Cambridge, UK: Polity Press, 2014).

Meier, Heinrich. *Carl Schmitt und Leo Strauss: The Hidden Dialogue* (Chicago: University of Chicago Press 1995).

Meier, Heinrich, *The Lessons of Carl Schmitt: Four Chapters on the Distinction between Political Theology and Political Philosophy* (Chicago: University of Chicago Press 1998).

Meinecke, Friedrich. *Machiavellism: The Doctrine of Raison d'état and Its Place in Modern History* (New Haven: Yale University Press 1962).

Mommsen, Hans. *Alternatives to Hitler: German Resistance under the Third Reich* (Princeton: Princeton University Press 2003).

Nagel, Anne C. *Johannes Popitz (1884–1945) Görings Finanzminister und Verschwörer gegen Hitler: Eine Biographie* (Cologne: Böhlau Verlag, 2015).

Neumann, Volker. *Carl Schmitt als Jurist* (Tübingen: Mohr Siebeck 2015).

Nunan, Timothy, Translator's Introduction to Carl Schmitt, *Writings on War* (Malden Ma: Polity Press 2011), 1–26.

Rasch, William, 'Human Rights as Geopolitics: Carl Schmitt and the Legal Form of American Supremacy'. *Cultural Critique* 54 (Spring 2002), 120–147.

Roberts, Aaron B. 'Carl Schmitt – Political Theologian'. *The Review of Politics*, 77, 3 (Summer 2015), 449–474.

Rosler, Andrés, "It Had to Be You: Carl Schmitt on Exclusion and Political Reasoning," *Philosophies* 9, 48(April 2024), 1–26.

Schmitt, Carl. *Antworten in Nürnberg*, ed. Helmuth Quaritsch (Berlin: Duncker & Humblot 2000).

Schmitt, Carl, 'Behemoth, Leviathan und Genf: Vom Wandel der Herrschaftsformen'. *Deutsche Kolonialzeitung* 55 (1943), 30–33.

Schmitt, Carl, 'Cambio de Estructura del Instituto de Estudios Politicos'. Instituto de Estudios Politicos (Madrid 1943).

Schmitt, Carl, Huber, Ernst Rudolf. *Carl Schmitt-Ernst Rudolf Huber Briefwechsel, 1926–1981* (Berlin: Duncker & Humblot 2014).
Schmitt, Carl. *Das internationale Verbrechen des Angriffskrieges und der Grundsatz "Nullum crimen, nulla poena sine lege"*, ed. Helmut Quaritsch (Berlin: Duncker & Humblot 1994).
Schmitt, Carl. *Die Kernfrage des Völkerbundes* (Berlin: Dummler, 1926).
Schmitt, Carl, 'Die letzte globale Linie'. *Marine-Rundschau*, 8 (1943), 521–527.
Schmitt, Carl, 'Die Letzte Globale Linie'. *Völker und Meer: Aufsätze und Vorträge*, ed. Egmont Zechlin (Leipzig: Verlag Otto Harrassowitz 1944), 342–349.
Schmitt, Carl. *Die Militärzeit 1915 bis 1919*, ed., Ernst Hüsmert and Gerd Giesler (Berlin: Akademie Verlag, 2005).
Schmitt, Carl. *Die Wendung zum diskriminierenden Kriegsbegriff* (Munich: Duncker & Humblot 1938).
Schmitt, Carl, *Ex Captivitate Salus*, eds. Andreas Kalyvas and Federico Finchelstein (Cambridge, UK: Polity Press 2017).
Schmitt, Carl, 'Francisco de Vitoria und die Geschichte seines Ruhmes'. *Die Neue Ordnung: Zeitschrift für Religion, Kultur, Gesellschaft* 3, 4 (July 1949).
Schmitt, Carl. *Glossarium: Aufzeichnungen der Jahre 1947–1951*, ed. Eberhard Freiherr von Medem (Berlin: Duncker & Humblot 1991).
Schmitt-Hans Speidel Correspondence, 1947–1978, Carl Schmitt Nachlass, RW 265, 15553–15576, Landesarchiv, Nordrhein-Westfalen, Duisburg.
Schmitt, Carl. *On the Three Types of Juristic Thought*, trans. Joseph W. Bendersky (Westport, CT: Praeger 2004).
Schmitt, Carl. *Staat, Bewegung, Volk: Die Dreigliederung der politischen Einheit* (Hamburg: Hanseatische Verlagsanstalt 1933).
Schmitt, Carl. *Staatsgefüge und Zusammenbruch des Zweiten Reiches: Der Sieg des Bürgers über den Soldaten* (Hamburg: Hanseatische Verlagsanstalt 1934).
Schmitt, Carl. *Tagebücher, Oktober 1912 bis Februar 1915*, ed., Ernst Hüsmert (Berlin: Akademie Verlag, 2003).
Schmitt, Carl, 'the Forming of the French Spirit via the Legists', in *The Tyranny of Values & Other Texts*, eds. Russell Berman & Samuel Zeitlin (Candor, NY: Telos Press Publishing 2018), 51–90.
Schmitt, Carl. *Tagebücher 1925 bis 1929*, ed. Martin Tielke and Gert Giesler (Berlin: Duncker & Humblot 2018).
Schmitt, Carl. *Tagebücher 1930 bis 1934*, ed. Wolfgang Schuller (Berlin: Akademie Verlag 2010).
Schmitt, Carl. *The Concept of the Political*, trans. George Schwab (Chicago: University of Chicago Press, expanded ed. 2007).
Schmitt, Carl. *The Nomos of the Earth in the International Law of the Jus Publicum Europaeum*. Trans. G. L. Ulmen (New York: Telos Press 2003).

Schmitt, Carl, 'Über des Verhältnis der Begriffe Krieg und Feind (1938)', in *Positionen und Begriff im Kampf mit Weimar – Genf – Versailles, 1923–1939* (Hamburg: Hanseatische Verlagsanstalt 1940), 244–251.

Schmitt, Carl, 'USA Und die völkerrechtlichen Formen des modernen Imperialismus', in *Die Vereinigten Staaten von Amerika*, ed. Hans Rothfels (Köningsberg: Albertus-Universität 1933), 117–142

Schmitt, Carl. *Verfassungsrechtliche Aufsätz aus den Jahren 1924–1954: Materialien zu einer Verfassungslehre* (Berlin: Duncker & Humblot 1958).

Schröder, Peter, 'Carl Schmitt's Appropriation of the Early Modern European Tradition of Political Thought on the State and Interstate Relations'. *History of Political Thought* 33, 2 (Summer 2012), 348–371.

Smelser, Joshua, 'On the Use and Abuse of Francisco de Vitoria: James Brown Scott and Carl Schmitt'. *Journal of the History of International Law* 20, 3 (December 2018), 345–372.

Stirk, Peter, "Carl Schmitt's Völkerrechtliche Grossraumordnung', *History of Political Thought* 2 (Summer 1999), 357–374.

CHAPTER 14

'An Appropriate Alliance': Situating the Laws of Friendship in Vitoria, Schmitt, and the History of International Legal Thought

Daniel R. Quiroga-Villamarín

> There can be no doubt that fighting on behalf of allies and friends is a just cause of war [...] The confirmation of this is provided by the Romans, who extended their empire in just this way, by coming to the aid of their friends and allies, thereby taking possession of new provinces by the laws of war.[1]

> Should smaller and weaker states be unable to maintain their independence by virtue of an appropriate alliance, they may be forced, voluntarily or by necessity, to abdicate the [right to wage war].[2]

1 Introduction: Something We Used to Have

For most international lawyers, it seems that alliances – to paraphrase Kennedy's quip on religion – are 'something we used to have.'[3] Of course, there is a widespread sense that there was some point in the past in which inter-polity relations were marked by a morass of 'complicated legal procedures and alliances.'[4] In fact, the right of the princes that composed the Holy Roman Empire

1 Francisco de Vitoria, 'De Indes,' in Anthony Pagden and Jeremy Lawrance (eds.), *Political Writings* (Cambridge: Cambridge University Press 1991) 232–292, 289.

2 Carl Schmitt, The Concept of the Political, Expanded ed (Chicago: University of Chicago Press 2007) 46.

3 David Kennedy, 'Images of Religion in International Legal Theory,' in Mark W. Janis and Carolyn Evans (eds.) *Religion and International Law* (Leiden: Brill 2004) 145–153, 145.

4 Martti Koskenniemi, 'The Politics of International Law,' *European Journal of International Law* 1(1) (1990), 4–32, 5.

 | DOI:10.1163/9789004757448_015

to form alliances (and, accordingly, the right of external rulers to intervene in the Empire's affairs on behalf of their 'friends') was one of the central legal disputes that led to the Thirty Year's War and the famous treaties of Westphalia of 1648[5]– an event that led to the birth, in the eyes of many, of the field.[6]

Our discipline, however, has long been attuned to think that this all changed with the emergence of 'modern international law' in the twentieth century.[7] Had not this policy of legalized alliances, after all, led Europe and the world to 'sleepwalk' into the trenches of the Great War of 1914?[8] For that reason, it is not surprising that many of the architects of the post-war order sought to deny any legal or normative role to alliances – as they became increasingly associated with the bellicose tendencies of a previous period in international affairs.[9] If the Great War had truly been a 'war to end all wars,'[10] the international legal order that would follow suit should also effectively be one that abolished alliances as lawful practices.[11] For a brief moment, in the so-called 'interwar period,' there was hope that this might become true. With efforts such as the League of Nations and the 1928 General Treaty providing for the Renunciation of War as an Instrument of National Policy (also called the Briand–Kellogg pact or Pact of Paris in the historiography), it seemed that a sort of 'anti-alliance alliance' might emerge as a force of peace in international affairs.[12] With the eruption of a second even 'Greater War' in 1939, this inter-

---

5 Peter Schröder, 'The Constitution of the Holy Roman Empire after 1648: Samuel Pufendorf's Assessment in His Monzambano,' *The Historical Journal* 42, no. 4 (1999): 961–983; Ronald G. Asch, 'The Ius Foederis Re-Examined: The Peace of Westphalia and the Constitution of the Holy Roman Empire,' in Randall Lesaffer (ed.), *Peace Treaties and International Law in European History: From the Late Middle Ages to World War One* (Cambridge: Cambridge University Press 2004) 319–337.

6 Benno Teschke, *The Myth of 1648: Class, Geopolitics, and the Making of Modern International Relations* (London: Verso 2003); P. Fitzpatrick, 'Taking Place: Westphalia and the Poetics of Law,' *London Review of International Law* 2(1) (2014), 155–165.

7 Ole Spiermann, 'Twentieth Century Internationalism in Law,' *European Journal of International Law* 18(5) (2007), 785–814.

8 Christopher M. Clark, *The Sleepwalkers: How Europe Went to War in 1914* (London: Penguin 2013) 121–167; Olivier Wieviorka, *Histoire Totale de La Seconde Guerre Mondiale* (Paris: Perrin 2023), 21–27.

9 Bernadotte E. Schmitt, 'Triple Alliance and Triple Entente, 1902–1914,' *The American Historical Review* 29(3) (1924), 449–473; Ido Oren, 'The War Proneness of Alliances,' *The Journal of Conflict Resolution* 34(2) (1990), 208–233.

10 H. G. Wells, *War That Will End War* (Redditch: Read Books 2016 [1914]).

11 Arno Mayer, *Politics and Diplomacy of Peacemaking: Containment and Counterrevolution at Versailles, 1918–1919* (New York: Alfred A. Knopf 1967).

12 Oona Hathaway and Scott Shapiro, *The Internationalists: How a Radical Plan to Outlaw War Remade the World* (New York: Simon & Schuster 2017). 120–133. For a critique of this narrative, see Lauren Benton, *They Called It Peace: Worlds of Imperial Violence* (Princeton: Princeton University Press 2024), 3.

war project was eventually refurnished to become the banner of the newly formed 'United Nations Organization' in 1942 – which effectively functioned as a military alliance to end all alliances, waging a war to, this time hopefully, end all wars.[13]

As a result, with the establishment of the United Nations (UN) in 1945 – and the consecration of the 'prohibition of the use of force' as its 'cornerstone' – the question of alliances disappeared, by and large, from international legal discourse.[14] While the UN has developed into a truly universal international organization with global reach, its origins as a military alliance (which shines saliently, for instance, in the UN Charter's mention of 'peace-loving states' in Art. 4[15]) has conveniently been repressed or forgotten, or reduced to mere historical curiosity.[16] In fact, the complicated place of regional arrangements (many of them of a military nature) within the broader UN system was an issue of contention in the early years of this organization.[17] But in contemporary international legal scholarship and practice, these other regional entities have been redescribed as 'sister' international organizations and even those that have a patently defensive function (such as the North Atlantic Treaty Organization [thereafter, NATO]) are rarely read, *legally*, as alliances.[18] As

---

13 Inis L. Claude, *Swords into Plowshares: The Problems and Progress of International Organization*, 4. ed (New York: McGraw-Hill 1984).

14 Oliver Diggelmann, 'The Creation of the United Nations: Break with the Past or Continuation of Wartime Power Politics?,' *Die Friedens-Warte* 93(3–4) (2020), 371–389. See further ICJ, *Armed Activities on the Territory of the Congo (Democratic Republic of the Congo V. Uganda)*, Judgment of 19 December 2005, ICJ Reports 2005, 168. para 148.

15 Charles K. Webster, 'The Making of the Charter of the United Nations,' *History* 32(115) (1947), 16–38, 21; Ulrich Fastenrath, 'Membership, Article 4,' in Bruno Simma et al (eds.), *The Charter of the United Nations: A Commentary*, 3rd ed. (Oxford: Oxford University Press 2012) 341–362.

16 Simon Chesterman, Santiago Villapando, and David M. Malone, 'Introduction,' in Simon Chesterman, Santiago Villalpando, and David M. Malone (eds.), *The Oxford Handbook of United Nations Treaties* (New York: Oxford University Press 2019), 1–22, 6. Compare with Mark Mazower, *No Enchanted Palace: The End of Empire and the Ideological Origins of the United Nations* (Princeton: Princeton University Press 2009).

17 Nico Krisch and Christian Walter, 'Regional Arrangements, Introduction to Chapter VIII,' in Bruno Simma et al (eds.), *The Charter of the United Nations: A Commentary*, Third edition (Oxford: Oxford University Press 2012), 1429–1534; Daniel R. Quiroga-Villamarín, "Holding Fast to the Heritage of Freedom': The Grotian Moment(s) of the Universal Declaration of Human Rights and the Early United Nations (1941–1949),' *Grotiana* 44(1) (2023), 94–115.

18 David Nauta, *The International Responsibility of NATO and Its Personnel during Military Operations* (Leiden: Brill 2018), 86–107; Thomas D. Grant, 'NATO,' in Anne Van Aaken et al (eds.), *The Oxford Handbook of International Law in Europe* (Oxford: Oxford University Press 2023), 501–524.

Jennings and Watts noted in the 9th edition of *Oppenheim's International Law* – perhaps the last major textbook to include a chapter on treaties of alliance – 'insofar as it establishes a system of collective security, the [UN Charter ...] may also be considered an alliance.'[19] We, as a discipline, *may* consider alliances – but we would rather not! The result is that '[w]hen we public international lawyers look out the window, we see a world of nations-states and worry about war[; w]e remember the great wars of the twentieth century.' But we do not *see* alliances.[20] As Simpson aptly noted, '[f]riendship is not a regular stop in the international legal curriculum.'[21]

Our neighbouring fields of scholarship, conversely, have witnessed a resurgence of interest in inter-polity friendship and alliance in international affairs. In International Relations and international security studies, the upheavals of the post-Cold War period led to a sustained interested in alliances and their role in global order.[22] Economists and quantitatively oriented political scientists, in turn, have interrogated the variables that lead to alliance making and breaking.[23] Historians, in turn, have also examined the important role of alliances in inter-imperial competition[24] and intra-imperial consolida-

---

19 Robert Jennings and Arthur Watts, *Oppenheim's International Law. Vol. 1: Peace*, 9th ed (London: Oxford Univerity Press 2008), 1320 §664–666.

20 David Kennedy, 'One, Two, Three, Many Legal Orders: Legal Pluralism and the Cosmopolitan Dream,' *N.Y.U. Review of Law & Social Change* 31 (2006), 641–659, 650.

21 Gerry J. Simpson, *The Sentimental Life of International Law: Literature, Language, and Longing in World Politics* (Oxford: Oxford University Press 2021), 151.

22 Stephen M. Walt, *The Origins of Alliances* (Ithaca: Cornell University Press 1990); Glenn Herald Snyder, *Alliance Politics* (Ithaca: Cornell University Press 1997); Erich Reiter and Heinz Gärtner, eds., *Small States and Alliances* (Heidelberg: Springer 2001); Simon Koschut and Andrea Oelsner, eds., *Friendship and International Relations* (Basingstoke: Palgrave 2014); Evgeny Roschin, *Friendship among Nations* (Manchester: Manchester University Press 2017); Christina L. Davis, *Discriminatory Clubs: The Geopolitics of International Organizations* (Princeton: Princeton University Press 2023).

23 Brian Lai and Dan Reiter, 'Democracy, Political Similarity, and International Alliances, 1816–1992,' *The Journal of Conflict Resolution* 44(2) (2000), 203–227; Douglas M. Gibler and Meredith Reid Sarkees, 'Measuring Alliances: The Correlates of War Formal Interstate Alliance Dataset, 1816–2000,' *Journal of Peace Research* 41(2) (2004), 211–222; Douglas M. Gibler, *International Military Alliances, 1648–2008* (Washington, D.C: CQ Press 2009); Matthew O. Jackson and Stephen Nei, 'Networks of Military Alliances, Wars, and International Trade,' *Proceedings of the National Academy of Sciences* 112(50)(2015), 15277–15284; Charles H. Anderton and John R. Carter, *Principles of Conflict Economics: The Political Economy of War, Terrorism, Genocide, and Peace*, 2nd ed. (Cambridge: Cambridge University Press 2019).

24 Christine Isom-Verhaaren, *Allies with the Infidel: The Ottoman and French Alliance in the Sixteenth Century* (London: I.B. Tauris 2013); James W. Peterson, *American Foreign Policy: Alliance Politics in a Century of War, 1914–2014* (New York: Bloomsbury Academi

tion.[25] We can conclude, with Burton, that it is rather difficult to think about the project of international order without reflecting on the place of legal arguments surrounding relations of friendship and alliance between peoples in its constructions – from the days of the Roman Empire to the more recent centuries marked by the rise of powers which often claimed to be its legitimate successor.[26]

With this in mind, in this chapter I raise a my friendly amendment to Simpson's conclusion cited above: '[f]riendship is not[,]' *in our day and age,* 'a regular stop in the international legal curriculum.' For many centuries, in fact, questions of alliance and friendship occupied a central role in the European legal imagination.[27] If we go back to older traditions of international legal thought – for instance, what we now understand as the early modern 'Law of Nations,'[28] the long-eighteenth-century 'Public Law of Europe,'[29] or the *fin de*

2014); Peter R. Mansoor and Williamson Murray, eds., *Grand Strategy and Military Alliances* (Cambridge: Cambridge University Press 2018).

25 Lauren A. Benton, *Law and Colonial Cultures: Legal Regimes in World History, 1400–1900* (Cambridge: Cambridge University Press 2002); Michael R. Auslin, *Negotiating with Imperialism: The Unequal Treaties and the Culture of Japanese Diplomacy* (Cambridge: Harvard University Press 2006); Lauren A Benton, *A Search for Sovereignty: Law and Geography in European Empires, 1400–1900* (Cambridge: Cambridge University Press 2010); Brett Rushforth, *Bonds of Alliance: Indigenous and Atlantic Slaveries in New France* (Chapel Hill: University of North Carolina Press 2012); Lauren A. Benton and Lisa Ford, *Rage for Order: The British Empire and the Origins of International Law, 1800–1850* (Cambridge: Harvard University Press 2016); Lauren Benton, 'Made in Empire: Finding the History of International Law in Imperial Locations,' *Leiden Journal of International Law* 31(3) (2018), 473–478. See also Benton, *They Called It Peace.*

26 Paul J. Burton, *Friendship and Empire Roman Diplomacy and Imperialism in the Middle Republic (353–146 BC)* (Cambridge: Cambridge University Press 2016). See also Stefan Kadelbach, Thomas Kleinlein, and David Roth-Isigkeit (eds.), *System, Order, and International Law: The Early History of International Legal Thought from Machiavelli to Hegel* (New York: Oxford University Press 2017).

27 Martti Koskenniemi, *To the Uttermost Parts of the Earth: Legal Imagination and International Power, 1300–1870* (Cambridge: Cambridge University Press 2021).

28 Richard Tuck, *The Rights of War and Peace: Political Thought and the International Order from Grotius to Kant* (Oxford: Oxford University Press 2001); Valentina Vadi, *War and Peace: Alberico Gentili and the Early Modern Law of Nations* (Leiden: Brill Nijhoff 2020).

29 Raphaël Cahen, Frederik Dhondt, and Elisabetta Fiocchi Malaspina, 'Training, Ideas and Practices. The Law of Nations in the Long Eighteenth Century: An Introduction to the Focus Section,' *Journal of the History of International Law* 22(1) (2020), 45–49; Inge Van Hulle and Randall Lesaffer, 'Introduction,' in *International Law in the Long Nineteenth Century (1776–1914)* (Leiden: Brill, 2019), VII–IX. See also Frederik Dhondt, *Balance of Power and Norm Hierarchy: Franco-British Diplomacy after the Peace of Utrecht* (Leiden: Brill Nijhoff 2015).

siècle nineteenth-century 'classical international law'[30] – we would see that questions related to the law and practice of inter-polity alliance were central to legal discourse.[31] This mismatch between our contemporary lack of engagement with alliances *vis-à-vis* the central place these issues had historically in our discipline animates the two objectives of this chapter. In the one hand, I wish to recover (as a legal historian) the legacy of these forgotten traditions of legal thought, hoping that this will provide some insights on how to reread alliances back into the canon of contemporary general public international law. On the other hand, I seek to understand (as a legal theorist) how the international legal imagination came to repress or displace the *problématique* of alliance- making and -breaking from the central place it held. One can think, for instance, of how important questions of alliances were for Francisco de Vitoria (1483–1546)[32] or Hugo Grotius (1583–1645)[33] – two figures often credited with being the 'fathers' of the field[34] – compared to its now marginal position in international legal discourse.

An early – and, no doubt, problematic and somewhat self-serving – critic of this transition was Carl Schmitt (1888–1985). As an avid student of the 'classics' of international legal thought,[35] Schmitt came to lament the loss of the issue of 'alliances' as a legal question.[36] This is particularly clear in his critique of the League of Nations, which he not only saw as a deeply offensive military alliance because of its role in the suppression of German ambitions, but also because it did not dare to open embrace its 'particular' nature and instead wore a mantle

30 Martti Koskenniemi, *The Gentle Civilizer of Nations: The Rise and Fall of International Law 1870–1960* (Cambridge: Cambridge University Press 2009).

31 Lesaffer, 'Amicitia in Renaissance Peace and Alliance Treaties (1450–1530),' *Journal of the History of International Law* 4(1) (2002): 77–99; Randall Lesaffer, 'Treaties within the History of International Law,' in Michael J. Bowman and Dino Kritsiotis (eds.), *Conceptual and Contextual Perspectives on the Modern Law of Treaties* (Cambridge: Cambridge University Press 2018), 43–76; Randall Lesaffer, 'Alliance Treaties and the Political and Legal Order of Old Regime Europe,' n.d., https://opil.ouplaw.com/page/952.

32 Vitoria, 'De Indes.' 289–290.

33 Hugo Grotius, *The Rights of War and Peace, Book II*, Richard Tuck (ed.) (Indianapolis: Liberty Fund 2005), 817–847. See also Daniel R. Quiroga-Villamarín, '"Friendship between Unequals": The Brotherly Law of Alliances in Grotius and the Early Modern Law of Nations,' *Grotiana* Grotiana 46(1) (2025): 243–261.

34 Daniel R. Quiroga-Villamarín, 'Book Review: Worldmaking after Empire: The Rise and Fall of Self-Determination, Written by Adom Getachew,' *Journal of the History of International Law* 24(4) (2022), 589–595.

35 See de la Rasilla (in this volume).

36 Martti Koskenniemi, 'The Oxford Handbook of Carl Schmitt,' in Jens Meierhenrich and Oliver Simons (eds.) *Carl Schmitt and International Law* (Oxford: Oxford University Press 2015), 592–611, 599–600.

of fake 'universalism.'[37] Against it, he mobilized his notion of the 'friend/enemy' distinction in his *The Concept of the Political* (1932), shocking the sensibilities of those who thought friends and enemies were, like alliances, something we used to have in the past.[38] By reading Schmitt's intervention – which was published one year before Schmitt's adhesion to the Nazi Party – in tandem with Vitoria's thoughts on the relationship between law and alliances, I unearth the ways in which this early modern concern continues to reverberate in twentieth-century international legal thought. Placing these two, no doubt problematic, figures in conversation, we can see clearly that our field has traced an 'arc' for alliances in international legal thought – from their central place in earlier centuries to their disappearance in the twentieth century.

To do so, after this introduction, I provide an introduction (Section 2) to the place of alliances in the work of Vitoria (and the early law of nations, more broadly understood). Then, I turn (Section 3) to the disappearance of these institutions from the 'modern' international law that emerged out of the wreckage of the global conflagrations of the twentieth century. This allows me to (Section 4) conclude with some remarks on the place – or lack thereof – of alliances our contemporary challenges to the international legal order.

2 'For the Sake of Allies and Friends': Maybe the Real Empire Was Made along the Way

Vitoria's lecture 'On the American Indians' (*De Indis*) has been the focus of much commentary in international legal thought.[39] Along with the subsequent lecture 'On the Law of War' (*De Jure Belli*),[40] Vitoria's intervention on the legality – or lack thereof – of the Spanish Conquest of the Americas has been read, throughout time, in very different ways.[41] For the purposes of this

37 Carl Schmitt, *Positionen und Begriffe: im Kampf mit Weimar – Genf – Versailles, 1923–1939*, Vierte, korrigierte Auflage (Berlin: Duncker und Humblot 2014). In English, see Hjalmar Falk, 'Carl Schmitt and the Challenges of Interwar Internationalism. Against Weimar – Geneva – Versailles,' *Global Intellectual History* 7(4) (2022), 765–783.

38 Schmitt, *The Concept of the Political*. See also Wouter G. Werner, 'The Changing Face of Enmity: Carl Schmitt's International Theory and the Evolution of the Legal Concept of War,' *International Theory* 2(3) (2010), 351–380.

39 Vitoria, 'De Indes.'

40 Francisco de Vitoria, 'On the Law of War,' in Anthony Pagden and Jeremy Lawrance (eds.), *Political Writings* (Cambridge: Cambridge University Press 1991), 293–328.

41 See further Ignacio de la Rasilla, *In the Shadow of Vitoria: A History of International Law in Spain (1770–1953)*, Studies in the History of International Law (Leiden: Brill Nijhoff 2018). See also Daniel R. Quiroga Villamarín, 'Within International Law's Sistine Chapel: José

chapter, we need not to worry too much about locating 'the real Spanish contribution' of these lectures to the discipline.[42] Rather, I want to focus on a particular aspect of his intervention which has not received sufficient attention: the relationship between alliance, friendship, and empire. In particular, I argue that arguments surrounding the obligations to protect allies effectively opened a dent in what was otherwise a rather strict regime prohibiting the use of force save for specific, 'just,' causes.[43]

In his lectures, Vitoria starts by posing the question of whether it is lawful to forcibly baptise non-Christians. While this is a recurring question in Christian theology and governance, he noted that this thorny issue resurged with a vengeance in relation to the legal questions posed by the status 'of these barbarians in the New World, commonly called Indians, who came under the power of the Spaniards.'[44] For that reason, the lecture effectively entailed a comprehensive examination of the legality of the Conquest. And for that reason, it has provided plenty of materials for later interpretations that see his lectures either as a trenchant critique of the Spanish colonial venture or as an early – if somewhat confused – critique of European imperialism abroad.[45] This multiplicity of readings is partly caused by the fact that Vitoria discussed several grounds to dismiss the legality of the Conquest, dismissing some (for instance, Papal authority[46]) while embracing others (famously, the right of 'natural partnership and communication').[47] In particular, in this chapter I want to focus on the seventh just title he analysed: the acquisition of lands and the subjection of peoples 'for the sake of allies and friends.'[48]

María Sert y Badia's 'The Lesson of Salamanca' in, and as, International Legal History (1936),' *Max Planck Institute for Legal History and Legal Theory Research Paper Series* no. *2023–03*, 2023, https://doi.org/10.2139/ssrn.4375880.

42 Martti Koskenniemi, 'Empire and International Law: The Real Spanish Contribution,' *University of Toronto Law Journal* 61, no. 1 (2011): 1–36. See also Antony Anghie, *Imperialism, Sovereignty and the Making of International Law* (Cambridge: Cambridge University Press 2005) 13–31.

43 Tuck, *The Rights of War and Peace*. See further Vitoria, 'On the Law of War,' 302–304.

44 Vitoria, 'De Indes,' 233.

45 For an overview of this literature, see Pekka Niemelä, 'A Cosmopolitan World Order? Perspectives on Francisco de Vitoria and the United Nations,' *Max Planck Yearbook of United Nations Law Online* 12(1) (2008), 301–344, 309–313. See also Lewis Hanke, *The Spanish Struggle for Justice in the Conquest of the Americas* (Philadelphia: University of Pennsylvania Press 1949) 150–152.

46 Vitoria, 'De Indes,' 258–264. See also Daniel R. Quiroga-Villamarín, '*Vicarius Christi*: Extraterritoriality, Pastoral Power, and the Critique of Secular International Law,' *Leiden Journal of International Law* 34(3) (2021), 629–652.

47 Vitoria, 'De Indes,' 278–284.

48 Ibid, 289–290.

While his intervention is relatively short compared to that of other 'titles,' it is illustrative, I argue, of the central place that questions of alliance had in early modern legal thought. Drawing from Roman law and practice, Vitoria concludes (as noted in the epigraph) that 'there can no doubt that fighting on behalf of allies and friends is a just cause of war,' even if one's polity has not been directly 'injured.'[49] In fact, he notes that this is how the Roman Empire had actually developed, as it took 'possession of new provinces by the laws of war [...] by coming to the aid of their friends.'[50] He even notes that some argue that this might have actually justified certain parts of the Spanish Conquest, as it was said that the *conquistadores* signed a treaty with the Tlaxcaltecs against the Mexicans (Aztecs or Mexica).[51] Although Vitoria does not conclude if this was the case (which, in his mind, is an empirical question about the specific provisions of the alleged treaty), for him it is clear that legally there is an unequivocal right – and perhaps even an obligation – to assist allies. In turn, this also entails a claim to the spoils of war: conquered land and peoples included.[52] In principle, the wronged party can only claim an 'equitable satisfaction' that stands 'in proportion' to the original injury after its military victory over the wrongdoer.[53] But when it comes to the injured party's allies, Vitoria does not discuss any notion of proportionality.[54]

This is remarkable because it offers a way of subverting the rather strict rules that limited the recourse to war in the Christian tradition – a subject Vitoria explores at length in his other lecture.[55] In principle, Christians can only wage war in self-defence, and offensive warfare should only be undertaken 'to obtain

49 Ibid, 289.

50 Ibid. See further Vitoria, 'On the Law of War,' 325.

51 Ibid. Interestingly, the Aztec Empire is better understood as a Confederation (it is even called the 'Triple Alliance' in certain sources) than a singular polity. See Barry L. Isaac, 'The Aztec 'Flowery War': A Geopolitical Explanation,' *Journal of Anthropological Research* 39(4) (1983), 415–432.

52 Vitoria, 'On the Law of War,' 318; 322–325.

53 Ibid, 323.

54 This oversight could be justified on the relative brevity of the tract (see Ibid at 293). However, it is telling that in both lectures Vitoria discusses the legality of the Roman Empire noting its reliance on alliances as a mechanism of expansion without explicitly commenting on the limits of 'conquest by friendship' of both slaves and land. See Ibid at 325.

55 Vitoria, 'On the Law of War,' 302–304. See also Peter Haggenmacher, 'Just War and Regular War in Sixteenth Century Spanish Doctrine,' *International Review of the Red Cross* 32(290) (1992), 434–445, 436–437.

amends for a violation of right, 'iniuria accepta.'[56] And as he explicitly notes, the desire for 'imperial aggrandisement (*amplification imperii*)' cannot be used as a legitimate *casus belli* to declare an offensive war.[57] And yet, here is where the magic of friendship kicks in. Even if a given polity was not injured by the enemy, a violation of right to an ally might entitle such polity to wage legitimate war *as if* it had been the victim of an injury.

This justification had deep roots in Roman legal practice and was perhaps one of the ways in which European thought balanced the tension between what Haggenmacher has called the 'Christian doctrine of just war' and the Roman idea of regular war.[58] Indeed, the Roman Republic had first expanded by establishing (somewhat ambiguous, to be sure) treaties of alliances with its neighbouring allies (*socii*) – creating legal relations that straddled between vassalage and 'equal rights.'[59] Expansion beyond the Republic's province, moreover, usually started with the establishment of ambiguous legal relationships of 'friendship' with neighbouring polities. For example, in the Gallic campaigns it has been well established that the Romans celebrated treaties with the Aedui as 'friends of the roman people' (*frates populi Romani*).[60] While the treaty 'emphasized the perfect independence and equality of the high contracting parties, it left no doubt in the minds of other nations that the relation was little different form a clientage.'[61] As Benton notes, while often remember Roman warfare as a series of massive campaigns of conquest, it is worth nothing that these belligerent actions were preceded and superseded by 'smaller wars' which often led to '[c]onquest by agreement of pact of protection.'[62]

Legal relationships of alliance (either as military pacts subscribed between equal powers or as arrangements of quasi-vassalage and protection) were fun-

56 Vitoria, 'On the Law of War,' 303–304. Coleman Phillipson, 'Franciscus a Victoria (1480–1546). International Law and War,' *Journal of the Society of Comparative Legislation* 15(2) (1915), 175–197, 187.

57 Vitoria, 'On the Law of War,' 303; Phillipson, 'Franciscus a Victoria (1480–1546). International Law and War,' 189.

58 Haggenmacher, 'Just War and Regular War in Sixteenth Century Spanish Doctrine,' 437.

59 Controversies about the rights and duties of these allies famously led to the 'Social War' of the first century before the CE. See Elena Isayev, *Migration, Mobility and Place in Ancient Italy* (Cambridge: Cambridge University Press 2017), 311–359.

60 Antony Hostein, *La cité et l'empereur: les Éduens dans l'Empire romain d'après les Panégyriques latins* (Paris, Publications de la Sorbonne 2012) 347–377.

61 Max Radin, 'The International Law of the Gallic Campaigns,' *The Classical Journal* 12(1) (1916), 8–33, 13.

62 Benton, *They Called It Peace*, 32–33.

damental parts of the early modern world order.[63] Benton argues that during this period there was a broad shared understanding of certain patterns of 'legal action' around questions of jurisdiction, protection, and punishment that she calls the framework of 'interpolity law.'[64] In Europe, the Americas, and beyond, imperial powers – especially those that claimed the mantle of being Rome's legal successor – justified their intervention in wars that would have been technically 'unjust' for the sake of their injured allies or friends. The right to conclude alliances (and to intervene on behalf of those one had subscribed a treaty with) came to be an issue studied under the Latin expression of the *ius foederis*.[65] As I noted above, the right of the princes of the Holy Roman Empire to form alliances (and, accordingly, the right of external polities to intervene on behalf of their 'friends') was one of the central legal questions behind the violence of the Thirty Year's War.[66]

In this chapter, I do not want to offer a comprehensive theory and history of the place of the *ius foederis* in international law. Instead, my more modest aim is to show that Vitoria's lectures remind us that questions of alliance – especially as they neatly intersect with the broader thorny issues of protection and belligerent punishment – were at the heart of early modern interpolity law, both within and beyond Europe. And yet, they are largely unexplored in the contemporary literature on international law. While we might hear echoes of these discussions in current debates and international legal arrangements,[67] there is no longer a distinctive discursive or policy-space for alliances in the international legal imagination. This transformation, I argue, occurred slowly and surely in the twentieth century. And for that reason, Carl Schmitt was a first-hand witness and critique of this transformation. We turn to this now.

63 Bardo Fassbender, 'Ius Foederis (the Right to Conclude Alliances),' Encyclopedia of Early Modern History Online, 2019, https://doi.org/10.1163/2352-0272_emho_SIM_017889.

64 Benton, *They Called It Peace*, 12.

65 Ronald G. Asch, 'The Ius Foederis Re-Examined: The Peace of Westphalia and the Constitution of the Holy Roman Empire,' in Randall Lesaffer (ed.) *Peace Treaties and International Law in European History: From the Late Middle Ages to World War One* (Cambridge: Cambridge University Press 2004) 319–337.

66 Schröder, 'The Constitution of the Holy Roman Empire after 1648: Samuel Pufendorf's Assessment in His Monzambano,' 975–977.

67 As for example, Peters notes in relation to the *casus foederis* clause of the German Basic Law. See Anne Peters, 'Between Military Deployment and Democracy: Use of Force under the German Constitution,' *Journal on the Use of Force and International Law* 5(2) (2018), 246–294. Footnote 155 at 268.

3 The 'Janus-Face League': The Geneva Alliance and Humanity's Law

There was at least one burning question that haunted Vitoria and that would become crucial for Schmitt's own thought: who has the right to subscribe alliances (and more dramatically, wage war) on behalf of the 'polity.' While Vitoria would be quick to concede that every private person has the right to engage in self-defence (including *Conquistadores* that had not been provided with proper hospitality in the shores of the New World), for him only the 'commonwealth' had the right to avenge injury and wage war.[68] Fair enough. But how do we identify the 'commonwealth' as a political unit? This was, after all, pressing question for a world in which fluid jurisdictional boundaries were giving way into what would later be understood as the 'nation-state.'[69] Vitoria, drawing on the Aristotelian tradition, concludes that only 'perfect communities' can be considered as commonwealths, and offered Castile and Aragon as examples.[70] This included communities that were nominally subjects of the Holy Roman Emperor, but Vitoria concluded that they ought to have this capacity or otherwise they could not be considered proper 'self-sufficient' units. This did not apply, however, to 'princelings' that are clearly subject to the authority of a higher power.[71] That is, a 'sovereign.'

This line of reasoning will be, of course, familiar for readers of Schmitt. While Vitoria was trying to understand of the emergence of the sovereign nation-state in its early stages, Schmitt looked backwards, certainly with a degree of nostalgia, to understand how this institution entered a fatal crisis in his own lifetime. For him, the early modern age can be seen as an era of the consolidation of 'the sovereign state' as something that stood 'above society as a stable and distinct force.'[72] Indeed, what makes the state sovereign is that it can take existential decisions on behalf of the commonwealth – chief among them, waging war and tackling 'exceptional' situations.[73] This, in turn, places the sovereign state in the position of recognizing, 'in concrete clarity,' the commonwealth's 'enemy.'[74] This is why Schmitt places the friend/enemy distinction at the heart of this concept of 'the political' – which cannot, in his

68 Vitoria, 'On the Law of War,' 301.

69 Benton, *Law and Colonial Cultures*.

70 In other versions of this text, he added Venice or Milan too. Ibid.

71 Ibid.

72 Schmitt, *The Concept of the Political*, 22.

73 Ibid, 46.

74 Ibid, 67.

view, confused with the mere 'dealings and manipulations' called 'politics.'[75] To embrace 'the political' the polity, represented by a state that clearly stands above it and its divisions, must recognize when it must wage war to face an existential threat represented by another polity which is organised in an 'enemy' state.

Like Vitoria, Schmitt distinguishes here between the 'public enemy' and the 'public enemy' – in particular, using the Latin concept of *hostis* in contrast to *inimicus*.[76] While private parties could perhaps defend themselves from their *inimicus*, the decision to wage war against the *hostis* was exclusively reserved to the sovereign state.[77] And the struggle between these sovereign hostile states was not merely rhetorical: they had their root in the 'real possibility of physical killing.'[78] And yet, Schmitt's understanding of 'the political' (as anchored in this friend/enemy distinction) was not, he argued, one that favoured 'war nor militarism, neither imperialism nor pacifism.'[79] While war implied the possibility of the 'existential negation of the enemy,' it did not require it. All that mattered was for a polity to recognize that the possibility of its own 'existential negation' required it to embrace war as the last resort of the sovereign. The specific ways in which war could be waged responds to technological and strategic concerns, but its ultimate logic was that of 'the political' dichotomy.

As Schmitt would explain with more detail later in his monograph *The Nomos of the Earth*, this understanding of belligerency (which he called the 'non-discriminatory concept of war') was ultimately 'based on parity.'[80] The enemy was a *hostis*, but it was also a 'just' one. Or, as Schwab puts it, a 'clean' enemy.[81] In Schmitt's somewhat stylised reading of the early modern 'public law of Europe,' war was rarely waged to complete annihilate the enemy. Rather, the logic of the system was grounded 'in a balance spatial structure of

75 Ibid, 30. Another synonym of this which Schmitt despised was 'party politics.' See Ibid at 32.

76 Ibid, 28. He also refers to Greek notions employed by Plato in the *Republic* to make the same point.

77 To prove this, Schmitt even argued that the personal 'right of vendettas' ought to be suspended during time of 'public' warfare. Ibid at 47.

78 Ibid. 33.

79 Ibid.

80 Carl Schmitt, *The Nomos of the Earth in the International Law of the Jus Publicum Europaeum*, trans. G. L Ulmen (New York: Telos Press 2006) 153. See also Martti Koskenniemi, 'International Law as Political Theology: How to Read Nomos Der Erde?,' *Constellations* 11(4) (2004), 492–511.

81 George Schwab, 'Introduction,' in *The Concept of the Political*, by Carl Schmitt, trans. George Schwab, Expanded edition (Chicago: University of Chicago Press 2007), 3–16, 10.

self-contained states, each with defined territorial limits and fixed borders.'[82] Given that balance of power was a crucial element of the system, one's 'friends' and 'enemies' were rarely fixed.[83] Enmity was not rooted in other aesthetic, cultural, or economic considerations – as Schmitt considered all of these fields to be ultimately subservient to 'the political.' Accordingly, one's loyal ally today could be one's mortal foe tomorrow. And of course, early modern European history is replete of such instances of diplomatic shifts. The possibility of remaining neutral in European warfare, moreover, was also clearly recognized by this system.[84] Although, Schmitt insisted, adopting neutrality did not eliminate the logic of enmity, but it provided a strategy to engage with it. It was, like technological developments and strategic considerations, part of a 'grammar' that was ultimately anchored in the logic of 'the political.'[85]

This – to be sure, rather rosy and unduly nostalgic – picture of the early modern *jus belli*, however, had been slowly but surely eroded by the rise of liberalism as a political doctrine. In his later work, Schmitt traces this turn to Kant's introduction of a concept of an 'unjust enemy' in inter-polity warfare.[86] As the enemy-friend distinction is grounded in the possibility of the existential annihilation of any given polity, branding it as an 'unjust' combatant or denying its right to wage war was – for Schmitt – the same as robbing its people 'of their constituent power.'[87] It is in this sense that one of the most chilling statements of *The Concept of the Political* ought to be understood: '[i]f a people no longer possesses the energy or the will to maintain itself in the sphere of politics, the latter will not thereby vanish from the world. Only a weak people will disappear.'[88] This does not mean that such people will be surely 'annihilated,' but that by precluding any possibility of combative resistance they have effectively recognized that they are no longer sovereign in interpolity relations. Their state has been reduced merely to the status of what Vitoria would have called a 'princeling' – a vassal of truly sovereign power. This is why, in the sentence cited in the epigraph, Schmitt notes that for some minor states the only alternative to the abdication of the *jus belli* by

82 Schmitt, *The Nomos of the Earth in the International Law of the Jus Publicum Europaeum*, 167.

83 Schmitt, *The Concept of the Political*, 34–35. In this sense, Schmitt had a different perspective than other Nazi theorists who saw France as the 'natural enemy' of the German state.

84 Ibid, 35.

85 Ibid, 37.

86 Schmitt, *The Nomos of the Earth in the International Law of the Jus Publicum Europaeum*, 168–171.

87 Ibid, 171.

88 Schmitt, *The Concept of the Political*. 53.

defeat might be to subject themselves to the authority of a Greater Power through 'an appropriate alliance.'[89] This was compounded by the fact that he, rightly, anticipated that the rising costs of warfare 'will perhaps only a few states to survive, i.e., those whose industrial potential would allow them to wage a promising war.'[90] But regardless of whether sovereignty is ceded by defeat or by alliance, the result was ultimately the same. Either a polity is sovereign (and, accordingly, can wage war on its terms), or it has been reduced to serving as another's vassal – either by force or by a treaty of 'friendship.'

This was, in his view, the problem with the 'Janus-faced' League in Geneva.[91] This 'incongruous organization,' which he clarified was neither universal neither even international, was in fact a sort of disguised *anti-alliance alliance.*[92] Despite its rhetorical commitment to pacifism and the abolition of war as an instrument of foreign policy,[93] the League did not in fact eliminate the *jus belli.*[94] Instead, it partially transferred the right to the alliance, as such. And given that the League in fact was 'a certain means of control and management that two leading European Great Powers, England and France, exercised over smaller and medium-sized European states,'[95] this effectively nullified their right to wage war through a bond of alliance. Of course, Schmitt was chiefly concerned with the consequences this had for Germany as one of these 'medium-sized' vassals.[96] As the vanquished power after the Great War of 1914, the fledgling German Republic had not only agreed provide the victors a series of payments as reparations (which Schmitt insinuated should rather be seen as a

---

89 Ibid, 46.

90 Ibid. Think, for instance, of the costs of being a nuclear great power today.

91 Most of his early essays on the League have been reproduced in Schmitt, *Positionen und Begriffe*. 'Die Rheinlande als Objekt internationaler Politik,' 'Das Doppelgesicht des Genfer Völkerbundes,' and 'Der Völkerbund und Europa' are some of the most important ones. The expression of a 'Janus-faced' League comes from this second essay. On the occupation of the Rhineland, see further Joshua Smeltzer and Duncan Kelly, 'Carl Schmitt on the Theory and Practice of Occupation and Dictatorship,' in Annabel Brett, Megan Donaldson, and Martti Koskenniemi (eds.), *History, Politics, Law* (Cambridge: Cambridge University Press 2021) 160–188.

92 Schmitt, *The Concept of the Political*, 55–57. It is telling that he contrasts the League with the Communist Third International, which is much more 'international' in his view.

93 Something that he discussed more extensively in relation to the Briand–Kellogg treaty, See Schmitt. 50–52.

94 Ibid, 57.

95 Schmitt, *The Nomos of the Earth in the International Law of the Jus Publicum Europaeum*, 242.

96 A point he makes most clearly in 1933 in Carl Schmitt, 'Forms of Modern Imperialism in International Law,' in *Spatiality, Sovereignty and Carl Schmitt: Geographies of the Nomos*, ed. Stephen Legg, trans. Matthew Hannah, Interventions (London: Routledge 2011) 29–45.

'tribute') but also accepted a series of limitations to its internal and external capabilities of acting as a truly 'sovereign' state.[97]

This development was not a given under the existing logic of Europe's public laws of war. In his view, the Great War of 1914 began as 'a state war in the old style' – that is, in the same way in which 'clean' wars between 'just' enemies were waged in the early modern era.[98] By the end of the Great War, however, there had been a substantive transformation on 'the Meaning of War' with legal consequences for both victors and vanquished. The Versailles Treaty of 1919–1920 had effectively 'juridified' the right to wage war, famously declaring the former German Kaiser as the 'only defendant of this new type of international crime.'[99] This effectively entailed an abandonment of the old logic of 'the doctrine of *justus hostis*' and instead, in the years that followed, led to a series of measures (within and beyond the League) to operationalize a new form of 'humanity's law' that prescribed aggressive war.[100] But, as it is well-known, Schmitt found this lofty language to be highly problematic – and frankly hypocritical. Given that 'humanity' as such did not have an enemy, the Franco-British invocation of it was merely an attempt to 'usurp a universal concept against its military opponent.'[101] For that reason, the 'solemn declaration of outlawing war does not abolish the friend-enemy distinction, but on the contrary, opens new possibilities by giving an international *hostis* declaration new content and new vigor.'[102]

In sum, the war's outcome had led to Germany's reduction to a 'unjust enemy.' This had, in fact, limited its capability to face its 'enemies,' hence questioning whether it was truly a 'sovereign' state. But for Schmitt, even the way in which this was done was problematic – Germany's 'vassalage' was shrouded in a hypocritical 'humanitarian' rhetoric that occluded the League's true nature as a military alliance. His polity had found itself in the situation he had theoretically lamented: when a 'smaller and weaker state' is unable to maintain their independence and has to subject through 'an appropriate alliance […] voluntarily or by necessity' to abdicate the *jus belli*.[103] As a historical

97 Schmitt, *The Concept of the Political*, Footnote 12 at 31.

98 Schmitt, *The Nomos of the Earth in the International Law of the Jus Publicum Europaeum*, 259.

99 Schmitt. 262. See also Gerry J. Simpson, *Law, War and Crime: War Crimes Trials and the Reinvention of International Law* (Cambridge: Polity 2007).

100 To use, in somewhat anachronical manner, the language of Ruti G. Teitel, *Humanity's Law* (Oxford: Oxford University Press 2011).

101 Schmitt, *The Concept of the Political*, 54.

102 Ibid, 51.

103 Ibid, 47.

example of this, he looked, across the ocean, to the Western Hemisphere. Since 1823, the US proclamation of the Monroe Doctrine had effectively done this same operation at the continental scale – reducing the republics south of the *Río Grande* into 'appropriate allies' whose legal status oscillated widely between equal military partners and bona fide 'vassals' depending on the particular needs of the regional hegemon.[104]

In a way, rehearsing Schmitt's critique of the League – and of liberal international order, more broadly understood – is not particularly novel in our field.[105] What I want to stress, however, in this chapter is the ways in which notions of alliances (understood not only as 'political' agreements but as veritable legal relationships) are central to his argument. The League's legal significance, in his view, could not be properly addressed unless we have a vocabulary to make sense of how military covenants intersected with the laws of war. And in this sense, we see a resonance in the themes argued by between Vitoria and Schmitt. In a way, what the latter wanted to do was precisely defend what he saw as the 'old logic' of early modern European warfare that he thought Vitoria and others had painstaking created against the encroachment of a new 'modern' understanding of international law.[106] In that old framework, as we have seen, alliances had a pivotal function.

And perhaps they still do. Of course, we can sympathise with the feeling of healthy scepticism I introduced earlier in the introduction in relation to the problematic relation of alliances and war in interpolity affairs. This is, after all, the reason why many peoples and states in the twentieth century opted to pursue 'non-alignment' as a political project precisely because of their suspicion to the belligerent tendencies of alliances in worldly politics.[107] But the fact

---

104 Schmitt, *The Nomos of the Earth in the International Law of the Jus Publicum Europaeum*, 281–294. See also Artur Simonyan, 'Science of International Law and Regional Orders: A Critical Appraisal of Alejandro Alvarez and Carl Schmitt,' *Revista Tribuna Internacional* 12(24) (2023): 19–40.

105 Especially given the resurgence of interest in Schmitt in the English-speaking worlds, from both the left and the right, since the US invasion of Iraq in 2003. See generally Benno Gerhard Teschke, 'Fatal Attraction: A Critique of Carl Schmitt's International Political and Legal Theory,' *International Theory* 3(2) (2011), 179–227; Samuel Moyn, 'Concepts of the Political in Twentieth-Century European Thought,' in Jens Meierhenrich and Oliver Simons (eds.), *The Oxford Handbook of Carl Schmitt* (Oxford: Oxford University Press 2014) 291–311. See also William E. Scheueman, *The End of Law: Carl Schmitt in the Twenty-First Century*, 2nd ed. (Lanham: Rowman & Littlefield International 2020).

106 On Schmitt's reading of Vitoria, see Schmitt, *The Nomos of the Earth in the International Law of the Jus Publicum Europaeum*, 101–125.

107 Daniel R. Quiroga Villamarín, 'Ghosts of Alignments Past: Understanding Latin American Proposals for 'Mediation' in the War against Ukraine,' *Bulletin of Latin American Research* 43 (4) (2024), 269–299.

that one would prefer not to live in a world ruled by military alliances does not mean, in fact, that such a world exists – nor that it came into being magically in 1919–1920s. For all his flaws, Schmitt is right insofar that even if one desires that the antithesis of friend/enemy between nations 'will one day vanish from the world' or other 'hopes and pedagogic ideals,' it serves badly these utopian purposes to simply pretend that was the case after the Great War of 1914.[108] This is where Schmitt's discussion of the Briand – Kellogg treaty is particularly helpful.[109] While the 'general rule' established by the treaty was the abolition of war, the plethora of reservations and conditions raised by states to its ratification (chiefly those related to the protection of 'allies' and self-defence) effectively opened a dent in what was a rather strict 'just war' and 'unjust enemy' system. In his words, these reservations (for instance, the protection of the second Polish Republic as a 'friend') were 'not peripheral but essential exceptions; they [gave] the treaty its real content.'[110] This would prefigure later conversations on the prohibition of force under the UN system.

This is why I have placed Vitoria and Schmitt in conversation – as they remind us that, despite our lofty rhetoric about modern international law's role in the abolition of war and alliances, we still remain in a world in which legal notions of 'friendship' or 'enmity' effectively open pathways for violence in contravention of rather 'strict' regimes against war. Alliances are not merely something 'we used to have.' From the early days of the Roman Republic to the Spanish Conquest of the Americas all the way to the current conflagrations between rival polities that claim to inherit Rome's mantle, the protection of allies has played a crucial role in the legal justification of warfare and empire. In 2026, this point seems rather obvious as we are living through a period marked by wars being waged (at least rhetorically) for the 'sake of allies and friends' in Eastern Europe, Western Asia, and beyond.[111] And yet, as a discipline, we no longer have the legal vocabulary to question these legal relationships – and their ominous, and violent, consequences.

4 Concluding Remarks: With Friends Like These…

Friendship, alas, is a famously ambiguously 'category.'[112] The languages I speak are full of idioms related to the relatively thin barrier between friendship *vis-à-*

108 Schmitt, *The Concept of the Political*, 28.

109 See also Schmitt, 'Forms of Modern Imperialism in International Law,' 43–44.

110 Schmitt, *The Concept of the Political*, 51.

111 To use, again, Vitoria's legal title. See Vitoria, 'De Indes,' 289–290.

112 Jacques Derrida, *The Politics of Friendship* (London: Verso 2020).

vis love – and/or hate. Another recurrent expression relates to the possibility of those who are nominally our 'friends' really act more like foes, eliminating the need of having enemies proper ('with friends like these'; *avec des amis comme ca; con amigos como estos*). I wonder if this what, perhaps, what the Aedui thought as they saw the Roman legions march into Gaul. Perhaps the same is true of Schmitt, as he saw the armies of 'humanity' marching into the occupied Rhineland. It is little comfort to know that these actions were undertaken by 'friends' or in times of 'peace.' It also offers little respite for the occupied party to be reminded that it formally consented to these operations – often, through the formal celebration of a treaty that ended 'hostilities.' Allies and friends could be as abusive as enemies, but they also add insult to injury by doing so operating under a complete different legal regime than that of open warfare. Indeed, this is a central ambiguity that lies at the heart of treaties of 'alliance': is our bond one of a relationship of equal military partners or is it a vertical obligation of vassalage in return for protection?

If the latter was true, in Schmitt's view, then the minor 'ally' had effectively renounced its sovereignty. As '*protego ergo obligo* is the *cogito ergo sum* of the state,' once a polity had placed its military defence under the purview of another power, it could no longer claim to really be a true state.[113] The 'simplest expression' of this operation could be found in an institution long recognized by public international law: the protectorate.[114] In this way, a horizontal treaty of alliance between equals could effectively become a vertical instrument of empire-making. But as Benton notes, this was not entirely clear to those 'smaller' polities who subscribed to these pacts – especially, as until quite recently, the overwhelming military superiority of European states was not a given for treaty-negotiators in interpolity relations.[115] And yet, this expansive ambiguity has been rarely explored in the contemporary literature. How did the same treaty permit yesterday's allies to be today's vassals? How would this historical role of alliance treaties help us engage with contemporary debates – say, about debates on 'vassalization' in, and beyond, Europe?[116]

This is why, I believe, we ought to engage with Vitoria and Schmitt in our times. This, at least for me, is not a given. In fact, given the problematic engage-

113 Schmitt, *The Concept of the Political*, 52.

114 Ibid, 52–53. See further Mieke van der Linden, 'The Neglected Colonial Root of the Fundamental Right to Property African Natives' Property Rights in the Age of New Imperialism and in Times Thereafter,' *ZaöRV* 75 (2015), 791–822.

115 Benton, *They Called It Peace*. See further Rushforth, *Bonds of Alliance*.

116 Jennifer Rankin, 'Macron Sparks Anger by Saying Europe Should Not Be 'Vassal' in US-China Clash,' *The Guardian*, 10 April 2023, https://www.theguardian.com/world/2023/apr/10/emmanuel-macron-sparks-anger-europe-vassal-us-china-clash.

ment of these two figures with the political constellations of their own times – to say nothing of their dark legacies throughout the decades – I am sympathetic to the voices of those who would rather have us 'forget' Vitoria or Schmitt.[117] Indeed, having written parts of this chapter in Germany (based in an institution deeply divided by corrosive debates around the uses and abuses of antisemitism in the context of an ongoing war raging in former colony the British Empire was 'mandated' to 'protect') and finalised it in Austria, I cannot disregard the position of those who have argued for us to forcefully 'cancel' Schmitt.[118] Not long ago, in my own institution in Geneva, I felt the need to provide a justification on the pertinence of reading Schmitt's *Political Theology* for a reading group session on secularization.[119] Across the board, 'former' empires are coming to terms with the painful roots of modern academia in the fruits – intellectual, material, and symbolic – of colonialism. As statutes and stained-glass windows depicting slaves fall left and right, should we also dethrone these two shadowy figures from the 'canon'?

And yet, I do think that is something to be gained from engaging with their work. But not because I think we can separate their work from their times and clinically isolate their insights from their imperial entanglements. On the contrary, I suggest we should engage with Vitoria's and Schmitt's work on the laws

---

117 As Baudrillard once suggested we do with Foucault, see Jean Baudrillard, *Forget Foucault*, trans. Sylvère Lotringer (Los Angeles: Semiotext(e), 2007). On Vitoria's ultimately useful function for the Spanish Conquest, see Koskenniemi, 'Empire and International Law.' On his many 'revivals' throughout history (including those that were aligned with Fascism and the European far right) see Rasilla, *In the Shadow of Vitoria*; Quiroga Villamarín, 'Within International Law's Sistine Chapel.' On Schmitt's antisemitism and adhesion to the Nazi Party, see Peter C. Caldwell, 'Controversies over Carl Schmitt: A Review of Recent Literature,' *The Journal of Modern History* 77(2) (2005), 357–387; Tracey B. Strong, 'Foreword: Dimensions of the New Debate around Carl Schmitt,' in *The Concept of the Political*, Carl Schmitt, trans. George Schwab, Expanded edition (Chicago: University of Chicago Press 2007), ix–xxxi; Raphael Gross, *Carl Schmitt and the Jews: The 'Jewish Question,' the Holocaust, and German Legal Theory* (Madison: University of Wisconsin Press, 2007).

118 See, in this regard, the debate at the *EJIL* blog and subsequent letters to the editors. J. H. H. Weiler, 'Cancelling Carl Schmitt?,' EJIL: Talk!, August 13, 2021, https://www.ejiltalk.org/cancelling-carl-schmitt/. See also the replies by Freddy Sourgens and Tara Van Ho at https://academic.oup.com/ejil/article/32/3/729/6433405; https://academic.oup.com/ejil/article/32/3/730/6433408.

119 Schmitt, Carl, *Political Theology, Four Chapters on the Concept of Sovereignty* (Chicago: University of Chicago Press 2005). In that sense, I thank the editors of this volume for allowing to produce a, somewhat belated, reply here in print to that important conversation.

of friendship *not despite, but because* of their colonial significance.[120] For these two figures remind us, in different ways, of what Mayer has called (in another context) the 'persistence of the Old Regime' in modern European history.[121] Domestic and international legal history is often presented as a progressive and irenic narrative linked to the rise of the modern liberal, and secular state – and its corresponding rights-bearing subject.[122] Vitoria was writing at the outset of this transformation, Schmitt at its dusk. But neither was particularly convinced of its inevitability. And the latter, in fact, was quite concerned with recent developments. As such, they remind us that despite modernity's grand promises of a new time, today's castles are built out of the debris of the past. The 'feudal order,' for Schmitt, was not a thing we used to have.[123] Instead, he argued that relationships of vassalage, tribute, and unequal alliance were the building blocks of international (dis)order. That regime was not, in any meaningful way, *Ancien*. Nothing, if anything, 'happened to unequal treaties.'[124] Alas, we still live in a world of friends/enemies, allies/vassals, and empires/princelings. Wars are still waged – and arguments in favour of the legality of conquest are raised – for the 'sake of friends and allies.' With friends like these, I wonder, who needs enemies?

Bibliography

Anderton, Charles H., and John R. Carter. *Principles of Conflict Economics: The Political Economy of War, Terrorism, Genocide, and Peace*. 2nd ed. Cambridge University Press, 2019. https://doi.org/10.1017/9781316875506.

Anghie, Antony. *Imperialism, Sovereignty and the Making of International Law*. Cambridge University Press, 2005.

Asch, Ronald G. "The Ius Foederis Re-Examined: the Peace of Westphalia and the Constitution of the Holy Roman Empire." In *Peace Treaties and International Law in European History: From the Late Middle Ages to World War One*, edited by

120 I've tried to make a similar point elsewhere, see Daniel R. Quiroga-Villamarín, 'Enforcement,' in *Public International Law: A Multi-Perspective Approach*, ed. Sué González Hauck, Raffaela Kunz, and Max Milas (Abingdon: Routledge, 2024), 47–53.

121 Arno J. Mayer, *The Persistence of the Old Regime: Europe to the Great War* (London: Verso 2010).

122 Quiroga-Villamarín, '*Vicarius Christi*.' See also T. Altwicker and O. Diggelmann, 'How Is Progress Constructed in International Legal Scholarship?,' *European Journal of International Law* 25(2) (2014), 425–444.

123 Schmitt, *The Concept of the Political*, 52.

124 Matthew Craven, 'What Happened to Unequal Treaties? The Continuities of Informal Empire,' *Nordic Journal of International Law* 74, no. 3–4 (2005), 335–382.

Randall Lesaffer. Cambridge University Press, 2004. Cambridge Core. https://doi.org/10.1017/CBO9780511494239.015.

Auslin, Michael R. *Negotiating with Imperialism: The Unequal Treaties and the Culture of Japanese Diplomacy*. Harvard University Press, 2006.

Baudrillard, Jean. *Forget Foucault*. Translated by Sylvère Lotringer. Semiotext(e), 2007.

Benton, Lauren. "Made in Empire: Finding the History of International Law in Imperial Locations." *Leiden Journal of International Law* 31, no. 03 (2018): 473–478. https://doi.org/10.1017/S0922156518000237.

Benton, Lauren. *They Called It Peace: Worlds of Imperial Violence*. Princeton University Press, 2024.

Benton, Lauren A. *A Search for Sovereignty: Law and Geography in European Empires, 1400–1900*. Cambridge University Press, 2010.

Benton, Lauren A. *Law and Colonial Cultures: Legal Regimes in World History, 1400–1900*. Cambridge University Press, 2002.

Benton, Lauren A., and Lisa Ford. *Rage for Order: The British Empire and the Origins of International Law, 1800–1850*. Harvard University Press, 2016.

Burton, Paul J. *Friendship and Empire Roman Diplomacy and Imperialism in the Middle Republic (353–146 BC)*. Cambridge University Press, 2016.

Cahen, Raphaël, Frederik Dhondt, and Elisabetta Fiocchi Malaspina. "Training, Ideas and Practices. The Law of Nations in the Long Eighteenth Century: An Introduction to the Focus Section." *Journal of the History of International Law* 22, no. 1 (2020): 45–49. https://doi.org/10.1163/15718050-12340141.

Caldwell, Peter C. "Controversies over Carl Schmitt: A Review of Recent Literature." *The Journal of Modern History* 77, no. 2 (2005): 357–387. https://doi.org/10.1086/431819.

Chesterman, Simon, Santiago Villapando, and David M. Malone. "Introduction." In *The Oxford Handbook of United Nations Treaties*, edited by Simon Chesterman, Santiago Villalpando, and David M. Malone. Oxford University Press, 2019.

Clark, Christopher M. *The Sleepwalkers: How Europe Went to War in 1914*. Penguin, 2013.

Claude, Inis L. *Swords into Plowshares: The Problems and Progress of International Organization*. 4. ed. McGraw-Hill, 1984.

Craven, Matthew. "What Happened to Unequal Treaties? The Continuities of Informal Empire." *Nordic Journal of International Law* 74, nos. 3–4 (2005): 335–382. https://doi.org/10.1163/157181005774939896.

Davis, Christina L. *Discriminatory Clubs: The Geopolitics of International Organizations*. Princeton University Press, 2023.

Derrida, Jacques. *The Politics of Friendship*. Verso, 2020.

Dhondt, Frederik. *Balance of Power and Norm Hierarchy: Franco-British Diplomacy after the Peace of Utrecht*. Brill Nijhoff, 2015.

Diggelmann, Oliver. "The Creation of the United Nations: Break with the Past or Continuation of Wartime Power Politics?" *Die Friedens-Warte* 93, nos. 3–4 (2020): 371–89. https://doi.org/10.35998/fw-2020-0015.

Diggelmann, Oliver, and Tilmann Altwicker. "How Is Progress Constructed in International Legal Scholarship?" *European Journal of International Law* 25, no. 2 (2014): 425–44. https://doi.org/10.1093/ejil/chu035.

Falk, Hjalmar. "Carl Schmitt and the Challenges of Interwar Internationalism. Against Weimar – Geneva – Versailles." *Global Intellectual History* 7, no. 4 (2022): 765–783. https://doi.org/10.1080/23801883.2020.1830497.

Fassbender, Bardo. "Ius Foederis (the Right to Conclude Alliances)." Encyclopedia of Early Modern History Online, 2019. https://doi.org/10.1163/2352-0272_emho_SIM_017889.

Fastenrath, Ulrich, and Donald Riznik. "Membership, Article 4." In *The Charter of the United Nations: A Commentary*, Fourth edition, edited by Bruno Simma, Andreas Paulus, Georg Nolte, and Daniel-Erasmus Khan. Oxford. Oxford University Press, 2024.

Fitzpatrick, P. "Taking Place: Westphalia and the Poetics of Law." *London Review of International Law* 2, no. 1 (2014): 155–165. https://doi.org/10.1093/lril/lru003.

Genin, Vincent. "The Institute of International Law's Crisis in the Wake of the Franco-Prussian War (1873–1899)." In *International Law in the Long Nineteenth Century (1776–1914)*, edited by Inge Van Hulle and Randall Lesaffer. Brill | Nijhoff, 2019.

Gibler, Douglas M. *International Military Alliances, 1648–2008*. CQ Press, 2009.

Gibler, Douglas M., and Meredith Reid Sarkees. "Measuring Alliances: the Correlates of War Formal Interstate Alliance Dataset, 1816–2000." *Journal of Peace Research* 41, no. 2 (2004): 211–222. JSTOR.

Grant, Thomas D. "Nato." In *The Oxford Handbook of International Law in Europe*, edited by Anne Van Aaken, Pierre d'Argent, Lauri Mälksoo, and Johann Justus Vasel. Oxford>; Oxford University Press, 2023. 501–524. https://doi.org/10.1093/oxfordhb/9780198865315.013.23.

Gross, Raphael. *Carl Schmitt and the Jews: The "Jewish Question," the Holocaust, and German Legal Theory*. University of Wisconsin Press, 2007.

Grotius, Hugo. *The Rights of War and Peace, Book II*. Edited by Richard Tuck. Natural Law and Enlightenment Classics. Liberty Fund, 2005.

Haggenmacher, Peter. "Just War and Regular War in Sixteenth Century Spanish Doctrine." *International Review of the Red Cross* 32, no. 290 (1992): 434–445. https://doi.org/10.1017/S0020860400070960.

Hanke, Lewis. *The Spanish Struggle for Justice in the Conquest of the Americas*. University of Pennsylvania Press, 1949.

Hathaway, Oona, and Scott Shapiro. *The Internationalists: How a Radical Plan to Outlaw War Remade the World*. Simon & Schuster, 2017.

Hostein, Antony. "La cité et l'empereur: les Éduens dans l'Empire romain d'après les 'Panégyriques latins.'" Histoire ancienne et médiévale 117. Publications de la Sorbonne, 2012.

Isaac, Barry L. "The Aztec 'Flowery War': a Geopolitical Explanation." *Journal of Anthropological Research* 39, no. 4 (1983): 415–432. JSTOR.

Isayev, Elena. *Migration, Mobility and Place in Ancient Italy*. Cambridge University Press, 2017.

Isom-Verhaaren, Christine. *Allies with the Infidel: The Ottoman and French Alliance in the Sixteenth Century*. I.B. Tauris, 2013.

Jackson, Matthew O., and Stephen Nei. "Networks of Military Alliances, Wars, and International Trade." *Proceedings of the National Academy of Sciences* 112, no. 50 (2015): 15277–84. https://doi.org/10.1073/pnas.1520970112.

Jennings, Robert, and Arthur Watts. *Oppenheim's International Law. Vol. 1: Peace*. 9th ed. Oxford Univerity Press, 2008.

Kadelbach, Stefan, Thomas Kleinlein, and David Roth-Isigkeit, eds. *System, Order, and International Law: The Early History of International Legal Thought from Machiavelli to Hegel*. Oxford University Press, 2017.

Kennedy, David. "Images of Religion in International Legal Theory." In *Religion and International Law*, edited by Mark W. Janis and Carolyn Evans. Brill, 2004. https://doi.org/10.1163/9789047413400_013.

Kennedy, David. "One, Two, Three, Many Legal Orders: Legal Pluralism and the Cosmopolitan Dream." *N.Y.U. Review of Law & Social Change* 31 (July 2006): 641–659.

Koschut, Simon, and Andrea Oelsner, eds. *Friendship and International Relations*. Palgrave, 2014.

Koskenniemi, Martti. "Empire and International Law: The Real Spanish Contribution." *University of Toronto Law Journal* 61, no. 1 (2011): 1–36. https://doi.org/10.3138/utlj.61.1.001.

Koskenniemi, Martti. "International Law as Political Theology: How to Read Nomos Der Erde?" *Constellations* 11, no. 4 (2004): 492–511. https://doi.org/10.1111/j.1351-0487.2004.00391.x.

Koskenniemi, Martti. *The Gentle Civilizer of Nations: The Rise and Fall of International Law 1870–1960*. Cambridge University Press, 2009.

Koskenniemi, Martti. "The Oxford Handbook of Carl Schmitt." In *Carl Schmitt and International Law*, edited by Jens Meierhenrich and Oliver Simons. Oxford University Press, 2015. https://doi.org/10.1093/oxfordhb/9780199916931.013.020.

Koskenniemi, Martti. "The Politics of International Law." *European Journal of International Law* 1, no. 1 (1990): 4–32. https://doi.org/10.1093/oxfordjournals.ejil.a035781.

Koskenniemi, Martti. *To the Uttermost Parts of the Earth: Legal Imagination and International Power, 1300–1870*. Cambridge University Press, 2021.

Lai, Brian, and Dan Reiter. "Democracy, Political Similarity, and International Alliances, 1816–1992." *The Journal of Conflict Resolution* 44, no. 2 (2000): 203–227. JSTOR.

Lesaffer, Randall. "Alliance Treaties and the Political and Legal Order of Old Regime Europe." https://opil.ouplaw.com/page/952.

Lesaffer, Randall. "Amicitia in Renaissance Peace and Alliance Treaties (1450–1530)." *Journal of the History of International Law / Revue d'histoire Du Droit International* 4, no. 1 (2002): 77–99. https://doi.org/10.1163/15718050220957143.

Lesaffer, Randall. "Treaties within the History of International Law." In *Conceptual and Contextual Perspectives on the Modern Law of Treaties*, edited by Michael J. Bowman and Dino Kritsiotis. Cambridge University Press, 2018. https://doi.org/10.1017/9781316179031.005.

Linden, Mieke van der. "The Neglected Colonial Root of the Fundamental Right to Property African Natives' Property Rights in the Age of New Imperialism and in Times Thereafter." *ZaöRV* 75 (2015): 791–822.

Mansoor, Peter R., and Williamson Murray, eds. *Grand Strategy and Military Alliances*. Cambridge University Press, 2018.

Mayer, Arno. *Politics and Diplomacy of Peacemaking: Containment and Counterrevolution at Versailles, 1918–1919*. Alfred A. Knopf, 1967.

Mayer, Arno J. *The Persistence of the Old Regime: Europe to the Great War*. Verso, 2010.

Mazower, Mark. *No Enchanted Palace: The End of Empire and the Ideological Origins of the United Nations*. Princeton University Press, 2009.

Moyn, Samuel. "Concepts of the Political in Twentieth-Century European Thought." In *The Oxford Handbook of Carl Schmitt*, edited by Jens Meierhenrich and Oliver Simons. Oxford University Press, 2014. https://doi.org/10.1093/oxfordhb/9780199916931.013.003.

Nauta, David. *The International Responsibility of NATO and Its Personnel during Military Operations*. Brill, 2018.

Niemelä, Pekka. "A Cosmopolitan World Order? Perspectives on Francisco de Vitoria and the United Nations." *Max Planck Yearbook of United Nations Law Online* 12, no. 1 (2008): 301–344. https://doi.org/10.1163/18757413-90000026a.

Oren, Ido. "The War Proneness of Alliances." *The Journal of Conflict Resolution* 34, no. 2 (1990): 208–233. JSTOR.

Peters, Anne. "Between Military Deployment and Democracy: Use of Force under the German Constitution." *Journal on the Use of Force and International Law* 5, no. 2 (2018): 246–294. https://doi.org/10.1080/20531702.2018.1521066.

Peterson, James W. *American Foreign Policy: Alliance Politics in a Century of War, 1914–2014*. Bloomsbury Academic, 2014.

Phillipson, Coleman. "Franciscus a Victoria (1480–1546). International Law and War." *Journal of the Society of Comparative Legislation* 15, no. 2 (1915): 175–97. JSTOR.

Quiroga Villamarín, Daniel R. "Ghosts of Alignments Past: Understanding Latin American Proposals for 'Mediation' in the War against Ukraine." *Bulletin of Latin American Research* 43(4) (2024): 296–299.

Quiroga Villamarín, Daniel R. "Within International Law's Sistine Chapel: José María Sert y Badia's 'The Lesson of Salamanca' in, and as, International Legal History (1936)." *Max Planck Institute for Legal History and Legal Theory Research Paper Series No. 2023–03*, ahead of print, 2023. https://doi.org/10.2139/ssrn.4375880.

Quiroga-Villamarín, Daniel R. "Book Review: Worldmaking after Empire: the Rise and Fall of Self-Determination, Written by Adom Getachew." *Journal of the History of International Law* (Leiden, The Netherlands) 24, no. 4 (2022): 589–595. https://doi.org/10.1163/15718050-12340212.

Quiroga-Villamarín, Daniel R. "Enforcement." In *Public International Law: A Multi-Perspective Approach*, edited by Sué González Hauck, Raffaela Kunz, and Max Milas. Routledge, 2024.

Quiroga-Villamarín, Daniel R. "'Holding Fast to the Heritage of Freedom': The Grotian Moment(s) of the Universal Declaration of Human Rights and the Early United Nations (1941–1949)." *Grotiana* 44, no. 1 (2023): 94–115. https://doi.org/10.1163/18760759-20230013.

Quiroga-Villamarín, Daniel R. "*Vicarius Christi*: Extraterritoriality, Pastoral Power, and the Critique of Secular International Law." *Leiden Journal of International Law* 34, no. 3 (2021): 629–52. https://doi.org/10.1017/S0922156521000285.

Quiroga-Villamarín, Daniel R. "'Friendship between Unequals": The Brotherly Law of Alliances in Grotius and the Early Modern Law of Nations,' *Grotiana* (forthcoming).

Radin, Max. "The International Law of the Gallic Campaigns." *The Classical Journal* 12, no. 1 (1916): 8–33. JSTOR.

Rankin, Jennifer. "Macron Sparks Anger by Saying Europe Should Not Be 'Vassal' in US-China Clash." The Guardian, April 10, 2023. https://www.theguardian.com/world/2023/apr/10/emmanuel-macron-sparks-anger-europe-vassal-us-china-clash.

Rasilla, Ignacio de la. *In the Shadow of Vitoria: a History of International Law in Spain (1770–1953)*. Studies in the History of International Law, volume 22. Brill Nijhoff, 2018.

Reiter, Erich, and Heinz Gärtner, eds. *Small States and Alliances*. Springer, 2001.

Roschin, Evgeny. *Friendship among Nations*. Manchester University Press, 2017. JSTOR. http://www.jstor.org/stable/j.ctv18b5g18.

Rushforth, Brett. *Bonds of Alliance: Indigenous and Atlantic Slaveries in New France.* With Omohundro Institute of early American history and culture. University of North Carolina Press, 2012.

Scheueman, William E. *The End of Law: Carl Schmitt in the Twenty-First Century.* 2nd ed. Rowman & Littlefield International, 2020.

Schmitt, Bernadotte E. "Triple Alliance and Triple Entente, 1902–1914." *The American Historical Review* 29, no. 3 (1924): 449. https://doi.org/10.2307/1836520.

Schmitt, Carl. "Forms of Modern Imperialism in International Law." In *Spatiality, Sovereignty and Carl Schmitt: Geographies of the Nomos*, edited by Stephen Legg, translated by Matthew Hannah. Interventions. Routledge, 2011.

Schmitt, Carl. *Political Theology, Four Chapters on the Concept of Sovereignty*. University of Chicago Press, 2005.

Schmitt, Carl. *Positionen und Begriffe: im Kampf mit Weimar – Genf – Versailles, 1923 – 1939*. Vierte, Korrigierte Auflage. Duncker und Humblot, 2014.

Schmitt, Carl. *The Concept of the Political*. Expanded ed. University of Chicago Press, 2007.

Schmitt, Carl. *The Nomos of the Earth in the International Law of the Jus Publicum Europaeum*. Translated by G. L Ulmen. Telos Press, 2006.

Schröder, Peter. "The Constitution of the Holy Roman Empire after 1648: Samuel Pufendorf's Assessment in His Monzambano." *The Historical Journal* 42, no. 4 (1999): 961–983. JSTOR.

Schwab, George. "Introduction." In *The Concept of the Political*, Expanded ed, by Carl Schmitt, translated by George Schwab. University of Chicago Press, 2007.

Simonyan, Artur. "Science of International Law and Regional Orders: A Critical Appraisal of Alejandro Alvarez and Carl Schmitt." *Revista Tribuna Internacional* 12, no. 24 (2023): 19–40. https://doi.org/10.5354/0719-482X.2023.72106.

Simpson, Gerry J. *Law, War and Crime: War Crimes Trials and the Reinvention of International Law*. Polity, 2007.

Simpson, Gerry J. *The Sentimental Life of International Law: Literature, Language, and Longing in World Politics*. Oxford University Press, 2021.

Smeltzer, Joshua, and Duncan Kelly. "Carl Schmitt on the Theory and Practice of Occupation and Dictatorship." In *History, Politics, Law*, 1st ed., edited by Annabel Brett, Megan Donaldson, and Martti Koskenniemi. Cambridge University Press, 2021. https://doi.org/10.1017/9781108903516.010.

Snyder, Glenn Herald. *Alliance Politics*. Cornell University Press, 1997.

Spiermann, Ole. "Twentieth Century Internationalism in Law." *European Journal of International Law* 18, no. 5 (2007): 785–814. https://doi.org/10.1093/ejil/chm045.

Strong, Tracey B. "Foreword: Dimensions of the New Debate around Carl Schmitt." In *The Concept of the Political*, Expanded ed, by Carl Schmitt, translated by George Schwab. University of Chicago Press, 2007.

Teitel, Ruti G. *Humanity's Law*. Oxford University Press, 2011.

Teschke, Benno. *The Myth of 1648: Class, Geopolitics, and the Making of Modern International Relations*. Verso, 2003.

Teschke, Benno Gerhard. "Fatal Attraction: A Critique of Carl Schmitt's International Political and Legal Theory." *International Theory* 3, no. 2 (2011): 179–227. https://doi.org/10.1017/S175297191100011X.

Tuck, Richard. *The Rights of War and Peace: Political Thought and the International Order from Grotius to Kant*. Oxford University Press, 2001.

Vadi, Valentina. *War and Peace: Alberico Gentili and the Early Modern Law of Nations*. Brill Nijhoff, 2020.

Vitoria, Francisco de. "de Indes." In *Political Writings*, edited by Anthony Pagden and Jeremy Lawrance. Cambridge Texts in the History of Political Thought. Cambridge University Press, 1991.

Vitoria, Francisco de. "on the Law of War." In *Political Writings*, edited by Anthony Pagden and Jeremy Lawrance. Cambridge Texts in the History of Political Thought. Cambridge University Press, 1991.

Walt, Stephen M. *The Origins of Alliances*. Cornell University Press, 1990.

Walter, Christian. "Regional Arrangements, Introduction to Chapter Viii." In *The Charter of the United Nations: A Commentary*, Fourth edition, edited by Bruno Simma, Georg Nolte, Daniel-Erasmus Khan, and Andreas Paulus. Oxford University Press, 2024.

Webster, Charles K. "The Making of the Charter of the United Nations." *History* 32, no. 115 (1947): 16–38. JSTOR.

Weiler, J. H. H. "Cancelling Carl Schmitt?" EJIL: Talk!, August 13, 2021. https://www.ejiltalk.org/cancelling-carl-schmitt/.

Wells, H. G. *War That Will End War*. Read Books, 2016.

Werner, Wouter G. "The Changing Face of Enmity: Carl Schmitt's International Theory and the Evolution of the Legal Concept of War." *International Theory* 2, no. 3 (2010): 351–80. Cambridge Core. https://doi.org/10.1017/S1752971910000163.

Wieviorka, Olivier. *Histoire Totale de La Seconde Guerre Mondiale*. Perrin, 2023.

CHAPTER 15

Displacing Vitoria? Carl Schmitt on Emer de Vattel in the History of Modern *Ius Gentiums*

Maximiliano Hernández Marcos

1 Vitoria and Vattel in Schmitt's Perspective

In *Der Nomos der Erde* (1950), Carl Schmitt presents the thought of the Swiss jurist Emer de Vattel (1714–1767) as the theoretical culmination – brought about by the clarity of his Enlightenment spirit – of the historical process that led to the formation of the modern *ius gentium europaeum*. This process began at the end of the sixteenth century and culminated in the development of the concept of humanised war. The great merit of the author of *Le Droit des Gens* (1758), in this respect, lies, on the one hand, in the firm confinement of war to European territories spatially organised according to the system of equilibrium between sovereign states, and, on the other hand, in its regulation and rationalisation as an armed conflict governed by the principle of 'legal equality' between those states, recognised as *iusti hostes*.[1]

This new restrictive conception of war as an exclusively inter-state relationship based on the legal equality of belligerents – historically grounded in the *nomos* of European political equilibrium – was developed by Vattel through the concept of 'war in due form'. This concept put an end to the scholastic-medieval doctrine of 'just war' in the sense of 'just cause', and introduced legal limitations to warfare that contributed to its humanisation, thereby avoiding the danger of exterminating or annihilating the enemy – risks to which the traditional conception of *bellum iustum* remained exposed.

If, in Schmitt's historical reconstruction, the jurist from Neuchâtel is celebrated as the final and fully lucid thinker in the development of the modern law of nations from the sixteenth to the eighteenth centuries, the theologian from Salamanca, Francisco de Vitoria, appears, by contrast, at the beginning of this trajectory. In his efforts to resolve the problem of the legal and spatial delimitation of war, he is portrayed as the last representative of the law of

1 See Carl Schmitt, *The Nomos of the Earth in the International Law of the Jus Publicum Europaeum* (New York: Telos Press 2003) 165–166.

 | DOI:10.1163/9789004757448_016

nations of the medieval *Respublica Christiana*, with its spatial organisation based on the distinction between Christian and non-Christian peoples. Vitoria justified the Spanish conquest of the Americas indirectly, through the hypothetical construction of a 'just war', whose concrete basis was the papal commission of the evangelising mission.[2]

What lies behind this interpretation – which is debatable in itself – is undoubtedly Schmitt's attempt to undermine the image of Vitoria as the founder of modern international law, an image that had begun to spread after the First World War. In this respect, he questions the contemporary appropriation of Vitoria's theory of *iustum bellum* as a spurious and anachronistic use of his thought to legitimise, in the twentieth century, a new discriminatory and criminalising conception of just war – one that disregards the heterogeneity of their respective historical and conceptual frameworks.[3]

For in any war that invokes a material just cause – this is Schmitt's thesis – there is 'a latent tendency to discriminate against the unjust opponent and, thus, to eliminate war as a legal institution'.[4] This not only means that the enemy is stigmatised and reduced to the status of a criminal or outlaw, thereby legitimising war as a punitive action, but also that war itself is removed from the domain of *ius gentium* and becomes total war – an unrestrained struggle for the extermination and annihilation of the opponent.

This danger – the exclusion of any legal regulation of war and of the enemy, and thus their elimination as concepts of the law of nations – was, however, neutralised in the medieval Christian *ius gentium* by the 'institutional foundations' that sustained the *bellum iustum* (the spiritual authority of the Pope, the feudal-estate right of self-defence, and theological-moral assumptions). These foundations safeguarded both the equality of the contenders and the legal course of armed conflict. The disappearance of this institutional framework in the modern era, and the organisation of international relations around independent sovereign states – exclusively entitled to both *ius belli* and *ius puniendi* – implies, on the other hand, that any recourse to a just cause to justify armed action can only lead to the criminalisation of the enemy and the authorisation of total war, outside the bounds of legal norms. This is precisely what, according to Schmitt, occurred in the two great wars of the twentieth century.

To avert this threat and preserve war as a legal concept – specifically, as a concept within the *ius gentium* – modern international thought, from Baltha-

2 Ibid., 111–112, 121.

3 Ibid., 119–120, 123–124.

4 Ibid.

zar Ayala (1548–1584) to Emer de Vattel, via Alberico Gentili, Hugo Grotius, and Cornelis van Bynkershoek (1673–1743), among others, defended the formal *aequalitas* of belligerents as *iusti hostes*. To this end, it gradually replaced the traditional idea of just war with the concept of 'war in due form'.

There is thus no doubt that Schmitt, disappointed by the world order that emerged after the Second World War and the creation of the United Nations, invokes Vitoria and Vattel in an intellectual strategy aimed at excluding them from the conceptual foundations of this new 'liberal internationalism' – albeit in different ways. He repositions the father of the School of Salamanca within the still-medieval historical-conceptual context of the *Respublica Christiana*, in which the risk of criminalising 'just war' was mitigated. As for the jurist from Neuchâtel, Schmitt elevates him as the great modern theorist of the concept of 'war in due form' between equal sovereign states – one that eliminated any discriminatory or punitive tendency of the *bellum iustum*. In this way, by relocating Vitoria to his concrete Christian-medieval roots, Schmitt sought to deprive the new international law promoted by American liberalism of the abstract, humanitarian-universalist legitimacy derived from its presumed founder.

At the same time, by claiming Vattel – rather than Kant – as the culmination of the *ius gentium europaeum*, Schmitt aimed to justify his failed project, conceived in the context of Hitler's expansionism, for a new world order based on the balance of strong and equal powers, each exercising regional influence. In such a world, Germany would dominate its own *Mitteleuropa* without external interference, just as the United States did in the Americas and the USSR in Eastern Europe.[5] This plan was presented as the continuation (and salvation) of the classical law of nations based on state sovereignty and the neutrality of war – both of which, Schmitt contends, were violated by the victors of 1945

---

5 It is well known that Schmitt called for the application of the Monroe Doctrine in Europe in the sense of non-interference by other powers foreign to the continent, in order to ensure the new German Reich its domain in the Central European 'great space', first against the expansive policy of the USSR and then against American intervention. See José Luis Villacañas, *Poder y conflicto. Ensayos sobre Carl Schmitt* (Madrid: Biblioteca Nueva 2008) 248–253; and José María Beneyto, 'Camilo Barcia Trelles on Francisco de Vitoria: At the Crossroads of Carl Schmitt's Grossraum and James Brown Scott's "Modern International Law"', *The European Journal of International Law* 31 (4) (2021), 1483, 1485–1486, https://doi.org/10.1093/ejil/chab005. With this interpretation, Schmitt was making an ideological and falsifying use of a doctrine originally intended, in 1823, to preserve the incipient democratic and free republics of America against the colonisation and despotism of the old Restorationist Europe.

through American interventionism and the criminal prosecution of a defeated Germany for war crimes, crimes against humanity, and genocide.[6]

Schmitt thus appears to identify, in the Swiss jurist's rigorous formulation of a modern *ius gentium* grounded in state sovereignty, an anchor point for advocating a new international *nomos* of neutrality among continental powers – one that would permit Germany to freely organise its own European *Grossraum*. Yet in doing so, he overlooks the essential difference between the old and new *ius*: the transformation of the concept and historical form of sovereignty brought about by the shift from the limited classical state to the contemporary 'total state' – a shift that Schmitt himself had already recognised in the late 1920s.

An analysis of the undoubtedly central, but not yet absolute, role of sovereignty in Vattel's internationalist thought will serve both to highlight this omission and to demonstrate the shortcomings of Schmitt's interpretation of the author of *Le Droit des Gens* (1758). At the same time, it will show the extent to which Schmitt, in this case, failed to apply the very historical-conceptual methodology that had enabled him, in contrast, to relocate Vitoria to the late Middle Ages.

The aim of this chapter is to question – or at least substantially qualify – Schmitt's reading of Vattel in two ways. First, it will show that the common order of coexistence between independent states based on their sovereign equality, which Schmitt supports in *Der Nomos der Erde*, is, for the Neuchâtel jurist, possible only within certain limits. These limits are set by the law of nations on the international exercise of sovereignty and stem from the absolute requirement to preserve human society and the community of nations above the arbitrary and unlimited will of any single state. Second, it will be recalled that the idea of an international legal order grounded in the strict independence of each nation results from the combination of the two founda-

6 The nostalgic farewell to the *ius publicum europaeum*, which, as the end of global modern Eurocentrism, is narrated in *The Nomos of the Earth*, undoubtedly constitutes in Schmitt an apologetic and self-exculpatory intellectual operation, and thus clearly ideological, insofar as it is presented as the sad song of those defeated in 1945 'before the altar of jurisprudence'. In this respect, Villacañas has shown the conceptual and practical contradictions of this intended prolongation of the classical law of nations, based on the European balance of sovereign and equal states exercising their dominion over the rest of the world, in the international order of equilibrium between great spaces of power defended by Schmitt, in which the prominence and independence of the European area would supposedly be preserved through the hegemony in Mitteleuropa of a 'total state' like that of Hitler's new Reich, which enforced a policy of violating the sovereignty of the other states and practised discriminatory and 'total war' against which the old *ius gentium* would rise (Villacañas, *Poder y conflicto*, 235–236, 245–246, 255–256, 259).

tional principles of *iusnaturalism* on which Vattel builds his system of *ius gentium*: individual liberty and natural sociability. Their internationalist counterparts are state sovereignty and the aforementioned society of nations.

Yet in his reading of the Swiss jurist, Schmitt makes no mention of the latter – as if the *socialitas* of the human being and its normative implications were irrelevant to Vattel's conception of the law of nations. In the following two sections, these two deficiencies in Schmitt's account of the Swiss internationalist will be addressed as critical observations, beginning with the second.

2 The Basic Pillars of Vattel's *Le Droit des Gens*: Sovereignty and Mutual Assistance

This section begins with an overview of the reception of the two *iusnaturalist* principles found in Vattel's *Law of Nations* – sovereignty and mutual assistance. It then examines each principle in turn, before concluding with a discussion of the dialectical relationship between them.

1. There appears to be little doubt that the most recent scholarship on *Le Droit des Gens* (1758) concurs with Schmitt in holding that Emer de Vattel's historical significance lies in his establishment of classical international law as an autonomous discipline. This was achieved through his scientific and systematic elaboration of a legal-normative order among equal and independent states, thereby culminating a developmental process of nearly two centuries.[7]

Likewise, there is broad agreement that the defining feature of this scientific elaboration was the central role Vattel assigned to state sovereignty within the system of international relations. More contested, however, is the actual scope and function of sovereignty in his system, and how this has shaped the subsequent history of international law.

Until the final third of the twentieth century, the prevailing interpretation was that promoted by Vattel's detractors in the aftermath of the First World War. According to this view, the Swiss jurist, in advocating the sovereign will of the state as 'the source and condition for the application of the law of nations', effectively severed the natural law heritage of his modern predeces-

7 Emmanuelle Jouannet, *Emer de Vattel et l'émergence doctrinale du droit international classique* (Paris: Pedone 1998) 9, 16. The same thesis, although with less emphasis, in Horatia Muir-Watt, 'Droit naturel et souveraineté de l'État dans la doctrine de Vattel', *Archives de philosophie du droit* 32 (1987), 74; and Peter Haggenmacher, 'Le modèle de Vattel et la discipline du droit international', in Vincent Chétail – Peter Haggenmacher (eds.), *Vattel's International Law in a XXIst Century Perspective* (Leiden / Boston: M. Nijhoff 2011) 8.

sors in favour of an 'individualistic and voluntarist', even 'exacerbated positivism'[8] – thereby supporting a foreign policy grounded in power, which ultimately contributed to the outbreak of the First World War.

In this respect, the most extreme and defamatory version of this interpretation was advanced by its Dutch originator, Cornelis van Vollenhoven. In a pamphlet-like text published in 1919, he went so far as to accuse Vattel of justifying the impunity of the criminal state and of endorsing the right to declare war without any restriction, solely for reasons of self-interest – in the name of a conception of sovereignty as 'the arbitrary despotism of the statesman' and as absolute freedom 'to commit a crime or some other injustice'.[9]

What underpins this positivist interpretation of Vattel – beyond the satirical tone and, at times, denigrating rhetoric employed by some of his critics – is the belief that, if state sovereignty is the sole pillar of the international community, then the international legal order teeters on the brink of collapse into the arbitrariness of states, subject only to fluctuating power dynamics and the competing interests of great powers within their respective spheres of influence.

Schmitt, in attributing to the Neuchâtel jurist the scientific merit of founding the *ius gentium europaeum* on the sovereign equality of all states, appears to share this positivist theory, which prevailed during his time.[10] However, his

---

8 Jouannet, *Emer de Vattel*, 11, 142; see Muir-Watt, 'Droit naturel', 72, who argues this interpretation.

9 Cornelis van Vollenhoven, *The Three Stages in the Evolution of the Law of Nations* (The Hague: M. Nijhoff 1919) 26–35, here 28. In his wake, three years later the Belgian Antoine Pillet accused Vattel of having 'deprived international law of any rational basis, both in war and in peace, by making it a matter of the personal consent' of sovereigns (*La guerre et le droit* (Louvain: Uystpruyst-Dieudonné 1922) 33). This critical interpretation, detracting even from Vattel's, was supported by many of the participants in the courses at the Académie de Droit International de La Haye in the 1920s (J. S. Reeves, G. Gidel, L. Le Fur, A. Verdross…), who, faced with the anarchy in international relations during the interwar period, called for objective legal rules to ensure peace between states and therefore welcomed the natural law of authors such as H. Grotius or F. de Vitoria. Its continuation, with less virulence, until the end of the twentieth century is witnessed, for example, by Peter P. Rémec, *The Position of the Individual in International Law according to Grotius and Vattel* (The Hague: M. Nijhoff 1960) 239, for whom Vattel is 'partly responsible for the extreme positivistic conceptions'. On this interpretation, see Jouannet, *Emer de Vattel*, 11–12 note 12; and Gabriella Silvestrini, 'Justice, War and Inequality. The Unjust Aggressor and the Enemy of the Human Race in Vattel's Theory of the Law of Nations', *Grotiana* 31 (2010), 47–49.

10 Schmitt cites the classic volume edited by Antoine Pillet, *Les fondateurs du droit international* (Paris: V. Giard & E. Brière 1904) on two occasions in *The Nomos of the Earth*: first, to polemicise with J. Barthélemy's study published there on Francisco de Vitoria and his new reception, and then, in his brief presentation of A. Gentile, to rely on the

assessment and its purpose diverge fundamentally from those of Vattel's critics: the author of *The Nomos of the Earth* embraces this development rather than deploring it. He does not seek to establish a universal legal-normative order to which all states would be subject, but rather – as already noted – to secure, in the aftermath of the Second World War, an international framework based on neutrality among large spheres of influence under hegemonic powers.

But was Emer de Vattel truly the figure who introduced positivism into classical international law? And to what extent, and in what sense, did he elevate state sovereignty to the cornerstone of modern *ius gentium*?

In contrast to the twentieth-century reception of *Le Droit des Gens* (1758) – a view shared both by Vattel's detractors and by followers such as Schmitt – a re-evaluation of his thought has been under way since the end of the last century. While acknowledging Vattel's contribution to positivism, this reassessment situates him within the historical-conceptual tradition of Central European *ius gentium*, extending from Grotius to Wolff, to whom he remains indebted.[11]

Within this framework, two core claims have emerged. First, that Vattel – following in the footsteps of his teacher, Christian Wolff – did not advocate

---

corresponding chapter by H. Nézard on the Italian jurist. There is no mention, however, of André Mallarmé's contribution, 'Emer de Vattel (1714–1767)' (in Pillet, *Les fondateurs*, 481–601), in which he could have found a broader and more complex view of the Swiss internationalist than that offered by Schmitt himself or by Vattel's interwar detractors. Even his disciple Reinhart Koselleck, *Critique and Crisis: Enlightenment and the Pathogenesis of Modern Society* (Cambridge, Mass.: MIT Press 1988) 41–50, when in 1959 he developed the Schmittian thesis on the Swiss jurist in terms of the political neutralisation of natural law by the 'voluntary law of nations', recognised the importance of Vattel's *iusnaturalism* for its function as a critical reserve for the moralisation of international relations. This is precisely the counter-image of Schmitt's Vattel recently proposed: a defence of the just war that would have led to 'total war' during the French Revolution (see David A. Bell, *The First Total War: Napoleon's Europe and the Birth of Warfare as We Know It* (Boston / New York: Houghton Mifflin 2007); and Dan Edelstein, *The Terror of Natural Right: Republicanism, the Cult of Nature, and the French Revolution* (Chicago: University of Chicago Press 2008)). This interpretation, consistent with the general thesis of Koselleck's book, has rightly been questioned from the point of view of Vattel's reception in the revolutionary era by Isaac Nakhimovsky, 'Carl Schmitt's Vattel and the "Law of Nations" between Enlightenment and Revolution', *Grotiana* 31 (2010), 141–164.

11 In addition to the aforementioned works by Muir-Watt, 'Droit naturel', Jouannet, *Emer de Vattel*, Haggenmacher, 'Le modèle de Vattel', and Silvestrini, 'Justice', or that of Francesco Mancuso, *Diritto, stato, sovranità. Il pensiero giuridico-politico di Emer de Vattel tra assolutismo e rivoluzione* (Naples: ESI 2002), decisive milestones in this revaluation of Vattel's work and role in the history of international law include the two colloquia held in

an exclusively positive *ius gentium*. Rather, he reasserted *iusnaturalism* at a moment when contractualist political thought was in decline, projecting it onto international relations in a way that integrated positive law into his system as an extension or concrete elaboration of natural law, which he regarded as the ultimate foundation of the *ordo inter gentes*. The jurist from Neuchâtel thus appears as a kind of final synthesis of the Grotian and Pufendorfian traditions, inasmuch as he accepted 'the existence of the positive law of nations alongside that of the natural law of nations'.[12]

Second, Vattel's application of *iusnaturalism* to international relations – while taking into account the essential distinction between the *status naturalis* of states and that of individuals – led him to place state sovereignty at the centre of his system and to protect it as a fundamental natural law. This move significantly altered the scope of the normative content of the natural law of nations: the natural duties of nations towards one another lost the binding character they still retained in the work of Grotius. No longer *ius cogens*, they were reinterpreted as mere '[subjective] rights or permissions', so that their non-fulfilment was no longer punishable. As a result, *ius naturae* was deprived of its earlier function of limiting 'the arbitrariness of states, which the tradition of the School of natural law and the law of nations had attributed to it'.[13]

2. There is no doubt that Vattel's aim, following in the footsteps of his master Christian Wolff, is to restore to the *ius gentium* its *iusnaturalist* foundation by asserting the principle that it 'is originally nothing more than the law of nature

---

Geneva and Neuchâtel in 2008, on the occasion of the 250th anniversary of the publication of *Le Droit des Gens* (1758), initiated by P. Haggenmacher and E. Jouannet respectively, which resulted in two collective volumes: the one by V. Chétail – P. Haggenmacher (eds.), *Vattel's International Law in a XXIst Century Perspective*; and Yves Sandoz (ed.), *Réflexions sur l'impact, le rayonnement et l'actualité du 'Droit des Gens' d'Emer de Vattel – Reflections on the Impact, Influence and Continuing Relevance of Emer de Vattel's 'Law of Nations'* (Bruxelles: Bruylant 2010); as well as the *Grotiana* special issue of 2010. A precedent for this revaluation from a historical perspective is the earlier work by A. Mallarmé already cited, which, however, tends to emphasise the Grotian rather than the Pufendorfian debt of Wolff–Vattel (Mallarmé, 'Emer de Vattel', 481–482, 585–586).

12 Jouannet, *Emer de Vattel*, 27. This sort of historical synthesis between a quasi-'positivist' and a strictly *iusnaturalist* conception of modern *ius gentium* is what has led historiographical attention to focus on the relationship between natural law and positive law in Vattel, emphasising one side or the other, or highlighting its problematic and even dialectical character (see Ernst Reibstein, 'Die Dialektik der souveränen Gleichheit bei Vattel', *Zeitschrift für ausländisches öffentliches Recht und Völkerrecht* 19 (4) (1958), 614–615).

13 Muir-Watt, 'Droit naturel', 73.

applied to nations'.[14] In this *iusnaturalist* framework, there is no place for the positive law of treaties or the customs in force in international relations, since such an 'arbitrary law of nations' belongs to history, not to the systematic body of general principles and rules derived from natural law for the coexistence and agreements between states. These positive norms are seen instead as concrete adaptations of natural law, from which they derive all their legitimacy.[15]

By tracing international law back to its original source in human nature, Vattel seeks to establish a common legal order binding on all nations – an order that stands above the will or consent of any individual state. Yet this theoretical position encounters a decisive historical obstacle: by the time of the final decline of the Holy Roman Empire in the Westphalian era, and with the proliferation of independent states across Europe, there was no longer any superior or impartial authority capable of guaranteeing, or acting as the spokesperson for, the supposed natural law of nations. In the absence of such authority, no institution remained to ensure its effective enforcement.

For Vattel, the only way to establish a European legal order under these conditions is to naturalise, to a certain extent, this historical situation – a multiplicity of politically free and autonomous states – by elevating their constitutive principle, sovereignty, to the status of the fundamental law of the new international order. In doing so, a contingent *factum* becomes general and obligatory *ius*. In this way, the principle of freedom and equality among individuals in the natural state finds its specifically differentiated equivalent

14 Emer de Vattel, *The Law of Nations, or, Principles of the Law of Nature, Applied to the Conduct and Affairs of Nations and Sovereigns*, eds. Béla Kapossy – Richard Whatmore (Indianapolis: Liberty Fund 2008), Preliminaries §6. Citations of Vattel from this English edition (new, revised, and enriched from London: G. G. and J. Robinson 1797) will henceforth include only the author and short title, followed by book in roman numerals, chapter number, paragraph, or, where appropriate, page of this edition.

15 Vattel, *Law of Nations*, Preface, 17; Preliminaries §§24–25. For Vattel, positive law is based on natural law, of which it is, according to the ancient Roman view, its adaptation 'to the given concrete circumstances' (Reibstein, 'Die Dialektik', 611). As a basis, natural law must serve as a general guide for customs and new treaties that are formalised, as well as for questioning their legitimacy and that of existing treaties, without these ceasing to be valid for the signatory states, since positive law, as a concrete determination of natural law, abstract in itself, can modify it (Vattel, *Law of Nations*, Preliminaries §9). This priority validity of positive law, as *ius cogens*, over natural law – on which, however, it is based – when they differ, may seem 'paradoxical' today (Haggenmacher, 'Le modèle de Vattel', 20), but it is consistent with Wolff's ontological-rationalist view of the world of law as a unitary and open system of progressive and differentiated stratification of the positions and functions of the legal subject (see Damiano Canale, *La costituzione delle differenze* (Torino: G. Giappichelli, 2000) 39 ff.).

in the *ius gentium* in what Vattel calls 'the second general law of the society of nations'. This principle establishes the respect and preservation of all that pertains to state sovereignty (freedom and independence, autonomous judgement, natural equality) as a common, sacred, and inalienable duty in international relations.[16]

By naturalising sovereignty as the fundamental law of the international community, Vattel thus makes the sovereign independence of the state the central object of the law of nations – the foundational principle governing relations between peoples. Internally, at the constitutional level, the sphere of sovereignty is regulated through the set of duties (and rights) of a nation towards itself, which constitute the core tasks of good government: the preservation and perfection of the country and its state.[17] Vattel devotes the first and most extensive book of his *Le Droit des Gens* to this internal dimension.

Externally, in the domain properly belonging to *ius inter gentes*, the legal preservation of national sovereignty is expressed above all in the right to security and the corresponding obligation of non-interference in the affairs of other nations.[18] International justice, in this view, consists precisely in the equal freedom and independence of all states.[19] The centrality of *ius securitatis* as guarantor of state sovereignty in international relations is confirmed by the fact that any violation of it – any offence, external interference, or territorial aggression – is sufficient cause, and indeed the only cause, for a just war.

Conversely, the peaceful order of the international community would be ensured by the scrupulous respect of all nations for the independence of each state. The second natural law of the society of nations thus functions in

16 Vattel, *Law of Nations*, Preliminaries §§15–16, §18–19. Vattel does not mention state sovereignty expressly here but refers instead to the attributes typically associated with it in international relations: those of the self-government of a nation as a 'moral person', 'without dependence on any foreign power' (Vattel, *Law of Nations*, I, 1, §§4–5), capable, therefore, of entering freely into relations with others.

17 Vattel, *Law of Nations*, I, 2 use consistently same size font for 'Vattel, *Law of Nations*'. §14. The distinction 'preservation/perfection', which he also applies, in Book II, to duties towards other nations, is taken by Vattel – like most of his ideas (including the structure of his work) – from Christian Wolff, *Jus Gentium methodo scientifica pertractatum* (Halle: Renger 1749), ch. 1, §§28–29 ff.

18 Vattel, *Law of Nations*, II, 4, §§49–62. The prohibition of interference is the application of the principle *neminem laedere* to the relationship between states (Vattel, *Law of Nations*, II, 1, §§18–19), which follows from the natural law principle of respect for sovereignty.

19 Vattel, *Law of Nations*, II, 5, §§63–69. Although the distributive justice ('give to each his own') invoked there by Vattel has a broader sense – it includes mutual assistance between nations (§63) – in relation to what is required by the *ius securitatis* it is reduced to this sovereign equality of 'non-interference', of 'do no harm', i.e. to mere formal and negative justice (§64 ff.).

Vattel's system as a genuine principle of pre-established harmony – a kind of invisible hand of international justice – inasmuch as its observance would lead to peace and coexistence among peoples through a political balance resulting solely from each state being left free to exercise its natural liberty in its own affairs.[20]

This theory of the balance of power – or of a republic constituted by the freedom of its independent members – which the Swiss jurist presents as his normative model of inter-state justice in Europe, undoubtedly forms the basis of Schmitt's interpretation of Vattel's *ius gentium*. It also supports Schmitt's attempt to transpose the Vattelian model, in a certain way, into the mid-twentieth century by promoting a new world order founded on the neutrality – or *laissez-faire* – of sovereign states within large spheres of influence.

For Vattel, however, this theory still represents a rationalist ideal: the ideal of a community of virtuous sovereigns who always act in accordance with the natural laws of justice, producing order and peace automatically, without deviation, as the result of a natural mechanism that functions properly only when each part adheres strictly to its programmed role. This normative vision might be plausible if the international order depended solely on the regulation of sovereignty as an object of law. Yet the true significance – and indeed the problematic character – of sovereignty as the foundational pillar of Vattel's *Le Droit des Gens* (1758) lies in the fact that sovereignty also constitutes the subject of international law. In fact, the legal-objective preservation of the independence of each state – understood as the fundamental law of the international community – serves precisely to enable sovereignty to assume this new role as the sole subject of *ius gentium*.[21]

The importance of this conceptual *novum* for classical international law must be clarified. In the Vattelian model, the significance of sovereignty as a subject does not lie in its role as a source of international norms, since the positive law of treaties and international customs – 'conventional law' and 'customary law' – that is, the historical 'arbitrary law of nations', voluntarily agreed upon by some or most sovereign states, is excluded from the system.

20 Vattel himself represents this idea of international justice as a concord of mere sovereign abstention or neutrality in Europe with the image of a republic of the balance of independent powers (*Law of Nations*, III, 3, §47), which translates to the level of the law of nations the doctrine of the pre-established harmony between the isolated monads of Leibniz (see Haggenmacher, 'Le modèle de Vattel', 33), whose philosophy he fervently advocated.

21 Haggenmacher, 'Le modèle de Vattel', 24–26, underlines that this conversion of sovereignty – hitherto reduced to the supreme power within a state – into a subject of international law is the great novelty of Vattel in comparison with his modern predecessors.

Rather, sovereignty plays a central role as the subject of application of the natural law of nations: that 'necessary and immutable' law of the 'just and good in itself', which 'nations and sovereigns are bound to respect and follow in all their actions' because it 'immediately comes from nature'.[22]

Instead of paving the way for positivism *tout court* by making the sovereign will of individual states the exclusive source of international law, Vattel seeks to subordinate that will to a minimum framework of common rules. These rules would, in his view, put an end to the anarchy prevailing in international power relations after the Peace of Westphalia (1648) and allow for the creation of a genuine legal order of coexistence among nations. He places his trust in the revival of the old natural law and its set of universal rights and duties applicable to all states. However, he entrusts the execution and interpretation of these norms to the sovereign will of each individual state, which thus becomes the exclusive interpreter and unchallengeable judge of these general and abstract principles in their application to specific historical or empirical situations.

In this way, sovereigns are afforded a wide margin of flexibility in acting in accordance with natural law, with the resulting risk of arbitrary or even manifestly unjust decisions. This is not merely an empirical problem – dependent on the degree of wisdom and enlightened education of each prince – but, above all, a structural one inherent to Vattel's own theory. It leaves the concrete definition of the natural duties and rights between states entirely at the mercy of the sovereign will.

Vattel indeed maintains that the natural law of nations binds each nation only to the extent that it is consciously accepted, and therefore he qualifies it as 'internal law', borrowing an expression from Grotius. Since every state is free and independent, each possesses full autonomy of judgement in interpreting and applying the rights and duties derived from natural law. In every situation, it may decide for itself what its duty requires, and 'what it is proper or improper for it to do', without any other state being entitled to compel it to act otherwise – or even to judge the 'intrinsic justice' of its conduct, as such a judgement would infringe upon its sovereign freedom.[23]

This radically individualistic subjectivisation applies not only to the duties of each nation towards itself but also to its duties towards others. Compliance

22 Vattel, *Law of Nations*, Preface, 17; see also Preliminaries §7.

23 Vattel, *Law of Nations*, Preliminaries §16, §§20–21. The abstention from judgement on the unjust conduct of another nation is a restriction imposed by the 'voluntary law of nations', which binds not in conscience but, like positive law, on the basis of what is agreed with others – enforceable by the will of others ('external law') (Vattel, *Law of Nations*, Preliminaries §17).

or non-compliance with such duties likewise depends entirely on the sovereign judgement of the state in question. No other state – whether the one requesting assistance or a third party – has the right to compel or sanction it. In the same vein, all states must endure, without the possibility of intervention, even those acts committed by a sovereign against its own people that they consider 'unjust and condemnable in themselves'.

With this 'unilateral and discretionary regime' in the application of the natural *ius gentium* by sovereign princes, the Hobbesian state of nature – in which each individual is the sole judge of his own actions – is reproduced at the international level. And, as in the domestic state of nature, the arbitrariness of sovereign decisions and the likelihood of conflict between states over their competing interpretations of rights, or alleged violations of them, are equally foreseeable – especially in cases where the *ius securitatis* of each state is at stake.[24]

3. That said, alongside sovereignty as the second fundamental law of *ius gentium* – the unfolding of which reveals the Hobbesian aspect of Vattel's *iusnaturalist* system – the *Preliminaries* to *Le Droit des Gens* (1758) also establish another foundational principle. This is presented as the 'first general law' of the natural society of nations: the principle of mutual assistance, according to which 'each individual nation is bound to contribute with everything in its power to the happiness and perfection of all the others'.[25]

This fundamental obligation of mutual aid – referred to in modern terminology as the duty or 'law of solidarity' – has been largely overlooked, or even marginalised, in the reception of Vattel's thought within international legal scholarship. That reception has focused almost exclusively – as shown above – on the centrality of the principle of sovereignty, arguably shaped by the power politics that have defined relations between states during the era of so-called 'classical international law'.[26]

24 On this unilateral regime of specific determination of what is just and unjust, and its potential for conflict due to the frequent confusion between one's own right and self-interest, see Haggenmacher, 'Le modèle de Vattel', 37–38; Muir-Watt, 'Droit naturel', 78.

25 Vattel, *Law of Nations*, Preliminaries §§13 and 12.

26 Only recently has its importance in Vattel's *ius gentium* been emphasised and defended by the work of Heinhard Steiger, 'Solidarität und Souveränität oder Vattel reconsidered', in H. Steiger, *Von der Staatengesellschaft zur Weltrepublik? Aufsätze zur Geschichte* (Baden-Baden: Nomos Verlag 2009) 133–141; and Petter Korkman, 'L'amour universel du genre humain comme fondement des relations internationales chez de Vattel', in Sandoz (ed.), *Réflexions sur l'impact*, 23–29.

Schmitt does not mention this principle at all in *The Nomos of the Earth*. Yet it constitutes not only a central object of the law of nations – inasmuch as it underpins and delimits the principal domain of international regulation, namely, the duties and rights of nations towards one another, to which Vattel devotes the second book of his treatise[27] – but also the final aim of his *ius gentium*: the material purpose that gives meaning to the very existence of a legal order among states, that is, a genuine 'natural society of nations'.

It is important, therefore, to highlight this teleological function of the *iusnaturalist* law of mutual assistance and to clarify its implications for the international order Vattel envisions, as a principle grounded in human nature itself.

Whereas the law of sovereignty translates into inter-state relations the natural freedom of individuals – modified, of course, to suit the distinct character of states – the law of mutual assistance, by contrast, reproduces at the international level the corresponding obligation that arises from the inherently social existence of human beings. It may therefore be described as the law of sociability – both of human nature and of the international community. It is not without reason that Vattel refers to this as the law of 'the natural society established among the human race'. Following his teacher Wolff, he attributes to it both ontological and ethical significance: it is grounded, on the one hand, in the social being or destiny of humankind and, on the other, it is formulated

27 For Vattel, *ius inter gentes* consists of two types of duties: the merely negative or prohibitive ones (duties/rights of non-interference), linked to the 'right of security' or sovereignty of each nation, which result from the application of the principle *neminem laedere* to interstate relations and which are, strictly speaking, the 'voluntary law of nations' (Vattel, *Law of Nations*, II, 1, §§18–19; II, 4, §§49 ff.); and the properly *iusnatural* and positive ones, which command actions of aid to other countries in relation to the two fundamental duties of each nation towards itself: preservation and perfection. Aid to preservation consists of duties both of defending any unjustly attacked neighbouring state and of offering humanitarian assistance in cases of natural or social catastrophe (Vattel, *Law of Nations*, II, 1, §§4–5), as well as the duty/right of mutual trade (II, 2, §§21–34). Aid to perfection involves the duty to contribute, if required, to the civilisation of another nation by providing educational means, by serving as a virtuous example for imitation, by safeguarding its public glory and honour (II, 1, §§6–14), and by respecting its 'dignity' and 'majesty' as an equally sovereign nation (II, 3, §§35 ff.). In addition, there is another series of international mutual duties/rights which we might call – Vattel does not – 'cosmopolitan', relating to the movement and residence of human beings and the common use of things (rights of foreigners, right of necessity, right of innocent use) (II, 8–10).

as a normative imperative to cultivate and promote the 'universal society of the human race'.[28]

At the same time, this law of sociability – universally binding on human beings – is also the foundational law of the 'natural society of nations'. This is not only because states inherit a large portion of the natural rights and obligations of individuals through the social contract, but also because states themselves, as 'moral persons', must relate to other states – and to the individuals within them – according to the same natural laws that govern relations within human society. Hence, the *inter gentes* rights and duties derived from the first natural law of the society of nations are also – explicitly and by name – designated as the 'offices and rights of humanity'.[29]

The significance of this first *iusnaturalist* principle must be considered in order to understand the ultimate aim pursued by the Swiss thinker's law of nations. The fact that the law which regulates and enables social life among individuals becomes the fundamental norm governing relations between nations indicates that Vattel conceives *ius gentium* as a normative order of solidarity between peoples. Its aim is to strengthen mutual sociability and to consolidate the shared bonds of interdependence and cooperation.

This vision implies a shift both in the epistemological conception of the law of nations and in the very meaning of the international legal order. From a scientific standpoint, the epistemic object of *ius gentium* in Vattel – its material content – is broader than that of its first classical referent, Hugo Grotius. It

---

28 Vattel, *Law of Nations*, Preliminaries §§10–12. Unlike Hobbes, for Vattel the state of nature is intrinsically social – not because of a sociable instinct linked to human rationality (as in H. Grotius), but because of biological neediness: individuals must enter into society to obtain help in achieving the natural end of their own happiness, including the satisfaction of both physical (preservation) and intellectual (perfection) needs (*Law of Nations*, Preliminaries §6 note, §10; see Preface, 14). Thus, the final foundation of all obligations and virtues is self-love (or desire for happiness) and utility, broadly understood as that which contributes to one's general perfection (see Emer de Vattel, 'Essay on the Foundation of Natural Law and on the First Principle of the Obligation Men Find Themselves Under to Observe Laws', §§20–21, in *Law of Nations*, 753–754). Sociability, love, and moral laws serve egoism, but the individual's own good is in turn inseparable from the collective good. For Vattel, helping others and showing solidarity is the intelligent form of selfishness. On this relationship between sociability and self-love, see Korkman, 'L'amour universel', 24–27; Jouannet, *Emer de Vattel*, 147–149; Haggenmacher, 'Le modèle de Vattel', 29–30. Vattel follows Wolff on this point, from whom he also borrows the notions of the 'society of the human race' (*societas naturalis magna inter homines instituta* – Christian Wolff, *Jus naturae methodo scientifica pertractatum* (Halle: Renger 1747), VII, ch. 1, §142 ff.) and the 'natural society of nations' (*societas a natura inter gentes instituta* – Wolff, *Jus gentium*, Prolegomena §7).

29 Vattel, *Law of Nations*, II, 1, §2.

is no longer centred on war, but rather on the regulation of what Vattel calls the 'most normal order of relations between nations', in which war appears as an exceptional situation: a temporary disruption of peaceful relations that, in Vattel's treatment, requires only one of the four books of *Le Droit des Gens* – Book III.[30]

In turn, from a normative perspective, the 'international normality' addressed by this new science is not merely conceived as a minimal order of monadological coexistence between sovereign states. Instead, it is envisaged as a more qualified order of cooperation – one that enables the formation of a common society oriented towards the 'welfare, development, and perfection' of all nations and of the human race as a whole.[31]

The aim is not merely to achieve a legal order that, by applying the principle of *neminem laedere* to international relations, protects the security rights of each sovereign state and channels armed conflicts towards the restoration of stability. In contrast to this minimalist conception of *ius gentium* as a system of formal and negative justice – focused on preserving independence and equality among nations, avoiding harm and interference, and adhering to the principle of sovereignty – the *iusnaturalist* law of mutual assistance calls for a legal order of material and positive justice. Through the rights and duties of solidarity, such an order would collectively ensure mutual aid, exchange, and communication between all states (and their citizens), based on the needs and resources of each.

Just as the scrupulous observance of the second natural law of the 'society of nations' leads Vattel, in Book III, to depict the preventive justice of war through the image of a European republic founded on the balance of power, so too does the implementation of the first natural law of solidarity evoke, in Book II, the image of a worldwide republic of fraternity. This republic would express social justice among peoples by linking, as Cicero suggests, the particular good of each state with the common good of international society.[32]

That this is a normative ideal of *ius gentium*, grounded in the inherently social nature of the human being, is confirmed by Vattel's own admission

30 Mallarmé, 'Emer de Vattel', 587–588; see Steiger, 'Solidarität', 141.

31 Steiger, 'Solidarität', 140–141. Vattel's international law is thus not limited to the logic of 'coexistence'; contra Haggenmacher, 'Le modèle de Vattel', 46.

32 Vattel, *Law of Nations*, II, 1, §16; II, 6, §72. Vattel aspires to an equitable justice between peoples – the basis of all human society – which materially realises the principle *suum cuique tribuere*. It is not by chance that the law of mutual assistance is the application, within the *ius gentium* and following Wolff, of the idea of justice as *caritas sapientis*, with which Leibniz sought to ground a Christian natural law of love for one's neighbour; see Steiger, 'Solidarität', 138–140.

that it remains a 'beautiful dream' – distant from the realities of power politics among the European princes of his time.[33] Indeed, this ideal of an international *ius gentium* based on cooperation – rather than mere coexistence – could only become a reality if nations were to conduct their relations under the benevolent impulse of the two inseparable passions that sustain sociability and mutual assistance: love and friendship.[34]

4. The invocation of love not only as the foundation or source of the legal order of cooperation between nations, demanded by human nature, but above all as the essential condition for achieving it – without which the ultimate goal of *ius gentium*, however necessary and normative, remains a beautiful utopia – reveals the tragic dimension of Emer de Vattel's internationalist vision.[35]

This tragedy arises not so much from theory as from praxis. It is rooted less in the normative structure that governs relations between nations – based on two natural principles and passions that are difficult to reconcile, though inseparable (the law of sociability and the law of individual liberty, altruism and self-love) – than in the practical execution of the two types of duties and rights derived from them.

At the level of their application, there emerges a fundamental asymmetry between the two principles and their respective spheres of legal regulation. In the absence of an authority superior to the plurality of nations, the subject responsible for complying with the law of nations and ensuring its fulfilment – namely, the individual state – is structurally predisposed to favour one of the principles. That subject belongs to the legal sphere defined by the law of sovereignty and is therefore subject to it above all. In other words, for any sovereign state, the duties a nation owes to itself always take precedence over the duties it owes to others when these come into conflict or tension.[36]

In such cases, the specific determination of priority – and the fulfilment or non-fulfilment of a given duty – depends entirely on the sovereign's own judgement. This judgement, in turn, is shaped by a range of empirical variables, among which the personal management of individual passions and the perception of national interest play a decisive role.

33 Vattel, *Law of Nations*, II, 1, §16; see §1.

34 Vattel, *Law of Nations*, II, 1, §§11–12.

35 See Korkman, 'L'amour universel', 28–29.

36 Vattel, *Law of Nations*, Preliminaries §14. This priority certainly reflects the primacy of egoism over altruism in human nature (see note 28), but it is also due to the fact that states, as *societates perfectae*, are almost self-sufficient and thus require mutual assistance less than individuals (Vattel, *Law of Nations*, II, 1, §3; see Preface, 15).

The tragedy of a law of nations intended to regulate peaceful and fraternal collaboration among peoples – but which, in practice, is reduced to preserving the balance of power, if not outright to justifying war – lies, for Vattel, in the intrinsic dialectic between the sociable law of mutual assistance and the individualistic law of state sovereignty. Yet the resolution of this dialectic is tragic not because the two duties are logically incompatible, but because of the asymmetry in their practical realisation, which stems from the partiality of the subject entrusted with enforcing both principles.

Yet this tragic outcome does not negate or invalidate the duties of solidarity.[37] On the contrary, they retain their legal-normative force for international actors as the ideal *telos* and ultimate meaning of *ius gentium*. In practice, however, they remain in this state of ideality in an almost Sisyphean fashion, constrained by the inescapable tragic structure imposed by the historical reality of the law of sovereignty. This outcome results not only from the *iusnaturalist* priority of each nation's duties towards itself over those owed to others, but even more from the non-coercive nature of the latter.

The fulfilment of mutual assistance among nations depends not only on the sovereign will of each individual state, but also on the fact that no nation can be compelled by force to carry out such duties. For Vattel, these duties constitute an *ius imperfectum*, meaning that any state in need has only a 'right to request' aid from others, not a right to compel them to provide it. Failure to fulfil such duties, therefore, is not considered an injustice, but merely a lack of equity.[38]

By contrast, the duties and rights associated with the respect for each state's sovereign freedom – which, in international relations, are governed by the principle of *neminem laedere* and make up the 'right of security' – constitute

37 This insuperable tension between solidarity and sovereignty constitutes the genuine radical, *iusnaturalist* dialectic of Vattel's law of nations; the supposed dialectic between natural and positive law (Reibstein, 'Die Dialektik') is such only for sovereignty (it concerns the 'voluntary law of nations'), and is, strictly speaking, simply an expression of the Wolffian-Vattelian conception of the legal order as a unitary process of differentiated stratification, including specific variation and modification (see note 15).

38 Vattel, *Law of Nations*, II, 1, §§8–10; Preliminaries §17. It is not correct to interpret the distinction *ius imperfectum/perfectum* from Pufendorf in terms of a moral/law difference, as is often done, neither from the historical-conceptual perspective nor in terms of what is delimited in each case, because it does not correspond to the distinction 'internal/external', but is rather a distinction about the enforceability of the law itself (Steiger, 'Solidarität', 137). Hence, it is not only plausible, but even a normative-historical task of states – such would be the political effect of the solidarity/sovereignty dialectic – to turn 'imperfect' duties of humanity into 'perfect' international duties through their positivisation, as Steiger suggests (Steiger, 'Solidarität', 137, 141).

an *ius perfectum*, or strict right. Non-compliance in this domain is regarded as *iniuria* or 'injustice', and therefore grants the injured party a legitimate power to resort to external coercion, including war, against the offending state.

Through this distinction between 'perfect and imperfect rights', Vattel underscores the difference in enforceability between the law of sovereign power and the law of solidarity. In doing so, he reveals the extent to which his noble attempt to formulate an international legal order of cooperation – under historical conditions dominated by the exclusive regime of state sovereignty – is ultimately threatened by failure.

Does the recognition of state sovereignty as the sole subjective and unilateral agent for the realisation of the natural *ius gentium* therefore imply that international relations are left entirely to the arbitrary and unlimited despotism of each state – to the ambition for power of its prince and his desire for hegemonic expansion, as Vattel's detractors have claimed? Or, on the contrary, are there limits to the exercise of sovereign power set by the law of nations itself?

Does the principle of mutual assistance – beyond its ideal character and its potential to humanise international relations – also function as an effective legal restraint? Might it serve as a counterbalance within the natural law dialectic between solidarity and sovereignty, so that the tragic realism commonly associated with individualistic state sovereignty is not the sole outcome, but rather finds its counterpart in a solidarity capable of restraining the abuses of sovereign power in the conduct of international affairs?

This would seem to be the case. Vattel's law of nations also envisages a practical path out of this dialectic on the side of the law of solidarity – not in response to the ordinary and legitimate non-fulfilment of particular 'offices of humanity' by states, but in the exceptional case of a systematic and general violation of the *ius gentium* itself. Such a violation would not merely jeopardise its normative goal, but would threaten its minimum onto-anthropological foundation, which is safeguarded by the natural principle of solidarity: namely, the survival of the 'natural society of nations' and of the 'universal society of the human race'.

But this is the subject of the next section.

3 The International Limits of Sovereignty

In his brief account of Vattel's role within the *ius gentium europaeum*, Carl Schmitt omits any mention of the principle of mutual assistance – as already noted – and of its dialectical relationship with the law of sovereignty, which constitutes the backbone of the Swiss jurist's internationalist vision. Schmitt also overlooks the fact that, although state sovereignty is the sole subject of international law, its exercise is not without *iusnaturalist* limits. These limits are imposed by the law of nations itself and are derived from the principle of solidarity, understood as the natural law of sociability both among human beings and within the international community.

However, these limits are not established to guarantee the normative aim of solidarity (that is, cooperation between peoples), but rather to protect the very conditions of its possibility: the preservation of the 'natural society of nations' and of the 'universal society of the human race'. Therefore, when the exercise of sovereignty reaches the point of threatening all social relations between states – and even between human beings – when a state's conduct flagrantly violates the basic legal constraints that sustain international sociability, these limits must be invoked, defended, and restored by, or on behalf of, the community of nations, through punitive action against the offending state. There is thus no international impunity for a sovereign state that fails to respect the *ius gentium*.

But what, then, are the limits on a nation's sovereign will? In Vattel, two fundamental types can be identified: the first arises from a voluntary self-limitation by states, undertaken precisely to secure their own sovereign independence as a means of safeguarding the natural society of nations; the second stems from an externally imposed limitation, which restricts or even nullifies state sovereignty in order to protect the international community or the universal society of humankind.

The first type corresponds to what Vattel calls the 'voluntary law of nations'. This involves a necessary modification, exception, or restriction of the natural law of nations in its differentiated application to individual states, with the aim of enabling the fulfilment of natural law itself – in this case, the fundamental law of the freedom and independence of each nation. Respect for this national freedom requires that states voluntarily limit their own exercise of sovereignty in such a way that sovereign equality among all nations is preserved – without which international society is impossible.

Vattel refers to all these (self-)restrictions of sovereignty, undertaken to ensure its preservation within a society of equal sovereign states, as the voluntary law of nations. This is not because it has been expressly agreed to by treaty among all free states, but because its binding force derives from the 'presumed consent' that all nations necessarily give to the principle of sovereignty and to the legal rules its exercise entails.[39]

Two main sets of rules fall within this category. In normal international conditions, these include the application of the principle of *neminem laedere* – specifically, the prohibition on interference in the internal affairs of other states, and the associated duty to refrain from passing judgement on the presumed injustice of another state's conduct, giving rise to the maxim of non-intervention. In exceptional circumstances, such as armed conflict, the voluntary law of nations includes the legal formalities that ensure sovereign equality between belligerents. These formalities define what Vattel terms a 'war in due form' and serve to neutralise, in the eyes of other nations and in relation to the restoration of peace, any judgement regarding the justice of the cause or the conduct of hostilities.[40]

The voluntary law of nations thus demonstrates that, in international relations, the sovereignty of each state is not absolute, nor can it be sustained without these restrictive rules on its exercise – rules which enable the formation and preservation of a natural society of sovereign nations. The dialectic between the particular freedom of states and their unavoidable sociability finds reconciliation here through a deviation from itself: that of the *ius gentium voluntarium*, which nature tolerates in order to enforce (rather than infringe) its own laws in a world marked by the plurality of sovereign states.

This voluntary self-limitation is therefore best understood as a supplementary adaptation of natural law – an accommodation that renders possible an international order in which sovereignty may be exercised legitimately. It constitutes a legal order that can thus be regarded as emanating from the collective will of all sovereigns: the general act of sovereignty itself in its concrete application.

Schmitt, although he does not refer to it explicitly, is undoubtedly invoking this 'voluntary law of nations' when he praises Vattel for having constructed a legal system of European spatial equilibrium – a society of states based on mere coexistence and grounded in the principle of mutual neutrality. What Schmitt fails to address, however, are those cases of international intervention that disrupt these neutral relations – cases which override or suspend the *ius gentium voluntarium* in the name of the *ius gentium naturale*, and which chal-

---

39 Vattel, *Law of Nations*, Preface, 16–17; Preliminaries §21 and §§27–28; III, 12, §§189, 192. We cannot enter here into this thorny concept of the 'voluntary law of nations', midway between natural and positive law, so important and debated in Vattel's reception and in his positivist interpretation (see Reibstein, 'Die Dialektik', 609, 615 ff.; and especially Jouannet, *Emer de Vattel*, 141 ff.).

40 On 'war in due form', see Vattel, *Law of Nations*, III, 4, §§51–68; 12, §§158–162.

lenge sovereignty not to assert it, but to protect instead the natural sociability of nations and of human beings.

It is precisely these cases of externally imposed limitations that deserve emphasis here, for in their exceptionality, they provide the clearest resolution of the dialectic between the two natural principles of the law of nations in favour of the law of solidarity. They also reveal, with particular force, the properly *iusnaturalist* limits on the exercise of sovereignty – limits that Schmitt overlooks in his account of the Vattelian model.

Whereas the voluntary self-restriction of sovereignty responds to the need to regulate its legitimate use (in accordance with the *ius gentium*) in international relations, its violent limitation or interruption by external powers is justified only in cases of illegitimate, arbitrary exercise of sovereign freedom. Such conduct constitutes a violation of the *ius gentium* in both its natural and voluntary forms and threatens human sociability and the shared benefits it secures.

This illegitimacy is manifest in a systematic and flagrant transgression of the fundamental laws of justice and humanity – laws that make peaceful coexistence possible both among peoples and among individuals, or, in Vattel's terms, that uphold the 'natural society of nations' and the 'universal society of the human race'. When a sovereign state notoriously violates these norms in its international conduct, it becomes an 'unjust enemy', or even an 'enemy of mankind'. In such cases, all other nations are authorised to unite against it to repress, punish, and even annihilate it (as a body politic).[41]

---

41 Although not entirely separable, two types of cases are discernible in which a nation deserves the legitimate punishment of the international community, depending on whether it only violates justice among sovereign states and the 'society of nations' or whether it attacks humanity itself and the 'society of the human race'. The first type corresponds to a mischievous nation, which 'by her constant maxims' and sustained conduct of injuring others and exciting 'domestic disturbances' within them, proves a pernicious disposition to despise and flout justice among peoples and thus becomes an 'unjust enemy', so that all other nations, united, are authorised to repress, punish, and even annihilate it (as a body politic) for the good of the society of nations and 'the safety of the human race' (Vattel, *Law of Nations*, II, 5, &70). The right of punishment by the community of nations here is founded on the systematic violation of formal justice *inter gentes*: the natural *ius securitatis* and the corresponding principle of non-interference established by the *ius gentium voluntarium*, without the observance of which there can be no society of equal states. The second type attacks humanity and the 'society of the human race' more than justice as such, because it questions every sociable form of friendship, trust, and fraternity, and thereby removes the foundation of the first law of the natural law of nations and of its civilising purposes; hence the countries which act in this way, rather than being 'unjust' enemies (they are also unjust, since justice is the basis

For by acting against the law of nations, such a state places itself outside that law. It is thereby reduced – whether as an 'unjust enemy' or as a 'monster' – to the status of a 'criminal', and may be treated accordingly by the society of nations. Collective action against it, though clearly legitimate, is thus not grounded in a right of intervention, which, strictly speaking, does not and cannot exist within the *ius gentium voluntarium*. Rather, it is based on a right of punishment which, in such cases, is authorised by the law of sociability and activates the *ius gentium naturale*. It is the responsibility of the society of nations to exercise this right.

The recognition of an *iusnaturalist* limit on the conduct of sovereign states in their mutual relations shows that, for the jurist from Neuchâtel, sovereignty is not a shield against international impunity – as Schmitt sought to suggest in his interpretation of Vattel. Indeed, Schmitt was clearly intent on presenting Vattel's law of nations as free from any loophole that might lead to a potential criminalisation of the 'unjust enemy'. To this end, he focused metonymically on the *ius gentium voluntarium*, as though it constituted the entire system, and as though it did not in fact rest upon the deeper foundation of the *ius gentium naturale*.

The dominant image of Vattel in Schmitt's time – as a positivist responsible for elevating state sovereignty into the sole source and bulwark of international relations – also served Schmitt's purpose. Yet it is worth correcting this view, and suggesting instead that the author of *Le Droit des Gens* (1758) may be more aptly criticised for his excessive fidelity to natural law, and for exposing the fragility of his otherwise well-intentioned proposals.

For while Vattel does indeed acknowledge a right of punishment on the part of the international community against a state that flagrantly violates the legal norms governing relations between peoples, he fails to propose any

---

of society), become properly 'enemies of mankind'. This is the case with the so-called warlike peoples, who fight for delight and ferocity, without just cause or useful motive, revealing with this barbarous behaviour a spirit of cruelty and brutality, which is incompatible with the sociability of human beings and peoples; they are, in fact, 'monsters, unworthy the name of men', and therefore 'enemies to the human race' (Vattel, *Law of Nations*, III, 3, §34). Similarly, there are nations that employ illegitimate means against the enemy in a war or outside of it (murder by treason, poisoning of weapons or water, mistreatment and rape of unarmed civilians in a war, killing of prisoners of war or enslavement of them…) that attack humanity or undermine the foundations of human society in general (Vattel, *Law of Nations*, III, 8, §§136–159). Likewise with the manifestly 'monstrous' conduct of a tyrant towards his people: when the latter resist or revolt against him and demand help, a foreign nation or the international community may intervene, but only by virtue of a 'right of succour' to the people, not of punishment of the oppressive sovereign (Vattel, *Law of Nations*, II, 4, §56).

concrete institutional mechanism to give that right effective force. Beyond a general appeal to a vague and informal 'natural society of nations', or to the concerted action of individual states acting on its behalf, the responsibility for executing justice is effectively left – paradoxically – to the good legal conscience of nations and to their mutual love, or else to the shifting interests and potential imperial ambitions of the most powerful actors.

In such an *iusnaturalist* configuration of international relations, the ideal of a cooperative society of nations risks becoming little more than a legal utopia. For without enforceable guarantees, it is difficult to aspire to anything beyond a fragile balance of power among sovereign states.

Bibliography

Bell, David A. *The First Total War: Napoleon's Europe and the Birth of Warfare as We Know It* (Boston / New York: Houghton Mifflin Co., 2007).

Beneyto, José María. 'Camilo Barcia Trelles on Francisco de Vitoria: At the Crossroads of Carl Schmitt's *Grossraum* and James Brown Scott's "Modern International Law"'. *The European Journal of International Law* 31(4) (2021): 1477–1492. https://doi.org/10.1093/ejil/chab005.

Canale, Damiano. *La costituzione delle differenze* (Torino: G. Giappichelli, 2000).

Edelstein, Dan. *The Terror of Natural Right: Republicanism, the Cult of Nature, and the French Revolution* (Chicago: University of Chicago Press, 2008).

Haggenmacher, Peter. 'Le modèle de Vattel et la discipline du droit international'. In *Vattel's International Law in a XXIst Century Perspective*, eds. Vincent Chétail and Peter Haggenmacher (Leiden/Boston: M. Nijhoff, 2011), 3–49.

Jouannet, Emmanuelle. *Emer de Vattel et l'émergence doctrinale du droit international classique* (Paris: Pedone, 1998).

Korkman, Petter. 'L'amour universel du genre humain comme fondement des relations internationales chez de Vattel'. In *Réflexions sur l'impact, le rayonnement et l'actualité du 'Droit des Gens' d'Emer de Vattel – Reflections on the Impact, Influence and Continuing Relevance of Emer de Vattel's 'Law of Nations'*, ed. Yves Sandoz (Bruxelles: Bruylant, 2010), 23–29.

Koselleck, Reinhart. *Critique and Crisis: Enlightenment and the Pathogenesis of Modern Society* (Cambridge, Mass.: MIT Press, 1988).

Mallarmé, André. 'Emer de Vattel (1714–1767)'. In *Les fondateurs du droit international*, ed. Antoine Pillet (Paris: V. Giard & E. Brière, 1904), 481–601.

Mancuso, Francesco. *Diritto, stato, sovranità: Il pensiero giuridico-politico di Emer de Vattel tra assolutismo e rivoluzione* (Naples: ESI, 2002).

Muir-Watt, Horatia. 'Droit naturel et souveraineté de l'État dans la doctrine de Vattel'. *Archives de philosophie du droit* 32 (1987): 71–83.

Nakhimovsky, Isaac. 'Carl Schmitt's Vattel and the "Law of Nations" between Enlightenment and Revolution'. *Grotiana* 31 (2010): 141–164.

Pillet, Antoine. *La guerre et le droit* (Louvain: Uystpruyst-Dieudonné, 1922).

Pillet, Antoine, ed. *Les fondateurs du droit international* (Paris: V. Giard & E. Brière, 1904).

Reibstein, Ernst. 'Die Dialektik der souveränen Gleichheit bei Vattel'. *Zeitschrift für ausländisches öffentliches Recht und Völkerrecht* 19 (4) (1958): 607–635.

Rémec, Peter P. *The Position of the Individual in International Law according to Grotius and Vattel* (The Hague: M. Nijhoff, 1960).

Sandoz, Yves, ed. *Réflexions sur l'impact, le rayonnement et l'actualité du 'Droit des Gens' d'Emer de Vattel – Reflections on the Impact, Influence and Continuing Relevance of Emer de Vattel's 'Law of Nations'* (Bruxelles: Bruylant, 2010).

Schmitt, Carl. *The Nomos of the Earth in the International Law of the Jus Publicum Europaeum* (New York: Telos Press, 2003).

Silvestrini, Gabriella. 'Justice, War and Inequality: The Unjust Aggressor and the Enemy of the Human Race in Vattel's Theory of the Law of Nations'. *Grotiana* 31 (2010): 44–68.

Steiger, Heinhard. 'Solidarität und Souveränität oder Vattel reconsidered'. In *Von der Staatengesellschaft zur Weltrepublik? Aufsätze zur Geschichte* (Baden-Baden: Nomos Verlag, 2009), 133–141.

Vattel, Emer de. *The Law of Nations, or, Principles of the Law of Nature, Applied to the Conduct and Affairs of Nations and Sovereigns*, eds. Béla Kapossy and Richard Whatmore (Indianapolis: Liberty Fund, 2008).

Vattel, Emer de. 'Essay on the Foundation of Natural Law and on the First Principle of the Obligation Men Find Themselves under to Observe Laws'. In *The Law of Nations, or, Principles of the Law of Nature, Applied to the Conduct and Affairs of Nations and Sovereigns*, eds. Béla Kapossy and Richard Whatmore (Indianapolis: Liberty Fund, 2008), 747–771.

Villacañas, José Luis. *Poder y conflicto: Ensayos sobre Carl Schmitt* (Madrid: Biblioteca Nueva, 2008).

Vollenhoven, Cornelis van. *The Three Stages in the Evolution of the Law of Nations* (The Hague: M. Nijhoff, 1919).

Wolff, Christian. *Jus naturae methodo scientifica pertractatum* (Halle: Renger, 1747).

Wolff, Christian. *Jus gentium methodo scientifica pertractatum* (Halle: Renger, 1749).

CHAPTER 16

Schmitt vs. Vitoria on the Digital Battlefield: Free Flow of Information, Digital Sovereignty, and the Neutrality of Technology

Johannes Thumfart

1 Introduction

Schmitt and Vitoria are two highly problematic theorists who arrived at fundamentally opposing conclusions. Although this perception of the differences between the accounts of Vitoria and Schmitt is to some extent attributable to Schmitt's distorted description of Vitoria in *The Nomos of the Earth*, the following juxtaposition is still valid: Vitoria and Schmitt embody the productive and problematic aspects of both liberalism and realism in particularly drastic ways. Vitoria is a proto-liberal internationalist who emphasized international norms and international exchange; but he is also highly problematic because he instrumentalized a neutral understanding of international norms to justify Spanish colonialism. Schmitt, too, is a highly problematic author. He defended German fascism as a form of resistance against what he regarded as the incoherence of neutral liberal norms.[1] Beyond his specific historical context, Schmitt can be benevolently understood as a proto-realist[2] who emphasized the importance of territorially limited 'enclosures' of power in order to prevent the escalation of regional conflicts to the global level.

This juxtaposition of Vitoria and Schmitt is also relevant to the contemporary debate about the exercise of state sovereignty in the context of digital technologies. Vitoria's *ius communicationis* ('right of communication') is a forerunner of the modern doctrine of the liberal 'free flow of information', which constitutes the central liberal concept of the digital age.[3] Similar to

1 Carl Schmitt, 'Staat, Bewegung, Volk. Die Dreigliederung der Politischen Einheit.', in *Gesammelte Schriften 1933–1936: Mit Ergänzenden Beiträgen aus Der Zeit des Zweiten Weltkriegs* (Berlin: Duncker und Humblot 2021), 76–115; Carl Schmitt, 'Der Führer schützt das Recht. Zur Reichstagsrede Adolf Hitlers Vom 13. Juli 1934', *Deutsche Juristen-Zeitung* 39, no. 15 (1934).

2 Matthew G. Specter, *The Atlantic Realists: Empire and International Political Thought between Germany and the United States* (Stanford: Stanford University Press 2022), pp. 68ff.

3 José María Desantes Guanter, *Francisco de Vitoria, Precursor Del Derecho de La Información* (Madrid: Fundación de la Comunicación Social 1999).

 | DOI:10.1163/9789004757448_017

the problematic aspects of Vitoria, the digital free flow of information has been criticized as promoting 'digital colonialism'[4] due to the economic dominance of Silicon Valley's 'platform economy'[5] and the intrusive nature of the US 'cyber-industrial complex'.[6]

In turn, Schmitt has been cited as the intellectual foundation of attempts to combat such 'digital colonialism' through the establishment of 'digital sovereignty', which implies national control over digital technologies, infrastructure, information, and services.[7] In this context, the authoritarian Schmitt is particularly relevant to powers such as China and Russia, which follow their approaches of 网络主权 ('cyber sovereignty'), 信息主权 ('information sovereignty'), and *Суверенный интернет* ('sovereign internet') and which are heavily engaged in economic nationalism, surveillance, and censorship. Particularly, Russia's Eurasia ideologues are strongly influenced by Schmittian ideas, also regarding the digital.[8] But even in the EU, Schmitt has been cited to make the case for *sovereignté numérique* ('digital sovereignty'), combining the demand for the rule of law regarding privacy and antitrust with an agenda of economic protectionism toward US Big Tech.[9]

---

4 Nick Couldry and Ulises Ali Mejias. 'The Decolonial Turn in Data and Technology Research: What Is at Stake and Where Is It Heading?' *Information, Communication & Society* 26, no. 4 (12 March 2023): 786–802; Renata Avila Pinto, 'Digital Sovereignty or Digital Colonialism?', *Sur – International Journal on Human Rights* 27 (16 July 2018); Michael Kwet, 'Digital Colonialism: US Empire and the New Imperialism in the Global South', *Race & Class* 60, no. 4 (April 2019): 3–26.

5 Cristiano Codagnone, Athina Karatzogianni, and Jacob Matthews, *Platform Economics: Rhetoric and Reality in the 'Sharing Economy'* (Leeds: Emerald Publishing 2019); José Van Dijck, Thomas Poell, and Martijn De Waal, *The Platform Society*, vol. 1 (Oxford: Oxford University Press 2018).

6 Jerry Brito and Tate Watkins, 'Loving the Cyber Bomb? The Dangers of Threat Inflation in Cybersecurity Policy', Mercatus Center, 10 April 2012, available at: https://www.mercatus.org/publications/technology-and-innovation/loving-cyber-bomb-dangers-threat-inflation-cybersecurity.

7 Johannes Thumfart, 'The Norm Development of Digital Sovereignty between China, Russia, the EU and the US: From the Late 1990s to the Covid-Crisis 2020/21 as Catalytic Event', in Dara Hallinan, Ronald Leenes, and Paul de Hert (eds.) *Enforcing Rights in a Changing World* (London: Hart Publishing 2021), 1–44.

8 Leonid Savin, Номос Киберпространства и суверенный Интернет, *Pluriversum*, December 30, 2019, https://pluriversum.org/opinion/cyberspace/nomos-kiberprostranstva-i-suverennyj-internet/; Leonid Savin, Суверенный Интернет – дело принципиальной важности для национальной безопасности, *News Front*, December 30, 2019, https://news-front.info/2019/12/30/suverennyj-internet-delo-princzipialnoj-vazhnosti-dlya-naczionalnoj-bezopasnosti/; Timothy Snyder, *The Road to Unfreedom: Russia, Europe, America* (New York: Tim Duggan Books 2018).

9 Pierre Bellanger, 'De la souveraineté numérique'. *Le Débat* 170 (2012/3): 149–159.

The politicization of technology in the context of digital sovereignty challenges what is, according to Schmitt, one of the basic convictions of liberalism, namely that technology is politically neutral and has a neutralizing and depoliticizing effect. According to Schmitt's *The Age of Neutralizations and Depoliticizations* from 1929, modern liberalism is only the most recent form of an 'elemental impulse that has been decisive for centuries, i.e., the striving for a neutral domain'.[10] For Schmitt, the historical process of neutralization consists of the continuous search for new means to neutralize and, thereby, pacify the political conflicts within the state. This historical process of neutralization inevitably tends toward technology as a non-human instance supposedly embodying absolute neutrality. He wrote: 'The absolute and ultimate neutral ground has been found in technology since apparently there is nothing more neutral'.[11]

However, for Schmitt, the historical process of neutralization collapses precisely when societies enter the 'technological age' and become universally technology-driven. For Schmitt, due to its aspired neutrality, the modern state is, in its essence, always a proto-technological '*machina machinarum*'.[12] Nevertheless (or exactly because of that), for Schmitt, technology is precisely nothing on which a state can be built:

> You cannot represent in front of automatons and machines, as little as they can represent or be represented. And when the state has turned into the Leviathan, it vanished from the world of the representative.[13]

In the technological age, when technology is used for neutralization and depoliticization, the modern state is, therefore, confronted with its own lack of substance. When taken to its extreme, instead of having a neutralizing effect, technology reveals the original antagonistic power of the political. Schmitt noted that 'every type of culture, every people and religion, every war and peace can use technology as a weapon'.[14] As a result, according to Schmitt, the liberal ideal of technological neutrality collapses, and the state is forced

10 Carl Schmitt, "The Age of Neutralizations and Depoliticizations' in *The Concept of the Political: Expanded Edition* (Chicago, University of Chicago Press 2007), 80–96, 89.

11 Ibid. 90.

12 Carl Schmitt, *Gespräch über die Macht und den Zugang zum Machthaber* (Stuttgart: Klett Cotta 1954), 26.

13 Carl Schmitt, *Römischer Katholizismus und Politische Form* (Hellerau: Jakob Hegner 1923), 36.

14 Schmitt, 'The Age of Neutralizations and Depoliticizations', 91.

to abandon the concept of neutrality, to become non-neutral and radically partisan, to transcend the modern idea of the state.

Most problematically, it seems that for Schmitt, totalitarian and hyper-partisan National Socialism was the answer to the collapse of liberal neutrality in the technological age, as he underlined in his *Staat, Bewegung, Volk* from 1933 and *Der Führer schützt das Recht* from 1934.[15] Schmitt's critique of liberal neutrality is a continuous feature of Schmitt's thought; it equally characterizes its Weimar phase, Schmitt's personal involvement in Nazi Fascism, and his postwar thought on international law. Precisely because of this continuity and consistency, Schmitt's Nazism rather constitutes a logical conclusion than an opportunistic lapsus. Precisely because Schmitt justified his Nazism with the collapse of liberal neutrality, his assessment of the political implications of technology constitutes a stark warning: if Schmitt's thought is used today to justify notions of digital sovereignty that fundamentally oppose liberal neutrality in the form of the neutrality of technology, this creates the specter of a limitless Leviathan controlling technological infrastructure, free expression, and the economy. Such a non-neutral state in the digital age could monitor and control every aspect of its citizens' lives under the guise of national self-determination. From the perspective of Schmitt's decisionism, the introduction of AI systems into administrative and legal decision-making processes (to be discussed in Section 3)[16] makes clear that no further level of neutralization through technologization is possible than the outsourcing to machines of this most elementary level of the state. The non-neutral state of the twentieth century used the technologies of the industrial age to commit unspeakable atrocities. It remains to be seen what the non-neutral state of the digital age will do with its infinitely more advanced technologies.

This chapter discusses the problem complex of the free flow of information, digital sovereignty, and the neutrality of technology in light of the opposition between Vitoria's colonialist proto-liberalism and Schmitt's fascist proto-realism. Section 2 demonstrates how Vitoria's 'right of communication' and its colonial effect provided the ground for the postwar 'free flow of information' doctrine and its contemporary version of the 'free internet' doctrine, which

15 Schmitt, 'Staat, Bewegung, Volk'; Schmitt, 'Der Führer schützt das Recht'.

16 Prime Minister of Australia. 'Australian Government Collaboration with Microsoft on Artificial Intelligence'. 16 November 2023, available at: https://www.pm.gov.au/media/australian-government-collaboration-microsoft-artificial-intelligence; Straton Papagianneas and Adam Knight, 'The Stumbling Smart State Fragmented Policy Experimentation and Dubious Consolidation', in Rogier Creemers, Straton Papagianneas, and Adam Knight (eds.), *The Emergence of China's Smart State* (Blue Ridge Summit: Rowman & Littlefield 2023), 35–52.

developed similarly colonial effects. Section 3 elaborates on the connection between the contemporary digital sovereignty discourse and Schmitt's critique of liberal neutrality and the neutrality of technology in particular. Section 4 discusses several concrete EU policies and demonstrates how the development of digital sovereignty constitutes a symptom of the decay of liberalism in the digital age. This is followed by a brief summary.

2 Vitoria and UNESCO's Free Flow of Information: A Liberal Justification for Colonialism

Vitoria's *ius communicationis* is the first modern legal principle of global free trade, including the circulation of ideas, goods, and people. Of course, what Vitoria euphemized as 'free exchange' was, in fact, unidirectional exploitation and highly profitable to the colonizing power. Most importantly, the *ius communicationis* served as a justification for colonialism since Vitoria argued that the Spaniards had the right to defend themselves if the Amerindians were to hinder them from enjoying their 'right of communication'.[17]

Of course, it was only formally, and not actually, possible for the Native Americans to enjoy the same rights in Europe. Vitoria's *ius communicationis* is, therefore, a prime example of the hypocritical aspect of the 'majestic equality' (to quote Anatole France) of liberal norms: The *ius communicationis* allowed all peoples to cross the oceans and participate in maritime trade, although Vitoria was well aware that only the European side, which was making these supposedly neutral claims, could de facto enjoy this right, since, at that time, only Europe had the military and technological resources to do so.

Vitoria's *ius communicationis* is also a prime example of liberal norms as it is underpinned by a lofty, multi-layered philosophical legitimization that closely resembles liberal cosmopolitanism and has often been equated with it.[18] For instance, Vitoria makes the case that there is a community of humankind, which requires and legitimates global free commerce.[19] Furthermore, he poi-

17 Francisco de Vitoria, 'On the American Indians', in *Political Writings*, ed. Anthony Pagden and Jeremy Lawrence, Cambridge Texts in the History of Political Thought (Cambridge: Cambridge University Press 1991), 231–292, 280.

18 Please note that the word *resembles* is decisive here. In my deeper readings of Vitoria, I underlined that this ultimately represents a misreading of Vitoria. Johannes Thumfart, 'Francisco de Vitorias Philosophie: globalpolitisch, nicht kosmopolitisch', in Kirstin Bunge, Anselm Spindler, and Andreas Wagner (eds.), *Die Normativität des Rechts bei Francisco de Vitoria* (Stuttgart: Frommann-Holzboog 2011), 229–254.

19 Francisco de Vitoria, 'On the American Indians', 278, 280.

nts toward the material nature of running water, the open sea, and rivers, which makes them difficult to control, and which he, following Roman Law, understands as commons.[20] Finally, anticipating Milton's truth justification of free speech, he argues that the free intercourse of ideas will inevitably lead to the triumph of the most reasonable ones.[21]

Also, Vitoria's Thomism, which might be interpreted as a medieval remnant in his thought, is, in fact, very close to modern liberal discourse ethics. In Aquinas's commentary on Aristotle's politics, it says that

> The political community is a kind of communication (agreement) because it is contrary to the definition (reason) of a political community that citizens do not communicate at all (agree on nothing) – *civitas est quaedam communicatio. Unde contra rationem civitatis esset quod cives in nullo communicarent.*[22]

This is also true regarding the Thomist Vitoria, to whom the ideas of global communication and the global society of humankind are tightly intertwined, forming a single title of *ius societatis et communicationis* ('right of partnership/society and communication').[23] Undoubtedly, this makes sense from an argumentative perspective: since global communication is the condition of the possibility of the international legal order, upholding global communication constitutes the most important norm of international law.

The universal nature of Vitoria's arguments made it possible that the far more modern and more liberal Dutch thinker Hugo Grotius appropriated them for the rivaling Dutch to formulate a free trade doctrine against the Portuguese and Spanish claims to a monopoly on trade with his *De jure praedae* of 1605 and the subsequent *Mare Liberum* of 1609.[24] With this appropri-

20 Ibid., 279.

21 He does so regarding the question of whether one could communicate with unbelievers, which is not part of the English translation of *De Indis*. Vitoria argues that Christianity, since to him it is the more reasonable belief, would inevitably triumph in open discourse with Muslims. Francisco de Vitoria, De Indis, III, II, Articulus II (IX) Utrum cum infidelibus possit communicari: "*Non est dubium quin converteremus ad fidem Christi maiorem partem saracenorum, si cum eius haberemus familiaritatem, quia in secta sua non habent nisi meras fabulas et meras nugas*'. See also: Johannes Thumfart, *Die Begründung der Globalpolitischen Philosophie: Francisco de Vitorias Vorlesung über die Entdeckung Amerikas im ideengeschichtlichen Kontext* (Berlin: Kulturverlag Kadmos 2012), 157–164.

22 Aquinas. Sententia Politicorum. II, 1, 6; https://www.corpusthomisticum.org/cpo.html.

23 Desantes Guanter, *Francisco de Vitoria, Precursor Del Derecho de La Información*, 24.

24 Johannes Thumfart, 'On Grotius's Mare Liberum and Vitoria's De Indis, Following Agamben and Schmitt', *Grotiana* 30, no. 1 (2009): 65–87.

ation by Grotius, who was one of the most important sources of English liberalism, the *ius communicationis* transformed into the root of the modern liberal internationalist free trade doctrine.

As such, the proto-liberal *ius communicationis* was also a conceptual origin of the liberal norm of the 'free flow of information' institutionalized in the UNESCO constitution from 1945. Vitoria's texts and their appropriation by Grotius were common knowledge among international lawyers in the twentieth century, particularly in the context of the Carnegie Endowment for International Peace, which connected these ideas to global market liberalization.[25]

However, most importantly, the resurgence of explicitly or implicitly Vitorian ideas in the period following the Second World War was owed to international security concerns. Considering the atrocities of the Nazi regime against culture and science – 'the murder of teachers, artists, scientists, and intellectual leaders; the burning of books'[26] – the argument was made that the international exchange of information is vital to prevent wars. The preamble to the UNESCO constitution argued that 'wars begin in the minds of men' and that the Second World War was 'made possible by the (...) propagation (...) of the doctrine of the inequality of men and races'. The UNESCO constitution, therefore, promoted the 'free exchange of ideas and knowledge' and underlined that the drafters will 'develop and (...) increase the means of communication between their peoples and (...) employ these means for the purposes of mutual understanding (...)'.[27]

Despite these reasonable and seemingly neutral layers of legitimization, similar to the *ius communicationis,* UNESCO's free flow of information was instrumental in promoting the particular interests of hegemonic powers. An important contextual factor determining UNESCO's free flow of information doctrine was the US interest in replacing the British Empire as the global information superpower. For example, in 1944, the chairman of the US Federal Communications Commission criticized that 'Great Britain owns the major portion of the cables of the world' and condemned this 'control of communication facilities by one country with preferential services and rates to its own

25 Paolo Amorosa, *Rewriting the History of the Law of Nations: How James Brown Scott Made Francisco de Vitoria the Founder of International Law* (Oxford: Oxford University Press 2019), p. 317; Carl Schmitt, *The Nomos of the Earth in the International Law of the Jus Publicum Europaeum* (New York: Telos Press 2003), 119.

26 H. H. Krill De Capello, 'The Creation of the United Nations Educational, Scientific and Cultural Organization', *International Organization* 24, no. 1 (1970): 1–30, 11 FN 47.

27 UNESCO. 'UNESCO Constitution'. 4 November 1946.

nationals'.[28] Correspondingly, in 1946, the US Assistant Secretary of State outlined the government's position, which was, at that time, not directed against dictatorships but rather against European competitors in the global media economy.

> The State Department (...) plans to do everything within its power along political or diplomatic lines to help break down the artificial barriers to the expansion of private American news agencies, magazines, motion pictures, and other media of communication throughout the world (...). Freedom of the press – and freedom of exchange of information generally – is an integral part of our foreign policy.[29]

US norm entrepreneurship was ultimately successful. The European powers were weakened by the war and were willing to cooperate due to their fear of the Soviet Union.[30] The US position regarding information freedom heavily influenced UNESCO's position on this matter.[31] An attempt to achieve a 'decolonization of information'[32] at UNESCO resulted in the UK and the US leaving this organization in the 1980s.

Next to its security aspect and its economic dimension, the free flow of information has a geopolitical aspect, as exemplified by the founding of the Voice of America, Radio Free Europe, and Radio Liberty during the propaganda battles of the Second World War and the Cold War.[33] The fall of the Soviet Union at the end of the twentieth century was, to a certain degree, facilitated by Western media and by the free distribution of information by dissidents.[34] These events led the global dominant power, the US, to the conviction that the free flow of information was desirable because it inherently

---

28 Herbert I. Schiller, 'Genesis of the Free Flow of Information Principles: The Imposition of Communications Domination', *Instant Research on Peace and Violence* 5, no. 2 (1975): 75–86, 77.

29 Ibid.

30 Ibid.

31 Ibid.

32 UNESCO. *Many Voices, One World: Communication and Society Today and Tomorrow; towards a New More Just and More Efficient World Information and Communication Order*. London: Kogan Page 1980, 37.

33 Ralph A. Uttaro, 'The Voices of America in International Radio Propaganda', *Law and Contemporary Problems* 45, no. 1 (1982): 103–122.

34 Evgenij V. Morozov, *The Net Delusion: The Dark Side of Internet Freedom*, 1. ed (New York: Public Affairs 2011), 35.

promoted democratization and liberalization.[35] The characteristic ideas of this period in this regard are best summarized by a speech that Ronald Reagan gave even shortly before the fall of the Berlin Wall. In it, he emphasized the crucial role of digital technologies in the triumph of liberal democracy:

> More than arms, more than diplomacy, the communications revolution will be the greatest force for advancement of freedom in the world (…). Information is the oxygen of the information age. (…) It seeps through walls topped with barbed wire and wafts across borders. (…) The Goliath of totalitarian control will rapidly be brought down by the David of the microchip.[36]

During these years, which saw the development of digital technologies and the internet, the free flow of information was increasingly disconnected from human agency or intersubjective communication and related to technology alone, a process to which I have referred as a 'reification of liberalism in digital technologies'.[37] Information technologies alone were expected to weaken the authority of non-democratic governments. A particularly clear expression of this idea is an essay by Bill Clinton's foreign policy advisor, Joseph Nye, and US Navy Admiral William A. Owens from 1996. The article titled *America's Information Edge* was published in *Foreign Affairs* and argues that information technology is enough to liberalize societies. It reads:

> The beauty of information as a power resource is that, while it can enhance the effectiveness of raw military power, it ineluctably democratizes societies. The communist and authoritarian regimes that hoped to maintain their centralized authority while still reaping the economic

35 Daniel R. McCarthy, *Power, Information Technology, and International Relations Theory: The Power and Politics of US Foreign Policy and the Internet*, Palgrave Studies in International Relations (New York: Palgrave Macmillan 2015), 84.

36 David S. Broder, 'Reagan: Spread of Ideas Can Outdate Nato', *Washington Post* (14 June 1989), availabe at: https://www.washingtonpost.com/archive/politics/1989/06/14/reagan-spread-of-ideas-can-outdate-nato/d6c12735-902c-452a-b005-58790e2c0c7d/; 'Reagan Urges "Risk" on Gorbachev : Soviet Leader May Be Only Hope for Change, He Says', *Los Angeles Times* (13 June 1989), available at https://www.latimes.com/archives/la-xpm-1989-06-13-mn-2300-story.html.

37 Johannes Thumfart, *The Liberal Internet in the Postliberal Era: Digital Sovereignty, Private Government, and Practices of Neutralization* (Basingstoke: Palgrave Macmillan 2024).

> and military benefits of information technologies discovered they had signed a Faustian bargain.[38]

In the same year, 1996, John Perry Barlow published his famous *Declaration of the Independence of Cyberspace*, which presented similar concepts in the language of popular culture and was centered around the idea that digital technologies inherently contested state sovereignty. He wrote:

> Governments of the Industrial World, you weary giants of flesh and steel, I come from Cyberspace, the new home of Mind. You have no sovereignty where we gather.[39]

While Barlow's declaration arose out of a concrete conflict between internet activists and the US government pushing for internet regulation,[40] countercultural claims and the US official doctrine, in fact, fundamentally coincided. Both parts of US society, the new digital tech counterculture and the liberal establishment (led by so-called 'Atari Democrats'), believed that information technologies would corrode sovereignty and weaken state power, and through this techno-deterministic course of inevitable events, democracy would automatically triumph.

The same conviction is displayed in Clinton's famous quote from 2000, which, once more, directly attributed a democratizing effect to technology and not to human agency:

> We know how much the Internet has changed America, and we are already an open society. Imagine how much it could change China. Now, there's no question China has been trying to crack down on the Internet. Good luck! That's sort of like trying to nail Jell-O to the wall.[41]

---

38 Joseph S. Nye and William A. Owens, 'America's Information Edge', *Foreign Affairs* 75, no. 2 (1996): 20, 35.

39 John Perry Barlow, 'A Declaration of the Independence of Cyberspace', Electronic Frontier Foundation, 1996, available at: https://www.eff.org/de/cyberspace-independence.

40 Andy Greenberg, 'It's Been 20 Years since John Perry Barlow Declared Cyberspace Independence', *Wired* (2 August 2016), available at: https://www.wired.com/2016/02/its-been-20-years-since-this-man-declared-cyberspace-independence/.

41 'Clinton's Words on China: Trade Is the Smart Thing', *The New York Times* (9 March 2000), available at: https://www.nytimes.com/2000/03/09/world/clinton-s-words-on-china-trade-is-the-smart-thing.html.

Although slightly more balanced in tone, this conviction also found its expression in the Obama administration's 'Internet Freedom' Doctrine of 2010, which was introduced by Hillary Clinton as Secretary of State.[42] Displaying a form of 'infrastructural globalism',[43] Clinton sketched the utopia (or dystopia?) that 'the spread of information networks is forming a new nervous system for our planet'.[44]

Such beliefs can be understood as an amalgam of the US intellectual tradition based on Lockean natural rights and characteristically US-American techno-optimism. It makes liberal democracy look like a natural kind of government that merely requires the right neutral circumstances provided by information technologies to prosper. An early critic remarked that visions of free cyberspace equate 'the imposition of the American polity's unique right to free speech on all the world's polities' and that 'vacant freedom, in practice, unfolds as wars between gangs over turf'.[45]

In reality, which is hardly surprising, virtually all of the revolutions based on the mobilization of civil societies through digital media have failed. Of course, destabilization does not lead 'naturally' to democracy as this amalgam of natural right theories from seventeenth-century Europe and Californian techno-ideology suggests.[46] The 'color revolutions' from 2003 to 2005 around the territory of the former Soviet Union in Georgia ('Rose', 2003), Ukraine ('Orange', 2004), and Kyrgyzstan ('Tulip', 2005) all failed due to a lack of institutionalization,[47] and so did the Iranian 'Twitter Revolution' of 2009. In turn, the 'Arab Spring' of 2011, the apex of the 'Internet Freedom' doctrine, was even connected with the destabilization of a whole region through the rise of religious extremism, chaos, and even tighter forms of dictatorship.[48]

42 Hillary Clinton, 'Remarks on Internet Freedom', U.S. Department of State, 21 January 2010, available at: //2009–2017.state.gov/secretary/20092013clinton/rm/2010/01/135519.htm.

43 Paul N. Edwards, 'Meteorology as Infrastructural Globalism', *Osiris* 21, no. 1 (January 2006): 229–250.

44 Clinton, 'Remarks on Internet Freedom'.

45 Reilly Jones, 'A Critique of Barlow's "A Declaration of the Independence of Cyberspace"', *Extropy #17* 8, no. 2 (2nd Half 1996), available at: http://people.morrisville.edu/~reymers/readings/STS316/Barlow-Declaration-Critique_by_Jones.pdf.

46 Richard Barbrook and Andy Cameron, 'The Californian Ideology', *Science as Culture* 6, no. 1 (January 1996): 44–72.

47 Melinda Haring Cecire Michael, 'Why the Color Revolutions Failed', *Foreign Policy* (18 March 2013), available at: https://foreignpolicy.com/2013/03/18/why-the-color-revolutions-failed/.

48 Jack L. Goldsmith, 'The Failure of Internet Freedom', Emerging Threats (Knight First Amendment Institute, 2018), available at: http://kfai-documents.s3.amazonaws.com/documents/0f969b7a13/The-Failure-of-Internet-Freedom.pdf.

Furthermore, with the Snowden revelations of 2013, the world learned that the internet freedom agenda was accompanied by an unprecedented push of the US to establish a global digital hegemony that did not promote democratization but unprecedented global mass surveillance.[49]

However, it was in 2016 that the downside of the free flow of information became most apparent in the West: Russia used digital media to take revenge for US global surveillance and interfered in US elections and Brexit.[50] This, in turn, pushed Western democracies and US tech giants toward constructing barriers to the global free flow of information, which primarily includes laws against disinformation and restrictions for foreigners regarding the placement of ads with political content on platforms such as Facebook.[51] Under the impression of this catalytic event, the West abandoned the paradigm of the free flow of information and developed forms of territorial digital sovereignty, which will be discussed further in Section 4. In November 2020, history had come full circle when former President Obama, once a promoter of internet freedom and brought into power by an unprecedented use of digital media in his Presidential campaign, characterized the internet as 'the single biggest threat to our democracy'.[52]

There are striking parallels between the cynical aspects of the free flow of information and the internet freedom agenda and Vitoria's *ius communicationis*. By promoting global exchange, Vitoria secured Spanish trade interests and provided a cosmopolitan legitimization to colonialism in Latin America. In turn, the promotion of the free flow of information weakened states and brought about a lawless global cyberspace, which increased the power of the dominant player up to a point where 'cyber anarchy'[53] led to 'digital colonialism'.[54] Furthermore, as initially mentioned, for Vitoria, the *ius communicationis* implicitly served to promote Christianity since Vitoria knew that the Amerindians did not have the technological edge to travel to Europe. Analogously, US propagation of the free flow of information was implicitly intended only to

---

49 Zygmunt Bauman et al., 'After Snowden: Rethinking the Impact of Surveillance', *International Political Sociology* 8, no. 2 (June 2014): 121–144.

50 Ivan Krastev and Stephen Holmes, *The Light That Failed: A Reckoning* (London: Allen Lane 2019), E-book at 118.

51 Thumfart, 'The Norm Development of Digital Sovereignty'.

52 Jeffrey Goldberg, 'Why Obama Fears for Our Democracy', *The Atlantic* (16 November 2020), available at: https://www.theatlantic.com/ideas/archive/2020/11/why-obama-fears-for-our-democracy/617087/.

53 Jack L. Goldsmith, 'Against Cyberanarchy', *The University of Chicago Law Review* Vol. 65, no. No. 4 (Autumn) (1998): 1199–1250.

54 Couldry and Mejias. 'The Decolonial Turn in Data and Technology Research'; Avila Pinto, 'Digital Sovereignty or Digital Colonialism?'; Kwet, 'Digital Colonialism'.

promote Western liberal ideas. This supposedly neutral liberal norm was fundamentally put in question as soon as other powers learned to use it to further their political agendas.

3 Schmitt, Liberal Neutrality, and the Neutrality of Technology

The previous section established an analogy between the free flow of information and the later doctrine of internet freedom as justifying digital colonialism and Vitoria's *ius communicationis* as justifying historical colonialism. In turn, the debate about digital sovereignty (to be specified in Section 4) is primarily a pushback against the US use of the free flow of information to solidify its digital hegemony but also against the unwanted side effects of this doctrine from a Western point of view, which became clear with the US general election and Brexit in 2016. Considering this conceptual conflict, it does not come as a surprise that Schmitt's *Nomos of the Earth* plays a role in the debate about digital sovereignty. After all, within international legal theory and/or the theory of international relations, the proto-realist Schmitt is the counterpart to the proto-liberal Vitoria par excellence.

It is useful to add some paragraphs regarding the opposition between Vitoria and Schmitt before coming to Schmitt's account of the relationship between liberal neutrality and technology, which is crucial to this chapter. On the one hand, the opposition between Schmitt and Vitoria is characterized by the distortion and abuse of historical arguments guided by the political context and interests of historiographers. For instance, Brown Scott's hagiographic account (published by the liberal Carnegie Endowment) presented Vitoria, partly inaccurately, as the spiritual father of the global liberal order.[55] Schmitt clearly took this propagandistic distortion at face value; in his not historically exact but rather revanchist *The Nomos of the Earth* from 1950, Vitoria served as the genealogical centerpiece and was clearly abused as a proto-liberal straw man representing the Western-led postwar international liberal order, which Schmitt opposed.

On the other hand, Schmitt was aware of the ahistorical character of this genealogical narrative and added a crucial caveat. He argued that, in contrast to later liberalism, Vitoria only instrumentalized the appearance of neutrality in order to promote Christian mission. He insisted that Vitoria was 'no advocate of the absolute humanity fashionable in the 18th and 19th centuries'.[56] He

55 Amorosa, *Rewriting the History of the Law of Nations.*

56 Schmitt, *The Nomos of the Earth*, 114.

stated accurately that 'Christian mission' is 'the limit of the absolute neutrality of Vitoria's arguments, as well as of the general reciprocity and reversibility of his concepts'. According to Schmitt, later liberals made the mistake of taking Vitoria's proto-liberal appearance of neutrality at face value. Their 'objectivity doomed his theses and definitions to be misused and paved the way for completely heterogeneous aims'.[57]

Schmitt's critique of the international liberal order in *The Nomos of the Earth* is relevant beyond his obvious revanchist intentions. His critique of a purely formal, liberal understanding of international law became a recognized part of international legal scholarship with Koskenniemi's *From Apology to Utopia,* first published in 1989.[58] Schmitt's arguments entered scholarship closer to Vitoria with Anghie's *Imperialism, Sovereignty and the Making of International Law* from 2005,[59] which did not cite Schmitt directly but was heavily influenced by Koskenniemi.

Beyond raising the obvious issue of Vitoria's institutional embeddedness in the Catholic Church and the concomitant hypocritical aspects of his 'objective' and 'neutral' claims, Schmitt makes a more complex argument, which is particularly important regarding the afterlife of Vitoria's *ius communicationis.*

According to Schmitt, seemingly 'objective' and 'neutral' claims regarding global norms are problematic because they deny the inevitable existential belongingness to a political community of those who formulate these seemingly 'objective' and 'neutral' norms. According to Schmitt, there is clearly no such thing as *pouvoir neutre,*[60] but all legal norms are born out of political partisanship and are 'secondary to factual decision'.[61] It is worth noting that Schmitt's skepticism toward neutrality is clearly one of the theoretical issues connecting Schmitt, the more or less respected theorist of international law and international relations, with Schmitt, the reviled Nazi. It is precisely in his most problematic texts from 1933 and 1934 that Schmitt is most explicitly engaging in a deconstruction of liberal neutrality. In his *Staat, Bewegung, Volk* from 1933, he paradoxically and irrationally argues that it represents a 'scientific' (in the sense of racist pseudo-science) truth that German law can only be assessed by 'racially Aryan' (whatever that may be) lawyers.

57 Ibid. 115.

58 Martti Koskenniemi, *From Apology to Utopia: The Structure of International Legal Argument: Reissue with a New Epilogue* (Cambridge: Cambridge University Press 2005).

59 Antony Anghie, *Imperialism, Sovereignty, and the Making of International Law* (Cambridge: Cambridge University Press 2005).

60 Schmitt, 'The Age of Neutralizations and Depoliticizations', 90.

61 Koskenniemi, *From Apology to Utopia*, 226.

> Only those are able to see facts correctly, (...) who participate in the law-creating community in a way determined by their being and species and existentially belong to it. (...) No matter how (...) an alien of a species may behave and how astutely he may try (...), he is of a different nature, and in every decisive train of thought he remains within the existential conditions of his own species. This is the objective reality of "objectivity".[62]

Accordingly, it is precisely in his infamously apologetic *Der Führer schützt das Recht* from 1934 that Schmitt stressed that Weimar liberalism 'destroyed itself in this neutral legality and left itself at the mercy of its own enemies' and that the failure of Weimar demonstrated the 'contrast between a substantial law not separated from morality and justice and the empty legality of an untrue neutrality'.[63]

It is evident that the rejection of the neutrality of law connects all three phases of Schmitt's work: the Weimar period, the Nazi period, and the postwar period. It is also evident that it constitutes a free pass for all kinds of racist or nationalist identity politics. On the one hand, Schmitt's core concept in this regard is simply a performative contradiction along the line of the paradox of the Cretan Epimenides claiming that all Cretans are liars. Similar to one of his sources, Nietzsche, Schmitt tells us that, objectively and neutrally speaking, there are no objective or neutral claims. This constitutes an irrationalist carte blanche for all kinds of statements, which runs even deeper as the fight against rationalist intellectualism is one of the core aspects of Schmitt's work during all its phases.[64] On the other hand, Schmitt can be considered the founder of postmodern reasoning because he was one of the earliest figures in Social Sciences and Legal Studies to emphasize the social constructedness of norms and the crucial role of identity in discourses.

For Schmitt, the hubris of global, neutral, and universal norms lies precisely in the fact that they must be understood as the expression of a concrete social structure and specific interests, but they claim to be universal in nature and to apply to the whole globe. As these norms are understood to be 'universal', their validity is not related to a political entity with a territorial 'enclosure'[65] but, at the same time, unsupported by de facto power and potentially limitless. That is why, for Schmitt, a civilizational 'Großraum' connected to a clearly

---

62 Schmitt, 'Staat, Bewegung, Volk', 114f.

63 Schmitt, 'Der Führer schützt das Recht'.

64 Thumfart, *The Liberal Internet in the Postliberal Era*. Section 5.4.

65 Schmitt, *The Nomos of the Earth*, 74.

defined region or continent is preferable over the global order of international liberalism.[66]

According to Schmitt, due to its conflicted nature, liberalism's universalistic un-limitation of norms does not create a cosmopolitan utopia by abolishing the possibility of normative ambivalence but rather a global civil war which 'makes the enemy a felon (…)': 'the action taken against him is no more war than a police action against a gangster'.[67] In a prototypically realist way, Schmitt argues that the threshold to enact such 'police actions' becomes correspondingly low, and international security is rather threatened than stabilized by universal norms since these norms not only legitimize countless interventions but ultimately make permanent interventions necessary. In his *Großraum versus Universalism* from 1939, he wrote:

> A universalistic world principle encompassing the entire Earth and all of humanity (…) leads naturally to the interference of everyone in everything. While the spatial idea involves a perspective of delimitation and distribution and thus constructs a legal ordering principle, the universalistic claim to world-interference [*Welt-Einmischungsanspruch*] obliterates any reasonable delimitation and distinction.[68]

For Schmitt, which is particularly interesting in this context, liberal neutrality is also closely connected with technology. In his speech on *The Age of Neutralizations and Depoliticizations,* he argues that liberalism's obsession with neutrality historically tends toward granting technology an ever-greater significance in society. Because of its non-human nature, technology is expected to produce real neutrality untainted by human belongingness to a specific political community and its interests. He wrote:

> The absolute and ultimate neutral ground has been found in technology, since, apparently, there is nothing more neutral.[69]

However, according to Schmitt, in the technological age, i.e., just when liberal neutrality has reached its ultimate destination, it becomes apparent that the

---

66 Carl Schmitt, 'Großraum versus Universalism: The International Legal Struggle over the Monroe Doctrine', in Stephen Legg (ed.), *Spatiality, Sovereignty and Carl Schmitt: Geographies of the Nomos* (London: Routledge 2011), 46–54.

67 Schmitt, *The Nomos of the Earth*, 124.

68 Schmitt, 'Großraum versus Universalism', 46.

69 Schmitt, 'The Age of Neutralizations and Depoliticizations', 90.

neutrality of technology is devoid of any substance that could contribute to maintaining the state by pacifying internal conflicts. He wrote that

> You cannot represent in front of automatons and machines, as little as they can represent or be represented. And when the state has turned into the Leviathan, it vanished from the world of the representative.[70]

This is precisely problematic because, according to Schmitt, the modern, rationalistic, and neutral state is, in its essence, a technology as well:

> The well-functioning European modern state was the first machine and, at the same time, the concrete precondition of all later machines. It was the machine of machines, the *machina machinarum*.[71] [It constituted] (...) not only an essential intellectual or sociological precondition for the technical-industrial age (...) but also the (...) prototypical work of the new technological era.[72]

In the attempted neutralization and depoliticization through technology, the modern state is, therefore, confronted with its own void and is no longer able to pacify the tension of the political within its own borders. From this perspective, it is clear that the neutrality of technology cannot have the depoliticizing effect that liberalism is expecting it to have but collapses into its reversal, a total politicization of everything:

> (...) The neutrality of technology is something other than the neutrality of all former domains. Technology is always only an instrument and weapon; precisely because it serves all, it is not neutral (...). Every type of culture, every people and religion, every war and peace can use technology as a weapon (...). Consequently, no conclusions which usually can be drawn from the central domains of spiritual life can be derived from pure technology as nothing but technology.[73]

In retrospect, Schmitt's thesis of the collapse of liberal neutrality prefigures exactly what happened in the post–Cold War era, when the US and its allies

70 Schmitt, *Römischer Katholizismus und Politische Form*, 36.

71 Schmitt, *Gespräch über Die Macht und den Zugang zum Machthaber*, 26.

72 Carl Schmitt, *The Leviathan in the State Theory of Thomas Hobbes: Meaning and Failure of a Political Symbol* (Westport: Greenwood Press 1996), 34.

73 Schmitt, 'The Age of Neutralizations and Depoliticizations', 91.

increasingly began to interpret the civilizing effect of the 'free flow of information' as the civilizing effect of the 'free internet'. As I argue elsewhere, in this process, liberal neutrality became increasingly disassociated from human elements and reified in the infrastructure of the internet, which was, due to its neutrality, supposed to achieve liberal democracy worldwide automatically.[74]

4 Digital Sovereignty as Postliberalism

The awakening from the illusion that liberal neutrality can be effectively reified in the internet happened in two phases. With the Snowden revelations in 2013, the world learned that – similar to Vitoria's instrumentalization of the supposedly neutral *ius communicationis* for colonialism – the US had continuously abused the free flow of information doctrine at least since 2001 and the Patriot Act. In this phase, the concept of 'digital sovereignty' emerged in Russia and the EU.[75] Shocked by the extent of US surveillance activities, both actors demanded independence from transnational digital networks. However, while the EU tried to counter US digital hegemony foremost through regulations such as the GDPR, which came into force in 2016, and similar regulations with an economic scope, such as the DSA and the DMA, Russia also started to develop aggressive capacities in the digital realm, which corresponds to Moscow's realist understanding of sovereignty.[76]

Second, after the Russian election meddling in 2016 in the EU and the US, the US and its allies themselves realized that the neutrality of technology was not necessarily contributing to liberalism but was treacherous. In Schmitt's words, 'every type of culture, every people and religion, every war and peace can use technology as a weapon'. Not only US could use the internet to project power, but Russia and its allies could also use it.

In this norm development of digital sovereignty, China remains the great outlier because it implemented digital sovereignty long before the Snowden revelations. The theoretical discourse in China started independently of Schmitt in 1996.[77] One of the first theorists of information sovereignty, Wenxiang Gong, denounced 网络霸权 ('cyber-hegemony') and 网络殖民主义 ('cyber-

74 Thumfart, *The Liberal Internet in the Postliberal Era*.

75 Thumfart, 'The Norm Development of Digital Sovereignty'.

76 Johannes Thumfart, 'Digital Sovereignty in China, Russia and India: From NWICO to SCO and BRICS', in Luca Belli and Min Jiang (eds.), *Digital Sovereignty in the BRICS Countries* (Cambridge: Cambridge University Press 2024).

77 Wanshu Cong and Johannes Thumfart, 'A Chinese Precursor to the Digital Sovereignty Debate: Digital Anti-Colonialism and Authoritarianism from the Post–Cold War Era to

colonialism') in 1998. Putting the finger where it hurts, he directly attacked the supposed neutrality of the free flow of information.

> Whilst the information superpowers sing the hymns of 'international freedom of communication' and 'information without borders', many developing countries feel that their rights are being taken away and even their national security is being threatened.[78]

The practical implementation of these ideas was the development of the Great Firewall starting in 1999. China constitutes the exception to post–Cold War liberal theory, which assumed that technologization and integration into global networks automatically caused liberalism by neutralizing authoritarian political power. Contrary to liberal expectations, China did not democratize during its ascendance in the world economy and its increasing technological development. On the contrary, under Xi, the country became more authoritarian. And, of course, one reason for this development is that Beijing found ways to use digital technologies not only to censor the internet but also for surveillance, propaganda, and the projection of power. China's Xinjiang province, in particular, serves today as a showcase of digital authoritarianism, and it is, at the same time, closely linked to US-Chinese entanglement in the private tech sector.[79] Demonstrating the inability of liberalism to defend its own interests, the Chinese Great Firewall was even partly custom-built by the US American firm Cisco.[80] Rather than constituting an authoritarian exception, China today must be understood within a global complex of authoritarian surveillance practices that includes international Big Tech. Such a comparative view 'does not render these developments any less dystopian, but rather more so' since it emphasizes China's embeddedness into a 'general authoritarian shift' connected with digitalization.[81]

---

the Tunis Agenda', *Global Studies Quarterly* 2, no. 4 (October 2022), https://doi.org/10.1093/isagsq/ksac059.

78 Wenxiang Gong (龚文庠), 'International Communication in the Information Age: New Issues Facing International Relations (信息时代的国际传播:国际关系面临的新问题)'. *Studies of Intenational Politics* (国际政治研究) 2 (1998): 45.

79 Ivan Franceschini and Nicholas Loubere, *Global China as Method* (Cambridge: Cambridge University Press 2022), 29ff.

80 Nate Cardozo and Sophia Cope, 'Cisco's Latest Attempt to Dodge Responsibility for Facilitating Human Rights Abuses: Export Rules', *Electronic Frontier Foundation*, 18 April 2016, available at: https://www.eff.org/de/deeplinks/2016/04/ciscos-latest-attempt-dodge-responsibility-facilitating-human-rights-abuses-export.

81 Franceschini and Loubere, *Global China as Method*, 28, 9.

In Europe, digital sovereignty is still far from being brought to such extremes and has positive aspects. Particularly from the point of view of Schmittian decisionism, Article 22 of the GDPR represents a milestone since it guarantees the right not to be subject to a decision based solely on automated processing (if this decision has significant effects).[82] One must consider the full ontological depth of Article 22. While algorithmic decision-making is connected with drastic forms of discrimination,[83] it might very well be that sophisticated automated decisions will one day be more neutral and less biased than human decisions, which would realize the liberal utopia of full neutralization and depoliticization through technology. Even in this case, and this is precisely the point of the debate between realist voluntarism and liberal intellectualism,[84] Article 22 would grant the right to a *human decision.* Human decisions might be preferable simply because they are human, even if they are less neutral, less rational, and worse in all other aspects. The state in the digital age should certainly be partisan and non-neutral in the sense that it is decidedly positively biased toward humans in general and 'specieist' in that sense.

However, particularly in Europe, the clash of a liberal, neutral attitude toward technology and reasonable demands for digital sovereignty to prevent foreign interference developed a number of highly problematic tendencies. First, as the EU's sovereignty rests with the member states, the continent's approach to digital sovereignty remains fractured. For example, while justified worries regarding increasing Chinese influence triggered the debate about the exclusion of the Chinese infrastructure provider Huawei from access to European markets, such protectionist policies are difficult to reconcile with Europe's export-orientation. The result is an uneven approach to the Huawei ban, which was much easier to implement in the US.[85]

Furthermore, the EU is pursuing several infrastructural projects to increase its digital independence, but these projects, too, would require the abandonment of liberal free trade norms such as competitive tendering. A good example of this indecisiveness is the EU's project to pursue the development of the sovereign cloud infrastructure Gaia-X. Already in 2017, France and Germany celebrated a bizarre 'Cloud Independence Day' without real consequences.[86]

82 Thumfart, *The liberal internet in the postliberal era,* Section 9.8.

83 Ibid., Section 8.5.

84 Ibid. Section 5.4.

85 'Eleven EU Countries Took 5G Security Measures to Ban Huawei, ZTE', *Euronews* (12 August 2024), available at: https://www.euronews.com/next/2024/08/12/eleven-eu-countries-took-5g-security-measures-to-ban-huawei-zte.

86 Federal Office for Information Security. 'Cloud Independence Day: BSI und ANSSI stellen European Secure Cloud Label vor,' Press Release, June 6, 2017, available at: https://www.

In 2019, the European Cloud project Gaia-X was revealed and promoted by industry representatives to 'strengthen Europe's digital sovereignty'.[87] One year later, it was announced that Chinese and US tech firms would participate in the EU's digital sovereignty flagship project,[88] and, consequently, the EU has been accused of mere 'sovereignty-washing'.[89] During 2021, the project increasingly disintegrated.[90] The same year, it was announced that Google and Deutsche Telekom would partner to construct a so-called 'sovereign cloud' for Germany's public and private sectors.[91] In 2022, Amazon published its 'digital sovereignty pledge', promoting a liberal understanding of digital sovereignty, which emphasizes not the national, but the individual control over data.[92] The same year, the German government partially cut funding for Gaia-X. A network of domestic cloud providers summarized:

> The positive statements on digitalization and the strategy regarding digital sovereignty are insufficiently followed by deeds. The consequences are unfortunately bitter: some of the tender plants that appear suitable for advancing digitalization in public administration and shaping this in a sovereign manner (…) would thus unfortunately wither before they could grow.[93]

---

bsi.bund.de/DE/Presse/Kurzmeldungen/Meldungen/news_Cloud_Independence_Day_06062017.html.

87 Bitkom. 'A sovereign cloud and data infrastructure for Germany and Europe,' Position Paper, November 15, 2019, available at: https://www.bitkom.org/EN/List-and-detailpages/Publications/A-sovereign-cloud-and-data-infrastructure-for-Germany-and-Europe.

88 Philipp Grüll and Samuel Stolton, "US and Chinese tech giants welcomed into 'EU sovereign' cloud project,' *Euractiv* (October 15, 2020), available at: https://www.euractiv.com/section/digital/news/us-and-chinese-tech-giants-welcomed-into-eu-sovereign-cloud-project/.

89 Evgeny Morozov. Tweet October 17, 2020, 12:06 PM, https://twitter.com/evgenymorozov/status/1317406673749815297?s=20

90 'Inside Gaia-X: How Chaos and Infighting Are Killing Europe's Grand Cloud Project', *POLITICO* (26 October 2021), available at: https://www.politico.eu/article/chaos-and-infighting-are-killing-europes-grand-cloud-project/.

91 Deutsche Telekom AG. 'T-Systems and Google Cloud Partner to Deliver Sovereign Cloud for Germany', 08/2021, available at: https://www.telekom.com/en/media/media-information/archive/sovereign-cloud-from-t-systems-and-google-cloud-635314.

92 Amazon Web Services. 'AWS Digital Sovereignty Pledge: Control without Compromise'. 27 November 2022, available at: https://aws.amazon.com/blogs/security/aws-digital-sovereignty-pledge-control-without-compromise/.

93 Sovereign Cloud Stack, 'The Gaia-X Foundation Is Solid', Sovereign Cloud Stack, 31 March 2022, available at: https://scs.community/2022/03/31/future-of-gaiax/.

Unsurprisingly, this demonstrates that liberal societies are not capable of effectively contesting the liberal norms on which they are built, among which is the illusion of the neutrality of technology. However, this weakness does not mean that liberalism is triumphing. Given the discrepancy between their rhetoric on digital sovereignty, which is also underpinned by the actual need to defend European self-determination against the US and China, and the numerous obstacles to the realization of digital sovereignty, EU policymakers are nudged into engaging in a dangerous form of compensation. As the EU's almost exclusively regulatory focus already suggests, purely prohibitive approaches are used to symbolically camouflage the inability to achieve actual infrastructural or economic sovereignty in this area.

The area of freedom of expression on the internet is a relatively inexpensive field for governments to stage digital sovereignty and the 'taking back of control'. For example, in August 2024, EU Commissioner Thierry Breton publicly warned Musk not to violate EU law when he interviewed US-Presidential candidate Trump on his US-based platform X (formerly known as Twitter).[94] This rhetoric confirmed the widespread criticism that the EU is engaging in 'regulatory imperialism' with extraterritorial effects.[95] In the most drastic demonstration yet of a heavy-handed approach to platform regulation, French officials temporarily arrested *Telegram* founder Pavel Durov the same month as part of an inquiry in relation to a lack of moderation on the messaging app.[96] It is crucial to know that Durov is a tenacious enemy of the Russian government, which unsuccessfully attempted in 2018 to shut down *Telegram*.[97] Comparable to similar measures by India's authoritarian nationalist government, the EU Commission has already discussed social media shutdowns on the grounds of 'incendiary statements'.[98]

These measures are not to be entirely viewed from a critical perspective. Even more tragically, they might even be necessary in the digital age, which

94 'EU Takes Shot at Musk over Trump Interview – and Misses', *POLITICO* (13 August 2024), available at: https://www.politico.eu/article/eu-elon-musk-donald-trump-interview-thierry-breton-letter-social-media/.

95 Anu Bradford, *Digital Empires: The Global Battle to Regulate Technology* (Oxford University Press: New York 2023)

96 'Telegram CEO Pavel Durov Says His Arrest Is "Misguided"', *BBC* (6 September 2024), available at: https://www.bbc.com/news/articles/c78lgzl919g0.

97 'Russia Lifts Ban on Telegram Messaging App after Failing to Block It', *Reuters* (18 June 2020), available at: https://www.reuters.com/article/technology/russia-lifts-ban-on-telegram-messaging-app-after-failing-to-block-it-idUSKBN23P2DY/.

98 Thumfart, Johannes. 'Digital Rights and the State of Exception. Internet Shutdowns from the Perspective of Just Securitization Theory'. *Journal of Global Security Studies*, 2024, https://doi.org/10.1093/jogss/ogad024.

is characterized by a fundamental challenge to state power posed by technologies that are not neutral at all but can be highly destabilizing. By producing the real or perceived need to infringe deeply on the freedom of expression, digital technologies force the liberal state to undermine its own foundation. As legal scholar Bradford writes, the current digital sovereignty discourse in liberal countries 'may even lend legitimacy to the more extreme variants of digital sovereignty that authoritarian governments such as China and Russia are pursuing'.[99] The German NetzDG, which influenced the DSA's provisions regarding disinformation and fake news, inspired authoritarian and semi-authoritarian regimes all over the globe, including Singapore, Russia, the Philippines, and Venezuela, which explicitly mentioned the German NetzDG as model legislation.[100] Last but not least, the EU itself counts an illiberal member in Hungary. The Orbán government's approach to platform regulation illustrates how digital sovereignty measures presented in Brussels as neutral instruments to uphold the rule of law can instead be deployed as tools of state pressure on the public.[101]

5 Conclusion

In this chapter, I juxtaposed the proto-liberal Vitoria and the proto-realist Schmitt in regard to their significance to the contemporary discourse about digital sovereignty. In the second section, I demonstrated how Vitoria's proto-liberal *ius communicationis* was legitimized by universalistic arguments but constituted a tool of colonial exploitation. Due to their universalistic underpinning, Vitoria's arguments could be appropriated in Grotius's doctrine of Free Trade and later constituted one of the sources of UNESCO's 'free flow of information' doctrine.

Also, in regard to its historical context, the doctrine of the free flow of information is comparable to Vitoria's *ius communicationis*. On the one hand, it is based on universalistic, supposedly neutral arguments that are typical of lib-

99 Bradford, *Digital Empires*, Ebook at 652.

100 Jacob Mchangama and Joelle Fiss, 'The Digital Berlin Wall: How Germany (Accidentally) Created a Prototype for Global Online Censorship' (Copenhagen: Justitia, November 2019), available at: https://globalfreedomofexpression.columbia.edu/wp-content/uploads/2019/11/Analyse_The-Digital-Berlin-Wall-How-Germany-Accidentally-Created-a-Prototype-for-Global-Online-Censorship.pdf.

101 Asya Metodieva, 'Digital sovereignty contested: Hungary's strategic use of EU platform regulations'. *Journal of Contemporary European Studies* (2025), 1–18.

eralism, and, on the other hand, it can be clearly identified as an instrument for promoting global US-American dominance in the global media economy.

I demonstrated that the notion of the free flow of information was radicalized by the US with the advent of digital technologies in the post–Cold War era, when information technologies were imagined as destabilizing authoritarian regimes and spreading democracy by themselves. This liberal concept proved particularly wrong in 2016 when digital technologies were used by the Russians to interfere with democratic processes in the US and in Europe. Speaking with Schmitt, it then became evident that the digital free flow of information is not inherently liberal or neutral from the perspective of liberal societies, but that 'every type of culture, every people and religion, every war and peace can use technology as a weapon'.

I have demonstrated that the development of digital sovereignty constitutes a reaction to the political effects of digital technologies. Extreme forms of digital sovereignty were established by the US's geopolitical competitors, Russia and China. Moderate forms were established by the US's Western allies in the EU. In Russia and France alike, the turn toward digital sovereignty has been underpinned by citations of Schmitt's *The Nomos of the Earth,* which emphasizes the importance of territorial enclosures of power and the destabilizing tendencies of liberal universalism.

However, the politicization of digital technologies through liberal states is highly problematic as it challenges what is, according to Schmitt, one of the most important pillars of liberalism: its belief in the neutralizing and depoliticizing effect of technology. According to Schmitt, this belief cannot be maintained during the technological age, and the state is forced to abandon the idea of neutrality that characterizes the modern state and to find another form. For Schmitt, totalitarian National Socialism was an answer to the erosion of neutrality in the technological age. Not only from this perspective, liberal states' turn toward digital sovereignty is highly problematic. I have shown how specific policies that restrict the freedom of expression may be necessary due to the ubiquity of digital technologies, but such policies ultimately undermine the credibility of the liberal state. China's digital authoritarianism may be the future of the non-neutral state in the digital age. However, one should not make the mistake of viewing China as an exception, but rather understand that China's illiberal digital sovereignty is a symptom of the general decline of liberal neutrality under digital conditions, which I refer to elsewhere as 'postliberalism'.[102] As other countries followed China in terms of

102 Thumfart, *The Liberal Internet in the Postliberal Era.*

digital sovereignty, the country may well just be the first to establish a non-neutral state in the digital age.

Bibliography

'Clinton's Words on China: Trade Is the Smart Thing' *The New York Times* (9 March 2000), available at: https://www.nytimes.com/2000/03/09/world/clinton-s-words-on-china-trade-is-the-smart-thing.html.

'Eleven EU Countries Took 5G Security Measures to Ban Huawei, ZTE' *Euronews* (12 August 2024), available at: https://www.euronews.com/next/2024/08/12/eleven-eu-countries-took-5g-security-measures-to-ban-huawei-zte.

'EU Takes Shot at Musk over Trump Interview – and Misses', *POLITICO* (13 August 2024), available at: https://www.politico.eu/article/eu-elon-musk-donald-trump-interview-thierry-breton-letter-social-media/.

'Inside Gaia-X: How Chaos and Infighting Are Killing Europe's Grand Cloud Project'. *POLITICO* (26 October 2021), available at: https://www.politico.eu/article/chaos-and-infighting-are-killing-europes-grand-cloud-project/.

'Reagan Urges "Risk" on Gorbachev : Soviet Leader May Be Only Hope for Change, He Says'. *Los Angeles Times* (13 June 1989), available at: https://www.latimes.com/archives/la-xpm-1989-06-13-mn-2300-story.html.

'Russia Lifts Ban on Telegram Messaging App after Failing to Block It'. *Reuters* (18 June 2020), available at: https://www.reuters.com/article/technology/russia-lifts-ban-on-telegram-messaging-app-after-failing-to-block-it-idUSKBN23P2DY/.

'Telegram CEO Pavel Durov Says His Arrest Is "Misguided"', *BBC* (6 September 2024), available at: https://www.bbc.com/news/articles/c78lgzl919go.

'The Gaia-X Foundation Is Solid', *Sovereign Cloud Stack* (31 March 2022), available at: https://scs.community/2022/03/31/future-of-gaiax/.

Amazon Web Services. 'AWS Digital Sovereignty Pledge: Control without Compromise', 27 November 2022, available at: https://aws.amazon.com/blogs/security/aws-digital-sovereignty-pledge-control-without-compromise/.

Amorosa, Paolo. *Rewriting the History of the Law of Nations: How James Brown Scott Made Francisco de Vitoria the Founder of International Law*. Oxford: Oxford University Press 2019.

Anghie, Antony. *Imperialism, Sovereignty, and the Making of International Law*. Cambridge: Cambridge University Press 2005.

Avila Pinto, Renata. 'Digital Sovereignty or Digital Colonialism?' *Sur – International Journal on Human Rights* 27 (16 July 2018), available at: https://sur.conectas.org/en/digital-sovereignty-or-digital-colonialism/.

Barbrook, Richard, and Andy Cameron. 'The Californian Ideology'. *Science as Culture* 6, no. 1 (January 1996): 44–72.

Barlow, John Perry. 'A Declaration of the Independence of Cyberspace'. *Electronic Frontier Foundation*, 8 February 1996, available at: https://www.eff.org/de/cyberspace-independence.

Bauman, Zygmunt, Didier Bigo, Paulo Esteves, Elspeth Guild, Vivienne Jabri, David Lyon, and R. B. J. Walker. 'After Snowden: Rethinking the Impact of Surveillance'. *International Political Sociology* 8, no. 2 (June 2014): 121–144.

Bellanger, Pierre. 'De La Souveraineté Numérique'. *Le Débat* 170, no. 3 (2012): 149–59.

Bitkom. 'A Sovereign Cloud and Data Infrastructure for Germany and Europe'. 15 November 2019, available at: https://www.bitkom.org/EN/List-and-detailpages/Publications/A-sovereign-cloud-and-data-infrastructure-for-Germany-and-Europe.

Bradford, Anu. *Digital Empires: The Global Battle to Regulate Technology*. New York: Oxford University Press, 2023.

Brito, Jerry, and Tate Watkins. 'Loving the Cyber Bomb? The Dangers of Threat Inflation in Cybersecurity Policy'. Mercatus Center, 10 April 2012, available at: https://www.mercatus.org/publications/technology-and-innovation/loving-cyber-bomb-dangers-threat-inflation-cybersecurity.

Broder, David S. 'Reagan: Spread of Ideas Can Outdate Nato'. *Washington Post* (14 June 1989), available at: https://www.washingtonpost.com/archive/politics/1989/06/14/reagan-spread-of-ideas-can-outdate-nato/d6c12735-902c-452a-b005-58790e2c0c7d/.

Cecire, Melinda Haring, Michael. 'Why the Color Revolutions Failed'. *Foreign Policy* (18 March 2013), available at: https://foreignpolicy.com/2013/03/18/why-the-color-revolutions-failed/.

Clinton, Hillary. 'Remarks on Internet Freedom'. U.S. Department of State, 21 January 2010, available at: //2009-2017.state.gov/secretary/20092013clinton/rm/2010/01/135519.htm.

Codagnone, Cristiano, Athina Karatzogianni, and Jacob Matthews. *Platform Economics: Rhetoric and Reality in the 'Sharing Economy'*. Leeds: Emerald Publishing 2019.

Cong, Wanshu, and Johannes Thumfart. 'A Chinese Precursor to the Digital Sovereignty Debate: Digital Anti-Colonialism and Authoritarianism from the Post–Cold War Era to the Tunis Agenda'. *Global Studies Quarterly* 2, no. 4 (October 2022). https://doi.org/10.1093/isagsq/ksac059.

Couldry, Nick, and Ulises Ali Mejias. 'The Decolonial Turn in Data and Technology Research: What Is at Stake and Where Is It Heading?' *Information, Communication & Society* 26, no. 4 (12 March 2023): 786–802.

De Capello, H. H. Krill. 'The Creation of the United Nations Educational, Scientific and Cultural Organization'. *International Organization* 24, no. 1 (1970): 1–30.

Desantes Guanter, José María. *Francisco de Vitoria, Precursor Del Derecho de La Información*. Madrid: Fundación de la Comunicación Social 1999.

Deutsche Telekom AG. 'T-Systems and Google Cloud Partner to Deliver Sovereign Cloud for Germany', 08/2021. https://www.telekom.com/en/media/media-information/archive/sovereign-cloud-from-t-systems-and-google-cloud-635314.

Federal Office for Information Security. 'Cloud Independence Day: BSI und ANSSI stellen European Secure Cloud Label vor', June 6, 2017, available at: https://www.bsi.bund.de/DE/Presse/Kurzmeldungen/Meldungen/news_Cloud_Independence_Day_06062017.html.

Franceschini, Ivan, and Nicholas Loubere. *Global China as Method*. Cambridge: Cambridge University Press 2022.

Goldberg, Jeffrey. 'Why Obama Fears for Our Democracy'. *The Atlantic* (16 November 2020), available at: https://www.theatlantic.com/ideas/archive/2020/11/why-obama-fears-for-our-democracy/617087/.

Goldsmith, Jack L. 'Against Cyberanarchy'. *The University of Chicago Law Review* Vol. 65, No. 4 (Autumn) (1998): 1199–1250.

Goldsmith, Jack L. 'The Failure of Internet Freedom'. Emerging Threats. Knight First Amendment Institute, 2018, available at: http://kfai-documents.s3.amazonaws.com/documents/0f969b7a13/The-Failure-of-Internet-Freedom.pdf.

Gong, Wenxiang. 信息时代的国际传播: 国际关系面临的新问题 [International Communication in the Information Age: News Problems Faced by International Relations].' 国际政治研究 [*International Politics Studies*] 2 (1998): 41–46.

Greenberg, Andy. 'It's Been 20 Years since John Perry Barlow Declared Cyberspace Independence'. *Wired* (2 August 2016), available at: https://www.wired.com/2016/02/its-been-20-years-since-this-man-declared-cyberspace-independence/.

Grüll, Philipp, and Samuel Stolton. 'US and Chinese Tech Giants Welcomed into "EU Sovereign" Cloud Project'. www.euractiv.com (15 October 2020), available at: https://www.euractiv.com/section/digital/news/us-and-chinese-tech-giants-welcomed-into-eu-sovereign-cloud-project/.

Jones, Reilly. 'A Critique of Barlow's "A Declaration of the Independence of Cyberspace"'. *Extropy* #17 8, no. 2 (2nd Half 1996), available at: http://people.morrisville.edu/~reymers/readings/STS316/Barlow-Declaration-Critique_by_Jones.pdf.

Koskenniemi, Martti. *From Apology to Utopia: The Structure of International Legal Argument: Reissue with a New Epilogue*. Cambridge: Cambridge University Press 2005.

Krastev, Ivan, and Stephen Holmes. *The Light That Failed: A Reckoning*. London: Allen Lane 2019.

Kwet, Michael. 'Digital Colonialism: US Empire and the New Imperialism in the Global South'. *Race & Class* 60, no. 4 (April 2019): 3–26.

McCarthy, Daniel R. *Power, Information Technology, and International Relations Theory: The Power and Politics of US Foreign Policy and the Internet.* New York: Palgrave Macmillan 2015.

Mchangama, Jacob and Joelle Fiss, 'The Digital Berlin Wall: How Germany (Accidentally) Created a Prototype for Global Online Censorship' (Copenhagen: Justitia, November 2019), available at: https://globalfreedomofexpression.columbia.edu/wp-content/uploads/2019/11/Analyse_The-Digital-Berlin-Wall-How-Germany-Accidentally-Created-a-Prototype-for-Global-Online-Censorship.pdf.

Metodieva, Asya. 'Digital sovereignty contested: Hungary's strategic use of EU platform regulations'. *Journal of Contemporary European Studies* (2025), 1–18.

Morin-Desailly, Catherine. 'Rapport d'information, Fait Au Nom de La Commission Des Affaires Européennes', 20 March 2013, available at: www.senat.fr/notice-rapport/2012/r12-443-notice.html.

Morozov, Evgenij V. *The Net Delusion: The Dark Side of Internet Freedom.* New York: Public Affairs 2011.

Morozov, Evgeny. Tweet October 17, 2020, 12:06, available at: https://twitter.com/evgenymorozov/status/1317406673749815297?s=20

Nye, Joseph S., and William A. Owens. 'America's Information Edge'. *Foreign Affairs* 75, no. 2 (1996): 20–36.

Papagianneas, Straton, and Adam Knight. 'the Stumbling Smart State Fragmented Policy Experimentation and Dubious Consolidation'. In Rogier Creemers, Straton Papagianneas, and Adam Knight (eds.), *The Emergence of China's Smart State*, edited by, 35–52. Blue Ridge Summit: Rowman & Littlefield 2023.

Powell, Jamie. 'Europe's Digital Infrastructure Issue'. *Financial Times* (2 September 2019), available at: https://www.ft.com/content/d409ef42-5e61-3654-86fc-d70286a899b2.

Prime Minister of Australia. 'Australian Government Collaboration with Microsoft on Artificial Intelligence', 16 November 2023, available at: https://www.pm.gov.au/media/australian-government-collaboration-microsoft-artificial-intelligence.

Savin, Leonid. 'Номос Киберпространства исуверенный Интернет'. *Плюриверсум* (blog), 30 December 2019. https://pluriversum.org/opinion/cyberspace/nomos-kiberprostranstva-i-suverennyj-internet/.

Savin, Leonid. 'Суверенный Интернет – Дело Принципиальной Важности Для Национальной Безопасности'. *News Front* (30 December 2019), available at: https://news-front.info/2019/12/30/suverennyj-internet-delo-princzipialnoj-vazhnosti-dlya-naczionalnoj-bezopasnosti/.

Schiller, Herbert I. 'Genesis of the Free Flow of Information Principles: The Imposition of Communications Domination'. *Instant Research on Peace and Violence* 5, no. 2 (1975): 75–86.

Schmitt, Carl. 'Der Führer schützt das Recht. Zur Reichstagsrede Adolf Hitlers Vom 13. Juli 1943.' *Deutsche Juristen-Zeitung* 39, no. 15 (1934).

Schmitt, Carl. 'Großraum versus Universalism: the International Legal Struggle over the Monroe Doctrine'. In Stephen Legg (ed.), *Spatiality, Sovereignty and Carl Schmitt: Geographies of the Nomos*, 46–54. London: Routledge 2011.

Schmitt, Carl. 'Staat, Bewegung, Volk. Die Dreigliederung der Politischen Einheit.' In *Gesammelte Schriften 1933–1936: Mit ergänzenden Beiträgen aus der Zeit des Zweiten Weltkriegs*, 76–115. Berlin: Duncker und Humblot 2021.

Schmitt, Carl. 'the Age of Neutralizations and Depoliticizations'. In *The Concept of the Political*, 80–96. Chicago: University of Chicago Press 2007.

Schmitt, Carl. *Gespräch über die Macht und den Zugang zum Machthaber*. Stuttgart: Klett Cotta 1954.

Schmitt, Carl. *Römischer Katholizismus Und Politische Form*. Hellerau: Jakob Wegner 1923.

Schmitt, Carl. *The Leviathan in the State Theory of Thomas Hobbes: Meaning and Failure of a Political Symbol*. Westport, Conn: Greenwood Press 1996.

Schmitt, Carl. *The Nomos of the Earth in the International Law of the Jus Publicum Europaeum*. New York: Telos Press 2003.

Snyder, Timothy. *The Road to Unfreedom: Russia, Europe, America*. New York: Tim Duggan Books 2018.

Specter, Matthew. *The Atlantic Realists: Empire and International Political Thought between Germany and the United States*. Stanford, California: Stanford University Press 2022.

Thumfart, Johannes. 'Digital Rights and the State of Exception. Internet Shutdowns from the Perspective of Just Securitization Theory'. *Journal of Global Security Studies* 9, no. 1 (9 January 2024): https://doi.org/10.1093/jogss/ogad024.

Thumfart, Johannes. 'Francisco de Vitorias Philosophie: Globalpolitisch, Nicht Kosmopolitisch'. In Kirstin Bunge, Anselm Spindler, and Andreas Wagner (eds.), *Die Normativität des Rechts bei Francisco de Vitoria*, 229–254. Stuttgart: Frommann-Holzboog 2011.

Thumfart, Johannes. 'On Grotius's Mare Liberum and Vitoria's De Indis, Following Agamben and Schmitt'. *Grotiana* 30, no. 1 (2009): 65–87. https://doi.org/10.1163/016738309X12537002674286.

Thumfart, Johannes. 'the Norm Development of Digital Sovereignty between China, Russia, the Eu and the Us: from the Late 1990s to the Covid-Crisis 2020/21 as Catalytic Event'. In Dara Hallinan, Ronald Leenes, and Paul de Hert (eds.), *Enforcing Rights in a Changing World*, 1–44. London: Hart Publishing 2021.

Thumfart, Johannes. *Die Begründung der Globalpolitischen Philosophie: Francisco de Vitorias Vorlesung Über Die Entdeckung Amerikas Im Ideengeschichtlichen Kontext*. Kaleidogramme, Bd. 44. Berlin: Kulturverlag Kadmos 2012.

Thumfart, Johannes. 'Digital Sovereignty in China, Russia and India: from Nwico to Sco and Brics', in Luca Belli and Min Jiang (eds.), *Digital Sovereignty in the BRICS Countries*. Cambridge: Cambridge University Press 2024.

Thumfart, Johannes. *The Liberal Internet in the Postliberal Era: Digital Sovereignty, Private Government, and Practices of Neutralization*. Basingstoke: Palgrave Macmillan 2024.

UNESCO. 'UNESCO Constitution', 1945.

UNESCO. *Many Voices, One World: Communication and Society Today and Tomorrow ; towards a New More Just and More Efficient World Information and Communication Order*. London: Kogan Page 1980.

Uttaro, Ralph A. 'The Voices of America in International Radio Propaganda'. *Law and Contemporary Problems* 45, no. 1 (1982): 103–122.

Van Dijck, José, Thomas Poell, and Martijn De Waal. *The Platform Society*. Vol. 1. Oxford: Oxford University Press 2018.

Vitoria, Francisco de. 'on the American Indians'. In Anthony Pagden and Jeremy Lawrance (eds.), *Political Writings*, 231–292. Cambridge: Cambridge University Press 1991.

PART 5

Vitoria and Schmitt in the Canon of International Law

CHAPTER 17

'Ancora tu?' Questioning Carl Schmitt's Place in the Canon of International Law

Paolo Amorosa and Ville Suuronen

1 Introduction

Que faire de Carl Schmitt?, wondered Jean-Francois Kervégan in a 2011 book bearing the question as its title.[1] It is a valid and difficult question, one that has been asked numerous times and received divergent answers across academic disciplines and fields of thought. International law is no exception.

Schmitt's association with the Nazi regime and ideology accounts for why he was very rarely mentioned in post-war literature on international law,[2] though his unacknowledged intellectual influence could be easily found in major works such as Wilhelm Grewe's *The Epochs of International Law*.[3] Schmitt has resurfaced to the mainstream of international legal literature at the turn of the twenty-first century.[4] As the United States and its allies inaugurated a global War on Terror, Schmitt's reflections on exceptionalism and the hypocrisy of humanitarian discourse in a liberal vein were recovered as intellectual fodder for critiques by international lawyers from the left of the political spectrum.[5] Although left-wing Schmittianism has been a constant feature of Schmitt's intellectual heritage,[6] this Schmittian revival has continued to

1 Jean-Francois Kervégan, *Que faire de Carl Schmitt?* (Paris: Gallimard, 2011).

2 On Schmitt's influence see Dirk Van Laak, *Gespräche in der Sicherheit des Schweigens. Carl Schmitt in der politischen Geistesgeschichte der frühen Bundesrepublik* (Berlin: Akademie Verlag, 2002); Jan-Werner Müller, *A Dangerous Mind: Carl Schmitt in Post-War European Thought* (New Haven: Yale University Press, 2003).

3 Wilhelm Grewe, *The Epochs of International Law* (Berlin: De Gruyter 2000 [1988]).

4 e.g., Martti Koskenniemi, *The Gentle Civilizer of Nations: The Rise and Fall of International Law 1870–1960* (Cambridge, 2004), 413–509; Louiza Odysseos and Fabio Petito, eds., *The International Political thought of Carl Schmitt: Terror, Liberal War and the Crisis of Global Order* (London, 2007).

5 See in the same sense Koskenniemi, 'Carl Schmitt and International Law' in Jens Meienrich and Oliver Simons (eds.), *The Oxford Handbook of Carl Schmitt*, (Oxford: Oxford University Press 2013), 605–606.

6 Ellen Kennedy, "Carl Schmitt and the Frankfurt School" *Telos* (71)1987: 37–66; Hubertus Buchstein, "The Godfather of Left-Schmittianism? Otto Kirchheimer and Carl Schmitt after

 | DOI:10.1163/9789004757448_018

develop approaches one might consider antithetical to his legacy. More recently, some have gone as far as suggesting the reading of Schmitt through a post-colonial lens.[7] Under these ambivalent circumstances, it is hardly surprising that international lawyers have been reckoning with Schmitt's place within the disciplinary tradition. Most of these conversations take a shape that is particularly familiar in post-*Me too* times, where nebulous talk over the prevalence of a cancel culture[8] and of an 'illiberal liberalism' defining the contemporary left is rife.[9] The central question is whether one can separate the art from the artist, as the expression goes. As long as Schmitt's association with the Nazi regime and his sustained antisemitism are duly acknowledged,[10] both poles of the debate, that of the intellectual significance of Schmitt, beyond his horrific ideological flaws and that of the full rejection of his work as too tainted to be of any use to us today, appear to have a place in contemporary international law discourse.

Recently, Schmitt's legacy was debated in two short contributions by Joseph Weiler and Tara van Ho, which appeared on outlets of the *European Journal of International Law* (EJIL).[11] Weiler articulates, in the detail allowed by a short text, the reprehensible features of Schmitt's politics and work. However, it is telling that Weiler's indictment is construed as a justification of why he 'add[s] a metaphorical plaque to the intellectual statue of Schmitt', making a point of reminding his 'reader who the man was.' This dovetails with the assertion that the 'seriousness of [Schmitt's] failings, both in thought and deed [...] are integral to a not insignificant part of his work' and only 'in some respects'. In other words, the text posits the assumption that a significant part of Schmitt's intel-

1945". *Redescriptions: Political Thought, Conceptual History and Feminist Theory* 24(1): 4–26.

7 Stephen Legg, 'Interwar spatial chaos? Imperialism, internationalism and the League of Nations' in Stephen Legg (ed.), Spatiality, Sovereignty and Carl Schmitt Geographies of the Nomos (London: Routledge, 2011), 106–124; Andreas Kalyvas, 'Carl Schmitt's Postcolonial Imagination', *Constellations* 25 (2018), 35–53. For an astute critique of these perspectives, see for instance Robert J. C. Young, 'Mythmaking: The Nomos of Postcoloniality' in Caroline S. Hau and Pheng Cheah (Eds.), *Siting Postcoloniality: Critical Perspectives from the East Asian Sinosphere* (Durham, NC: Duke University Press, 2022), 33–52.

8 The pitfalls of 'cancel culture' discourse are brilliantly outlined in Amia Srinivasan, 'Cancelled', *London Review of Books*, Vol. 45 no. 13, 29 June 2023.

9 Frank Furedi, "Illiberal Liberalism: A Genealogy," *The Journal of Illiberalism Studies*. 2(2) 2022: 19–36.

10 See in the same sense, Martti Koskenniemi, 'Letter to the Editors', *Chinese Journal of International Law*, 12 (2013), 201–202.

11 Joseph Weiler, 'Cancelling Carl Schmitt?', EJIL:Talk, 13 August 2021, available at ejiltalk.org/cancelling-carl-schmitt/; Tara Van Ho, 'Cancelling Schmitt', *European Journal of International Law*, 32 (2021), 730–731.

lectual production would be untainted by his ideology. In line with this decoupling, Weiler never entertains the idea that one might simply and legitimately decide to forgo Schmitt as an intellectual reference: ' "cancelling" Schmitt from public law and political theory scholarly discourse [i]s an idea or policy I could not support.' Referring to the leading academic reviews he has been Editor-in-Chief of for many years, Weiler curtly states: 'We are journals of public law, so it would be odd if Schmitt did not pop up regularly.'

Weiler's text reflects a shared position within international legal academia: debates might take place on whether the 'plaque' on Schmitt's 'statue' is sufficiently clear and big, or whether it has been placed prominently enough. At the other end of this debate, Van Ho critiques Weiler's decoupling position, 'parsing Schmitt's intellectual contributions so as to deem only some of his work unacceptable.' Instead, she submits, 'his core beliefs were written into his scholarship [and a]ny attempt to engage [him] is a choice to forgive his sins and find value in him.' Yet, Despite Weiler's evocation of 'cancel culture,' apart from Tara van Ho, virtually nobody has been vocally trying to topple Schmitt's metaphorical statue or remove it from our epistemic living space. However, it seems there is not even a point in articulating *why* the statue is there, to begin with: it is accepted as self-evident, it would be 'odd' otherwise.

Instead of analysing this topic through the problematic lens of 'cancelling,' Schmitt's position in the canon of international law can also be approached by examining the issue of canonicity as such.[12] By problematizing the idea of the canon as a monolithic monument that would, by essence, be relatively static and offer membership on the basis of some objective or generally recognized form of intellectual achievement, it is crucial to recognize the functioning of the canon as a fluid historical artefact, whose making and reproduction heavily depends on contingent choices, political convenience and – often unreflective – serial repetition. Understanding canons as active creations, rather than self-evident objects, evokes our responsibility in the making and constant re-making of the canon, and therefore also our ability to change them.

This point was already made by novelist Jorge Luis Borges in his short essay on Franz Kafka: 'The fact is that every writer *creates* his own precursors. His work modifies our conception of the past, as it will modify the future.'[13] By using the work of another author, one reinterprets and re-invokes the importance of one's precursors in a novel historical context, a logic operating also in the international legal canon. By problematizing the essentialist canonical

12 See Paolo Amorosa and Claire Vergerio, 'Canon-Making in the History of International Legal and Political Thought', *Leiden Journal of International Law*, 35 (2022), 469–478.

13 Jorge Luis Borges, 'Kafka and His Precursors', in *Labyrinths. Selected Stories and Other Writings* (New York: New Directions, 1964), 201.

lens, it is possible to glean again the forms of structural bias that characterize international law – such as its Eurocentrism and gendered nature – and to discover how such structures contribute to the preservation of Schmitt's prominence within the field. Read in this light, the question whether we should use Schmitt in our disciplinary discourse not only appears generally justified but also acquires a direct political relevance.

In this essay, we explore this question by examining Schmitt's work, focusing especially on his reading of Francisco de Vitoria and his legacy in the twentieth century – a reading that directly engages the politics of canonicity. As we will see, in Schmitt's work, Vitoria emerges as one of the canonical figures, who allow him to rewrite the history of international law from a radically anti-liberal perspective and to whitewash his own Nazi engagement. In the following sections, we begin with a close analysis of Vitoria's role in Schmitt's oeuvre. We argue that by criticizing the liberal appropriations of Vitoria in the twentieth century – especially that of James Brown Scott (1866–1943) – Schmitt not only offers a counter-reading of the history of European international law, but also reiterates, in a veiled form, core arguments at the heart of his own Nazi writings – in particular, the idea that liberalism must be blamed for the breakdown of classical European political rationalism and thus for the major catastrophes of the twentieth century.

Secondly, we assess Schmitt's role in the international legal discourse of recent decades through a canonical perspective. We analyse the reasons and choices sustaining the Schmittian revival of the twenty-first century to disclose the implications of canon-making as a political phenomenon. This operation is crucial to the self-image of the discipline beyond Schmitt, to express precisely and with awareness the fundamental values we aim to convey by relying on past thinkers.

2 Schmitt as a Scholar of International Law and His Discovery of Vitoria

Schmitt's 1936 downfall in the ranks of the Nazi party[14] has often been seen as the crucial event turning his work more clearly towards questions of international law. However, as the subtitle of Schmitt's 1940 essay collection high-

---

14 C.f., Andreas Koenen, *Der Fall Carl Schmitt. Sein Aufstieg zum "Kronjuristen des Dritten Reiches"* (Darmstadt: Wissenschaftliche Buchgesellschaft, 1995), 651–764; Dirk Blasius, *Carl Schmitt. Preußischer Staatsrat in Hitlers Reich* (Göttingen: Vandenhoeck und Ruprecht, 2001), 153–180; Reinhard Mehring, *Carl Schmitt: Aufstieg und Fall* (München: C.H. Beck, 2009), 378–380.

lights, his self-proclaimed 'battle with Weimar, Geneva, Versailles' incorporated both questions of constitutional and international law already by 1923/1924.[15] Of his numerous essays on international law from the Weimar-era,[16] of special importance is Schmitt's *Die Rheinlande als Objekt internationaler Politik* (1925), which offers a critique of the Rheinland occupation. Schmitt's most important contribution to international law from the 1920s, *Die Kernfrage des Völkerbundes* (1926), describes the League of Nations as suffering from a 'principled lack of principles' and aims to de-mask it as an instrument of indirect Anglo-American imperialism.[17] Also his *magnum opus, Verfassungslehre* (1928), offers a 'constitutional theory of a league' and sketches what a true league of nations would look like if based on the sovereignty of nation-states.[18]

In 1930, Schmitt edited a collection of legal documents pertaining to the League of Nations as well as the Holy Alliance and the Monroe Doctrine titled *Der Völkerbund und das politische Problem der Friedenssicherung*. A specifically National Socialist edition of this work was published in 1934 and included an array of Hitler's and Mussolini's speeches, which Schmitt portrays as documents testifying to the end of utopian universalism and pacifism – the ideals of the League of Nations – in the international realm.[19] The republication of this collection was closely related to Schmitt's book *Nationalsozialismus und Völkerrecht* (1934), which Michael Stolleis describes as the first attempt at developing a specifically Nazi approach to international law.[20] After 1933, Schmitt wrote numerous essays on different particular questions of international law,[21] comparative essays on the different legal systems and ideologies of Nazi Germany, Fascist Italy and the Soviet Union,[22] and a long essay on how the Nazi racial legislation would affect international private law.[23] Emblemat-

---

15 Carl Schmitt, *Positionen und Begriffe. Im Kampf mit Weimar–Genf–Versailles, 1923–1939* (Berlin: Duncker & Humblot, 2014).

16 See Carl Schmitt, *Frieden oder Pazifismus? Arbeiten zum Völkerrecht und zur internationalen Politik*, ed. Günter Maschke (Berlin: Duncker and Humblot, 2005), 1–25, 26–50, 51–72, 240–254, 255–273, 274–280, 333–348, 349–377.

17 Carl Schmitt, *Die Kernfrage des Völkerbundes* (Berlin: Dümmler, 1926).

18 Carl Schmitt, *Verfassungslehre* (Berlin: Duncker & Humblot, 2010), 363–91.

19 Carl Schmitt, *Der politische Problem der Friedenssicherung* (Leipzig-Berlin, 1934).

20 Michael Stolleis, *Geschichte des öffentlichen Rechts in Deutschland. Weimarer Republik und Nationalsozialismus* (München: Piper, 2002), 384.

21 Carl Schmitt, *Gesammelte Schriften 1933–1936. Mit ergänzenden Beiträgen aus der Zeit des Zweiten Weltkriegs* (Berlin: Duncker & Humblot, 2021), 207–211, 212–223, 233–237, 238–243, 325–329, 364–368, 386–402.

22 Schmitt, *Gesammelte Schriften*, 333–334, 335–349.

23 Schmitt, *Gesammelte Schriften*, 369–385.

ically, Schmitt also became an editor of the journal 'Zeitschrift für ausländisches öffentliches Recht und Völkerrecht' in 1934.[24]

All of this *precedes* what is often one-sidedly and misleadingly described as Schmitt's 'turn' in 1936. Most importantly, although Schmitt did turn increasingly towards international law, this cannot be described simply as Schmitt's personal decision stemming from his downfall:[25] it was a defining feature of *all of Nazi legal science*. As Stolleis emphasizes, constitutional law was increasingly perceived as a 'substantially empty and dangerous area,' whose decisive questions had already been settled. This 'loss of meaning' was compensated by the growing importance of international law.[26] Schmitt's later central works on international law – including *Der Leviathan* (1938), *Die Wendung zum diskriminierenden Kriegsbegriff* (1938), *Völkerrechtliche Großraumordnung* (1939ff.), *Land und Meer* (1942), *Völkerrecht – Ein Repertorium* (1948–1950, published only posthumously) and *Die Lage der europäischen Rechtswissenschaft* (1950), as well as his later *magnum opus Der Nomos der Erde* (1950), of which the two latter were by and large written already during World War II – must be understood in this broader historical context.

How does Vitoria appear in these writings? The contents of Schmitt's personal library and his publications indicate that Schmitt likely familiarized himself with Vitoria during the late 1930s.[27] The library includes a collection of Vitoria's writings published in Spanish between 1933 and 1935[28] as well as two books on Vitoria: Teodoro Andrés Marcos's *Vitoria y Carlos V en la soberanía hispano-americana*[29] and Günther Krauß's planned habilitation *Homo homini homo. Zwölf Kapitel zur Relectio de Indis des Francisco de Vitoria* from 1952, which was rejected and never published.[30] As Günther Maschke notes, Schmitt's views on Vitoria were decisively influenced by contemporary Spanish authors and Krauss,[31] who was Schmitt's student and Nazi-era assistant.

24 Stolleis, *Geschichte*, 393.

25 c.f., Joseph Bendersky, *Carl Schmitt. Theorist for the Reich* (Princeton: Princeton University Press, 1983), 248.

26 Stolleis, *Geschichte*, 381, 318, 254–235.

27 https://www.carl-schmitt.de/wp-content/uploads/CSG_Bibliothek_H2_2021.pdf

28 Francisco de Vitoria, *Relecciones teológicas. Edición crítica, con facsimil de códices y ediciones príncipes, variantes, versión castellana, notas e introducción.* Ed. Luis G. Alonso Getino, Tomo 1–3, Madrid 1933–1935.

29 Also cited in Schmitt, *Der Nomos der Erde*, 77, 87.

30 Montserrat Herrero in Carl Schmitt und Álvaro d'Órs, *Briefwechsel*. Edited by Montserrat Herrero. (Berlin, Duncker & Humblot, 2004), *111 fn 9*.

31 Günter Maschke in Schmitt, *Frieden oder Pazifismus?*, 671ff. For the Spanish authors mentioned by Schmitt, see fn 31.

Also, Schmitt's *Glossarium* as well as the correspondence with Álvaro d'Órs testify to an intensive reflection on Vitoria in the 1940s and 1950s.[32]

Schmitt's first passing references to Vitoria date back to presentations in Nürnberg in February 1941[33] and in Madrid, on 1 June 1943.[34] However, the only comprehensive analysis of Vitoria in Schmitt's *oeuvre* has its roots in a series of lectures given in Spain and Portugal in 1943/44.[35] This presentation was published anonymously in 1949 in the journal *Die Neue Ordnung* with the title 'Francisco de Vitoria und die Geschichte seines Ruhmes' and in Spanish translation (with Schmitt's authorship acknowledged) during the same year. This essay was then included as a chapter in *Der Nomos der Erde*.[36]

Although Schmitt's treatment of Vitoria has a very limited space in his *oeuvre*, a holistic understanding of his works on international law is crucial for grasping how and why Schmitt discovers Vitoria in the 1940s. Although Schmitt would describe his article on Vitoria as a 'meticulously considered, subject-specific essay,'[37] his focus and polemical criticism of Vitoria's legacy in the twentieth century testifies to the story being more complex. While Schmitt was certainly interested in Vitoria as a central author of late Spanish scholasticism as such, his main target of criticism in the chapter concerns the twentieth-century liberal appropriations of Vitoria. The politics of canons are at the heart of Schmitt's interest in Vitoria; by criticizing James Brown Scott for depicting Vitoria as the father of modern international law,[38] Schmitt aims to offer a counter-reading of Vitoria in support of his own historical depiction of international law.

---

32 Carl Schmitt, *Glossarium. Aufzeichnungen aus den Jahren 1947 bis 1958*. Ed. Gerd Giesler and Martin Tielke (Berlin: Duncker & Humbolt, 2015), 19, 72, 129–130, 141, 148, 151, 154, 197, 201, 207, 210, 213, 269, 281, 371ff, 397; Schmitt und Álvaro d'Órs, *Briefwechsel*, 66–68, 72–75, 78–81, 85–98, 108–111, 119–123, 129–131. Schmitt was also involved in planning an international conference on Vitoria, but this plan never came to fruition (Mehring, *Aufstieg und Fall*, 471–472).

33 Carl Schmitt, *Staat, Grossraum, Nomos. Arbeiten aus den Jahren 1916–1969*, ed. Günter Maschke (Berlin: Duncker & Humblot, 1995), 410.

34 Schmitt, *Frieden oder Pazifismus*, 664.

35 Carl Schmitt, *Antworten in Nürnberg*. Ed. Helmut Quaritsch. (Berlin: Duncker and Humblot, 2000), 24fn45.

36 Schmitt, *Der Nomos der Erde im Völkerrecht des Jus Publicum Europaeum* [hereafter NdE] (Berlin: Duncker & Humblot, 2011), 69–96.

37 Carl Schmitt and Ernst Rudolf Huber, *Briefwechsel 1926–1981*, ed. Ewald Grothe (Berlin: Duncker & Humblot, 2014), 353.

38 While Schmitt also mentions the works of Ernst Nys, Camilio Barcia Trelles, Alejandro Alvarez and Fernandez Prida as promoting Vitoria as the founder of modern international law (NdE, 88), we will focus on Scott as Schmitt's polemical criticism is most clearly directed against his work.

As we will see, Schmitt read Vitoria's reception among Western legal scholars in the twentieth century in light of his earlier theories, developed *in nuce* already in the 1920s. For Schmitt, the problematic reception of Vitoria's work among American and European theorists of international law in support of just war, the League of Nations and the championing of 'peace through justice' more generally, begin to appear as *ex post facto* confirmations of his own critiques of pacifism, universalism and especially, the League of Nations – all themes that were also at the core of Schmitt's Nazi writings on international law. Engaging in a specifically canonical politics, Schmitt's confrontation with Vitoria's heritage forms one of the historical foils against which he legitimized his own far-right readings of the history of international law and whitewashed his previous involvement with the Nazi regime. In what follows, we will analyse both Schmitt's treatment of Vitoria and the canonical politics involved in this reading.

3 Vitoria and the Politics of Canons in *Der Nomos der Erde*

As Schmitt noted in 1963, 'the epoch of statehood is reaching its end.' Although the European nation-state and its monopoly of sovereignty were now being 'dethroned,' the conceptual framework of this previous epoch was sustained by theorists of international law.[39] This created an 'intermediate situation,' in which it was becoming impossible to know what war and peace still meant in practice.[40] As Schmitt emphasizes, *Der Nomos der Erde* was an attempt to address this intermediate situation and to offer 'a historical retrospection… that reflects systematically on the great era of the *jus publicum Europaeum* and its concepts of state and war and just enemy in constant awareness of their systematicity.'[41]

In *Der Nomos der Erde*, Schmitt argues that modern international law was born in the wake of the European colonization of the Americas and the confessional religious wars in Europe. Analysing the major European peace conferences of 1648, 1713, 1814/1815, 1856, 1878 and 1885, plus other central sources, he aimed to show that European international law and order was consolidated by the Treaties of Westphalia in 1648 and the Treaty of Utrecht in 1713.[42] The

39 Carl Schmitt, *Der Begriff des Politischen. Text von 1932 mit einem Vorwort und drei Corollarien* (Berlin: Duncker & Humblot, 2009), 10.
40 Ibid, 12.
41 Ibid, 16.
42 NdE, 162; c.f., 156–157.

most crucial historical development consists of the birth of modern sovereign nation states, for which Thomas Hobbes's *Leviathan* (1651) offers 'the first philosophical-systematic grounding.'[43] With Hobbes, the right to wage war (*jus belli*) becomes an inseparable part of international politics. Going beyond medieval theories of just war, modern international law distinguishes clearly between moral and political questions. These changes allow for what Schmitt calls the 'bracketing of war' (*Hegung des Krieges*): The limitation of warfare to a matter of foreign policy between states and the protection of civilians from violence, which form the central essence of European public law and represent the greatest achievement of occidental political rationalism.[44] This 'bracketing' presupposes the unlimited warfare of European nations in the colonized and free territories as well as the freedom of the seas, forming a new Eurocentric global order and creating a multifaceted balance of power in continental Europe between sovereign nation-states and the English sea empire.[45] For Schmitt, the golden age of the *jus publicum Europaeum* is situated between 1713 and 1914,[46] during which Europe forms the centre of the world and civilization means essentially European civilization.[47]

What is Vitoria's role in this historical narrative? For Schmitt, Vitoria was a theological author, who was writing in the context of the medieval *Respublica Christiana*, preceding the birth of modern international law.[48] According to Schmitt, Vitoria's *Relecciones de Indis et de Jure Belli* (1538/9) provide the one and only 'systematic' treatment concerning the question of 'the European land-grabbing as a whole.'[49] As Schmitt shows, by engaging in a debate with the humanist Juan Gines Sepúlveda (1490–1573), Vitoria's analysis of the Conquista takes a stance against the central theses defended by other Spanish and later European authors. Drawing on Aristotle's *Politics* and the idea that some individuals are by nature slaves, Sepulveda had argued that the indigenous peoples of Southern America should be seen as barbarians and savages, whom Europeans could conquer with self-evident legitimacy.[50] For Vitoria, like for Augustine, it was as self-evident that also indigenous people had an

43 NdE, 134.
44 NdE, 89–96, 112–135, 156–158.
45 NdE, 54–5, 112–3, 144–6, 156.
46 NdE, 155–156.
47 NdE, 54.
48 NdE, 25–30, 79–83.
49 NdE, 70.
50 NdE, 71.

immortal soul, which led him to polemically reject Sepulveda's Aristotelian argumentation as essentially 'pagan.'[51]

However, Schmitt emphasizes that Vitoria was by no means a modern secular jurist but a theologian, and his arguments cannot be read in light of later non-theological jurists, such as Balthasar Ayala, Albericus Gentilis or Richard Zouche.[52] The Spanish Dominican spoke and wrote as a 'counselor of conscience (*Gewissensberater*)' for future theologians and political actors.[53] Vitoria's analysis on the legitimacy of the *Conquista* was not posed in legal terms, but rather as a matter of moral theology. Vitoria too took for granted that a war between Christian nations was something essentially different than a war between Christians and non-Christians, arguing also that indigenous peoples required 'guidance.'[54] Relying on the medieval doctrine of just war, Vitoria supported the legitimacy of the *Conquista* by recognizing the Pope as the ultimate authority, who could grant missionary orders to wage just wars against non-Christian peoples. As a theologian, Vitoria is speaking as an organ of the Roman Catholic Church under which the crown of Castille had received the authority for its mission.[55] What differentiates Vitoria from later theorists of the law of nations is precisely the crucial difference of historical contexts: medieval Christendom vs. later-secularized international law.[56]

Aiming to 'purify [Vitoria's] image from false overpainting (*Übermalungen*) and to give back his words their true sense,'[57] Schmitt's essay then turns toward analysing the different legacies and interpretations of Vitoria's work, which 'have their own history.'[58] Although the '[t]ransferring of arguments and concepts to other situations is not unusual in itself and occurs frequently in history,'[59] in the case of Vitoria, the 'exploitation' (*Verwertung*)[60] of his arguments in historically different situations actually grounds the basis of his contemporary 'fame.'[61] Schmitt discovers the first example of such a decontextualized use of Vitoria from Hugo Grotius's *Mare Liberum* (1609), in which Grotius argues that, in terms of international law, the sea is *terra nul-*

51 NdE, 73.
52 NdE, 79.
53 NdE, 79.
54 NdE, 73.
55 NdE, 74, 78, 80–82.
56 NdE, 84.
57 NdE, 96.
58 NdE, 70.
59 NdE, 85.
60 NdE, 89.
61 NdE, 85.

lius. Transforming Vitoria's argumentation from the defence of the Conquista to a legitimation for the Dutch and English protestants to seize territories from Portugal and Spain, Grotius offers an early example of a politicized use of Vitoria in which ideas formed in the historical context of medieval Christendom are transferred to the modern realm of secular international law.[62] However, beyond examining such historical examples, Schmitt asks how and why a 'Vitoria renaissance' would begin after World War I, making Vitoria a 'world-famous' and 'globally-celebrated' author.[63]

While it was Ernest Nys, who laid the basis for the twentieth-century renaissance of Vitoria, Schmitt is especially interested in James Brown Scott, whose work reflects an entirely new epoch in the history of Vitoria's 'exploitation.'[64] Painting Vitoria and Suarez as the founders of modern international law without any sense for the crucial historical differences between the medieval *Respublica Christiana* and the later secularized international law between sovereign nation states, it was Scott's 'great enthusiasm' that laid the foundations for Vitoria's contemporary fame in the twentieth century.[65]

For Schmitt, Scott's liberal thought represented everything that was wrong with modern international law after World War I. Schmitt argues that by using Vitoria to justify a 'return to older and healthier conceptions of war' and to an epoch of 'just' wars,[66] Scott was misconceptualizing the nature of classical European international law and its notion of 'bracketed' wars. For Schmitt, the Versailles Treaties represented the perversion of modern international law, as they destroyed the idea of national sovereignty, incorporating *jus belli* and the perception of the enemy as a *justus hostis*. Against Scott, Schmitt would argue that by condemning Germany and its Kaiser as responsible for the outbreak of World War I, the Versailles Treaties reflected *a new form of just wars*, not a return to Vitoria and the era of medieval Christendom.[67] In this context, Schmitt cites Scott's and Robert Lansing's memorandum concerning the responsibility of the Central Powers in causing World War I. Scott and Lansing would speak of a 'moral crime against humanity' and claim that the initiators of this war needed to go down in history as 'stigmatized.'[68] For

62 NdE, 86.

63 NdE, 87.

64 NdE, 87–89; c.f., Schmitt, *Glossarium*, 129–130.

65 NdE, 89. On Scott's uses of Vitoria, see Paolo Amorosa, *Rewriting the History of the Law of Nations. How James Brown Scott Made Francisco de Vitoria the Founder of International Law* (Oxford: Oxford University Press, 2019).

66 NdE, 89.

67 NdE, 232–233.

68 NdE, 239.

Schmitt, this was nothing but a legitimization of a new kind of liberal imperialism against Germany and the central powers, which would destroy the concrete balance of powers on which classical European international law was based.

Similarly, Schmitt's stance on the League of Nations was diametrically opposed to that of Scott's. For Schmitt, the League did not establish a new form of global pacifism and universalism but was rather established 'as an ideological instrument' that served the purposes of 'imperialism.'[69] As Schmitt had noted already in his 1926 book on the League, from the perspective of classical European international law, 'it is not international law that brings peace, but rather a true peace is the foundation of international law.'[70] For Schmitt, no such thing as 'peace through law' can exist; 'in reality, law is only possible through peace.'[71] In *Der Nomos der Erde*, this 'true peace' then becomes identical with the Eurocentric balance of power and the notion of bracketed wars, which Schmitt describes as the great achievement of European political rationalism.

For Schmitt, Scott exemplifies a thinker exploiting and falsifying Vitoria's ideas by arguing for 'peace through justice' and capturing universalistic terminology for particularistic purposes. While Scott interpreted what Schmitt called the modern 'turn to the discriminatory concept of war' as a return to the Christian-theological doctrines of just war,[72] Schmitt argues that such an interpretation is nothing but an ideological exploitation of Vitoria's name for entirely different purposes. It is precisely in this sense that Schmitt claims that his Vitoria analysis had 'broken through' a 'ring of freemasonic pacifism.'[73] Instead of reflecting a humanization of warfare, the development of a new kind of just war doctrine was actually a function of the development of modern technology and unforeseen weapons of mass destruction. It is in this new historical situation that 'one needs a just war in order to legitimate the use of such means of destruction (*Vernichtungsmittel*).'[74]

What are Schmitt's motivations for criticizing Scott and his canonical uses of Vitoria? As we will see in the following section, the shadow of Schmitt's Nazi engagement is clearly present in his reading of the history of international law and the legacy of Vitoria in *Der Nomos der Erde* (1950).

---

69 Schmitt, *Der Begriff des Politischen*, 52.

70 Schmitt, *Die Kernfrage*, 7.

71 Ibid., 60–61, footnote 55.

72 NdE, 298.

73 Mehring, *Aufstieg und Fall*, 413.

74 NdE, 299.

4 The Shadow of Schmitt's National Socialism in *Der Nomos der Erde*

It is against Scott and others advocating for the return of just wars that Schmitt describes himself as the 'last conscious representative of the *jus publicum Europaeum*.'[75] Styling himself a defender of classical European political rationalism, Schmitt in fact used Vitoria's legacy polemically in order to *accuse liberalism of destroying classical European public law*. Not European colonial violence or the rise of far-right and nationalist politics, but rather the liberal-humanitarian hypocrisies of the Allied Powers were to be blamed for the catastrophes of the twentieth century.

As Schmitt had noted already in his *Begriff des Politischen*, 'whoever invokes humanity, wants to cheat.'[76] *Der Nomos der Erde* offers the concrete historical depiction for the process through which liberalism had supposedly systematically deformed all major political concepts and notions since the nineteenth century.[77] Placing himself on the side of Vitoria, Schmitt traced an intellectual history of the development of this kind of non-political and humanitarian argumentation, as first developed by Sepulveda, and later by Francis Bacon (1561–1626) and Jean Barbeyrac (1674–1744).

For Schmitt, it is by no means a 'paradox that humanists and humanitarians put forward such inhumane argumentation' as Sepulveda, for the concept of humanity itself 'has two sides.'[78] With the development of a 'philosophy of absolute humanity' in the eighteenth century, liberal thinkers inaugurated an era in which the 'sub-human' is introduced into the history of mankind as the 'hostile twin' of this humanitarianism itself.[79] In his later work *Die Tyrannei der Werte* (1959), Schmitt would go as far as arguing that this liberal in/humanization was also apparent in the notorious book by Karl Binding and Alfred Hoche, *Die Freigabe der Vernichtung lebensunwerten Lebens* (1920) – a key source for the legitimization of Nazi policies of destruction.[80]

Der Nomos der Erde also portrays the Versailles Treaties as embodying this dualistic spirit of liberal humanitarianism. Throughout his Weimar-era works, Schmitt – like the great majority of German jurists[81] – perceived the Versailles

75 Carl Schmitt, *Ex Captivitate Salus. Erfahrungen aus der Zeit 1945/47* (Berlin: Duncker & Humblot, 2002), 75; Reinhart Koselleck and Carl Schmitt, *Der Briefwechsel*, ed. Jan Eike Dunkhase (Berlin: Suhrkamp, 2019), 330.

76 Schmitt, *Der Begriff des Politischen*, 51–52.

77 Ibid, 63.

78 NdE, 72.

79 NdE, 72–73.

80 Carl Schmitt, *Die Tyrannei der Werte* (Berlin: Duncker & Humblot, 2011), 52.

81 Stolleis, *Geschichte*, 63; c.f., 87.

treaties as an injustice against Germany. While Schmitt portrayed the Weimar republic as a compromise formed under the Versailles Treaties, he nevertheless recognized the validity of the Weimar constitution as an authentic decision of the German people.[82] However, in his Nazi works, these historical circumstances appear in a radically different light. In *Nationalsozialismus und Völkerrecht* (1934), Schmitt speaks openly of the '*Kriegsschuldlüge*', the lie concerning Germany being responsible for World War I, referring to article 231 of the Versailles Treaties.[83] Elsewhere, Schmitt praises Hitler for pulling Germany out of the League of Nations and for overcoming the false ideals of pacifism with a vision for a true peace in Europe.[84] Further, in his *Staatsgefüge und Zusammenbruch des zweiten Reiches* (1934), Schmitt portrays Hitler as the leader who rescued Germany from the impasses of essentially non-German Western liberalism.[85]

In Schmitt's Nazi works, the issue of canonicity also takes on an openly political profile. As Schmitt abandoned his 'decisionism' in favour of racist 'concrete order thought,'[86] he would also discover new precursors to his own Nazi era legal theory. Engaging in a historical battle against Jewish influences in Germany, Schmitt would begin to criticize the reception of Roman law in favor of restoring a true Germanic legal science.[87] Further, aiming to 'purify' the German legal literature from the Jewish 'infection,'[88] Schmitt would organize a conference on 'Jewishness in Legal Science' in Berlin in late 1936 and engage in a racialist politics of canons by demanding that Jewish authors would be cited as Jews. As Schmitt notes here: 'The problem of citations is… a fundamental problem. It is possible to recognize a single author in the way he cites.'[89] By 1935, Schmitt was defending the Nuremberg laws as the new 'constitution of freedom' in Germany, celebrating the fact that 'German blood and German honor' had once again become 'main concepts' of German law.[90] That

82 Schmitt, *Verfassungslehre*, 23–24, 72.

83 Schmitt, *Gesammelte Schriften*, 187, 192.

84 Ibid, 51–53.

85 Carl Schmitt, *Staatsgefüge und Zusammenbruch des zweiten Reiches: Der Sieg des Bürgers über den Soldaten* (Berlin: Duncker & Humblot, 2011).

86 Ville Suuronen, 'Carl Schmitt as a theorist of the 1933 Nazi revolution: "The difficult task of rethinking and recultivating traditional concepts"'. *Contemporary Political Theory* 20(2): 341–363

87 Ville Suuronen, "Mobilizing the western tradition for present politics: Carl Schmitt's polemical uses of roman law, 1923–1945". *History of European Ideas* 47: 748–772.

88 Schmitt, *Gesammelte Schriften*, 484.

89 Ibid, 487–488.

90 Ibid, 282–284.

the idea of race forms the core of Schmitt's Nazi thought is also testified in detail by his speculations on how the new German racial legislation would affect international private law.[91]

To be sure, *Der Nomos der Erde* does not repeat these racial arguments, but rather openly states that its *nomos*-philosophy has nothing to do with biological conceptions of law and order.[92] Despite such self-serving statements, as has been argued in previous research,[93] Schmitt's post-war thought is defined by a form of cultural and structural racism that offers an unapologetic vision of international law formed under European hegemony. Especially the idea that the Versailles Treaties represent the deformation of European public law remains a core feature of Schmitt's historical narrative. Any historical event that could question this revanchist take, such as the imperialist Brest-Litovsk Treaty (1918), forced by Germany upon Russia, are not mentioned in Schmitt's work.

Further, *Der Nomos der Erde* also includes an open defence of the colonial aspects of European public law as a necessary and founding element of occidental political rationalism. This is also clearly apparent in the way Schmitt describes the 'heroes of the Conquista' and portrays the 'discovery' of America as the 'last great heroic act (*Heldentat*) of European peoples.'[94] Schmitt was worried that '[t]he great work of the Spanish conquistadores is today being set under a judgment of condemnation (*Verdammungsurteil*), which concerns European colonialism as such.'[95] For Schmitt, such a self-destructive approach had its roots in the 'centuries long propaganda against the Spanish Conquista, in the *Leyenda Negra*.' What astonishes Schmitt the most is that today, there are Europeans who seek to free themselves from the 'odium' of colonialism by 'apologizing for the heroic deeds of their ancestors.'[96] In essence, for Schmitt, 'anti-colonialism is nothing else but the liquidation of a historical past at the cost of European nations' – nothing but 'anti-European propaganda.'[97]

As Schmitt distanced himself from Nazism in the late 1930s and early 1940s, he would actively try to whitewash his Nazi engagement through a specific kind of canonical politics, rediscovering figures he had formerly criticized in

91 Ibid, 369–385.

92 NdE, 39.

93 Ville Suuronen, "The Rise of the Homme Machine: Carl Schmitt's Critique of Biotechnology and Utopias". *Political Theory* 48:5, 2020, 615–643.

94 Schmitt, *Staat, Grossraum, Nomos*, 585.

95 Ibid, 585.

96 Ibid, 585.

97 Ibid, 596, 594; c.f., Schmitt, *Glossarium*, 213.

his Nazi writing, including Savigny.[98] This reversal is apparent in Schmitt's uses of Vitoria and in his previously mentioned polemics against Scott in *Der Nomos der Erde* (1950). By styling himself as the 'last conscious representative of the *jus publicum Europaeum*' and by portraying himself as the 'brother' of Jean Bodin and Thomas Hobbes,[99] Schmitt was consciously situating himself in a continuum with classical Western thinkers, aiming to distance himself from his Nazi involvement. Claiming that he had 'always only spoken and written as a jurist'[100] and that his intellectual 'home' was 'in two areas of legal science, in international law and in constitutional law,'[101] Schmitt was not only trying to 'purify' Vitoria's legacy from the illegitimate uses of liberals, but also offering an alternative history of international law, which was, at the same time, an attempt to whitewash his own Nazi cooperation through a broad historical foil.

Many of these aspects were already noted by contemporary commentators that reacted critically to Schmitt's anonymous publication of his Vitoria essay in Germany in 1949.[102] And it is also significant that Schmitt's friend, Álvaro d'Órs, would console him by stating that his work on Vitoria could find 'a better "climate" in Francoist Spain than it could "at the moment in Germany",'[103] which was also reflected in the fact that Schmitt's Vitoria essay was published with his own name in Spain. And yet, the canonical politics involved in Schmitt's reading of Vitoria have not been recognized with the clarity they deserve. Instead, many of the earlier commentators on Schmitt's Nazi engagement, such as George Schwab and Joseph Bendersky, would largely repeat Schmitt's own deeply apologetic self-stylizations and historical narratives that served to obfuscate the complex intellectual moves inherent in Schmitt's writings on international law. For them, Schmitt had never been a true Nazi, but rather was simply paying 'lip service to Nazi views by inserting the odd anti-Semitic remark into his publications.'[104] Coming up with the most creative explanations as to why Schmitt's references to blood and racial

98 e.g., Carl Schmitt, "Die Lage der europäischen Rechtswissenschaft", in Carl Schmitt, *Verfassungsrechtliche Aufsätze aus den Jahren 1924–1954. Materialien zu einer Verfassungslehre* (Berlin: Duncker & Humblot, 2003), 386–429. For context, see Suuronen, "Mobilizing the western tradition for present politics".

99 Schmitt, *Ex Captivitate Salus*, 63–64.

100 Schmitt, *Glossarium*, 13–14.

101 Schmitt, *Ex Captivitate Salus*, 55.

102 See Mehring, *Aufstieg und Fall*, 470–480.

103 Schmitt und Álvaro d'Órs, Briefwechsel 89, 92.

104 Bendersky, *Theorist for the Reich*, 207–208.

homogeneity supposedly 'did not follow the Nazi line,'[105] they bequeathed a problematic image of Schmitt's Nazi engagement that took Schmitt's own narratives for granted. If one were to critically paraphrase the apologetic interpretations of Schwab and Bendersky that downplay Schmitt's racism in terms of the politics of canons and Vitoria, one could argue that it is the name of Vitoria that is 'artificially placed within the text'[106] of *Der Nomos der Erde*.[107]

5 Schmitt's Revival and the Politics of the International Legal Canon

Established now that Schmitt's use of Vitoria and his broader history of international law cannot be decoupled from his far-right ideology and from the whitewashing of his own Nazi past, we move to the second leg of our argument. To interrogate the place Schmitt has come to hold in our disciplinary canon is particularly difficult because its motivation is normally not articulated but assumed as self-evident. Of course, there is a large amount of insightful scholarship relying on Schmitt's work as inspiring and still topical today. But the phenomenon we are pointing at regards the widespread defensive reflex that surfaces in many legal scholars, whenever an argument for sidelining Schmitt as an intellectual reference is brought up. That instinctive reply that giving up Schmitt would be, as Weiler put it, 'odd' and a 'policy [one] could not support.'

We submit that the widespread reflex defending Schmitt's canonical position can be explained – and demystified – through two known profiles relating canonicity and a discipline's shared imagination: a vision of the canon as a cultural monument based on objective standards; the canon as a shorthand articulation of what an academic tradition and the epistemic community which identifies with it stand for.

In the first place, the reflexive defence of Schmitt's canonical status seems to be based on a shared recognition of an objective intellectual stature. This stance reflects a clear position in the long-standing debate in literary studies over the nature of canons.[108] Simplifying, canonical texts would be selected

105 George Schwab, *The Challenge of the Exception: An Introduction to the Political Ideas of Carl Schmitt Between 1921 and 1936* (Berlin: Duncker and Humblot, 1970), 101.

106 Bendersky, *Theorist for the Reich*, 208.

107 In utilizing Vitoria in a self-serving manner, Schmitt fit well into the broader political climate of Spain during this time. For context, see Ignacio de la Rasilla, 'The Fascist Mimesis of Spanish International Law and its Vitorian Aftermath', *Journal of the History of International Law*, 14 (2012).

108 On this understanding of the nature of canons, see Amorosa and Vergerio, cit., 4–5.

for enduring relevance either for their intrinsic value, as the defenders of Schmitt's self-evident canonicity seem to assume, or as a function of various hierarchies of power. However, a careful reading of the debate, as most famously articulated in the Canon Wars of the 1990s, shows how even the supporters of the intrinsic value of canonical texts as their main defining quality put significant focus on the canon as a series of subjective receptions. Harold Bloom's *The Western Canon*,[109] the key articulation of the 'intrinsic value' argument, depicts the relation of authors with canonical works as a process of influence, necessarily entailing both imitation and overcoming. Imitation of canonical standards establishes belonging to a certain discourse or tradition and the borrowing of its pedigree. Overcoming the canonical models determines the individuation and original contribution of the author to the literary space or scholarly field concerned. The canon is what results from the constant repetition of this dual process. In other words, even the theory of canon-making that places most importance on some objective intellectual quality of the work at hand submits that the canon is a fluid, ever-changing artefact made and remade by each generation in order to leave their mark according to their choices and values. In this light, leaving the propriety of Schmitt's inclusion in the canon of international law to an unarticulated assumption over the brilliance of his writings cannot be enough. The controversy surrounding his figure and ideology demands, at the very least, an explanation of why we, as an epistemic community, consider him an essential part of our shared disciplinary heritage today. This issue becomes even more pressing, given that Schmitt had disappeared from international law literature in the post-war period, without rising cries over a supposed cancelling. The fact that the Schmittian revival in international law can be dated to the twenty-first century, makes such recovery very close in time to us, demanding a deeper analysis.

This links to the second profile, the restatement of the international legal tradition, entailed even by the mere mention of a canonical figure. Indeed, reference to historical figures associated with the discipline and its fundamental principles is often performative. Nods in works of a fundamentally doctrinal nature to, say, Grotius or Vitoria – but also to figures closer to us in time, like Schmitt or Lauterpacht – tend to simply signal a mark of belonging of the author to the disciplinary tradition, rather than something specific about its content and meaning. Such is the staying power of the canon, once it is acknowledged as received wisdom. But canons are also necessarily sites of contestation and constant reinterpretation. To explore the canon of inter-

109 Harold Bloom, *The Western Canon* (New York: Harcourt Brace & Company, 1994).

national law, as it stands, and argue for its evolution in a certain direction, it is crucial to unearth the wider assumptions founding Schmitt's canonical inclusion in the international legal literature that relies directly on his intellectual production.

What is then the tradition that is reflected in the invocation of Schmitt as a figure in the disciplinary canon by a twenty-first international lawyer?

To answer this question, let's assume in the first place that the defensive reflex over Schmitt's place in the canon is based on the assertion of a constructive value in his work. By this, we mean that the instinctive assignment of contemporary relevance to Schmitt's ideas is not limited to a negative connotation, to the role of an intellectual sparring partner, whose function is only to be *a priori* defeated. In current international legal literature, it is patent that Schmitt is not only used that way: it seems more common to encounter texts that think with him than against him. Then, what are the purported inspiring elaborations found in Schmitt's work and rooting a vision of the international legal order resonating with the profession today?

While early twenty-first-century international law re-engagements with Schmitt revolved around his theory of decisionism and exceptional powers in the context of the War on Terror,[110] that wave of contributions has since subsided. Currently, we identify three main interrelated macro-themes international lawyers adopt in thinking with Schmitt. First, there is what we could call the legal-theoretical contribution of his critique of formalist and positivist approaches to international law. According to Schmitt, these were tools aimed at depoliticizing the 'tyranny of values,' founding, for instance, the discriminatory concept of war placed at the core of the universalist global order and weaponized by the liberal leading powers. And indeed, secondly, many point to the normative contribution of Schmitt acting as 'an antidote to an overdose of liberal optimistic internationalism'[111] and its attendant ideological corollaries, such as a progressive vision of history. Thirdly, there is the geopolitical contribution by Schmitt as a theorist of multipolarity, primarily based on his theory of *Grossraum*, particularly topical in a historical phase, where rivalries among regional powers, seeking to re-expand their sphere of influence and control, are running high. These three contributions come together to form a wide-ranging critique of the universalist-liberal international legal order that developed in the twentieth century under the impulse of the United States of

110 See, for instance, Fleur Johns, 'Guantánamo Bay and the Annihilation of the Exception', *European Journal of International Law*, 16 (2005), 613–635.

111 Bardo Fassbender, 'Carl Schmitt (1888–1985)', in Bardo Fassbender and Anne Peters (eds.), *The Oxford Handbook of the History of International Law*, (Oxford: Oxford University Press 2012), 1178.

America as a hegemonic global power. The sharing of this target is a key circumstance in Schmitt's current fortune with scholars on the political left, including international lawyers.

Of course, this is a simplification and generalization of engagements with Schmitt in current international law literature. However, we submit that this characterization does cover a large ground of Schmitt's uses in relevant publications. Within this literature, one finds reasoned explanations of the relevance of Schmitt's work for one's argument or theoretical elaboration[112] but this is not always the case. Way too often, Schmitt is treated as the obvious interlocutor, an act underwritten by the unspoken assumption we have already encountered: it would be 'odd' otherwise. Whether consciously or not, these authors are operating in a space where the imitation side in the canonical process of influence – that is the borrowing of influence from the canonical figure or text – is necessarily the preponderant motivation for choosing to engage Schmitt. Indeed, if the conversation with Schmitt was primarily geared towards a deep engagement with his ideas and the production of original contributions, then the intellectual reasons for choosing to discuss his work and not that of another author would organically be part of the articulation of the new argument. *A contrario*, default selections of Schmitt rely on what he can bring to the table as a canonical figure. The value of engaging Schmitt in this sense can be articulated through two interconnected concepts crucial in describing the dynamics of canon-making: pedigree and serial repetition.

In terms of pedigree, Schmitt carries with him the imposing – and ambivalent – tradition of the German legal academia, which since the first half of the nineteenth century and on the wings of the influential work of Friedrich Carl Savigny, has established itself as an intellectual model for modern jurisprudence in continental Europe and beyond. Schmitt has been and still is generally considered a towering figure of twentieth-century German jurisprudence. Being able to harness the weight of the association to the tradition of German jurisprudence is not a small reward. After all, as Martti Koskenniemi has suggested with a touch of provocation, there is a case to be made for international law to be called a German discipline[113] in genealogic terms.

This reward is also not the easiest to get in the English-speaking academia. Access to the primary sources might be difficult either for limited availability –

112 e.g., Walter Rech, 'Eschatology and Existentialism: Carl Schmitt's Historical Understanding of International Law and Politics', in Matilda Arvidsson, Leila Brännstöm, and Panu Minkkinen (eds.), *The Contemporary Relevance of Carl Schmitt. Law, Politics, Theology*, (New York: Routledge 2016), 161.

113 Martti Koskenniemi, 'Between Coordination and Constitution. International Law as a German Discipline', *Redescriptions*, 15 (2011), 45–70.

especially with regard to less known authors or minor works – or lack of knowledge of the German language. With the interest in Schmitt revived across law and the social sciences, these problems have ceased to exist. Most of his works and all the major ones have been published by now in English translation, with the relevant exception of his Nazi writings. However, one might assume that the recent republication of his Nazi writings in German (in 2021) will induce more critique toward his oeuvre in the coming years.

But Schmitt has not only been translated, he has also been digested for a global audience. The industrial amount of secondary literature produced on Schmitt in the 21st century,[114] that is the serial repetition that established him as a canonical figure in current international legal discourse, favours the future persistence of this status quo. Under certain circumstances, it may make it a safe choice, especially for young or less established scholars, to choose Schmitt as interlocutor. If so many in the discipline are working on/with Schmitt – the reasoning might go – then work engaging him will surely be recognized as relevant, as intervening in the ongoing disciplinary discourse. The process leading to this outcome, be it conscious or unconscious, might also take a less instrumental route. If large numbers of international lawyers routinely discuss Schmitt – or say Kelsen, Lauterpacht, etc. – then it might follow that engaging with those same authors is simply the language in which the international law tribe speaks its history and intellectual heritage. To speak the canon can simply be intended as the form taken by participation in the social practices of the professional community one has chosen to enter. Indeed, the main perks of claiming the pedigree carried by canonical figures in an academic–professional setting are the facilitation of inclusion and mutual recognition.

However, the serial repetition of engaging with a canonical figure also affects the originality of the arguments that are produced. Schmitt's arguments have been repeated and streamlined so many times that they appear routinely in a standardized and decontextualized form, apparently with little sense of the historical events and ideological milieu in which they were forged. This routinization and thinning of Schmitt's arguments – or their 'exploitation', were one to use Schmitt's own terminology in relation to Vitoria – through the sidelining of context, making his ideas less charged and more pliable to versatile uses and interpretations, is a feature of the canon. It is the type of process that allows us, for instance, to link Vitoria or Grotius with

114 See, in this book, Ignacio de la Rasilla, 'Carl Schmitt and Francisco de Vitoria through the Mirror of the Classics of International Law', Ch. 21, pp. 27–28.

current doctrines and institutions that would not have been conceivable within their early-modern horizon of experiences.

Nonetheless, the resulting pragmatist adoption of simplified and decontextualized ideas runs against the stated intentions set out for Schmitt's earliest post-WWII revival in the 1990s. When Chantal Mouffe and other leading figures of political theory like Slavoj Zizek came together to reconsider Schmitt's legacy[115] they did so with purpose, convinced of the specific relevance of his work to the challenges posed by the political climate in the West after the end of the Cold War. At that same time Francis Fukuyama was proclaiming the 'end of history' and with it, many surmised, of politics altogether. Mouffe and collaborators instead submitted 'that, at th[at] juncture, Schmitt's thought serve[d] as a warning against the dangers of complacency that a triumphant liberalism entails'.[116] The contributions in the book represent an engagement with Schmitt's work in meaningful critical fashion. They acknowledge Schmitt's insight in articulating crucial questions for the analysis of contemporary politics while pointing out the fundamental theoretical – not just ideological – shortcomings of his ideas. They recognize the value of his work in reflecting over the peculiar challenges of the 1990s in global politics while identifying the flaws and dangers in his solutions to those very challenges. In other words, Mouffe and the contributors chose Schmitt as their interlocutor with a reasoned and detailed sense of his suitability to the situation at hand. They went for an author that, at that point, was not an obvious or safe choice, but a business that while inconvenient, even disturbing, was pressing and needed to be taken care of. They found what they considered the most productive interlocutor to develop original and relevant ideas. They did not reach for the canon as it stood, quite the contrary: they contributed to reshape it by placing Schmitt at the forefront again, but with the clear idea that this was a necessary intellectual move to save the liberal democracy of the 90s from its complacent, self-congratulating self. Three decades later, the diagnoses concerning the failures of liberalism as well as the broad contemporary far-right backlash against it have become much more commonplace; and also here, the discussion with Schmitt and his ensuing, problematic relevance continues.

As discussed, not every use of canon carries intention and purpose with it. As Schmitt came back in 'fashion', alongside the reflective attempts aimed at taking in his work with all its disturbing aspects in order to neutralize it, came the publications, which took the neutralization as the starting point. By this we mean that the canonical Schmitt that came to flood international legal

115 Chantal Mouffe (ed.), *The Challenge of Carl Schmitt*, (London: Verso 1999).
116 Ibid., 2.

literature, pre-packaged in the few simplified and context-deprived versions of his doctrines outlined above, appears as a more fluid thinker, easier to adapt to support one's arguments and, overall, a less ominous figure.

It is only in this canonical context that the idea of adding a plaque warning about Schmitt's Nazi affiliation and his antisemitism to his intellectual statue can make sense: because the most disturbing implications of his ideas, made obvious by their context, have been removed in the normalizing serialized transmission of the canon. Now, this common dynamic of thinning in canon-making, of canonical figures becoming increasingly vague signifiers, almost-empty canvases on which we paint our disciplinary history as an exercise of (re-)creation of professional identity, works very well with authors farther in time from us. For instance, associating the work of contemporary international organizations to ideas developed by Grotius or Kant, while patently anachronistic and requiring several logical leaps, is less problematic and more constructive than working with a neutralized Schmitt. Reconstructing the stakes of the projects and controversies that thinkers from centuries ago were involved in is, of course, of extreme interest and importance, surely for how it enables us to see our own situation and thereby favor imaginative approaches to present challenges. This distance, at the same time, makes it easier to appreciate the narratives built on those reconstructions for what they are. It should be obvious that to link Grotius with the United Nations or the regulation of the use of force in the twenty-first century requires a significant interpretive stretch. But in that reaching back across the centuries lies a symbolic – and political – value that goes way beyond the ability to construe more cogent historical arguments, something many international lawyers who embarked in such revival projects – including Schmitt with his use of Vitoria – have shown to know and exploit.

With a purposeful canonization of Schmitt, critical thinking must operate differently. The political phenomena he discussed are too directly recognizable for us, part of our imaginary and social experience. Moreover, the hateful political preferences, which Schmitt baked into his intellectual production, and which seemed defeated in the aftermath of World War II, have returned to haunt Europe, as bloody imperial conflicts are fought on the continent and its immediate neighbourhoods, racially motivated violence is on the rise and far-right politicians keep strengthening their hold on power in an increasing number of European nations.

As Mouffe and her collaborators understood, the topicality and relevance of Schmitt's ideas meant that their neutralization had to be the endpoint of a meaningful reflection, not the starting point, the canonical, almost-empty canvas made more pliable by the passing of time and changing of historical conditions. The latter option, the one often pursued in current canonical uses of Schmitt in international law literature, involves, by default, too much loss of meaning to produce tenable arguments. Take for instance efforts to employ Schmitt's theory of large political spaces (*Grossräume*), the establishment of regional spheres of influence around a continental hegemonic power, as a basis for emancipation from the oppressiveness entailed in a universalist unipolar global order. In abstract, this might sound like an idea worth exploring, especially to somebody legitimately seeking to counteract the detrimental effects of the dominant influence of the United States and its allies on global politics. However, the moment one reconsiders the theory in the sobering historical context in which it was conceived, leading up to the subjugation of large swathes of continental Europe and North Africa by Nazi Germany, and within Schmitt's larger ideological horizon of 'concrete order thought', the perspective must necessarily shift. *Grossraum* thinking replaces the existing hierarchy in the international power structure with different hierarchies, whereby regional hegemons would not have to be bothered even by the most limited understanding of states' equality and minorities' rights. Replying to an article engaged in this sort of exercise, Koskenniemi has expressed this criticism in forceful terms: 'Whatever may have been [the author]'s intention in celebrating the wisdom of this dead Nazi, there is certainly no reason to wish the resuscitation of the age-old idea that authority emerges from physical power, and that the only alternative for those who fall within its range is either to succumb or to be destroyed.'[117] Seen in this light, the availability of a Schmittian argument neutralized by serial canonical transmission is more of an obstacle creating blind spots rather than the intended springboard towards original and effective solutions.

Something else has changed since Schmitt's revival. In the current global political situation, liberal democracy is surely not complacent but acutely aware of its fragility. And maybe this helps to explain why, beyond pedigree and serialized repetition, Schmitt resonates so much with international lawyers today. Even in the most neutralized versions of his arguments, his fundamental idea that law is a function of live and continuous political conflict remains at the core. And as political oppositions grow increasingly fraught both within national communities and on the international stage, Schmitt's themes seem more and more to apply to our current predicament. Clearly, Schmitt is a legal thinker for polarized times.

117 Martti Koskenniemi, Letter to the Editors, *supra* fn 5, 202.

6 Concluding Remarks: *Que faire?*

In this era of rise of far-right politics and authoritarianism on a global scale, Schmitt should be handled with much more care than he has been till now. His canonical revival has made it possible even for the best-intentioned author to peddle a Schmitt-inspired plan only to miss its discriminatory implications and the whitewashing of his own Nazi engagement, as analysed above in relation to Schmitt's analysis of Vitoria and his intellectual legacy. From this perspective, calls for reconsidering Schmitt's canonical footprint should be pondered and not met with the prevalent defensive reflex. Indeed, as seen throughout this chapter, canons reside in a seriality of choices across time where agency, contingency, creativity and immediate convenience mix with cultural inertia, habit and status quo politics within established epistemic communities. Using this complexity to deflect responsibility for our own choices in sustaining and/or modifying the existing canon is problematic, especially when dealing with the legacy of a thinker strongly associated with ideologies that are currently undermining communal life in our societies. Even less available should be justifications based on unarticulated intrinsic value or canonical status quo. Instead of going in the direction of explicitly linking the canon to our choices, they erase that connection by expressing a sort of fatalist circularity: 'Schmitt's statue should be there, because it is there.'

The taking of responsibility for canonical choices does not necessarily entail the 'forgetting' of Schmitt in international legal literature, in our view. But it does require the direct facing of the most controversial aspects of Schmitt's figure and work, rather than their smoothing over for more palatable consumption. It is in those aspects that the key cognitive value of engaging him lies, in the potential for articulation and analysis of political issues that are disturbing yet pressing, keeping at the forefront an acute sense of the existential dangers they entail. In other words, to think productively and responsibly *with* Schmitt is to also think *against* him[118] in one unified analytical process.

The 'forgetting' of Schmitt is a responsible choice too. The accusations of censorship, entailed in the concept of 'cancelling', fall the moment one understands the canon in its choice- and value-dependent fluidity and selectivity. Indeed, choosing to engage with a certain author – or choosing not to – is simply the way in which the canon is made and remade, the way in which an epistemic community and the individuals within it seek to express its shared heritage and vision of knowledge and society. Seen in this sense,

118 See in the same sense Mouffe, 'Introduction', cit., 5–6.

canon-formation reflects acts of individual agency to establish what Antonio Gramsci would have called cultural hegemony within the group. As such, any purposeful addition or remotion responding to the canonical agent's values and vision of international law is by definition part of the contested process that makes the canon. In this light, there are several profiles under which the 'forgetting' of Schmitt could be seen as a valuable project towards the construction of a canon expressing emancipation and inclusivity as values sustaining international law.

In the first place, 'forgetting' Schmitt could be seen as contributing to the ongoing efforts of expanding the canon, bringing to the forefront of and rewriting into the history of international law the contribution of marginalized human groups, in the past and in the present. Expanding the canon to be more representative and inclusive in the face of ongoing structural bias and routine discrimination within academia is a formidable tool to change, in the long term, the culture towards more just outcomes. If the current 'forgetting' of marginalized scholars is an unjustifiable form of injustice, the picture would be different with the purposeful 'forgetting' or reduction of use of some of the dead Western white men that have dominated the canon of international law up to this day, especially in relation to someone like Schmitt who not only celebrated the Nuremberg laws as the 'constitution of freedom', but also advocated the erasing of other authors on the basis of their ethnicity. This 'forgetting' would be directly aimed at establishing a measure of just and equal representation and, at the same time, represent a basic dynamic of the canon-making process.

Of course, the rebalancing of the canon towards a more representative make-up is not an issue that regards specifically Schmitt, but other valid motivations for his 'forgetting' have a closer connection to his legacy. Even more in the current political climate, an author might seek to avoid any ambiguity that she might share any part of his disdain for any aspiration towards genuine universalist ethics. While a key social function of academia is to offer nuance, this does not mean embracing ambiguity too. We do have a responsibility to denounce legal doctrines and projects aimed at feeding hate and fear of the Other, rather than addressing real social needs. Avoiding association altogether with a leading Nazi lawyer might be a blunt instrument but surely an effective one in the direction of clarity of stance. At the very least, we should do our best to make sure that the fashion of fanciful engagements with the normalized canonical Schmitt passes as soon as possible.

Lastly, avoiding Schmitt could favour forms of engagement that effectively face the current predicament of global politics by looking beyond it. As discussed above, the most productive engagements think both *with* and *against* him. They are fuelled by a need to cut through the utopias to unearth the pitfalls of our political systems and 'fix' them. They require a realist attitude that relies on what was undoubtedly Schmitt's most refined skill: the insight and ability to spell out the implications, the 'quiet parts' of liberal ideologies. But international law lives of utopias too. Creating space for canonical figures who might be seen not just as insightful but also inspiring, can favour the pursuit of conversations with those authors that operate effectively as just *with* engagements. With international law and global politics currently in an existential crisis, it is crucial to deal with problems and potential solutions embedded in our current systems but also to imagine the better world beyond it we aspire to. In this sense, moving beyond Schmitt might help us see farther.

After all, a responsible stance towards the canonicity of Schmitt requires little more than a moment of reflection in the face of the blinding routinized discourse created by canonical transmission. A moment to stop and ask oneself: what do we have to learn from a man who poured so much of his hate into his lifework and ideas? This question, we think, should be seriously pondered in each engagement with the legacy of Carl Schmitt. Crossing that threshold before discussing his ideas once more would go a long way towards the most meaningful use of his work in international legal literature.

Bibliography

Amorosa, Paolo. *Rewriting the History of the Law of Nations. How James Brown Scott Made Francisco de Vitoria the Founder of International Law.* (Oxford: Oxford University Press, 2019).

Amorosa, Paolo, and Claire Vergerio. 'Canon-Making in the History of International Legal and Political Thought'. *Leiden Journal of International Law* 35 (2022): 469–478.

Bendersky, Joseph. *Carl Schmitt. Theorist for the Reich.* (Princeton: Princeton University Press, 1983).

Blasius, Dirk. *Carl Schmitt. Preußischer Staatsrat in Hitlers Reich.* (Göttingen: Vandenhoeck und Ruprecht, 2001).

Bloom, Harold. *The Western Canon.* (New York: Harcourt Brace & Company, 1994).

Borges, Jorge Luis. 'Kafka and His Precursors'. In *Labyrinths. Selected Stories and Other Writings* (New York: New Directions, 1964), 199–202.

Buchstein, Hubertus. 'The Godfather of Left-Schmittianism? Otto Kirchheimer and Carl Schmitt after 1945'. *Redescriptions: Political Thought, Conceptual History and Feminist Theory* 24, no. 1 (2021): 4–26.

Fassbender, Bardo. 'Carl Schmitt (1888–1985)'. In *The Oxford Handbook of the History of International Law*, edited by Bardo Fassbender and Anne Peters (Oxford: Oxford University Press, 2012), 1174–1179.

Furedi, Frank. 'Illiberal Liberalism: A Genealogy'. *The Journal of Illiberalism Studies* 2, no. 2 (2022): 19–36.

Grewe, Wilhelm. *The Epochs of International Law*. (Berlin: De Gruyter, 2000).

Johns, Fleur. 'Guantánamo Bay and the Annihilation of the Exception'. *European Journal of International Law* 16, no. 4 (2005): 613–635.

Kalyvas, Andreas. 'Carl Schmitt's Post-colonial Imagination'. *Constellations* 25, no. 1 (2018): 35–53.

Kennedy, Ellen. 'Carl Schmitt and the Frankfurt School'. *Telos* 71 (1987): 37–66.

Kervégan, Jean-Francois. *Que faire de Carl Schmitt?* (Paris: Gallimard, 2011).

Koenen, Andreas. *Der Fall Carl Schmitt. Sein Aufstieg zum "Kronjuristen des Dritten Reiches"*. (Darmstadt: Wissenschaftliche Buchgesellschaft, 1995).

Koskenniemi, Martti. 'Between Coordination and Constitution. International Law as a German Discipline'. *Redescriptions* 15 (2011): 45–70.

Koskenniemi, Martti. 'Carl Schmitt and International Law'. In *The Oxford Handbook of Carl Schmitt*, edited by Jens Meienrich and Oliver Simons (Oxford: Oxford University Press, 2013), 592–610.

Koskenniemi, Martti. *The Gentle Civilizer of Nations: The Rise and Fall of International Law 1870–1960*. (Cambridge: Cambridge University Press, 2004).

Koskenniemi, Martti. 'Letter to the Editors'. *Chinese Journal of International Law* 12, no. 1 (2013): 201–202.

Legg, Stephen. 'Interwar Spatial Chaos? Imperialism, Internationalism and the League of Nations'. In *Spatiality, Sovereignty and Carl Schmitt Geographies of the Nomos*, edited by Stephen Legg (London: Routledge, 2011), 106–124.

Mehring, Reinhard. *Carl Schmitt: Aufstieg und Fall*. (München: C.H. Beck, 2009).

Mouffe, Chantal, ed. *The Challenge of Carl Schmitt*. (London: Verso, 1999).

Müller, Jan-Werner. *A Dangerous Mind: Carl Schmitt in Post-War European Thought*. (New Haven: Yale University Press, 2003).

Odysseos, Louiza, and Fabio Petito, eds. *The International Political thought of Carl Schmitt: Terror, Liberal War and the Crisis of Global Order*. (London: Routledge, 2007).

Rasilla, Ignacio de la. 'Carl Schmitt and Francisco de Vitoria through the Mirror of the Classics of International Law'. In this book, Chapter 21.

Rasilla, Ignacio de la. 'The Fascist Mimesis of Spanish International Law and its Vitorian Aftermath'. *Journal of the History of International Law* 14, no. 2 (2012): 207–36.

Rech, Walter. 'Eschatology and Existentialism: Carl Schmitt's Historical Understanding of International Law and Politics'. In *The Contemporary Relevance of Carl Schmitt. Law, Politics, Theology*, edited by Matilda Arvidsson, Leila Brännstöm, and Panu Minkkinen (New York: Routledge, 2016), 160–174.

Schmitt, Carl. *Antworten in Nürnberg*. Edited by Helmut Quaritsch. (Berlin: Duncker and Humblot, 2000).

Schmitt, Carl. *Der Begriff des Politischen. Text von 1932 mit einem Vorwort und drei Corollarien.* (Berlin: Duncker & Humblot, 2009).

Schmitt, Carl. *Der Nomos der Erde im Völkerrecht des Jus Publicum Europaeum.* (Berlin: Duncker & Humblot, 2011).

Schmitt, Carl. *Der politische Problem der Friedenssicherung.* (Leipzig-Berlin, 1934).

Schmitt, Carl. *Die Kernfrage des Völkerbundes.* (Berlin: Dümmler, 1926).

Schmitt, Carl. *Die Lage der Europäischen Rechtswissenschaft.* In Carl Schmitt, *Verfassungsrechtliche Aufsätze aus den Jahren 1924–1954. Materialien zu einer Verfassungslehre.* (Berlin: Duncker & Humblot, 2003).

Schmitt, Carl. *Die Tyrannei der Werte.* (Berlin: Duncker & Humblot, 2011).

Schmitt, Carl. *Ex Captivitate Salus. Erfahrungen aus der Zeit 1945/47.* (Berlin: Duncker & Humblot, 2002).

Schmitt, Carl. *Frieden oder Pazifismus? Arbeiten zum Völkerrecht und zur internationalen Politik.* Edited by Günter Maschke. (Berlin: Duncker and Humblot, 2005).

Schmitt, Carl. *Gesammelte Schriften 1933–1936. Mit ergänzenden Beiträgen aus der Zeit des Zweiten Weltkriegs.* (Berlin: Duncker & Humblot, 2021).

Schmitt, Carl. *Glossarium. Aufzeichnungen aus den Jahren 1947 bis 1958.* Edited by Gerd Giesler and Martin Tielke. (Berlin: Duncker & Humbolt, 2015).

Schmitt, Carl. *Positionen und Begriffe. Im Kampf mit Weimar–Genf–Versailles, 1923–1939.* (Berlin: Duncker & Humblot, 2014).

Schmitt, Carl. *Staat, Grossraum, Nomos. Arbeiten aus den Jahren 1916–1969.* Edited by Günter Maschke. (Berlin: Duncker & Humblot, 1995).

Schmitt, Carl. *Staatsgefüge und Zusammenbruch des zweiten Reiches: Der Sieg des Bürgers über den Soldaten.* (Berlin: Duncker & Humblot, 2011).

Schmitt, Carl. *Verfassungslehre.* (Berlin: Duncker & Humblot, 2010).

Schmitt, Carl, and Ernst Rudolf Huber. *Briefwechsel 1926–1981.* Edited by Ewald Grothe. (Berlin: Duncker & Humblot, 2014).

Schmitt, Carl, and Álvaro d'Ors. *Briefwechsel.* Edited by Montserrat Herrero. (Berlin: Duncker & Humblot, 2004).

Schmitt, Carl, and Reinhart Koselleck. *Der Briefwechsel.* Edited by Jan Eike Dunkhase. (Berlin: Suhrkamp, 2019).

Schwab, George. *The Challenge of the Exception: An Introduction to the Political Ideas of Carl Schmitt Between 1921 and 1936.* (Berlin: Duncker and Humblot, 1970).

Srinivasan, Amia. 'Cancelled'. *London Review of Books* 45, no. 13 (29 June 2023).

Stolleis, Michael. *Geschichte des öffentlichen Rechts in Deutschland. Weimarer Republik und Nationalsozialismus.* (München: Piper, 2002).

Suuronen, Ville. 'Carl Schmitt as a theorist of the 1933 Nazi revolution: 'The difficult task of rethinking and recultivating traditional concepts'. *Contemporary Political Theory* 20, no. 2 (2021): 341–363.

Suuronen, Ville. 'Mobilizing the western tradition for present politics: Carl Schmitt's polemical uses of roman law, 1923–1945'. *History of European Ideas* 47, no. 5 (2021): 748–72.

Suuronen, Ville. 'The Rise of the Homme Machine: Carl Schmitt's Critique of Biotechnology and Utopias'. *Political Theory* 48, no. 5 (2020): 615–643.

Van Ho, Tara. 'Cancelling Schmitt'. *European Journal of International Law* 32, no. 2 (2021): 730–731.

Van Laak, Dirk. *Gespräche in der Sicherheit des Schweigens. Carl Schmitt in der politischen Geistesgeschichte der frühen Bundesrepublik.* (Berlin: Akademie Verlag, 2002).

Vitoria, Francisco de. *Relecciones teológicas. Edición crítica, con facsimil de códices y ediciones príncipes, variantes, versión castellana, notas e introducción.* Edited by Luis G. Alonso Getino. Tomo 1–3. (Madrid, 1933–1935).

Weiler, Joseph. 'Cancelling Carl Schmitt?'. *EJIL:Talk!* (blog), 13 August 2021.

Young, Robert J. C. 'Mythmaking: the Nomos of Postcoloniality'. In *Siting Postcoloniality: Critical Perspectives from the East Asian Sinosphere*, edited by Caroline S. Hau and Pheng Cheah (Durham, NC: Duke University Press, 2022), 33–52.

CHAPTER 18

Carl Schmitt and Francisco de Vitoria: Classics of International Law?

Ignacio de la Rasilla

> A delicate question, to which somewhat diverse solutions might be given according to times and seasons.
>
> C.A. SAINT BEUVE, *'What Is a Classic?'* (1850)

1 Introduction

In his *The Nomos of the Earth in the International Law of Jus Publicum Europaeum*, Carl Schmitt (1888–1985) wrote that "the history of how Vitoria's arguments have been used in international law from the 16th century until now offers striking examples of unexpected transformations and reinterpretations,"[1] and furthermore, he suggested that "Vitoria's reputation has its own history and requires special treatment."[2] These remarks and, by extension, Schmitt's own contribution to the genealogy of Francisco de Vitoria's "unexpected transformations and reinterpretations" in international law should be read as a reaction and a counterpoint to James Brown Scott's (1866–1943) "presentist" reading of Vitoria in the light of the tenets of liberal internationalism in the interwar period.[3] In Schmitt's view, Scott's interpretations were one of "the false overpaintings" from which Schmitt wanted to "purify [Vitoria's] portrait" in order "to return to his words their true sense."[4]

1 Carl Schmitt, *The Nomos of the Earth in the International Law of the Jus Publicum Europaeum* (New York: Telos Press 2003) 125. Originally published as Carl Schmitt, *Der Nomos der Erde im Völkerrecht des Jus Publicum Europaeum* (Berlin: Duncker & Humblot 1950).

2 Ibid., 115.

3 Joshua Smeltzer, 'On the Use and Abuse of Francisco de Vitoria: James Brown Scott and Carl Schmitt'. *Journal of the History of International Law* 20 (2018), 345–72.

4 Ibid., 346.

 | DOI:10.1163/9789004757448_019

Schmitt's above remarks followed in the wake of Vitoria's status already being well-established as a "classic" of international law at the time of his writing. In the interwar years, Vitoria's reputation among international lawyers had grown exponentially, largely due to Scott's championing of the sixteenth-century Spanish Dominican friar as the "founding father" of international law.[5] Schmitt built on the boost that Scott, whose work on Vitoria can be retraced back to the early 1900s" as part of his plans for *The Classics of International Law* (1911–1950) collection, and in particular, Camilo Barcia Trelles (1888–1977)[6] had given to Vitoria's intellectual fame in the interwar period.

However, Schmitt's *The Nomos of the Earth* would go on to crystallize Vitoria's classic status in the modern sense. Schmitt did this by identifying in Vitoria, a distinguishing feature that all classics in all intellectual disciplines share, namely that their works have received multiple interpretations over time. It is from this modern acknowledgment that follows the ensuing need to scholarly unravel the classics' intellectual hermeneutic genealogy as a precondition for engaging with their works anew. This unravelling may be carried out with a particular polemical and normative purpose, as Schmitt himself intended and did in *The Nomos* and other works. Or it may, instead, be historiographically conceived as a diachronically contextualized investigation of the uses, misuses, and abuses to which the classic's works have been put with attention to the successive historical contexts that lent inspiration to each of them and to their respective intellectual gravitational pulls over time. An abridged intellectual history along these "serial contextualization" lines of the uses, misuses, and abuses of Vitoria's arguments in international law over time, including Schmitt's contribution to the many interpretative twists and turns they have undergone, has been offered elsewhere.[7] This chapter offers instead an assessment of Carl Schmitt's engagement with Francisco de Vitoria (c 1483–1546) in the light of ten distinguishing characteristics that underlie the rise of Francisco de Vitoria as a global "classic" of international law.

---

5 Paolo Amorosa, *Rewriting the History of the Law of Nations. How James Brown Scott Made Francisco de Vitoria the Founder of International Law* (Oxford: Oxford University Press 2019).

6 According to Schmitt, 'Camilo Barcia Trelles's lectures constituted the strongest breakthrough for the world at large,' *The Nomos of the Earth*, 118. Highlighting the influence beyond strictly Vitorian themes of Barcia Trelles on Schmitt's *The Nomos of the Earth*, see J.M. Beneyto, 'Camilo Barcia Trelles on Francisco de Vitoria: At the Crossroads of Carl Schmitt's Grossraum and James Brown Scott's "Modern International Law"'. *European Journal of International Law* 4 (2020), 1477–1492.

7 More recently in Ignacio de la Rasilla, 'The Three Revivals of Francisco de Vitoria in the History of International Law', in J. M. Beneyto (ed.), *Empire, Humanism and Rights. Collected Essays on Francisco de Vitoria* (Cham: Springer 2021) 73–93.

These ten proposed features of Vitoria as a classic of international law are that Vitoria's work has been used as a lens to address larger historical themes; his central position in the intellectual canon and as a landmark in the historical periodization of international law; Vitoria's broad interdisciplinary appeal; the fact that Vitoria has become identified as the first expounder of international legal ideas and doctrines; the multiple interpretations and reinterpretations to which Vitoria's oeuvre has been subjected; that he has been used as a shortcut in an intellectual tradition of thinking about the international; the fact that he has been turned into an intellectual symbol of cultural patriotism over time; Vitoria, in part, hegemonically induced universal appeal; the more recent diachronical use to which his works have been put to contextually investigate episodes in the history of international law from the nineteenth century up to the present; and, last but not least, the semi-industrial quantity of academic commentary Vitoria has attracted over time. The chapter provides an analysis of the interfaces between this proposed tenfold list of what makes a global classic of international law and Schmitt's engagement with Vitoria, and complements further this analysis with references to Schmitt's own contemporary status as a classic legal and political thinker of the twentieth century with regard to each of them. The conclusion considers the role of Western classics as transmission belts to pass on a deep intellectual disciplinary tradition and its embedded critiques to incoming generations of international legal thinkers.

2 Vitoria and Schmitt: A Match Made in Heaven and Hell

2.1 *The Classic as a Lens to Address Larger Historical Themes*

The first feature of Francisco de Vitoria as a global classic of international law is that his works have been widely used as a way to address larger historical themes and as a lens through which to look at events and processes unleashed in the times in which his intellectual works are embedded. The sixteenth-century prima professor of theology at the University of Salamanca and Dominican friar, Francisco de Vitoria, offers a textbook illustration of this intellectual pattern in which landmark historical events and the work of an author become intermingled. Although Vitoria addressed questions touching on *ius gentium* in several works, his two *relectiones De indis noviter inventis* (On the Recently Discovered Indians) and *De indis sive de iure belli hispanorum in barbaros* (On the Indies, or the Law Governing the Spaniards' War with the Barbarians), both from 1539, have been widely used to symbolize the new role of *ius naturae et gentium* in tackling the moral, legal, and practical dilemmas that emerged in the wake of the discovery, conquest, and management of the *novus orbis*. These *relectiones*, which, as Martti Koskenniemi notes, have traditionally been seen as "critical of the conduct of the Conquista" and which "actively propagated domestic and universal laws to control and direct its course,"[8] established Vitoria's reputation in the late nineteenth century as a seminal representative of a humanitarian international legal sensibility that subsequent generations of modern international lawyers would see, and claim, as their own. However, this received interpretation of Vitoria's significance in international law, which began to take shape in the late nineteenth century in the positive appraisals of his works made by some of the early members of the *Institut de droit international*,[9] would, as we shall later see, in time become challenged by postcolonial international law scholars.[10]

Schmitt was squarely drawn to this dimension of Vitoria's work as a lens through which to look at historical events and processes unleashed by what he called "a legendary and unforeseen discovery of a new world" from which the "traditional Eurocentric order of international law" arose.[11] This "unrepeatable historical event" was, in Schmitt's view, "the basic event in the history of European international law," both "in terms of legal history and legal philosophy" since it enabled "the land appropriation of a new world."[12] Consonant with the central role that Schmitt attributed to locating the "intellectual place of the present in the process of history,"[13] he saw the aftermath of WWII as the moment of the ultimate "foundering" of *ius publicum europaeum* (the public law of Europe), the trajectory of dissolution of which had already been anticipated in the universal geographical inclusiveness of the Second Hague Peace Conference and further confirmed in the post-Versailles system. This *le droit public de l'Europe* had, in Schmitt's view, been founded over a European imperial overseas spatial order – a "nomos of the earth"[14] – that had the effect

8 Martti Koskenniemi, 'Empire and international law: the real Spanish contribution'. *University of Toronto Law Journal* 1 (2011) 1–36, 4.

9 Elsewhere, I've called this the 'first Vitorian revival.' See, briefly, De la Rasilla, 'The Three Revivals', 7.

10 Antony Anghie, *Imperialism, Sovereignty, and the Making of International Law* (Cambridge: Cambridge University Press 2005).

11 Schmitt, *The Nomos of the Earth*, 39.

12 Schmitt, *The Nomos of the Earth*, 83.

13 Jens Meierhenrich and Oliver Simons, '"A Fanatic of Order in an Epoch of Confusing Turmoil" The Political, Legal, and Cultural Thought of Carl Schmitt', in Meierhenrich and Simons (eds.), *The Oxford Handbook of Carl Schmitt* (Oxford: Oxford University Press 2016) 3–70, 3, 4.

14 Schmitt, *The Nomos of the Earth*, 83. 'The Greek word for the first measure of all subsequent measures, for the first land-appropriation understood as the first partition and

of bracketing warfare among equal sovereigns in Europe[15] and relegating violence, instead, to the colonies.[16]

Schmitt's works on international law have also been used as lenses to address a larger historical theme associated with the times in which his intellectual works are embedded. This is particularly the case regarding the study of international law under the Third Reich,[17] to which Schmitt contributed as a theorist of Nazi expansionism, with his elaborations on the centrality of empire in international law and the concept of *Großraum* – a greater territorial space or Germanic pan-region – inspired by the Monroe doctrine, which buttressed Adolf Hitler's aggressive quest for a "Lebensraum" (living space).[18] In recent years, the study of international law under Nazism has benefitted from a broader historiographical move oriented to revisiting the "darker legacies of law in Europe" in international legal history[19] and this has in turn bolstered a renewed attention to some of Schmitt's polemical contributions in their historical context.[20]

2.2 *A Classic's Preeminent Place in the Intellectual Canon and the Periodization of International Law*

A second feature distinguishing Vitoria as a classic of international law is the preeminent place his works occupy in the historical canon of international law, and by extension, in its intellectual periodization. Vitoria's *relectiones,* in which, in 1539, he organized Spain's legitimate and illegitimate claims for

classification of space, for the primeval division and distribution, is nomos', in Schmitt, *The Nomos of the Earth,* 67.

15 Martti Koskenniemi, 'The Past according to International Law. A Practice of History and Histories of a Practice', in Annabel Brett, Megan Donaldson, and Martti Koskenniemi (eds.), *History, Politics, Law: Thinking through the International* (Cambridge: Cambridge University Press 2021) 49–68.

16 See, on the basis of Hannah Arendt's marginalia in her copy of *The Nomos of the Earth,* Anna Jurkevics, 'Hannah Arendt reads Carl Schmitt's The Nomos of the Earth: A dialogue on law and geopolitics from the margins'. *European Journal of Political Theory* 3 (2017) 345–66.

17 See early on Detlev. F. Vagts, 'International Law in the Third Reich'. *The American Journal of International Law* 3 (1990) 661–704.

18 Beneyto, 'Camilo Barcia Trelles on Francisco de Vitoria'.

19 Christian Joerges and N. S. Ghaleigh (eds.) (with a prologue by Michael Stolleis and an epilogue by JHH Weiler), *Darker Legacies of Law in Europe. The Shadow of National Socialism and Fascism over Europe and Its Legal Traditions* (Oxford: Hart 2003).

20 See e.g. in this volume the chapter by Joseph W. Bendersky, 'The Mind Has…Its Ineluctable Freedom…Even in the Claws of the Leviathan.' Vitoria As Clue to Schmitt's Concepts of Grossraum, Race, And War During World War II'.

entitlement to American lands and discussed just and unjust wars remain a focal point in the historical intellectual canon of international law. This position was further reinforced by the fact that he was the presiding figure in the neo-Thomist school of moral and legal theologians that came to be known as the "School of Salamanca." Moreover, the fact that Vitoria's works have been widely used as an intellectual gateway to a macro context-shifting event in the history of the international order has fostered their status as a companion milestone in a dominantly Eurocentric periodization of the discipline[21] that is often framed by a succession of Western diplomatic conferences and international treaties.[22] This centrality of Vitoria in the Western intellectual canon and the Western-centric historical periodization of the discipline also accounts for Vitoria having become one of the key foci in alternative intellectual periodizations of the discipline that put emphasis on the exclusion of non-Western intellectual figures and the perspectives of those subjected to Western imperial events and colonial processes.[23]

Schmitt's focus on Vitoria, both built on and further contributed to Vitoria's canonical status in the Western intellectual tradition, and by extension, his centrality in the Western-centric historical periodization of international law. Schmitt contributed to anchoring Vitoria as a focal point in the narrative of the origin of the "traditional Eurocentric order of international law," including above Hugo Grotius, who Schmitt discusses in his genealogy of appropriators who misconstrued Vitoria's thinking as a "polemical jurist in a hostile country," who adopted Vitoria's arguments "as propaganda in European trade wars."[24] With his work, Schmitt also indirectly contributed to a heterogeneous Schmittian periodization of the history of international law, hinging on the definitive collapse of the Eurocentric order in the aftermath of WWII and the advent of an era of American hegemony. In doing so, Schmitt somewhat anticipated the tensions in the still West-centric yet increasingly globalized international legal order that ensued in the wake of the decolonization process. Moreover, Schmitt's periodization with its focus on the pivotal role

---

21 Oliver Diggelmann, 'The Periodization of the History of International Law', in Bardo Fassbender and Anne Peters (eds.), *The Oxford Handbook of the History of International Law* (Oxford: Oxford University Press 2012) 997–1011.

22 e.g. the Treaty of Tordesillas (1493), The Treaty of Westphalia (1648), The Congress of Vienna (1815), The Congress of Berlin (1885), The Treaty of Versailles (1919), and the Conference of San Francisco (1945).

23 De la Rasilla, 'The Problem of Periodization in the History of International Law'. *Law and History Review* 1 (2019) 275–308.

24 Schmitt, *The Nomos of the Earth*, 116.

of European imperialism in the development of international law has had much influence on, and found corollaries in, ulterior post-colonial meta-periodizations of international law.[25]

It is true, on the other hand, that Schmitt's works have provided him with a prominent place in the twentieth-century intellectual canons of the disciplines of political theory, constitutional law, and legal philosophy. However, in international law circles, Schmitt's post-Cold War revival in political theory has had, in particular, a clear influence on the international legal thought of Martti Koskenniemi,[26] a particularly prolific critic of international legal liberalism and, perhaps, also the closest to a living international law classic-to-be in international legal scholarship today. The influence of Schmitt on Koskenniemi, whose engagement with and often reliance on and borrowing from Schmitt's analytical framework, including by scattering some of Schmitt's most oft quoted lines in some of his works, has done wonders to introduce the latter in international legal scholarship. Koskenniemi's influence may therefore have had some degree of influence in Schmitt's featuring in the otherwise extremely Eurocentric and male-dominated series of bio-intellectual portraits included in *The Oxford Handbook of the History of International Law* (2012).[27] However, the inclusion of Schmitt in this unofficial canon of great figures in international law was largely done at the expense of non-Western authors, despite the fact that this multiauthored volume was presented as a contribution "toward a global history of international law,"

25 De la Rasilla, 'The Problem of Periodization'.

26 This constitutes an interesting topic for another time. Koskenniemi has devoted extensive intellectual energy to works on Schmitt in a chapter in his *The Gentle Civilizer of Nations, The Rise and Fall of International Law* (Cambridge: Cambridge University Press 2002) 413–509, which elaborates on Schmitt's influence on Hans Morgenthau, and Martti Koskenniemi, 'International Law as Political Theology How to Read the Nomos der erde'. *Constellations* 4 (2004), 492–511, republished in *Forum Historiae Iuris* (2006). Martti Koskenniemi, 'Carl Schmitt and international law', in *The Oxford Handbook of Carl Schmitt*, 592–611. See also Martti Koskenniemi, 'Letter in Response to Michael Salter's Recent Paper on Carl Schmitt's Grossraum'. *Chinese Journal of International Law* 12 (2013), 201–202 as an *'aperitif'* for *'le plat de consistance'* offered in response to it by Michael Salter's 'A Reply to Koskenniemi's Letter'. *Chinese Journal of International Law* 12 (2013), 203–210. See also, engaging repeatedly with Schmitt, Martti Koskenniemi, 'By Their Acts You Shall Know Them… (and Not by Their Legal Theories)'. *European Journal of International Law* 4 (2004), 839–851.

27 Bardo Fassbender, 'Carl Schmitt', in Bardo Fassbender and Anne Peters (eds.), *The Oxford Handbook of the History of International Law* (Oxford: Oxford University Press 2012) 1173–1178.

roughly up to WWII.[28] Moreover, other non-Western authors, far more qualified than Schmitt in intra-disciplinary terms to feature in such a list, were not included.[29]

Therefore, and despite Schmitt being presented there as someone who "also had a strong influence on the jurisprudence of international law,"[30] one should not read from his inclusion a generalized endorsement of his canonical status among international lawyers.[31] Instead, his presence may instead be accounted for as an oblique effect of German cultural patriotism, which, although of a particularly troubled variety in the case of Schmitt, is, as we shall see below, also a feature shared by Vitoria as a classic of international law. This noted, it is, nonetheless, undeniable that Schmitt nowadays features in an extended interdisciplinary canon of international law which has been further expanding toward thinkers and "classics" in political theory, economics, political economy, history, philosophy, and history and which, once again, Koskenniemi has done much to promote.[32] However, unlike Vitoria, Schmitt does not occupy a preeminent place in the traditional periodization of international law, but instead he belongs together with other Nazi theorists of international law in the dark shadow of a dominant Western chronological division of time in the history of international law.[33]

---

28 Bardo Fassbender and Anne Peters, 'Introduction: towards a global history of international law', in Bardo Fassbender and Anne Peters (eds.), *The Oxford Handbook of the History of International Law* (Oxford: Oxford University Press 2012) 1–24.

29 Indeed, *The Oxford Handbook of the History of International Law* ignored African, Asian, Latin-American and female authors almost altogether in the 22-short bio-intellectual 'portraits' section it included. Indeed, the eighth-century author Muhammad al-Shaybani, who, in fact, only became known to Western erudite legal historians under the title of 'the Islamic Grotius,' and Bertha von Suttner, who was the first woman to receive the Nobel Peace Prize in 1905, remain the only concessions to racial, gender and geographical diversity in the section devoted to providing an intellectual gallery of eminent international law scholars contained in the multi-authored volume.

30 Fassbender, 'Carl Schmitt'.

31 Koskenniemi also touches on this, offering his own explanation of why 'the booming Schmitt commentary of the past two decades has not spread into international law as much as one might have expected'. Martti Koskenniemi, 'Carl Schmitt and international law', in *The Oxford Handbook of Carl Schmitt*, 592–611.

32 Martti Koskenniemi, 'Law of Nations and the "Conflict of the Faculties"'. *History of the present* 1 (2018), 4–28.

33 See also in this volume Paolo Amorosa and Ville Suuronen, '"Ancora tu?" Questioning Carl Schmitt's Place in the Canon of International Law', in *Francisco de Vitoria and Carl Schmitt: Crossroads in the History of International Law and Political Theory* (Leiden: Brill 2025).

2.3 *A Classic's Broad Interdisciplinary Appeal*

A third, related, distinguishing feature of a classic of international law that Vitoria epitomizes is its broad interdisciplinary appeal. While Vitoria occupies a seminal position in the intellectual historical canon of international law, he also occupies a remarkable place in historical intellectual canons of other disciplines. Vitoria's work features in a diversity of academic curricula, including those of international relations, the history of political thought,[34] political theory,[35] human rights,[36] global history,[37] global legal history,[38] and many other areas in the social sciences. This is partly due to the fact that Vitoria, who arguably bequeathed to "international lawyers up to our time not only a language but also a specific conceptual structure ridden with dualisms,"[39] wrote on subject matters that also fit squarely within the scope of many other intellectual disciplinary traditions. Moreover, interdisciplinary migration can also be considered an offspring of what Koskenniemi calls "the way legal authority migrates between different disciplines"[40] and the great intellectual influence that comes in its wake. As Brett et al. note, it is indeed "difficult to find a major figure in the history of European political thought who would not have attempted to say something about how authority emerges, or is justified and critiqued in the world beyond the single polity";[41] and, one may add, who in order to do so has not, therefore, regarded Vitoria as a valuable source of reference and inspiration.

34 Terry Nardin and Nicholas Rengger (eds.), *International Relations in Political Thought: Texts from the Ancient Greeks to the First World War* (Cambridge: Cambridge University Press 2002); Martin Wight, *International Theory: The Three Traditions* (Leicester: Leicester U.P. for the Royal Institute of International Affairs 1991).

35 Anthony Pagden and Jeremy Lawrance (eds.), *Vitoria: Political Writings* (Cambridge: Cambridge University Press 1991).

36 R. L. Soriano, *Historia tematica de los derechos humanos* (Madrid: Editorial MAD 2009).

37 David Armitage, *Foundations of Modern International Thought* (Cambridge: Cambridge University Press 2013).

38 Thomas Duve, J. L. Egío and Christiane Birr (eds.), *The School of Salamanca: A Case of Global Knowledge Production Max Planck Studies in Global Legal History of the Iberian Worlds* (Leiden: Brill 2021).

39 J. M. Beneyto, 'Conquest, Empire, and Peace: Vitoria, Charles V, Erasmus and the Foundations of the Law of Nations', in J. M. Beneyto (ed.), *Empire, Humanism and Rights. Collected Essays on Francisco de Vitoria* (Leiden: Springer 2021) 1–47, 1.

40 Martti Koskenniemi, *To the Uttermost Parts of the Earth: Legal Imagination and International Power, 1300–1870* (Cambridge: Cambridge University Press 2021) 5.

41 Annabel Brett, 'Between history, politics and law: History of political thought and history of international law', in Annabel Brett, Megan Donaldson, and Martti Koskenniemi (eds.), *History, Politics, Law: Thinking through the International* (Cambridge: Cambridge University Press 2021) 19–48.

Schmitt's engagement with Vitoria furthermore contributed to his interdisciplinary appeal. Indeed, if, as Schmitt notes, "J.B. Scott's zeal succeeded in making Vitoria's name well known and even popular in circles far beyond the scholarly disciplines of history and international law."[42] Schmitt's works on Vitoria have been a bridge across which Vitoria has become an object of interest for readers in other disciplinary traditions.[43] Second, while Schmitt is now arguably part of the modern intellectual canon of legal and political thought in the twentieth century, he is also, as was noted above, part of the "extended interdisciplinary intellectual canon of other disciplinary traditions, including more recently international law."[44] In what constitutes yet further proof – as if the present case of a Dominican friar and a Nazi theorist was not proof enough – that international legal theory does, indeed, make strange bedfellows, this recent inclusion has been, to a great extent due, as noted above, to the intellectual influence of the Marxist-inspired international law scholar Martti Koskenniemi.[45]

2.4 *A Classic as a First Expounder of International Legal Theories or Doctrines*

A fourth, related, characteristic of Vitoria as a Western classic of international law is having been identified as the author of the first formulation of one or more international legal theories or doctrines. That the classic's ideas and formulations have migrated across time and space and in doing so have become a substratum of further legal discussions and adaptations is reminiscent of the feeling of déjà vu one experiences with all "classics." Calvino

42 Schmitt, *The Nomos of the Earth*, 119.

43 David Chandler, 'Revival of Carl Schmitt in International Relations: The Last Refuge of Critical Theorists?'. *Millennium: Journal of International Studies* 1(2008) 27–48.

44 Robert Howse, 'Schmitt, Schmitteanism and Contemporary International Legal Theory', in Anne Orford and Florian Hoffmann (eds.), *The Oxford Handbook of the Theory of International Law* (Oxford: Oxford University Press 2016) 212–230.

45 A detailed study of the main foci and topoi of Koskenniemi's opus on international law would identify many Marxist legacies in it in particular connected to how the Soviet Theory of International Law was interpreted across socialist developing countries, including China, during the decolonization period; see further Ignacio de la Rasilla, 'China's International Law and the Third World during the Revolutionary Period (1949–1978)', in Ignacio de la Rasilla, Jiangyu Wang and Congyan Cai (eds.), *Histories of International Law in China. All Under Heaven* (Oxford: Oxford University Press forth. 2025). See, also, Martti Koskenniemi. 'What Should International Lawyers Learn from Karl Marx?'. *Leiden Journal of International Law* 2(2004) 229–246; and Martti Koskenniemi, 'What Should International Lawyers Learn from Karl Marx?', in Susan Marks (ed.), *International Law on the Left: Re-Examining Marxist Legacies* (Cambridge: Cambridge University Press 2008) 30–52.

evoked this as one of the criteria identifying a "classic," when noting that "a classic is a book which even when we read it for the first time gives the sense of re-reading something we have read before"'[46] This association of the classics as the first expounders of a theory or doctrine has been regularly buttressed by the uses contemporary authors make of them. David Kennedy in his study of "primitive international legal scholarship" also refers to this form of juridical presentism in remarking that "many contemporary authors use historic texts either to demonstrate that the author's contemporary vision is fully present, if in a nascent form, or that modern doctrinal and systemic developments are foreshadowed in the historical texts."[47]

A classic example is provided by Vitoria's oft-quoted first elaboration of the relevance of the notion of the "international community" in international law in his *relectio De potestate civili* of 1528, in which he associated *ius gentium* with the notion of *totus orbis* (the whole world). This, Vitoria argued, "in a certain manner is a republic" (*qui aliquo modo est una respublica*) and as such "has the power to enact laws which are just and convenient to all men; and these make up the law of nations" (*potestate ferendi leges aequast et convenientes omnibus, quales sunt in iure gentium*). This idea gained further credentials after the first World War with the establishment of the League of Nations, when most of the fundamental international legal doctrines and their system of legal sources were established. It would subsequently underlie multiple international legal theorizations of the "international community" as an international law-making entity of sorts, and it has indeed over time been associated with contemporary international legal doctrines, such as norms of *ius cogens*, also known as non-derogable peremptory norms of international law, and *erga omnes* international law obligations.[48] A similar liberal "globalist" orientation would again take hold in the post-Cold War period with the rise of revamped "international constitutionalist" theorizations[49] underlying notions in international law thinking, such as that of global governance and global law. These, with their stress on interdependence as the backbone of a legal "international community," undergirded by cosmopolitan notions of justice, would be once again retraced to the intellectual foundations provided by Vitoria and the School of Salamanca.

46 Italo Calvino, 'Why Read the Classics?'. *The New York Review* (9 October 1986).

47 D. W. Kennedy, 'Primitive legal scholarship'. *Harvard International Law Journal* 1(1986) 1–98.

48 See e.g. Antonio Robledo, 'Le ius cogens international: sa genèse, sa nature, ses fonctions'. *Collected Courses of The Hague Academy of International Law* 172 (1981) 13–217.

49 Jan Klabbers, Anne Peters, and Geir Ulfstein, *The Constitutionalization of International Law* (Oxford: Oxford University Press 2009).

Schmitt's engagement with Vitoria predates many of the conceptual normative implications in international law (including the theorization and normative fleshing out notion of *ius cogens* as a sort of supra-positive safeguard of community interests) of the theorization of a supranational international community based on community values providing the basis for a minimum public international order in the fashion of a domestic constitutional order, extrapolated to the international realm. However, Schmitt's early critique of the abstract universalism of the post-Versailles international system and the instrumentalization of its theoretical premises in the hands of an emerging great power under the cloak of humanity extends to some of its corollaries, in particular, as we shall see below, the "criminalization of war," although without targeting Vitoria's contribution to the underlying premise or the subsequently added international constitutional dimension. The criminalization of war naturally derives from the domestic analogy, which is foundational to modern international law, as this ensues from the – albeit always imperfect – transposition of the Western liberal constitutional state model to the international domain in an attempt to provide a semblance of order among sovereign states.

Schmitt has, on the other hand, been credited with the introduction of influential concepts in the fields of politics and law, including that of "political theology," understood as the assertion that "all significant concepts in the modern theory of the state are secularized theological concepts, not only because of their historical development – in which they were transferred from theology to the theory of the state ... but also because of their systematic structure."[50] Schmitt is also well known for his "theory of decisionism," as opposed to normativism *à la* Kelsen as the basis on which the "legal system rests." It is from this theoretical understanding that is derived his oft-quoted axiom through his theorization of the "state of exception" that the "sovereign is he who decides on the exception"[51] and his vaunted "friend/enemy distinction" as the fundamental distinction in (or even) the definition of politics itself.

2.5 *Multiple Interpretations and Reinterpretations of the Classic*

A fifth feature of the classics of international law is that their work has been interpreted and reinterpreted multiple times. Indeed, presentism, broadly understood among historians as "a term of abuse conventionally deployed to

50 Miguel Vatter, 'The Political Theology of Carl Schmitt Oxford', in *The Oxford Handbook of Carl Schmitt*, 245–268, 245.

51 Stanley Paulson, 'Hans Kelsen and Carl Schmitt Growing Discord, Culminating in the "Guardian" Controversy of 1931', in *The Oxford Handbook of Carl Schmitt*, 510–546, 511.

describe an interpretation of history that is biased towards and colored by present-day concerns, preoccupations, and values,"[52] recurs around the interpretation of Vitoria's opus. This has become the object of different interpretations and re-interpretations, in the light of different strategic circumstances and the rise and fall of political ideologies and trends in international legal thought over time. An illustration is provided by JB Scott, who became a highly influential champion of Vitoria in the "contest over the founding fathers of international law," which, partly pervaded by nationalist and religious prejudices (the Protestant Grotius vs the Catholic Vitoria) had developed since the late nineteenth century. Scott, for whom Grotius was a "popularizer in the best sense of the word" and therefore "a member of the Vitorian or, as it is more usually termed, the Spanish school"[53] also saw in Vitoria's reputation a vehicle for "a dominant pan-American liberal international and imperial legal approach, based on US legal and political values, which shaped the emergence of international law as a modern discipline in Latin America and the US."[54]

The most recent and dramatically apparent example of this recurrent tendency is a "post-colonial" critical reading of Vitoria that proposes substituting his long-established late nineteenth-century classical representation as a humanist critic of empire with an opposite depiction of him as a legitimizer of the Spanish *conquista*.[55] According to the highly influential reading by Antony Anghie, who depicts Vitoria as an early precursor of a juridical mode of discourse that has been subsequently pursued in imperialist projects up to the present day, Vitoria's work may "be read as a particularly insidious justification of conquest, precisely because it is presented in the language of liberality and even equality."[56] Anghie's stress that "international law was created out of the unique issues generated by the encounter between the Spanish and the Indians"[57] has contributed to setting Vitoria as a landmark in a post colonial periodization of the history of international law. However, it has also led to multiple charges that Anghie's was a revisionist anachronist reading informed

52 David Armitage, In Press, 'In Defense of Presentism', in D. M. McMahon (ed.), *History and Human Flourishing* (New York: Oxford University Press 2023) 44–69, 47.

53 J. B. Scott, *The Spanish Origin of International Law: Francisco de Vitoria and his Law of Nations* (Oxford: The Clarendon Press 1934) 10a.

54 J. P. Scarfi, 'The Latin American politics of international law: Latin American countries' engagements with international law and their contradictory impact on the liberal international order'. *Cambridge Review of International Affairs* 2(2021), 1–18.

55 On the relatively little explored positions of Schmitt on European colonialism and colonial warfare, see in this volume Jochen von Bernstorff, 'Carl Schmitt on Imperialism and International Law'.

56 Anghie, *Imperialism, Sovereignty, and the Making of International Law*, 28.

57 Ibid., 15.

by presentist concerns,[58] which in turn has fostered methodological debates among historians, legal historians, and critical international law scholars on the relationship between history and international law and the proper role, and limitations, of contextual methods in capturing it.[59]

Carl Schmitt, as was anticipated in the introduction, was particularly aware of this dimension and elaborated *in extenso* on "Vitoria's place in legal history and the scholarly uses of his much-cited lectures, the interpretation of which has its own history,"[60] furthermore considering that "few authors have had their arguments transplanted in such a way, and few names have become so famous as a result."[61] Schmitt began his genealogy of appropriators who misconstrued Vitoria's thinking with Grotius, highlighting in particular Grotius' appropriation of Vitoria's arguments in his *Mare liberum*, at a time when "these arguments meant something completely different," thus "neutrali [zing] the specifically Catholic character of Vitoria's intentions" with his "Protestant instrumentalisation."[62] However, while Schmitt also noted that "it was [Ernst] Nys who broke the ground and paved the way"[63] for this revival in the late nineteenth century as a "function of his [Nys's] faith in humanitarian civilization and progress,"[64] his main focus of interest was "the renaissance of Vitoria and late Spanish scholasticism" in the aftermath of WWI. This is, according to Schmitt, when "the Spanish Dominican's arguments were inserted, in an even more astonishing manner, into a system of thought completely foreign to him."[65]

In order to support this view, Schmitt focuses on James Brown Scott, according to Schmitt, "dedicated himself to becoming the official exponent of Vitoria's fame"[66] and whose "efforts also marked a new stage in the instrumentalization of Vitoria's arguments, which has reached the point of political myth-making."[67] For Schmitt, this instrumentalization or misconstruction

58 Georg Cavallar, 'Vitoria, Grotius, Pufendorg, Wolff and Vattel: accomplices of European colonialism and exploitation or true cosmopolitans?'. *Journal of the History of International Law* 2(2008), 181–209.

59 Martti Koskenniemi, 'Vitoria and us: thoughts on critical histories of international law'. *Rechtsgeschichte* 22(2014), 119–138; Anne Orford, *International Law and the Politics of History* (Cambridge: Cambridge University Press 2021).

60 Schmitt, *The Nomos of the Earth*, 102.

61 Ibid., 115.

62 Ibid., 116.

63 Ibid., 118.

64 Ibid., 118.

65 Ibid., 116.

66 Ibid., 118.

67 Ibid., 119.

revolved, above all, on the use of Vitoria to enable a "return to older" concepts of just war, with their discriminatory consequences for the criminalization and even demonization of the adversary in the name of the appropriated concept of humanity. This, in Schmitt's view, made the theory of "justus hostis" ("just enemy") run amok since it was, originally, based on equal sovereignty among European powers that served as a cornerstone of *ius publicum europaeum*[68] in the service of regulating limited legal warfare within Europe, while outsourcing unlimited war to the extra-European world. Instead, a according to Schmitt, with the collapse of "*le droit public de l'Europe*," the thinking of Vitoria "is misconstrued" in an "essentially different intellectual milieu of untheological purely moral or purely juridical expositions"[69] to produce a concept of discriminatory war and a form of liberal universalism at the service of the rising hegemony of the United States from the post-Versailles system onward.

Second, Schmitt's opus has itself been the object of multiple interpretations and reinterpretations, in particular, since its rediscovery and certain intellectual rehabilitation in the field of political theory in the late 1980s. In international legal scholarship, some of Schmitt's concepts were indeed repackaged by exponents of a certain strand of "Left-Schmittianism"[70] in a critique of the liberal American empire, which gained salience in assessing instances of humanitarian intervention in the late 1990s, and, in particular, in the aftermath of 9–11, the launch of the "war on terror" and the Iraq War. This, and its translation into English[71] (and also into French and Spanish),[72] provided the context for a rediscovery of *The Nomos of the Earth,* which, as was noted above, Koskenniemi largely heralded in international legal scholarship.[73]

Moreover, the parallel interdisciplinary turn to the history of international law and the attention devoted to Vitoria in this particular context have in turn

---

68 Ibid., 119.

69 Ibid., 115.

70 Matthew G. Specter, 'What's "Left" in Schmitt? From Aversion to Appropriation in Contemporary Political Theory', in *The Oxford Handbook of Carl Schmitt*, 426–454.

71 Carl Schmitt *Der Nomos der Erde* was translated into English by the Critical Theory-based Telos Press as part of a leftist Schmitt vogue for his critique, if from the extreme right, of liberalism (Carl Landauer, 'Lather, Rinse, Repeat. The Historical Returns of International Law'. *Jus Gentium: Journal of International Legal History* 2 (2024), 329–370.

72 *Le nomos de la terre dans le droit des gens du jus publicum europaeum*, par Carl Schmitt, traduit de l'allemand par Lilyane Deroche-Gurcel, revisé, présenté et annoté par Peter Haggenmacher (Paris: PUF 2001). Carl Schmitt, *El nomos de la tierra en el derecho de gentes del 'ius publicum europaeum'*, traduccion de Dora Schilling. Edicion y estudio preliminar "Soberania y orden internacional en Carl Schmitt", de Jose Luis Monereo Perez (Granada: Editorial Comares 2002).

73 Martti Koskenniemi, 'International Law as Political Theology'.

further promoted engagement with Schmitt's *The Nomos of the Earth* among international legal historians applying diachronical lenses to the different revivals of Vitoria over time and among those interested in unearthing the genealogy of the historiography of international law.

2.6 *A Classic as a Flag-bearer of an Intellectual Tradition*

Connected to the multiple reinterpretations his works have received and Vitoria's broad interdisciplinary appeal, Vitoria has become a historical flag-bearer of an ever-reinterpreted (and partly ever-reinvented) intellectual tradition in international law. Indeed, Vitoria is paradigmatic in the sense that his works have grown to be commonly regarded as embodiments of a conceptual world view underlying the theories and methodology of international law. In this, he is second to none and perhaps only comparable to Grotius. Indeed, the epithet "Grotian" is understood as an intellectual crossroads between natural law and positivism in a state-centered international system, and as such it is often classically opposed to the conceptual world view of international legal positivism. This, which is traditionally retraced to the formulations of Emer de Vattel (1714–1767) in his highly influential *Le droit des gens* (1758), does not recognize any legal or axiological superior authority over the always retractable expression of state sovereign consent, either in its tacit (custom) or explicit (treaty) forms, as a source of international legal obligations.[74]

This conventional characterization of what the epithet "Grotian" stands for owes volumes to the interpretation that Hersch Lauterpacht (1897–1960), a judge on the bench of the International Court of Justice (1955–1960) and a long-standing holder of the Whewell Chair of international law at Cambridge, gave of what he termed the "Grotian tradition in international law,"[75] on the third centenary of Grotius's death in the aftermath of WW II. Lauterpacht's re-interpretation of the Grotian tradition, which he divided into eleven tenets, proceeded by making him an emblem of the international rule of law and even an early predecessor of international human rights law, which was a nascent international legal regime,[76] to which Lauterpacht was also seminally contributing at the time of his writing.[77]

---

74 Emmanuelle Jouannet, *Vattel and the Emergence of Classic International Law* (Gina Bellande and Robert Howse trans.) (Oxford: Hart 2009).

75 Hirsch Lauterpacht, 'The Grotian Tradition in International Law'. *British Yearbook of International Law*, 23 (1946), 1–53.

76 Ibid., 51.

77 Hersch Lauterpacht, *An International Bill of the Rights of Man* (New York, 1945).

Over time, international lawyers have widely adopted Lauterpacht's broadly re-updated "Grotian tradition,"[78] which he considered had provided "international law with unprecedented dignity and authority by making it part not only of a general system of jurisprudence but also of a universal moral code"[79] and a shortcut for the main features of a liberal international order. The most apparent consequence is that the epithet "Grotian" has been applied as an identifier of authority to many contemporary international legal doctrines that Grotius is interpreted as being (even if vaguely) associated with.[80] It has also been used to conjugate the moniker "Grotian moments," on which a certain strand of international legal literature has also emerged, to describe "rapid crystallizations of new rules and doctrines of customary international law."[81] Meanwhile, Francisco de Vitoria, who stood up against the excesses of his own country's imperialism, has over time become a symbol of the humanist universal natural law tradition. This tradition of international legal thought with the international community as its core is, as was seen above, retraced back to Vitoria and other members of the School of Salamanca, like Francisco de Suarez, who according to Lauterpacht laid the "foundations of the jurisprudential treatment of the problem of the international community as a whole."[82]

Schmitt, as was seen above, does not directly focus his critique on the contribution of Vitoria and the School of Salamanca to the theorization of the "international community" in international law but focuses instead on what he considers the misconstruction of Vitoria's doctrine to enable a return to the doctrine of just war. On the other hand, Schmitt may himself be considered a flag bearer of an anti-liberal democratic parliamentarist tradition in legal political thought. This connection with authoritarianism worked wonders in fostering his intellectual reception in Spain, where, through some of his disciples, his thought largely contributed to the legal architecture of the Franco regime. This emerged from the ashes of a civil war waged by an alliance of Catholic conservatives and proto-fascist factions against a democratically elected gov-

78 Ignacio de la Rasilla, 'Grotian Revivals in the History and Theory of International Law', in Randall Lesaffer and Janne Nijman (eds.), *The Cambridge Companion to Hugo Grotius* (Cambridge: Cambridge University Press 2021) 578–596.

79 Lauterpacht, above, n. 70.

80 See e.g. John Parry, 'What is the Grotian Tradition in International Law?', *University of Pennsylvania Journal of International Law*, 35:2 (2014), 299–377.

81 See, more recently, Tom Sparks and Mark Somos, 'Grotian Moments: An Introduction', *Grotiana*, 42:2 (2021), 179–191, introducing a symposium on the concept of 'Grotian moments'.

82 Lauterpacht, *An International Bill of the Rights of Man*, 17.

ernment. Schmitt's representativeness of a conceptually acute form of anti-liberalism has made him, unsurprisingly, appealing across "the political spectrum from the extreme left to the extreme right."[83]

2.7 *A Classic's Relationship with Cultural Patriotism*

The seventh characteristic of Vitoria as a global classic is the role played by cultural patriotism in both the making and the upholding of his classic status and in promoting the national, and in some cases by extension the international, institutionalization of his figure over time. Although this may often be overlooked given the global reputation a classic has gained over time, a classic never comes from nowhere. Instead, underlying the rise of a classic, there is more often than not a sustained national effort claiming the classic's intellectual prowess as an iconic representative of the nation, which takes pride by association. Likewise, Spanish institutions and academics have strongly backed the reputation of Francisco de Vitoria and the School of Salamanca in innumerable publications, with the establishment of national and international associations[84] bearing the name of Vitoria and also homonymous yearbooks,[85] by erecting public statues, setting up research centers, and even by giving his name to universities. This nationalistic glorification of the classics is not without a dark side. In the case of Vitoria, Francoist international lawyers went as far as using Vitorian doctrines to justify the *coup d'etat* against the Spanish Second Republic, which initiated the Spanish Civil War, and later in its aftermath, made the School of Salamanca stand as a nationalist purist and intellectually regressive symbol of Franco's national-Catholicist dictatorial regime.[86]

Schmitt largely contributed to this dimension of Spanish cultural patriotism in relationship to Vitoria, including by being the most prominent foreign contributor to the "Vitorian aftermath of the fascist mimesis" of international law in Spain.[87] This, which began in the early–mid 1940s when the Francoist intelligentsia began its strategically ideological realignment in the face of Ger-

83 Specter, 'What's "Left" in Schmitt?', 426–454.

84 Association Internationale Vitoria-Suarez (ed.), *Vitoria et Suarez: Contribution des théologiens au droit international moderne* (Paris: Pedone 1939).

85 Anuario de la Asociacion Francisco de Vitoria, see Julia Bühner, 'Histories Hidden in the Shadow: Vitoria and the International Ostracism of Francoist Spain'. *Journal of the History of International Law* 2–3 (2020), 421–445.

86 Ignacio de la Rasilla, *In the Shadow of Vitoria: A History of International Law in Spain 1770–1953* (Leiden: Brill Nijhoff 2017).

87 Ignacio de la Rasilla, 'The Fascist Mimesis of Spanish International Law and its Vitorian Aftermath, 1939–1953'. *Journal of the History of International Law* 2 (2012), 207–236.

many losing ground in WWII, would spread its intellectual effects for decades in the works of Spanish international lawyers.[88] Paradoxically perhaps, however, the good fame of Vitoria, far from being tainted by his association with a dictatorial national-Catholicist regime's intellectual elite, has largely survived intact in post-democratic Spain. On the other hand, unlike Vitoria, Schmitt's troubling personal political biography, idiosyncratic work, and life-long anti-semitism make him the antithesis of what contemporary Germany would embrace as an intellectual symbol of cultural patriotism. However, this has not detracted from the fact that his intellectual prestige as one of the "German greats" has been supported by the interest his German co-nationals – and also intellectual Germanophiles, like Koskenniemi himself, as was seen above – have shown in his scholarship over time. This pseudo- "rehabilitation" of Schmitt has been surrounded by debates and polemics, including among international lawyers, on the possibility or impossibility of detaching the possible contemporary relevance of his intellectual insights from his extremely troubling political and personal biography.[89]

2.8 *A Classic's Universality*

An eighth characteristic of a classic of international law is its universality, or if preferred, its "great staying power across both time and space." However, unlike the great classics of literature, the universalization of Vitoria has not only hinged on his works' intellectual quality or even on the fact that they "focus on matters of great importance, identifying fundamental human problems and providing some sort of guidance for dealing with them."[90] By contrast, in international law, the elevation of a classic has much to do with its canonical position in the dominant Western intellectual tradition and accompanying Western-centric periodization of international law and its subsequent cultural export in the wake of different waves of Western imperialism and colonization around the globe. In this context, the reception of a Western classic may be part of a process of "strategic appropriation" of international law by peripheral and semi-peripheral international law elites,[91] as is shown for instance, in the Chinese translations of Western international law text-

88 Ignacio de la Rasilla, 'Beyond the Spanish classics: The ephemeral awakening of the history of international law in pre-democratic Spain'. *Monde(s)* 1 (2015), 135–154.

89 Among international law scholars, see, interestingly, on this, Salter, 'A Reply to Koskenniemi's Letter', more recently, Joseph Weiler, 'Cancelling Schmitt', Editorial. *European Journal of International Law* 2 (2021), 393–395.

90 R. J. Smith, *The I Ching: A Biography* (Princeton: Princeton University Press 2012) 5.

91 A. Becker Lorca, *Mestizo International Law: A Global Intellectual History 1842–1933* (Cambridge: Cambridge University Press 2015).

books produced in the nineteenth century to argue against "unequal treaties."[92] However, this reception also remains a symptom of constrained "acculturation" to the tenets of the international legal tradition embodied by Western foreign powers and a symbol of the enduring quality of their cultural hegemony over time.

Schmitt's influential reading of Vitoria at the heart of the historical events that inaugurated the "Eurocentric tradition of international law" largely presupposes Vitoria's universalism and further contributed to it. Ironically, perhaps, in doing so, Schmitt also pointed the way, as was seen above, to postcolonial historical reinterpretations of Vitoria's significance in international law.[93] Second, Schmitt has gained over time his own "universal" appeal as a critic of parliamentary democracy, a theorist of authoritarianism, and as a critic of international legal liberalism, in particular, regarding an American form of morally inspired universalism.

2.9 *A Classic's Diachronical Uses*

A ninth and more recent feature of the global classics of international law is that they have become vehicles for the study of the history of international law in different times and periods. Study of the genealogy of interpretations and reinterpretations of the classics over time has in turn nurtured a parallel array of new investigations into the lives, times, and works of those who contributed to the classics' modern fame in international law and the historical, legal, political, and biographical contexts underlying these re-readings and re-interpretations. It is indeed perhaps the most enduring testament to the status of a classic as a classic when this becomes a sort of Ariadna's thread in the study of altogether different historical periods. One of those times was the interwar period, when the establishment of the League of Nations as the first universal permanent international organization and the parallel efforts to tame the excesses of the absolute sovereignty conceptions underlying the horrors of World War I largely contributed to a revival of the natural law tradition among international lawyers. This in turn fostered a trend of interwar presentist reinterpretations of Vitoria[94] and later a reaction penned by Schmitt[95] to

92 M. A. Carrai, *Sovereignty in China: A Genealogy of a Concept since 1840* (Cambridge: Cambridge University Press 2019).

93 Anghie, *Imperialism, Sovereignty, and the Making of International Law.*

94 C. Barcia Trelles 'Francisco de Vitoria et l'école moderne'. *Collected Courses of Hague Academy of International Law* 17 (1928), 109–342; J. B. Scott, *The Catholic Conception of International Law* (Washington: Lawbook Exchange 2014).

95 Schmitt, *The Nomos of the Earth.*

some of them in the immediate aftermath of WW II. "Vitorian" revivals,[96] which are themselves constitutive building blocks in the construction of a classic, are increasingly studied in their own detailed contextual terms, with specific attention to the works, lives, and times of their protagonists,[97] including in the case of the second of them, J. B. Scott, C. Barcia Trelles and C. Schmitt. A similar genealogy of revivals can be predicated of Grotius with, in this case, Hersch Lauterpacht playing a pivotal role. It is also thanks to the use of historical diachronical perspectives that both Grotius and Vitoria have also indirectly provided new lenses through which to look diachronically into the historical development of international, and also national, traditions of international law at different times.[98]

Schmitt himself indirectly inaugurated, as we have seen above, a diachronical perspective on the uses and misuses of Vitoria's works. Since Schmitt was one of the members of the "influential Vitorian triangle," who largely contributed to Vitoria's enduring modern fame in international law in the interwar years and their aftermath,[99] it is therefore apposite that a contemporary dimension of the interest in Schmitt's intellectual engagement with the works of Vitoria would fit squarely within a contextualized diachronical historical framework. Second, since Schmitt is still a relatively modern twentieth-century author, in particular when compared to the almost 500 years elapsed since Vitoria delivered his *relectio* on the Indians in 1539, diachronical study of the subsequent uses to which his works have been put against the background provided by different circumstances and trends in international legal thought in different historical periods may not possibly be too extended yet. However, it is already incipient, and considering the intellectual patterns that underpin the survival of the classics, we may be sure to see more of it in the future.

2.10 *A Classic as a Generator of an Industry of Academic Commentary*

A tenth and more apparent feature ensuing from all the previous characteristics that one can distil from the case of Vitoria as a prototypical global classic of international law is that the "classics" generate an industry of academic commentary around them. From the sixteenth century to the present day, there is

---

96 De la Rasilla, 'The Three Revivals', n.7.

97 Amorosa, *Rewriting the History of the Law of Nations.*

98 M. Van Ittersum, 'Hugo Grotius: the making of a founding father of the history of international law', in Anne Orford and Florian Hoffmann (eds.), *The Oxford Handbook of the Theory of International Law* (Oxford: Oxford University Press 2016) 82–100; and De la Rasilla, 'Grotian Revivals', n.78.

99 See, further, Ignacio de la Rasilla, 'Camilo Barcia Trelles in and Beyond Vitoria's Shadow (1888–1977)', *European Journal of International Law* 4 (2020), 1433–1449.

indeed an extremely vast body of literature on the opus of Vitoria and, by extension, his life and times,[100] and also on the School of Salamanca.[101] Even within the narrow confines of international legal scholarship, there have been multiple editions of their works and translations into numerous languages, research monographs, edited volumes, innumerable journal articles, and book chapters, and also of course several Hague Academy courses, with new additions to the large literature that continue appearing every year.[102] If to these one adds Vitoria's presence in all international law textbooks and the overall number of variously accumulated citations in various fields, the overall "impact factor" of Vitoria is indeed simply off the charts.

Schmitt contributed to the intellectual industry of academic production on Vitoria, first in his own right, having dedicated several works to Vitoria. However, far more quantitatively important are the multiple publications bearing on Vitoria that take their cue from Carl Schmitt's engagement with the Spanish Dominican friar. Second, Schmitt himself has been translated into many languages, with Spanish being the language more of his works were translated into by the end of Franco's 40-year authoritarian regime in Spain.[103] Moreover, numerous monographs, edited volumes, journal articles, chapters, PhD theses in different fields, and even a voluminous multiauthored handbook have already been dedicated to him, with, as a consequence, the number of citations of his works growing exponentially across different fields. If Vitoria, as elaborated on elsewhere,[104] has undergone three revivals in the intellectual history of international law, less than 40 years since Schmitt's death in 1985, one may also speak of a first Schmittian revival, which is itself the first stage in the making of a classic. Considering the academic spillover effect that revivals generate, one may also be certain that more Schmittian revivals will follow in the future.

---

100 See e.g. Jean-Paul Coujou & Idoya Zorroza Mª, *Bibliografía vitoriana* Cuadernos de Pensamiento Español Nº 52 (Pamplona, 2014).

101 See e.g. C. A. Ramírez Santos and José Luis Egío, *Conceptos, autores, instituciones Revisión crítica de la investigación reciente sobre la Escuela de Salamanca (2008–19) y bibliografía multidisciplinar* (Madrid: Dykinson, S.L. 2020). See also Antonio Fernandez Sanchez' Spanish School of International Law (16th and 17th centuries)'. Oxford Bibliographies of International Law (Oxford. Oxford University Press, 2016)

102 Just in 2021. See e.g. J. M. Beneyto (ed.), *Empire, Humanism and Rights. Collected Essays on Francisco de Vitoria* (Cham: Springer 2021); also, Koskenniemi, 'To the Uttermost Parts' n. 40.

103 J. M. Beneyto, *Politische Theologie als politische Theorie: Eine Untersuchung zur Rechts- und Staatstheorie Carl Schmitts und zu ihrer Wirkungsgeschichte in Spanien* (Berlin: Duncker & Humblot 1983).

104 De la Rasilla, 'The Three Revivals'.

3 Conclusion

The ten characteristics of a global classic of international law, distilled from Francisco Vitoria, may be applied and so tested by reference to other classic authors of international law, beginning with Hugo Grotius, whether independently or in combination with Vitoria himself. Likewise, one may envisage applying this proposed ten-fold standards of classicism in international law to the likes of Suarez, Gentili, Pudendorf, Vattel, and others, again independently or in combination with any other usual suspects in the traditional Western, and also in the emerging non-Western and/or now interdisciplinarily extended canon of international law and/or also in combination with some of their more modern commentators.[105] However, the closer the arrow of time approaches the global massive levels of today's academic professionalized field of international law, and its far more expanded and diversified contemporary specialized international legal regimes, each of which is in turn divided into multiple layers of international legal expertise, the less likely it is that international law scholars will continue meeting all the distilled criteria and characteristics of a traditional global classic of international law *à la Vitoria*. This noted, this ten-fold list may perhaps be also still applied with some fortune as a litmus test of sorts to some or other aspiring classics-to-be in international law in our day and age.

Study of the works of the Western classics will continue intriguing, inspiring, and broadening intellectual horizons, beyond the habits of conformity of new incoming generations to the discipline. In doing so, the Western classics will continue performing the functions of transmission belts to pass on a deep intellectual disciplinary tradition and its embedded critiques, on which classic thinkers have left their influential imprint and into which incoming generations around the globe have been, continue, and will, indeed, continue to be professionally socialized. Notwithstanding this, one may, however, welcome less of the inflated hyper-protagonism gained by the Western "classics" and the thematically overlapping reiterative intellectual energy and no less accompanying mystification that has historically been – and continues to be – spent in deciphering each of the interpretations they have received over time. Instead, more intellectual energy may instead be devoted to a myriad other authors who have remained in the shadow of the hegemonically induced appeal of the Western classics under conditions of cultural hegemony

105 For instance, the pair made by Hugo Grotius and Hersch Lauterpacht comes naturally to mind.

and to other members of an interdisciplinary extended canon of international law. By the same token, far more academic attention should ideally also be devoted to multiple other "minor" historical figures, including, in particular, women, so as to unearth a truly globally inclusive history of international law from under the largely overgrown shadow of the Western classics of international law ... and their commentators.

Bibliography

Amorosa, Paolo. Rewriting the History of the Law of Nations. How James Brown Scott Made Francisco de Vitoria the Founder of International Law (Oxford: Oxford University Press 2019).

Anghie, Antony. *Imperialism, Sovereignty, and the Making of International Law* (Cambridge: Cambridge University Press 2005).

Armitage, David. 'In Defense of Presentism', in D. M. McMahon (ed.), History and Human Flourishing (New York: Oxford University Press 2023) 44–69.

Armitage, David. Foundations of Modern International Thought (Cambridge: Cambridge University Press 2013).

Association Internationale Vitoria-Suarez (ed.), Vitoria et Suarez: Contribution des théologiens au droit international moderne (Paris: Pedone 1939).

Barcia Trelles, Camilo 'Francisco de Vitoria et l'école moderne'. *Collected Courses of Hague Academy of International Law* 17 (1928), 109–342.

Beneyto, Jose Maria. (ed.), *Empire, Humanism and Rights. Collected Essays on Francisco de Vitoria* (Cham: Springer 2021).

Beneyto, Jose Maria. 'Conquest, Empire, and Peace: Vitoria, Charles V, Erasmus and the Foundations of the Law of Nations', in J. M. Beneyto (ed.), *Empire, Humanism and Rights. Collected Essays on Francisco de Vitoria* (Leiden: Springer 2021) 1–47.

Beneyto, Jose Maria. 'Camilo Barcia Trelles on Francisco de Vitoria: At the Crossroads of Carl Schmitt's Grossraum and James Brown Scott's "Modern International Law"'. *European Journal of International Law* 4 (2020), 1477–1492.

Beneyto, Jose Maria. *Politische Theologie als politische Theorie: Eine Untersuchung zur Rechts- und Staatstheorie Carl Schmitts und zu ihrer Wirkungsgeschichte in Spanien* (Berlin: Duncker & Humblot 1983).

Becker, Arnulf. Mestizo International Law: A Global Intellectual History 1842–1933 (Cambridge: Cambridge University Press 2015).

Brett, Annabel. 'Between history, politics and law: History of political thought and history of international law', in Annabel Brett, Megan Donaldson, and Martti Koskenniemi (eds.), *History, Politics, Law: Thinking through the International* (Cambridge: Cambridge University Press 2021) 19–48.

Bühner, Julia. 'Histories Hidden in the Shadow: Vitoria and the International Ostracism of Francoist Spain'. *Journal of the History of International Law* 2–3 (2020), 421–445.

Carrai, Maria *Sovereignty in China: A Genealogy of a Concept since 1840* (Cambridge: Cambridge University Press 2019).

Calvino, Italo. 'Why Read the Classics?'. The New York Review (9 October 1986).

Cavallar, George. 'Vitoria, Grotius, Pufendorg, Wolff and Vattel: accomplices of European colonialism and exploitation or true cosmopolitans?'. *Journal of the History of International Law* 2(2008), 181–209.

Chandler, David. 'Revival of Carl Schmitt in International Relations: The Last Refuge of Critical Theorists?'. Millennium: Journal of International Studies 1(2008) 27–48.

Cojou, Jean Paul and María Idoya Zorroza-Huarte, (eds.), Bibliografia Vitoriana (Pamplona: Universidad de Navarra 2014).

De la Rasilla, Ignacio. 'China's International Law and the Third World during the Revolutionary Period (1949–1978)', in Ignacio de la Rasilla, Jiangyu Wang and Congyan Cai (eds.), Histories of International Law in China. All Under Heaven (Oxford: Oxford University Press forth. 2026).

De la Rasilla, Ignacio. 'Grotian Revivals in the History and Theory of International Law', in Randall Lesaffer and Janne Nijman (eds.), The Cambridge Companion to Hugo Grotius (Cambridge: Cambridge University Press 2021) 578–596.

De la Rasilla, Ignacio. 'Camilo Barcia Trelles in and Beyond Vitoria's Shadow (1888–1977)', European Journal of International Law 4 (2020), 1433–1449.

De la Rasilla, Ignacio. 'The Problem of Periodization in the History of International Law'. Law and History Review 1 (2019) 275–308.

De la Rasilla, Ignacio. 'The Three Revivals of Francisco de Vitoria in the History of International Law', in J. M. Beneyto (ed.), Empire, Humanism and Rights. Collected Essays on Francisco de Vitoria (Cham: Springer 2021) 73–93.

De la Rasilla, Ignacio. In the Shadow of Vitoria: A History of International Law in Spain 1770–1953 (Leiden: Brill Nijhoff 2017).

De la Rasilla, Ignacio. 'Beyond the Spanish classics: The ephemeral awakening of the history of international law in pre-democratic Spain'. Monde(s) 1 (2015), 135–154.

De la Rasilla, Ignacio 'The Fascist Mimesis of Spanish International Law and its Vitorian Aftermath, 1939–1953'. *Journal of the History of International Law* 2 (2012), 207–236.

Diggelmann, Oliver. 'The Periodization of the History of International Law', in Bardo Fassbender and Anne Peters (eds.), The Oxford Handbook of the History of International Law (Oxford: Oxford University Press 2012) 997–1011.

Duve, Thomas and Jose Luis Egío and Christiane Birr (eds.), *The School of Salamanca: A Case of Global Knowledge Production Max Planck Studies in Global Legal History of the Iberian Worlds* (Leiden: Brill 2021).

Fassbender, Bardo and Anne Peters, 'Introduction: towards a global history of international law', in Bardo Fassbender and Anne Peters (eds.), *The Oxford Handbook of the History of International Law* (Oxford: Oxford University Press 2012) 1–24.

Fassbender, Bardo. 'Carl Schmitt', in Bardo Fassbender and Anne Peters (eds.), The Oxford Handbook of the History of International Law (Oxford: Oxford University Press 2012) 1173–1178.

Fernandez Sanchez, Antonio. 'Spanish School of International Law (16th and 17th Centuries)'. Oxford Bibliographies of International Law (Oxford: Oxford University Press, 2016).

Howse, Robert. 'Schmitt, Schmitteanism and Contemporary International Legal Theory', in Anne Orford and Florian Hoffmann (eds.), The Oxford Handbook of the Theory of International Law (Oxford: Oxford University Press 2016) 212–230.

Joerges, Christian and N. S. Ghaleigh (eds.) (with a prologue by Michael Stolleis and an epilogue by JHH Weiler), *Darker Legacies of Law in Europe. The Shadow of National Socialism and Fascism over Europe and Its Legal Traditions* (Oxford: Hart 2003).

Jouannet, Emmanuelle. Vattel and the Emergence of Classic International Law (Gina Bellande and Robert Howse trans.) (Oxford: Hart 2009).

Jurkevics, Anna. 'Hannah Arendt reads Carl Schmitt's The Nomos of the Earth: A dialogue on law and geopolitics from the margins'. *European Journal of Political Theory* 3 (2017), 345–366.

David, Kennedy. 'Primitive legal scholarship'. *Harvard International Law Journal* 1-(1986) 1–98.

Klabbers, Jan, Anne Peters, and Geir Ulfstein, *The Constitutionalization of International Law* (Oxford: Oxford University Press 2009).

Martti Koskenniemi, *To the Uttermost Parts of the Earth: Legal Imagination and International Power, 1300–1870* (Cambridge: Cambridge University Press 2021).

Koskenniemi, Martti. 'the past According to International Law. a Practice of History and Histories of a Practice', in Annabel Brett, Megan Donaldson, and Martti Koskenniemi (eds.), *History, Politics, Law: Thinking through the International* (Cambridge: Cambridge University Press 2021) 49–68.

Martti Koskenniemi, 'Law of Nations and the "Conflict of the Faculties"'. *History of the present* 1 (2018), 4–28.

Koskenniemi, Martti. 'Carl Schmitt and International Law', in *The Oxford Handbook of Carl Schmitt'* in Jens Meierhenrich and Oliver Simons (eds.), The Oxford Handbook of Carl Schmitt (Oxford: Oxford University Press 2016) 592–611.

Koskenniemi, Martti 'Vitoria and us: thoughts on critical histories of international law'. *Rechtsgeschichte* 22(2014), 119–138.

Koskenniemi, Martti. 'Letter in Response to Michael Salter's Recent Paper on Carl Schmitt's Grossraum'. *Chinese Journal of International Law* 12 (2013), 201–202.

Koskenniemi, Martti. 'Empire and international law: the real Spanish contribution'. *University of Toronto Law Journal* 1 (2011), 1–36.

Koskenniemi, Martti. 'International Law as Political Theology How to Read the Nomos der erde'. *Constellations* 4 (2004), 492–511.

Koskenniemi, Martti. 'By Their Acts You Shall Know Them… (and Not by Their Legal Theories)'. *European Journal of International Law* 4 (2004), 839–851.

Koskenniemi, Martti. The Gentle Civilizer of Nations, The Rise and Fall of International Law (Cambridge: Cambridge University Press 2002).

Landauer, Carl. 'Lather, Rinse, Repeat. The Historical Returns of International Law'. *Jus Gentium: Journal of International Legal History* 2 (2024), 329–370.

Lauterpacht, Hersch. 'The Grotian Tradition in International Law'. *British Yearbook of. International Law*, 23 (1946), 1–53.

Lauterpacht, Hersch. *An International Bill of the Rights of Man* (New York, 1945).

Meierhenrich, Jens and Oliver Simons, '"A Fanatic of Order in an Epoch of Confusing Turmoil" the Political, Legal, and Cultural Thought of Carl Schmitt', in Jens Meierhenrich and Oliver Simons (eds.), *The Oxford Handbook of Carl Schmitt*, (Oxford: Oxford University Press 2016) 3–70.

Nardin, Terry and Nicholas Rengger (eds.), *International Relations in Political Thought: Texts from the Ancient Greeks to the First World War* (Cambridge: Cambridge University Press 2002).

Orford, Anne. *International Law and the Politics of History* (Cambridge: Cambridge University Press 2021).

Pagden, Anthony and Jeremy Lawrance (eds.), *Vitoria: Political Writings* (Cambridge: Cambridge University Press 1991).

Parry, John. 'What is the Grotian Tradition in International Law?', University of Pennsylvania Journal of International Law, 35:2 (2014), 299–377.

Ramírez Santos C.A. and José Luis Egío, *Conceptos, autores, instituciones Revisión crítica de la investigación reciente sobre la Escuela de Salamanca* (2008–19) *y bibliografía multidisciplinar* (Madrid: Dykinson, S.L. 2020).

Robledo, Antonio. 'Le ius cogens international: sa genèse, sa nature, ses fonctions'. *Collected Courses of The Hague Academy of International Law* 172 (1981) 13–217.

Paulson, Stanley, 'Hans Kelsen and Carl Schmitt Growing Discord, Culminating in the "Guardian" Controversy of 1931', in Jens Meierhenrich and Oliver Simons (eds.), The Oxford Handbook of Carl Schmitt (Oxford: Oxford University Press 2016) 510–546.

Salter, Michael. 'A Reply to Koskenniemi's Letter'. *Chinese Journal of International Law* 12 (2013), 203–210.

Scarfi, Juan Pablo. 'The Latin American politics of international law: Latin American countries' engagements with international law and their contradictory impact on the liberal international order'. *Cambridge Review of International Affairs* 2(2021), 1–18.

Schmitt, Carl. The Nomos of the Earth in the International Law of the Jus Publicum Europaeum (New York: Telos Press 2003)

Schmitt, Carl. Der Nomos der Erde im Völkerrecht des Jus Publicum Europaeum (Berlin: Duncker & Humblot 1950).

Scott, James Brown. The Spanish Origin of International Law: Francisco de Vitoria and his Law of Nations (Oxford: The Clarendon Press 1934)

Scott, James Brown. *The Catholic Conception of International Law* (Washington D.C.: Georgetown University Press, 1934).

Smeltzer, Joshua. 'On the Use and Abuse of Francisco de Vitoria: James Brown Scott and Carl Schmitt'. *Journal of the History of International Law* 20 (2018), 345–372.

Smith, R.J., The I Ching: A Biography (Princeton: Princeton University Press 2012)

Soriano, Ramon Luis. *Historia tematica de los derechos humanos* (Madrid: Editorial MAD 2009).

Sparks, Tom and Mark Somos, 'Grotian Moments: An Introduction', Grotiana, 42:2 (2021), 179–191

Specter, Matthew G. 'What's "Left" in Schmitt? from Aversion to Appropriation in Contemporary Political Theory', in Jens Meierhenrich and Oliver Simons (eds.), The Oxford Handbook of Carl Schmitt (Oxford: Oxford University Press 2016) 426–454.

Vagts, Detlev. F. 'International Law in the Third Reich'. *The American Journal of International Law* 3 (1990), 661–704.

Van Ittersum, Martinne, 'Hugo Grotius: the Making of a Founding Father of the History of International Law', in Orford, Anne and Florian Hoffmann (eds.), The Oxford Handbook of the Theory of International Law (Oxford: Oxford University Press 2016) 82–100.

Vatter, Miguel. 'the Political Theology of Carl Schmitt Oxford', in Jens Meierhenrich and Oliver Simons (eds.), The Oxford Handbook of Carl Schmitt (Oxford: Oxford University Press 2016) 245–268.

Weiler, Joseph. 'Cancelling Schmitt', 32 *European Journal of International Law* 2 (2021), 393–395.

Wight, Martin. *International Theory: The Three Traditions* (Leicester: Leicester U.P. for the Royal Institute of International Affairs 1991).

Index